A-Level
Chemistry

Exam Board: OCR A

Revising for Chemistry exams is stressful, that's for sure — even just getting your notes sorted out can leave you needing a lie down. But help is at hand...

This brilliant CGP book explains **everything you'll need to learn** (and nothing you won't), all in a straightforward style that's easy to get your head around. We've also included **exam questions** to test how ready you are for the real thing.

There's even a free Online Edition you can read on your computer or tablet!

How to get your free Online Edition

Go to **cgpbooks.co.uk/extras** and enter this code...

1051 7320 2494 8781

This code only works for one person. If somebody else has used this book before you, they might have already claimed the Online Edition.

A-Level revision? It has to be CGP!

Published by CGP

Editors:
Katie Braid, Gordon Henderson, Emily Howe, Paul Jordin, Rachel Kordan, Sarah Pattison and Sophie Scott.

Contributors:
Antonio Angelosanto, Mike Bossart, Robert Clarke, Vikki Cunningham, Ian H. Davis, John Duffy, Max Fishel, Emma Grimwood, Lucy Muncaster, Derek Swain, Paul Warren and Christopher Workman.

ISBN: 978 1 78294 302 0

With thanks to Jamie Sinclair for the proofreading.
With thanks to Jan Greenway for the copyright research.

With thanks to NASA / Goddard Space Flight Center / Science Photo Library for permission to reproduce the photograph used on page 106.

Graph to show trend in atmospheric CO_2 Concentration and global temperature on page 108 based on data by EPICA Community Members 2004 and Siegenthaler et al 2005.

Cover Photo **Laguna Design**/Science Photo Library

Clipart from Corel®
Printed by Elanders Ltd, Newcastle upon Tyne.

Based on the classic CGP style created by Richard Parsons.

Contents

If you're revising for the **AS exams**, you'll need Modules 1-4.
If you're revising for the **A-Level exams**, you'll need the whole book.

Module 4: Section 1 — Basic Concepts and Hydrocarbons (AS)

Module 4: Section 2 — Alcohols, Haloalkanes & Analysis (AS)

Module 5: Section 1 — Rates, Equilibrium & pH

Module 5: Section 2 — Energy

Module 5: Section 3 — Transition Elements

Module 6: Section 1 — Aromatic Compounds & Carbonyls

Module 6: Section 2 — Nitrogen Compounds, Polymers & Synthesis

Module 6: Section 3 — Analysis

Do Well In Your Exams

The Scientific Process

'How Science Works' is all about the scientific process — how we develop and test scientific ideas. It's what scientists do all day, every day (well except at coffee time — never come between scientists and their coffee).

Scientists Come Up with **Theories** — Then **Test Them**...

Science tries to explain **how** and **why** things happen. It's all about seeking and gaining **knowledge** about the world around us. Scientists do this by **asking** questions and **suggesting** answers and then **testing** them, to see if they're correct — this is the **scientific process**.

1) **Ask** a question — make an **observation** and ask **why or how** whatever you've observed happens.
   E.g. Why does sodium chloride dissolve in water?
2) **Suggest** an answer, or part of an answer, by forming a **theory** or a **model** (a possible **explanation** of the observations or a description of what you think is happening actually happening).
   E.g. Sodium chloride is made up of charged particles which are pulled apart by the polar water molecules.
3) Make a **prediction** or **hypothesis** — a **specific testable statement**, based on the theory, about what will happen in a test situation.
   E.g. A solution of sodium chloride will conduct electricity much better than water does.
4) Carry out **tests** — to provide **evidence** that will support the prediction or refute it.
   E.g. Measure the conductivity of water and of sodium chloride solution.

A theory is only scientific if it can be tested.

...Then They **Tell** Everyone About Their **Results**...

The results are **published** — scientists need to let others know about their work. Scientists publish their results in **scientific journals**. These are just like normal magazines, only they contain **scientific reports** (called papers) instead of the latest celebrity gossip.

1) Scientific reports are similar to the **lab write-ups** you do in school. And just as a lab write-up is **reviewed** (marked) by your teacher, reports in scientific journals undergo **peer review** before they're published.

   Scientists use standard terminology when writing their reports. This way they know that other scientists will understand them. For instance, there are internationally agreed rules for naming organic compounds, so that scientists across the world will know exactly what substance is being referred to. See page 85.
2) The report is sent out to **peers** — other scientists who are experts in the **same area**. They go through it bit by bit, examining the methods and data, and checking it's all clear and logical. When the report is approved, it's **published**. This makes sure that work published in scientific journals is of a **good standard**.
3) But peer review **can't guarantee** the science is **correct** — other scientists still need to **reproduce** it.
4) Sometimes **mistakes** are made and bad work is published. Peer review **isn't perfect** but it's probably the best way for scientists to self-regulate their work and to publish **quality reports**.

...Then **Other Scientists** Will **Test** the Theory Too

1) Other scientists read the published theories and results, and try to **test the theory** themselves. This involves:
   - Repeating the **exact same experiments**.
   - Using the theory to make **new predictions** and then testing them with **new experiments**.
2) If all the experiments in the world provide evidence to back it up, the theory is thought of as **scientific 'fact'**.
3) If **new evidence** comes to light that **conflicts** with the current evidence the theory is questioned all over again. More rounds of **testing** will be carried out to try to find out where the theory **falls down**.

This is how the **scientific process works** — **evidence** supports a theory, loads of other scientists read it and test it for themselves, eventually all the scientists in the world **agree** with it and then bingo, you get to **learn** it.

This is how scientists arrived at the structure of the atom (see p.16-17) — and how they came to the conclusion that electrons are arranged in shells and orbitals. As is often the case, it took years and years for these models to be developed and accepted.

The Scientific Process

*If the **Evidence** Supports a Theory, It's **Accepted** — for Now*

Our currently accepted theories have survived this '**trial by evidence**'. They've been tested **over and over again** and each time the results have backed them up. **BUT**, and this is a big but (teehee), they never become totally indisputable fact. Scientific **breakthroughs** or **advances** could provide new ways to question and test the theory, which could lead to **changes and challenges** to it. Then the testing starts all over again...

And this, my friend, is the **tentative nature of scientific knowledge** — it's always **changing** and **evolving**.

For example, when CFCs were first used in fridges in the 1930s, scientists thought they were problem-free — there was no evidence to say otherwise. It was decades before anyone found out that CFCs were actually making a massive hole in the ozone layer. See p 106.

***Evidence** Comes From **Lab Experiments**...*

1) Results from **controlled experiments** in **laboratories** are **great**.
2) A lab is the easiest place to **control variables** so that they're all **kept constant** (except for the one you're investigating).
3) This means you can draw meaningful **conclusions**.

For example, if you're investigating how temperature affects the rate of a reaction, you need to keep everything but the temperature constant, e.g. the pH of the solution, the concentration of the solution, etc.

*...But You **Can't** Always do a Lab Experiment*

There are things you **can't** study in a lab. And outside the lab controlling the variables is tricky, if not impossible.

- *Are increasing CO_2 emissions causing climate change?*
  There are other variables which may have an effect, such as changes in solar activity. You can't easily rule out every possibility. Also, climate change is a very **gradual process**. Scientists won't be able to tell if their predictions are correct for donkey's years.
- *Does drinking chlorinated tap water increase the risk of developing certain cancers?*
  There are always differences between groups of people. The best you can do is to have a **well-designed study** using **matched groups** — **choose two groups** of people (those who drink tap water and those who don't) which are **as similar as possible** (same mix of ages, same mix of diets etc). But you still can't rule out every possibility. Taking new-born identical twins and treating them identically, except for making one drink gallons of tap water and the other only pure water, might be a fairer test, but it would present huge **ethical problems**.

Samantha thought her study was very well designed — especially the fitted bookshelf.

*Science Helps to Inform **Decision-Making***

Lots of scientific work eventually leads to **important discoveries** that **could** benefit humankind — but there are often **risks** attached (and almost always **financial costs**). **Society** (that's you, me and everyone else) must weigh up the information in order to **make decisions** — about the way we live, what we eat, what we drive, and so on. Information can also be used by **politicians** to devise policies and laws.

- **Chlorine** is added to water in **small quantities** to disinfect it. Some studies link drinking chlorinated water with certain types of cancer (see page 65). But the risks from drinking water contaminated by nasty bacteria are far, far greater. There are other ways to get rid of bacteria in water, but they're heaps **more expensive**.
- Scientific advances mean that **non-polluting hydrogen-fuelled cars** can be made. They're better for the environment, but are really expensive. And it'd cost a lot to adapt filling stations to store hydrogen.
- Pharmaceutical drugs are really expensive to develop, and drug companies want to make money. So they put most of their efforts into developing drugs that they can sell for a good price. Society has to consider the **cost** of buying new drugs — the **NHS** can't afford the most expensive drugs without **sacrificing** something else.

So there you have it — how science works...

Hopefully these pages have given you a nice intro to how science works. You need to understand it for the exam, and for life. Once you've got it sussed it's time to move on to the really good stuff — the chemistry. Bet you can't wait...

Planning Experiments

As well as doing practical work in class, you can get asked about it in your exams too. Harsh I know, but that's how it goes. You need to be able to plan the perfect experiment and make improvements to ones other people have planned.

Make Sure You **Plan** Your **Experiment Carefully**

It's really important to plan an experiment well if you want to get accurate and precise results. Here's how to go about it...

Have a peek at page 12 to find out more about accurate and precise results.

1) Work out the **aim** of the experiment — what are you trying to find out?
2) Identify the **independent**, **dependent** and other **variables** (see below).
3) Decide what **data** to collect.
4) Select **appropriate equipment** which will give you accurate results.
5) Make a **risk assessment** and plan any safety precautions.
6) Write out a **detailed method**.
7) Carry out **tests** — to gather **evidence** to address the aim of your experiment.

Make it a **Fair Test** — Control your **Variables**

You probably know this all off by heart but it's easy to get mixed up sometimes. So here's a quick recap:

Variable — A variable is a **quantity** that has the **potential to change**, e.g. mass.
There are two types of variable commonly referred to in experiments:

- **Independent variable** — the thing that you **change** in an experiment.
- **Dependent variable** — the thing that you **measure** in an experiment.

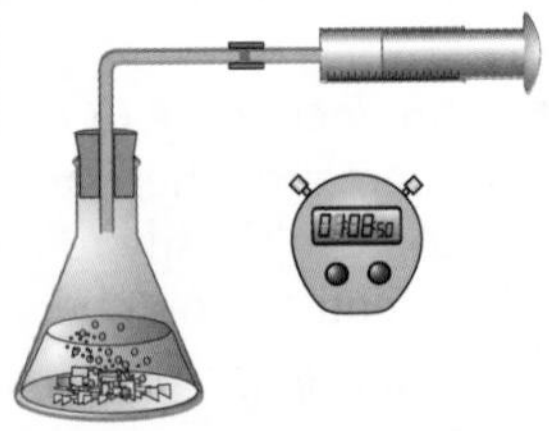

As well as the independent and dependent variables, you need to think of all the other variables in your experiment and plan ways to keep each of those the same.

For example, if you're investigating the effect of **temperature** on rate of reaction using the apparatus on the right, the variables will be:

Independent variable	Temperature
Dependent variable	Volume of gas produced — you can measure this by collecting it in a gas syringe.
Other variables	E.g. concentration and volume of solutions, mass of solids, pressure, the presence of a catalyst and the surface area of any solid reactants.

You MUST control your other variables so they're always the same.

Collect the Appropriate **Data**

Experiments always involve collecting **data** and you need to decide what data to collect.

1) There are different types of data, so it helps to know what they are:
   - **Discrete** — you get discrete data by **counting**. E.g. the number of bubbles produced in a reaction.
   - **Continuous** — a continuous variable can have **any value** on a scale. For example, the volume of gas produced. You can never measure the exact value of a continuous variable.
   - **Categoric** — a categoric variable has values that can be sorted into **categories**. For example, the colours of solutions might be blue, red and green.
2) You need to make sure the data you collect is appropriate for your experiment.

Example: A student suggests measuring the rate of the following reaction by observing how conductivity changes over the course of the reaction:
$NaOH_{(aq)} + CH_3CH_2Br_{(l)} \rightarrow CH_3CH_2OH_{(l)} + NaBr_{(aq)}$
Suggest what is wrong with the student's method, and how it could be improved.

You couldn't collect data about how the **conductivity changes** over the course of the reaction, because there are **salts** in both the reactants and the products.

Instead you could use a **pH meter** to measure how the **pH changes** from basic (due to sodium hydroxide) to neutral.

Planning Experiments

Choose *Appropriate* Equipment — Think about *Size* and *Sensitivity*

Selecting the right apparatus may sound easy but it's something you need to think carefully about.

1) The equipment has to be **appropriate** for the specific experiment.

   For example, if you want to measure the volume of gas produced in a reaction, you need to make sure you use apparatus which will collect the gas, without letting any escape.

2) The equipment needs to be the right **size**.

   For example, if you're using a gas syringe to collect a gas, it needs to be big enough to collect **all** the gas produced during the experiment, or the plunger will just fall out the end. You might need to do some **calculations** to work out what size of syringe to use.

3) The equipment needs to be the right level of **sensitivity**.

   If you want to measure 10 cm^3 of a liquid, it will be more accurate to use a measuring cylinder that is graduated to the nearest 0.5 cm^3 than to the nearest 1 cm^3. A burette would be most accurate though (they can measure to the nearest 0.1 cm^3).

Risk Assessments Help You to Work *Safely*

1) When you're planning an experiment, you need to carry out a **risk assessment**. To do this, you need to identify:
   - All the **dangers** in the experiment, e.g. any hazardous compounds or naked flames.
   - **Who** is at **risk** from these dangers.
   - What can be done to **reduce the risk**, such as wearing goggles or working in a fume cupboard.
2) You need to make sure you're working **ethically** too. This is most important if there are other people or animals involved. You have to put their welfare first.

Methods Must be *Clear* and *Detailed*

When **writing** or **evaluating** a method, you need to think about all of the things on these two pages. The method must be **clear** and **detailed** enough for anyone to follow — it's important that **other people** can recreate your experiment and get the **same** results. Make sure your method includes:

1) All **substances** and **quantities** to be used.
2) How to **control** variables.
3) The exact **apparatus** needed (a diagram is usually helpful to show the set up).
4) Any **safety precautions** that should be taken.
5) What **data** to collect and **how** to collect it.

Practice Questions

Q1 Briefly outline the steps involved in planning an experiment.

Q2 What three things should you consider when choosing the best apparatus for your experiment?

Exam Question

Q1 A student carries out an experiment to investigate how the rate of the following reaction changes with the concentration of hydrochloric acid: $Mg_{(s)} + 2HCl_{(aq)} \rightarrow MgCl_{2\,(aq)} + H_{2\,(g)}$

The student decides to measure how the pH changes over time using litmus paper.
Explain why this method of measuring pH is unsuitable, and suggest an alternative method. [2 marks]

Revision time — independent variable. Exam mark — dependent variable...

I wouldn't advise you to investigate the effect of revision on exam marks. Just trust me — more revision = better marks. But if you were to investigate it, there are all manner of variables that you'd need to control. The amount of sleep you had the night before, how much coffee you drank in the morning, your level of panic on entering the exam hall...

Practical Techniques

The way you carry out your experiment is important, so here's a nice round up of some of the techniques chemists use all the time. You've probably met some of them before, which should hopefully make it all a bit easier. Hopefully... :-)

Results Should be *Precise*

1) **Precise** results are **repeatable** and **reproducible**. **Repeatable** means that if the **same** person does the experiment again using the same methods and equipment, they'll get the same results. **Reproducible** means that if someone **else** does the experiment, or a different **method** or piece of **equipment** is used, the results will still be the same.
2) To make sure your results are precise, you need to **minimise** any **errors** that might sneak into your data. This includes:
   - using **apparatus** and **techniques** correctly,
   - taking **measurements** correctly,
   - **repeating** your experiments and calculating a **mean**.

Make Sure You **Measure** Substances **Correctly**

The **state** (solid, liquid or gas) that your substance is in will determine **how** you decide to measure it.

1) You weigh **solids** using a **balance**. Here are a couple of things to look out for:
   - Put the container you are weighing your substance into on the balance, and make sure the balance is set to exactly zero before you start weighing out your substance.
   - If you need to **transfer** the solid into another container, make sure that it's **all** transferred. For example, if you're making up a standard solution you could wash any remaining solid into the new container using the solvent. Or, you could **reweigh** the weighing container after you've transferred the solid so you can work out **exactly** how much you added to your experiment.
2) There are a few methods you might use to measure the volume of a liquid. Whichever method you use, always read the volume from the **bottom** of the **meniscus** (the curved upper surface of the liquid) when it's at **eye level**.

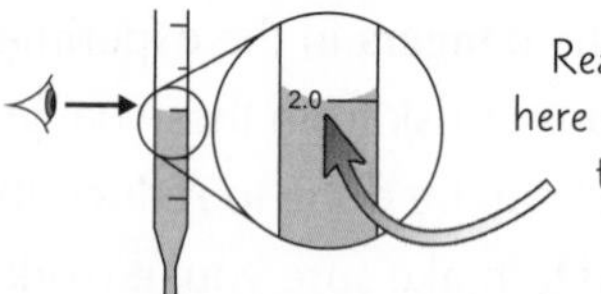

Pipettes are long, narrow tubes that are used to **suck up** an **accurate volume** of liquid and transfer it to another container. They are often **calibrated** to allow for the fact that the last drop of liquid stays in the pipette when the liquid is ejected. This reduces transfer errors.

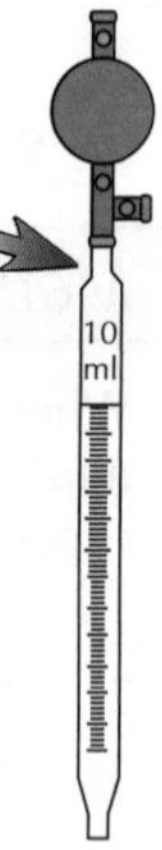

Burettes measure from **top** to **bottom** (so when they are **full**, the scale reads **zero**). They have a **tap** at the bottom which you can use to release the liquid into another container (you can even release it drop by drop). To use a burette, take an **initial reading**, and once you've released as much liquid as you want, take a **final reading**. The **difference** between the readings tells you how much liquid you used.

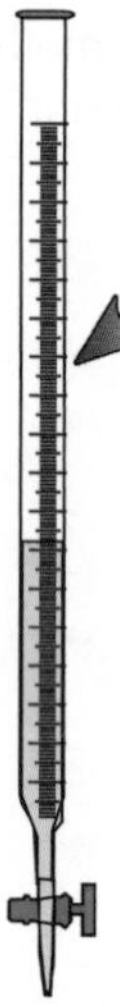

Burettes are used a lot for titrations. There's loads more about titrations on pages 30-33.

Volumetric flasks allow you to **accurately** measure a very **specific** volume of liquid. They come in various **sizes** (e.g. 100 ml, 250 ml) and there's a **line** on the neck that marks the volume that they measure. They're used to make **accurate dilutions** and **standard solutions**. To use them, first measure out and add the liquid or solid that is being diluted or dissolved. Rinse out the measuring vessel into the volumetric flask with a little solvent to make sure everything's been transferred. Then fill the flask with solvent to the **bottom** of the neck. Fill the neck **drop by drop** until the bottom of the meniscus is **level** with the line.

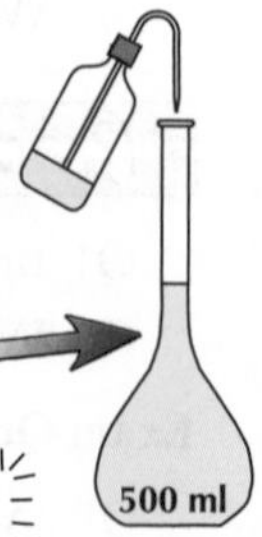

A standard solution is a solution with a precisely known concentration. You can find out how they're made and used on page 31.

3) Gases can be measured with a **gas syringe**. They should be measured at **room temperature** and **pressure** as the **volume** of a gas **changes** with temperature and pressure. Before you use the syringe, you should make sure it's completely **sealed** and that the **plunger** moves **smoothly**.

Once you've measured a quantity of a substance you need to be careful you don't **lose** any. In particular, think about how to minimise losses as you transfer it from the measuring equipment to the reaction container.

Practical Techniques

Measure **Temperature** Accurately

I'm sure you've heard this before, so I'll be quick... You can use a **thermometer** or a **temperature probe** to measure the temperature of a substance (a temperature probe is like a thermometer but it will always have a **digital display**).

- Make sure the **bulb** of your thermometer or temperature probe is **completely submerged** in any mixture you're measuring.
- Wait for the temperature to **stabilise** before you take an initial reading
- If you're using a thermometer with a scale, read off your measurement at **eye level** to make sure it's accurate.

Qualitative Tests Can be Harder to **Reproduce**

Qualitative tests measure **physical qualities** (e.g. colour) while **quantitative** tests measure numerical data, (e.g. mass). So if you carried out a reaction and noticed that heat was produced, this would be a **qualitative** observation. If you **measured** the temperature change with a thermometer, this would be **quantitative**.

Qualitative tests can be harder to **reproduce** because they're often **subjective** (based on **opinion**), such as describing the **colour** or **cloudiness** of a solution. There are ways to **reduce** the subjectivity of qualitative results though. For example:

- If you're looking for a **colour change**, put a **white background** behind your reaction container.
- If you're looking for a **precipitate** to form, mark an **X** on a piece of paper and place it under the reaction container. Your solution is 'cloudy' when you can **no longer see** the X.

There are Specific Techniques for Synthesising **Organic Compounds**

Synthesis is used to **make** one **organic compound** from another. There are a number of techniques that chemists use to help them make and purify their products. For example:

These techniques are covered in more detail on pages 112-113.

1) **Reflux** — heating a reaction mixture in a flask fitted with a **condenser** so that any materials that **evaporate**, condense and drip back into the mixture.
2) **Distillation** — gently heating a mixture so that the compounds evaporate off in order of **increasing boiling point** and can be collected separately. This can be done **during** a reaction to collect a product as it forms, or **after** the reaction is **finished** to purify the mixture.
3) **Removing water soluble impurities** — adding **water** to an organic mixture in a separating funnel. Any **water soluble impurities** move out of the organic layer and dissolve in the aqueous layer. The layers have different **densities** so are easy to separate.

More techniques for organic synthesis are covered on pages 198 and 199.

Practice Questions

Q1 Give three ways that you could improve the precision of an experiment.

Q2 How would you measure out a desired quantity of a solid? And a gas?

Q3 How could you make the results of an experiment measuring time taken for a precipitate to form less subjective?

Exam Question

Q1 A student dilutes a 1 mol dm^{-3} solution of sodium chloride to 0.1 mol dm^{-3} as follows:

He measures 10 cm^3 of 1 mol dm^{-3} sodium chloride solution in a pipette and puts this into a 100 cm^3 volumetric flask. He then tops up the volumetric flask with distilled water until the top of the meniscus is at 100 cm^3.

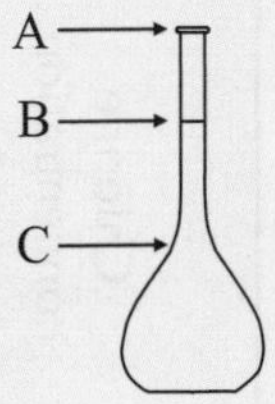

a) What has the student done incorrectly? What should he have done instead? [1 mark]

b) Which of the arrows in the diagram on the right indicates the level to which you should fill a volumetric flask? [1 mark]

Reflux, take it easy...

It might seem like there's a lot to do to make sure your results are accurate, but you should get lots of practice in practicals. Before long you'll be measuring temperatures and volumes with your eyes shut (metaphorically speaking).

Presenting Results

Once you've collected the data from your experiment, it's not time to stop, put your feet up and have a cup of tea — you've got some presenting to do. Results tables need converting into graphs and other pretty pictures.

Organise Your Results in a **Table**

It's a good idea to set up a table to **record** the **results** of your experiment in. When you draw a table, make sure you **include** enough **rows** and **columns** to **record all of the data** you need. You might also need to include a column for **processing** your data (e.g. working out an average).

Make sure each **column** has a **heading** so you know what's going to be recorded where.

The **units** should be in the **column heading**, not the table itself.

Temperature (°C)	Time (s)	Volume of gas evolved (cm^3)			Average volume of gas evolved (cm^3)
		Run 1	Run 2	Run 3	
20	10	8.1	7.6	8.5	(8.1 + 7.6 + 8.5) ÷ 3 = 8.1
	20	17.7	19.0	20.1	(17.7 + 19.0 + 20.1) ÷ 3 = 18.9
	30	28.5	29.9	30.0	(28.5 + 29.9 + 30.0) ÷ 3 = 29.5

You'll need to repeat each test **at least three** times to check your results are **precise**.

You can find the **mean result** by **adding up** the data from each repeat and **dividing** by the number of repeats.

Graphs: **Line, Bar or Scatter** — Use the **Best Type**

You'll often need to make a **graph** of your results.
Graphs make your data **easier to understand** — so long as you choose the right type.

When drawing graphs, the dependent variable should go on the y-axis, the independent on the x-axis.

Line graphs are best when you have **two sets of continuous data**. For example:

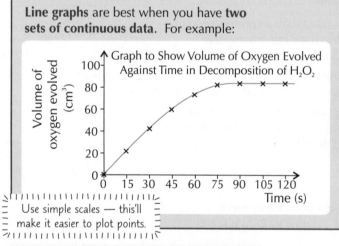

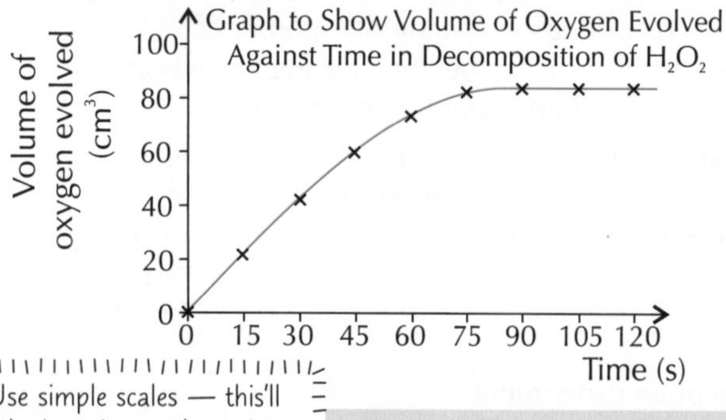

Use simple scales — this'll make it easier to plot points.

Scatter plots are great for showing how two sets of data are related (or **correlated**). Don't try to join all the points — draw a **line of best fit** to show the **trend**.

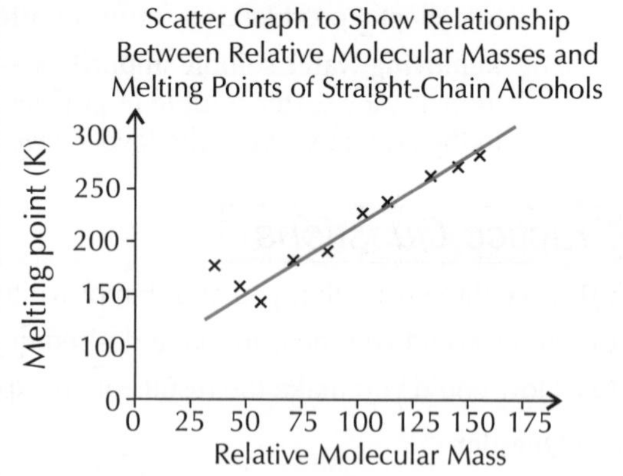

You should use a **bar chart** when one of your data sets is **categoric**. For example:

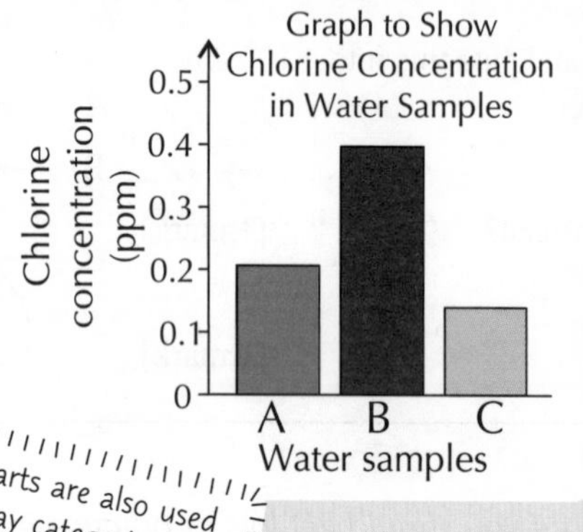

Pie charts are also used to display categoric data.

Apple and blackberry was number one on Jane's pie chart

Whatever type of graph you make, you'll ONLY get full marks if you:

- Choose a sensible **scale** — don't do a tiny graph in the corner of the paper, or massive axes where the data only takes up a tiny part of the graph.
- **Label** both **axes** — including units.
- Plot your points accurately — use a **sharp pencil**.

Sometimes you might need to work out the gradient of a graph, e.g. to work out the rate of a reaction. There are details of how to do this on pages 78 and 79.

Presenting Results

Don't Forget About **Units**

Units are really important — 10 g is a bit different from 10 kg, so make sure you don't forget to add them to your **tables** and **graphs**. It's often a good idea to write down the units on each line of any **calculations** you do — it makes things less confusing, particularly if you need to convert between two different units.

Here are some useful examples:

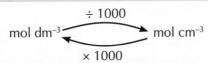

Concentration can be measured in **mol dm^{-3}** (M) and **mol cm^{-3}**.

mol dm^{-3} → ÷ 1000 → mol cm^{-3}

mol cm^{-3} → × 1000 → mol dm^{-3}

Example: Write 2 mol dm^{-3} in mol cm^{-3}.

To convert 0.2 mol dm^{-3} into mol cm^{-3} you divide by 1000.

0.2 mol dm^{-3} ÷ 1000 = **2 × 10^{-4} mol cm^{-3}**

Standard form is useful for writing very big or very small numbers.

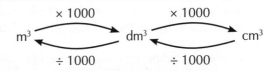

Volume can be measured in **m^3**, **dm^3** and **cm^3**.

m^3 → × 1000 → dm^3 → × 1000 → cm^3

cm^3 → ÷ 1000 → dm^3 → ÷ 1000 → m^3

Example: Write 6 dm^3 in m^3 and cm^3.

To convert 6 dm^3 into m^3 you divide by 1000.

6 dm^3 ÷ 1000 = 0.006 m^3 = **6 × 10^{-3} m^3**

To convert 6 dm^3 into cm^3 you multiply by 1000.

6 dm^3 × 1000 = 6000 cm^3 = **6 × 10^3 cm^3**

Round to the **Lowest Number** of **Significant Figures**

The first significant figure of a number is the first digit that isn't a zero. The second, third and fourth significant figures follow on immediately after the first (even if they're zeros).

You always need to be aware of **significant figures** when working with data.

1) The rule is the same for when doing calculations with the results from your experiment, or when doing calculations in the exam — you have to round your answer to the **lowest number of significant figures** (s.f.) given in the question.
2) It always helps to write down the number of significant figures you've rounded to after your answer — it shows you really know what you're talking about.
3) If you're converting between **standard** and **ordinary form**, you have to keep the **same number** of significant figures. For example, 0.0060 mol dm^{-3} is the same as 6.0 × 10^{-3} mol dm^{-3} — they're both given to 2 s.f..

Example: 13.5 cm^3 of a 0.51 mol dm^{-3} solution of sodium hydroxide reacts with 1.5 mol dm^{-3} hydrochloric acid. Calculate the volume of hydrochloric acid required to neutralise the sodium hydroxide

No. of moles of NaOH: (13.5 cm^3 × 0.51 mol dm^{-3}) ÷ 1000 = 6.885 × 10^{-3} mol

(3 s.f.) (2 s.f.)

You don't need to round intermediate answers. Rounding too early will make your final answer less accurate.

Volume of HCl: (6.885 × 10^{-3}) mol × 1000 ÷ 1.5 mol dm^{-3} = 4.59 cm^3 = **4.6 cm^3 (2 s.f.)**

Final answer should be rounded to 2 s.f.

Make sure all your units match when you're doing calculations.

Practice Questions

Q1 Why is it always a good idea to repeat your experiments?

Q2 How would you convert an answer from m^3 to dm^3?

Q3 How do you decide how many significant figures you should round your answer to?

Exam Question

Q1 10 cm^3 sodium hydroxide solution is titrated with 0.50 mol dm^{-3} hydrochloric acid to find its concentration. The titration is repeated three times and the volumes of hydrochloric acid used are: 7.30 cm^3, 7.25 cm^3, 7.25 cm^3.

a) What is the mean volume of hydrochloric acid recorded in dm^3? [1 mark]

b) What is the concentration of hydrochloric acid in mol cm^{-3}? [1 mark]

Significant figures — a result of far too many cream cakes...

When you draw graphs, always be careful to get your axes round the right way. The thing you've been changing (the independent variable) goes on the x-axis, and the thing you've been measuring (the dependent variable) is on the y-axis.

Analysing Results

You're not quite finished yet... there's still time to look at your results and try and make sense of them. Graphs can help you to see patterns but don't try and read too much in to them — they won't tell you what grade you're going to get.

Watch Out For **Anomalous** Results

1) Anomalous results are ones that **don't fit** in with the other values and are likely to be wrong.
2) They're often due to **random errors**, e.g. if a drop in a titration is too big and shoots past the end point, or if a syringe plunger gets stuck whilst collecting gas produced in a reaction.
3) When looking at results in tables or graphs, you always need to look to see if there are any anomalies — you need to **ignore** these results when calculating means or drawing lines of best fit.

There's more about random errors on pages 12 and 13.

Example: Calculate the mean volume from the results in the table below.

Titration Number	1	2	3	4
Titre Volume (cm^3)	15.20	15.30	15.25	15.50

Titre **4** isn't **concordant** (doesn't match) the other results so you need to ignore it and just use the other three:

$$\frac{15.20 + 15.30 + 15.25}{3} = \mathbf{15.25\ cm^3}$$

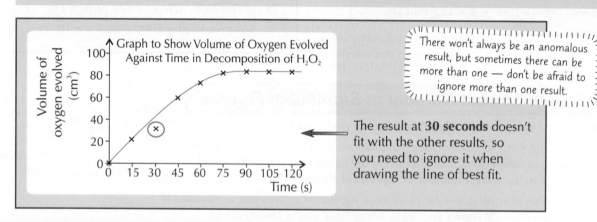

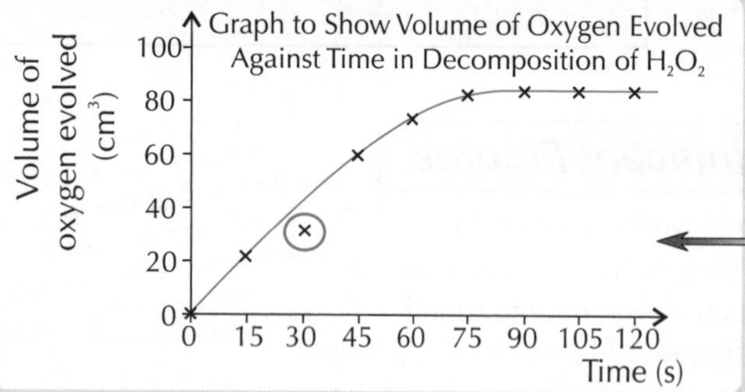

There won't always be an anomalous result, but sometimes there can be more than one — don't be afraid to ignore more than one result.

The result at **30 seconds** doesn't fit with the other results, so you need to ignore it when drawing the line of best fit.

Scatter Graphs Show The **Relationship** Between Variables

Correlation describes the **relationship** between two variables — the independent one and the dependent one. Data can show:

1) **Positive correlation**
As one variable **increases** the other **increases**.

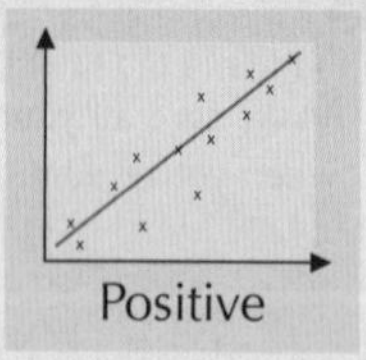

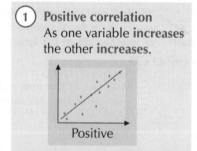

2) **Negative correlation**
As one variable **increases** the other **decreases**.

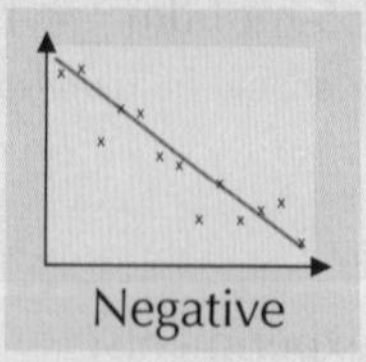

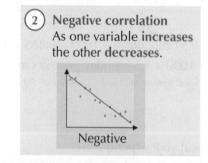

3) **No correlation**
There is **no relationship** between the two variables.

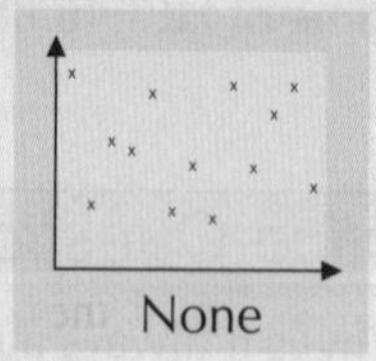

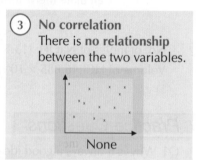

Correlation **Doesn't** Mean **Cause** — Don't Jump to Conclusions

1) Ideally, only **two** quantities would **ever** change in any experiment — everything else would remain **constant**.
2) But in experiments or studies outside the lab, you **can't** usually control all the variables. So even if two variables are correlated, the change in one may **not** be causing the change in the other. Both changes might be caused by a **third variable**.

Example:

Some studies have found a correlation between **drinking chlorinated tap water** and the risk of developing certain cancers. So some people argue that water shouldn't have chlorine added.

BUT it's hard to control all the **variables** between people who drink tap water and people who don't. It could be due to other lifestyle factors.

Or, the cancer risk could be affected by something else in tap water — or by whatever the non-tap water drinkers drink instead...

Analysing Results

Don't Get **Carried Away** When Drawing Conclusions

The **data** should always **support** the conclusion. This may sound obvious but it's easy to **jump** to conclusions. Conclusions have to be **specific** — not make sweeping generalisations.

Example:

1) The rate of an enzyme-controlled reaction was measured at **10 °C, 20 °C, 30 °C, 40 °C, 50 °C** and **60 °C**. All other variables were kept constant, and the results are shown in the graph below.

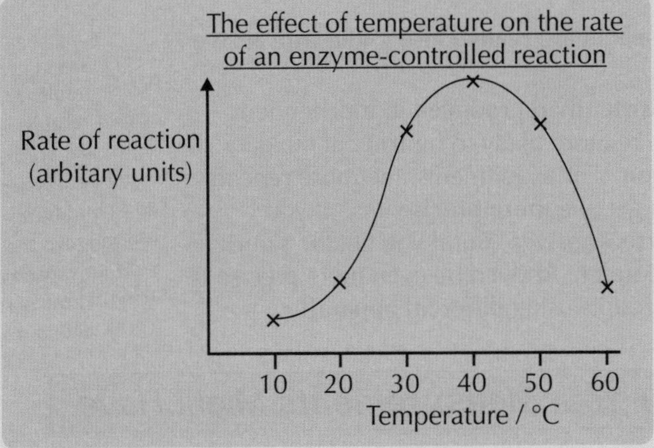

2) A science magazine **concluded** from this data that enzyme X works best at **40 °C**.
3) The data **doesn't** support this. The enzyme **could** work best at 42 °C or 47 °C but you can't tell from the data because **increases** of **10 °C** at a time were used. The rate of reaction at in-between temperatures **wasn't** measured.
4) All you know is that it's faster at **40 °C** than at any of the other temperatures tested.
5) The experiment **ONLY** gives information about this particular enzyme-controlled reaction. You can't conclude that **all** enzyme-controlled reactions happen faster at a particular temperature — only this one. And you can't say for sure that doing the experiment at, say, a different constant pressure, wouldn't give a different optimum temperature.

Practice Questions

Q1 How do you treat anomalous results when calculating averages? And when drawing lines of best fit?

Q2 What is negative correlation?

Exam Question

Q1 A student carried out an investigation to study how the rate of a reaction changed with temperature. He plotted his results on the graph shown on the right.

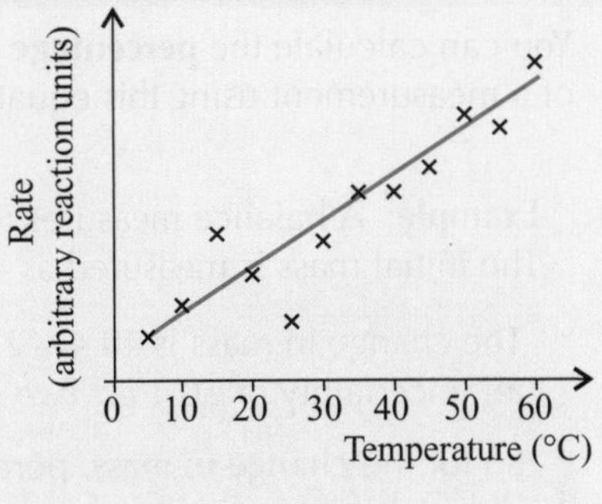

a) Give the temperatures at which any anomalous results occurred. [1 mark]

b) What type of correlation is there between temperature and rate of reaction? [1 mark]

c) Which of the following statements are appropriate conclusions to draw from this experiment?

1 The rate of the reaction is highest at 60 °C.
2 Increasing the temperature causes the rate of the reaction to increase.
3 Between 5 °C and 60 °C, the rate of the reaction increased as temperature increased.

A Statements 1, 2 and 3.
B Statements 2 and 3 only.
C Statement 3 only.
D Statement 2 only.

[1 mark]

Correlation Street — my favourite programme...

Watch out for bias when you're reading about the results of scientific studies. People often tell you what they want you to know. So a bottled water company might say that studies have shown that chlorinated tap water can cause cancer, without mentioning any of the doubts in the results. After all, they want to persuade you to buy their drinks.

Evaluating Experiments

So you've planned an experiment, collected your data (no less than three times, mind you) and put it all onto a lovely graph. Now it's time to sit back, relax and... work out everything you did wrong. That's science, I'm afraid.

You Need to Look **Critically** at Your Experiment

There are a few terms that'll come in handy when you're evaluating how convincing your results are...

1) **Valid results** — Valid results answer the **original question**. For example, if you haven't **controlled all the variables** your results won't be valid, because you won't be testing just the thing you wanted to.

2) **Accurate results** — Accurate results are those that are **really close** to the **true** answer.

3) **Precise results** — **Precise** results can be **consistently reproduced** in independent experiments. If results are reproducible they're more likely to be **true**. If the data isn't precise you **can't draw** a valid **conclusion**. For experiments, the **more repeats** you do, and the closer together the data you get, the **more precise** it is. If you get the **same result** twice, it could be the correct answer. But if you get the same result **20 times**, it's much more likely to be correct. And it'd be even more precise if everyone in the class gets about the same results using **different apparatus**.

Precise results are sometimes called reliable results. So, just like precise results, reliable results are repeatable and reproducible, and you can improve the reliability of an experiment by taking repeat readings and calculating a mean.

Uncertainty is the Amount of **Error** Your **Measurements** Might Have

1) Any measurements you make will have **uncertainty** in them due to the limits to the **sensitivity** of the equipment you used.
2) If you use a weighing scale that measures to the nearest 0.1 g, then the **true** weight of any substance you weigh could be up to 0.05 g **more than** or **less than** your reading. Your measurement has an **uncertainty** (or error) of ±0.05 g in either direction.
3) The ± sign tells you the **range** in which the true value could lie. The range can also be called the **margin of error**.
4) For any piece of equipment you use, the uncertainty will be **half** the **smallest increment** the equipment can measure, in either direction.
5) If you're **combining measurements**, you'll need to combine their **uncertainties**. For example, if you're calculating a temperature change by measuring an initial and a final temperature, the **total** uncertainty for the temperature change will be the uncertainties for both measurements added together.

The **Percentage Error** in a Result Should be Calculated

You can calculate the **percentage error** of a measurement using this equation:

$$\text{percentage error} = \frac{\text{uncertainty}}{\text{reading}} \times 100$$

Percentage error is sometimes called percentage uncertainty.

Example: A balance measures to the nearest 0.2 g, and is used to measure the **change in mass** of a substance. The initial mass is measured as 40.4 g. The final mass is measured as 22.0 g. Calculate the percentage error.

The change in mass is 40.4 – 22.0 = 18.4 g. The balance measures to the nearest 0.2 g, so **each reading** has an uncertainty of ±0.1 g. **Two** readings have been combined, so the **total uncertainty** is 0.1 × 2 = 0.2 g.

So for the **change in mass**, percentage error = $\frac{0.2}{18.4} \times 100 = \mathbf{1.1\%}$

The percentage error for each reading is just 0.1 ÷ reading × 100. E.g. for the initial mass it's 0.1 ÷ 40.4 × 100 = 0.2%

You Can **Minimise** the Percentage Error

1) One obvious way to **reduce errors** in your measurements is to use the most **sensitive equipment** available to you.
2) A bit of clever **planning** can also improve your results. If you measure out **5 cm³** of liquid in a measuring cylinder that has increments of 0.1 cm³ then the percentage error is (0.05 ÷ 5) × 100 = **1%**.
But if you measure **10 cm³** of liquid in the same measuring cylinder the percentage error is (0.05 ÷ 10) × 100 = **0.5%**. Hey presto — you've just halved the percentage error.
So the percentage error can be reduced by planning an experiment so you use a **larger volume** of liquid.
3) The general principle is that the **smaller** the measurement, the **larger** the percentage error.

Evaluating Experiments

Errors Can Be Systematic or Random

1) **Systematic errors** are the same every time you repeat the experiment. They may be caused by the **set-up** or **equipment** you used. For example, if the 10.00 cm^3 pipette you used to measure out a sample for titration actually only measured 9.95 cm^3, your sample would have been about 0.05 cm^3 too small **every time** you repeated the experiment.
2) **Random errors** vary — they're what make the results a bit **different** each time you repeat an experiment. The errors when you make a reading from a burette are random. You have to estimate or round the level when it's between two marks — so sometimes your figure will be **above** the real one, and sometimes it will be **below**.
3) **Repeating an experiment** and finding the mean of your results helps to deal with **random errors**. The results that are a bit high will be **cancelled out** by the ones that are a bit low. So your results will be more **precise** (reliable). But repeating your results won't get rid of any **systematic errors**, so your results won't get more **accurate**.

This should be a photo of a scientist. I don't know what happened — it's a random error...

Think About How the Experiment Could Be Improved

In your evaluation you need to think about anything that you could have done differently to improve your results. Here are some things to think about...

1) **Whether your method gives you valid results.**
   - Will the data you collected answer the question your experiment aimed to answer?
   - Did you control all your variables?

2) **How you could improve the accuracy of your results.**
   - Was the apparatus you used on an appropriate scale for your measurements?
   - Could you use more sensitive equipment to reduce the random errors and uncertainty of your results?

3) **Whether your results are precise.**
   - Did you repeat the experiment, and were the results you got similar?

Practice Questions

Q1 What's the difference between the accuracy and precision of results?

Q2 What's the uncertainty of a balance that reads to the nearest 0.1 g?

Q3 How do you calculate percentage error?

Q4 Give two ways of reducing percentage error.

Q5 How can you reduce the random errors in your experiments?

Exam Question

Q1 A student carried out an experiment to determine the temperature change in the reaction between citric acid and sodium bicarbonate using the following method:

1. Measure out 25.0 cm^3 of 1.00 mol dm^{-3} citric acid solution in a measuring cylinder and put it in a polystyrene cup.
2. Weigh out 2.10 g sodium bicarbonate and add it to the citric acid solution.
3. Place a thermometer in the solution and measure the temperature change over one minute.

a) The measuring cylinder the student uses measures to the nearest 0.5 cm^3. What is the percentage error of the student's measurement? [1 mark]

b) The student's result is different to the documented value. How could you change the method to give a more accurate measurement for the change in temperature of the complete reaction? [2 marks]

Repeat your results: Your results, your results, your results, your results...

So there you have it, folks. All you need to know about planning, carrying out and analysing experiments. Always look out for where errors could be creeping in to your experimental methods. And make sure you're confident at working out uncertainties and percentage errors. Have another read of that bit if you're feeling a bit... well... uncertain.

The Atom

This stuff about atoms and elements should be ingrained in your brain from GCSE. You do need to know it perfectly though if you are to negotiate your way through the field of man-eating tigers which is Chemistry.

Atoms are made up of Protons, Neutrons and Electrons

Atoms are the stuff **all** elements and compounds are made of.
They're made up of 3 types of **subatomic** particle — **protons**, **neutrons** and **electrons**.

Electrons

1) Electrons have **–1** charge.
2) They whizz around the nucleus in **orbitals**. The orbitals take up most of the **volume** of the atom.

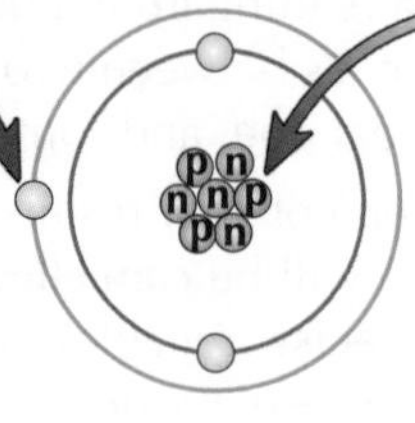

Nucleus

1) Most of the **mass** of the atom is concentrated in the nucleus.
2) The **diameter** of the nucleus is rather titchy compared to the whole atom.
3) The nucleus is where you find the **protons** and **neutrons**.

The mass and charge of these subatomic particles are **tiny**, so **relative mass** and **relative charge** are used instead.

Subatomic particle	Relative mass	Relative charge
Proton	1	+1
Neutron	1	0
Electron, e^-	$\frac{1}{2000}$	–1

The mass of an electron is negligible compared to a proton or a neutron — this means you can usually ignore it.

Nuclear Symbols Show Numbers of Subatomic Particles

You can figure out the **number** of protons, neutrons and electrons from the **nuclear symbol**.

$$^{A}_{Z}\mathrm{X}$$

Mass (nucleon) number (A)
This tells you the **total** number of **protons** and **neutrons** in the nucleus.

Element symbol (X)

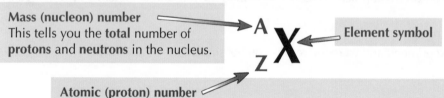

Atomic (proton) number (Z)

1) This is the number of **protons** in the nucleus — it identifies the element.
2) **All** atoms of the same element have the **same** number of protons.

Sometimes the atomic number is left out of the nuclear symbol, e.g. ^{7}Li. You don't really need it because the element's symbol tells you its value.

1) For **neutral** atoms, which have no overall charge, the number of electrons is **the same as** the number of protons.
2) The number of neutrons is just **mass number minus atomic number**, i.e. 'top minus bottom' in the nuclear symbol.

Nuclear Symbol	Atomic Number	Mass Number	Protons	Electrons	Neutrons
$^{7}_{3}\mathrm{Li}$	3	7	3	3	7 – 3 = 4
$^{19}_{9}\mathrm{F}$	9	19	9	9	19 – 9 = 10
$^{24}_{12}\mathrm{Mg}$	12	24	12	12	24 – 12 = 12

"Hello, I'm Newt Ron..."

Ions have Different Numbers of Protons and Electrons

Negative ions have **more electrons** than protons...

F^-

The negative charge means that there's 1 more electron than there are protons. F has 9 protons (see table above), so F^- must have 10 electrons. The overall charge = +9 – 10 = –1.

...and **positive** ions have **fewer electrons** than protons.

Mg^{2+}

The 2+ charge means that there are 2 fewer electrons than there are protons. Mg has 12 protons (see table above), so Mg^{2+} must have 10 electrons. The overall charge = +12 – 10 = +2.

The Atom

Isotopes are Atoms of the *Same Element* with Different Numbers of *Neutrons*

Make sure you **learn** this definition and totally **understand** what it means —

Isotopes of an element are atoms with the same number of protons but different numbers of neutrons.

35 – 17 = 18 neutrons ← **Different** mass numbers mean different masses and different numbers of neutrons. → **37 – 17 = 20 neutrons**

$^{35}_{17}Cl$ The **atomic numbers** are the same. **Both** isotopes have 17 protons and 17 electrons. $^{37}_{17}Cl$

Chlorine-35 and chlorine-37 are examples of isotopes.

1) It's the **number** and **arrangement** of electrons that decides the **chemical properties** of an element. Isotopes have the **same configuration of electrons**, so they've got the **same** chemical properties.
2) Isotopes of an element do have slightly different **physical properties** though, such as different densities, rates of diffusion, etc. This is because **physical properties** tend to depend more on the **mass** of the atom.

Here's another example — naturally occurring **magnesium** consists of 3 isotopes.

^{24}Mg (79%)	^{25}Mg (10%)	^{26}Mg (11%)
12 protons	12 protons	12 protons
12 neutrons	**13** neutrons	**14** neutrons
12 electrons	12 electrons	12 electrons

The periodic table gives the atomic number for each element. The other number isn't the mass number — it's the relative atomic mass (see page 18). They're a bit different, but you can often assume they're equal — it doesn't matter unless you're doing really accurate work.

Practice Questions

Q1 Draw a diagram showing the structure of an atom, labelling each part.

Q2 Where is the mass concentrated in an atom, and what makes up most of the volume of an atom?

Q3 Draw a table showing the relative charge and relative mass of the three subatomic particles found in atoms.

Q4 Using an example, explain the terms 'atomic number' and 'mass number'.

Q5 Define the term 'isotopes' and give examples.

Exam Questions

Q1 Hydrogen, deuterium and tritium are all isotopes of each other.

a) Identify one similarity and one difference between these isotopes. [2 marks]

b) Deuterium can be written as ^{2}H. Determine the number of protons, neutrons and electrons in a neutral deuterium atom. [1 mark]

c) Write a nuclear symbol for tritium, given that it has 2 neutrons. [1 mark]

Q2 This question relates to the atoms or ions A to D: A. $^{32}_{16}S^{2-}$, B. $^{40}_{18}Ar$, C. $^{30}_{16}S$, D. $^{42}_{20}Ca$.

a) Identify the similarity for each of the following pairs.

i) A and B. [1 mark]

ii) A and C. [1 mark]

iii) B and D. [1 mark]

b) Which two of the atoms or ions are isotopes of each other? Explain your reasoning. [2 marks]

Got it learned yet? — Isotope so...

This is a nice straightforward page just to ease you in to things. Remember that positive ions have fewer electrons than protons, and negative ions have more electrons than protons. Get that straightened out or you'll end up in a right mess. There's nowt too hard about isotopes neither. They're just the same element with different numbers of neutrons.

Atomic Models

Things ain't how they used to be, you know. Take atomic structure, for starters.

*The **Accepted Model** of the **Atom** Has **Changed** Throughout History*

The model of the atom you're expected to know (the one on page 14) is the currently **accepted model**. It fits all the observations and evidence we have so far, so we **assume it's true** until someone shows that it's **incomplete or wrong**. In the past, completely different models were accepted, because they fitted the evidence available at the time:

1) Some **ancient Greeks** thought that all matter was made from **indivisible particles**.
2) At the start of the 19th century John Dalton described atoms as **solid spheres**, and said that different types of sphere made up the different elements.
3) But as scientists did more experiments, our currently accepted models began to emerge, with modifications or refinements being made to take account of new evidence.

The Greek word atomos means 'uncuttable'.

Experimental Evidence** Showed that Atoms **Weren't Solid Spheres

In 1897 J J Thomson did a whole series of experiments and concluded that atoms **weren't** solid and indivisible.

1) His measurements of **charge** and **mass** showed that an atom must contain even smaller, negatively charged particles. He called these particles 'corpuscles' — we call them **electrons**.
2) The 'solid sphere' idea of atomic structure had to be changed. The new model was known as the **'plum pudding model'** — a positively charged sphere with negative electrons embedded in it.

positively charged 'pudding'
delicious pudding

Rutherford** Showed that the **Plum Pudding** Model Was **Wrong

1) In 1909 Ernest Rutherford and his students Hans Geiger and Ernest Marsden conducted the famous **gold foil experiment**. They fired **alpha particles** (which are positively charged) at an extremely thin sheet of gold.
2) From the plum pudding model, they were expecting **most** of the alpha particles to be deflected **very slightly** by the positive 'pudding' that made up most of an atom.
3) In fact, most of the alpha particles passed **straight through** the gold atoms, and a very small number were deflected **backwards** (through more than 90°). This showed that the plum pudding model **couldn't be right**.
4) So Rutherford came up with a model that **could** explain this new evidence — the **nuclear model** of the atom:

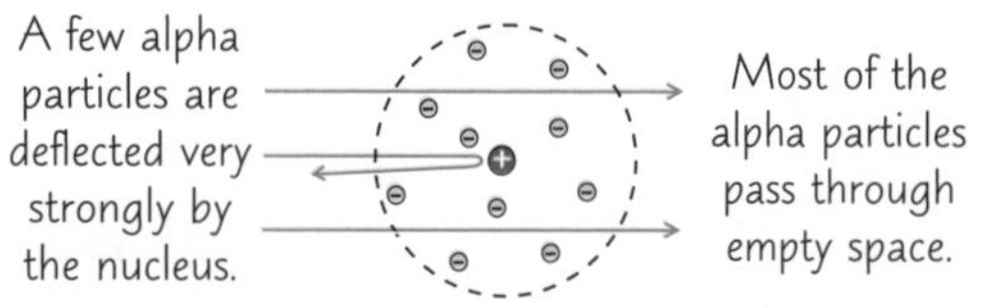
A few alpha particles are deflected very strongly by the nucleus.
Most of the alpha particles pass through empty space.

1) There is a **tiny, positively charged nucleus** at the centre of the atom, where most of the atom's mass is concentrated.
2) The nucleus is surrounded by a **'cloud'** of **negative electrons**.
3) Most of the atom is **empty space**.

*Rutherford's **Nuclear Model** Was **Modified** Several Times*

Rutherford's model seemed pretty convincing, but (there's always a but)... the scientists of the day didn't just say, "Well done Ernest old chap, you've got it", then all move to Patagonia to farm goats. No, they stuck at their experiments, wanting to be sure of the truth. (And it's just conceivable they wanted some fame and fortune too.)

1) Henry Moseley discovered that the charge of the nucleus **increased** from one element to another in units of one.
2) This led Rutherford to investigate the nucleus further. He finally discovered that it contained **positively charged** particles that he called **protons**. The charges of the nuclei of different atoms could then be explained — the atoms of **different elements** have a **different number of protons** in their nucleus.
3) There was still one problem with the model — the nuclei of atoms were **heavier** than they would be if they just contained protons. Rutherford predicted that there were other particles in the nucleus, that had **mass but no charge** — and the **neutron** was eventually discovered by James Chadwick.

This is nearly always the way scientific knowledge develops — **new evidence** prompts people to come up with **new, improved ideas**. Then other people go through each new, improved idea with a fine-tooth comb as well — modern **'peer review'** (see p.2) is part of this process.

Atomic Models

The **Bohr Model** Was a Further Improvement

1) Scientists realised that electrons in a '**cloud**' around the nucleus of an atom would **spiral down** into the nucleus, causing the atom to **collapse**. Niels Bohr proposed a new model of the atom with four basic principles:

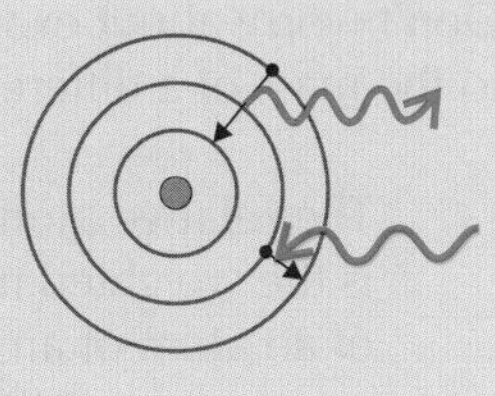

- Electrons can only exist in **fixed orbits**, or **shells**, and not anywhere in between.
- Each shell has a **fixed energy**.
- When an electron moves between shells **electromagnetic radiation** is **emitted** or **absorbed**.
- Because the energy of shells is fixed, the radiation will have a **fixed frequency**.

2) The frequencies of radiation emitted and absorbed by atoms were already known from experiments. The Bohr model fitted these observations — it looked good.
3) The Bohr model also explained why some elements (the noble gases) are **inert**. He said that the shells of an atom can only hold **fixed numbers of electrons**, and that an element's reactivity is due to its electrons. Atoms will react in order to gain full shells of electrons. When an atom has **full shells** of electrons it is **stable** and does not react.

There's **More Than One** Model of Atomic Structure in Use Today

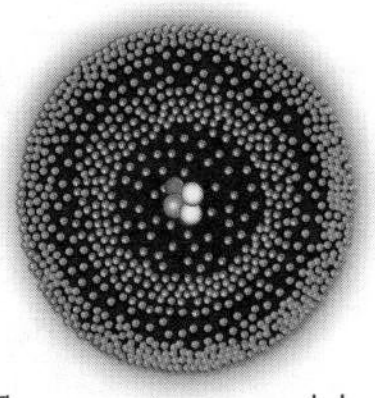

The quantum model of an atom with two shells of electrons. The denser the dots, the more likely an electron is to be there.

1) We now know that the Bohr model is **not perfect** — but it's still widely used to describe atoms because it's simple and explains many **observations** from experiments, like bonding and ionisation energy trends.
2) The most accurate model we have today involves complicated quantum mechanics. Basically, you can never **know** where an electron is or which direction it's going in at any moment, but you can say **how likely** it is to be at any particular point in the atom. Oh, and electrons can act as **waves** as well as particles (but you don't need to worry about the details).
3) This model might be **more accurate**, but it's a lot harder to get your head round and visualise. It **does** explain some observations that can't be accounted for by the Bohr model though. So scientists use whichever model is most relevant to whatever they're investigating.

Practice Questions

Q1 What particle did J J Thomson discover?

Q2 Describe the model of the atom that was adopted because of Thomson's work.

Q3 Who developed the 'nuclear' model of the atom? What evidence did they have for it?

Exam Question

Q1 Scientific theories are constantly being revised in the light of new evidence. New theories are accepted if they have been successfully tested by experiments or because they help to explain certain observations.

a) Niels Bohr thought that the model of the atom proposed by Ernest Rutherford did not describe the electrons in an atom correctly. Why did he think this and how was his model of the atom different from Rutherford's? [2 marks]

b) According to the Bohr model, what happens when electrons in an atom move from one shell to another? [1 mark]

c) How did Bohr explain the lack of reactivity of the noble gases? [2 marks]

These models are tiny — even smaller than size zero, I reckon...

The process of developing a model to fit the evidence available, looking for more evidence to show if it's correct or not, then revising the model if necessary is really important. It happens with all new scientific ideas. Remember, scientific 'facts' are only accepted as true because no one's proved yet that they aren't. It might all be bunkum.

Relative Mass

Relative mass... What? Eh?... Read on...

Relative Masses** are Masses of Atoms Compared to **Carbon-12

The actual mass of an atom is **very**, **very tiny**.
Don't worry about exactly how tiny for now, but it's far **too small** to weigh. So, the mass of one atom is compared to the mass of a different atom. This is its **relative mass**. Here are some **definitions** for you to learn:

The **relative atomic mass**, A_r, is the weighted **mean mass** of an atom of an element, compared to 1/12th of the mass of an atom of **carbon-12**.

Relative isotopic mass is the mass of an atom of an **isotope**, compared with 1/12th of the mass of an atom of **carbon-12**.

1) Relative atomic mass is an **average**, so it's not usually a whole number.
2) Relative isotopic mass is usually a **whole number**.

E.g. a natural sample of chlorine contains a mixture of ^{35}Cl (75%) and ^{37}Cl (25%), so the relative isotopic masses are **35** and **37**. But its relative atomic mass is **35.5**.

Jason's shirt was isotropical...

Relative Molecular Masses** are Masses of **Molecules

The **relative molecular mass** (or **relative formula mass**), M_r, is the average mass of a **molecule** or **formula unit**, compared to 1/12th of the mass of an atom of **carbon-12**.

Don't worry, this is one definition that you **don't** need to know for the exam.
But... you **do** need to know how to **work out** the **relative molecular mass**, and the **relative formula mass**, so it's probably best if you **learn** what they mean anyway.

1) **Relative molecular mass** is used when referring to **simple molecules**.
2) To find the relative molecular mass, just **add up** the **relative atomic mass values** of all the atoms in the molecule.

E.g. $M_r(C_2H_6O) = (2 \times 12) + (6 \times 1) + 16 = \mathbf{46}$

1) **Relative formula mass** is used for compounds that are **ionic** (or **giant covalent**, such as SiO_2).
2) To find the relative formula mass, **add up** the **relative atomic masses (A_r)** of all the ions in the formula unit. (A_r of ion = A_r of atom. The electrons make no difference to the mass.)

E.g. $M_r(CaF_2) = 40 + (2 \times 19) = \mathbf{78}$

*A_r Can Be Worked Out from **Isotopic Abundances***

You need to know how to calculate the **relative atomic mass** (A_r) of an element from its **isotopic abundances**.

1) Different isotopes of an element occur in different quantities, or isotopic abundances.
2) To work out the relative atomic mass of an element, you need to work out the **average** mass of all its atoms.
3) If you're given the isotopic abundances in **percentages**, all you need to do is follow these two easy steps:

Step 1: Multiply each **relative isotopic mass** by its **% relative isotopic abundance**, and **add up** the results.
Step 2: Divide by **100**.

Example: Find the relative atomic mass of boron given that 20.0 % of the boron atoms found on Earth have a relative isotopic mass of 10.0, while 80.0 % have a relative isotopic mass of 11.0.

Step 1: $(20 \times 10) + (80 \times 11) = 1080$

Step 2: $1080 \div 100 = \mathbf{10.8}$

Relative Mass

Mass Spectrometry Can Tell Us About *Isotopes*

Mass spectra are produced by mass spectrometers — devices which are used to find out what samples are made up of by measuring the masses of their components. Mass spectra can tell us dead useful things, e.g. the **relative isotopic masses and abundances** of different elements.

This is the mass spectra for chlorine.

The **y-axis** gives the **abundance of ions**, often as a percentage. For an element, the **height** of each peak gives the **relative isotopic abundance**.

The **x-axis** units are given as a **'mass/charge'** ratio (you may sometimes see it written as **m:z**). Since the charge on the ions is mostly **+1**, you can often assume the x-axis is simply the **relative isotopic mass**.

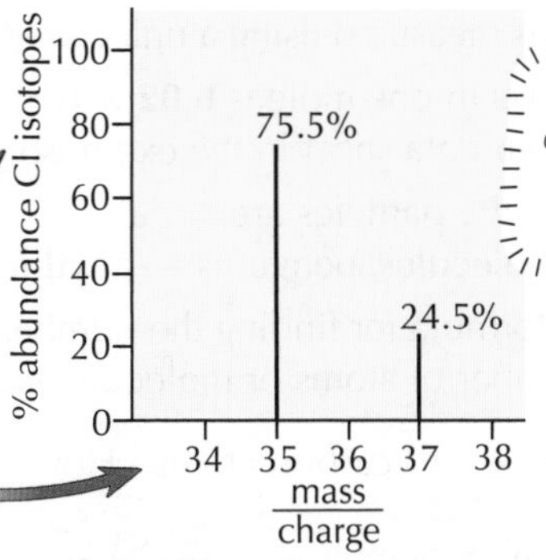

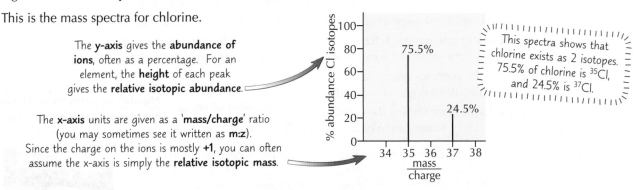

This spectra shows that chlorine exists as 2 isotopes. 75.5% of chlorine is ^{35}Cl, and 24.5% is ^{37}Cl.

Mass spectra can be used to work out the relative atomic masses of different elements.

The method for working out the relative atomic mass from a graph is a bit different to working it out from percentages, but it starts off in the same way.

Step 1: Multiply each **relative isotopic mass** by its **relative isotopic abundance**, and **add up** the results.
Step 2: Divide by the **sum** of the isotopic abundances.

Example: Use the data from this mass spectrum to work out the relative atomic mass of neon. Give your answer to 1 decimal place.

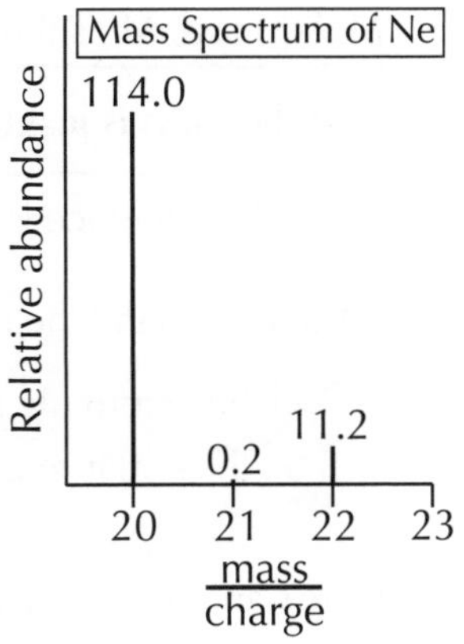

Step 1: (20 × 114.0) + (21 × 0.2) + (22 × 11.2) = 2530.6

Step 2: (114.0 + 0.2 + 11.2 = 125.4)
2530.6 ÷ 125.4 = **20.2**

Practice Questions

Q1 Explain what relative atomic mass (A_r) and relative isotopic mass mean.

Q2 Explain the difference between relative molecular mass and relative formula mass.

Q3 Explain what relative isotopic abundance means.

Exam Questions

Q1 Copper exists in two main isotopic forms, ^{63}Cu and ^{65}Cu.

a) Calculate the relative atomic mass of copper using the information from the mass spectrum. [2 marks]

b) Explain why the relative atomic mass of copper is not a whole number. [2 marks]

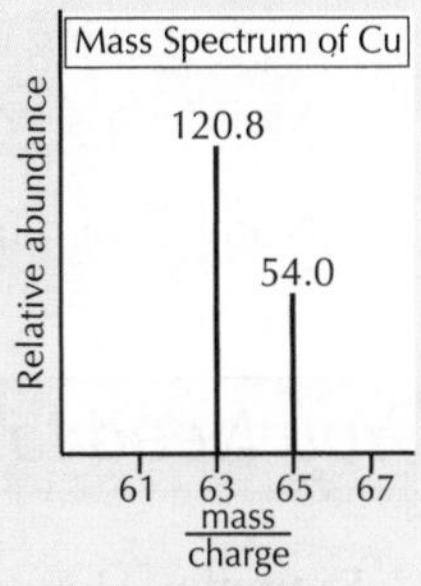

Q2 The percentage make-up of naturally occurring potassium is:
93.1% ^{39}K, 0.120% ^{40}K and 6.77% ^{41}K.
Use the information to determine the relative atomic mass of potassium. [2 marks]

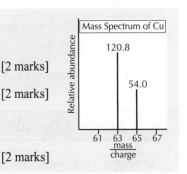

You can't pick your relatives, you just have to learn them...

Isotopic masses are a bit frustrating. Why can't all atoms of an element just be the same? But the fact is they're not, so you're going to have to learn how to use those spectra to work out the relative atomic masses of different elements. The actual maths is pretty simple. A pinch of multiplying, a dash of addition, some division to flavour and you're away.

The Mole

It'd be handy to be able to count out atoms — but they're way too tiny. You can't even see them, never mind get hold of them with tweezers. But not to worry — using the idea of relative mass, you can figure out how many atoms you've got.

*A **Mole** is Just a (Very Large) **Number of Particles***

Chemists often talk about 'amount of substance'. Basically, all they mean is 'number of particles'.

1) Amount of substance is measured using a unit called the **mole** (or **mol**). The number of moles is given the symbol **n**.
2) The number of **particles** in one mole is **6.02 × 10²³**. This number is **the Avogadro constant, N_A**.
   It's given to you on your data sheet in the exam, so don't worry about learning its value, just what it means.
3) It **doesn't matter** what the particles are.
   They can be atoms, molecules, penguins — **anything**.
4) Here's a nice simple formula for finding the number of moles from the number of atoms or molecules:

$$\text{Number of moles} = \frac{\text{Number of particles you have}}{\text{Number of particles in a mole}}$$

Example: I have 1.50×10^{24} carbon atoms. How many moles of carbon is this?

$$\text{Number of moles} = \frac{1.50 \times 10^{24}}{6.02 \times 10^{23}} \approx \mathbf{2.49\ moles}$$

Molar Mass is the Mass of One Mole

Molar mass, M, is the mass of **one mole** of something. Just remember:

Molar mass is just the same as the relative molecular mass, M_r.

That's why the mole is such a ridiculous number of particles (6.02×10^{23}) — it's the number of particles for which the weight in g is the same as the relative molecular mass.

The only difference is it has units of 'grams per mole', so you stick a 'g mol⁻¹' on the end...

Example: Find the molar mass of $CaCO_3$.

Relative formula mass, M_r, of $CaCO_3$ = 40.1 + 12.0 + (3 × 16.0) = 100.1
So the molar mass, M, is **100.1 g mol⁻¹**. — i.e. 1 mole of $CaCO_3$ weighs 100.1 g.

Here's another formula.
This one's really important — you need it **all the time**:

$$\text{Number of moles} = \frac{\text{mass of substance}}{\text{molar mass}}$$

You can re-arrange this equation using this formula triangle:

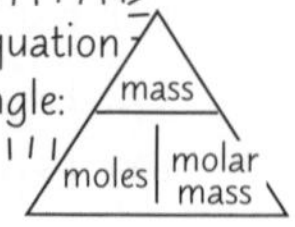

Example: How many moles of aluminium oxide are present in 5.1 g of Al_2O_3?

Molar mass, M, of Al_2O_3 = (2 × 27.0) + (3 × 16.0) = 102.0 g mol⁻¹

Number of moles of Al_2O_3 = $\frac{5.1}{102.0}$ = **0.05 moles**

Example: How many moles of chlorine molecules are present in 71.0 g of chlorine gas?

We're talking chlorine **molecules** (not chlorine atoms), so it's Cl_2 we're interested in.
Molar mass, M, of Cl_2 = (2 × 35.5) = 71.0 g mol⁻¹

Number of moles of Cl_2 = $\frac{71.0}{71.0}$ = **1 mole**

But note that it would be 2 moles of chlorine atoms, since chlorine atoms have a molar mass of 35.5 g mol⁻¹.

*You Need to be able to work out the **Number** of **Atoms** in Something*

Example: How many atoms are in 8.5 g of H_2S?

Molar mass, M, of H_2S = 1.0 + 1.0 + 32.1 = 34.1 g mol⁻¹
Number of moles of H_2S = $\frac{8.5}{34.1}$ = 0.249 moles
Number of molecules of H_2S = 0.249 × 6.02 × 10^{23} = 1.50 × 10^{23}
There are 3 atoms in 1 molecule of H_2S so, total no. atoms = 1.50 × 10^{23} × 3 = **4.5 × 10²³** (2 s.f)

Multiplying moles by Avogadro's constant gives you the number of molecules/particles.

The Mole

All Gases Take Up the **Same Volume** under the Same Conditions

The space that one mole of a gas occupies at a certain temperature and pressure is known as the **molar gas volume**. It has units of **$dm^3\ mol^{-1}$**.
If temperature and pressure stay the same, **one mole** of **any** gas always has the **same volume**.
At **room temperature and pressure** (r.t.p.), this happens to be **$24\ dm^3\ mol^{-1}$** (r.t.p is 298 K (25 °C) and 101.3 kPa).
Here's the formula for working out the number of moles in a volume of gas.

$$\text{Number of moles} = \frac{\text{Volume in dm}^3}{\text{Molar gas volume}}$$

At r.t.p, just substitute $24\ dm^3\ mol^{-1}$ into this equation as the molar gas volume.

Example: How many moles are there in $6.0\ dm^3$ of oxygen gas at r.t.p.?

$$\text{Number of moles} = \frac{6.0}{24} = \mathbf{0.25\ moles\ of\ oxygen\ molecules}$$

This is oxygen molecules, not atoms, as gaseous oxygen exists as O_2, not lone O atoms.

Ideal Gas equation — pV = nRT

In the real world, it's not always room temperature and pressure.
The **ideal gas equation** lets you find the **number of moles** in a certain volume at **any temperature and pressure**.

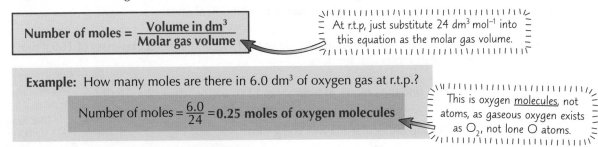

pV = nRT Where: p = pressure (Pa)
V = volume (m^3)
n = number of moles
R = $8.314\ J\ K^{-1}\ mol^{-1}$
T = temperature (K)

$1\ cm^3 = 1 \times 10^{-6}\ m^3$
$1\ dm^3 = 1 \times 10^{-3}\ m^3$

R is the gas constant. Don't worry about what it means. Just learn it.

K = °C + 273

Example: At a temperature of 60.0 °C and a pressure of 250 kPa, a gas occupied a volume of $1100\ cm^3$ and had a mass of 1.60 g. Find its relative molecular mass.

1 kPa = 1000 Pa

$1100\ cm^3 = 1.1 \times 10^{-3}\ m^3$

$$n = \frac{pV}{RT} = \frac{(250 \times 10^3) \times (1.1 \times 10^{-3})}{8.314 \times 333} = 0.0993 \text{ moles}$$

If 0.0993 moles is 1.60 g, then 1 mole $= \frac{1.60}{0.0993} = 16.1$ g. So the relative molecular mass (M_r) is **16.1**.

Practice Questions

Q1 How many molecules are there in one mole of ethane molecules?

Q2 What is the equation for working out the number of moles of something from a given mass?

Q3 What volume does 1 mole of gas occupy at r.t.p.?

Exam Questions

Q1 How many atoms are in 7.3 g of HCl? [2 marks]

Q2 Calculate the mass of 0.360 moles of ethanoic acid, CH_3COOH. [2 marks]

Q3 At what temperature will 1.28 g of chlorine gas occupy $98.6\ dm^3$, at a pressure of 175 Pa? [2 marks]

Q4 What volume will be occupied by 88 g of propane gas (C_3H_8) at r.t.p.? [2 marks]

Put your back teeth on the scale and find out your molar mass...

You need this stuff for loads of calculation questions. You'll almost definitely need to use all the formulae to find out things like the volume of a gas or the number of moles in a volume of gas. Before tackling a question, sit down and see what information you have, what equations you can use and how you can rearrange them to get the answer.

Empirical and Molecular Formulae

Here's another page piled high with numbers — it's all just glorified maths really.

Empirical and **Molecular** Formulae are **Ratios**

You have to know what's what with empirical and molecular formulae, so here goes...

1) The **empirical formula** gives the smallest whole number ratio of atoms of each element in a compound.
2) The **molecular formula** gives the **actual** numbers of atoms of each type of element in a molecule.
3) The molecular formula is made up of a **whole number** of empirical units.

Example: A molecule has an empirical formula of $C_4H_3O_2$, and a molecular mass of 166 g mol^{-1}. Work out its molecular formula.

Compare the empirical and molecular masses.

First find the **empirical mass**: $(4 \times 12.0) + (3 \times 1.0) + (2 \times 16.0)$
$= 48.0 + 3.0 + 32.0 = 83.0$ g mol^{-1}

Empirical mass is just like the relative formula mass... (if that helps at all...).

But the **molecular mass** is 166 g mol^{-1},

so there are $\frac{166}{83.0} = 2$ empirical units in the molecule.

The molecular formula must be the **empirical formula × 2**,
so the molecular formula = $\mathbf{C_8H_6O_4}$. So there you go.

Empirical Formulae are Calculated from **Experiments**

You need to be able to work out empirical formulae from **experimental results** too.

Example: When a hydrocarbon is burnt in excess oxygen, 4.4 g of carbon dioxide and 1.8 g of water are made. What is the empirical formula of the hydrocarbon?

First work out how many moles of the products you have.

$$\text{No. of moles of } CO_2 = \frac{\text{mass}}{M} = \frac{4.4}{12.0 + (2 \times 16.0)} = \frac{4.4}{44.0} = 0.10 \text{ moles}$$

1 mole of CO_2 contains 1 mole of carbon atoms, so you must have started with **0.10 moles of carbon atoms**.

$$\text{No. of moles of } H_2O = \frac{1.8}{(2 \times 1.0) + 16.0} = \frac{1.8}{18.0} = 0.10 \text{ moles}$$

1 mole of H_2O contains 2 moles of hydrogen atoms (H), so you must have started with **0.20 moles of hydrogen atoms**.

Ratio C : H = 0.10 : 0.20 . Now you divide both numbers by the **smallest** — here it's 0.10.
So, the ratio C : H = 1 : 2. So the empirical formula must be $\mathbf{CH_2}$.

This works because the only place the carbon in the carbon dioxide and the hydrogen in the water could have come from is the hydrocarbon.

As if that's not enough, you also need to know how to work out empirical formulae from the **percentages** of the different elements.

Example: A compound is found to have percentage composition 56.5% potassium, 8.70% carbon and 34.8% oxygen by mass. Calculate its empirical formula.

These answers are given to 3 significant figures.

In **100 g** of compound there are:

Use $n = \frac{\text{mass}}{M}$

$\frac{56.5}{39.1} = 1.45$ moles of K $\frac{8.70}{12.0} = 0.725$ moles of C $\frac{34.8}{16.0} = 2.18$ moles of O

Divide each number of moles by the **smallest number** — in this case it's 0.725.

K: $\frac{1.45}{0.725} = 2.00$ C: $\frac{0.725}{0.725} = 1.00$ O: $\frac{2.18}{0.725} = 3.01$

The ratio of K : C : O ≈ 2 : 1 : 3. So you know the empirical formula's got to be $\mathbf{K_2CO_3}$.

Empirical and Molecular Formulae

Molecular Formulae are Calculated from **Experimental Data** Too

Once you know the empirical formula, you just need a bit more info and you can work out the **molecular formula** too.

Example:

When 4.6 g of an alcohol, with molar mass 46 g mol^{-1}, is burnt in excess oxygen, it produces 8.8 g of carbon dioxide and 5.4 g of water.
Calculate the empirical formula for the alcohol and then its molecular formula.

Alcohols contain C, H and O.

The carbon in the CO_2 and the hydrogen in the H_2O must have come from the alcohol — work out the number of moles of each of these.

No. of moles of $CO_2 = \frac{\text{mass}}{M} = \frac{8.8}{44} = 0.2$ moles

1 mole of CO_2 contains 1 mole of C. So, 0.2 moles of CO_2 contains **0.2 moles of C.**

No. of moles $H_2O = \frac{\text{mass}}{M} = \frac{5.4}{18} = 0.3$ moles

1 mole of H_2O contains 2 moles of H. So, 0.3 moles of H_2O contains **0.6 moles of H.**

Mass of C = no. of moles × M = 0.2 × 12.0 = 2.4 g

Mass of H = no. of moles × M = 0.6 × 1.0 = 0.6 g

Mass of O = 4.6 – (2.4 + 0.6) = 1.6 g

Number of moles O = $\frac{\text{mass}}{M} = \frac{1.6}{16.0} = 0.1$ moles

Now work out the mass of carbon and hydrogen in the alcohol. The rest of the mass of the alcohol must be oxygen — so work out that too. Once you know the mass of O, you can work out how many moles there are of it.

When you know the number of moles of each element, you've got the molar ratio. Divide each number by the smallest.

Molar Ratio = C : H : O = 0.2 : 0.6 : 0.1 = 2 : 6 : 1

Empirical formula = C_2H_6O

Mass of empirical formula = (2 × 12.0) + (6 × 1.0) + 16.0 = 46.0 g

In this example, the mass of the empirical formula equals the molecular mass, so the empirical and molecular formulae are the same.

Molecular formula = C_2H_6O

Compare the empirical and molecular masses.

Practice Questions

Q1 Define 'empirical formula'.

Q2 What is the difference between a molecular formula and an empirical formula?

Exam Questions

Q1 Hydrocarbon X has a molecular mass of 78 g. It is found to have 92.3% carbon and 7.7% hydrogen by mass. Calculate the empirical and molecular formulae of X. [3 marks]

Q2 When 1.2 g of magnesium ribbon is heated in air, it burns to form a white powder, which has a mass of 2 g. What is the empirical formula of the powder? [2 marks]

Hint: organic acids contain C, H and O.

Q3 When 19.8 g of an organic acid, A, is burnt in excess oxygen, 33.0 g of carbon dioxide and 10.8 g of water are produced.
Calculate the empirical formula for A and hence its molecular formula, if $M_r(A) = 132$. [4 marks]

The Empirical Strikes Back...

With this stuff, it's not enough to learn a few facts parrot-fashion, to regurgitate in the exam — you've gotta know how to use them. The only way to do that is to practise. Go through all the examples on these two pages again, this time working the answers out for yourself. Then test yourself on the exam questions. It'll help you sleep at night — honest.

Equations and Calculations

Balancing equations'll cause you a few palpitations — as soon as you make one bit right, the rest goes pear-shaped.

Balanced Equations have **Equal Numbers** of each Atom on **Both Sides**

1) Balanced equations have the **same number** of each atom on **both** sides. They're... well... you know... balanced.
2) You can only add more atoms by adding **whole reactants** or **products**. You do this by putting a number **in front** of a substance or changing one that's already there. You **can't** mess with formulae — ever.

Example: Balance the equation: $C_2H_6 + O_2 \rightarrow CO_2 + H_2O$.

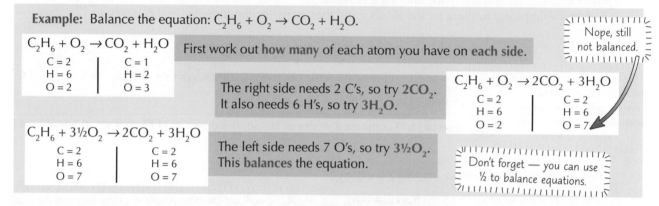

$C_2H_6 + O_2 \rightarrow CO_2 + H_2O$

Left	Right
C = 2	C = 1
H = 6	H = 2
O = 2	O = 3

First work out **how many** of each atom you have on **each side**.

The right side needs 2 C's, so try $2CO_2$. It also needs 6 H's, so try $3H_2O$.

$C_2H_6 + O_2 \rightarrow 2CO_2 + 3H_2O$

Left	Right
C = 2	C = 2
H = 6	H = 6
O = 2	O = 7

Nope, still not balanced.

The left side needs 7 O's, so try $3\frac{1}{2}O_2$. This **balances** the equation.

$C_2H_6 + 3\frac{1}{2}O_2 \rightarrow 2CO_2 + 3H_2O$

Left	Right
C = 2	C = 2
H = 6	H = 6
O = 7	O = 7

Don't forget — you can use ½ to balance equations.

Ionic Equations Only Show the **Reacting Particles**

1) You can also write an **ionic equation** for any reaction involving **ions** that happens **in solution**.
2) In an ionic equation, only the **reacting particles** (and the **products** they form) are included.

Example: Here is the **full balanced equation** for the reaction of **nitric acid** with **sodium hydroxide**:

$$HNO_3 + NaOH \rightarrow NaNO_3 + H_2O$$

The **ionic** substances in this equation will **dissolve**, breaking up into ions in solution. You can rewrite the equation to show all the **ions** that are in the reaction mixture:

$$H^+ + NO_3^- + Na^+ + OH^- \rightarrow Na^+ + NO_3^- + H_2O$$

Leave anything that <u>isn't</u> an ion in solution (like the H_2O) as it is.

To get from this to the ionic equation, just cross out any ions that appear on **both sides** of the equation — in this case, that's the sodium ions (Na^+) and the nitrate ions (NO_3^-).

An ion that's present in the reaction mixture, but doesn't get involved in the reaction is called a <u>spectator ion</u>.

So the **ionic equation** for this reaction is:

$$\mathbf{H^+ + OH^- \rightarrow H_2O}$$

3) When you've written an ionic equation, check that the **charges** are **balanced**, as well as the atoms — if the charges don't balance, the equation isn't right.

In the example above, the **net charge** on the left hand side is +1 + −1 = **0** and the net charge on the right hand side is **0** — so the charges balance.

Balanced Equations can be used to Work out **Masses**

Balanced equations show the **reaction stoichiometry** (see page 32). The reaction stoichiometry tells you the ratios of reactants to products, i.e. how many moles of product are formed from a certain number of moles of reactants.

Example: Calculate the mass of iron oxide produced if 28 g of iron is burnt in air. $2Fe + \frac{3}{2}O_2 \rightarrow Fe_2O_3$

The molar mass, M, of Fe = 55.8 g mol⁻¹, so the number of moles in 28 g of Fe = $\frac{\text{mass}}{M} = \frac{28}{55.8} = 0.50$ moles.

From the equation: 2 moles of Fe produces 1 mole of Fe_2O_3, so 0.50 moles of Fe produces 0.25 moles of Fe_2O_3.

M of $Fe_2O_3 = (2 \times 55.8) + (3 \times 16) = 159.6$ g mol^{-1}

Mass of Fe_2O_3 = no. of moles × M = 0.25 × 159.6 = **40 g (2 s.f)**

Once you know the number of moles and the molar mass (M) of Fe_2O_3, it's easy to work out the mass.

Equations and Calculations

That's not all... Balanced Equations can be used to Work Out Gas Volumes

It's pretty handy to be able to work out **how much gas** a reaction will produce, so that you can use **large enough apparatus**. Or else there might be a rather large bang.

Example: How much gas is produced when 15 g of sodium is reacted with excess water at r.t.p.?

$$2Na_{(s)} + 2H_2O_{(l)} \rightarrow 2NaOH_{(aq)} + H_{2\,(g)}$$

Excess water means you know all the sodium will react.

M of Na = 23,0 g mol^{-1}, so number of moles in 15 g of Na = $\frac{15}{23.0}$ = 0.65 moles

From the equation, 2 moles Na produces 1 mole H_2,
so you know 0.65 moles Na produces $\frac{0.65}{2}$ = 0.325 moles H_2.

So the volume of H_2 = 0.325 × 24 = **7.8 dm³**

The reaction happens at room temperature and pressure, so you know 1 mole takes up 24 dm³ (p. 21).

State Symbols Give a bit More Information about the Substances

State symbols are put after each reactant and product in an equation. They tell you what **state of matter** things are in.

s = solid **l = liquid** **g = gas** **aq = aqueous (solution in water)**

To show you what I mean, here's an example —

$CaCO_{3\,(s)}$	+	$2HCl_{(aq)}$	→	$CaCl_{2\,(aq)}$	+	$H_2O_{(l)}$	+	$CO_{2\,(g)}$
solid		solution		solution		liquid		gas

Practice Questions

Q1 What is the difference between a molecular equation and an ionic equation?

Q2 What is the state symbol for a solution of hydrochloric acid?

Exam Questions

Q1 Balance the following equation.

$$KI_{(aq)} + Pb(NO_3)_{2\,(aq)} \rightarrow PbI_{2\,(s)} + KNO_{3\,(aq)}$$ [1 mark]

Q2 Use the equation given to calculate the mass of ethene required to produce 258 g of chloroethane, C_2H_5Cl.

$$C_2H_4 + HCl \rightarrow C_2H_5Cl$$ [2 marks]

Q3 What volume of oxygen is required, at room temperature and pressure for the complete combustion of 3.50×10^{-2} mol of butane (C_4H_{10})? [2 marks]

Q4 15.0 g of calcium carbonate is heated strongly so that it fully decomposes. $CaCO_{3\,(s)} \rightarrow CaO_{(s)} + CO_{2\,(g)}$

a) Calculate the mass of calcium oxide produced. [2 marks]

b) Calculate the volume of gas produced. [1 mark]

Don't get in a state about equations...

You're probably completely fed up with all these equations, calculations, moles and whatnot... well hang in there — there are just a few more pages coming up. I've said it once, and I'll say it again — practise, practise, practise... it's the only road to salvation (by the way, where is salvation anyway?). Keep going... you're nearly there.

Formulae of Ionic Compounds

Ahh — ions. My favourite topic. In fact, the only things better than ions are probably ionic compounds, and here's a page all about them. It's like Christmas has come early...

Ions** are made when **Electrons** are **Transferred

1) Ions are formed when electrons are **transferred** from one atom to another.
2) The simplest ions are single atoms which have either lost or gained electrons so as to have a **full outer shell**.

A sodium atom (Na) **loses** 1 electron to form a sodium ion (Na^+)	$Na \rightarrow Na^+ + e^-$
A magnesium atom (Mg) **loses** 2 electrons to form a magnesium ion (Mg^{2+})	$Mg \rightarrow Mg^{2+} + 2e^-$
A chlorine atom (Cl) **gains** 1 electron to form a chloride ion (Cl^-)	$Cl + e^- \rightarrow Cl^-$
An oxygen atom (O) **gains** 2 electrons to form an oxide ion (O^{2-})	$O + 2e^- \rightarrow O^{2-}$

3) You **don't** have to remember what ion **each element** forms — nope, you just look at the Periodic Table.
4) Elements in the same **group** all have the same number of **outer electrons**. So they have to **lose or gain** the same number to get the full outer shell that they're aiming for. And this means that they form ions with the **same charges**.

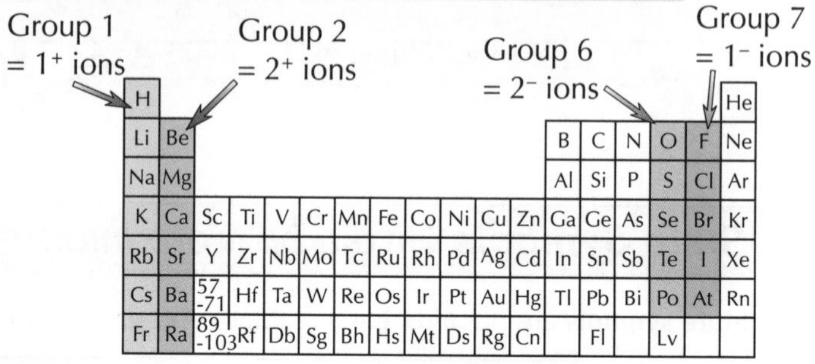

*Not all **Ions** are Made from **Single Atoms***

There are lots of ions that are made up of a group of atoms with an overall charge. These are called **molecular ions**.
You need to remember the formulae and the names of these ions:

Name	Formula
Nitrate	NO_3^-
Carbonate	CO_3^{2-}
Sulfate	SO_4^{2-}
Hydroxide	OH^-
Ammonium	NH_4^+
Zinc Ion	Zn^{2+}
Silver Ion	Ag^+

Amanda had a large overall charge.

Don't forget to learn the charge on each ion too.

Charges in Ionic Compounds** Always **Balance

1) **Ionic compounds** are made when positive and negative ions **bond** together. They do this through **ionic bonding**, but that's another story (see pages 42-43).
2) The charges on an **ionic compound** must always balance out to zero. For example...
   - In **NaCl**, the +1 charge on the Na^+ ion balances the –1 charge on the Cl^- ion.
   - In **$MgCl_2$**, the +2 charge on the Mg^{2+} ion balances the two –1 charges on the two Cl^- ions.

Example: What is the formula of potassium sulfate?

Potassium is in Group 1 of the periodic table, so will therefore form ions with a +1 charge: **K^+**.
The formula for the sulfate ion is **SO_4^{2-}**.
For every **one** sulfate ion, you will need **two** potassium ions to balance the charge: $(+1 \times 2) + (-2) = 0$.
So the formula is **K_2SO_4**.

Formulae of Ionic Compounds

Salts are *Ionic Compounds*

1) When **acids** and **bases** react, they form **water** and a **salt** (p. 28-29).
2) **Salts** are **ionic compounds**. All solid salts consist of a **lattice** of positive and negative ions. In some salts, **water molecules** are incorporated in the lattice too.
3) The water in a lattice is called **water of crystallisation**. A solid salt containing water of crystallisation is **hydrated**. A salt is **anhydrous** if it doesn't contain water of crystallisation.
4) **One mole** of a particular hydrated salt always has the **same number of moles** of water of crystallisation — its **formula** shows **how many** (it's always a whole number).
5) For example, **hydrated copper sulfate** has **five** moles of water for every mole of the salt. So its formula is **$CuSO_4.5H_2O$**. ⟵ Notice that there's a dot between $CuSO_4$ and $5H_2O$.
6) Many hydrated salts **lose** their water of crystallisation **when heated**, to become **anhydrous**. If you know the mass of the salt when hydrated and anhydrous, you can work its formula out like this:

Here's a tiny part of the lattice in a hydrated salt.

Water molecules are **polar** (see p. 48). They're held in place in the lattice because they're attracted to the ions.

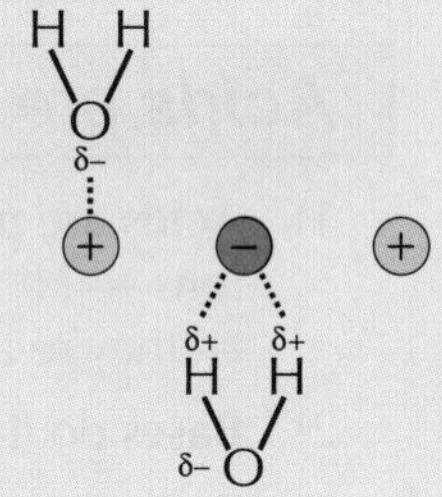

Example: Heating 3.210 g of hydrated magnesium sulfate, $MgSO_4$.**X**H_2O, forms 1.567 g of anhydrous magnesium sulfate. Find the value of **X** and write the formula of the hydrated salt.

First you find the number of moles of water lost.

Mass of water lost:	3.210 – 1.567 = 1.643 g
Number of moles of water lost:	mass ÷ molar mass = 1.643 g ÷ 18 g mol^{-1} = **0.09127 moles**

Then you find the number of moles of anhydrous salt.

Molar mass of $MgSO_4$:	24.3 + 32.1 + (4 × 16.0) = 120.4 g mol^{-1}
Number of moles (in 1.567 g):	mass ÷ molar mass = 1.567 g ÷ 120.4 g mol^{-1} = **0.01301 moles**

Now you work out the ratio of moles of anhydrous salt to moles of water in the form 1:n.

From the experiment, **0.01301 moles of salt : 0.09127 moles of water,**

So, **1 mole of salt :** $\frac{\mathbf{0.09127}}{\mathbf{0.01301}}$ **= 7.015 moles of water.**

You might be given the percentage of the mass that is water — use the method on page 22.

X must be a whole number, and some errors are to be expected in any experiment, so you can safely round off your result — so the formula of the hydrated salt is **$MgSO_4.7H_2O$**.

Practice Questions

Q1 What charge do the ions formed by Group 7 elements have?

Q2 What is the formula for the hydroxide ion?

Q3 Why can water molecules become fixed in an ionic lattice?

Exam Questions

Q1 What is the formula of scandium sulfate, given that the scandium ion has a charge of +3? [1 mark]

Q2 Use the periodic table to work out the formula of sodium oxide. [1 mark]

Q3 A sample of hydrated calcium sulfate, $CaSO_4.XH_2O$, was prepared by reacting calcium hydroxide with sulfuric acid. 1.883 g of hydrated salt was produced. This was then heated until all the water of crystallisation was driven off and the product was then reweighed. Its mass was 1.133 g.

a) How many moles of anhydrous calcium sulfate were produced? [2 marks]

b) Calculate the value of X in the formula $CaSO_4.XH_2O$. (X is a whole number.) [3 marks]

Ioning — every scientist's favourite household chore...

I prefer dusting personally. But even if you're a fan of vacuuming or sweeping, make sure you take the time to learn the rules for working out the charges on different ions. The periodic table is great for working out the charges of the ions of elements in groups 1, 2, 6 and 7, but the best way to remember the charges on molecular ions is to just learn them.

Acids and Bases

Acid's a word that's thrown around willy-nilly — but now for the truth...

Acids are all about *Hydrated Protons*

1) Acids are **proton donors**. When mixed with **water**, all acids **release hydrogen ions** — H^+ (these are just **protons**, but you never get them by themselves in water — they're always combined with H_2O to form hydroxonium ions, H_3O^+).
2) **Bases** do the opposite — they're proton acceptors and want to **grab H^+ ions**.
3) Bases that are soluble in water are known as **alkalis**. They release **OH^-** ions in solution.

Acids produce $H^+_{(aq)}$ ions in an aqueous solution.
Alkalis produce $OH^-_{(aq)}$ ions in an aqueous solution.

4) Some common acids are: **HCl** (hydrochloric acid), **H_2SO_4** (sulfuric acid), **HNO_3** (nitric acid) and **CH_3COOH** (ethanoic acid).
5) And some common bases are: **NaOH** (sodium hydroxide), **KOH** (potassium hydroxide) and **NH_3** (ammonia).

You'll need to learn the formulae and names of these acids and bases.

Acids and *Bases* Can Be *Strong* or *Weak*

1) The reaction between acids and water, and bases and water is **reversible**, so at any one point in time, both the forwards and backwards reactions will be happening.

Acids: $HA + H_2O \rightleftharpoons H_3O^+ + A^-$

Bases: $B + H_2O \rightleftharpoons BH^+ + OH^-$

These are really reversible reactions, but the equilibrium lies extremely far to the right.

2) For **strong acids**, e.g. HCl, very little of the reverse reaction happens, so nearly all the acid will dissociate (or ionise) in water, and **nearly all** the H^+ ions are released.

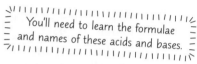

$HCl_{(aq)} \rightarrow H^+_{(aq)} + Cl^-_{(aq)}$

3) The same thing applies with **strong bases**, e.g. NaOH. Again, the forwards reaction is favoured, so nearly all the base dissociate in water and **lots** of OH^- ions are released.

$NaOH_{(aq)} \rightarrow Na^+_{(aq)} + OH^-_{(aq)}$

4) For **weak acids**, e.g. CH_3COOH, the backwards reaction is favoured, so only a small amount of the acid will dissociate in water and **only a few** H^+ ions are released.

$CH_3COOH_{(aq)} \rightleftharpoons CH_3COO^-_{(aq)} + H^+_{(aq)}$

5) Again, **weak bases**, such as NH_3, ionise only slightly in water. The backwards reaction is favoured so only a small amount of the base dissociates and **only a few** OH^- ions are released.

$NH_{3\,(aq)} + H_2O_{(l)} \rightleftharpoons NH_4^+{}_{(aq)} + OH^-_{(aq)}$

Acids React to Form *Neutral Salts*

Acids and **bases neutralise** each other. In the **neutralisation** reaction between acids and alkalis, a **salt** and **water** are produced.

1) It's the hydrogen ions released by the acid and the hydroxide ions released by the alkali that combine to form water.

$H^+_{(aq)} + OH^-_{(aq)} \rightleftharpoons H_2O_{(l)}$

2) You get a **salt** when the hydrogen ions in the acid are replaced by **metal ions** or **ammonium (NH_4^+) ions** from the alkali.

E.g. $HCl_{(aq)} + KOH_{(aq)} \rightarrow KCl_{(aq)} + H_2O_{(l)}$

3) Different acids produce **different salts** — sulfuric acid (H_2SO_4) produces salts called **sulfates**, hydrochloric acid (HCl) produces **chlorides**, and nitric acid (HNO_3) produces **nitrates**.

Ammonia is a bit of an exception as it doesn't directly produce hydroxide ions, but **aqueous ammonia** is still an **alkali**. This is because the reaction between ammonia and water produces hydroxide ions. Ammonia accepts a hydrogen ion from water molecules, forming an ammonium ion and a hydroxide ion. In this way, ammonia can **neutralise acids**.

$NH_{3\,(aq)} + H_2O_{(l)} \rightleftharpoons NH_4^+{}_{(aq)} + OH^-_{(aq)}$

Acids and Bases

Acids React with Metals and Metal Compounds

1) As you've seen, when **acids** react with **bases**, they **neutralise** each other and produce a **salt**.
2) **Metal oxides**, **metal hydroxides** and **metal carbonates** are all common bases that'll react with acids. **Metals** will also react with acids.

Metal + Acid → Metal Salt + Hydrogen

E.g. $Mg_{(s)} + H_2SO_{4\,(aq)} \rightarrow MgSO_{4\,(aq)} + H_{2\,(g)}$

Or the ionic equation: $Mg_{(s)} + 2H^+_{(aq)} \rightarrow Mg^{2+}_{(aq)} + H_{2\,(g)}$

Metal Oxide + Acid → Salt + Water

E.g. $ZnO_{(s)} + 2HCl_{(aq)} \rightarrow ZnCl_{2\,(aq)} + H_2O_{(l)}$

Ionic equation: $ZnO_{(s)} + 2H^+_{(aq)} \rightarrow Zn^{2+}_{(aq)} + H_2O_{(l)}$

Metal Hydroxide + Acid → Salt + Water

E.g. $KOH_{(aq)} + HCl_{(aq)} \rightarrow KCl_{(aq)} + H_2O_{(l)}$

Ionic equation: $OH^-_{(aq)} + H^+_{(aq)} \rightarrow H_2O_{(l)}$

Metal Carbonate + Acid → Metal Salt + Carbon Dioxide + Water

E.g. $Na_2CO_{3\,(s)} + 2HCl_{(aq)} \rightarrow 2NaCl_{(aq)} + CO_{2\,(g)} + H_2O_{(l)}$

Ionic equation: $Na_2CO_{3\,(s)} + 2H^+_{(aq)} \rightarrow 2Na^+_{(aq)} + CO_{2\,(g)} + H_2O_{(l)}$

The metal ions take the place of the hydrogen ions of the acid to form salts.

The O^{2-} ion accepts two H^+ ions which have been donated by the acid.

The ionic equation shows that a proton is transferred from the acid to the hydroxide ion. This ionic equation is the same for all reactions between metal hydroxides and acids.

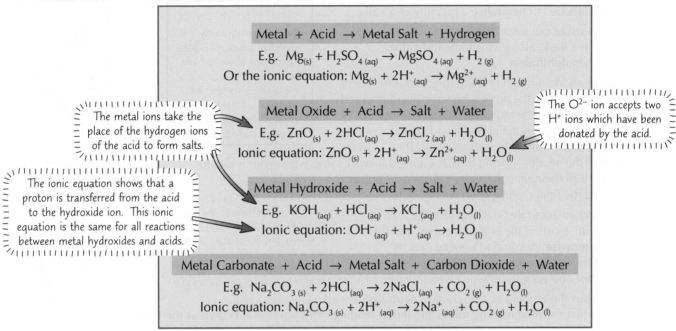

Ammonia reacts with Acids to make Ammonia Salts

The reaction of ammonia with nitric acid produces ammonium nitrate. Ammonium sulfate is made if ammonia reacts with sulfuric acid.

Ammonia + Acid → Ammonium salt

E.g. $NH_{3\,(aq)} + HNO_{3\,(aq)} \rightarrow NH_4NO_{3\,(aq)}$

Ionic equation: $NH_{3\,(aq)} + H^+_{(aq)} \rightarrow NH_4^+{}_{(aq)}$

This reaction is actually: $NH_4^+ + OH^- + HNO_3 \rightarrow NH_4NO_3 + H_2O$ as the reactant is aqueous ammonia.

Practice Questions

Q1 Define an acid, a base and an alkali.

Q2 Name three common acids.

Q3 What products are formed when an acid and an alkali react?

Exam Questions

Q1 A solution of magnesium chloride can be made in the laboratory using dilute hydrochloric acid.

a) Name a compound that could be used, with hydrochloric acid, to make magnesium chloride. [1 mark]

b) Write a balanced equation for this reaction. [1 mark]

Q2 Sodium hydroxide reacts with nitric acid at room temperature to produce water and a soluble salt.

a) Write a balanced equation, including state symbols for this reaction. [1 mark]

b) What is the name given to this type of reaction? [1 mark]

It's a stick-up — your protons or your life...

All acids have protons to give away and bases just love to take them. It's what makes them acids and bases. It's like how bus drivers drive buses... it's what makes them bus drivers. Learn the formulae for the common acids — hydrochloric, sulfuric, nitric and ethanoic, and the common alkalis — sodium hydroxide, potassium hydroxide and aqueous ammonia.

Titrations

Titrations are used to find out the concentrations of acid or alkali solutions. They're a bit fiddly to set up, but all titrations are kind of similar, so once you can do one, you can pretty much do them all.

Titrations Let You Work Out *Neutralisation Quantities*

1) **Titrations** allow you to find out **exactly** how much acid is needed to **neutralise** a quantity of alkali.
2) You measure out some **alkali** using a pipette and put it in a flask, along with some **indicator**, e.g. **phenolphthalein**.
3) First of all, do a rough titration to get an idea where the **end point** is (the point where the alkali is **exactly neutralised** and the indicator changes colour). To do this, take an initial reading to see how much acid is in the burette to start off with. Then, add the **acid** to the alkali — giving the flask a regular **swirl**. Stop when your indicator shows a permanent colour change (the end point). Record the final reading from your burette.
4) Now do an **accurate** titration. Run the acid in to within 2 cm^3 of the end point, then add the acid **dropwise**. If you don't notice exactly when the solution changed colour you've **overshot** and your result won't be accurate
5) **Work out** the amount of acid used to **neutralise** the alkali. This is just the **final reading minus the initial reading**. This volume is known as the **titre**.
6) It's best to **repeat** the titration a few times, making sure you get a similar answer each time — your readings should be within 0.1 cm^3 of each other. Then calculate a **mean**, ignoring any anomalous results. Remember to wash out the conical flask between each titration to remove any acid or alkali left in it.

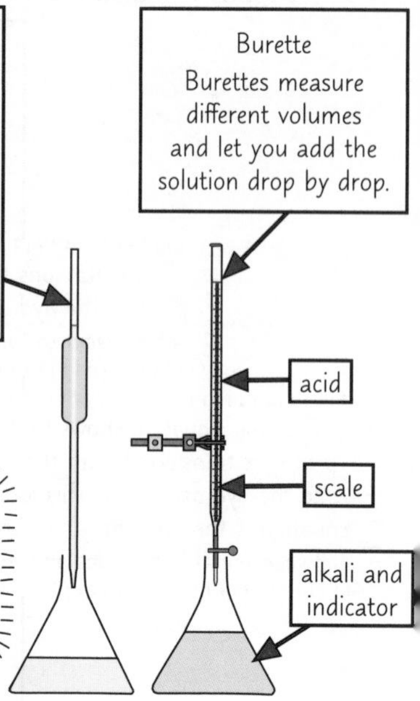
Pipette
Pipettes measure only one volume of solution. Fill the pipette just above the line, then take the pipette out of the solution (or the water pressure will hold up the level). Now drop the level down carefully to the line.
Burette
Burettes measure different volumes and let you add the solution drop by drop.
acid
scale
alkali and indicator

You can also do titrations the other way round — adding alkali to acid. You usually put the analyte in the conical flask and the solution of known concentration in the burette.

Titrations need to be done Accurately

1) When doing a titration, it's really important that you take your readings accurately.
2) When taking a reading from a burette, you should read from the bottom of the **meniscus**.
3) You don't have to read to the smallest graduation, e.g. 0.1 cm^3. You can make your readings **more accurate** by taking readings to the nearest 0.05 cm^3.

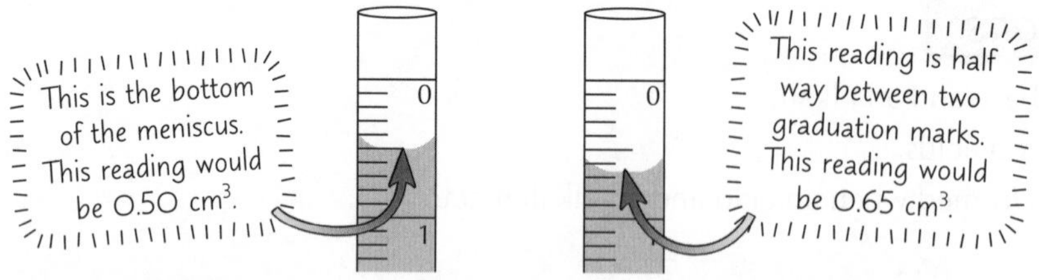
This is the bottom of the meniscus. This reading would be 0.50 cm³.
0
1
0
This reading is half way between two graduation marks. This reading would be 0.65 cm³.

Indicators Show you when the Reaction's *Just Finished*

Indicators change **colour**, as if by magic. In titrations, indicators that change colour quickly over a **very small pH range** are used so you know **exactly** when the reaction has ended.

Universal indicator is no good here — its colour change is too gradual.

The main two indicators for **acid/alkali reactions** are —

> **methyl orange** — turns **yellow** to **red** when adding acid to alkali.
> **phenolphthalein** — turns **pink** to **colourless** when adding acid to alkali.

When you're doing a titration where the end point is marked by a colour change, it's a good idea to carry out your titration on a white tile, or a sheet of white paper. That way, it's much easier to see exactly when the end point is.

Choppy seas made it difficult for Captain Blackbird to read the burette accurately.

Titrations

Titrations are done with **Standard Solutions**

1) In a titration, you have **one unknown concentration** to work out. To work out the concentration of the unknown solution, known as the **analyte**, you have to know the concentration of the solution you're titrating it against.
2) A solution that has a precisely known concentration is called a **standard solution**. Standard solutions are made by dissolving a **known amount** of **solid** in a known amount of **water** to create a known concentration.
3) To make up a standard solution, follow these steps:

> 1) Using a **precise** balance, carefully weigh out the required mass of solid onto a watch glass.
> 2) Transfer this solid to a beaker. Use some water to **wash** any bits of solid from the watch glass into the beaker.
> 3) Add water to the beaker to **completely dissolve** the solid. Use a glass rod to **stir** the solution to help the solid dissolve.
> 4) Once the solid has dissolved, transfer the solution into a **volumetric flask**. You'll need to use a volumetric flask that's the same size as the volume of solution you want to make up. **Rinse** the beaker and glass rod with water, transferring this water into the volumetric flask.
> 5) Use water to fill the volumetric flask up to the **graduation line**. Use a **pipette** to add the final few drops to make sure you don't add too much water and overshoot the graduation line.
> 6) Put the lid on the flask and turn the flask over a few times to thoroughly **mix** the solution.

When making up standard solutions, you should use distilled water. This is just pure water with nothing else in it.

In a Solution the **Concentration** is Measured in **mol dm^{-3}**

1) The **concentration** of a solution is how many **moles** are dissolved per **1 dm^3** of solution. Units are **mol dm^{-3}**.
2) Here's the formula to find the **number of moles**, (**n**).

$$\textbf{Number of moles} = \frac{\textbf{Concentration} \times \textbf{volume (in cm}^3\textbf{)}}{\textbf{1000}} \quad \text{or} \quad \textbf{Number of moles = Concentration} \times \textbf{Volume (in dm}^3\textbf{)}$$

1 dm^3 = 1000 cm^3 = 1 litre

3) To make a standard solution, you often have to calculate the mass of solid you'll need from a given volume and concentration.

Example: What mass of solid sodium carbonate, Na_2CO_3, is needed to make 250 cm^3 of 0.300 mol dm^{-3} sodium carbonate solution?

Start by working out how many **moles** of Na_2CO_3 are needed using the equation:

moles = concentration × volume ⟹ $n = 0.300 \times (\frac{250}{1000}) = 0.0750$ moles

Use mass = moles × M to work out the mass of Na_2CO_3 required.

mass = 0.0750 × [(2 × 23.0) + 12.0 + (3 × 16.0)] = 0.0750 × 106 = **7.95 g**

Make sure all your values are in the correct units — here, the concentration is given in mol dm^{-3} so you need to convert the volume to dm^3.

Practice Questions

Q1 Describe the procedure for doing a titration.

Q2 What colour change would you expect to see if you added an excess of hydrochloric acid to a conical flask containing sodium hydroxide and methyl orange?

Exam Questions

Q1 What mass of solid sodium hydrogen sulfate ($NaHSO_4$) would be required to make up 250 cm^3 of a standard solution of sodium hydrogen sulfate of concentration 0.600 mol dm^{-3}? [2 marks]

Q2* Describe how indicators are used and explain the importance of selecting an appropriate indicator when carrying out a titration. Include examples of indicators that would and would not be suitable for use in titrations. [6 marks]

Burettes and pipettes — big glass things, just waiting to be dropped...

Titrations are all about being accurate and precise. Make sure you're really careful when measuring out solutions, and reading values off your burette. An error in your experiment means you'll have errors all through your calculations.

* The quality of your extended response will be assessed for this question.

Titration Calculations

There's far more to a titration than just simply doing it.
Once you've got all those readings, there's a whole load of calculations to carry out. You've been warned...

You can Calculate **Concentrations** from Titrations

Example: 25.0 cm^3 of 0.500 mol dm^{-3} HCl was used to neutralise 35.0 cm^3 of NaOH solution. Calculate the concentration of the sodium hydroxide solution in mol dm^{-3}.

First write a **balanced equation** and decide **what you know** and what you **need to know**:

$$\underset{\substack{25.0\text{ cm}^3\\0.500\text{ mol dm}^{-3}}}{HCl} + \underset{\substack{35.0\text{ cm}^3\\?}}{NaOH} \rightarrow NaCl + H_2O$$

Now work out how many **moles of HCl** you have. You'll need to use the equation linking no. moles, concentration and volume — have a look back at the last page if you can't remember it.

$$\text{No. of moles of HCl} = \frac{\text{concentration} \times \text{volume (cm}^3)}{1000} = \frac{0.500 \times 25.0}{1000} = 0.0125 \text{ moles}$$

You need to be able to work out concentration in g dm^{-3} too. To do this, just convert moles into mass and use:

$$\text{Conc} = \frac{\text{mass (g)} \times 1000}{\text{volume (cm}^3)}$$

From the equation, you know 1 mole of HCl neutralises 1 mole of NaOH.
So 0.0125 moles of HCl must neutralise **0.0125** moles of NaOH.
Now it's a doddle to work out the **concentration of NaOH**.

$$\text{Concentration of NaOH} = \frac{\text{moles of NaOH} \times 1000}{\text{volume (cm}^3)} = \frac{0.0125 \times 1000}{35.0} = \mathbf{0.36\ mol\ dm^{-3}}$$

You have to account for **Reaction Stoichiometry**

I'll show them who's unbalanced...

1) A balanced equation will tell you the **reaction stoichiometry** — this is how many moles of one reactant react with how many moles of another reactant.
2) In titration calculations, you have to use the **balanced equation** when working out **concentrations**, as the stoichiometry of a reaction affects the ratios between each of the reactants and products in your reaction.

Example: This equation shows the reaction between sodium hydroxide and sulfuric acid:

$$2NaOH + H_2SO_4 \rightarrow Na_2SO_4 + 2H_2O$$

Given that it takes 19.1 cm^3 of 0.200 mol dm^{-3} NaOH to completely neutralise 25.0 cm^3 of the acid, calculate the concentration of the sulfuric acid.

First, work out the number of moles of NaOH in 19.1 cm^3 of 0.200 mol dm^{-3} NaOH solution.

$$\text{moles} = \text{concentration} \times \text{volume (dm}^3)$$
$$n = 0.200 \times (19.1 \div 1000) = 0.00382 \text{ moles}$$

This reaction doesn't happen as a 1:1 molar reaction, but happens in a **2:1 ratio** of NaOH : H_2SO_4.
For every 2 moles of NaOH, you only require 1 mole of H_2SO_4 for the reaction to happen.
So, you have half the number of moles of H_2SO_4 as you have NaOH.

$$\text{moles } H_2SO_4 = \text{moles of NaOH} \div 2$$
$$= 0.00382 \div 2 = 0.00191 \text{ moles}$$

$$\text{So, concentration of } H_2SO_4 = \frac{\text{moles of } H_2SO_4 \times 1000}{\text{volume (cm}^3)} = \frac{0.00191 \times 1000}{25.0} = \mathbf{0.0764\ mol\ dm^{-3}}$$

Titration Calculations

Polyprotic Acids donate *More* than *One Proton*

You may have to do calculations that involve acids that donate **more** than **one proton**. These are known as **polyprotic acids**.

- Diprotic acids donate two protons, e.g. sulfuric acid (H_2SO_4), carbonic acid (H_2CO_3) and hydrogen sulfide (H_2S).
- Triprotic acids donate three protons, e.g. phosphoric acid (H_3PO_4).

Compared to a monoprotic acid, you'll need **double** the number of moles of base to neutralise a **diprotic acid**. You'll need to **triple** the number of moles of base to neutralise a **triprotic acid** compared to a monoprotic acid. So, remember to take this into account when you're working out these sorts of titration calculations.

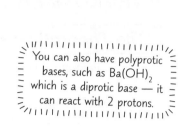

You can also have polyprotic bases, such as $Ba(OH)_2$ which is a diprotic base — it can react with 2 protons.

You can Calculate *Volumes* for Reactions from *Moles* and *Concentrations*

Example: 20.4 cm³ of a 0.500 mol dm⁻³ solution of sodium carbonate reacts with 1.50 mol dm⁻³ nitric acid. Calculate the volume of nitric acid required to neutralise the sodium carbonate.

First write a **balanced equation** for the reaction and decide **what you know** and what you **want to know**:

Na_2CO_3	+	$2HNO_3 \rightarrow 2NaNO_3 + H_2O + CO_2$
20.4 cm³		**?**
0.500 mol dm⁻³		**1.50 mol dm⁻³**

Calculating volumes for reactions is useful when you're planning quantities to use in titration experiments.

Now work out how many **moles** of Na_2CO_3 you've got:

$$\text{No. of moles of } Na_2CO_3 = \frac{\text{concentration} \times \text{volume (cm}^3)}{1000} = \frac{0.500 \times 20.4}{1000} = 0.0102 \text{ moles}$$

The reaction happens in a 1 : 2 molar ratio of $Na_2CO_3 : HNO_3$.
1 mole of Na_2CO_3 neutralises 2 moles of HNO_3, so 0.0102 moles of Na_2CO_3 neutralises **0.0204 moles of HNO_3**.
Now you know the number of moles of HNO_3 and the concentration, you can work out the **volume**:

$$\text{Volume of } HNO_3 \text{ (cm}^3) = \frac{\text{number of moles} \times 1000}{\text{concentration}} = \frac{0.0204 \times 1000}{1.50} = \mathbf{13.6\ cm^3}$$

Practice Questions

Q1 What equation links the number of moles, concentration and volume (in cm³)?

Exam Questions

Q1 Calculate the concentration (in mol dm⁻³) of a solution of ethanoic acid, CH_3COOH, if 25.4 cm³ of it is neutralised by 14.6 cm³ of 0.500 mol dm⁻³ sodium hydroxide solution.

$CH_3COOH + NaOH \rightarrow CH_3COONa + H_2O$ [3 marks]

Q2 You are supplied with 0.750 g of calcium carbonate and a solution of 0.250 mol dm⁻³ sulfuric acid. What volume of acid will be needed to neutralise the calcium carbonate?

$CaCO_3 + H_2SO_4 \rightarrow CaSO_4 + H_2O + CO_2$ [3 marks]

Q3 In a titration, 17.1 cm³ of 0.250 mol dm⁻³ hydrochloric acid neutralises 25.0 cm³ calcium hydroxide solution.

a) Write out a balanced equation for this reaction. [1 mark]

b) Work out the concentration of the calcium hydroxide solution. [3 marks]

DJs can't do titrations — they just keep on dropping the base...

This looks like a horrible load of calculations, but it's really not that bad. Just remember the equation linking concentration, volume (in cm³ and dm³) and moles and you'll be able to work out pretty much everything.

Atom Economy and Percentage Yield

How to make a subject like chemistry even more exciting — introduce the word 'economy'...

The **Theoretical Yield** of a Product is the **Maximum** you could get

1) The **theoretical yield** is the **mass of product** that **should** be made in a reaction if **no** chemicals are **'lost'** in the process. You can use the **masses of reactants** and a **balanced equation** to calculate the theoretical yield for a reaction.
2) The **actual** mass of product (the **actual yield**) is always **less** than the theoretical yield. Some chemicals are always 'lost', e.g. some solution gets left on filter paper, or is lost during transfers between containers.
3) The **percentage yield** is the **actual** amount of product you collect, written as a percentage of the theoretical yield. You can work out the percentage yield with this formula:

$$\text{percentage yield} = \frac{\text{actual yield}}{\text{theoretical yield}} \times 100\%$$

Example: Ethanol can be oxidised to form ethanal: $C_2H_5OH + [O] \rightarrow CH_3CHO + H_2O$
9.2 g of ethanol was reacted with an oxidising agent in excess and 2.1 g of ethanal was produced. Calculate the theoretical yield and the percentage yield.

[O] is just the symbol for any oxidising agent.

Number of moles = mass of substance ÷ molar mass

Moles of $C_2H_5OH = 9.2 \div [(2 \times 12.0) + (5 \times 1.0) + 16.0 + 1.0] = 9.2 \div 46.0 = 0.2$ moles

1 mole of C_2H_5OH produces 1 mole of CH_3CHO, so 0.2 moles of C_2H_5OH will produce 0.2 moles of CH_3CHO.

M of $CH_3CHO = (2 \times 12.0) + (4 \times 1.0) + 16.0 = 44.0\ \text{g mol}^{-1}$

Theoretical yield (mass of CH_3CHO) = number of moles × M = 0.2 × 44.0 = **8.8 g**

So, if the actual yield was 2.1 g, the percentage yield $= \frac{\text{actual yield}}{\text{theoretical yield}} \times 100\% = \frac{2.1}{8.8} \times 100\% \approx$ **24%**

Atom Economy is a Measure of the **Efficiency** of a Reaction

1) The **percentage yield** tells you how wasteful the **process** is — it's based on how much of the product is lost because of things like reactions not completing or losses during collection and purification.
2) But percentage yield doesn't measure how wasteful the **reaction** itself is. A reaction that has a 100% yield could still be very wasteful if a lot of the atoms from the **reactants** wind up in **by-products** rather than the **desired product**.
3) **Atom economy** is a measure of the proportion of reactant **atoms** that become part of the desired product (rather than by-products) in the **balanced** chemical equation. It's calculated using this formula:

$$\%\ \text{atom economy} = \frac{\text{molecular mass of desired product}}{\text{sum of molecular masses of all products}} \times 100\%$$

4) In an **addition reaction**, the reactants **combine** to form a **single product**. The atom economy for addition reactions is **always 100%** since no atoms are wasted.

E.g. ethene (C_2H_4) and hydrogen react to form ethane (C_2H_6) in an addition reaction: $C_2H_4 + H_2 \rightarrow C_2H_6$
The **only product** is ethane (the desired product). No reactant atoms are wasted so the atom economy is **100%**.

5) A **substitution reaction** is one where some atoms from one reactant are **swapped** with atoms from another reactant. This type of reaction **always** results in **at least two products** — the desired product and at least one by-product.

An example is the reaction of bromomethane (CH_3Br) with sodium hydroxide (NaOH) to make methanol (CH_3OH): $CH_3Br + NaOH \rightarrow CH_3OH + NaBr$
This is **more wasteful** than an addition reaction because the Na and Br atoms aren't part of the desired product.

$$\%\ \text{atom economy} = \frac{\text{molecular mass of desired product}}{\text{sum of molecular masses of all products}} \times 100\%$$

$$= \frac{M_r(CH_3OH)}{M_r(CH_3OH) + M_r(NaBr)} \times 100\%$$

$$= \frac{(12.0 + (3 \times 1.0) + 16.0 + 1.0)}{(12.0 + (3 \times 1.0) + 16.0 + 1.0) + (23.0 + 79.9)} \times 100\% = \frac{32.0}{32.0 + 102.9} \times 100\% = \mathbf{23.7\%}$$

Always make sure you're using a balanced equation.

Atom Economy and Percentage Yield

Reactions can Have **High Percentage Yields** and **Low Atom Economies**

Example: 0.475 g of CH_3Br reacts with an excess of NaOH in this reaction: $CH_3Br + NaOH \rightarrow CH_3OH + NaBr$
0.153 g of CH_3OH is produced. What is the percentage yield?

Number of moles = mass of substance ÷ molar mass

Moles of CH_3Br = 0.475 ÷ (12 + (3 × 1) + 79.9) = 0.475 ÷ 94.9 = **0.00501 moles**

The reactant : product ratio is 1 : 1, so the maximum number of moles of CH_3OH is **0.00501**.

Theoretical yield = 0.00501 × M(CH_3OH) = 0.00501 × (12.0 + (3 × 1.0) + 16.0 + 1.0) = 0.00501 × 32 = **0.160 g**

$$\text{percentage yield} = \frac{\text{actual yield}}{\text{theoretical yield}} \times 100\% = \frac{0.153}{0.160} \times 100\% = \mathbf{95.6\%}$$

So this reaction has a very high percentage yield, but, as you saw on the previous page, the atom economy is low.

It's Important to Develop Reactions that are **Sustainable**

1) Companies in the chemical industry will often choose to use reactions with high atom economies. High atom economy has **environmental** and **economic benefits**.
2) A **low atom economy** means there's lots of **waste** produced. It costs money to **separate** the desired product from the waste products and more money to dispose of the waste products **safely** so they don't harm the environment.
3) **Reactant chemicals** are usually costly. It's a **waste of money** if a high proportion of them end up as useless products.
4) Reactions with low atom economies are **less sustainable**. Many raw materials are in **limited supply**, so it makes sense to use them efficiently so they last as long as possible. Also, waste has to go somewhere — it's better for the environment if less is produced.
5) Reactions conditions with **high energy demands**, e.g. **high temperatures** and **high pressures**, cost a lot to maintain. **Lower temperatures** and **pressures** are cheaper to run and better for the environment.
6) Raw materials that come from **renewable sources**, e.g. plants, enzymes, are better for the environment than materials from **non-renewable sources**, e.g. crude oil, coal.

Fermentation is an example of a sustainable reaction.

Practice Questions

Q1 How many products are there in an addition reaction?

Q2 Why do reactions with high atom economy save chemical companies money and cause less environmental impact?

Exam Questions

Q1 Reactions 1 and 2 below show two possible ways of preparing the compound chloroethane (C_2H_5Cl):

1 $C_2H_5OH + PCl_5 \rightarrow C_2H_5Cl + POCl_3 + HCl$

2 $C_2H_4 + HCl \rightarrow C_2H_5Cl$

a) Which of these is an addition reaction? [1 mark]

b) Calculate the atom economy for reaction 1. [2 marks]

c) Reaction 2 has an atom economy of 100%. Explain why this is, in terms of the products of the reaction. [1 mark]

Q2 Phosphorus trichloride (PCl_3) reacts with chlorine to give phosphorus pentachloride (PCl_5):

$PCl_3 + Cl_2 \rightarrow PCl_5$

a) 0.275 g of PCl_3 reacts with an excess of chlorine. What is the theoretical yield of PCl_5? [2 marks]

b) When this reaction is performed 0.198 g of PCl_5 is collected. Calculate the percentage yield. [1 mark]

c) Changing conditions such as temperature and pressure will alter the percentage yield of this reaction. Will changing these conditions affect the atom economy? Explain your answer. [2 marks]

I knew a Tommy Conomy once... strange bloke...

These pages shouldn't be too much trouble — you've survived worse already. Make sure that you get plenty of practice using the percentage yield and atom economy formulae. And whatever you do, don't get mixed up between percentage yield (which is to do with the process) and atom economy (which is to do with the reaction).

Oxidation Numbers

This double page has more occurrences of "oxidation" than the Beatles' "All You Need is Love" features the word "love".

Oxidation Numbers *Tell you how Many* **Electrons Atoms** *have*

When atoms **react** or **bond** to other atoms, they can **lose** or **gain** electrons. The **oxidation number** tells you how many electrons an atom has donated or accepted to form an **ion**, or to form part of a **compound**.
There are certain rules you need to remember to help you assign oxidation numbers. Here they are...

1) All uncombined elements have an oxidation number of **0**. This means they haven't accepted or donated any electrons. Elements that are bonded to identical atoms will also have an oxidation number of **0**.

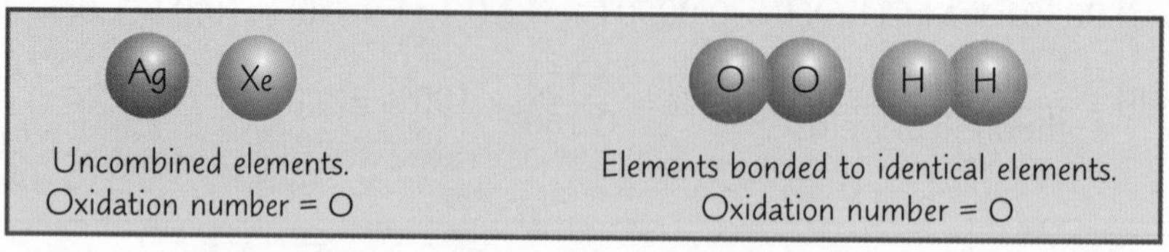

2) The oxidation number of a simple, monatomic ion (that's an ion consisting of just one atom) is the same as its **charge**.

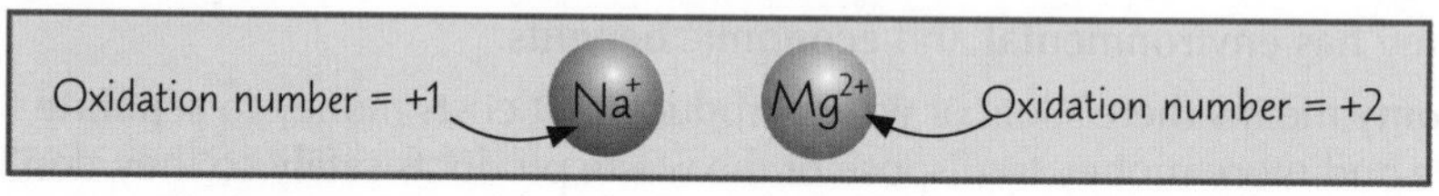

3) For **molecular ions** (see page 26), the sum of the oxidation numbers is the same as the overall charge of the ion. So each of the constituent atoms will have an oxidation number of its own, which will add up to the **overall charge**.

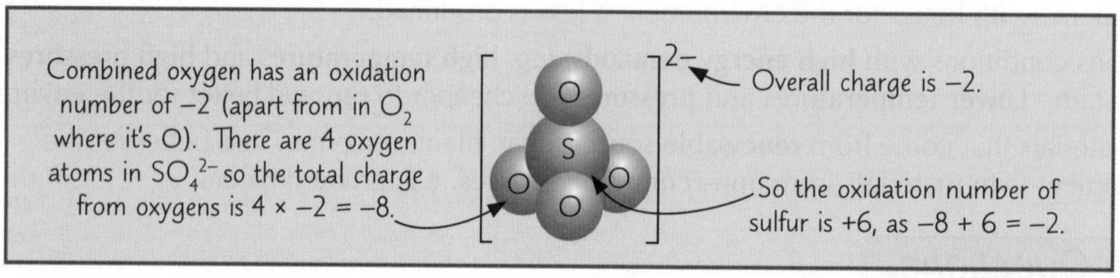

Combined oxygen has an oxidation number of −2 (apart from in O_2 where it's 0). There are 4 oxygen atoms in SO_4^{2-} so the total charge from oxygens is 4 × −2 = −8.
Overall charge is −2.
So the oxidation number of sulfur is +6, as −8 + 6 = −2.

4) For a neutral compound, the overall oxidation number is **0**. If the compound is made up of more than one element, each element will have its own oxidation number.

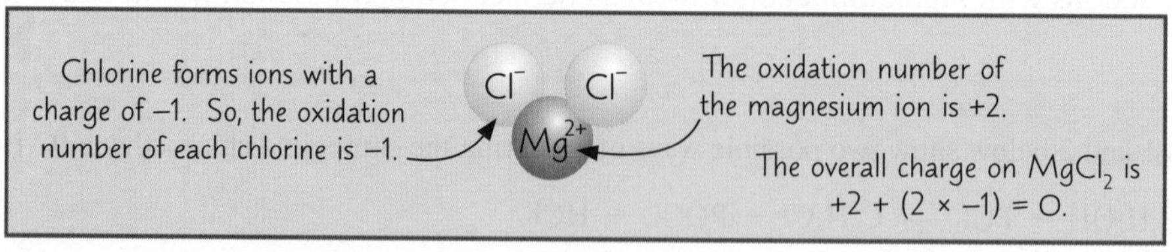

Chlorine forms ions with a charge of −1. So, the oxidation number of each chlorine is −1.
Cl^-
Cl^-
Mg^{2+}
The oxidation number of the magnesium ion is +2.
The overall charge on $MgCl_2$ is +2 + (2 × −1) = 0.

5) You'll need to **learn** these oxidation numbers.

- **Oxygen** nearly always has an oxidation number of **−2**, except in **peroxides** (O_2^{2-}) where it's **−1**, and **molecular oxygen** (O_2) where it's **0**.
- **Hydrogen** always has an oxidation number of **+1**, except in **metal hydrides** (MH_x, where M = metal) where it's **−1** and in **molecular hydrogen** (H_2) where it's **0**.

Roman Numerals *tell you the* **Oxidation Number**

If an element can have **multiple** oxidation numbers, or **isn't** in its 'normal' oxidation state, its oxidation number can be shown by using **Roman numerals**, e.g. (I) = +1, (II) = +2, (III) = +3 and so on. The Roman numerals are written after the name of the element they correspond to.

E.g. In iron(II) sulfate, iron has an oxidation number of +2. Formula = $FeSO_4$
In iron(III) sulfate, iron has an oxidation number of +3. Formula = $Fe_2(SO_4)_3$

Hands up if you like Roman numerals...

Oxidation Numbers

-ate Compounds Contain Oxygen and Another Element

1) Ions with names ending in -ate (e.g. sulfate, nitrate, chlorate, carbonate) contain **oxygen** and another element. For example, sulfates contain sulfur and oxygen, nitrates contain nitrogen and oxygen... and so on.
2) Sometimes the 'other' element in the ion can exist with different oxidation numbers, and so form different '-ate ions'. In these cases, the oxidation number is attached as a Roman numeral **after** the name of the -ate compound.
The roman numerals correspond to the **non-oxygen** element in the -ate compound.
E.g. In sulfate(VI) ions, the **sulfur** has oxidation number **+6** — this is the SO_4^{2-} ion.
In sulfate(IV) ions, the **sulfur** has oxidation number **+4** — this is the SO_3^{2-} ion.
In nitrate(III), **nitrogen** has an oxidation number of **+3** — this is the NO_2^- ion.

If there are no oxidation numbers shown, assume nitrate = NO_3^- and sulfate = SO_4^{2-}.

You Can Work Out Oxidation Numbers from Formulae or Systematic Names

You might need to **work out** the oxidation numbers of different elements in a compound from its **formula** or **systematic name**. You'll also need to be able to work out the formulae of compounds from their systematic names and visa versa.

Example: What is the formula of iron(III) sulfate?

From the systematic name, you can tell iron has an **oxidation number** of +3.
The formula of the sulfate ion is SO_4^{2-} and it has an **overall charge** of –2.
The overall charge of the compound is 0, so you need to find a ratio of $Fe^{3+}:SO_4^{2-}$ that will make the overall charge 0.

$(+3 \times 2) + (-2 \times 3) = 6 + -6 = 0$ The ratio of Fe : SO_4 is **2 : 3**.

So the formula is $\mathbf{Fe_2(SO_4)_3}$.

Example: What is the systematic name for ClO_2^-?

This formula contains **chlorine** and **oxygen**, so it's a **chlorate**.
Oxygen usually exists with an oxidation number of **–2**.
There are 2 oxygens, so this will make the total charge from oxygens $-2 \times 2 = -4$.
The overall charge on the molecule is –1, so chlorine must have an oxidation number of **+3**, since $-4 + 3 = -1$. So, the systematic name is **chlorate(III)**.

Practice Questions

Q1 What is the oxidation number of H in H_2?

Q2 What is the usual oxidation number for oxygen when it's combined with another element?

Q3 What is the oxidation number of sulfur in a sulfate(IV) ion?

Exam Questions

Q1 What is the systematic name of $Cr_2(SO_4)_3$? [1 mark]

Q2 What is the formula of iron(II) nitrate? [1 mark]

Q3 Lead sulfate can be formed by reacting lead oxide (PbO) with warm sulfuric acid in a ratio of 1:1.

a) What is the formula of lead sulfate? [1 mark]

b) Calculate the oxidation number of lead in:
i) lead oxide ii) lead sulfate [2 marks]

Sockidation number — a measure of how many odd socks are in my drawers...

There isn't any tricky maths involved with oxidation numbers, just a bit of adding, some subtracting... maybe a bit of multiplying if you're unlucky. The real trick is to learn the rules about predicting oxidation numbers for those elements and molecular ions that come up all the time, especially the ones for those pesky metal hydrides and peroxides.

Redox Reactions

Redox reactions can be tricky to get your head around at first. It will help you loads if you're confident about all the oxidation number stuff on the last two pages before you start tackling this.

If Electrons are Transferred, it's a ***Redox Reaction***

1) A **loss** of electrons is called **oxidation**. A **gain** in electrons is called **reduction**.
2) Reduction and oxidation happen **simultaneously** — hence the term "**redox**" reaction.
3) An **oxidising agent accepts** electrons and gets reduced.
4) A **reducing agent donates** electrons and gets oxidised.

$-e^-$

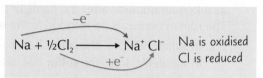

$$Na + \tfrac{1}{2}Cl_2 \longrightarrow Na^+ Cl^-$$

$+e^-$

Na is oxidised
Cl is reduced

Oxidation Numbers go ***Up*** *or* ***Down*** *as Electrons are* ***Lost*** *or* ***Gained***

1) The oxidation number for an atom will **increase by 1** for each **electron lost**.
2) The oxidation number will **decrease by 1** for each **electron gained**.
3) To work out whether something has been **oxidised** or **reduced**, you need to assign each element an oxidation number **before** the reaction, and **after** the reaction.
4) If the oxidation number has increased, then the element has **lost** electrons and been **oxidised**.
5) If the oxidation number has decreased, then the element has **gained** electrons and been **reduced**.

Check back at the rules for assigning oxidation numbers on page 36 if you're unsure about this.

Example: Identify the oxidising and reducing agents in this reaction: $4Fe + 3O_2 \rightarrow 2Fe_2O_3$

Iron has gone from having an oxidation number of 0, to an oxidation number of +3.
It's **lost electrons** and has been **oxidised**. This makes it the **reducing agent** in this reaction.

Oxygen has gone from having an oxidation number of 0, to an oxidation number of –2.
It's **gained electrons** and has been **reduced**. This means it's the **oxidising agent** in this reaction.

Example: Identify the oxidising and reducing agents in this reaction: $2Na + Cl_2 \rightarrow 2NaCl$

Sodium has gone from having an oxidation number of 0, to an oxidation number of +1.
It's **lost** an **electron** and has been **oxidised**, so it's a **reducing agent**.
Chlorine has gone from having an oxidation number of 0, to an oxidation number of –1. It's **gained** an **electron** and has been **reduced**, so it's an **oxidising agent**.

6) When **metals** form compounds, they generally **donate** electrons to form **positive ions** — meaning they usually have **positive oxidation numbers**.
7) When **non-metals** form compounds, they generally **gain** electrons — meaning they usually have **negative oxidation numbers**.

It can be quite difficult remembering all these rules.
So here's a helpful memory aid to make these oxidation and reduction rules a little bit easier. Just remember **OIL RIG**.

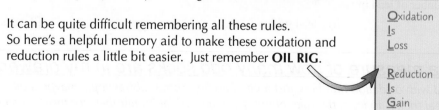

Oxidation
Is
Loss

Reduction
Is
Gain

PC Honey was a reducing agent where crime was concerned.

Redox Reactions

Metals** are **Oxidised** when they react with **Acids

1) On page 29 you saw how metals react with acids to produce a salt and hydrogen gas. Well this is a redox reaction:
   - The metal atoms are **oxidised**, losing electrons to form **positive metal ions** (in **salts**).
   - The hydrogen ions in solution are **reduced**, gaining electrons and forming hydrogen molecules.
2) For example, magnesium reacts with dilute hydrochloric acid like this:

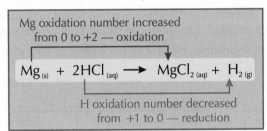

Mg oxidation number increased from 0 to +2 — oxidation

$$Mg_{(s)} + 2HCl_{(aq)} \rightarrow MgCl_{2\,(aq)} + H_{2\,(g)}$$

H oxidation number decreased from +1 to 0 — reduction

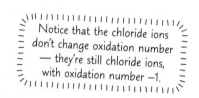

Notice that the chloride ions don't change oxidation number — they're still chloride ions, with oxidation number −1.

3) If you use **sulfuric acid** instead of hydrochloric acid, exactly the same processes of **oxidation** and **reduction** take place. For example, potassium is oxidised to K^+ ions:

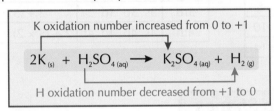

K oxidation number increased from 0 to +1

$$2K_{(s)} + H_2SO_{4\,(aq)} \rightarrow K_2SO_{4\,(aq)} + H_{2\,(g)}$$

H oxidation number decreased from +1 to 0

Practice Questions

Q1 Is an oxidising agent reduced or oxidised in a redox reaction?

Q2 Would the oxidation number of an element that is reduced get bigger, smaller, or stay the same?

Q3 What generally happens to the number of electrons a metal has when it forms a compound?

Q4 Describe what happens, in terms of oxidation and reduction, when metals react with acids.

Exam Questions

Q1 Nitric acid reacts with solid iron. What sort of a reaction is this? [1 mark]

Q2 Which of these equations shows a redox reaction?

A $HCl + NaOH \rightarrow NaCl + H_2O$ **B** $NaCl + AgNO_3 \rightarrow AgCl + NaNO_3$

C $BaBr_2 + H_2S \rightarrow BaS + 2HBr$ **D** $N_2 + O_2 \rightarrow 2NO$ [1 mark]

Q3 Concentrated sulfuric acid reacts with iron to produce iron(II) sulfate and one other product.

a) Write a balanced chemical equation for this reaction. [1 mark]

b) Use your answer to part a) to identify the oxidising agent and the reducing agent. [1 mark]

Q4 This equation shows the reaction of aluminium and iodine:

$$2Al_{(s)} + 3I_{2\,(g)} \rightarrow 2AlI_{3\,(s)}$$

Use oxidation numbers to show that aluminium has been oxidised. [1 mark]

Redox — relax in a lovely warm bubble bath...

*The thing here is to take your time. Questions on redox reactions aren't usually that hard, but they are easy to get wrong. So don't panic, take it easy, and get all the marks. Remember your nifty friend the **oil rig**. Oxidation Is Loss, Reduction Is Gain. Oxidation Is Loss, Reduction Is Gain. Oxidation Is Loss, Reduction Is Gain... Have you got it yet?*

Electronic Structure

Those little electrons prancing about like mini bunnies decide what'll react with what — it's what chemistry's all about.

Electron Shells are Made Up of Sub-Shells and Orbitals

1) In the currently accepted model of the atom, electrons have fixed energies.
2) They move around the nucleus in **shells** (sometimes called **energy levels**). These shells are all given numbers known as **principal quantum numbers**.
3) Shells **further** from the nucleus have a higher **energy** (and a larger principal quantum number) than shells closer to the nucleus.
4) Shells are divided up into **sub-shells**. Different electron shells have different numbers of sub-shells, each of which has a different energy. Sub-shells are called **s-**, **p-**, **d-** or **f-sub-shells**.
5) These sub-shells have different numbers of **orbitals**, which can each hold up to **2 electrons**.

You don't need to worry too much about the f-sub-shell, but it's good to know it's there.

This table shows the number of electrons that fit in each type of sub-shell.

Sub-shell	Number of orbitals	Maximum electrons
s	1	1 x 2 = 2
p	3	3 x 2 = 6
d	5	5 x 2 = 10
f	7	7 x 2 = 14

And this one shows the sub-shells and electrons in the first four energy levels.

Shell	Sub-shells	Total number of electrons	
1st	1s	2	= 2
2nd	2s 2p	2 + (3 × 2)	= 8
3rd	3s 3p 3d	2 + (3 × 2) + (5 × 2)	= 18
4th	4s 4p 4d 4f	2 + (3 × 2) + (5 × 2) + (7 × 2)	= 32

Orbitals Have Characteristic Shapes

There are a few things you need to know about orbitals... like what they are...

1) An orbital is the **bit of space** that an electron moves in. Orbitals within the same sub-shell have the **same energy**.
2) If there are two electrons in an orbital, they have to 'spin' in **opposite** directions — this is called **spin-pairing**.
3) s orbitals are **spherical** — p orbitals have **dumbbell shapes**. There are three p orbitals and they're at right angles to one another.

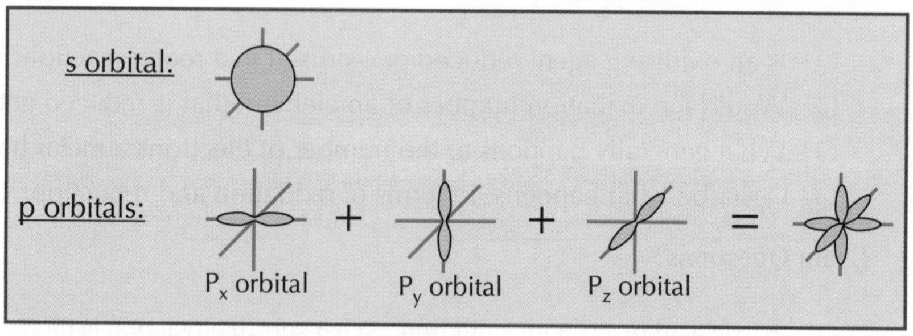

You Can Show Electron Configuration in Different Ways

The **number** of electrons that an atom or ion has, and how they are **arranged**, is called its **electron configuration**. Electron configurations can be shown in different ways. E.g. an atom of neon has 10 electrons — two in the 1s sub-shell, two in the 2s sub-shell and six in the 2p sub-shell. You can show this using...

Sub-shell notation:

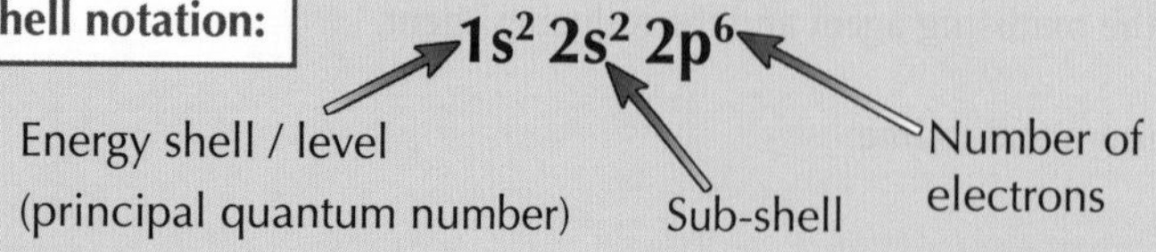

Electrons in boxes:

1) Each **box** represents one **orbital** and each **arrow** represents one **electron**.
2) The up and down arrows represent electrons **spinning** in opposite directions. Two electrons can only occupy the same orbital if they have **opposite** spin.

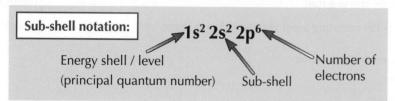

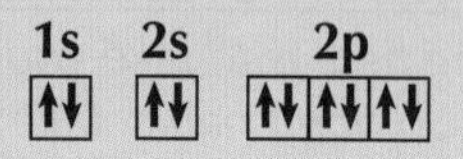

Electronic Structure

Work Out **Electron Configurations** by Filling the **Lowest** Energy Levels First

You can figure out most electron configurations pretty easily, so long as you know a few simple rules —

1) Electrons fill up the **lowest** energy sub-shells first.

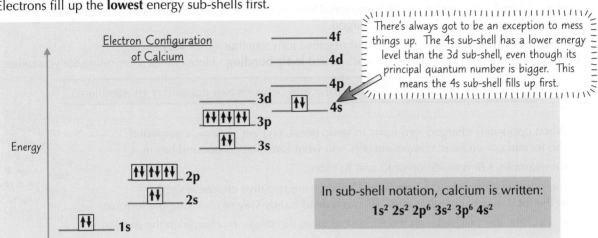

There's always got to be an exception to mess things up. The 4s sub-shell has a lower energy level than the 3d sub-shell, even though its principal quantum number is bigger. This means the 4s sub-shell fills up first.

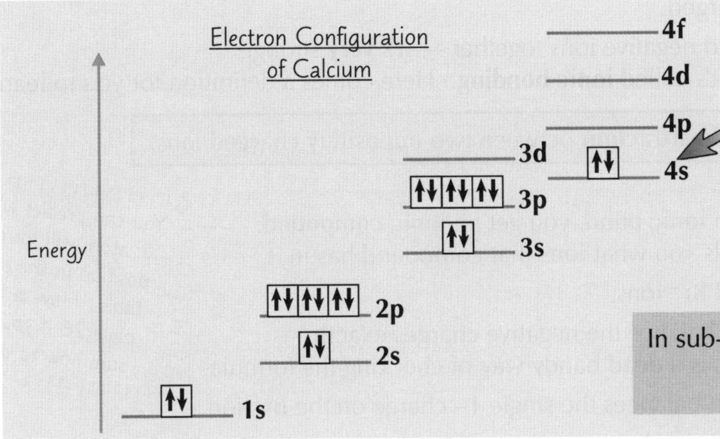

In sub-shell notation, calcium is written:
$1s^2\ 2s^2\ 2p^6\ 3s^2\ 3p^6\ 4s^2$

2) Electrons fill orbitals with the same energy **singly** before they start sharing.

3) For the configuration of **ions** from the **s** and **p** blocks of the periodic table, just **remove or add** the electrons to or from the highest-energy occupied sub-shell. E.g. $Mg^{2+} = 1s^2\ 2s^2\ 2p^6$, $Cl^- = 1s^2\ 2s^2\ 2p^6\ 3s^2\ 3p^6$.

Watch out — **noble gas symbols**, like that of argon (Ar), are sometimes used in electron configurations. For example, calcium ($1s^2\ 2s^2\ 2p^6\ 3s^2\ 3p^6\ 4s^2$) can be written as $[Ar]4s^2$, where $[Ar] = 1s^2\ 2s^2\ 2p^6\ 3s^2\ 3p^6$.

Practice Questions

Q1 How many electrons do full s, p and d sub-shells contain?

Q2 What is an atomic orbital?

Q3 Draw diagrams to show the shapes of an s and a p orbital.

Q4 Write down the sub-shells in order of increasing energy up to 4p.

Exam Questions

Q1 Potassium reacts with oxygen to form potassium oxide, K_2O.

a) Give the electron configurations of the K atom and K^+ ion using sub-shell notation. [2 marks]

b) Give the electron configuration of the oxide ion using 'electrons in boxes' notation. [1 mark]

Q2 This question concerns electron configurations in atoms and ions.

a) Identify the element with the 4th shell configuration of $4s^2\ 4p^2$. [1 mark]

b) Suggest the identity of an atom, a positive ion and a negative ion with the configuration $1s^2\ 2s^2\ 2p^6\ 3s^2\ 3p^6$. [3 marks]

c) Give the electron configuration of the Al^{3+} ion using sub-shell notation. [1 mark]

Q3 a) Write the electron configuration of a silicon atom using sub-shell notation. [1 mark]

b) How many orbitals contain an unpaired electron in a silicon atom? [1 mark]

She shells sub-sells on the shesore...

Electrons fill up the orbitals kind of like how strangers fill up seats on a bus. Everyone tends to sit in their own seat till they're forced to share. Except for the huge, scary man who comes and sits next to you. Make sure you learn the order that the sub-shells are filled up, so you can write electron configurations for any atom or ion they throw at you.

Ionic Bonding

There are two main types of bonding — ionic and covalent. You need to get them both totally sussed.

Ionic Bonding is when Ions are Stuck Together by Electrostatic Attraction

1) Ions are formed when electrons are **transferred** from one atom to another so as to have **full outer shells**. They may be positively or negatively charged.
2) **Electrostatic attraction** holds positive and negative ions together — it's **very** strong. When atoms are held together like this, it's called **ionic bonding**. Here comes a definition for you to learn...

An **ionic bond** is an **electrostatic attraction** between two **oppositely charged** ions.

When oppositely charged ions form an **ionic bond**, you get an **ionic compound**. The **formula** of an ionic compound tells you what **ions** that compound has in it.

For example, KBr is made up of K^+ and Br^- ions.

The positive charges in the compound **balance** the negative charges exactly — so the total overall charge is **zero**. This is a dead handy way of checking the formula.

- In **KBr**, the 1+ charge on the K^+ ion balances the single 1– charge on the Br^- ion.
- In **$MgBr_2$** the 2+ charge on the Mg^{2+} ion balances the two 1– charges on the two Br^- ions.

You can predict what ion an atom will form by its position in the periodic table. Have a look at page 26 if you're not sure how to do this.

Dot-and-Cross Diagrams Show Where the Electrons in a Bond Come From

Dot-and-cross diagrams show the **arrangement** of electrons in an atom or ion. Each electron is represented by a dot or a cross. They can also show which **atom** the electrons in a **bond** originally came from.

For example, **sodium chloride** is an ionic compound:

1) The formula of sodium chloride is **NaCl**. It tells you that sodium chloride is made up of **Na^+** and **Cl^- ions** in a 1:1 ratio.
2) A dot-and-cross diagram shows how ionic bonding works in sodium chloride —

Don't forget to include the charges of the ions on dot-and-cross diagrams.

Here, the dots represent the Na electrons and the crosses represent the Cl electrons (all electrons are really identical, but this is a good way of following their movement).

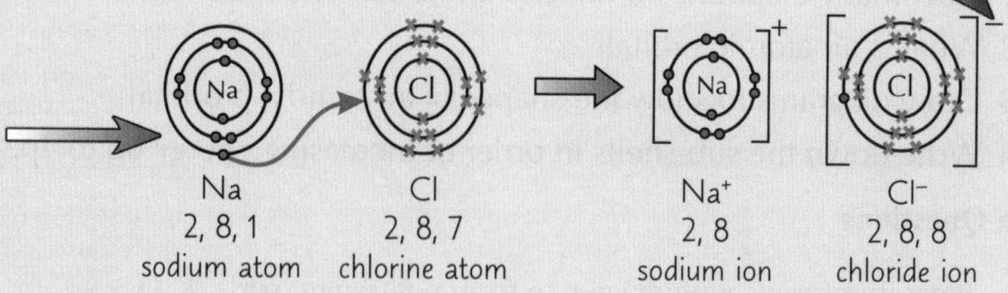

3) **Magnesium oxide**, MgO, is another good example:

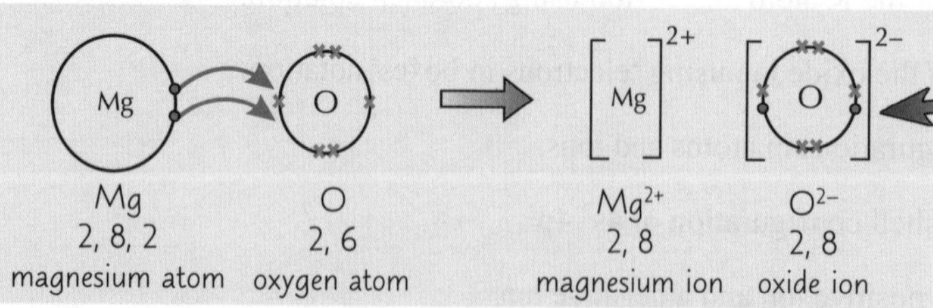

Here we've only shown the outer shells of electrons on the dot and cross diagram — it makes it much simpler to see what's going on.

4) When there's a 1:2 ratio of ions, such as in **magnesium chloride**, $MgCl_2$, you draw dot-and-cross diagrams like this:

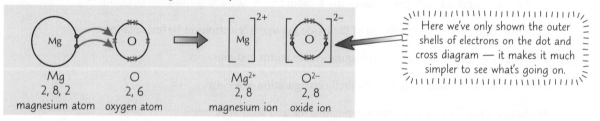

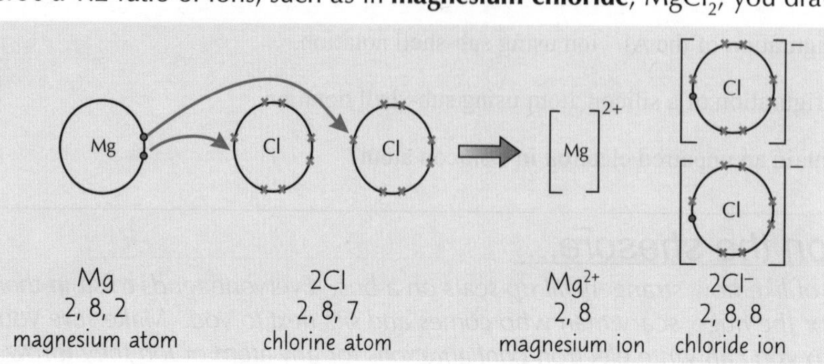

Dot
(cross)

Ionic Bonding

Sodium Chloride has a **Giant Ionic Lattice** Structure

1) In **sodium chloride**, the Na^+ and Cl^- ions are packed together alternately in a regular structure called a **lattice**.
2) The structure's called '**giant**' because it's made up of the same basic unit repeated over and over again.
3) It forms because each ion is electrostatically attracted in **all directions** to ions of the **opposite** charge.
4) The sodium chloride lattice is **cube** shaped — different ionic compounds have different shaped structures, but they're all still giant lattices.
5) Sodium chloride's got very strong **ionic bonds**, so it takes loads of **energy** to break up the lattice. This gives it a high melting point (801 °C).

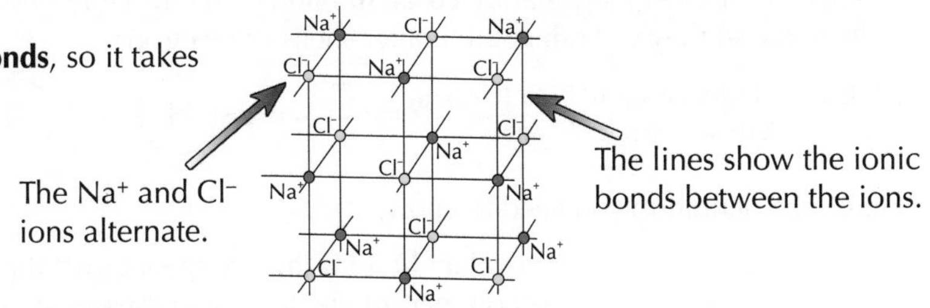

The Na⁺ and Cl⁻ ions alternate.
The lines show the ionic bonds between the ions.
Na⁺
Cl⁻

But it's not just melting points — the structure decides other **physical properties** too...

Ionic Structure Explains the **Behaviour** of Ionic Compounds

1) **Ionic compounds conduct electricity when they're molten or dissolved — but not when they're solid.** The ions in a liquid are mobile (and they carry a charge). In a solid they're fixed in position by the strong ionic bonds.
2) **Ionic compounds have high melting and boiling points.** The giant ionic lattices are held together by strong electrostatic forces. It takes loads of energy to overcome these forces, so their melting and boiling points are very high.
3) **Ionic compounds tend to dissolve in water.** Water molecules are polar — part of the molecule has a small negative charge, and the other bits have small positive charges (see p.48). The water molecules are attracted to the charged ions. They pull the ions away from the lattice and cause it to dissolve.

Practice Questions

Q1 How do ions form?

Q2 What is an ionic bond?

Q3 Draw a dot-and-cross diagram showing the bonding between magnesium and oxygen.

Q4 Why do many ionic compounds dissolve in water?

Exam Questions

Q1 a) What type of structure does sodium chloride have? [1 mark]

b) Would you expect sodium chloride to have a high or a low melting point? Explain your answer. [2 marks]

Q2 Calcium oxide is an ionic compound with ionic formula CaO.

a) Draw a dot-and-cross diagram to show the bonding in calcium oxide. Show the outer electrons only. [2 marks]

b) Solid calcium oxide does not conduct electricity, but molten calcium oxide does. Explain this with reference to ionic bonding. [3 marks]

The name's Bond... Ionic Bond... Electrons taken, not shared...

It's all very well learning the properties of ionic compounds, but make sure you can also explain why they do what they do. Remember — atoms are lazy. It's easier to lose two electrons to get a full shell than it is to gain six, so that's what an atom will do. And practise drawing dot-and-cross diagrams to show ionic bonding— they're easy marks in exams.

Covalent Bonding

And now for covalent bonding — this is when atoms share electrons with one another so they've all got full outer shells.

***Molecules** are Groups of Atoms **Bonded** Together*

Molecules form when **two or more** atoms bond together — it doesn't matter if the atoms are the **same** or **different**. Chlorine gas (Cl_2), carbon monoxide (CO), water (H_2O) and ethanol (C_2H_5OH) are all molecules.

Molecules are held together by **covalent bonds**. In covalent bonding, two atoms **share** electrons, so they've **both** got full outer shells of electrons.

E.g. two hydrogen atoms bond covalently to form a molecule of hydrogen.

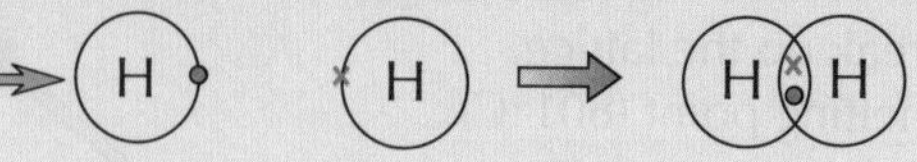

Covalent bonding happens between nonmetals. Ionic bonding is between a metal and a nonmetal.

Here's the definition you need to know:

A **covalent bond** is the strong **electrostatic attraction** between a **shared pair of electrons** and the **nuclei** of the bonded atoms.

*Make sure you can **Draw** the **Bonding** in these Molecules*

1) Dot-and-cross diagrams can be used to show how electrons behave in **covalent bonds**.
2) The bonded molecules are drawn with their outer atomic orbitals **overlapping**. The shared electrons that make up the covalent bond are drawn **within** the overlapping area.
3) To simplify the diagrams, not all the electrons in the molecules are shown — just the ones in the **outer shells**:

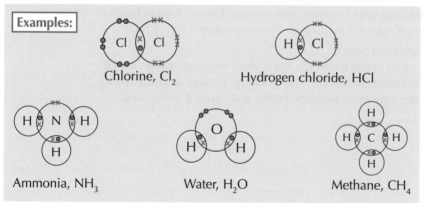

Examples:

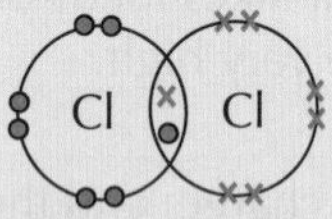

Chlorine, Cl_2

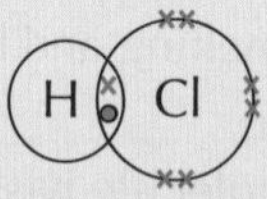

Hydrogen chloride, HCl

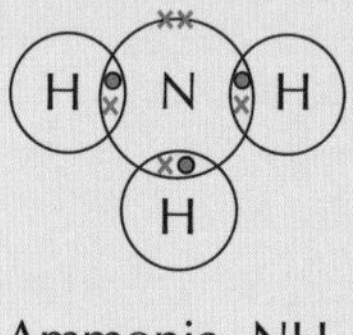

Ammonia, NH_3

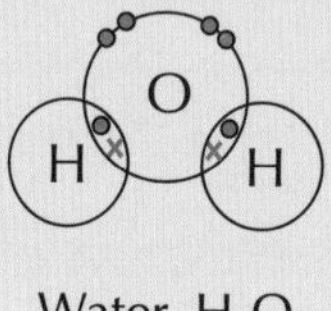

Water, H_2O

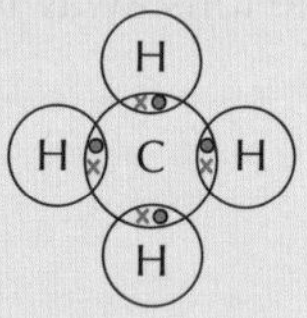

Methane, CH_4

4) Most of the time the central atom ends up with **eight electrons** in its **outer shell**. This is good for the atom — it's a very **stable** arrangement.

The outer electrons in hydrogen are in the first electron shell, which only needs two electrons to be filled.

*Some **Covalent** Compounds Are **Special Cases***

There are always a few pesky exceptions to make life that bit trickier...

A few compounds have **less** than 8 electrons in their outer shell...

In boron trifluoride, boron only has 6 electrons in its outer shell.

...and a few compounds can use d orbitals to '**expand the octet**'. This means they have **more** than 8 electrons in their outer shell.

In sulfur hexafluoride, sulfur has 12 electrons in its outer shell.

*The **Strength** of a Covalent Bond is Shown by its **Average Bond Enthalpy***

1) Average bond enthalpy measures the **energy** required to **break** a covalent bond.
2) The **stronger** a bond is, the more energy is required to break it, and so the **greater** the value of the average bond enthalpy.

There's loads more about enthalpy changes on pages 68-73.

Covalent Bonding

Some Atoms Share **More Than One Pair** of **Electrons**

1) Atoms don't just form single bonds — some can form **double** or even **triple covalent bonds.**
2) These multiple bonds contain **more than one** shared pairs of electrons between two atoms.
3) An example of a molecule that has a double bond is **oxygen**, O_2:

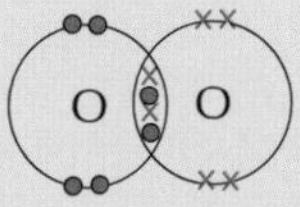

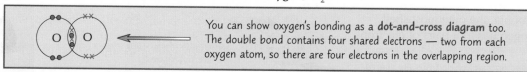

You can show oxygen's bonding as a **dot-and-cross diagram** too. The double bond contains four shared electrons — two from each oxygen atom, so there are four electrons in the overlapping region.

4) Nitrogen can triple bond, and carbon dioxide has two double bonds:

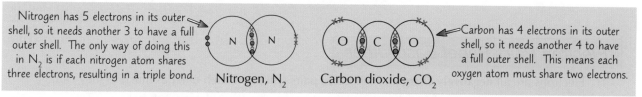

Nitrogen has 5 electrons in its outer shell, so it needs another 3 to have a full outer shell. The only way of doing this in N_2 is if each nitrogen atom shares three electrons, resulting in a triple bond.

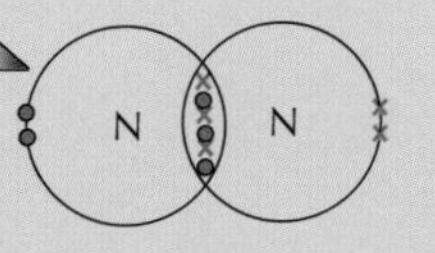

Nitrogen, N_2

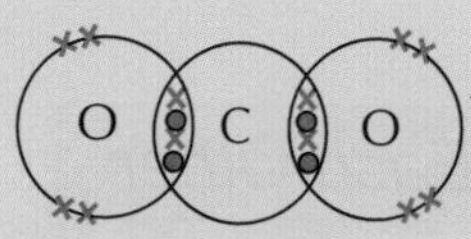

Carbon dioxide, CO_2

Carbon has 4 electrons in its outer shell, so it needs another 4 to have a full outer shell. This means each oxygen atom must share two electrons.

Dative Covalent Bonding is where **Both Electrons** come from **One Atom**

The **ammonium ion** (NH_4^+) is formed by dative covalent (or coordinate) bonding.
It forms when the nitrogen atom in an ammonia molecule **donates a pair of electrons** to a proton (H^+):

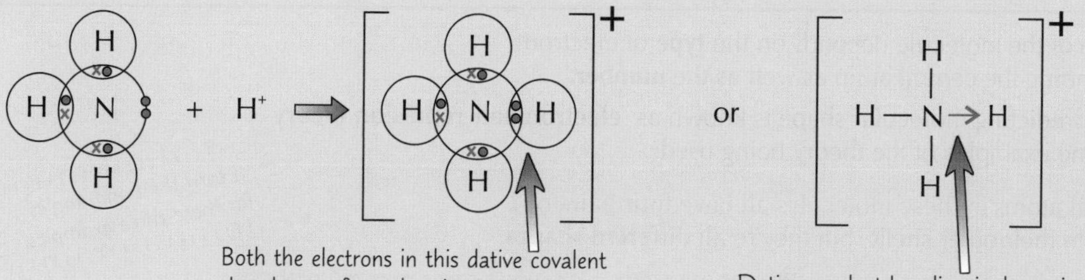

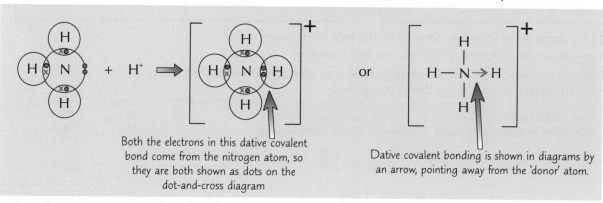

Both the electrons in this dative covalent bond come from the nitrogen atom, so they are both shown as dots on the dot-and-cross diagram

Dative covalent bonding is shown in diagrams by an arrow, pointing away from the 'donor' atom.

Practice Questions

Q1 Draw a dot-and-cross diagram to show the arrangement of the outer electrons in a molecule of hydrogen chloride.

Q2 How does the value of average bond enthalpy change as bond strength increases?

Q3 Name a molecule with a double covalent bond. Draw a diagram showing the outer electrons in this molecule.

Exam Questions

Q1 Carbon tetrachloride, CCl_4, is a covalently bonded molecule.

a) What is a covalent bond? [1 mark]

b) Draw a dot-and-cross diagram to show the electron arrangement in a molecule of carbon tetrachloride (CCl_4). [2 marks]

Q2 a) What type of bonding is present in the ammonium ion (NH_4^+)? [1 mark]

b) Explain how this type of bonding occurs. [1 mark]

Interesting fact #795 — $TiCl_4$ is known as 'tickle' in the chemical industry...

More pretty diagrams to learn here — practise till you get every single dot and cross in the right place. It's amazing to think of these titchy little atoms sorting themselves out so they've got full outer shells of electrons. Remember — covalent bonding happens between two nonmetals, whereas ionic bonding happens between a metal and a nonmetal.

Shapes of Molecules

Chemistry would be heaps more simple if all molecules were flat. But they're not.

Molecular Shape** depends on **Electron Pairs** around the **Central Atom

Molecules and molecular ions come in loads of **different shapes**.
The shape depends on the **number** of pairs of electrons in the outer shell of the central atom.

In ammonia, the outermost shell of nitrogen has four pairs of electrons.

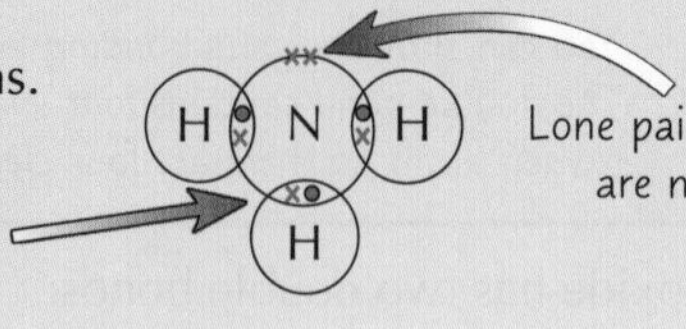
H
N
H
H
Bonding pairs of electrons are shared with another atom in a covalent bond.
Lone pairs of electrons are not shared.

A lone pear.

*Electron Pairs **Repel** Each Other*

1) Electrons are all **negatively charged**, so electron pairs will **repel** each other as much as they can.
2) This sounds straightforward, but the **type** of the electron pair affects **how much** it repels other electron pairs. Lone pairs repel **more** than bonding pairs.
3) This means the **greatest** angles are between **lone pairs** of electrons, and bond angles between bonding pairs are often **reduced** because they are pushed together by lone pair repulsion.

Lone pair/lone pair angles are the biggest.	Lone pair/bonding pair angles are the second biggest.	Bonding pair/bonding pair bond angles are the smallest.

4) So the shape of the molecule depends on the **type** of electron pairs surrounding the central atom as well as the **number.**
5) This way of predicting molecular shape is known as '**electron pair repulsion theory**'. Here are some examples of the theory being used:

Learn the bond angles for these three examples.

The central atoms in these molecules all have **four pairs** of electrons in their outer shells, but they're all **different shapes.**

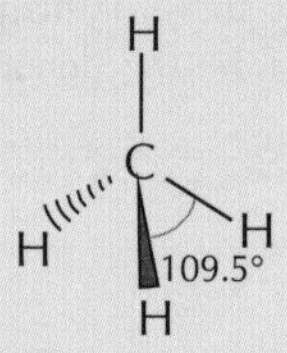
H
C
H
H
H
109.5°

Methane — no lone pairs.
All the bond angles are 109.5°.

The lone pair repels the bonding pairs

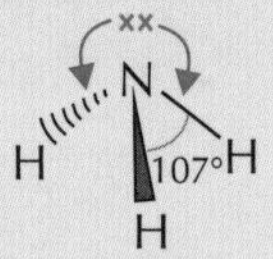
N
H
H
H
107°

Ammonia — 1 lone pair.
All three bond angles are 107°.

2 lone pairs reduce the bond angle even more

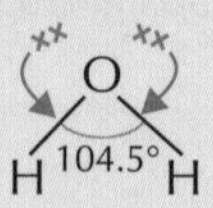
O
H
H
104.5°

Water — 2 lone pairs.
The bond angle is 104.5°.

To draw molecules in 3D, use solid wedges to show bonds pointing out of the page towards you, and broken lines to show bonds pointing into the page away from you.

*You Can Use **Electron Pairs** to **Predict** the Shapes of Molecules*

To predict the shape of a molecule, you first have to know how many bonding and non-bonding electron pairs are on the central atom. Here's how:

1) Find the **central atom** (the one all the other atoms are bonded to).
2) Work out the number of **electrons** in the **outer shell** of the central atom. Use the periodic table to do this.
3) The **molecular formula** tells you how many atoms the central atom is **bonded** to. From this you can work out how many electrons are **shared with** the central atom.
4) **Add up** the electrons and **divide by 2** to find the **number of electron pairs** on the central atom. If you have an ion remember to account for its **charge**.
5) **Compare** the number of **electron pairs** with the number of **bonds** to find the number of **lone pairs**.
6) You can then use the **number of electron pairs** and the number of **lone pairs** and **bonding centres** around the central atom to work out the **shape** of the molecule (see next page).

If there's a double bond, count it as two bonds.

Bonding centres are the atoms bonded to the central atom.

Shapes of Molecules

Practise **Drawing** these Molecules

Once you know how many electron pairs are on the central atom, you can use **electron pair repulsion theory** to work out the **shape** of the molecule.

These are the common shapes that you need to be able to draw:

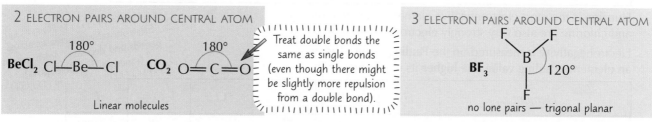

2 ELECTRON PAIRS AROUND CENTRAL ATOM

$BeCl_2$ 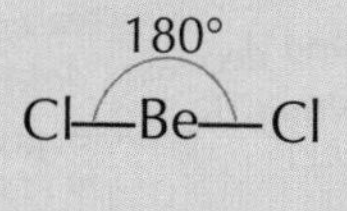

CO_2 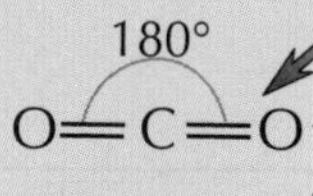

Linear molecules

Treat double bonds the same as single bonds (even though there might be slightly more repulsion from a double bond).

3 ELECTRON PAIRS AROUND CENTRAL ATOM

BF_3 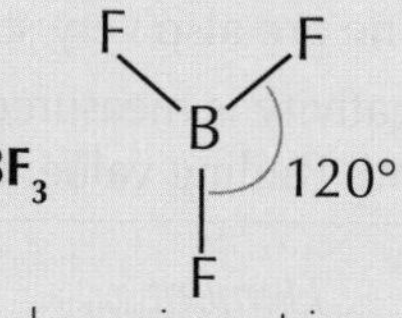

no lone pairs — trigonal planar

4 ELECTRON PAIRS AROUND CENTRAL ATOM

NH_4^+ 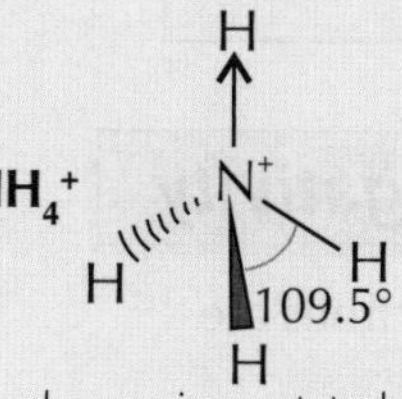

no lone pairs — tetrahedral

PF_3 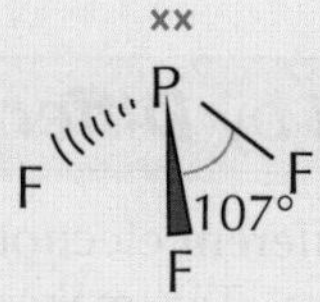

1 lone pair — trigonal pyramidal

H_2O 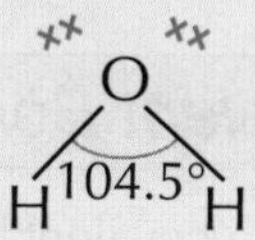

2 lone pairs — nonlinear or 'bent'

5 ELECTRON PAIRS AROUND CENTRAL ATOM

PCl_5 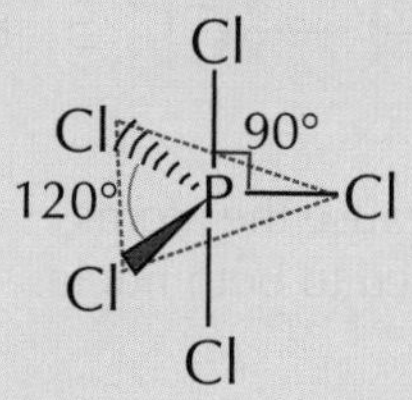

no lone pairs — trigonal bipyramidal

6 ELECTRON PAIRS AROUND CENTRAL ATOM

SF_6 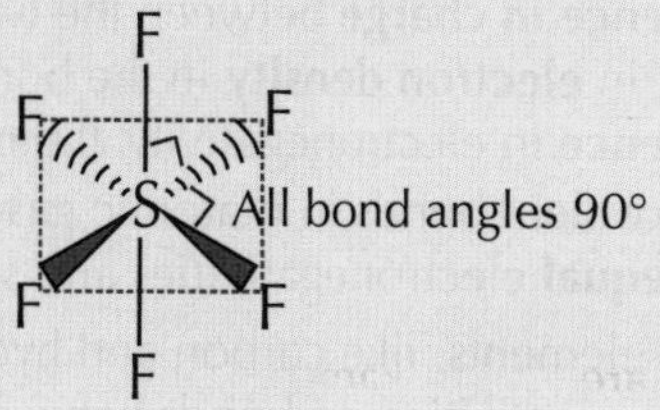

no lone pairs — octahedral

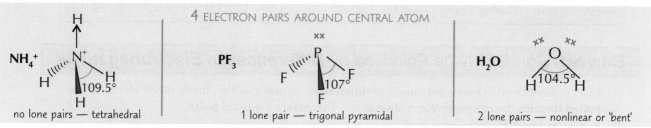

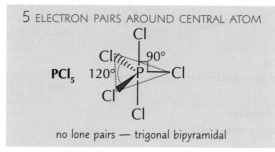

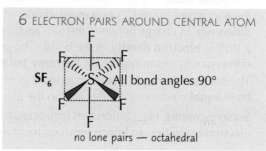

Practice Questions

Q1 What is a lone pair of electrons?

Q2 Write down the order of the strength of repulsion between different kinds of electron pair.

Q3 Explain why a water molecule is not linear.

Q4 Draw a tetrahedral molecule.

Exam Questions

Q1 a) Draw the shapes of the following molecules, showing the approximate values of the bond angles on the diagrams and naming each shape.

i) NCl_3 [3 marks]

ii) BCl_3 [3 marks]

b) Explain why the shapes of NCl_3 and BCl_3 are different. [3 marks]

Q2 The displayed formula of an organic compound is shown. Use electron pair repulsion theory to predict the shape and relevant bond angles of the bonds around atoms A, B and C. [3 marks]

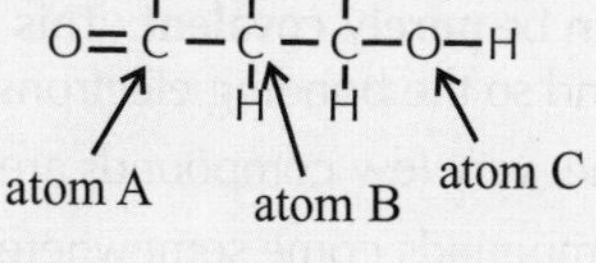

These molecules ain't square...

In the exam, those evil examiners might try to throw you by asking you for the shape of an unfamiliar molecule. Don't panic — you can use the steps on page 46 to work out the shape of any covalent molecule. So practise, practise practise until you can work out shapes and draw them while standing on your head. And don't forget the bond angles.

Polarity and Intermolecular Forces

This topic is a bit of a monster, I'm afraid, and it's full of some really important stuff that you need to get your head around. Don't worry though — we'll get through it together. First up, it's electronegativity and polar bonds.

Some Atoms **Attract** Bonding Electrons More than Other Atoms

An atom's ability to attract the electron pair in a covalent bond is called **electronegativity.**

Fluorine is the most electronegative element. Oxygen, nitrogen and chlorine are also very strongly electronegative.

Electronegativity is measured on the **Pauling Scale**. The greater an element's Pauling value, the **higher** its electronegativity.

Electronegativity increases across periods and decreases down groups (ignoring the noble gases).

Element	*H*	*C*	*N*	*Cl*	*O*	*F*
Electronegativity (Pauling Scale)	*2.1*	*2.5*	*3.0*	*3.0*	*3.5*	*4.0*

Covalent Bonds may be Polarised by **Differences** in **Electronegativity**

1) In a covalent bond between two atoms of **different** electronegativities, the bonding electrons are **pulled towards** the more electronegative atom. This makes the bond **polar**.
2) In a **polar bond**, the difference in electronegativity between the two atoms causes a **permanent dipole**. A dipole is a **difference in charge** between the two atoms caused by a shift in **electron density** in the bond. The greater the **difference** in electronegativity, the **more polar** the bond.

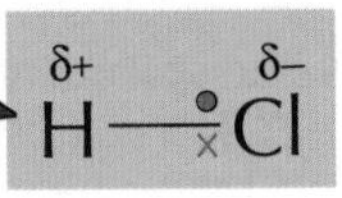

'δ' (delta) means 'slightly', so 'δ+' means 'slightly positive'.

3) The covalent bonds in diatomic gases (e.g. H_2, Cl_2) are **non-polar** because the atoms have **equal** electronegativities and so the electrons are equally attracted to both nuclei.

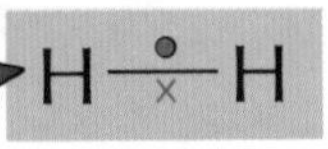

4) Some elements, like carbon and hydrogen, have pretty **similar** electronegativities, so bonds between them are essentially **non-polar**.

In Polar **Molecules**, Charge is Arranged **Unevenly**

Polar bonds have **permanent dipoles**. The **arrangement** of polar bonds in a molecule determines whether or not the **molecule** will have an **overall dipole**.

1) If the polar bonds are arranged **symmetrically** so that the dipoles **cancel** each other out, then the molecule has no overall dipole and is **non-polar**. E.g. carbon dioxide contains two polar bonds but has no overall dipole moment.

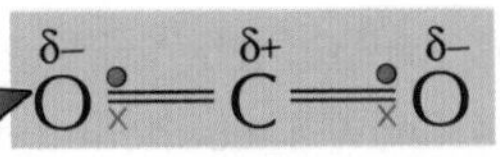

2) But if the polar bonds are arranged so that they **don't cancel** each other out then charge is arranged **unevenly** across the whole molecule, and it will have an **overall dipole**. Molecules with an overall dipole are **polar**. E.g. water is polar because the negative charge is positioned more towards the **oxygen** atom.

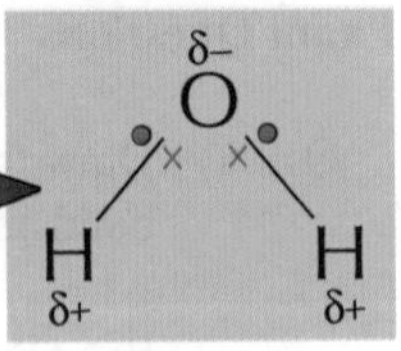

3) To work out whether a molecule has an overall dipole, first you need to draw it in **3D**. Then label the **partial charges** on each atom, and look to see if they cancel each other out.

There's a Gradual **Transition** from Ionic to Covalent Bonding

1) Only bonds between atoms of a **single** element, like diatomic gases such as hydrogen (H_2) or oxygen (O_2), can be **purely covalent**. This is because the **electronegativity difference** between the atoms is **zero** and so the bonding electrons are arranged completely **evenly** within the bond.
2) At the same time, very few compounds are completely ionic.
3) Really, most compounds come somewhere **in between** the two extremes — meaning they've often got ionic **and** covalent properties. E.g. covalent hydrogen chloride gas molecules dissolve to form hydrochloric acid, which is an ionic solution.

$$HCl_{(g)} \xrightarrow{H_2O} H^+_{(aq)} + Cl^-_{(aq)}$$

4) You can use electronegativity to **predict** what type of bonding will occur between two atoms. The higher the difference in electronegativity, the more ionic in character the bonding becomes.

Polarity and Intermolecular Forces

Intermolecular forces are the things that hold molecules together. They're weak, but important — without them we'd just be a cloud of gassy stuff. How polar a molecule is affects the type of intermolecular forces it will form. Onwards...

Intermolecular Forces are **Very Weak**

Intermolecular forces are forces between molecules. They're much **weaker** than covalent, ionic or metallic bonds. There are three types of intermolecular force you need to know about.

1) **Induced dipole-dipole** or **London (dispersion)** forces.
2) **Permanent dipole-dipole interactions.**
3) **Hydrogen bonding** (this is the strongest type).

Sometimes the term 'van der Waals forces' is used to refer to the first two types.

Induced Dipole-Dipole Forces are Found Between **All** Atoms and Molecules

Induced dipole-dipole forces cause **all** atoms and molecules to be **attracted** to each other. Even **noble gas atoms** are affected, despite not being at all interested in forming other types of bond. Here's why...

1) **Electrons** in charge clouds are always **moving** really quickly. At any particular moment, the electrons in an atom are likely to be more to one side than the other. At this moment, the atom would have a **temporary dipole**.
2) This dipole can cause **another** temporary (induced) dipole in the opposite direction on a neighbouring atom. The two dipoles are then **attracted** to each other.

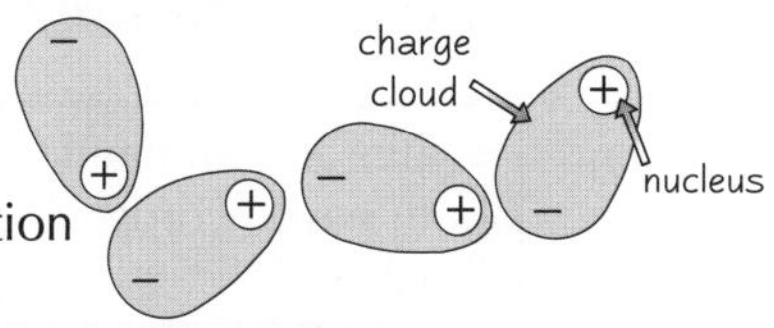

3) The second dipole can cause yet another dipole in a **third atom**. It's kind of like a domino rally.
4) Because the electrons are constantly moving, the dipoles are being **created** and **destroyed** all the time. Even though the dipoles keep changing, the **overall effect** is for the atoms to be **attracted** to each other.

Stronger **Induced Dipole-Dipole Forces** mean **Higher Boiling Points**

1) Not all induced dipole-dipole forces are the same strength — larger molecules have **larger electron clouds**, meaning **stronger** induced dipole-dipole forces. Molecules with greater **surface areas** also have stronger induced dipole-dipole forces because they have a **bigger exposed electron cloud**.
2) When you **boil** a liquid, you need to **overcome** the intermolecular forces, so that the particles can **escape** from the liquid surface. It stands to reason that you need **more energy** to overcome **stronger** intermolecular forces, so liquids with stronger induced dipole-dipole forces will have **higher boiling points**.
3) This graph of the boiling points of Group 4 hydrides shows the trend. As you go down the group, the induced dipole-dipole forces (and the boiling points) increase because the number of **shells** of electrons increases, and so atomic/molecular **size** increases.

Induced dipole-dipole forces affect other physical properties, such as melting point and viscosity, too.

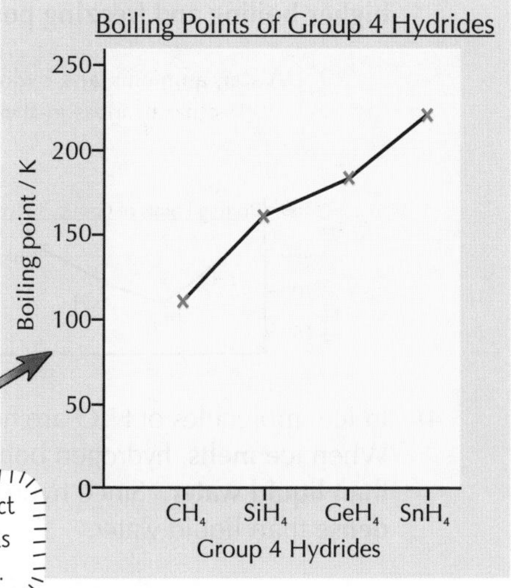

Induced Dipole-Dipole Forces Can Hold Molecules in a **Lattice**

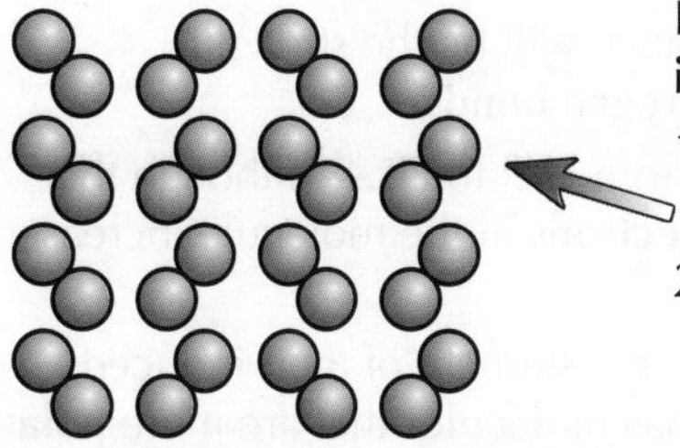

Induced dipole-dipole forces are responsible for holding **iodine** molecules together in a **lattice**.

1) Iodine atoms are held together in pairs by **strong** covalent bonds to form molecules of I_2.
2) But the molecules are then held together in a **molecular lattice** arrangement by **weak induced dipole-dipole** attractions.

Polarity and Intermolecular Forces

Two more types of intermolecular force for you to get under your belt. It must just be your lucky day.

Polar Molecules *Form* ***Permanent Dipole-Dipole*** *Interactions*

The δ+ and δ- charges on **polar molecules** cause **weak electrostatic forces** of attraction **between** molecules. These are called **permanent dipole-dipole interactions**.

E.g. hydrogen chloride gas has polar molecules.

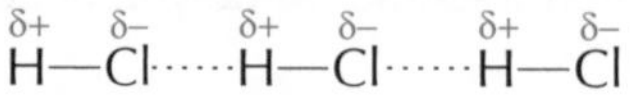

Permanent dipole-dipole interactions happen **in addition to** (not instead of) induced dipole-dipole interactions.

Permanent polar bonding.

Hydrogen Bonding *is the* ***Strongest*** *Intermolecular Force*

1) Hydrogen bonding can **only** happen when **hydrogen** is covalently bonded to **fluorine**, **nitrogen** or **oxygen**. Hydrogen has a **high charge density** because it's so small, and fluorine, nitrogen and oxygen are very **electronegative**. The bond is so **polarised** that a weak bond forms between the hydrogen of one molecule and a lone pair of electrons on the fluorine, nitrogen or oxygen in **another molecule**.
2) Molecules which have hydrogen bonding usually contain **–OH** or **–NH** groups.

Water and **ammonia** both have hydrogen bonding.

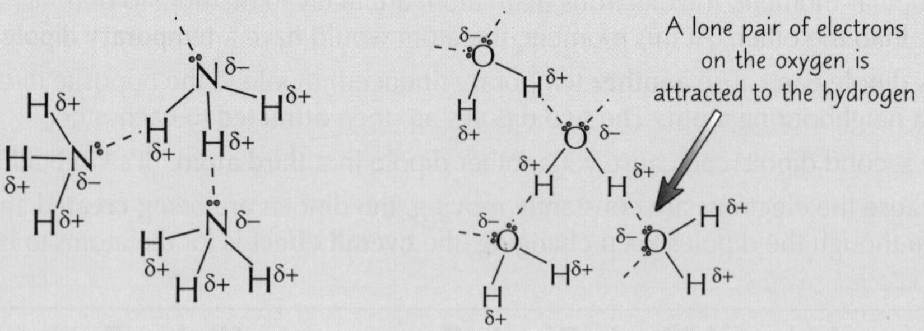

3) Hydrogen bonding has a huge effect on the properties of substances. They are **soluble** in water and have **higher boiling and freezing points** than molecules of a similar size that are **unable** to form hydrogen bonds.

Water, ammonia and hydrogen fluoride generally have the **highest boiling points** if you compare them with other hydrides in their groups, because of the **extra energy** needed to break the hydrogen bonds.

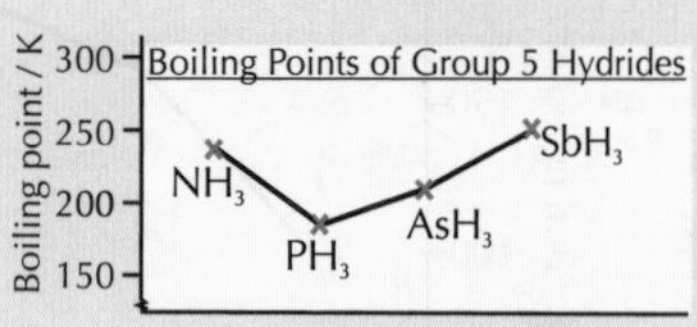

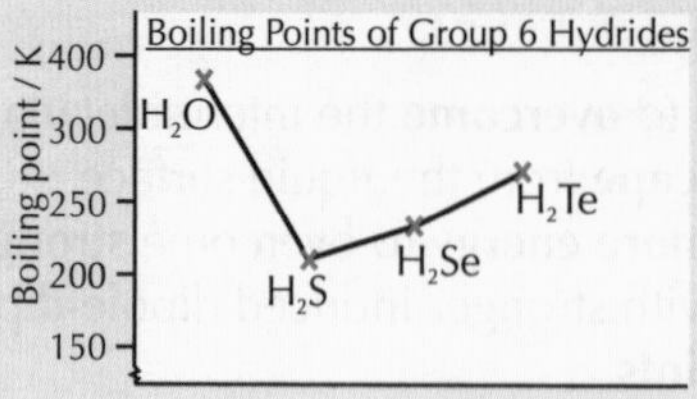

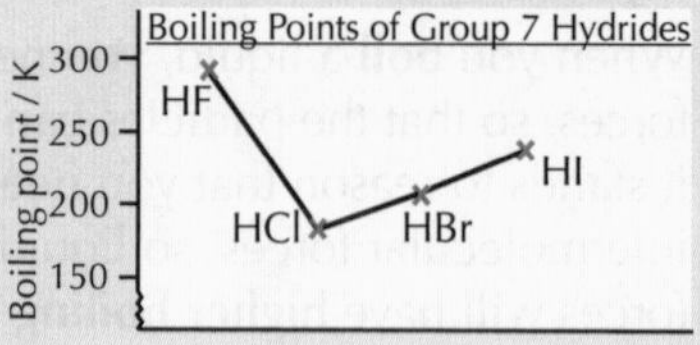

4) In ice, molecules of H_2O are held together in a **lattice** by hydrogen bonds. When ice **melts**, hydrogen bonds are **broken**, so ice has **more** hydrogen bonds than **liquid water**. Since hydrogen bonds are relatively **long**, this makes ice **less dense** than liquid water.

This is unusual... most substances get denser when they freeze.

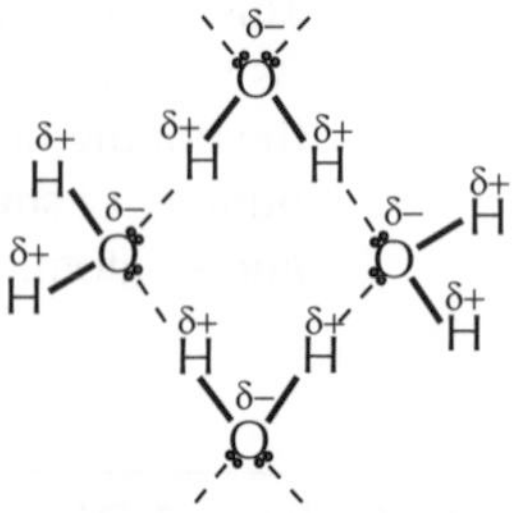

Intermolecular Forces Explain the ***Trends*** *in* ***Boiling Points***

1) In general, the **main factor** that determines the boiling point of a substance will be the strength of the **induced dipole-dipole forces** (unless the molecule can form **hydrogen bonds**).
2) This explains why the boiling points of the Group 7 hydrides **increase** from HCl to HI — although the permanent dipole-dipole interactions are **decreasing**, the **number of electrons** in the molecule increases, so the **strength** of the induced dipole-dipole interactions also **increases**.
3) But if you have two molecules with a **similar number** of electrons, then the strength of their induced dipole-dipole interactions will be **similar**. So if one of the substances has molecules that are more **polar** than the other, it will have stronger **permanent dipole-dipole** interactions and so a higher boiling point.

Polarity and Intermolecular Forces

Intermolecular Forces Explain the **Behaviour** of Simple Covalent Compounds

Simple covalent compounds have low melting and boiling points.

The intermolecular forces that hold together the molecules in simple covalent compounds are **weak** so don't need much energy to **break**. So the melting and boiling points are normally **low** — they are often **liquids** or **gases** at room temperature. As intermolecular forces get **stronger**, melting and boiling points **increase**.

Polar molecules are soluble in water.

Water is a **polar** molecule, so only tends to dissolve other polar substances. Compounds with **hydrogen bonds**, such as ammonia or ethanoic acid, can form hydrogen bonds with water molecules, so will be **soluble**. Molecules that only have induced dipole-dipole forces, such as methane, will be **insoluble**.

Simple covalent compounds don't conduct electricity.

Even though some covalent molecules have permanent dipoles, overall covalent molecules are **uncharged**. This means they can't conduct electricity.

Covalent Bonds **Don't** Break during **Melting** and **Boiling***

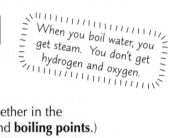

When you boil water, you get steam. You don't get hydrogen and oxygen.

This is something that confuses loads of people — get it sorted in **your** head now...

1) To **melt** or **boil** a simple covalent compound you only have to overcome the **intermolecular forces** that hold the molecules together.
2) You **don't** need to break the much stronger covalent bonds that hold the atoms together in the molecules. (That's why simple covalent compounds have relatively **low melting** and **boiling points**.)

Example: Chlorine, Cl_2, has **stronger** covalent bonds than bromine, Br_2. But under normal conditions, chlorine is a **gas** and bromine a **liquid**. Bromine has the higher boiling point because its molecules are **bigger**, giving stronger induced dipole-dipole forces.

*Except for giant molecular substances, like diamond.

Practice Questions

Q1 What is a dipole?

Q2 What is the only situation in which a bond is purely covalent?

Q3 Explain why induced dipole-dipole interactions are present even in inert atoms like argon.

Q4 How does the boiling point of a substance change if the strength of induced dipole-dipole interactions increases?

Q5 What atoms must be covalently bonded to hydrogen for hydrogen bonding to exist?

Q6 What types of forces must be overcome in order for a simple molecular substance to boil or melt?

Exam Questions

Q1 a) Define the term electronegativity. [1 mark]

b) Draw the shapes of the following molecules, marking any bond polarities clearly on your diagram:
i) Br_2 ii) H_2O iii) NH_3 [3 marks]

Q2 a) Name three types of intermolecular force. [3 marks]

b) Water, H_2O, boils at 373 K.

i) Explain why water's boiling point is higher than expected in comparison to other similar molecules. [2 marks]

ii) Draw a labelled diagram showing the intermolecular bonding that takes place in water. [2 marks]

May the force be with you...

Phew! You made it. You definitely deserve a break. Remember — induced dipole-dipole interactions occur between all molecules. Permanent dipole-dipole interactions only form if a molecule has an overall dipole, and you only need to think about hydrogen bonding if the molecule contains oxygen, nitrogen or fluorine covalently bonded to hydrogen.

The Periodic Table

As far as Chemistry topics go, the periodic table is a bit of a biggie. So much so that you really should know the history of it. So make yourself comfortable and I'll tell you a story that began... oh, about 200 years ago...

In the **1800s**, Elements Could Only Be Grouped by **Atomic Mass**

1) In the early 1800s, there were only two ways to categorise elements — by their **physical and chemical properties** and by their **relative atomic mass**. (The modern periodic table is arranged by **proton number**, but back then, they knew nothing about protons or electrons. The only thing they could measure was relative atomic mass.)

2) In 1817, Johann Döbereiner attempted to group similar elements — these groups were called **Döbereiner's triads**. He saw that **chlorine**, **bromine** and **iodine** had similar characteristics. He also realised that other properties of bromine (e.g. atomic weight) fell **halfway** between those of chlorine and iodine. He found other such groups of three elements (e.g. lithium, sodium and potassium), and called them **triads**. It was a start.

3) An English chemist called **John Newlands** had the first good stab at making a table of the elements in 1863. He noticed that if he arranged the elements in order of **mass**, similar elements appeared at regular intervals — every **eighth element** was similar. He called this the **law of octaves**, and he listed some known elements in rows of seven so that the similar elements lined up in columns.

Li	Be	B	C	N	O	F
Na	Mg	Al	Si	P	S	Cl

4) But the pattern broke down on the third row, with many transition metals like Fe, Cu and Zn messing it all up.

Dmitri Mendeleev Created the **First Accepted Version**

1) In 1869, Russian chemist **Dmitri Mendeleev** produced a better table, which wasn't far off the one we have today.

2) He arranged all the known elements by atomic mass, but left **gaps** in the table where the next element didn't seem to fit. That way he could keep elements with similar chemical properties in the same group.

3) He also predicted the properties of **undiscovered elements** that would go in the gaps.

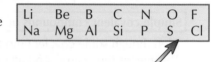

	Group 1	Group 2	Group 3	Group 4	Group 5	Group 6	Group 7
Period 1	H						
Period 2	Li	Be	B	C	N	O	F
Period 3	Na	Mg	Al	Si	P	S	Cl
Period 4	K Cu	Ca Zn	* *	Ti *	V As	Cr Se	Mn Br
Period 5	Rb Ag	Sr Cd	Y In	Zr Sn	Nb Sb	Mo Te	* I

4) When elements were **later discovered** (e.g. germanium, scandium and gallium) with properties that matched Mendeleev's predictions, it showed that clever old Mendeleev had got it right.

The **Modern Periodic Table** Arranges Elements by **Proton Number**

The modern periodic table is pretty much the one produced by Henry Moseley in 1914. He arranged the elements by **increasing atomic (proton) number** rather than by mass.

Grp 1	Grp 2													Grp 3	Grp 4	Grp 5	Grp 6	Grp 7	Grp 0
							1 H 1												4 He 2
7 Li 3	9 Be 4													11 B 5	12 C 6	14 N 7	16 O 8	19 F 9	20 Ne 10
23 Na 11	24 Mg 12													27 Al 13	28 Si 14	31 P 15	32 S 16	35.5 Cl 17	40 Ar 18
39 K 19	40 Ca 20	45 Sc 21	48 Ti 22	51 V 23	52 Cr 24	55 Mn 25	56 Fe 26	59 Co 27	59 Ni 28	63.5 Cu 29	65 Zn 30			70 Ga 31	73 Ge 32	75 As 33	79 Se 34	80 Br 35	84 Kr 36
86 Rb 37	88 Sr 38	89 Y 39	91 Zr 40	93 Nb 41	96 Mo 42	98 Tc 43	101 Ru 44	103 Rh 45	106 Pd 46	108 Ag 47	112 Cd 48			115 In 49	119 Sn 50	122 Sb 51	128 Te 52	127 I 53	131 Xe 54
133 Cs 55	137 Ba 56	139 La 57	179 Hf 72	181 Ta 73	184 W 74	186 Re 75	190 Os 76	192 Ir 77	195 Pt 78	197 Au 79	201 Hg 80			204 Tl 81	207 Pb 82	209 Bi 83	210 Po 84	210 At 85	222 Rn 86
223 Fr 87	226 Ra 88	227 Ac 89	261 Rf 104	262 Db 105	266 Sg 106	264 Bh 107	269 Hs 108	268 Mt 109	269 Ds 110	272 Rg 111	277 Cn 112			289 Uut 113	289 Fi 114	298 Uup 115	Lv 116	Uus 117	Uuo 118

140 Ce 58	141 Pr 59	144 Nd 60	145 Pm 61	150 Sm 62	152 Eu 63	157 Gd 64	159 Tb 65	163 Dy 66	165 Ho 67	167 Er 68	169 Tm 69	173 Yb 70	175 Lu 71
232 Th 90	231 Pa 91	238 U 92	237 Np 93	242 Pu 94	243 Am 95	247 Cm 96	245 Bk 97	251 Cf 98	254 Es 99	253 Fm 100	256 Md 101	254 No 102	257 Lr 103

f-block elements

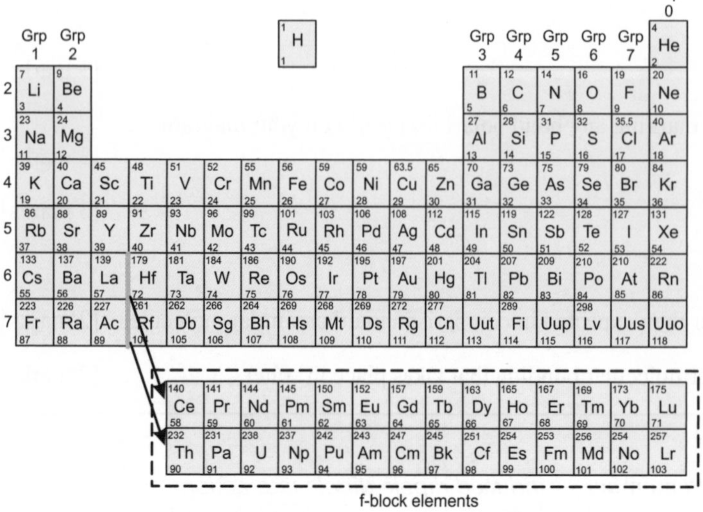

1) The periodic table is arranged into **periods** (rows) and **groups** (columns).

2) All the elements **within a period** have the same number of **electron shells** (if you don't worry about the sub-shells). The elements of Period 1 (hydrogen and helium) both have 1 electron shell, the elements in Period 2 have 2 electron shells, and so on... This means there are **repeating trends** in the physical and chemical properties of the elements across each period (e.g. decreasing atomic radius). These trends are known as **periodicity**.

3) All the elements **within a group** have the same number of **electrons in their outer shell**. This means they have **similar chemical properties**. The group number tells you the number of electrons in the outer shell, e.g. Group 1 elements have 1 electron in their outer shell, Group 4 elements have 4 electrons, etc... (Except for Group 0 elements — they have 8 electrons in their outer shell.)

The Periodic Table

You Can Use the Periodic Table to Work Out **Electron Configurations**

The periodic table can be split into an **s-block**, **d-block** and **p-block** like this: Doing this shows you which sub-shells all the electrons go into.

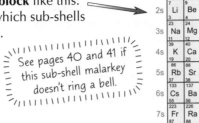

See pages 40 and 41 if this sub-shell malarkey doesn't ring a bell.

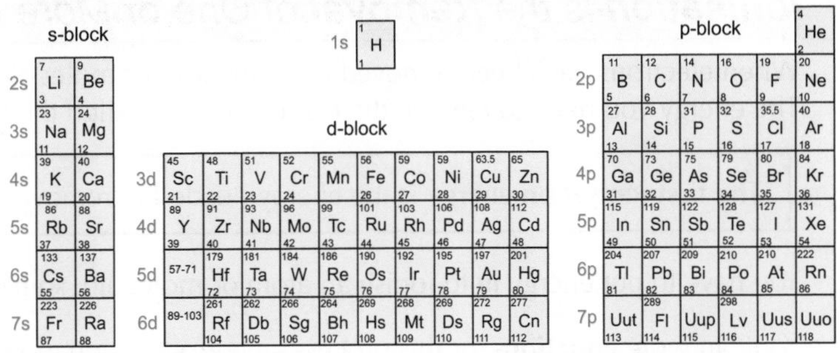

1) The **s-block** elements have an outer shell electron configuration of s^1 or s^2.

Example: Lithium ($1s^2$ $\mathbf{2s^1}$) and magnesium ($1s^2$ $2s^2$ $2p^6$ $\mathbf{3s^2}$)

I named my tortoise Neon — he's got a lovely, full shell.

2) The **p-block** elements have an outer shell electron configuration of s^2p^1 to s^2p^6.

Example: Chlorine ($1s^2$ $2s^2$ $2p^6$ $\mathbf{3s^2}$ $\mathbf{3p^5}$)

3) The **d-block** elements have electron configurations in which d sub-shells are being filled.

Example: Cobalt ($1s^2$ $2s^2$ $2p^6$ $3s^2$ $3p^6$ $\mathbf{3d^7}$ $4s^2$)

Even though the 3d sub-shell fills last in cobalt, it's not written at the end of the line.

When you've got the periodic table **labelled** with the **shells** and **sub-shells** like the one up there, it's pretty easy to read off the electron structure of any element. Just start with the first period and work your way across and down until you get to your element.

Example: Electron structure of phosphorus (P):

Period 1 — $1s^2$ ← Complete sub-shells
Period 2 — $2s^2$ $2p^6$
Period 3 — $3s^2$ $3p^3$ ← Incomplete outer sub-shell

So the electron structure is: $\mathbf{1s^2\ 2s^2\ 2p^6\ 3s^2\ 3p^3}$

Practice Questions

Q1 In what order are the elements set out in the modern periodic table?

Q2 What is the name given to the rows in the periodic table?

Q3 What is the name given to the columns in the periodic table?

Exam Questions

Q1 Which of the following is the electronic configuration of sodium?

A $1s^2$ $2s^2$ $2p^6$ $3p^1$ B $1s^2$ $2s^2$ $2p^6$ $3s^1$ C $1s^2$ $2p^6$ $3s^1$ D $1s^2$ $2s^2$ $2p^6$ $3s^2$ $3p^1$ [1 mark]

Q2 Which of the following is the electronic configuration of bromine?

A $1s^2$ $2s^2$ $2p^6$ $3s^2$ $3p^6$ $3d^{10}$ $4s^2$ $4p^3$ B $1s^2$ $2s^2$ $2p^6$ $3s^2$ $3p^6$ $3d^5$

C $1s^2$ $2s^2$ $2p^6$ $3s^2$ $3p^6$ $3d^{10}$ $4s^1$ D $1s^2$ $2s^2$ $2p^6$ $3s^2$ $3p^6$ $3d^{10}$ $4s^2$ $4p^5$ [1 mark]

Q3 State the block in the periodic table to which bromine belongs. [1 mark]

Q4 Explain, in terms of protons, why aluminium is placed directly after magnesium in the Periodic Table. [1 mark]

*Periodic — probably the best table in the world...**

Dropped History for Chemistry, did you? Ha, bet you're regretting that now... If so, you'll enjoy the free History lesson that you get here with the periodic table. Make sure you learn all the key details and particularly how to read electron configurations from the periodic table. That stuff is going to be popping up again later on...

**Excluding the Dinner and the Round, of course.*

Ionisation Energies

These pages get a trifle brain-boggling, so I hope you've got a few aspirin handy...

Ionisation** is the **Removal** of One or More **Electrons

When electrons have been removed from an atom or molecule, it's been **ionised**.
The energy you need to remove the first electron is called the **first ionisation energy**:

The **first ionisation energy** is the energy needed to remove **1 mole** of **electrons** from **1 mole** of **gaseous** atoms.

You have to put energy **in** to ionise an atom or molecule, so it's an **endothermic process**.

You can read all about endothermic reactions on p.68.

You can write **equations** for this process — here's the equation for the **first ionisation of oxygen**:

$$O_{(g)} \rightarrow O^+_{(g)} + e^- \qquad \text{1st ionisation energy} = +1314 \text{ kJ mol}^{-1}$$

Here are a few rather important points about ionisation energies:

1) You **must** use the gas state symbol, **(g)**, because ionisation energies are measured for gaseous atoms.
2) Always refer to **1 mole** of atoms, as stated in the definition, rather than to a single atom.
3) The **lower** the ionisation energy, the **easier** it is to form an ion.

*The **Factors** Affecting Ionisation Energy are...*

Nuclear charge — The **more protons** there are in the nucleus, the more positively charged the nucleus is and the **stronger the attraction** for the electrons.

Atomic radius — Attraction falls off very **rapidly with distance**. An electron **close** to the nucleus will be **much more** strongly attracted than one further away.

Shielding — As the number of electrons **between** the outer electrons and the nucleus **increases**, the outer electrons feel less attraction towards the nuclear charge. This lessening of the pull of the nucleus by inner shells of electrons is called **shielding**.

A **high ionisation energy** means there's a **strong attraction** between the **electron** and the **nucleus**, so **more energy** is needed to overcome the attraction and remove the electron.

*Ionisation Energy **Decreases** Down a Group*

1) As you **go down** a group in the periodic table, ionisation energies generally **fall**, i.e. it gets **easier** to remove outer electrons.
2) It happens because:
   - Elements further down a group have **extra electron shells** compared to ones above. The extra shells mean that the atomic radius is larger, so the outer electrons are **further away** from the nucleus, which greatly reduces their attraction to the nucleus.
   - The extra inner shells **shield** the outer electrons from the attraction of the nucleus.

The positive charge of the nucleus does increase as you go down a group (due to the extra protons), but this effect is overridden by the effect of the extra shells.

First ionisation energies of the first five elements of Group 1.

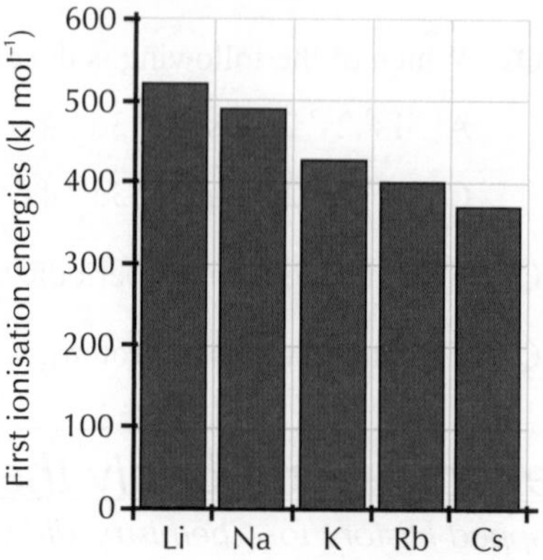

3) This provides **evidence** that electron shells **really exist** — a decrease in ionisation energy going down a group supports the Bohr model of the atom (see page 17).

Ionisation Energies

Ionisation Energy **Increases** Across a Period

The graph below shows the first ionisation energies of the elements in **Periods 2** and **3**.

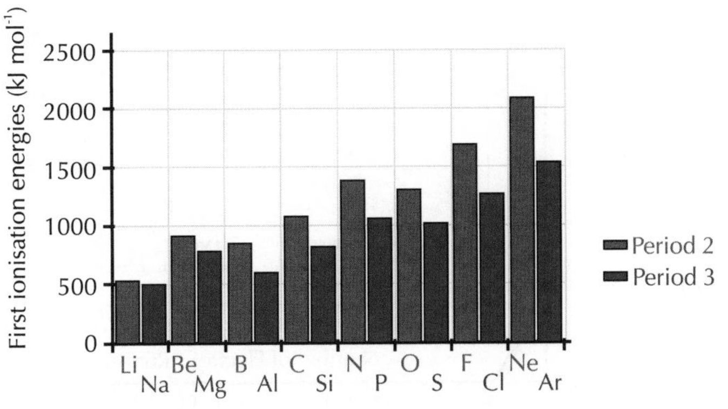

1) As you **move across** a period, the **general trend** is for the ionisation energies to **increase** — i.e. it gets harder to remove the outer electrons.
2) This is because the number of protons is increasing. As the **positive charge** of the nucleus increases, the electrons are **pulled closer** to the nucleus, making the atomic radius smaller.
3) The extra electrons that the elements gain across a period are added to the **outer energy level** so they don't really provide any extra shielding effect (shielding works with inner shells mainly).

There are **two exceptions** to the trend — the first ionisation energy **decreases** between Groups 2 and 3, and between Groups 5 and 6. On the graph, you can see this as **small drops** between those groups. Here's why...

The Drop Between Groups 2 and 3 is Due to **Sub-Shell Structure**

1) The outer electron in Group 3 elements is in a **p orbital** rather than an s orbital.
2) A p orbital has a **slightly higher** energy than an s orbital in the same shell, so the electron is, on average, to be found **further** from the nucleus.
3) The p orbital also has additional shielding provided by the **s electrons**.
4) These factors **override** the effect of the increased nuclear charge, resulting in the ionisation energy **dropping** slightly.

E.g.

	Electron structure	1st ionisation energy
Be	$1s^2 2s^2$	900 kJ mol^{-1}
B	$1s^2 2s^2 \mathbf{2p^1}$	801 kJ mol^{-1}

The Drop Between Groups 5 and 6 is Due to **p Orbital Repulsion**

1) In the Group 5 elements, the electron is being removed from a **singly-occupied** orbital (see page 41 for more on sub-shell filling).
2) In the Group 6 elements, the electron is being removed from an orbital containing **two electrons**.
3) The **repulsion** between two electrons in an orbital means that electrons are **easier to remove** from shared orbitals.

E.g.

	Electron structure	1st ionisation energy
N	$1s^2 2s^2 \mathbf{2p^3}$	1402 kJ mol^{-1}
O	$1s^2 2s^2 \mathbf{2p^4}$	1314 kJ mol^{-1}

Successive Ionisation Energies Involve Removing **Additional** Electrons

You can remove **all** the electrons from an atom, leaving only the nucleus.
Each time you remove an electron, there's a **successive ionisation energy**.

Example: The equation for the **second ionisation of oxygen** is:

$O^+_{(g)} \rightarrow O^{2+}_{(g)} + e^-$ 2nd ionisation energy = **+3388 kJ mol^{-1}**

Ionisation Energies

Successive Ionisation Energies Show **Shell Structure**

A **graph** of successive ionisation energies (like this one for sodium) provides evidence for the **shell structure** of atoms.

1) **Within each shell**, successive ionisation energies **increase**. This is because electrons are being removed from an **increasingly positive ion**, and there's also **less repulsion** amongst the remaining electrons. So the electrons are **held more strongly** by the nucleus.
2) The **big jumps** in ionisation energy happen when a new shell is broken into — an electron is being removed from a shell **closer** to the nucleus.

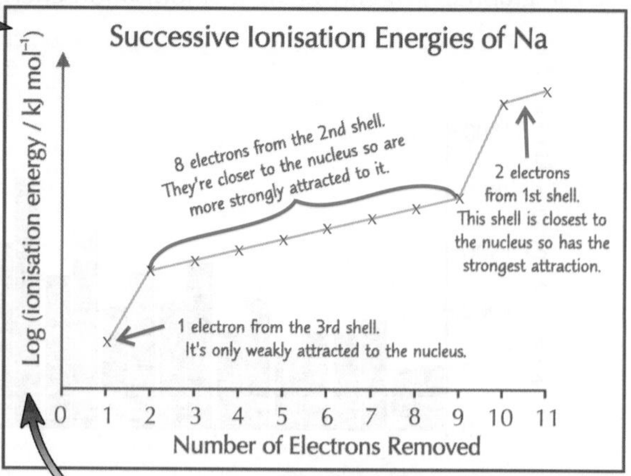

Successive Ionisation Energies of Na
Log (ionisation energy / kJ mol^{-1})
8 electrons from the 2nd shell. They're closer to the nucleus so are more strongly attracted to it.
2 electrons from 1st shell. This shell is closest to the nucleus so has the strongest attraction.
1 electron from the 3rd shell. It's only weakly attracted to the nucleus.
0 1 2 3 4 5 6 7 8 9 10 11
Number of Electrons Removed

Log scales are often used because the values have such a huge range.

1) Graphs like this can tell you which **group** of the periodic table an element belongs to. Just count **how many electrons are removed** before the first big jump to find the group number.

E.g. In the graph for sodium, **one electron** is removed before the first big jump — sodium is in **group 1**.

2) The graphs can also be used to predict the **electronic structure** of an element. Working from **right to left**, count how many points there are before each big jump to find how many electrons are in each shell, starting with the first.

E.g. The graph has **2 points** on the right-hand side, then a jump, then **8 points**, a jump, and **1 final point**. Sodium has **2 electrons** in the first shell, **8** in the second and **1** in the third.

Practice Questions

Q1 Write the definition of the first ionisation energy.

Q2 Name three factors which affect the size of an ionisation energy.

Q3 How does the first ionisation energy change as you go down a group?

Exam Questions

Q1 This graph shows the successive ionisation energies of a certain element.

a) To which group of the periodic table does this element belong? [1 mark]

b) Explain why it takes more energy to remove each successive electron. [2 marks]

c) What causes the sudden increases in ionisation energy? [1 mark]

d) What is the total number of shells of electrons in this element? [1 mark]

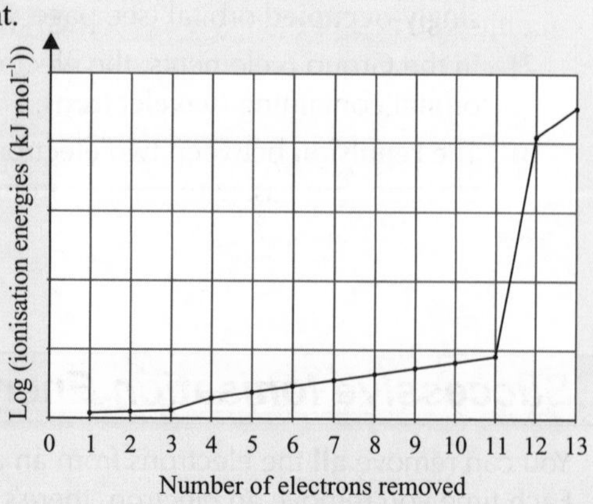

Log (ionisation energies (kJ mol^{-1}))
0 1 2 3 4 5 6 7 8 9 10 11 12 13
Number of electrons removed

Q2* State and explain the trend in the first ionisation energy across Period 3. [6 marks]

Shirt crumpled? Ionise it.

When you're talking about ionisation energies in exams, always use the three main factors — shielding, nuclear charge and atomic radius. Make sure you're comfortable interpreting the jumps in those graphs without getting stressed. And recite the definition of the first ionisation energy to yourself until you're muttering it in your sleep.

* The quality of your extended response will be assessed for this question.

Structure, Bonding and Properties

Atoms can form giant structures as well as piddling little molecules — well... 'giant' in molecular terms anyway. Compared to structures like the Eiffel Tower or even your granny's carriage clock, they're still unbelievably tiny.

Diamond, ***Graphite*** *and* ***Graphene*** *are Giant Covalent Lattices*

1) **Giant covalent lattices** are huge networks of **covalently** bonded atoms. (They're sometimes called **macromolecular structures** too.)
2) **Carbon** atoms can form this type of structure because they can each form four strong, covalent bonds.
3) Different forms of the **same element** in the **same state** are called **allotropes**. Carbon has several allotropes, but luckily you only need to know about three of them — **diamond**, **graphite** and **graphene**.

Diamond — not to be confused with a giant lettuce.

Diamond *is the* ***Hardest*** *known Substance*

In diamond, each carbon atom is **covalently bonded** to **four** other carbon atoms. The atoms arrange themselves in a **tetrahedral** shape — its crystal lattice structure.

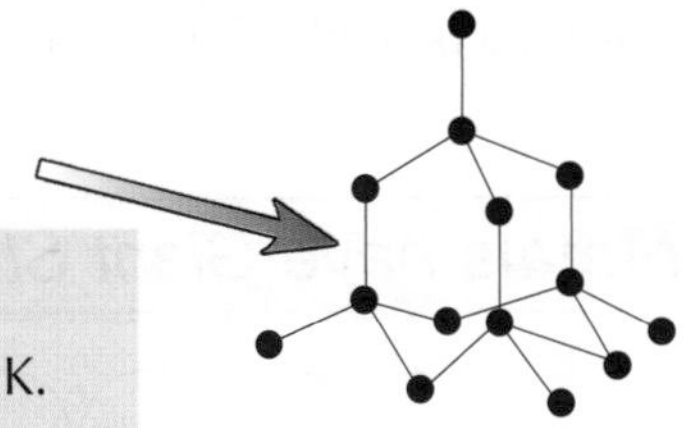

Because it has **lots** of **strong covalent** bonds:
1) Diamond has a **very high melting point** — it actually sublimes at over 3800 K.
2) Diamond is extremely **hard** — it's used in diamond-tipped drills and saws.
3) **Vibrations** travel easily through the stiff lattice, so it's a **good thermal conductor**.
4) It **can't conduct** electricity — all the outer electrons are held in localised bonds.
5) It won't dissolve in **any** solvent.

You can 'cut' diamond to form gemstones. Its structure makes it refract light a lot, which is why it sparkles.

'Sublimes' means it changes straight from a solid to a gas, skipping out the liquid stage.

Silicon (which is in the same periodic group as carbon) also forms a **crystal lattice** structure with **similar properties** to carbon. Each silicon atom is able to form **four** strong, covalent bonds.

Graphite *Has Loads of* ***Layers***

Graphite's **structure** means it has some **different properties** from diamond.

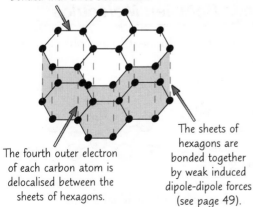

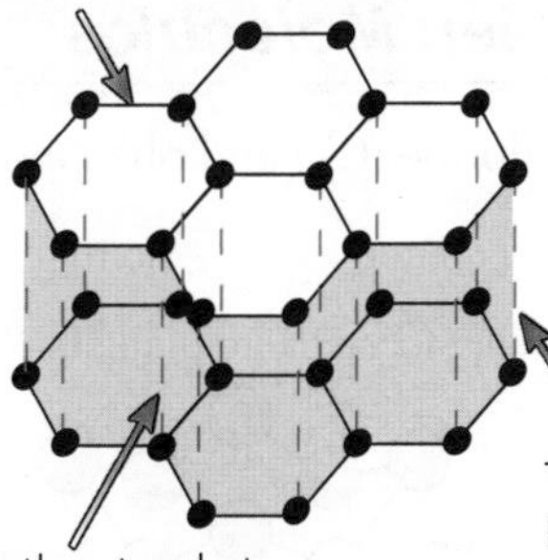

The carbon atoms are arranged in sheets of flat hexagons covalently bonded with three bonds each.
The fourth outer electron of each carbon atom is delocalised between the sheets of hexagons.
The sheets of hexagons are bonded together by weak induced dipole-dipole forces (see page 49).

1) The weak forces **between** the layers in graphite are easily broken, so the sheets can slide over each other — graphite feels **slippery** and is used as a **dry lubricant** and in **pencils**.
2) The '**delocalised**' electrons in graphite aren't attached to any particular carbon atom and are **free to move** along the sheets, so an **electric current** can flow.
3) The layers are quite **far apart** compared to the length of the covalent bonds, so graphite is **less dense** than diamond and is used to make **strong**, **lightweight** sports equipment.
4) Because of the **strong covalent bonds** in the hexagon sheets, graphite also has a **very high melting point** (it sublimes at over 3900 K).
5) Like diamond, graphite is **insoluble** in any solvent. The covalent bonds in the sheets are **too strong** to break.

Structure, Bonding and Properties

Graphene is One Layer of Graphite

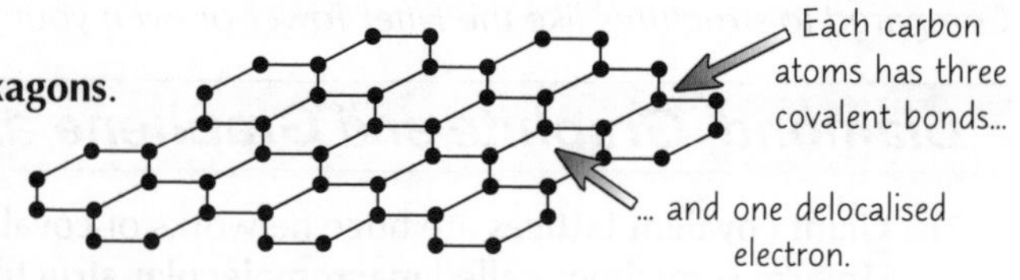
Each carbon atoms has three covalent bonds...
... and one delocalised electron.

Graphene is a **sheet** of carbon atoms joined together in **hexagons**. The sheet is just **one atom** thick, making it a **two-dimensional** compound.

Graphene's **structure** gives it some pretty **useful properties**.

1) Like in graphite, the **delocalised electrons** in graphene are **free to move** along the sheet. Without layers, they can move **quickly** above and below the sheet, making graphene the **best known** electrical conductor.
2) The **delocalised electrons** also strengthen the covalent bonds between the carbon atoms. This makes graphene extremely **strong**.
3) A single layer of graphene is **transparent** and incredibly **light**.

Like diamond and graphite, graphene has high melting and boiling points and it's insoluble due to its strong covalent bonds.

Due to its high strength, low mass, and good electrical conductivity, graphene has potential applications in **high-speed electronics** and **aircraft technology**. Its flexibility and transparency also make it a potentially useful material for **touchscreens** on smartphones and other electronic devices.

Metals have Giant Structures Too

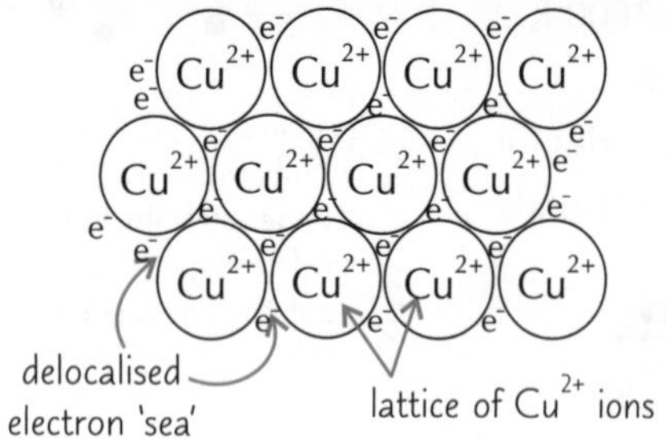
Cu2+
e-
delocalised electron 'sea'
lattice of Cu2+ ions

Metal elements exist as **giant metallic lattice structures**.

1) The electrons in the outermost shell of a metal atom are **delocalised** — the electrons are free to move about the metal. This leaves a positively charged **metal cation**, e.g. Na^+, Mg^{2+}, Al^{3+}.
2) The metal cations are **electrostatically attracted** to the delocalised negative electrons. They form a lattice of closely packed cations in a **sea** of delocalised electrons — this is **metallic bonding**.

Metallic bonding explains the properties of metals —

1) The **number of delocalised electrons per atom** affects the melting point. The **more** there are, the **stronger** the bonding will be and the **higher** the melting point. $\mathbf{Mg^{2+}}$ has **two** delocalised electrons per atom, so it's got a **higher melting point** than $\mathbf{Na^+}$, which only has **one**. The **size** of the metal ion and the **lattice structure** also affect the melting point. A smaller ionic radius will hold the delocalised electrons closer to the nuclei.
2) As there are **no bonds** holding specific ions together, the metal ions can slide past each other when the structure is pulled, so metals are **malleable** (can be hammered into sheets) and **ductile** (can be drawn into a wire).
3) The delocalised electrons can pass **kinetic energy** to each other, making metals **good thermal conductors**.
4) Metals are **good electrical conductors** because the **delocalised electrons** can move and carry a **current**.
5) Metals are **insoluble**, except in **liquid metals**, because of the **strength** of the metallic bonds.

Simple Molecular Structures Have Weak Bonds Between Molecules

1) Simple molecular structures contain only a **few** atoms — e.g. oxygen (O_2), chlorine (Cl_2) and phosphorous (P_4).
2) The covalent bonds **between** the atoms in the molecule are very strong, but the **melting** and **boiling points** of simple molecular substances depend upon the strength of the **induced dipole-dipole forces** (see p.49-51) **between** their molecules. These intermolecular forces are weak and easily overcome, so these elements have **low** melting and boiling points.
3) More atoms in a molecule mean stronger induced dipole-dipole forces. For example, in Period 3 sulfur is the **biggest molecule** (S_8), so it's got **higher** melting and boiling points than phosphorus or chlorine.

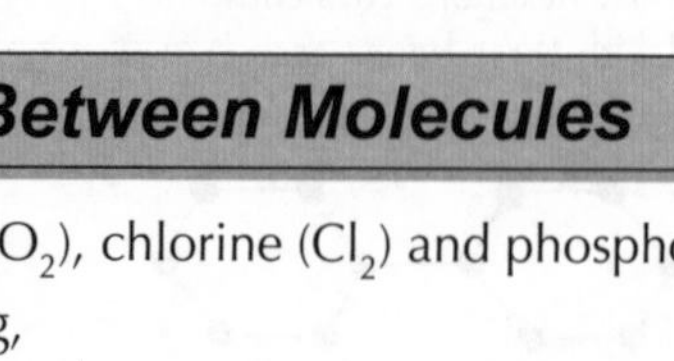

4) The noble gases have **very low** melting and boiling points because they exist as **individual atoms** (they're monatomic), resulting in **very weak** induced dipole-dipole forces.

Structure, Bonding and Properties

Bond Strength Affects Melting and Boiling Points Across a Period

As you go across a period, the **type** of bond formed between the atoms of an element **changes**. This affects the **melting** and **boiling points** of the element. The graph on the right shows the trend in boiling points across **Periods 2 and 3**.

1) For the **metals** (Li, Be, Na, Mg and Al), melting and boiling points **increase** across the period because the **metallic bonds** get stronger as the **ionic radius** decreases and the number of **delocalised electrons** increases.
2) The elements with **giant covalent lattice** structures (C and Si) have **strong covalent bonds** linking all their atoms together. **A lot** of energy is needed to break these bonds.
3) The elements that form **simple molecular structures** have only **weak intermolecular forces** to overcome between their molecules, so they have **low** melting and boiling points.
4) The noble gases (neon and argon) have the **lowest** melting and boiling points in their periods because they are held together by the **weakest** forces.

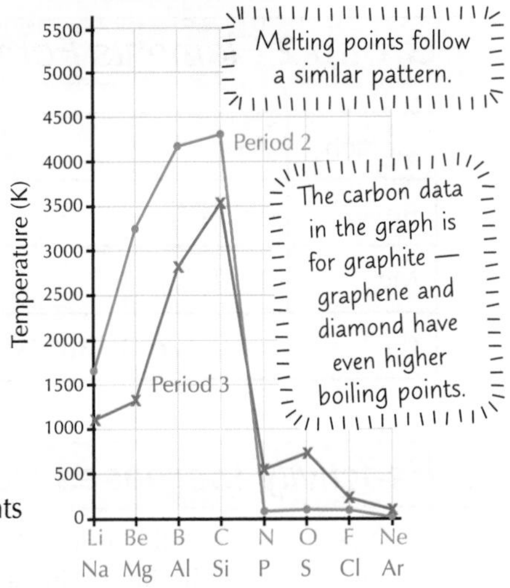

Bonding and Properties — A Quick Summary

Bonding	Examples	Melting and boiling points	Typical state at STP	Does solid conduct electricity?	Does liquid conduct electricity?	Is it soluble in water?
Ionic	NaCl $MgCl_2$	High	Solid	No (ions are held firmly in place)	Yes (ions are free to move)	Yes
Simple molecular (covalent)	CO_2 I_2 H_2O	Low (have to overcome induced dipole-dipole forces or hydrogen bonds, not covalent bonds)	Sometimes solid, usually liquid or gas (water is liquid because it has hydrogen bonds)	No	No	Depends on how polarised the molecule is
Giant covalent lattice	Diamond Graphite Graphene	High	Solid	No (except graphite and graphene)	— (will generally sublime)	No
Metallic	Fe Mg Al	High	Solid	Yes (delocalised electrons)	Yes (delocalised electrons)	No

Practice Questions

Q1 Diamond has a giant covalent lattice structure. Give two properties that it has as a result of this.

Q2 What forces exist between the carbon sheets in graphite?

Q3 Which element in Period 3 has the highest melting point? Which has the highest boiling point?

Exam Questions

Q1 Explain why the melting point of magnesium is higher than that of sodium. [3 marks]

Q2 This table shows the melting points for the Period 3 elements.

Element	Na	Mg	Al	Si	P	S	Cl	Ar
Melting point / K	371	923	933	1687	317	392	172	84

In terms of structure and bonding explain why:

a) silicon has a high melting point. [2 marks]

b) the melting point of sulfur is higher than that of phosphorus. [2 marks]

Q3* Compare and explain the electrical conductivities of diamond, graphite and graphene in terms of their structure and bonding. [6 marks]

Carbon is a girl's best friend...

Examiners love giving you questions on carbon structures. Close the book and do a quick sketch of each allotrope, together with a list of their properties — then look back at the page and see what you missed. And while you're at it, have a go at remembering all the stuff from that table up there — I can almost guarantee you'll need it at some point.

* The quality of your extended response will be assessed for this question.

Group 2 — The Alkaline Earth Metals

It would be easy for Group 2 elements to feel slightly inferior to those in Group 1. They're only in the second group, after all. That's why you should try to get to know and like them. They'd really appreciate it, I'm sure.

Group 2 Elements Form 2+ Ions

Element	Atom	Ion
Be	$1s^2\,2s^2$	$1s^2$
Mg	$1s^2\,2s^2\,2p^6\,3s^2$	$1s^2\,2s^2\,2p^6$
Ca	$1s^2\,2s^2\,2p^6\,3s^2\,3p^6\,4s^2$	$1s^2\,2s^2\,2p^6\,3s^2\,3p^6$

Group 2 elements all have two electrons in their outer shell (s^2).

They lose their two outer electrons to form **2+ ions**. Their ions then have every atom's dream electronic structure — that of a **noble gas.**

Reactivity Increases Down Group 2

Mr Kelly has one final attempt at explaining electron shielding to his students...

1) As you go down the group, the **ionisation energies** decrease. This is due to the **increasing atomic radius** and **shielding effect** (see p.54).
2) When Group 2 elements react they **lose electrons**, forming positive ions (**cations**). The easier it is to lose electrons (i.e. the lower the first and second ionisation energies), the more reactive the element, so **reactivity increases** down the group.

Group 2 Elements React with Water and Oxygen

When Group 2 elements react, they are **oxidised** from a state of **0** to **+2**, forming M^{2+} ions.

M just represents any Group 2 metal.

$$M \rightarrow M^{2+} + 2e^-$$
Oxidation number: **0** **+2**

Example: $\mathbf{Ca \rightarrow Ca^{2+} + 2e^-}$
0 **+2**

There are a few reactions of Group 2 elements that you need to know...

These are all redox reactions — see p.38 and 39 for more info.

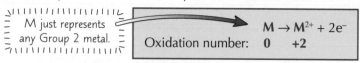

1 They react with WATER to produce HYDROXIDES.

The Group 2 metals react with water to give a **metal hydroxide** and **hydrogen.**

$$M_{(s)} + 2H_2O_{(l)} \rightarrow M(OH)_{2(aq)} + H_{2(g)}$$
Oxidation number: **0** **+2**

E.g. $Ca_{(s)} + 2H_2O_{(l)} \rightarrow Ca(OH)_{2(aq)} + H_{2(g)}$

Be	doesn't react
Mg	VERY slowly
Ca	steadily
Sr	fairly quickly
Ba	rapidly

2 They burn in OXYGEN to form OXIDES.

When Group 2 metals burn in oxygen, you get solid white **oxides.**

$$2M_{(s)} + O_{2(g)} \rightarrow 2MO_{(s)}$$
Oxidation number of metal: **0** **+2**
Oxidation number of oxygen: **0** **−2**

E.g. $2Ca_{(s)} + O_{2(g)} \rightarrow 2CaO_{(s)}$
0 **+2**
0 **−2**

3 They react with DILUTE ACID to produce a SALT and HYDROGEN.

When Group 2 metals react with dilute hydrochloric acid, you get a **metal chloride** and **hydrogen.**

$$M_{(s)} + 2HCl_{(aq)} \rightarrow MCl_{2(aq)} + H_{2(g)}$$
Oxidation number: **0** **+2**

E.g. $Ca_{(s)} + 2HCl_{(aq)} \rightarrow CaCl_{2(aq)} + H_{2(g)}$

Like with water, the reactions of Group 2 metals with dilute acid get more vigorous as you go down the group.

Different acids will produce different salts. E.g. if you use dilute sulfuric acid, you'll get a metal sulfate.

Group 2 — The Alkaline Earth Metals

Group 2 Oxides and Hydroxides are **Bases**

The **oxides** and **hydroxides** of Group 2 metals are **bases**. Most of them are **soluble** in water, so are also **alkalis**.

1) The **oxides** of the Group 2 metals react readily with **water** to form **metal hydroxides**, which dissolve. The **hydroxide ions, OH^-**, make these solutions **strongly alkaline** (e.g. pH 12 – 13).
2) Magnesium oxide is an exception — it only reacts slowly and the hydroxide isn't very soluble.
3) The oxides form **more strongly alkaline** solutions as you go down the group, because the hydroxides get more soluble.

$$CaO_{(s)} + H_2O_{(l)} \rightarrow Ca^{2+}_{(aq)} + 2OH^-_{(aq)}$$

An alkali is a base that's soluble in water.

Group 2 Compounds are used to **Neutralise Acidity**

Group 2 elements are known as the **alkaline earth metals**, and many of their common compounds are used for neutralising acids. Here are a couple of common examples:

1) Calcium hydroxide (slaked lime, $Ca(OH)_2$) is used in **agriculture** to neutralise acidic soils.

2) Magnesium hydroxide ($Mg(OH)_2$) and calcium carbonate ($CaCO_3$) are used in some indigestion tablets as **antacids**.

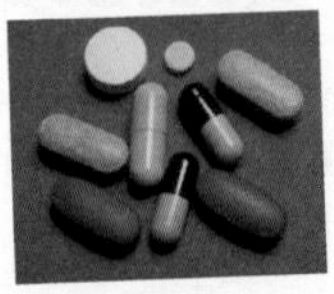

In both cases, the ionic equation for the neutralisation is $\mathbf{H^+_{(aq)} + OH^-_{(aq)} \rightarrow H_2O_{(l)}}$

Example: $Mg(\mathbf{OH})_{2(s)} + 2\mathbf{H}Cl_{(aq)} \rightarrow 2\mathbf{H_2O}_{(l)} + MgCl_{2(aq)}$

Daisy the cow*

Practice Questions

Q1 Which of the following increases in size down Group 2? A — atomic radius B — first ionisation energy

Q2 Which of these Group 2 metals is the least reactive? A — Mg B — Be C — Sr

Q3 Why does reactivity with water increase down Group 2?

Q4 Give a use of magnesium hydroxide.

Exam Questions

Q1 Calcium carbonate reacts with hydrochloric acid to produce a salt, carbon dioxide and water. Write an equation for this reaction. [1 mark]

Q2 Barium (Ba) can be burned in oxygen.

a) Write an equation for the reaction. [1 mark]

b) Show the change in oxidation state of barium. [1 mark]

c) Describe the pH of the solution formed when the product is added to water. [1 mark]

Q3 The table shows the atomic radii of three elements from Group 2.

Element	Atomic radius (nm)
X	0.105
Y	0.150
Z	0.215

a) Predict which element would react most rapidly with water. [1 mark]

b) Explain your answer. [2 marks]

I'm not gonna make it. You've gotta get me out of here, Doc...

We're deep in the dense jungle of Inorganic Chemistry now. Those carefree days of Module Two are well behind us. It's now an endurance test and you've just got to keep going. By now, all the facts are probably blurring into one. It's tough, but you've got to stay awake, stay focused and keep learning. That's all you can do.

*She wanted to be in the book. I said OK.

Group 7 — The Halogens

Now you can wave goodbye to those pesky s-block elements. Here come the halogens.

Halogens are the **Highly Reactive Non-Metals** of Group 7

The table below gives some of the main properties of the first 4 halogens.

halogen	formula	colour	physical state (at 20°C)	electronic structure
fluorine	F_2	pale yellow	gas	$1s^2\ 2s^2\ 2p^5$
chlorine	Cl_2	green	gas	$1s^2\ 2s^2\ 2p^6\ 3s^2\ 3p^5$
bromine	Br_2	red-brown	liquid	$1s^2\ 2s^2\ 2p^6\ 3s^2\ 3p^6\ 3d^{10}\ 4s^2\ 4p^5$
iodine	I_2	grey	solid	$1s^2\ 2s^2\ 2p^6\ 3s^2\ 3p^6\ 3d^{10}\ 4s^2\ 4p^6\ 4d^{10}\ 5s^2\ 5p^5$

The halogens exist as **diatomic** molecules (two atoms joined by a single covalent bond).

Their boiling and melting points **increase** down the group. This is due to the **increasing strength** of the **London** (induced dipole-dipole) **forces** as the size and relative mass of the atoms increases (see p.49-51 for more on intermolecular forces).

This trend is shown in the changes of **physical state** from chlorine (gas) to iodine (solid) — volatility **decreases** down the group. (A substance is said to be **volatile** if it has a low boiling point.)

The word halogen should be used when describing the atom (X) or molecule (X_2), but the word halide is used to describe the negative ion (X^-).

Halogens get **Less Reactive** Down the Group

1) Halogen atoms react by **gaining an electron** in their outer shell to form **1–** ions. This means they're **reduced**. As they're reduced, they **oxidise** another substance (it's a redox reaction) — so they're **oxidising agents**.

$X + e^- \rightarrow X^-$
ox. number: **0** → **–1**

2) As you go down the group, the atomic radii **increase** so the outer electrons are **further** from the nucleus. The outer electrons are also **shielded** more from the attraction of the positive nucleus, because there are more inner electrons. This makes it **harder** for larger atoms to attract the electron needed to form an ion (despite the increased charge on the nucleus), so larger atoms are less reactive.
3) Another way of saying that the halogens get **less reactive** down the group is to say that they become **less oxidising**.

Halogens **Displace** Less Reactive Halide Ions from Solution

1) The halogens' **relative oxidising strengths** can be seen in their **displacement reactions** with halide ions. For example, if you mix bromine water, $Br_{2(aq)}$, with potassium iodide solution ($KI_{(aq)}$), the bromine **displaces** the iodide ions (it oxidises them), giving iodine (I_2) and potassium bromide solution, $KBr_{(aq)}$.

Full equation: $Br_{2(aq)} + 2KI_{(aq)} \rightarrow 2KBr_{(aq)} + I_{2(aq)}$

Ionic equation: $Br_{2(aq)} + 2I^-_{(aq)} \rightarrow 2Br^-_{(aq)} + I_{2(aq)}$

Oxidation number of Br: 0 → –1
Oxidation number of I: –1 → 0

2) When these displacement reactions happen, there are **colour changes**.
3) You can make the changes easier to see by shaking the reaction mixture with an **organic solvent** like hexane. The halogen that's present will dissolve readily in the organic solvent, which settles out as a distinct layer above the aqueous solution.

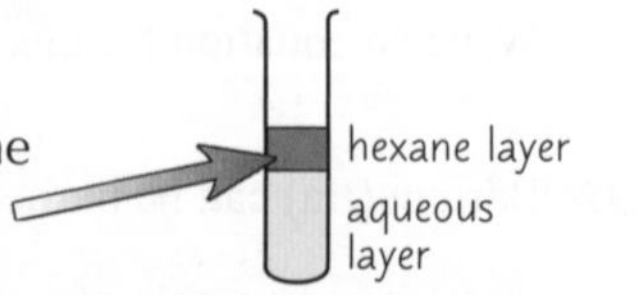

4) This table summarises the colour changes you'll see:

	$KCl_{(aq)}$ — colourless		$KBr_{(aq)}$ — colourless		$KI_{(aq)}$ — colourless	
	In aqueous solution	In organic solution	In aqueous solution	In organic solution	In aqueous solution	In organic solution
Chlorine water $Cl_{2(aq)}$ — colourless	no reaction	no reaction	yellow (**Br_2**)	orange (**Br_2**)	orange/brown (**I_2**)	purple (**I_2**)
Bromine water $Br_{2(aq)}$ — yellow	no reaction	no reaction	no reaction	no reaction	orange/brown (**I_2**)	purple (**I_2**)
Iodine Solution $I_{2(aq)}$ — orange/brown	no reaction	no reaction	no reaction	no reaction	no reaction	no reaction

Group 7 — The Halogens

Displacement Reactions Can Help to Identify Solutions

These displacement reactions can be used to help **identify** which halogen (or halide) is present in a solution.

A **halogen** will **displace a halide** from solution if the halide is **below it** in the Periodic Table, e.g.

You can also say a halogen will oxidise a halide if the halide is below it in the Periodic Table.

Periodic table	Displacement reaction	Ionic equation
Cl	chlorine (Cl_2) will displace bromide (Br^-) and iodide (I^-)	$Cl_{2(aq)} + 2Br^-_{(aq)} \rightarrow 2Cl^-_{(aq)} + Br_{2(aq)}$ $Cl_{2(aq)} + 2I^-_{(aq)} \rightarrow 2Cl^-_{(aq)} + I_{2(aq)}$
Br	bromine (Br_2) will displace iodide (I^-)	$Br_{2(aq)} + 2I^-_{(aq)} \rightarrow 2Br^-_{(aq)} + I_{2(aq)}$
I	no reaction with F^-, Cl^-, Br^-	

Silver Nitrate Solution is used to Test for Halides

The test for halides is dead easy. First you add **dilute nitric acid** to remove ions that might interfere with the test. Then you just add **silver nitrate solution** ($AgNO_{3(aq)}$). A **precipitate** is formed (of the silver halide).

$$Ag^+_{(aq)} + X^-_{(aq)} \rightarrow AgX_{(s)}$$ ...where X is Cl, Br or I

1) The **colour** of the precipitate identifies the halide.
2) Then to be extra sure, you can test your results by adding **ammonia solution**. (Each silver halide has a different solubility in ammonia — the larger the ion is, the more difficult it is to dissolve.)

Silver nitrate test for halide ions...

Chloride Cl^-: **white** precipitate, dissolves in dilute $NH_{3(aq)}$
Bromide Br^-: **cream** precipitate, dissolves in conc. $NH_{3(aq)}$
Iodide I^-: **yellow** precipitate, insoluble in conc. $NH_{3(aq)}$

Practice Questions

Q1 Describe the trend in boiling points as you go down Group 7.

Q2 Going down the group, the halogens become less reactive. Explain why.

Q3 What do you see when potassium iodide is added to bromine water?

Q4 Write the ionic equation for the reaction that happens when chlorine is added to a solution of iodide ions.

Exam Questions

Q1 a) Write an ionic equation for the reaction between iodine solution and sodium astatide (NaAt). [1 mark]

b) For the equation in a), deduce which substance is oxidised. [1 mark]

Q2 Dilute nitric acid and silver nitrate solution are added to a solution containing halide ions.
A yellow precipitate is formed that is insoluble in concentrated NH_3.
What is the formula of this precipitate?

A AgI   B Ag_2O C AgCl   D AgBr [1 mark]

Q3 Which two solutions would react to give a product that is purple when dissolved in an organic solvent?

A Iodine water and potassium chloride solution   B Chlorine water and potassium bromide solution

C Bromine water and potassium iodide solution   D Bromine water and potassium chloride solution [1 mark]

If you're not part of the solution, you're part of the precipitate...

This looks like a lot of tricky stuff, but really it all boils down to who's the best at nabbing that extra electron — the smaller the atom, the better it is. Make sure you remember all those pretty colour changes too — they're important.

Disproportionation and Water Treatment

Here comes another page jam-packed with golden nuggets of halogen fun. Oh yes, I kid you not. This page is the Alton Towers of Chemistry... white-knuckle excitement all the way...

Halogens Undergo **Disproportionation** with Alkalis

The halogens will react with cold dilute alkali solutions.
In these reactions, the halogen is simultaneously oxidised and reduced (called **disproportionation**)...

$$X_2 + 2NaOH \rightarrow NaXO + NaX + H_2O$$

Ionic equation: $X_2 + 2OH^- \rightarrow XO^- + X^- + H_2O$

Oxidation number of X: 0 (in X_2), +1 (in XO^-), −1 (in X^-)

The halogens (except fluorine) can exist in a wide range of oxidation states. E.g. chlorine can exist as:

−1	0	+1
Cl^-	Cl_2	ClO^-
chloride	chlorine	chlorate(I)

Chlorine and **Sodium Hydroxide** make Bleach

If you mix chlorine gas with cold, dilute aqueous sodium hydroxide, the above reaction takes place and you get **sodium chlorate(I) solution**, $NaClO_{(aq)}$, which just happens to be common household **bleach**.

$$2NaOH_{(aq)} + Cl_{2(g)} \rightarrow NaClO_{(aq)} + NaCl_{(aq)} + H_2O_{(l)}$$

Oxidation number of Cl: **0** (in Cl_2), **+1** (in NaClO), **−1** (in NaCl)

The oxidation number of Cl goes up and down so, you guessed it, it's disproportionation. Hurray.

The sodium chlorate(I) solution (bleach) has loads of uses — it's used in **water treatment**, to bleach **paper** and **textiles**... and it's good for **cleaning toilets**, too. Handy...

Chlorine is used to Kill Bacteria in Water

When you mix chlorine with water, it undergoes disproportionation.
You end up with a mixture of hydrochloric acid and **chloric(I) acid** (also called hypochlorous acid).

$$Cl_{2(g)} + H_2O_{(l)} \rightleftharpoons HCl_{(aq)} + HClO_{(aq)}$$

Oxidation number of Cl: **0** (in Cl_2), **−1** (in HCl, hydrochloric acid), **+1** (in HClO, chloric(I) acid)

Bromine and iodine also undergo disproportionation when mixed with water.

Aqueous chloric(I) acid **ionises** to make **chlorate(I) ions** (also called hypochlorite ions).

$$HClO_{(aq)} + H_2O_{(l)} \rightleftharpoons ClO^-_{(aq)} + H_3O^+_{(aq)}$$

Chlorate(I) ions **kill bacteria**.

So, **adding chlorine** (or a compound containing chlorate(I) ions) to water can make it safe to **drink** or **swim** in.

Crystal and Shane were thrilled to hear that the water was safe to swim in.

Disproportionation and Water Treatment

*Chlorine in Water — There are **Benefits**, **Risks** and **Ethical Implications***

1) Clean drinking water is amazingly important — around the world around **3.4 million people die** every year from waterborne diseases like cholera, typhoid and dysentery because they have to drink dirty water.
2) In the UK now we're lucky, because our drinking water is **treated** to make it safe. **Chlorine** is an important part of water treatment:

- It **kills disease-causing microorganisms** (see previous page).
- Some chlorine remains in the water and **prevents reinfection** further down the supply.
- It prevents the growth of **algae**, eliminating **bad tastes** and **smells**, and **removes discolouration** caused by organic compounds.

3) However, there are risks from using chlorine to treat water:

Chlorine gas is **very harmful** if it's breathed in — it irritates the **respiratory system**. **Liquid chlorine** on the skin or eyes causes severe **chemical burns**. Accidents involving chlorine could be really serious, or fatal.

Water contains a variety of organic compounds, e.g. from the decomposition of plants. Chlorine reacts with these compounds to form **chlorinated hydrocarbons**, e.g. chloromethane (CH_3Cl) — and many of these chlorinated hydrocarbons are carcinogenic (cancer-causing). However, this increased cancer risk is small compared to the risks from untreated water — a cholera epidemic, say, could kill thousands of people.

4) There are ethical considerations too. We don't get a **choice** about having our water chlorinated — some people object to this as forced 'mass medication'.
5) **Alternatives** to chlorine include:

Ozone (O_3) — a strong **oxidising** agent, which makes it great at **killing microorganisms**. However, it's **expensive** to produce and its **short half-life** in water means that treatment isn't permanent.

Ultraviolet light — it kills microorganisms by **damaging** their DNA, but it is **ineffective in cloudy water** and, like O_3, it won't stop the water being contaminated further down the line.

Practice Questions

Q1 How is common household bleach formed?

Q2 Write the equation for the reaction of chlorine with water. State underneath the oxidation numbers of the chlorine.

Q3 What are the benefits of adding chlorine to drinking water?

Exam Questions

Q1 If liquid bromine is mixed with cold, dilute potassium hydroxide, potassium bromate(I) is formed.

a) Give the ionic equation for the reaction. [1 mark]

b) What type of reaction is this? [1 mark]

Q2 Iodide ions react with chlorate(I) ions and water to form iodine, chloride ions and hydroxide ions.

a) Write a balanced equation for this reaction. [1 mark]

b) Show by use of oxidation states which substance has been oxidised and which has been reduced. [1 mark]

Remain seated until the page comes to a halt. Please exit to the right...

Oooh, what a lovely page, if I do say so myself. I bet the question of how bleach is made and how chlorine reacts with sodium hydroxide has plagued your mind since childhood. Well now you know. And remember... anything that chlorine can do, bromine and iodine can generally do as well. Eeee... it's just fun, fun, fun all the way.

Tests for Ions

If someone hands you a test tube and asks you what's in it, the last thing you should do is stick your finger in and taste the stuff. In fact, don't do that at all. Try these tests instead...

Hydrochloric Acid** Can Help Detect **Carbonates

To **test for carbonates** (CO_3^{2-}), add a **dilute acid** (e.g. dilute hydrochloric acid) to your mystery sample. If **carbonates** are present then **carbon dioxide** will be released.

The equation for the reaction is: $CO_3^{2-}{}_{(s)} + 2H^+{}_{(aq)} \rightarrow CO_{2(g)} + H_2O_{(l)}$

carbonate + acid → carbon dioxide + water

Example: $CaCO_{3(s)} + HCl_{(aq)} \rightarrow CO_{2(g)} + H_2O_{(l)} + CaCl_{2(aq)}$

You can **test** for carbon dioxide using **limewater**. Carbon dioxide turns limewater **cloudy** — just bubble the gas through a test tube of limewater and watch what happens.

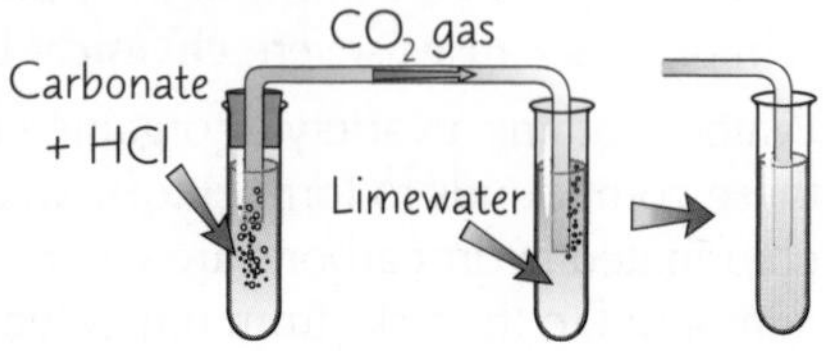

*Test for **Sulfates** with **HCl** and **Barium Chloride***

Most sulfates are soluble in water, but **barium sulfate** is **insoluble**. So, to test for a **sulfate** ion (SO_4^{2-}), add dilute HCl, followed by **barium chloride solution**, $BaCl_2$.
If you get a **white precipitate** it'll be **barium sulfate**, which tells you your mystery substance is a sulfate.

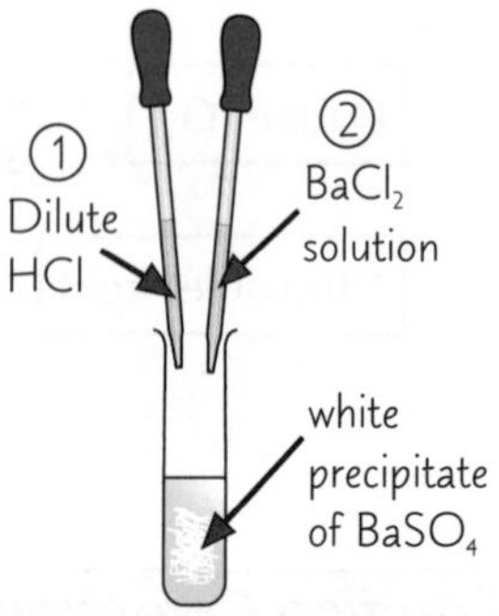

The equation for the reaction is: $Ba^{2+}{}_{(aq)} + SO_4^{2-}{}_{(aq)} \rightarrow BaSO_{4(s)}$

Example: $Na_2SO_{4(aq)} + BaCl_{2(aq)} \rightarrow BaSO_{4(s)} + 2NaCl_{(aq)}$

*Test for **Halides** with **Silver Nitrate***

As you may remember from page 63, to test for **halide ions** just add **nitric acid**, then **silver nitrate solution**.
If **chloride**, **bromide** or **iodide** is present, a **precipitate** will form.
The colour of the precipitate depends on the halide present:

Silver fluoride is soluble, so it won't give any precipitate.

Silver **chloride** (AgCl) is a **white precipitate**.
Silver **bromide** (AgBr) is a **cream precipitate**.
Silver **iodide** (AgI) is a **yellow precipitate**.

Nigel's favourite thing to test was Jen's patience.

You can test the **solubility** of these precipitates in **ammonia** to help you tell them apart.

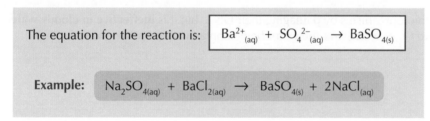

	Dissolves in dilute NH_3?	Dissolves in conc. NH_3?
AgCl	yes	yes
AgBr	no	yes
AgI	no	no

Tests for Ions

Use NaOH and Litmus Paper to Test for Ammonium Compounds

1) Ammonia gas (NH_3) is alkaline, so you can check for it using a damp piece of **red litmus paper**. If there's ammonia present, the paper will turn **blue**.
2) You can use this to **test** whether a substance contains **ammonium ions** (NH_4^+). Add some **sodium hydroxide** to your mystery substance in a test tube and **warm** the mixture. If there's ammonia given off this means there are ammonium ions in your mystery substance.

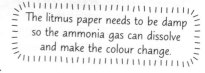

The litmus paper needs to be damp so the ammonia gas can dissolve and make the colour change.

$$NH_4^+{}_{(aq)} + OH^-{}_{(aq)} \rightarrow NH_{3(g)} + H_2O_{(l)}$$

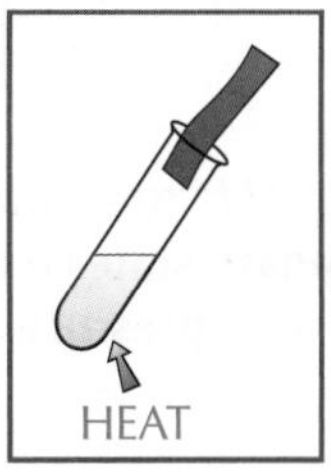

Example: $NH_4Cl_{(aq)} + NaOH_{(aq)} \rightarrow NH_{3(g)} + H_2O_{(l)} + NaCl_{(aq)}$

Watch Out for False Positives

1) As well as barium sulfate, barium carbonate and barium sulfite are also **insoluble**. So if you're testing for **sulfate ions**, you want to make sure that there are no **carbonate ions** or **sulfite ions** around first. (Otherwise your results won't mean much at all.)
2) Likewise, if you're testing for a **halide ion**, you want to rule out the presence of **sulfate ions** first. This is because sulfate ions will also produce a **precipitate** with silver nitrate.
3) A nifty way of getting round this is to first add a **dilute acid** to your test solutions. The acid will **get rid** of any lurking anions that you don't want.

The dilute acid mustn't interfere with the test you're doing — it's no good using HCl if you're testing for chloride ions.

4) You can also avoid mix-ups by doing your tests in this order:

(1) Test for carbonates —no CO_2→ (2) Test for sulfates —no precipitate→ (3) Test for halides

Practice Questions

Q1 Which halide ion will form a white precipitate when mixed with silver nitrate solution?

Q2 What colour will ammonia gas turn damp litmus paper?

Q3 Why should you add dilute HCl to a solution before carrying out the barium chloride test?

Exam Questions

Q1 Which of these would you expect to observe if you added dilute HCl to a solution containing carbonate ions?

A A white precipitate will form.
B Bubbles of gas will form.
C A yellow precipitate will form.
D No reaction will occur.

[1 mark]

Q2* You are given four test tubes, each containing one of the following solutions:

calcium carbonate **sodium sulfate** **ammonium carbonate** **magnesium chloride**

Describe the tests that you would carry out to identify each solution with a positive test result. Include any observations that you would expect and the conclusions that you would draw from them.

[6 marks]

It's easy to detect negative ions — they're the gloomy ones...

So here's another couple of pages covered in reactions that you've just got to learn, I'm afraid. Try closing the book and scribbling down what reagent you would use to test for each ion, and what the positive result would look like in each case. Keep going until they're all sorted out in your head. Then chill with a well-earned cuppa — you've earned it.

* The quality of your extended response will be assessed for this question.

Enthalpy Changes

A whole new section to enjoy — but don't forget, Big Brother is watching...

Chemical Reactions Often Have **Enthalpy Changes**

When chemical reactions happen, some bonds are **broken** and some bonds are **made**. More often than not, this'll cause a **change in energy**. The souped-up chemistry term for this is **enthalpy change**.

> **Enthalpy change**, ΔH (delta H), is the heat energy transferred in a reaction at **constant pressure**. The units of ΔH are **kJ mol^{-1}**.

You write $\Delta H^{\ominus}$ to show that the measurements were made under **standard conditions** and that the elements were in their **standard states** (i.e. their physical states under standard conditions). Standard conditions are **100 kPa** (about 1 atm) **pressure** and a temperature of **298 K** (25 °C). The next page explains why this is necessary.

Reactions can be either **Exothermic** or **Endothermic**

> **Exothermic** reactions **give out** energy. ΔH is **negative**.

In exothermic reactions, the temperature often goes **up**.

The symbols $\Delta_c H^{\ominus}$ and $\Delta_r H^{\ominus}$ (below) are explained on the next page.

Oxidation is usually exothermic. Here are 2 examples:

- The **combustion** of a fuel like methane:

  $CH_{4(g)} + 2O_{2(g)} \rightarrow CO_{2(g)} + 2H_2O_{(l)}$ $\quad \Delta_r H^{\ominus} = -890$ kJ mol^{-1} **exothermic**
- The oxidation of **carbohydrates**, such as glucose, $C_6H_{12}O_6$, in respiration.

Fabio heard an exothermic onesie would increase his hotness.

> **Endothermic** reactions **absorb** energy. ΔH is **positive**.

In these reactions, the temperature often **falls**.

- The **thermal decomposition** of calcium carbonate is endothermic:

  $CaCO_{3(s)} \rightarrow CaO_{(s)} + CO_{2(g)}$ $\quad \Delta_r H^{\ominus} = +178$ kJ mol^{-1} **endothermic**
- The main reactions of **photosynthesis** are also endothermic — sunlight supplies the energy.

Enthalpy Profile Diagrams Show Energy Change in **Reactions**

1) **Enthalpy profile diagrams** show you how the enthalpy (energy) changes during reactions.
2) The **activation energy**, E_a, is the minimum amount of energy needed to begin breaking reactant bonds and start a chemical reaction. (There's more on activation energy on page 74.)

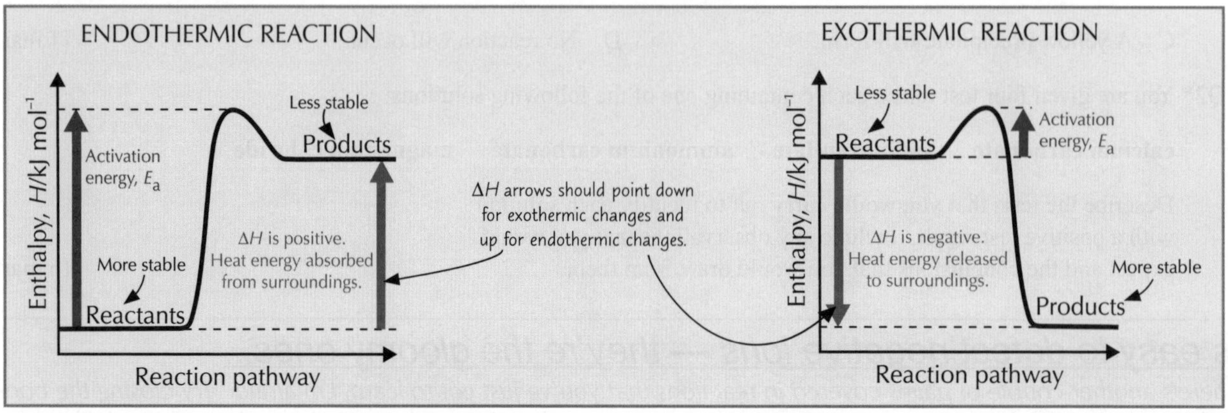

3) The **less enthalpy** a substance has, the **more stable** it is.

Enthalpy Changes

You Need to Specify the Conditions for Enthalpy Changes

1) You can't directly measure the **actual** enthalpy of a system. In practice, that doesn't matter, because it's only ever **enthalpy change** that matters. You can find enthalpy changes either by **experiment** or in **data books**.
2) Enthalpy changes you find in data books are usually **standard** enthalpy changes — enthalpy changes under **standard conditions** (**298 K** and **100 kPa**).
3) This is important because changes in enthalpy are affected by **temperature** and **pressure** — using standard conditions means that everyone can know **exactly** what the enthalpy change is describing.

There are Different Types of ΔH Depending On the Reaction

1) **Standard enthalpy change of reaction**, $\Delta_r H^\circ$, is the enthalpy change when the reaction occurs in the **molar quantities** shown in the **chemical equation**, under standard conditions.
2) **Standard enthalpy change of formation**, $\Delta_f H^\circ$, is the enthalpy change when **1 mole** of a **compound** is formed from its **elements** in their standard states, under standard conditions, e.g. $2C_{(s)} + 3H_{2(g)} + \frac{1}{2}O_{2(g)} \rightarrow C_2H_5OH_{(l)}$.
3) **Standard enthalpy change of combustion**, $\Delta_c H^\circ$, is the enthalpy change when **1 mole** of a substance is completely **burned in oxygen**, under standard conditions.
4) **Standard enthalpy change of neutralisation**, $\Delta_{neut} H^\circ$, is the enthalpy change when an **acid** and an **alkali** react together, under standard conditions, to form **1 mole of water**.

Practice Questions

Q1 Explain the terms exothermic and endothermic, giving an example reaction in each case.

Q2 Draw and label enthalpy profile diagrams for an exothermic and an endothermic reaction.

Q3 Define standard enthalpy of formation and standard enthalpy of combustion.

Exam Questions

Q1 Hydrogen peroxide, H_2O_2, can decompose into water and oxygen.

$$2H_2O_{2(l)} \rightarrow 2H_2O_{(l)} + O_{2(g)} \qquad \Delta H^\circ = -98 \text{ kJ mol}^{-1}$$

Draw an enthalpy profile diagram for this reaction. Mark on the activation energy, E_a, and ΔH. [3 marks]

Q2 Methanol, $CH_3OH_{(l)}$, when blended with petrol, can be used as a fuel. $\Delta_c H^\circ[CH_3OH] = -726 \text{ kJ mol}^{-1}$

a) Write an equation, including state symbols, for the standard enthalpy change of combustion of methanol. [1 mark]

b) Write an equation, including state symbols, for the standard enthalpy change of formation of methanol. [1 mark]

c) Petroleum gas is a fuel that contains propane, C_3H_8. Why does the following equation not represent a standard enthalpy change of combustion? [1 mark]

$$2C_3H_{8(g)} + 10O_{2(g)} \rightarrow 6CO_{2(g)} + 8H_2O_{(g)} \qquad \Delta_r H^\circ = -4113 \text{ kJ mol}^{-1}$$

Q3 Coal is mainly carbon. It is burned as a fuel. $\Delta_c H^\circ = -393.5 \text{ kJ mol}^{-1}$

a) Write an equation, including state symbols, for the standard enthalpy change of combustion of carbon. [1 mark]

b) Explain why the standard enthalpy change of formation of carbon dioxide will also be $-393.5 \text{ kJ mol}^{-1}$. [1 mark]

c) How much energy would be released when 1 tonne of carbon is burned? (1 tonne = 1000 kg) [2 marks]

Clap along if you feel like an enthalpy change without a roof...

Quite a few definitions here. And you need to know them all. If you're going to bother learning them, you might as well do it properly and learn all the pernickety details. They probably seem about as useful as a dead fly in your custard right now, but all will be revealed over the next few pages. Learn them now, so you've got a bit of a head start.

More on Enthalpy Changes

I bonded with my friend straight away. Now we're on the waiting list to be surgically separated.

Reactions are all about **Breaking** and **Making** Bonds

When reactions happen, **reactant bonds** are **broken** and **product bonds** are **formed**.

1) You **need** energy to break bonds, so bond breaking is **endothermic** (ΔH is **positive**).
2) Energy is **released** when bonds are formed, so this is **exothermic** (ΔH is **negative**).
3) The **enthalpy change** for a reaction is the **overall effect** of these two changes. If you need **more** energy to **break** bonds than is released when bonds are made, ΔH is **positive**. If you need **less**, ΔH is **negative**.

You need **Energy** to **Break** the **Attraction** between **Atoms** and **Ions**

1) In ionic bonding, **positive** and **negative ions** are attracted to each other. In covalent molecules, the **positive nuclei** are attracted to the **negative** charge of the shared electrons in a covalent bond.
2) You need energy to **break** this attraction — **stronger** bonds take more energy to break. The **amount of energy** you need per mole is called the **bond dissociation enthalpy**. (Of course it's got a fancy name — this is chemistry.)
3) Bond dissociation enthalpies always involve bond breaking in **gaseous compounds**. This makes comparisons fair.

Average Bond Enthalpies are **not Exact**

1) Water (H_2O) has **two O–H bonds**. You'd think it'd take the same amount of energy to break them both... but it **doesn't**.

   The **first** bond, $H–OH_{(g)}$: $E(H–OH) = +492 \text{ kJ mol}^{-1}$
   The **second** bond, $H–O_{(g)}$: $E(H–O) = +428 \text{ kJ mol}^{-1}$
   (OH^- is a bit easier to break apart because of the extra electron repulsion.)
   So, the **average** bond enthalpy is $(492 + 428) \div 2 = $ **+460 kJ mol⁻¹**.

2) The **data book** says the bond enthalpy for O–H is $+463 \text{ kJ mol}^{-1}$. It's a bit different because it's the average for a **much bigger range** of molecules, not just water. For example, it includes the O–H bonds in alcohols and carboxylic acids too.
3) So when you look up an **average bond enthalpy**, what you get is:

   The energy needed to break **one mole** of bonds in the **gas phase**, averaged over **many different** compounds.

You can find out **Enthalpy Changes** in the Lab

1) To measure the **enthalpy change** for a reaction you only need to know **two things** —
   - the **number of moles** of the stuff that's reacting,
   - the change in **temperature**.
2) How you go about doing the experiment depends on what type of reaction it is.

- To find the enthalpy of **combustion** of a **flammable liquid**, you burn it — using apparatus like this...

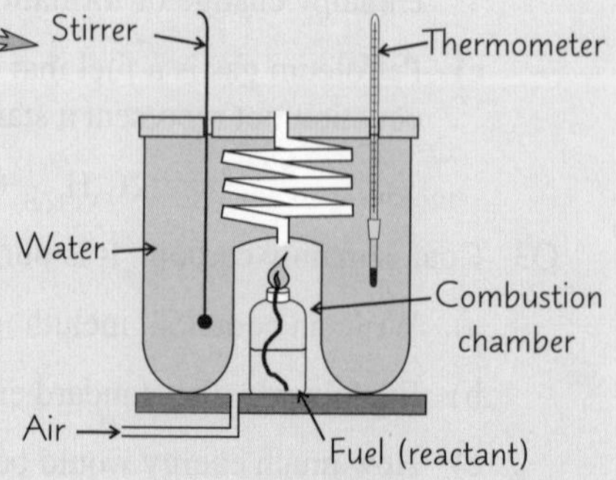

- As the fuel burns, it heats the water. You can work out the **heat absorbed** by the water if you know the **mass of water**, the **temperature change of the water** (ΔT), and the **specific heat capacity of water** ($= 4.18 \text{ J g}^{-1} \text{ K}^{-1}$). See the next page for all the details.
- Ideally **all** the heat given out by the fuel as it burns would be **absorbed** by the water — allowing you to work out the enthalpy change of combustion (see the next page). In practice though, you **always** lose some heat (as you heat the apparatus and the surroundings).

> The specific heat capacity of a substance is the amount of heat energy it takes to raise the temperature of 1 g of that substance by 1 K.

3) Similar methods to this (all known as calorimetry) can also be used to calculate an enthalpy change for a reaction that happens **in solution**, such as **neutralisation** or **displacement**. For a neutralisation reaction, combine known quantities of acid and alkali in an insulated container, and measure the temperature change. The **heat given out** can be calculated using the formula on the next page.

More on Enthalpy Changes

Calculate **Enthalpy Changes** Using the **Equation q = mcΔT**

It seems there's a snazzy equation for everything these days, and enthalpy change is no exception:

$q = mc\Delta T$ where, q = heat lost or gained (in joules). This is the same as the enthalpy change if the pressure is constant.
m = mass of water in the calorimeter, or solution in the insulated container (in grams).
c = specific heat capacity of water (4.18 J g^{-1} K^{-1}).
ΔT = the change in temperature of the water or solution (in K).

This is the same as the change in °C.

Example: In a laboratory experiment, 1.16 g of an organic liquid fuel was completely burned in oxygen. The heat formed during this combustion raised the temperature of 100 g of water from 295.3 K to 357.8 K. Calculate the standard enthalpy of combustion, $\Delta_c H^{\ominus}$, of the fuel. Its M_r is 58.0.

Remember — m is the mass of water, NOT the mass of fuel.

1. First off, you need to calculate the **amount of heat** given out by the fuel using $q = mc\Delta T$.

   $q = mc\Delta T$

   $q = 100 \times 4.18 \times (357.8 - 295.3) = 26\,125$ J

   $26\,125 \div 1000 = 26.125$ kJ

   If you're asked to calculate an enthalpy change, the answer should always be in kJ mol⁻¹. So change the amount of heat from J to kJ by dividing by 1000.

2. The standard enthalpy of combustion involves 1 mole of fuel. So next you need to find out **how many moles** of fuel produced this heat. It's back to the old $n = \text{mass} \div M_r$ equation.

   n = 1.16 ÷ 58.0 = 0.0200 mole of fuels

3. So the heat produced by 1 mole of fuel = –26.125 ÷ 0.0200

   ≈ **–1310 kJ mol⁻¹** (3 s.f.).

   This is the standard enthalpy change of combustion.

   It's negative because combustion is an exothermic reaction.

The actual $\Delta_c H^{\ominus}$ of this compound is –1615 kJ mol⁻¹ — lots of heat has been **lost** and not measured. For example, it's likely a bit would escape through the **calorimeter** and also the fuel might not **combust completely**.

Practice Questions

Q1 Briefly describe an experiment that could be carried out to find the enthalpy change of a reaction.

Q2 Why is the enthalpy change determined in a laboratory likely to be lower than the value shown in a data book?

Q3 What equation is used to calculate the heat change in a chemical reaction?

Exam Questions

Q1 A 50.0 cm^3 sample of 0.200 mol dm^{-3} copper(II) sulfate solution placed in a polystyrene beaker gave a temperature increase of 2.60 K when excess zinc powder was added and stirred. Calculate the enthalpy change when 1 mole of zinc reacts. Assume that the specific heat capacity for the solution is 4.18 J g^{-1} K^{-1}. Ignore the increase in volume due to the zinc.
The equation for the reaction is: $Zn_{(s)} + CuSO_{4(aq)} \rightarrow Cu_{(s)} + ZnSO_{4(aq)}$ [4 marks]

Q2 a) Explain why bond enthalpies determine whether a reaction is exothermic or endothermic. [2 marks]

b) Calculate the temperature change that should be produced when 1.000 kg of water is heated by burning 6.000 g of coal. Assume the coal is pure carbon.
[The specific heat capacity of water is 4.18 J g^{-1} K^{-1}. For carbon, $\Delta_c H^{\ominus} = -393.5$ kJ mol^{-1}] [3 marks]

Clap along if you feel like calorimetry is the truth...

Reactions are like pulling a model spaceship apart and building something new. Sometimes the bits get stuck together and you need to use loads of energy to pull 'em apart. Okay, so energy's not really released when you stick them together, but you can't have everything — and it wasn't that bad an analogy up till now.

Enthalpy Calculations

You can't always work out an enthalpy change by measuring a single temperature change. But there are other ways...

Hess's Law — the Total Enthalpy Change is Independent of the Route Taken

Hess's Law says that:

The **total enthalpy change** of a reaction is always **the same**, no matter **which route** is taken.

These handy diagrams are called enthalpy cycles.

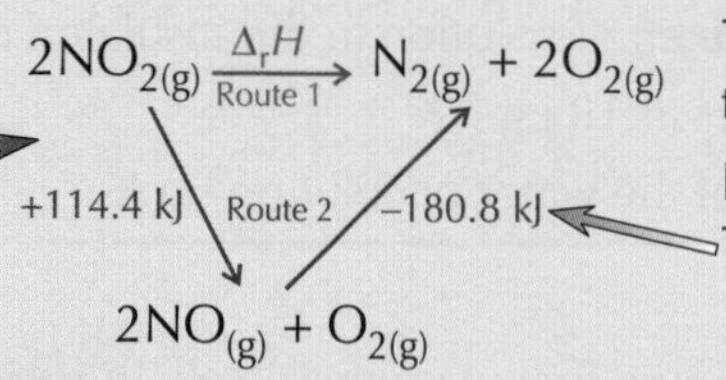

This law is handy for working out enthalpy changes that you **can't find directly** by doing an experiment.

Here's an example:

The **total enthalpy change** for route 1 is the **same as for route 2**.

So, $\Delta_rH = +114.4 + (-180.8) = \mathbf{-66.4\ kJ\ mol^{-1}}$.

Enthalpy Changes Can be Worked Out From Enthalpies of Formation

Enthalpy changes of formation are useful for calculating enthalpy changes you can't find directly.
You need to know Δ_fH° for **all** the reactants and products that are **compounds** — Δ_fH° for elements is **zero**.

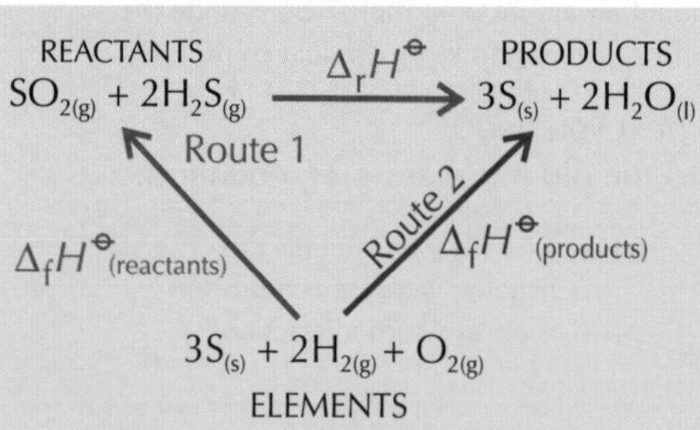

$\Delta_fH^\circ[SO_{2(g)}] = -297\ kJ\ mol^{-1}$
$\Delta_fH^\circ[H_2S_{(g)}] = -20.2\ kJ\ mol^{-1}$
$\Delta_fH^\circ[H_2O_{(l)}] = -286\ kJ\ mol^{-1}$

Here's how to calculate Δ_rH° for the reaction:

$$SO_{2(g)} + 2H_2S_{(g)} \rightarrow 3S_{(s)} + 2H_2O_{(l)}$$

Using **Hess's Law**: Route 1 = Route 2

Δ_rH° + the sum of Δ_fH°(reactants) = the sum of Δ_fH°(products)

So, Δ_rH° = the sum of Δ_fH°(products) – the sum of Δ_fH°(reactants)

Just plug the numbers given on the left into the equation above:

$\Delta_rH^\circ = [0 + (-286 \times 2)] - [-297 + (-20.2 \times 2)] = \mathbf{-235\ kJ\ mol^{-1}}$

Δ_fH° of sulfur is zero — it's an element.

There are 2 moles of H_2O and 2 moles of H_2S.

It **always** works, no matter how complicated the reaction... e.g. $2NH_4NO_{3(s)} + C_{(s)} \rightarrow 2N_{2(g)} + CO_{2(g)} + 4H_2O_{(l)}$

Using Hess's Law: Route 1 = Route 2

Δ_fH°(reactants) + Δ_rH° = Δ_fH°(products)

$(2 \times -365) + 0 + \Delta_rH^\circ = 0 + -394 + (4 \times -286)$

$\Delta_rH^\circ = -394 + (-1144) - (-730)$

$= \mathbf{-808\ kJ\ mol^{-1}}$

Remember... Δ_fH for any element is zero.

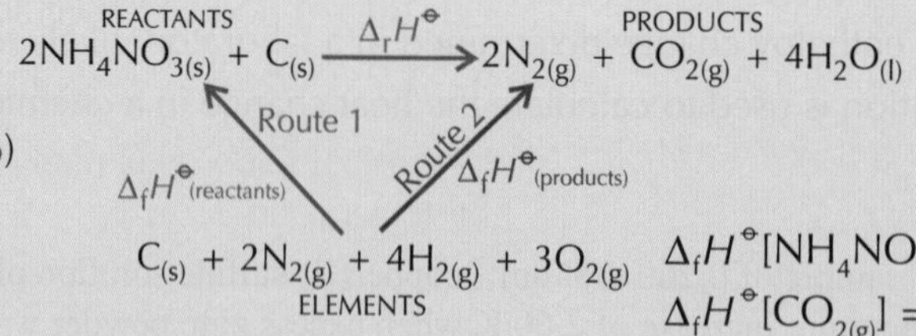

$\Delta_fH^\circ[NH_4NO_{3(s)}] = -365\ kJ\ mol^{-1}$
$\Delta_fH^\circ[CO_{2(g)}] = -394\ kJ\ mol^{-1}$
$\Delta_fH^\circ[H_2O_{(l)}] = -286\ kJ\ mol^{-1}$

Enthalpy Changes Can be Worked Out From Enthalpies of Combustion

You can use a similar method to find an enthalpy change from **enthalpy changes of combustion**.

Here's how to calculate Δ_fH° of $\mathbf{C_2H_5OH}$...

Using Hess's Law: Route 1 = Route 2

$\Delta_fH^\circ[C_2H_5OH] + \Delta_cH^\circ[C_2H_5OH] = 2\Delta_cH^\circ[C] + 3\Delta_cH^\circ[H_2]$

$\Delta_fH^\circ[C_2H_5OH] + (-1367) = (2 \times -394) + (3 \times -286)$

$\Delta_fH^\circ[C_2H_5OH] = -788 + -858 - (-1367) = \mathbf{-279\ kJ\ mol^{-1}}$

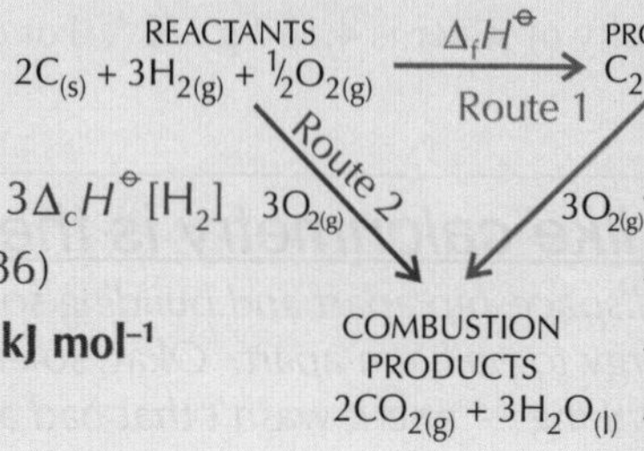

You need to add enough oxygen to balance the equations.

$\Delta_cH^\circ[C_{(s)}] = -394\ kJ\ mol^{-1}$
$\Delta_cH^\circ[H_{2(g)}] = -286\ kJ\ mol^{-1}$
$\Delta_cH^\circ[C_2H_5OH_{(l)}] = -1367\ kJ\ mol^{-1}$

Enthalpy Calculations

Enthalpy Changes Can Be Calculated using Average Bond Enthalpies

In any chemical reaction, energy is **absorbed** to **break bonds** and **given out** during **bond formation**. The difference between the energy absorbed and released is the overall **enthalpy change of reaction**:

Enthalpy Change of Reaction = Total Energy Absorbed – Total Energy Released

Example: Calculate the overall enthalpy change for this reaction: $N_{2(g)} + 3H_{2(g)} \rightarrow 2NH_{3(g)}$
Use the average bond enthalpy values in the table.

Bonds broken: 1 N≡N bond broken = 1 × 945 = 945 kJ mol^{-1}
3 H–H bonds broken = 3 × 436 = 1308 kJ mol^{-1}

Total Energy Absorbed = 945 + 1308 = **2253 kJ mol^{-1}**

Bonds formed: 6 N–H bonds formed = 6 × 391 = 2346 kJ mol^{-1}

Total Energy Released = **2346 kJ mol^{-1}**

Bond	Average Bond Enthalpy
N≡N	945 kJ mol^{-1}
H–H	436 kJ mol^{-1}
N–H	391 kJ mol^{-1}

Now you just subtract 'total energy released' from 'total energy absorbed':

Enthalpy Change of Reaction = 2253 – 2346 = **–93 kJ mol^{-1}**

Practice Questions

Q1 What is Hess's Law?

Q2 What is the standard enthalpy change of formation of any element?

Q3 Describe how you can make an enthalpy cycle to find the standard enthalpy change of a reaction using standard enthalpy changes of formation.

Exam Questions

Q1 Using the facts that the standard enthalpy change of formation of $Al_2O_{3(s)}$ is –1676 kJ mol^{-1} and the standard enthalpy change of formation of $MgO_{(s)}$ is –602 kJ mol^{-1}, calculate the enthalpy change of the following reaction.

$$Al_2O_{3(s)} + 3Mg_{(s)} \rightarrow 2Al_{(s)} + 3MgO_{(s)}$$

[2 marks]

Q2 Calculate the enthalpy change for the reaction below (the fermentation of glucose).

$$C_6H_{12}O_{6(s)} \rightarrow 2C_2H_5OH_{(l)} + 2CO_{2(g)}$$

Use the following standard enthalpies of combustion in your calculations:

$\Delta_c H^{\ominus}$(glucose) = –2820 kJ mol^{-1} $\Delta_c H^{\ominus}$(ethanol) = –1367 kJ mol^{-1} [2 marks]

Q3 Calculate the standard enthalpy of formation of propane from carbon and hydrogen. $3C_{(s)} + 4H_{2(g)} \rightarrow C_3H_{8(g)}$

Use the following data:

$\Delta_c H^{\ominus}$(propane) = –2220 kJ mol^{-1}, $\Delta_c H^{\ominus}$(carbon) = –394 kJ mol^{-1}, $\Delta_c H^{\ominus}$(hydrogen) = –286 kJ mol^{-1} [2 marks]

Q4 The table on the right shows some average bond enthalpy values.

Bond	C–H	C=O	O=O	O–H
Average Bond Enthalpy (kJ mol^{-1})	435	805	498	464

The complete combustion of methane can be represented by the following equation:

$$CH_{4(g)} + 2O_{2(g)} \rightarrow CO_{2(g)} + 2H_2O_{(l)}$$

Use the table of bond enthalpies above to calculate the enthalpy change for the reaction. [2 marks]

Clap along if you know what Hess's Law is to you...

To get your head around those enthalpy cycles, you're going to have to do more than skim them. It'll also help if you know the definitions for those standard enthalpy thingumabobs. I'd read those enthalpy cycle examples again and make sure you understand how the elements/compounds at each corner were chosen to be there.

Reaction Rates

The rate of a reaction is just how quickly it happens. Lots of things can make it go faster or slower.

Particles **Must** Collide to **React**

1) Particles in liquids and gases are **always moving** and **colliding** with **each other**. They **don't** react every time though — only when the **conditions** are right. A reaction **won't** take place between two particles **unless** —

- They collide in the **right direction**. They need to be **facing** each other the right way.
- They collide with at least a certain **minimum** amount of kinetic (movement) **energy**.

This stuff's called **Collision Theory**.

2) The **minimum amount of kinetic energy** particles need to react is called the **activation energy**. The particles need this much energy to **break the bonds** to start the reaction.
3) Reactions with **low activation energies** often happen **pretty easily**. But reactions with **high activation energies** don't. You need to give the particles extra energy by **heating** them.

To make this a bit clearer, here's an **energy profile diagram**.

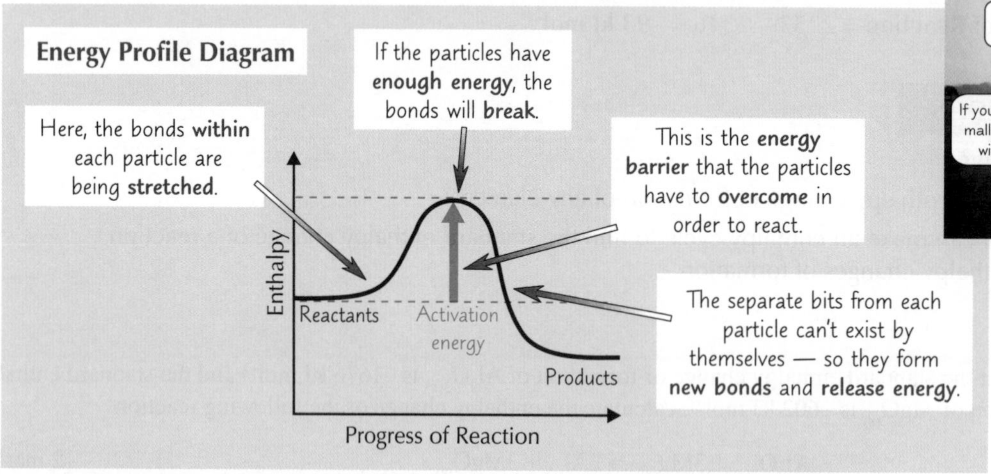

Molecules **Don't** all have the **Same Amount of Energy**

Imagine looking down on Oxford Street when it's teeming with people. You'll see some people ambling along **slowly**, some hurrying **quickly**, but most of them will be walking with a **moderate speed**. It's the same with the **molecules** in a liquid or gas. Some **don't have much kinetic energy** and move **slowly**. Others have **loads** of **kinetic energy** and **whizz** along. But most molecules are somewhere **in between**.

If you plot a **graph** of the **numbers of molecules** in a substance with different **kinetic energies** you get a **Boltzmann distribution**. It looks like this —

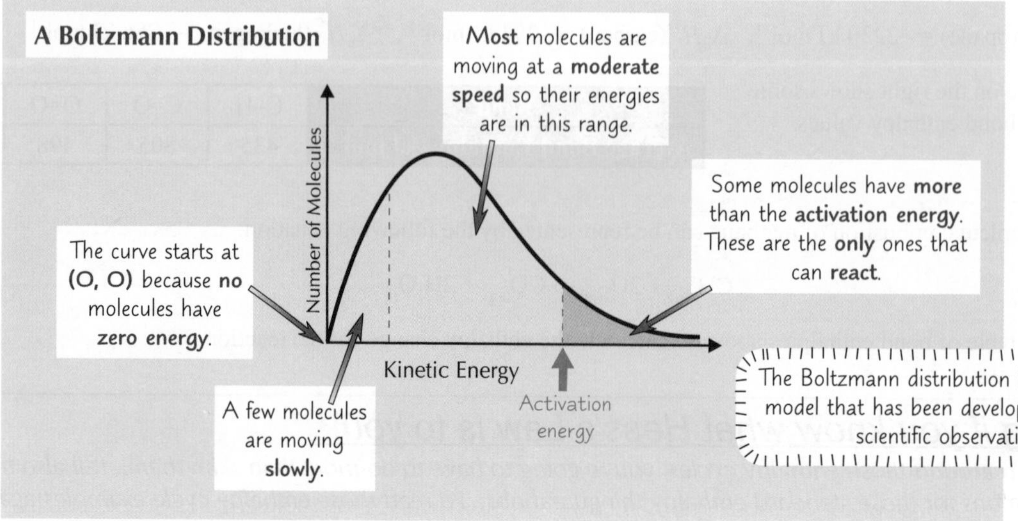

The Boltzmann distribution is a theoretical model that has been developed to explain scientific observations.

Reaction Rates

Increasing the *Temperature* makes Reactions *Faster*

1) If you increase the **temperature**, the particles will, on average, have more **kinetic energy** and will move **faster**.
2) So, a **greater proportion** of molecules will have at least the **activation energy** and be able to **react**. This changes the **shape** of the **Boltzmann distribution curve** — it pushes it over to the **right**.

The total number of molecules is still the same, which means the area under each curve must be the same.

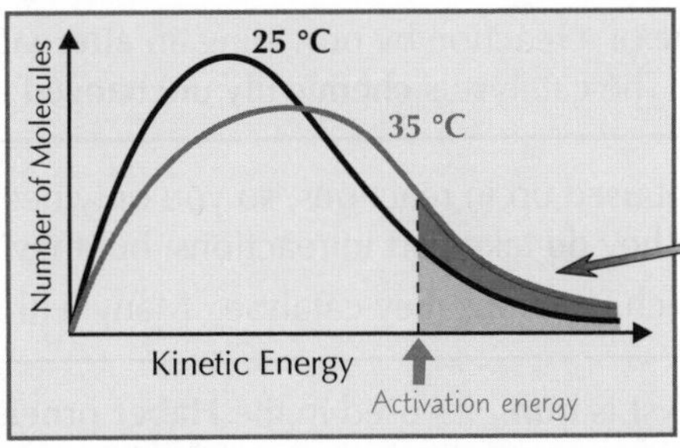

At higher temperatures, more molecules have at least the activation energy.

3) Because the molecules are flying about **faster**, they'll **collide more often**. This is **another reason** why increasing the temperature makes a reaction faster.

Concentration, *Pressure* and *Catalysts* also Affect the *Reaction Rate*

Increasing Concentration Speeds Up Reactions

If you increase the **concentration** of reactants in a **solution**, the particles will be **closer together**, on average. If they're closer, they'll **collide more frequently**. If there are **more collisions**, they'll have **more chances** to react.

Increasing Pressure Speeds Up Reactions

If any of your reactants are **gases**, increasing the **pressure** will increase the rate of reaction. It's pretty much the same as increasing the **concentration** of a solution — at higher pressures, the particles will be **closer together**, increasing the chance of **successful collisions**.

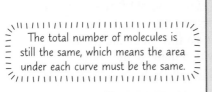

If one of the reactants is a solid, increasing its surface area makes the reaction faster too.

Catalysts Can Speed Up Reactions

Catalysts are really useful. They **lower the activation energy** by providing a **different way** for the bonds to be broken and remade. If the activation energy's **lower**, more particles will have **enough energy** to react. There's heaps of information about catalysts on the next two pages.

Practice Questions

Q1 Explain the term 'activation energy'.

Q2 Name four factors that affect the rate of a reaction.

Exam Questions

Q1 Nitrogen oxide (NO) and ozone (O_3) sometimes react to produce nitrogen dioxide (NO_2) and oxygen (O_2). How would increasing the pressure affect the rate of this reaction? Explain your answer. [2 marks]

Q2 On the right is a Boltzmann distribution curve for a sample of a gas at 25 °C.

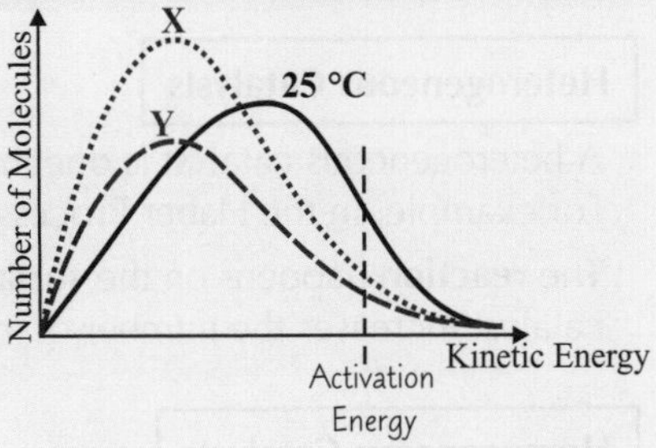

a) Which of the curves, X or Y, shows the Boltzmann distribution curve for the same sample at 15 °C ? [1 mark]

b) Explain how this curve shows that the reaction rate will be lower at 15 °C than at 25 °C. [1 mark]

Clap along if you feel like reaction rates are what you wanna do...

This page isn't too hard to learn — no equations, no formulas... what more could you ask for. The only tricky thing might be the Boltzmann thingymajiggle. Remember, increasing concentration and pressure do exactly the same thing. The only difference is, you increase the concentration of a solution and the pressure of a gas.

Catalysts

Catalysts were tantalisingly mentioned on the last page — here's the full story...

Catalysts Increase the Rate of Reactions

You can use **catalysts** to make chemical reactions happen **faster**. Learn this definition:

A **catalyst** increases the **rate** of a reaction by providing an **alternative reaction pathway** with a **lower activation energy**. The catalyst is **chemically unchanged** at the end of the reaction.

1) Catalysts are **great**. They **don't** get used up in reactions, so you only need a **tiny bit** of catalyst to catalyse a **huge** amount of stuff. They **do** take part in reactions, but they're **remade** at the end.
2) Catalysts are **very fussy** about which reactions they catalyse. Many will usually **only** work on a single reaction.

An example of a catalyst is **iron**. It's used in the **Haber process** to make ammonia.

$$N_{2(g)} + 3H_{2(g)} \underset{}{\overset{Fe_{(s)}}{\rightleftharpoons}} 2NH_{3(g)}$$

Enthalpy Profiles and Boltzmann Distributions Show Why Catalysts Work

If you look at an **enthalpy profile** together with a **Boltzmann Distribution**, you can see **why** catalysts work.

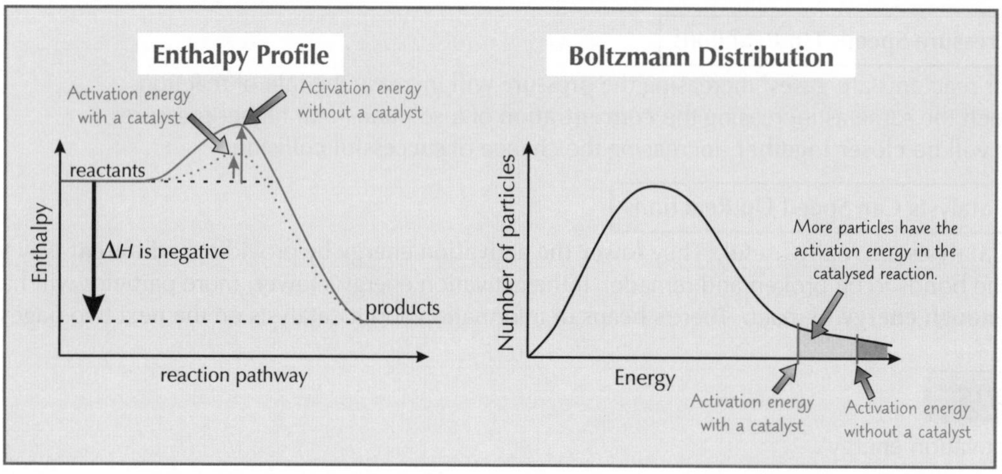

The 1985 Nobel Prize in Chemistry was awarded to Mr Tiddles for discovering catalysis.

The catalyst **lowers the activation energy**, meaning there are **more particles** with **enough energy** to react when they collide. So, in a certain amount of time, **more particles react**.

Catalysts can be Homogeneous or Heterogenous

Heterogeneous Catalysts

A heterogeneous catalyst is one that is in a **different phase** from the reactants — i.e. in a different **physical state**. For example, in the Haber Process (see above), **gases** are passed over a **solid iron catalyst**.

The **reaction** happens on the **surface** of the **heterogeneous catalyst**. So, **increasing** the **surface area** of the catalyst increases the number of molecules that can **react** at the same time, **increasing the rate** of the reaction.

Homogeneous Catalysts

Homogeneous catalysts are in the **same physical state** as the reactants.
Usually a **homogeneous** catalyst is an **aqueous catalyst** for a reaction between two **aqueous solutions**.

A homogeneous catalyst works by forming an **intermediate species**. The **reactants** combine with the **catalyst** to make an **intermediate species**, which then reacts to form the **products** and **reform the catalyst**.

Catalysts

Catalysts — Good for Industries...

Loads of industries rely on **catalysts**. They can dramatically lower production costs, give you more product in a shorter time and help make better products. Here are a few examples —

Iron is used as a catalyst in **ammonia** production. If it wasn't for the catalyst, the **temperature** would have to be raised loads to make the reaction happen **quick enough**. Not only would this be bad for the fuel bills, it'd **reduce the amount of ammonia** produced.

Using a catalyst can change the properties of a product to make it more useful, e.g. **poly(ethene)**.

	Made without a catalyst	Made with a catalyst (a Ziegler-Natta catalyst, to be precise)
Properties of poly(ethene)	less dense, less rigid	more dense, more rigid, higher melting point

...and for Environmental Sustainability

1) Using catalysts means that lower temperatures and pressures can be used. So energy is saved, meaning **less CO_2** is released, and fossil fuel reserves are preserved. Catalysts can also **reduce waste** by allowing a different reaction to be used with a better **atom economy**. (See page 34 for more on atom economy.)

For example, making the painkiller ibuprofen by the traditional method involves 6 steps and has an atom economy of 32%. Using catalysts, it can be made in **3 steps** with an **atom economy of 77%**.

2) **Catalytic converters** on cars are made from **alloys of platinum, palladium and rhodium**. They reduce the pollution released into the atmosphere by speeding up the reaction, $2CO + 2NO \rightarrow 2CO_2 + N_2$.

Practice Questions

Q1 Explain what a catalyst is.

Q2 Explain what the difference between a heterogeneous and a homogeneous catalyst is.

Q3 Describe three reasons why catalysts are useful for industry.

Exam Question

Q1 Sulfuric acid is manufactured by the contact process. In one of the stages, sulfur dioxide gas is mixed with oxygen gas and converted into sulfur trioxide gas. A solid vanadium(V) oxide (V_2O_5) catalyst is used. The enthalpy change for the uncatalysed reaction is -197 kJ mol^{-1}.

a) Write an equation for the catalysed reaction, including state symbols. [1 mark]

b) Which of the following enthalpy profile diagrams is correct for the catalysed reaction? [1 mark]

A

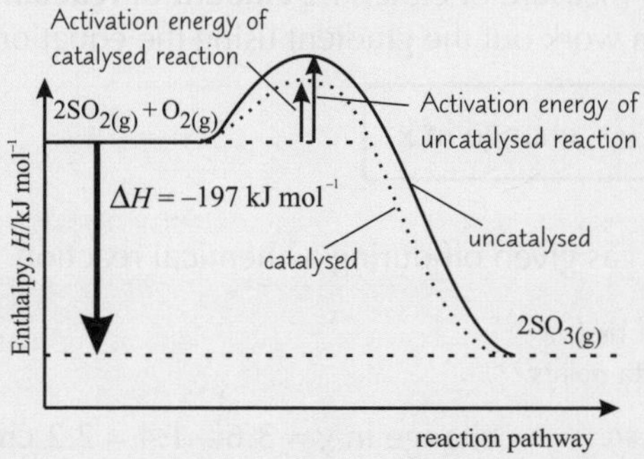

B

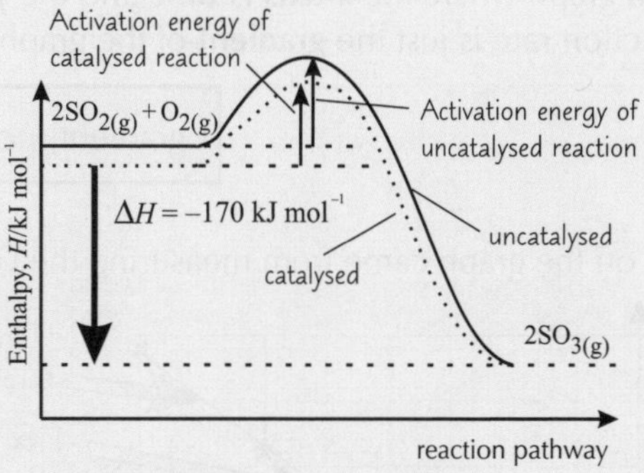

c) Is the vanadium(V) oxide catalyst heterogeneous or homogeneous? Explain your answer. [1 mark]

Catalysts and walking past bad buskers — increased speed but no change...

Whatever you do, don't confuse the Boltzmann diagram for catalysts with the one for a temperature change. Catalysts lower the activation energy without changing the shape of the curve. BUT, the shape of the curve does change with temperature. Get these mixed up and you'll be the laughing stock of the Examiners' tea room.

Calculating Reaction Rates

The rate of a reaction is just how quickly it happens. Seems simple enough, so let's crack on...

Reaction Rate is the Amount of Stuff Reacting Divided by Time

The **reaction rate** is the **rate** at which a **product is formed** or a **reactant is used up**. A simple equation for the rate of a chemical reaction is...

$$\text{rate of reaction} = \frac{\text{amount of reactant used or product formed}}{\text{time}}$$

There are Different ways to Investigate Reaction Rates

You can either measure how quickly the **reactants are used up** or how quickly the **products are formed** — it's usually **easier** to measure products forming. Here are a couple of ways to measure how quickly a product forms...

Change in mass

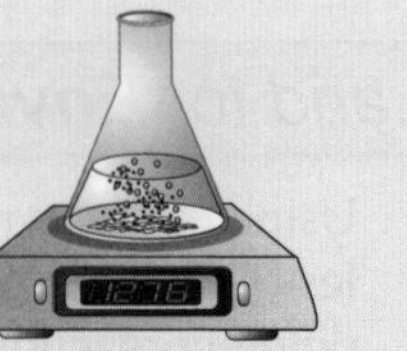

1) When the product is a **gas**, its formation can be measured using a **mass balance**.
2) The amount of product formed is the mass **disappearing** from the container.
3) When the reaction starts, you should start a **stop clock** or timer. Then take **mass measurements** at **regular time intervals**.
4) Make a **table** with a column for '**time**' and a column for '**mass**' and fill it in as the reaction goes on.
5) You'll know the reaction is **finished** when the reading on the mass balance **stops decreasing**.
6) This method is **very accurate** and easy to use but does **release gas** into the room, which could be **dangerous** if the gas is toxic or flammable.

Volume of gas given off

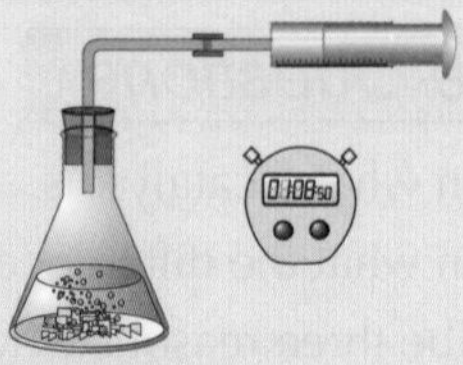

1) You can use a **gas syringe** to measure the **volume** of product formed.
2) The experiment is carried out the same way as above but you measure the **volume** of gas in the syringe rather than the mass from the balance.
3) This method is **accurate** but vigorous reactions can **blow the plunger** out of the syringe.

There are a few other ways to measure the amount of reactant used or product formed. For example, you can monitor **changes in pressure** (for gases), **changes in colour** (for solutions) or **changes in conductivity**. The best method **depends** on the **reaction** you're looking at.

You can Work out Reaction Rate from the Gradient of a Graph

If you have a graph where the **x-axis** is **time** and the **y-axis** is a measure of either the **amount of reactant** or **product**, then the reaction rate is just the **gradient** of the graph. You can work out the gradient using the equation...

$$\text{gradient} = \text{change in y} \div \text{change in x}$$

The data on the graph came from measuring the volume of gas given off during a chemical reaction.

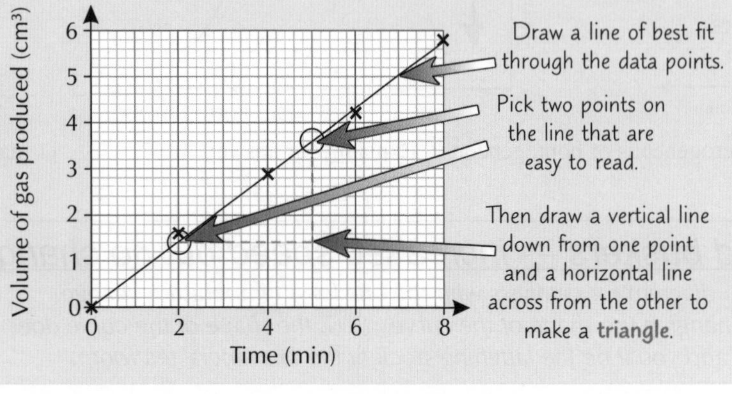
Volume of gas produced (cm³)
Time (min)
Draw a line of best fit through the data points.
Pick two points on the line that are easy to read.
Then draw a vertical line down from one point and a horizontal line across from the other to make a **triangle**.

change in y = 3.6 – 1.4 = 2.2 cm^3
change in x = 5.0 – 2.0 = 3.0 minutes
gradient = 2.2 ÷ 3.0 = 0.73 $cm^3\ min^{-1}$

So the rate of reaction = **0.73 $cm^3\ min^{-1}$**

Calculating Reaction Rates

You may need to Work out the Gradient from a Curved Graph

When the points on a graph lie in a **curve**, you can't draw a straight line of best fit through them. But you can still work out the gradient, and so the rate, at a **particular point** in the reaction by working out the **gradient of a tangent**.

Example: The graph below shows the mass of a reaction vessel measured at regular intervals during a chemical reaction. What is the rate of reaction at 3 mins?

1. Find the point on the curve that you need to look at. The question asks about the rate of reaction at 3 mins, so find 3 on the *x*-axis and go up to the curve from there.

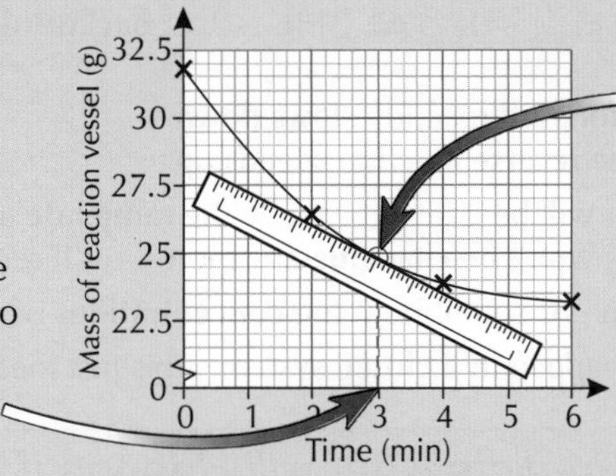

2. Place a ruler at that point so that it's just touching the curve. Position the ruler so that you can see the whole curve.
3. Adjust the ruler until the space between the ruler and the curve is equal on both sides of the point.

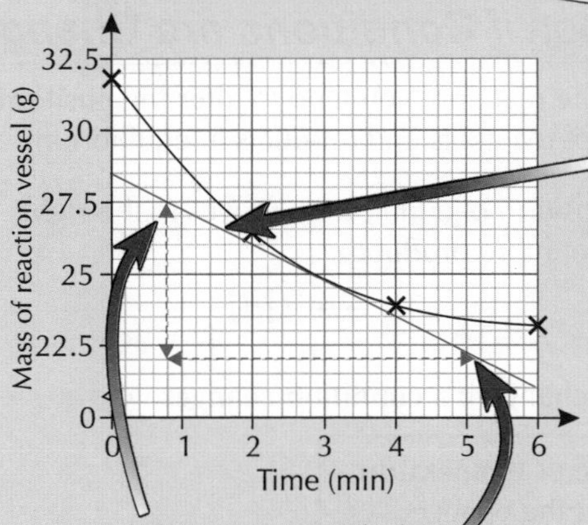

4. Draw a line along the ruler to make the tangent. Extend the line right across the graph — it'll help to make your gradient calculation easier as you'll have more points to choose from.
5. Calculate the gradient of the tangent to find the rate:

gradient = change in y ÷ change in x
= (27.50 – 22.00) ÷ (5.20 – 0.80)
= 5.50 cm^3 ÷ 4.40 mins = 1.25 $cm^3\ min^{-1}$

So, the rate of reaction at 3 mins was **1.25 $cm^3\ min^{-1}$**.

Don't forget the units — you've divided cm^3 by mins, so it's $cm^3\ min^{-1}$.

Practice Questions

Q1 Write the equation for reaction rate.

Q2 Describe how measuring a change in mass can help to work out the rate of a reaction.

Exam Question

Q1 Calcium and water react as in the equation below.

$$Ca_{(s)} + 2H_2O_{(l)} \rightarrow Ca(OH)_{2(aq)} + H_{2(g)}$$

a) From the graph on the right, work out the rate of reaction at 3 minutes. [3 marks]

b) Suggest how you would measure the volume of gas produced. [1 mark]

c) Explain why the method used here would be unsuitable for working out the rate of the reaction below.

$$6CO_{2(g)} + 6H_2O_{(l)} \rightarrow C_6H_{12}O_{6(aq)} + 6O_{2(g)}$$ [1 mark]

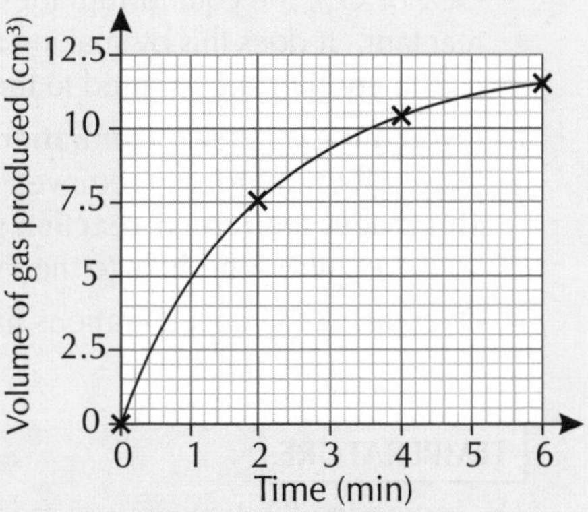

Calculate your reaction to this page. Boredom? How dare you...

Really, this stuff isn't too bad. Make sure you can write out the reaction rate equation in your sleep and that you understand what it means. It'll make handling the rest of the stuff on these pages easier. It might take a bit of practice to get the hang of these graphs but, as I'm sure you're tired of hearing, practice makes perfect. So get practising.

Dynamic Equilibrium

There's a lot of to-ing and fro-ing on this page. Mind your head doesn't start spinning.

Reversible Reactions Can Reach Dynamic Equilibrium

1) Lots of chemical reactions are **reversible** — they go **both ways**. To show a reaction's reversible, you stick in a $\rightleftharpoons$. Here's an example:

$$H_{2(g)} + I_{2(g)} \rightleftharpoons 2HI_{(g)}$$

This reaction can go in **either direction** —

forwards $H_{2(g)} + I_{2(g)} \rightleftharpoons 2HI_{(g)}$ ...or **backwards** $2HI_{(g)} \rightleftharpoons H_{2(g)} + I_{2(g)}$

2) As the **reactants** get used up, the **forward** reaction **slows down** — and as more **product** is formed, the **reverse** reaction **speeds up**.
3) After a while, the forward reaction will be going at exactly the **same rate** as the backward reaction, so the amounts of reactants and products **won't be changing** any more — it'll seem like **nothing's happening**.
4) This is called **dynamic equilibrium**. At equilibrium the **concentrations** of **reactants** and **products** stay **constant**.
5) A **dynamic equilibrium** can only happen in a **closed system**. This just means nothing can get in or out.

Le Chatelier's Principle Predicts what will Happen if Conditions are Changed

If you **change** the **concentration**, **pressure** or **temperature** of a reversible reaction, you tend to **alter** the **position of equilibrium**. This just means you'll end up with **different amounts** of reactants and products at equilibrium.

If the position of equilibrium moves to the **left**, you'll get more **reactants**.

$$H_{2(g)} + I_{2(g)} \rightleftharpoons 2HI_{(g)}$$

If the position of equilibrium moves to the **right**, you'll get more **products**.

$$H_{2(g)} + I_{2(g)} \rightleftharpoons 2HI_{(g)}$$

Le Chatelier's principle tells you how the **position of equilibrium** will change if a **condition changes**:

> If there's a change in **concentration**, **pressure** or **temperature**, the equilibrium will move to help **counteract** the change.

So, basically, if you **raise the temperature**, the position of equilibrium will shift to try to **cool things down**. And, if you **raise the pressure or concentration**, the position of equilibrium will shift to try to **reduce it again**.

Here Are Some Handy Rules for Using Le Chatelier's Principle

CONCENTRATION $2SO_{2(g)} + O_{2(g)} \rightleftharpoons 2SO_{3(g)}$

1) If you **increase** the **concentration** of a **reactant** (SO_2 or O_2), the equilibrium tries to **get rid** of the extra reactant. It does this by making **more product** (SO_3). So the equilibrium's shifted to the **right**.
2) If you **increase** the **concentration** of the **product** (SO_3), the equilibrium tries to remove the extra product. This makes the **reverse reaction** go faster. So the equilibrium shifts to the **left**.
3) **Decreasing** the concentrations has the **opposite effect**.

PRESSURE (this only affects **gases**)

1) **Increasing** the pressure shifts the equilibrium to the side with **fewer** gas molecules. This **reduces** the pressure.
2) **Decreasing** the pressure shifts the equilibrium to the side with **more** gas molecules. This **raises** the pressure again.

There are 3 moles on the left, but only 2 on the right. So, increasing the pressure shifts the equilibrium to the right.

$$2SO_{2(g)} + O_{2(g)} \rightleftharpoons 2SO_{3(g)}$$

TEMPERATURE

1) **Increasing** the temperature means **adding heat**. The equilibrium shifts in the **endothermic (positive ΔH) direction** to absorb this heat.
2) **Decreasing** the temperature **removes heat**. The equilibrium shifts in the **exothermic (negative ΔH) direction** to try to replace the heat.
3) If the forward reaction's **endothermic**, the reverse reaction will be **exothermic**, and vice versa.

This reaction's exothermic in the forward direction ($\Delta H = -197$ kJ mol^{-1}). If you increase the temperature, the equilibrium shifts to the left to absorb the extra heat.

Exothermic $\Longrightarrow$

$$2SO_{2(g)} + O_{2(g)} \rightleftharpoons 2SO_{3(g)}$$

$\Longleftarrow$ Endothermic

Dynamic Equilibrium

Catalysts **Don't Affect** The Position of Equilibrium

Catalysts have **NO EFFECT** on the **position of equilibrium.** They **speed up** the **forward AND reverse** reactions by the **same amount.** They **can't** increase **yield** — but they **do** mean equilibrium is reached **faster.**

Ethanol can be formed from **Ethene** and **Steam**

1) The industrial production of **ethanol** is a good example of why Le Chatelier's principle is important in **real life.**
2) Ethanol is produced via a **reversible exothermic reaction** between **ethene** and **steam**:

$$C_2H_{4(g)} + H_2O_{(g)} \rightleftharpoons C_2H_5OH_{(g)} \qquad \Delta H = -46\ \text{kJ mol}^{-1}$$

3) The reaction is carried out at a pressure of **60-70 atmospheres** and a temperature of **300 °C**, with a **phosphoric(V) acid** catalyst.

The **Conditions** Chosen are a **Compromise**

1) Because it's an **exothermic reaction**, **lower** temperatures favour the forward reaction. This means **more** ethene and steam are converted to ethanol at lower temperatures — you get a better **yield.**
2) But **lower temperatures** mean a **slower rate of reaction.** You'd be **daft** to try to get a **really high yield** of ethanol if it's going to take you 10 years. So the 300 °C is a **compromise** between **maximum yield** and **a faster reaction.**
3) **Higher pressures** favour the **forward reaction,** so a pressure of **60-70 atmospheres** is used — **high pressure** moves the reaction to the side with **fewer molecules of gas. Increasing the pressure** also increases the **rate** of reaction.
4) Cranking up the pressure as high as you can sounds like a great idea so far. But **high pressures** are **expensive** to produce. You need **stronger pipes** and **containers** to withstand high pressure. In this process, increasing the pressure can also cause **side reactions** to occur.
5) So the **60-70 atmospheres** is a **compromise** between **maximum yield** and **expense.** In the end, it all comes down to **minimising costs.**

Mr and Mrs Le Chatelier celebrate another successful year in the principle business

Practice Questions

Q1 Using an example, explain the terms 'reversible reaction' and 'dynamic equilibrium'.

Q2 If the equilibrium moves to the right, do you get more products or reactants?

Q3 A reaction at equilibrium is endothermic in the forward direction.
What happens to the position of equilibrium as the temperature is increased?

Exam Questions

Q1 Nitrogen and oxygen gases were reacted together in a closed flask and allowed to reach equilibrium, with nitrogen monoxide being formed. The forward reaction is endothermic.

$$N_{2(g)} + O_{2(g)} \rightleftharpoons 2NO_{(g)}$$

a) Explain how the following changes would affect the position of equilibrium of the above reaction:

i) Pressure is increased. [1 mark]

ii) Temperature is reduced. [1 mark]

iii) Nitrogen monoxide is removed. [1 mark]

b) What would be the effect of a catalyst on the composition of the equilibrium mixture? [1 mark]

Q2 Explain why moderate reaction temperatures are a compromise for exothermic reactions. [2 marks]

If it looks like I'm not doing anything, I'm just being dynamic... honest...

Equilibria never do what you want them to do. They always oppose you. Be sure you know what happens to an equilibrium if you change the conditions. About pressure — if there's the same number of gas moles on each side of the equation, you can raise the pressure as high as you like and it won't make a difference to the position of equilibrium.

The Equilibrium Constant

'Oh no, not another page on equilibria', I hear you cry... fair enough really.

K_c is the Equilibrium Constant

When you have a **homogeneous reaction** (where all the reactants and products are in the **same physical state**) that's reached **dynamic equilibrium**, you can work out the **equilibrium constant, K_c**, using the concentrations of the products and reactants at equilibrium. K_c gives you an idea of how far to the **left or right** the equilibrium is. Before you can calculate K_c, you have to write an **expression** for it. Here's how:

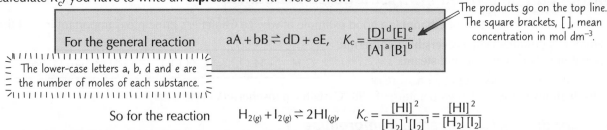

For the general reaction $aA + bB \rightleftharpoons dD + eE$, $K_c = \frac{[D]^d[E]^e}{[A]^a[B]^b}$

The products go on the top line. The square brackets, [ ], mean concentration in mol dm^{-3}.

The lower-case letters a, b, d and e are the number of moles of each substance.

So for the reaction $H_{2(g)} + I_{2(g)} \rightleftharpoons 2HI_{(g)}$, $K_c = \frac{[HI]^2}{[H_2]^1[I_2]^1} = \frac{[HI]^2}{[H_2][I_2]}$

Calculate K_c by Putting Numbers into the Expression

If you know the **equilibrium concentrations**, just put them in your expression. Then you can work out the **value** of K_c.

Example: What is the equilibrium constant for the hydrogen iodide example above, at 640 K? The equilibrium concentrations are:

[HI] = 0.80 mol dm^{-3}, $[H_2]$ = 0.10 mol dm^{-3}, and $[I_2]$ = 0.10 mol dm^{-3}.

Just stick the concentrations into the **expression** for K_c: $K_c = \frac{[HI]^2}{[H_2][I_2]} = \frac{0.80^2}{0.10 \times 0.10} = 64$

The **units** for K_c are a bit trickier — they **vary**, so you have to work them out after each calculation.
Here's how it's done...
Put the units in the expression instead of the number: $K_c = \frac{(\text{mol dm}^{-3})^2}{(\text{mol dm}^{-3})(\text{mol dm}^{-3})} = 0$

There's more on calculating units for K_c on page 126.

So there are **no units** for K_c because the concentration units cancel. So K_c for this reaction, at 640 K, is just **64**.

A **change in temperature** can change the **position of equilibrium** (see page 80) so K_c **varies** with temperature.

*You can **Estimate** the **Position of Equilibrium** Using the Value of K_c*

1) If K_c is **greater than 1**, there are **more products** than reactants and the equilibrium lies to the **right**. The higher above 1 K_c is, the **further to the right** equilibrium lies.
2) If K_c is **less than 1**, there are **more reactants** than products and the equilibrium lies to the **left**. The further below 1 K_c is, the **further to the left** equilibrium lies.

You can Investigate the Equilibrium Position with Changing Temperature...

In a closed system, the **brown** gas NO_2 exists in equilibrium with the **colourless** gas N_2O_4. This reversible reaction can be used to investigate the effect of **changing temperature** on **equilibrium position**. Here's how you do it...

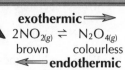

exothermic →
$2NO_{2(g)} \rightleftharpoons N_2O_{4(g)}$
brown — colourless
← **endothermic**

1) Place two **sealed** tubes containing the equilibrium mixture in water baths — one in a **warm** water bath and one in a **cool** water bath, and **observe** the **colours** of the mixtures.
2) The tube in the **warm** water bath will change to a **darker brown** colour as the **endothermic** reaction **speeds up** to absorb the extra heat, pushing **equilibrium to the left**.
3) The tube in the **cool** water bath will **lose colour** as the **exothermic** reaction **speeds up** to try and replace the lost heat, pushing **equilibrium to the right**.

The Equilibrium Constant

... and with Changing Concentration

Mixing **iron(III) nitrate** (yellow) and **potassium thiocyanate** (colourless) results in a **reversible reaction** where the product is **iron(III) thiocyanate** (blood red). You end up with the following equilibrium...

$$\underset{\text{yellow}}{Fe^{3+}_{(aq)}} + \underset{\text{colourless}}{3SCN^{-}_{(aq)}} \rightleftharpoons \underset{\text{blood red}}{Fe(SCN)_{3(aq)}}$$

The equilibrium mixture is a **reddish** colour. You can investigate what happens to the equilibrium position when the **concentrations** of reactants or products are changed by monitoring the **colour** of the solution.

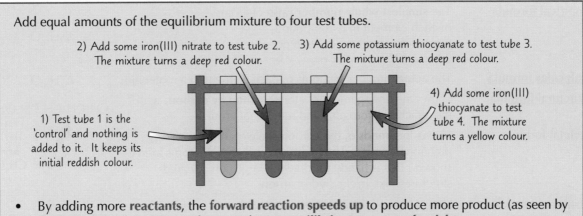

Add equal amounts of the equilibrium mixture to four test tubes.

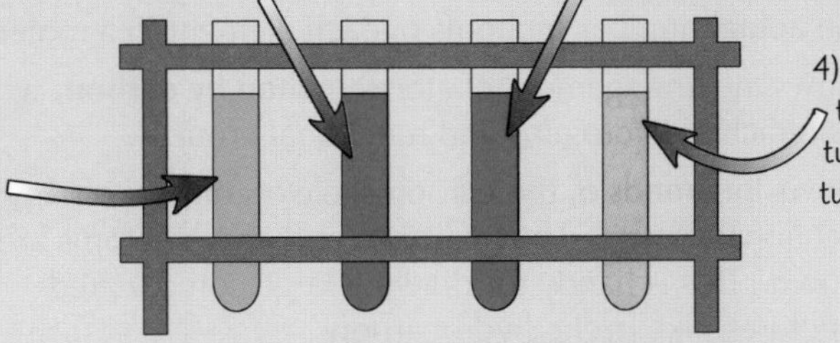
2) Add some iron(III) nitrate to test tube 2. The mixture turns a deep red colour.
3) Add some potassium thiocyanate to test tube 3. The mixture turns a deep red colour.
1) Test tube 1 is the 'control' and nothing is added to it. It keeps its initial reddish colour.
4) Add some iron(III) thiocyanate to test tube 4. The mixture turns a yellow colour.

- By adding more **reactants**, the **forward reaction speeds up** to produce more product (as seen by the deep red colour in test tubes 2 and 3) so **equilibrium moves to the right**.
- By adding more **product**, the **reverse reaction speeds up** to produce more reactants (as seen by the yellowish colour in test tube 4) so **equilibrium moves to the left**.

Practice Questions

Q1 Write an expression for the equilibrium constant of the reaction, $aA + bB \rightleftharpoons dD + eE$.

Q2 If K_c for a reaction has a value of 4, does the equilibrium lie to the right or the left?

Q3 What colour change would you expect in a NO_2/N_2O_4 gas mixture if you were to increase the temperature?

Q4 In which direction would equilibrium move if more product is added to a mixture?

Exam Questions

Q1 The concentrations of the species present in the following equilibrium mixture are 0.890 mol dm^{-3} N_2, 1.412 mol dm^{-3} H_2 and 1.190 mol dm^{-3} NH_3.

$$N_{2(g)} + 3H_{2(g)} \rightleftharpoons 2NH_{3(g)}$$

a) Calculate the equilibrium constant, K_c. [2 marks]

b) The forward reaction in the above equilibrium is exothermic. If the equilibrium mixture was placed in a cool water bath, describe what would happen to the concentration of NH_3. Explain your answer. [2 marks]

Q2 When a potassium chromate(VI) solution is mixed with sulfuric acid, the following equilibrium is established.

$$\underset{\text{yellow}}{2CrO_4^{2-}{}_{(aq)}} + 2H^+_{(aq)} \rightleftharpoons \underset{\text{orange}}{Cr_2O_7^{2-}{}_{(aq)}} + H_2O_{(l)}$$

Describe an experiment to establish the effect on the equilibrium position of changing the concentration of chromate and dichromate ions. Describe what the results of the experiment would be. [3 marks]

I'm constantly going on about equilibrium — that's what it feels like anyway...

Working out K_c is pretty straight forward once you've got the hang of it, although it may not seem like that to begin with. If you've not quite got it yet go back through these two pages until it all makes perfect sense. Once you've done that, there are just 6 more pages on equilibrium to go... ONLY JOKING! It's the end of the section. Hurrah hurrah hurrah :-)

Organic Chemistry — The Basics

This section's all about organic chemistry... carbon compounds, in other words. Read on...

*There are **Loads of Ways** of **Representing** Organic Compounds*

TYPE OF FORMULA	WHAT IT SHOWS YOU	FORMULA FOR BUTAN-1-OL
General formula	An algebraic formula that can describe **any member** of a family of compounds.	$C_nH_{2n+1}OH$ (for all alcohols)
Empirical formula	The **simplest whole number ratio** of atoms of each element in a compound (cancel the numbers down if possible). (So ethane, C_2H_6, has the empirical formula CH_3.)	$C_4H_{10}O$
Molecular formula	The **actual** number of atoms of each element in a molecule.	$C_4H_{10}O$
Structural formula	Shows the arrangement of atoms **carbon by carbon**, with the attached hydrogens and functional groups.	$CH_3CH_2CH_2CH_2OH$
Skeletal formula	Shows the **bonds** of the carbon skeleton **only**, with any functional groups. The hydrogen and carbon atoms aren't shown. This is handy for drawing large complicated structures, like cyclic hydrocarbons.	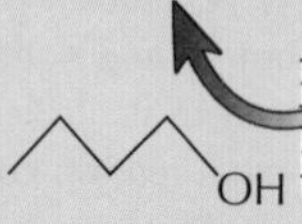
Displayed formula	Shows how all the atoms are **arranged**, and all the bonds between them.	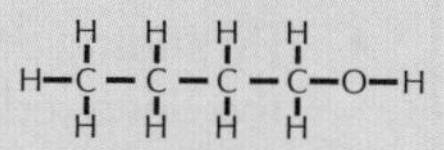

This could also be written as $CH_3(CH_2)_3OH$

*Members of **Homologous Series** Have the Same **General Formulas***

1) Organic chemistry is more about **groups** of similar chemicals than individual compounds.
2) These groups are called **homologous series**. A homologous series is a bunch of organic compounds that have the same **functional group** and **general formula**. Consecutive members of a homologous series differ by **$-CH_2-$**.

A functional group is a group of atoms in a molecule responsible for the characteristic reactions of that compound.

Example:
1) The simplest homologous series is the **alkanes**. They're **straight chain** molecules that contain only **carbon** and **hydrogen** atoms. There's a lot more about the alkanes on pages 88-91.
2) The **general formula** for alkanes is C_nH_{2n+2}. So the first alkane in the series is $C_1H_{(2 \times 1)+2} = CH_4$ (you don't need to write the 1 in C_1), the second is $C_2H_{(2 \times 2)+2} = C_2H_6$, the seventeenth is $C_{17}H_{(2 \times 17)+2} = C_{17}H_{36}$, and so on...

3) Here are the homologous series you need to know about:

HOMOLOGOUS SERIES	PREFIX OR SUFFIX	EXAMPLE
alkanes	–ane	propane — $CH_3CH_2CH_3$
branched alkanes	alkyl– (–yl)	methylpropane — $CH_3CH(CH_3)CH_3$
alkenes	–ene	propene — $CH_3CH{=}CH_2$
haloalkanes	chloro–/bromo–/iodo–	chloroethane — CH_3CH_2Cl
alcohols	–ol	ethanol — CH_3CH_2OH
aldehydes	–al	ethanal — CH_3CHO
ketones	–one	propanone — CH_3COCH_3
cycloalkanes	cyclo– ... –ane	cyclohexane C_6H_{12}
carboxylic acids	–oic acid	ethanoic acid — CH_3COOH
esters	alkyl– ... –anoate	methyl propanoate — $CH_3CH_2COOCH_3$

Don't worry if you don't recognise all these series yet — you'll meet them all by the end of the module.

Organic Chemistry — The Basics

There Are Different Types of Carbon Skeleton

1) All organic compounds contain a **carbon skeleton**. This can be either **aromatic** or **aliphatic**.
2) **Aromatic** compounds contain a **benzene** ring. You can **draw** benzene rings in two ways:

Like this:  or like this: 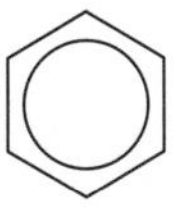

These are skeletal formulas — each point represents a carbon atom.

3) **Aliphatic** compounds contain carbon and hydrogen joined together in **straight** chains, **branched** chains or **non-aromatic rings**.
4) If an aliphatic compound contains a (non-aromatic) **ring**, then it can be called **alicyclic**.
5) Organic compounds may be saturated or unsaturated. **Saturated** compounds only contain carbon-carbon **single bonds** — like alkanes. **Unsaturated** compounds can have carbon-carbon **double** bonds, **triple** bonds or **aromatic** groups.
6) And finally... an **alkyl group** is a **fragment** of a molecule with general formula C_nH_{2n+1}.

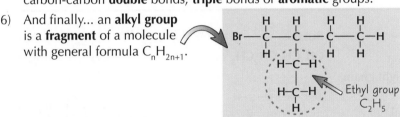

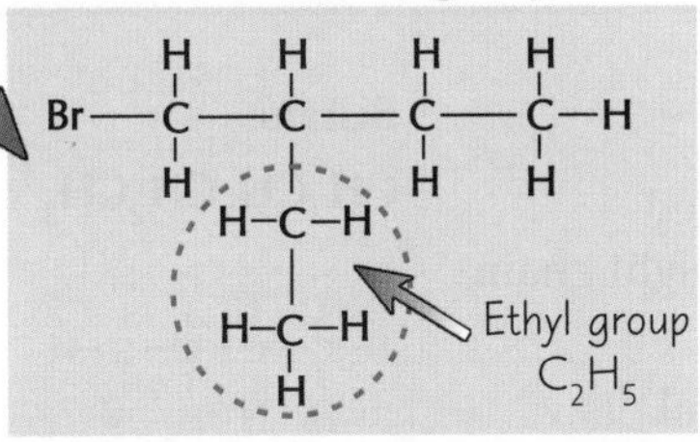

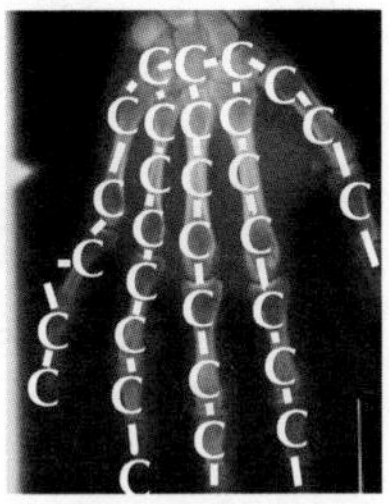

The X-ray revealed a break in Timothy's carbon skeleton.

Nomenclature is a Fancy Word for the Naming of Organic Compounds

Organic compounds used to be given whatever names people fancied, but these names led to **confusion** between different countries.

The **IUPAC** system for naming organic compounds was invented as an **international language** for chemistry. It can be used to give any organic compound a **systematic name** using these **rules** of nomenclature...

1) Count the carbon atoms in the **longest continuous chain** — this gives you the stem.

No. of Carbons	1	2	3	4	5	6	7	8	9	10
Stem	meth-	eth-	prop-	but-	pent-	hex-	hept-	oct-	non-	dec-

2) The **main functional group** of the molecule usually tells you what **homologous series** the molecule is in, and so gives you the **prefix** or **suffix** — see the table on page 84.
3) Number the **longest** carbon chain so that the main functional group has the lowest possible number. If there's more than one longest chain, pick the one with the **most side-chains**.
4) Any side-chains or less important functional groups are added as prefixes at the start of the name. Put them in **alphabetical** order, after the **number** of the carbon atom each is attached to.
5) If there's more than one **identical** side-chain or functional group, use **di-** (2), **tri-** (3) or **tetra-** (4) before that part of the name — but ignore this when working out the alphabetical order.

Example: $CH_3CH(CH_3)CH(CH_2CH_3)C(CH_3)_2OH$

1) The longest chain is **5** carbons. So the stem is **pent-**.
2) The main functional group is **-OH** So the name will be based on '**pentanol**'.
3) **Numbering** the longest carbon chain so that -OH has the **lowest** possible number (and you have most side chains) puts -OH on carbon 2, so it's some sort of **pentan-2-ol**.

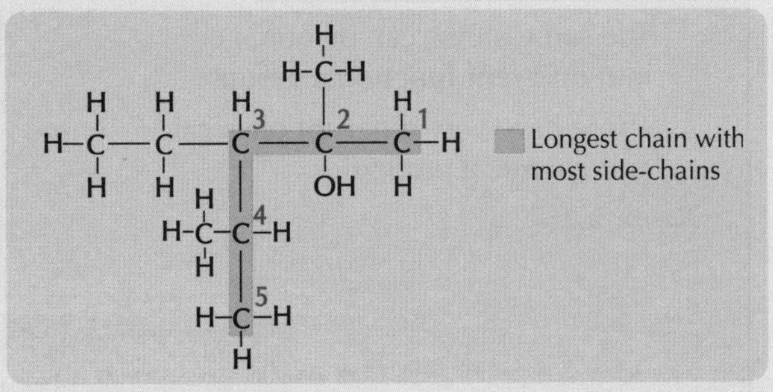

4) The other side chains are an **ethyl group** on carbon-3, and **methyl groups** on carbon-2 and carbon-4, so the **systematic name** for this molecule is: **3-ethyl-2,4-dimethylpentan-2-ol**.

Organic Chemistry — The Basics

Isomers Have the Same **Molecular Formula**

1) Two molecules are isomers of one another if they have the same **molecular formula** but the atoms are **arranged differently**.
2) There are two types of isomers you need to know about — **structural isomers** and **stereoisomers**. Structural isomers are coming right up, and you'll meet stereoisomers on pages 93-95.

Structural Isomers Have Different **Structural Arrangements** of Atoms

In structural isomers, the atoms are **connected** in different ways. So although the **molecular formula** is the same, the **structural formula** is different. There are **three** different types of structural isomer:

1. Chain Isomers

The **carbon skeleton** can be arranged differently — for example, as a **straight chain**, or **branched** in different ways.

These isomers have **similar chemical properties** — but their **physical properties**, like boiling point, will be **different** because of the change in shape of the molecule.

C_4H_{10}

Butane

$CH_3CH_2CH_2CH_3$

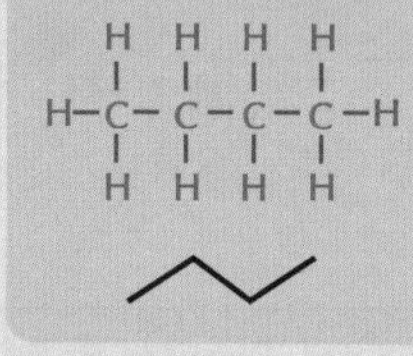

Methylpropane

$CH_3CH(CH_3)CH_3$

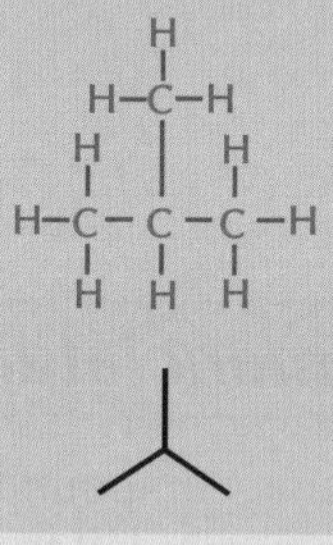

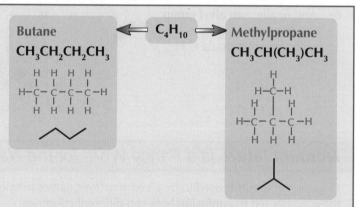

2. Positional Isomers

The **skeleton** and the **functional group** could be the same, only with the functional group attached to a **different carbon atom**.

These also have **different physical properties**, and the **chemical properties** might be **different** too.

$C_4H_{10}O$

Butan-1-ol

$CH_3CH_2CH_2CH_2OH$

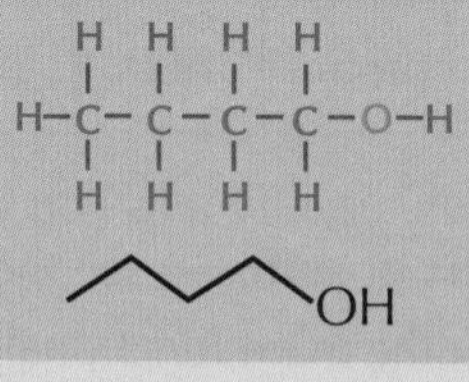

Butan-2-ol

$CH_3CH_2CHOHCH_3$

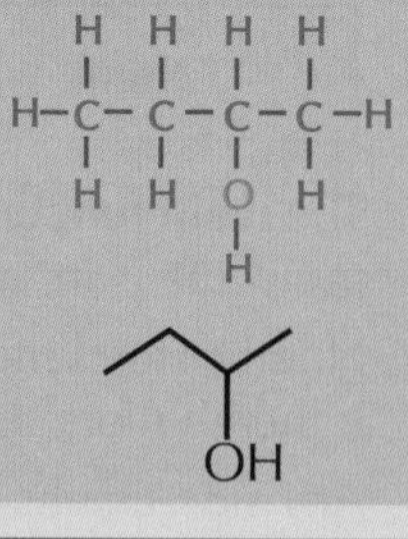

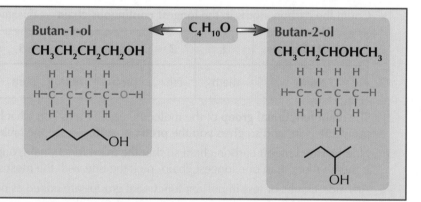

3. Functional Group Isomers

The same atoms can be arranged into **different functional groups**.

These have very **different physical** and **chemical** properties.

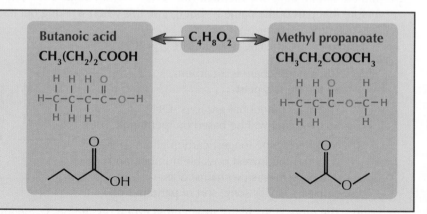

$C_4H_8O_2$

Butanoic acid

$CH_3(CH_2)_2COOH$

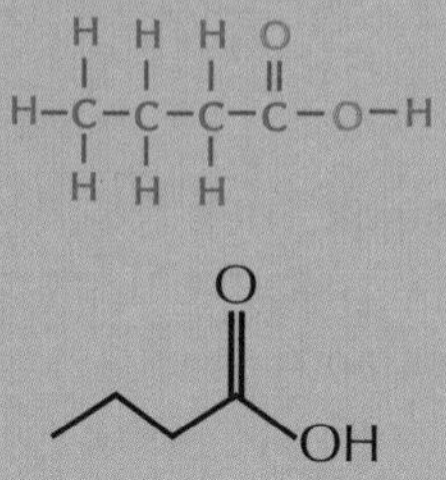

Methyl propanoate

$CH_3CH_2COOCH_3$

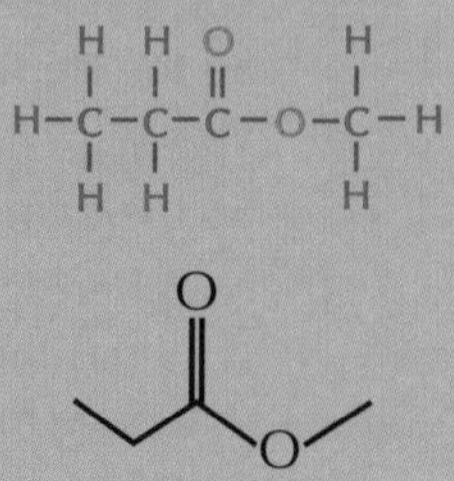

Organic Chemistry — The Basics

*Don't be Fooled — What Looks Like an Isomer Might **Not** Be*

Atoms can rotate as much as they like around single **C–C bonds**.
Remember this when you work out structural isomers — sometimes what looks like an isomer, isn't.

For example, there are **no chain** isomers and only **two positional** isomers of C_3H_7Br.

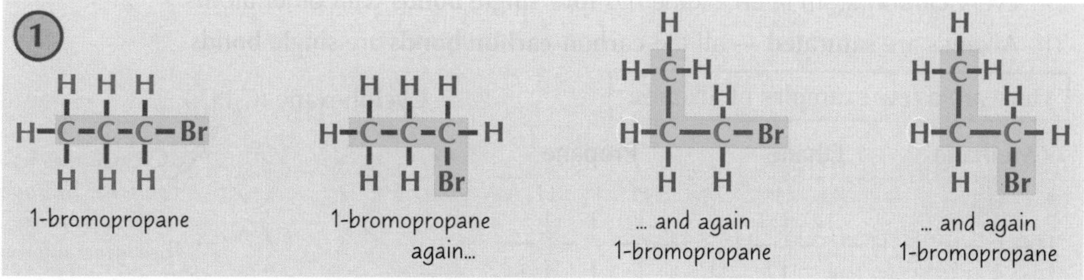

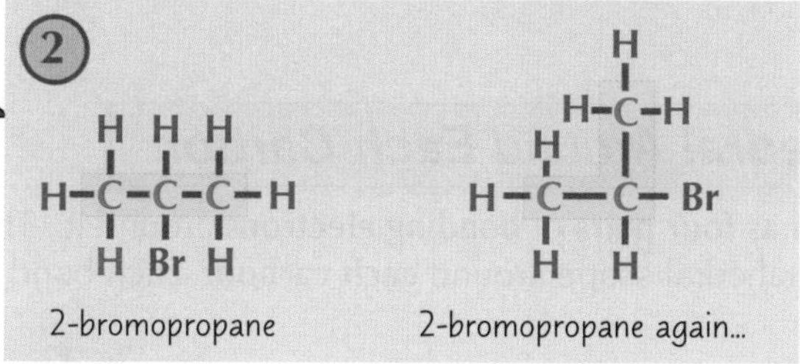

Practice Questions

Q1 Explain the difference between molecular formulas and structural formulas.

Q2 What is meant by the term 'homologous series'?

Q3 In what order should prefixes be listed in the name of an organic compound?

Q4 Draw the displayed formula of 3,4-diethylhexan-2-ol.

Q5 What are isomers?

Q6 Name the three types of structural isomerism.

Exam Questions

Q1 1-bromo-2-methylpentane is prepared from 2-methylpentan-1-ol in this reaction:

$$C_6H_{13}OH + NaBr + H_2SO_4 \rightarrow C_6H_{13}Br + NaHSO_4 + H_2O$$

a) Draw the displayed formulas for 1-bromo-2-methylpentane and 2-methylpentan-1-ol. [2 marks]

b) What is the functional group in 2-methylpentan-1-ol and why is it necessary to state its position on the carbon chain? [2 marks]

Q2 Give the systematic names of the following compounds.

a) 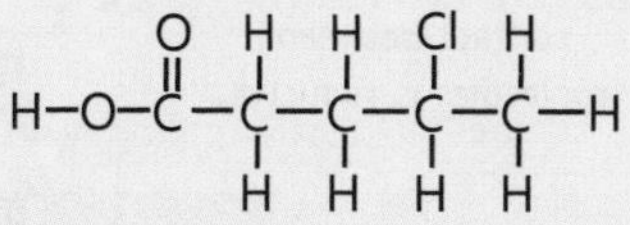

b) 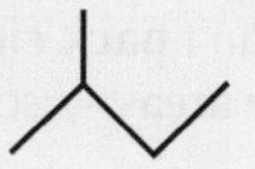

c) 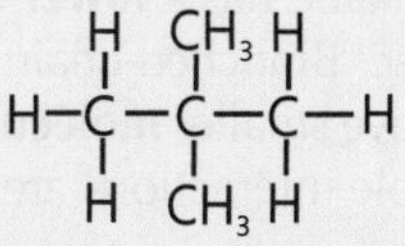

[3 marks]

Q3 a) How many chain isomers are there of the alkane C_6H_{14}?

A 4 **B** 5 **C** 6 **D** 7 [1 mark]

b) Explain what is meant by the term 'chain isomerism'. [2 marks]

Human structural isomers...

Alkanes

Alkanes are your basic hydrocarbons — like it says on the tin, they've got hydrogen and they've got carbon.

Alkanes are ***Saturated Hydrocarbons***

1) Alkanes have the **general formula C_nH_{2n+2}**. They've only got **carbon** and **hydrogen** atoms, so they're **hydrocarbons**.
2) Every carbon atom in an alkane has **four single bonds** with other atoms.
3) Alkanes are **saturated** — all the **carbon-carbon bonds** are **single bonds**.

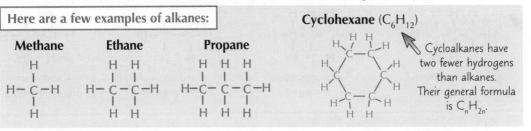

Here are a few examples of alkanes:

Methane

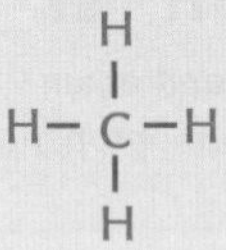

Ethane

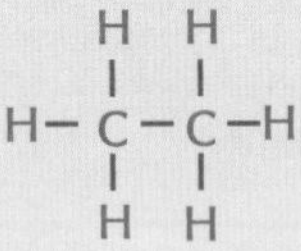

Propane

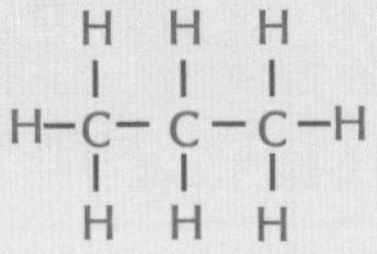

Cyclohexane (C_6H_{12})

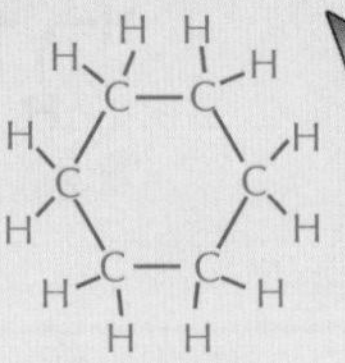

Cycloalkanes have two fewer hydrogens than alkanes. Their general formula is C_nH_{2n}.

Cyclohexane has the skeletal formula:

Alkane Molecules are ***Tetrahedral*** *Around* ***Each Carbon***

In an alkane molecule, each carbon atom has **four pairs** of **bonding electrons** around it. They all repel each other **equally**. So the molecule forms a tetrahedral shape around **each carbon**. Each bond angle is **109.5°**

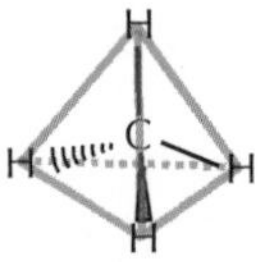

If you draw lines joining up the Hs in CH_4, the shape you get is a **tetrahedron**.

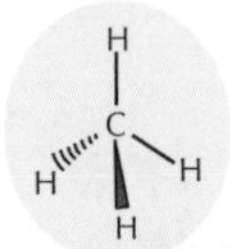

Methane
1 tetrahedral carbon

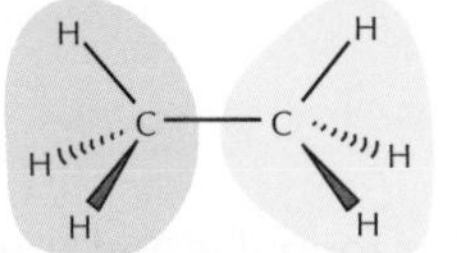

Ethane
2 tetrahedral carbons

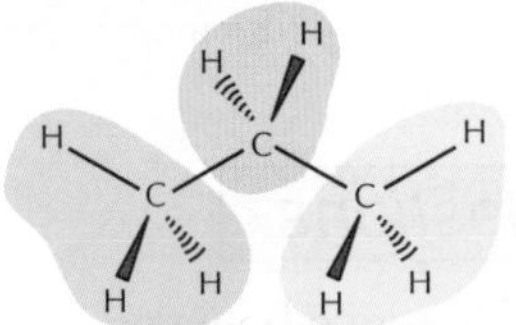

Propane
3 tetrahedral carbons

For more about the shapes of molecules, see pages 46-47.

The ***Boiling Point*** *of an Alkane Depends on its* ***Size*** *and* ***Shape***

The smallest alkanes, like methane, are **gases** at room temperature and pressure — they've got very low boiling points. Larger alkanes are **liquids** — they have higher boiling points.

1) Alkanes have **covalent bonds** inside the molecules. **Between** the molecules, there are **induced dipole-dipole** interactions (also called **London forces**) which hold them all together.
2) The **longer** the carbon chain, the **stronger** the induced dipole-dipole interactions. This is because there's **more surface contact** and more electrons to interact.
3) As the molecules get longer, it takes **more energy** to overcome the induced dipole-dipole interactions, and the boiling point **rises**.
4) A **branched-chain** alkane has a **lower** boiling point than its straight-chain isomer. Branched-chain alkanes can't **pack closely** together and they have smaller **molecular surface areas** — so the induced dipole-dipole interactions are reduced.

Example: Isomers of C_4H_{10}

Butane, boiling point = 273 K

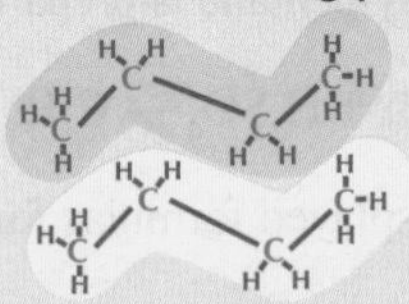

Molecules can pack closely so there is a lot of surface contact between them.

Methylpropane, boiling point = 261 K

Close packing isn't possible so surface contact between molecules is reduced

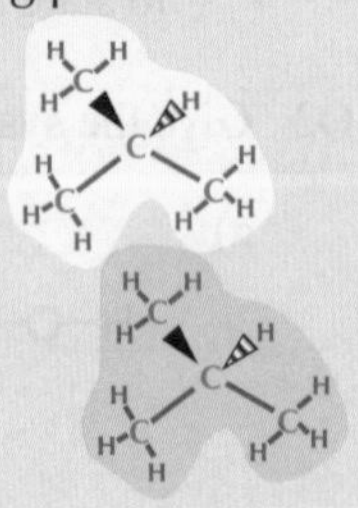

Alkanes Burn ***Completely*** *in Oxygen*

1) If you burn (**oxidise**) alkanes with **oxygen**, you get **carbon dioxide** and water — this is a **combustion reaction**.

Here's the equation for the combustion of propane — $C_3H_{8(g)} + 5O_{2(g)} \rightarrow 3CO_{2(g)} + 4H_2O_{(g)}$

2) Combustion reactions happen between **gases**, so liquid alkanes have to be **vaporised** first. Smaller alkanes turn into **gases** more easily (they're more **volatile**), so they'll **burn** more easily too.
3) Larger alkanes release heaps more **energy** per mole because they have more bonds to react.
4) Because they release so much energy when they burn, alkanes make excellent fuels.

Alkanes

You Can Use **Volumes** to Work Out **Combustion Equations**

Combustion reactions happen between **gases**. All gases at the same temperature and pressure have the same **molar volume**. This means you can use the **ratio** of the **volumes** of gases reacting together to calculate the **molar ratios**, and then work out what **hydrocarbon** is combusting.

Example: 30 cm³ of hydrocarbon X combusts completely with 240 cm³ oxygen. 150 cm³ carbon dioxide is produced. What is the molecular formula of hydrocarbon X?

- Using the volumes provided, the reaction equation can be written: $\mathbf{30X + 240O_2 \rightarrow 150CO_2 + ?H_2O}$.
- This can be simplified by dividing everything by 30: $\mathbf{X + 8O_2 \rightarrow 5CO_2 + nH_2O}$.
- 8 moles of oxygen reacts to form 5 moles of carbon dioxide and n moles of water. So any oxygen atoms that don't end up in CO_2 must be in H_2O. This means that $\mathbf{n = (8 \times 2) - (5 \times 2) = 6}$.
- This means the combustion equation is: $\mathbf{X + 8O_2 \rightarrow 5CO_2 + 6H_2O}$. You can use this to identify X.
- All the carbon atoms from X end up in carbon dioxide molecules, and all the hydrogen atoms from X end up in water, so the number of **carbon** atoms in X is **5** and the number of **hydrogen** atoms in X is **12**.
- The molecular formula of X is $\mathbf{C_5H_{12}}$.

Burning **Alkanes** In **Limited Oxygen** Produces **Carbon Monoxide**

1) If there isn't much oxygen around, the alkane will still burn, but it will produce **carbon monoxide** and water.

   For example, burning methane with not much O_2 — $\mathbf{2CH_{4(g)} + 3O_{2(g)} \rightarrow 2CO_{(g)} + 4H_2O_{(g)}}$

2) This is a problem because **carbon monoxide** is **poisonous**.
   1) The **oxygen** in your bloodstream is carried around by **haemoglobin**.
   2) **Carbon monoxide** is **better** at binding to haemoglobin than oxygen is, so it binds to the haemoglobin in your bloodstream **before** the oxygen can.
   3) This means that **less oxygen** can be carried around your body, leading to **oxygen deprivation**. At very high concentrations, carbon monoxide can be fatal.

Practice Questions

Q1 What's the general formula for alkanes?

Q2 What is the H-C-H bond angle in a molecule of methane?

Q3 What kind of intermolecular forces are there between alkane molecules?

Exam Questions

Q1 The alkane ethane is a saturated hydrocarbon.
It is mostly unreactive, but will react with oxygen in a combustion reaction.

a) What is a saturated hydrocarbon? [2 marks]

b) Write a balanced equation for the complete combustion of ethane. [2 marks]

Q2 Nonane is a hydrocarbon with the formula C_9H_{20}.

a) Which would you expect to have a higher boiling point, nonane or 2,2,3,3-tetramethylpentane? Explain your answer. [2 marks]

b) When nonane burns in a limited air supply, the products are carbon monoxide and water.

i) Write a balanced equation for the reaction. [1 mark]

ii) Explain why carbon monoxide is such a dangerous gas. [2 marks]

Tetrahedra — aren't they those monsters from Greek mythology...

Alkanes are the simplest organic compounds you're going to meet. They're very stable so they don't get up to much. Make sure you can explain why different alkanes can have different boiling points — even if their molecular formulas are the same. It's all about the strength of the intermolecular forces and how closely the molecules can pack together.

Reactions of Alkanes

Alkanes react with particles that have unpaired electrons (called free radicals). These reactions happen in several steps, and a mechanism breaks reactions down to show you the steps. Watch out, there are a few coming up...

There are **Two Types** of Bond Fission — **Homolytic** and **Heterolytic**

Breaking a covalent bond is called **bond fission**. A single covalent bond is a shared pair of electrons between two atoms. It can break in two ways:

Heterolytic Fission:

In heterolytic fission the bond breaks **unevenly** with one of the bonded atoms receiving **both** electrons from the bonded pair. **Two different** substances are formed — a positively charged **cation** (X^+), and a negatively charged **anion** (Y^-).

$$X{\div}Y \rightarrow X^+ + Y^-$$

('hetero' means 'different')

A curly arrows shows the movement of an electron pair.

Homolytic Fission:

In homolytic fission, the bond breaks evenly and each bonding atom receives **one electron** from the bonded pair. Two electrically uncharged **'radicals'** are formed. Radicals are particles that have an **unpaired electron**. They are shown in mechanisms by a big dot next to the molecular formula (the dot represents the unpaired electron.)

$$X{\div}Y \rightarrow X\bullet + Y\bullet$$

Because of the unpaired electron, radicals are very **reactive**.

Carl loved fission at the weekends.

Halogens React with **Alkanes**, Forming **Haloalkanes**

1) Halogens react with alkanes in **photochemical** reactions. Photochemical reactions are started by **light** — this reaction requires **ultraviolet light** to get going.
2) A hydrogen atom is **substituted** (replaced) by chlorine or bromine. This is a **free-radical substitution reaction**.

Example: Chlorine and **methane** react with a bit of a bang to form **chloromethane**:

$$CH_4 + Cl_2 \xrightarrow{UV} CH_3Cl + HCl$$

The **reaction mechanism** has three stages:

Initiation reactions — free radicals are produced.

1) Sunlight provides enough energy to break the Cl-Cl bond — this is **photodissociation**.

$$Cl_2 \xrightarrow{UV} 2Cl\bullet$$

2) The bond splits **equally** and each atom gets to keep one electron — **homolytic fission**. The atom becomes a highly reactive **free radical**, $Cl\bullet$, because of its **unpaired electron**.

Propagation reactions — free radicals are used up and created in a chain reaction.

1) $Cl\bullet$ attacks a **methane** molecule: $Cl\bullet + CH_4 \rightarrow \bullet CH_3 + HCl$
2) The new **methyl free radical**, $\bullet CH_3$, can attack another Cl_2 molecule: $\bullet CH_3 + Cl_2 \rightarrow CH_3Cl + Cl\bullet$
3) The new $Cl\bullet$ can attack **another** CH_4 molecule, and so on, until all the Cl_2 or CH_4 molecules are wiped out.

Termination reactions — free radicals are mopped up.

1) If two free radicals join together, they make a **stable molecule**.
2) There are **heaps** of possible termination reactions. Here are a couple of them to give you the idea:

$$Cl\bullet + \bullet CH_3 \rightarrow CH_3Cl$$
$$\bullet CH_3 + \bullet CH_3 \rightarrow C_2H_6$$

Some products formed will be trace impurities in the final sample.

The reaction between bromine and methane works in exactly the same way.

$$CH_4 + Br_2 \xrightarrow{UV} CH_3Br + HBr$$

Reactions of Alkanes

The Problem is — You End Up With a **Mixture of Products**

1) The big problem with free-radical substitution if you're trying to make a **particular product** is that you **don't only get** the product you're after, but a **mixture of products**.
2) For example, if you're trying to make chloromethane and there's **too much chlorine** in the reaction mixture, some of the remaining **hydrogen atoms** on the **chloromethane molecule** will be swapped for chlorine atoms. The propagation reactions happen again, this time to make **dichloromethane**.

$$Cl\bullet + CH_3Cl \rightarrow \bullet CH_2Cl + HCl$$

$$\bullet CH_2Cl + Cl_2 \rightarrow \mathbf{CH_2Cl_2} + Cl\bullet$$

dichloromethane

3) It doesn't stop there. Another substitution reaction can take place to form **trichloromethane**.

$$Cl\bullet + CH_2Cl_2 \rightarrow \bullet CHCl_2 + HCl$$

$$\bullet CHCl_2 + Cl_2 \rightarrow \mathbf{CHCl_3} + Cl\bullet$$

trichloromethane

4) **Tetrachloromethane** (CCl_4) is formed in the last possible substitution. There are no more hydrogens attached to the carbon atom, so the substitution process has to stop.
5) So the end product is a mixture of CH_3Cl, CH_2Cl_2, $CHCl_3$ and CCl_4. This is a nuisance, because you have to **separate** the **chloromethane** from the other three unwanted by-products.
6) The best way of reducing the chance of these by-products forming is to have an **excess of methane**. This means there's a greater chance of a chlorine radical colliding only with a **methane molecule** and not a **chloromethane molecule**.
7) Another problem with free radical substitution is that it can take place at any point along the **carbon chain**. So a mixture of **isomers** can be formed. For example, reacting **propane** with chlorine will produce a mixture of **1-chloropropane** and **2-chloropropane**.

Practice Questions

Q1 What's a free radical?

Q2 What's homolytic fission?

Q3 Write down the chemical equation for the free radical substitution reaction between methane and chlorine.

Q4 Write down three possible products, other than chloromethane, from the photochemical reaction between CH_4 and Cl_2.

Exam Question

Q1 When irradiated with UV light, methane gas will react with bromine to form a mixture of several organic compounds.

a) Name the type of mechanism involved in this reaction. [1 mark]

b) Write an overall equation to show the formation of bromomethane from methane and bromine. [1 mark]

c) Write down the two equations in the propagation step for the formation of CH_3Br. [2 marks]

d) i) Explain why a tiny amount of ethane is found in the product mixture. [1 mark]

ii) Name the mechanistic step that leads to the formation of ethane. [1 mark]

iii) Write the equation for the formation of ethane in this reaction. [1 mark]

e) Name the major product formed when a large excess of bromine reacts with methane in the presence of UV light. [1 mark]

This page is like... totally radical, man...

Mechanisms can be an absolute pain in the bum to learn, but unfortunately reactions are what Chemistry's all about. If you don't like it, you should have taken art — no mechanisms in that, just pretty pictures. Ah well, there's no going back now. You've just got to sit down and learn the stuff. Keep hacking away at it, till you know it all off by heart.

Alkenes

An alkene is like an alkane's wild younger brother. They look kinda similar, but alkenes are way more reactive.

Alkenes are **Unsaturated Hydrocarbons**

1) Alkenes have the **general formula C_nH_{2n}**. They're made of carbon and hydrogen atoms, so they're **hydrocarbons**.
2) Alkene molecules **all** have at least one **C=C double covalent bond**. Molecules with C=C double bonds are **unsaturated** because they can make more bonds with extra atoms in **addition** reactions.

Examples of alkenes:

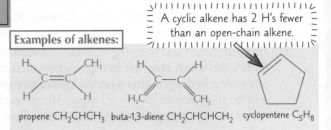

A cyclic alkene has 2 H's fewer than an open-chain alkene.

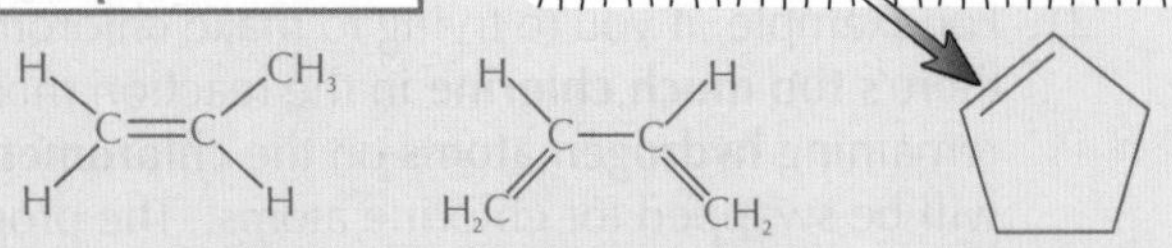

propene CH_2CHCH_3 buta-1,3-diene $CH_2CHCHCH_2$ cyclopentene C_5H_8

A **Double Bond** is made up of a **Sigma (σ) Bond** and a **Pi (π) Bond**

1) A σ **bond** (sigma bond) is formed when two **s orbitals overlap**.
2) The two s orbitals overlap in a straight line — this gives the **highest possible electron density** between the two nuclei. This is a **single** covalent bond.
3) The **high electron density** between the nuclei means there is a strong **electrostatic attraction** between the nuclei and the shared pair of electrons. This means that σ bonds have a high **bond enthalpy** — they are the **strongest** type of covalent bonds.

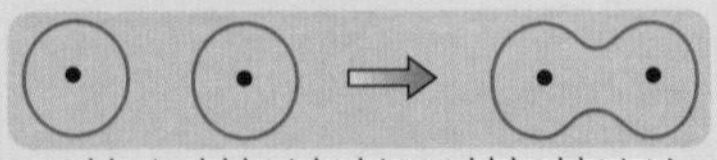

The C–C and C–H bonds in alkanes are all sigma bonds.

1) A π (pi) **bond** is formed by the sideways overlap of two adjacent **p orbitals**.
2) It's got **two parts** to it — one 'above' and one 'below' the molecular axis. This is because the p orbitals which overlap are **dumb-bell shaped**.
3) π bonds are much **weaker** than σ bonds because the electron density is **spread out** above and below the nuclei. This means that the **electrostatic attraction** between the nuclei and the shared pair of electrons is **weaker**, so π bonds have a **relatively low bond enthalpy**.

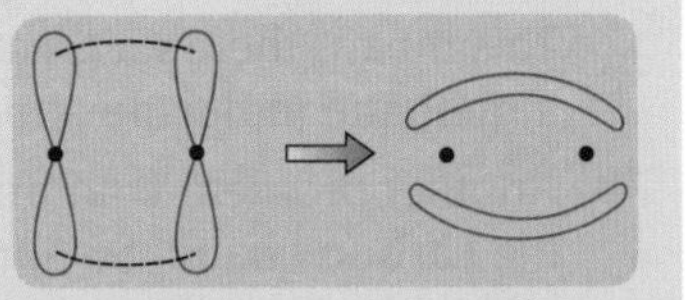

See page 40 for more on orbitals.

Alkenes are **Much More Reactive** than Alkanes

1) Alkanes only contain C–C and C–H σ **bonds**, which have a high bond enthalpy and so are difficult to break. The bonds are also **non-polar** so they don't attract **nucleophiles** or **electrophiles**. This means alkanes **don't react** easily.
2) Alkenes are **more reactive** than alkanes because the C=C bond contains both a σ bond and a π bond.
3) The C=C double bond contains four electrons so it has a **high electron density** and the π **bond** also sticks out above and below the rest of the molecule. These two factors mean the π **bond** is likely to be attacked by **electrophiles** (see p.96). The **low bond enthalpy** of the π bond also contributes to the reactivity of alkenes.
4) Because the double bond's so **reactive**, alkenes are handy **starting points** for making other organic compounds and for making **petrochemicals**.

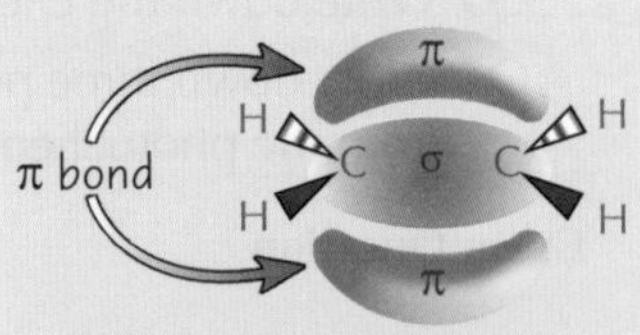

Each **double bond** is like a hot dog. The π **bond** is the bun and the σ **bond** is in the middle like the sausage.

Practice Questions

Q1 What is an alkene?

Q2 Describe the arrangement of electrons in a single bond and in a double bond.

Exam Question

Q1 Consider the hydrocarbons ethane and ethene.

a) Explain how the type of bonding differs in these two molecules. [2 marks]

b) Explain which of these molecules is more reactive. [2 marks]

Double, double toil and trouble. Alkene burn and pi bond bubble...

Double bonds are always made up of a σ bond and a π bond. So even though π bonds are weaker than σ bonds, double bonds will be stronger than single bonds because they have the combined strength of a σ and a π bond.

Stereoisomerism

The chemistry on these pages isn't so bad. And don't be too worried when I tell you that a good working knowledge of both German and Latin would be useful. It's not absolutely essential... and you'll be fine without.

Double Bonds Can't Rotate

1) Carbon atoms in a C=C double bond and the atoms bonded to these carbons all lie in the **same plane** (they're **planar**). Because of the way they're arranged, they're actually said to be **trigonal planar** — the atoms attached to each double-bonded carbon are at the corners of an imaginary equilateral triangle.

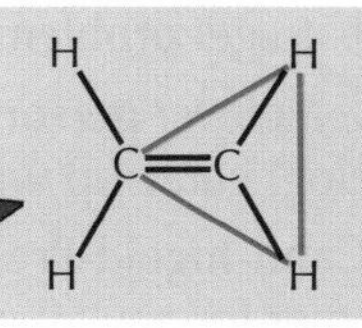

The bond angles in the planar unit are all 120°.

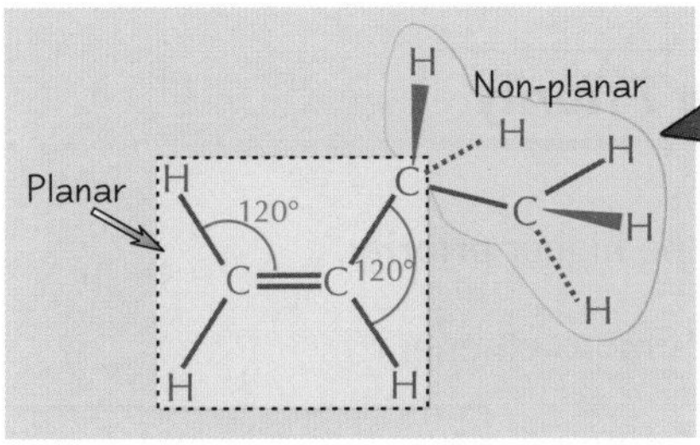

2) Ethene, C_2H_4 (like in the diagram above) is completely planar, but in larger alkenes, only the >C=C< unit is planar.
3) Another important thing about C=C double bonds is that atoms **can't rotate** around them like they can around single bonds (because of the way the p orbitals **overlap** to form a π **bond** — see p.92). In fact, double bonds are fairly **rigid** — they don't bend much either.
4) Even though atoms can't rotate about the **double bond**, things can still rotate about any **single bonds** in the molecule.
5) The **restricted rotation** around the C=C double bond is what causes **alkenes** to form **stereoisomers**.

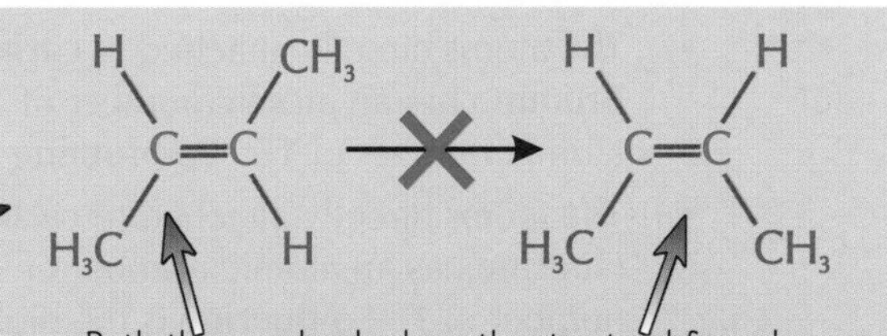

Both these molecules have the structural formula $CH_3CHCHCH_3$. The restricted rotation around the double bond means you can't turn one into the other so they are isomers.

E/Z isomerism is a Type of Stereoisomerism

1) **Stereoisomers** have the same structural formula but a **different arrangement** in space.
(Just bear with me for a moment... that will become clearer, I promise.)
2) Because of the **lack of rotation** around the double bond, some **alkenes** can have stereoisomers.
3) Stereoisomers occur when the two double-bonded carbon atoms each have two **different atoms** or **groups** attached to them.
4) One of these isomers is called the **'E-isomer'** and the other is called the **'Z-isomer'**, (hence the name E/Z isomerism).
5) The **Z-isomer** has the same groups either **both above** or **both below** the double bond, whilst the **E-isomer** has the same groups positioned **across** the double bond.

When you're naming stereoisomers, you need to put 'E' or 'Z' at the beginning of the name.

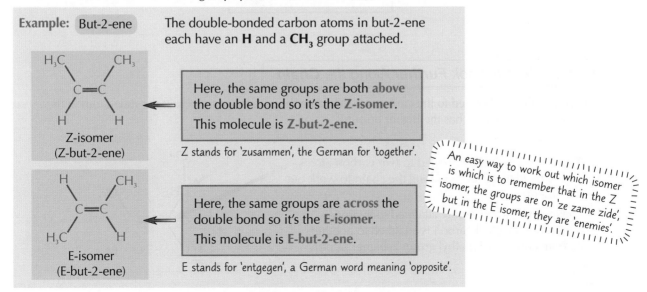

Example: But-2-ene

The double-bonded carbon atoms in but-2-ene each have an **H** and a $\mathbf{CH_3}$ group attached.

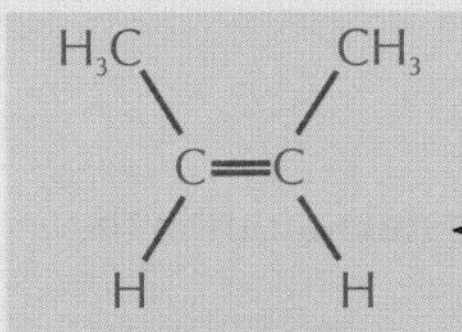

Z-isomer
(Z-but-2-ene)

Here, the same groups are both **above** the double bond so it's the **Z-isomer**.
This molecule is **Z-but-2-ene**.

Z stands for 'zusammen', the German for 'together'.

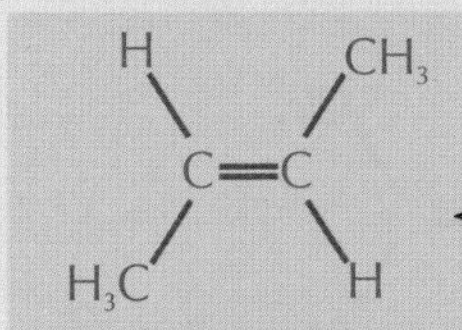

E-isomer
(E-but-2-ene)

Here, the same groups are **across** the double bond so it's the **E-isomer**.
This molecule is **E-but-2-ene**.

E stands for 'entgegen', a German word meaning 'opposite'.

An easy way to work out which isomer is which is to remember that in the Z isomer, the groups are on 'ze zame zide', but in the E isomer, they are 'enemies'.

Stereoisomerism

The E/Z System Works Even When All the Groups Are Different

1) When the carbons on either end of a double bond both have the **same groups** attached, then it's easy to work out which is the E-isomer and which is the Z-isomer (like in the example on page 93).
2) It only starts to get **problematic** if the carbon atoms both have **totally different groups** attached.
3) Fortunately, a clever person (well, three clever people — Mr Cahn, Mr Ingold and Mr Prelog) came up with a solution to this problem.
4) Using the **Cahn-Ingold-Prelog (CIP) rules** you can work out which is the E-isomer and which is the Z-isomer for any alkene. They're really simple, and they work every time.

Atoms With a Larger Atomic Number are Given a Higher Priority

1) Look at the atoms **directly bonded** to each of the C=C carbon atoms. The atom with the higher **atomic number** on each carbon is given the higher **priority**.

Example: Here's one of the stereoisomers of 1-bromo-1-chloro-2-fluoro-ethene:

- The atoms directly attached to **carbon-1** are bromine and chlorine. **Bromine** has an atomic number of **35** and **chlorine** has an atomic number of **17**. So **bromine** is the higher priority group.
- The atoms directly attached to **carbon-2** are fluorine and hydrogen. **Fluorine** has an atomic number of **9** and **hydrogen** has an atomic number of **1**. So **fluorine** is the higher priority group.

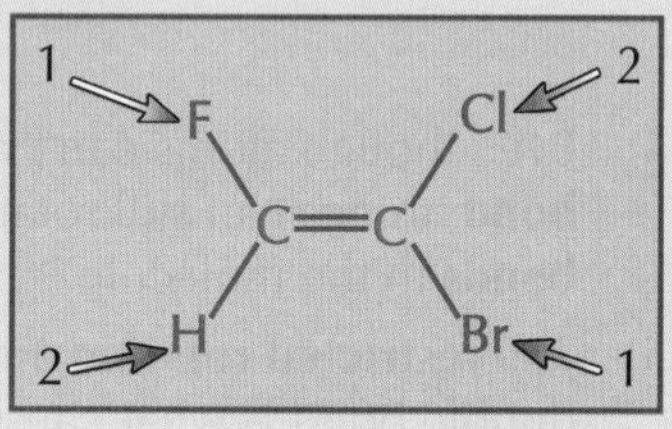

2) Now you can assign the isomers as E- and Z- as before, just by looking at how the groups of the **same priority** are arranged.

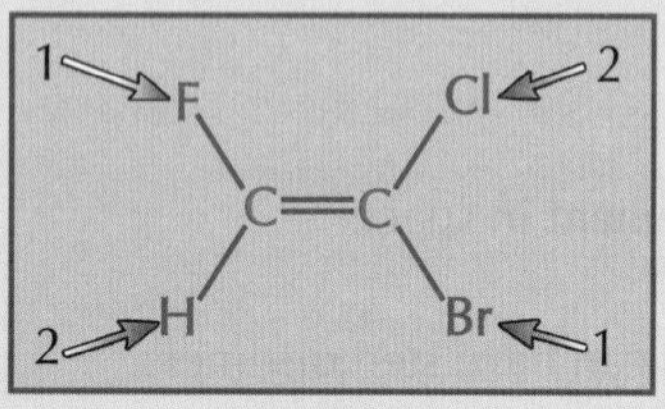

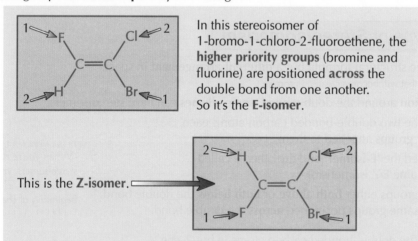

In this stereoisomer of 1-bromo-1-chloro-2-fluoroethene, the **higher priority groups** (bromine and fluorine) are positioned **across** the double bond from one another. So it's the **E-isomer**.

How come you always get to go first?
Because I'm bigger than you.

This is the **Z-isomer.**

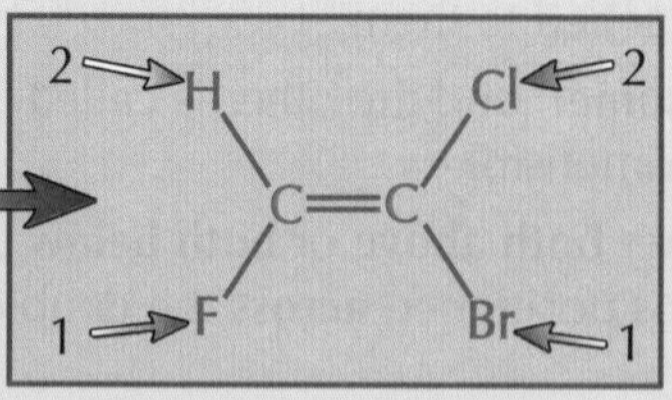

You May Have to Look Further Along the Chain

If the atoms **directly bonded** to the carbon are the **same** then you have to look at the **next** atom in the groups to work out which has the higher priority.

This carbon is directly bonded to **two carbon** atoms, so you need to go **further along** the chain to work out the ordering.

The methyl carbon is only attached to hydrogen atoms, but the ethyl carbon is attached to another carbon atom. So the **ethyl group** is higher priority.

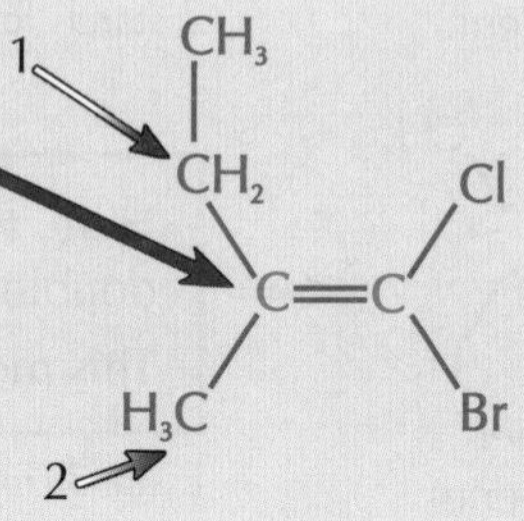

Stereoisomerism

E/Z Isomers Can Sometimes Be Called Cis-Trans Isomers

1) If the carbon atoms have at least **one group in common** (like in but-2-ene), then you can call the isomers '**cis**' or '**trans**' (as well as E- or Z-) where...
   - '**cis**' means the same groups are on the **same side** of the double bond,
   - '**trans**' means the same groups are on **opposite sides** of the double bond.

   So E-but-2-ene can be called **trans-but-2-ene**, and Z-but-2-ene can be called **cis-but-2-ene**.

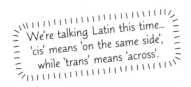

We're talking Latin this time... 'cis' means 'on the same side', while 'trans' means 'across'.

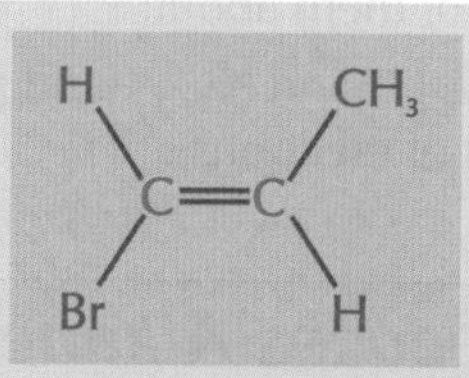

Here's an example:
The **H** atoms are on **opposite** sides of the double bond, so this is **trans-1-bromopropene**.
No problems there.

2) If the carbon atoms both have totally **different** groups attached to them, the cis-trans naming system can't cope.

Here, the **cis/trans** naming system doesn't work because the carbon atoms have **different groups** attached so there's no way of deciding **which isomer** is cis and which isomer is trans.

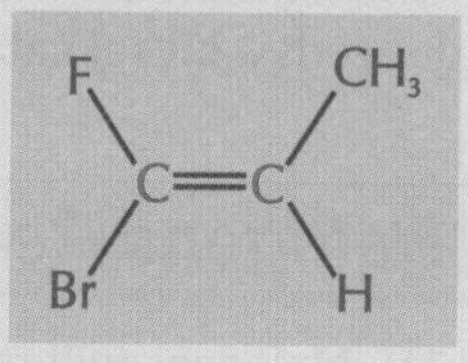

3) The E/Z system keeps on working though — in the E/Z system, Br has a **higher priority** than F, so the names depend on where the Br atom is in relation to the CH_3 group.

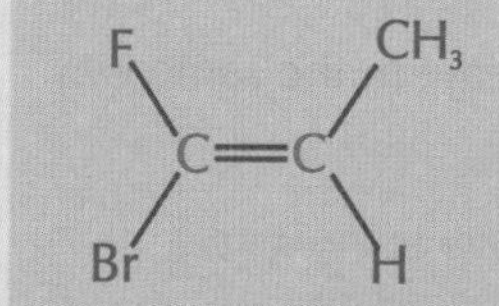

E-1-bromo-1-fluoropropene

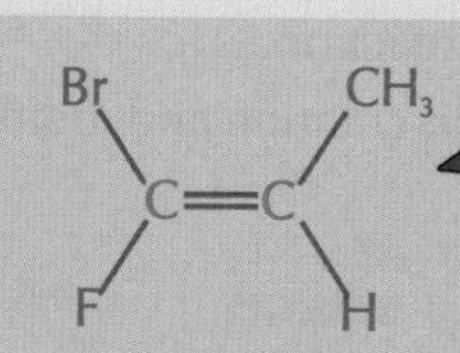

Z-1-bromo-1-fluoropropene

Practice Questions

Q1 Why is an ethene molecule said to be planar?

Q2 Define the term 'stereoisomers'.

Q3 Which of the following is the Z-isomer of but-2-ene?

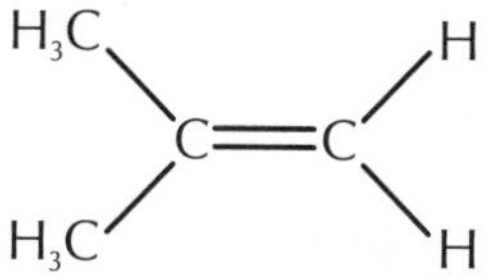

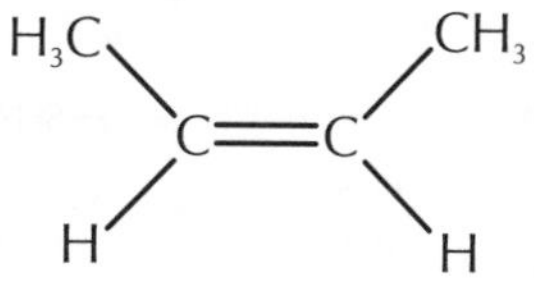

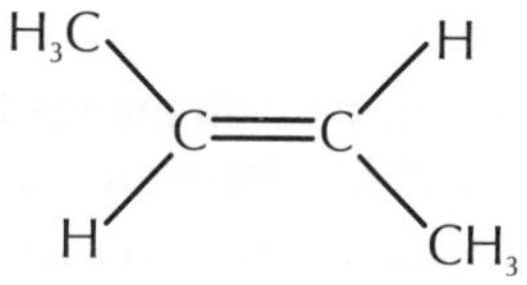

Q4 Is chlorine or bromine higher priority under the Cahn-Ingold-Prelog priority rules?

Q5 Which of the molecules in Question 3 is the trans-isomer of but-2-ene?

Exam Questions

Q1 a) Draw and name the E/Z isomers of pent-2-ene, using full systematic names. [2 marks]

b) Explain why alkenes can have E/Z isomers but alkanes cannot. [2 marks]

Q2 How many stereoisomers are there of the molecule $CH_3CH{=}CHCH_2CH{=}C(CH_3)_2$?

A. 1 B. 2 C. 3 D. 4 [1 mark]

You've reached the ausfahrt (that's German for exit)...

IMPORTANT FACT: If the two groups connected to one of the double-bonded carbons in an alkene are the same, then it won't have E/Z isomers. So neither propene nor but-1-ene have E/Z isomers. Try drawing them out if you're not sure. And then draw out all the structural isomers of butene. Just to prove you've got this completely sussed.

Reactions of Alkenes

I'll warn you now — some of this stuff gets a bit heavy — but stick with it, as it's pretty important.

Electrophilic Addition Reactions Happen to Alkenes

In an **electrophilic addition** reaction, the alkene **double bond** opens up and atoms are **added** to the carbon atoms.

1) Electrophilic addition reactions happen because the double bond has got plenty of **electrons** and is easily attacked by **electrophiles**.
2) **Electrophiles** are **electron-pair acceptors** — they're usually a bit short of electrons, so they're **attracted** to areas where there are lots of them about.
3) Electrophiles include **positively charged ions**, like H^+ and NO_2^+, and **polar molecules** (since the δ+ atom is attracted to places with lots of electrons).

Adding **Hydrogen** to C=C Bonds Produces **Alkanes**

Ethene will react with **hydrogen** gas in an addition reaction to produce ethane. It needs a **nickel catalyst** and a temperature of **150 °C** though.

$$H_2C{=}CH_2 + H_2 \xrightarrow[150\ ^\circ C]{Ni} CH_3CH_3$$

Halogens React With Alkenes to Form **Dihaloalkanes**

1) **Halogens** will react with alkenes to form **dihaloalkanes** — the halogens add **across** the **double bond**, and each of the carbon atoms ends up bonded to one halogen atom. It's an **electrophilic addition** reaction.

$$H_2C{=}CH_2 + X_2 \longrightarrow CH_2XCH_2X$$

2) Here's the mechanism — bromine is used as an example, but chlorine and iodine react in the same way.

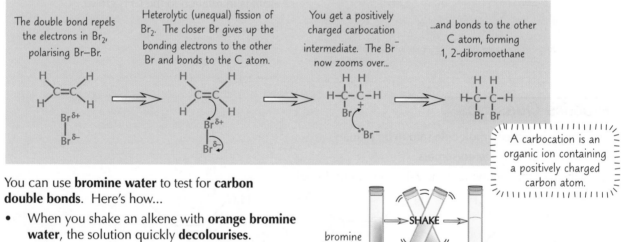

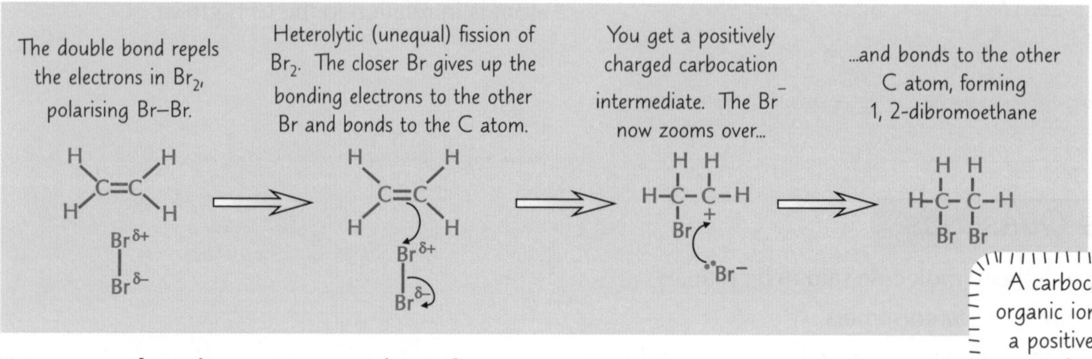
The double bond repels the electrons in Br2, polarising Br–Br.
Heterolytic (unequal) fission of Br2. The closer Br gives up the bonding electrons to the other Br and bonds to the C atom.
You get a positively charged carbocation intermediate. The Br⁻ now zooms over...
...and bonds to the other C atom, forming 1, 2-dibromoethane

A carbocation is an organic ion containing a positively charged carbon atom.

3) You can use **bromine water** to test for **carbon double bonds**. Here's how...
   - When you shake an alkene with **orange bromine water**, the solution quickly **decolourises**.
   - This is because bromine is added across the double bond to form a colourless **dibromoalkane**.

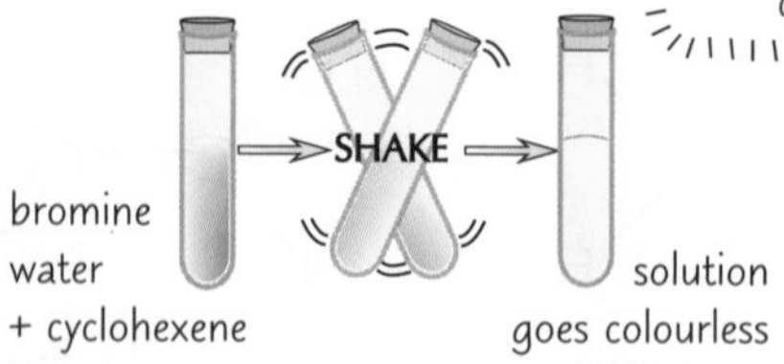
bromine water + cyclohexene
SHAKE
solution goes colourless

Alcohols Can be Made by **Steam Hydration**

1) Alkenes can be **hydrated** by **steam** at 300 °C and a pressure of 60-70 atm. The reaction needs a solid **phosphoric(V) acid catalyst**.
2) The reaction is used to manufacture **ethanol** from **ethene**:

$$H_2C{=}CH_{2(g)} + H_2O_{(g)} \underset{\substack{300\ ^\circ C \\ 60\ atm}}{\overset{H_3PO_4}{\rightleftharpoons}} CH_3CH_2OH_{(g)}$$

3) The reaction's **reversible** and the reaction yield is low — with ethene it's only about 5%. This sounds rubbish, but you can **recycle** the unreacted alkene gas, making the overall yield much better (you can get a yield of **95%** with ethene).

Reactions of Alkenes

Alkenes also Undergo **Addition** with **Hydrogen Halides**

Alkenes also undergo **addition** reactions with hydrogen halides — to form **haloalkanes**.
For example, this is the reaction between **ethene** and HBr: $H_2C{=}CH_2 + HBr \longrightarrow CH_2BrCH_3$

Adding **Hydrogen Halides** to **Unsymmetrical Alkenes** Forms **Two Products**

1) If the hydrogen halide adds to an **unsymmetrical** alkene, there are two possible products.
2) The amount of each product depends on how **stable** the **carbocation** formed in the middle of the reaction is.
3) Carbocations with more **alkyl groups** are more stable because the alkyl groups feed **electrons** towards the positive charge. The **more stable carbocation** is much more likely to form.

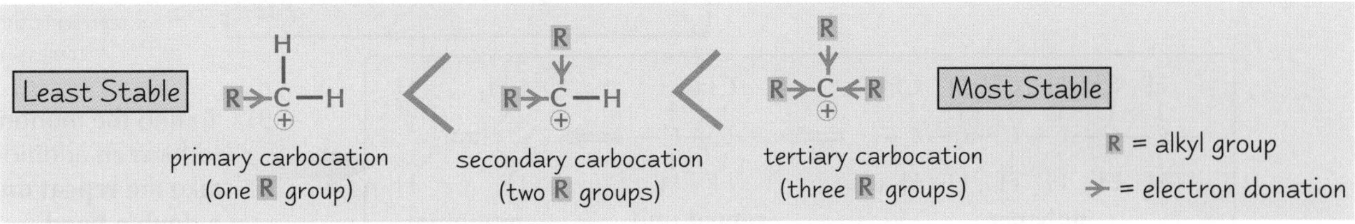

4) Here's how hydrogen bromide reacts with propene:

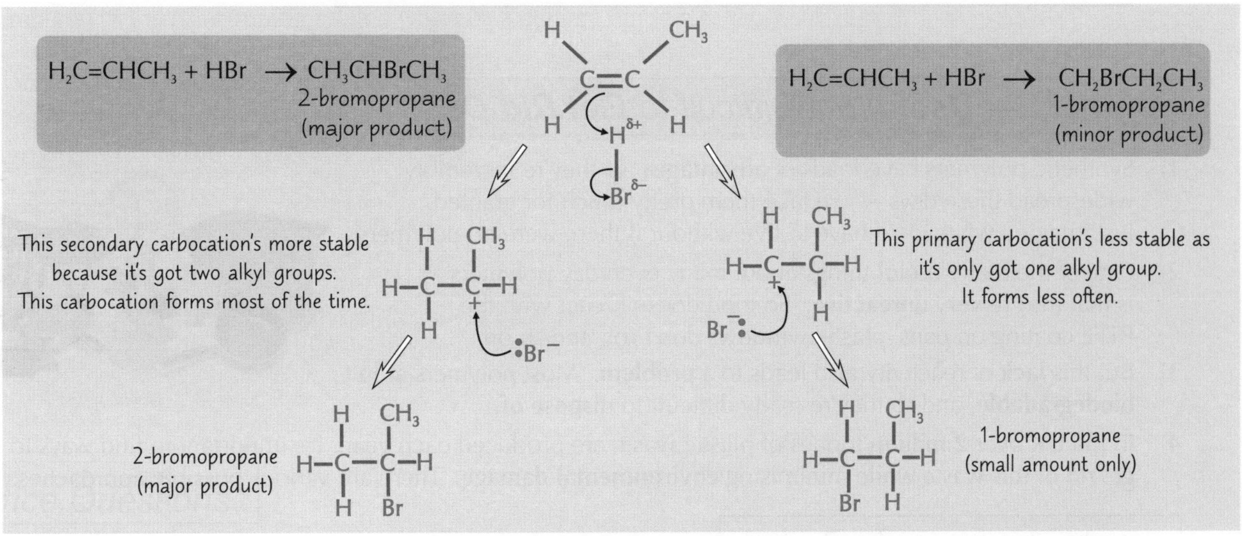

5) This can be summed up by **Markownikoff's rule** which says: The **major product** from addition of a hydrogen halide (HX) to an unsymmetrical alkene is the one where **hydrogen** adds to the carbon with the **most hydrogens** already attached.

Practice Questions

Q1 What is an electrophile?

Q2 Write an equation for the reaction of ethene with hydrogen.

Q3 What is Markownikoff's rule?

Exam Question

Q1 But-1-ene is an alkene. Alkenes contain at least one C=C double bond.

a) Describe how bromine water can be used to test for C=C double bonds. [2 marks]

b) Name the reaction mechanism involved in the above test. [1 mark]

c) Hydrogen bromide will react with but-1-ene by this mechanism, producing two isomeric products. Draw the displayed formulas of these two isomers and predict which will be the major product. [3 marks]

Electrophiles — they all want a piece of the pi...

Mechanisms are a classic that examiners just love. You need to know the electrophilic addition examples on these pages, so shut the book and scribble them out. And remember that sometimes the product has more than one isomer.

Polymers

Polymers are long, stringy molecules made by joining lots of alkenes together. They're made up of one unit repeated over and over and over and over and over and over and over and over again. Get the idea? OK, let's get started.

*Alkenes **Join Up** to form **Addition Polymers***

1) The **double bonds** in alkenes can open up and join together to make long chains called **polymers**. It's kind of like they're holding hands in a big line. The individual, small alkenes are called **monomers**.
2) This is called **addition polymerisation**. For example, **poly(ethene)** is made by the **addition polymerisation** of **ethene**.

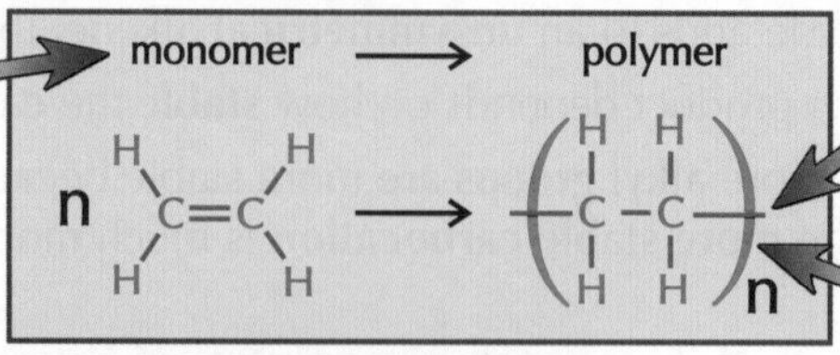

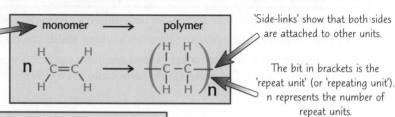

'Side-links' show that both sides are attached to other units.

The bit in brackets is the 'repeat unit' (or 'repeating unit'). n represents the number of repeat units.

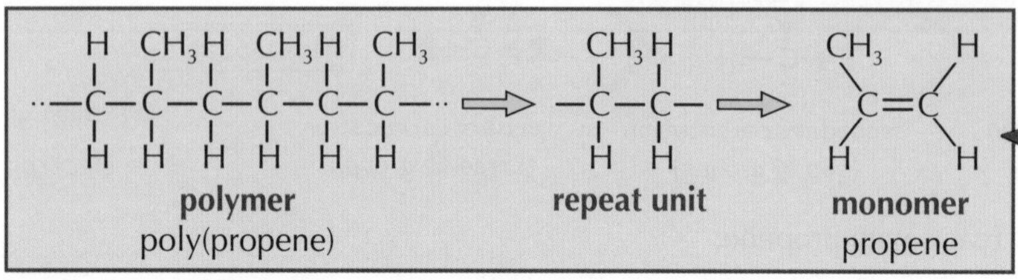

3) To find the **monomer** used to form an addition polymer, take the **repeat unit** and add a **double bond**.

*Polymers — **Useful** but Difficult to **Get Rid Of***

1) Synthetic polymers have loads of **advantages**, so they're incredibly widespread these days — we take them pretty much for granted. Just imagine what you'd have to live without if there were no polymers...
2) One of the really useful things about many everyday polymers is that they're very **unreactive**. So food doesn't react with the PTFE coating on pans, plastic windows don't rot, and so on.
3) But this **lack** of reactivity also leads to a **problem**. Most polymers aren't **biodegradable**, and so they're really difficult to **dispose of**.
4) In the UK over **2 million** tonnes of plastic waste are produced each year. It's important to find ways to get rid of this waste while minimising **environmental damage**. There are various possible approaches...

*Waste Plastics can be **Buried***

1) **Landfill** is one option for dealing with waste plastics. It's generally used when the plastic is:
   - difficult to separate from other waste,
   - not in sufficient quantities to make separation financially worthwhile,
   - too difficult technically to recycle.
2) But because the **amount of waste** we generate is becoming more and more of a problem, there's a need to **reduce** landfill as much as possible.

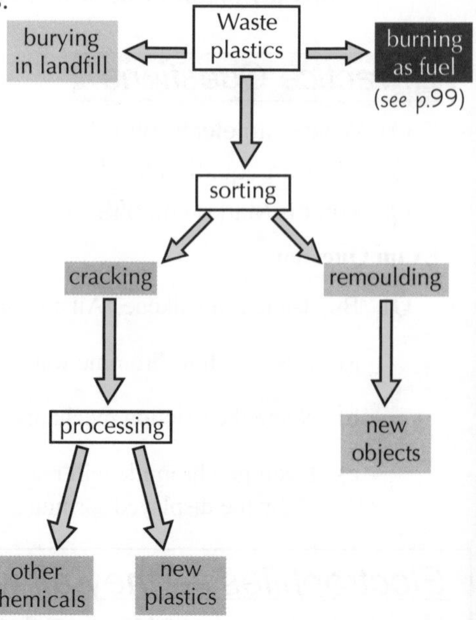

*Waste Plastics can be **Reused***

Many plastics are made from non-renewable **oil-fractions**, so it makes sense to reuse plastics as much as possible.

There's more than one way to reuse plastics. After **sorting** into different types:

- some plastics (poly(propene), for example) can be **recycled** by **melting** and **remoulding** them,
- some plastics can be **cracked** into **monomers**, and these can be used as an **organic feedstock** to make more plastics or other chemicals.

Polymers

Waste Plastics can be **Burned**

1) If recycling isn't possible for whatever reason, waste plastics can be burned — and the heat can be used to generate **electricity**.
2) This process needs to be carefully **controlled** to reduce **toxic** gases. For example, polymers that contain **chlorine** (such as **PVC**) produce **HCl** when they're burned — this has to be removed.
3) Waste gases from the combustion are passed through **scrubbers** which can **neutralise** gases such as HCl by allowing them to react with a **base**.

Rex and Dirk enjoy some waist plastic.

Biodegradable Polymers **Decompose** in the **Right Conditions**

Scientists can now make **biodegradable** polymers — ones that naturally **decompose**.

1) **Biodegradable polymers** decompose pretty quickly in certain conditions — because organisms can digest them.
2) Biodegradable polymers can be made from **renewable** raw materials such as **starch** (from maize and other plants) or **oil fractions**, such as from the hydrocarbon **isoprene** (2-methyl-1,3-butadiene). But at the moment they're more **expensive** than non-biodegradable equivalents.
3) Even though they're biodegradable, these polymers still need the right conditions before they'll decompose. You **couldn't** necessarily just put them in a landfill and expect them to perish away because there's a lack of **moisture** and **oxygen** under all that compressed soil. You need to chuck them on a big compost heap.
4) This means that you need to **collect** and **separate** the biodegradable polymers from non-biodegradable plastics.
5) There are various potential uses — e.g. plastic sheeting used to protect plants from the frost can be made from poly(ethene) with **starch grains** embedded in it. In time the starch is broken down by **microorganisms** and the remaining poly(ethene) crumbles into dust. There's no need to collect and dispose of the old sheeting.
6) Scientists have also started developing **photodegradable** polymers. These are polymers that decompose when exposed to **sunlight**.

Practice Questions

Q1 What is the name of the reaction that turns alkenes into polymers?

Q2 Draw the monomer used to make the polymer poly(propene).

Q3 Many plastics are unreactive. Describe one benefit and one disadvantage of this.

Q4 Describe three ways in which used polymers such as poly(propene) can be disposed of.

Q5 What is a biodegradable polymer?

Exam Questions

Q1 Waste plastics can be disposed of by burning.

a) Describe one advantage of disposing of waste plastics by burning. [1 mark]

b) Describe a disadvantage of burning waste plastic that contains chlorine. [1 mark]

Q2 Give two ways that waste polymers can be reused. [2 marks]

Q3 Chloroethene CH_2=CHCl forms the polymer poly(chloroethene), commonly known as PVC. Write an equation for the polymerisation of chloroethene, including a full displayed formula showing the repeating unit in poly(chloroethene). [2 marks]

Alkenes — join up today, your polymer needs YOU...

You may have noticed that all this recycling business is a hot topic these days. And not just in the usual places, such as Chemistry books. No, no, no... recycling even makes it onto the news as well. This suits examiners just fine — they like you to know how useful and important chemistry is. So learn this stuff, pass your exam, and do some recycling.

Alcohols

These two pages could well be enough to put you off alcohols for life...

Alcohols are **Primary**, **Secondary** or **Tertiary**

1) The alcohol homologous series has the **general formula $C_nH_{2n+1}OH$**.
2) An alcohol is **primary**, **secondary** or **tertiary**, depending on which carbon atom the **-OH** group is bonded to.

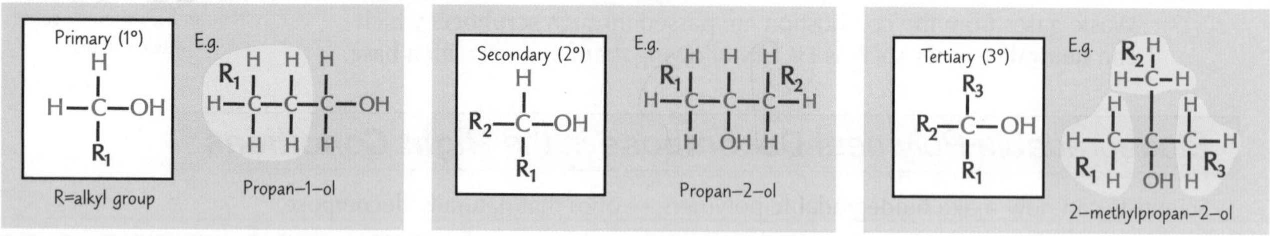

The Hydroxyl Group -OH Can Form **Hydrogen Bonds**

Alcohols are generally **polar molecules** due to the electronegative **hydroxyl group** which pulls the electrons in the C–OH bond **away** from the **carbon atom**.

$$\overset{\delta+}{R_1}-\overset{\delta-}{O}-\overset{\delta+}{H}$$

The electronegative oxygen in the polar hydroxyl group draws electron density away from the hydrogen, giving it a **slightly positive charge**. This positive charge can attract the **lone pairs** on an oxygen from a neighbouring molecule, forming hydrogen bonds (see page 50). This gives alcohols certain properties...

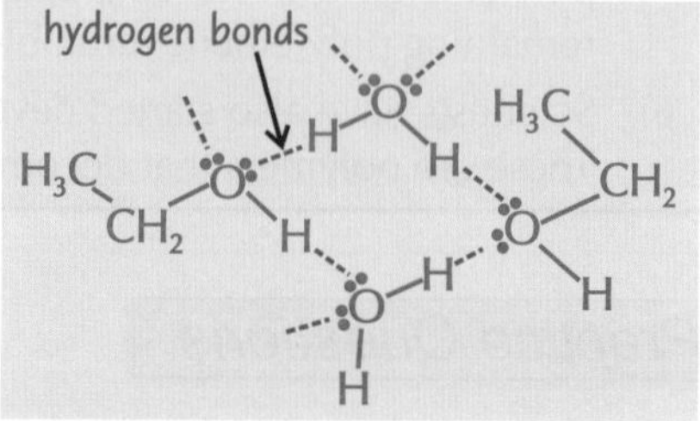

1) When you mix an alcohol with water, hydrogen bonds form between the **-OH** and **H_2O**. If it's a **small** alcohol (e.g. methanol, ethanol or propan-1-ol), hydrogen bonding lets it mix freely with water — it's **soluble** in water.
2) In **larger alcohols**, most of the molecule is a non-polar carbon chain, so there's less attraction for the polar H_2O molecules. This means that as alcohols **increase in size**, their solubility in water **decreases**.
3) Alcohols also form hydrogen bonds with **each other**. Hydrogen bonding is the **strongest** kind of intermolecular force, so it gives alcohols a relatively **low volatility** (they don't evaporate easily into a gas) compared to non-polar compounds, e.g. alkanes of similar sizes.

-OH can be **Swapped** for a Halogen to Make a **Haloalkane**

1) Alcohols will react with compounds containing **halide ions** (such as NaBr) in a **substitution reaction**.
2) The **hydroxyl** (-OH) group is **replaced** by the **halide**, so the alcohol is transformed into a **haloalkane**.
3) The reaction also requires an **acid catalyst**, such as H_2SO_4.

Example: To make 2-bromo-2-methylpropane you just need to shake 2-methylpropan-2-ol (a tertiary alcohol) with sodium bromide and concentrated sulfuric acid at room temperature.

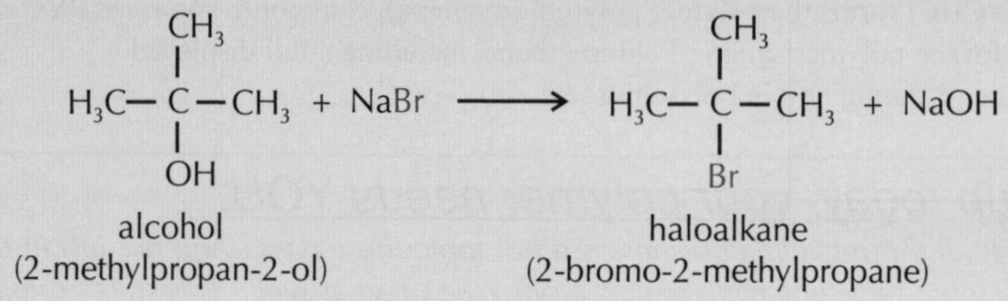

Alcohols

Alcohols can be **Dehydrated** to Form **Alkenes**

1) You can make alkenes by **eliminating** water from **alcohols** in an **elimination reaction**.
2) The alcohol is mixed with an **acid catalyst** — either **concentrated sulfuric acid** (H_2SO_4) or **concentrated phosphoric acid** (H_3PO_4). The mixture is then **heated**.
3) When an alcohol dehydrates it eliminates **water**.

> E.g. **Ethanol** dehydrates to form **ethene**.
> $C_2H_5OH \rightarrow CH_2{=}CH_2 + H_2O$

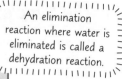

An elimination reaction where water is eliminated is called a dehydration reaction.

4) The water molecule is made up from the hydroxyl group and a hydrogen atom that was bonded to a carbon atom adjacent to the hydroxyl carbon.
5) This means that often there are **two possible** alkene products from one elimination reaction depending on **which side** of the hydroxyl group the **hydrogen** is **eliminated** from.
6) Also watch out for if any of the alkene products can form **E/Z isomers** (see pages 93-95) — if they can then a mixture of both isomers will form.

Example: When butan-2-ol is heated to 170 °C with concentrated phosphoric acid, it dehydrates to form a mixture of products. Give the names and structures of all the organic compounds in this mixture.

- Elimination can occur between the **hydroxyl group** and the hydrogen either on **carbon-1** or **carbon-3**. This results in **two** possible alkene products — **but-1-ene** and **but-2-ene**.
- In addition, **but-2-ene** can form **E/Z isomers**.
- So there are **3** possible products — but-1-ene, E-but-2-ene and Z-but-2-ene.

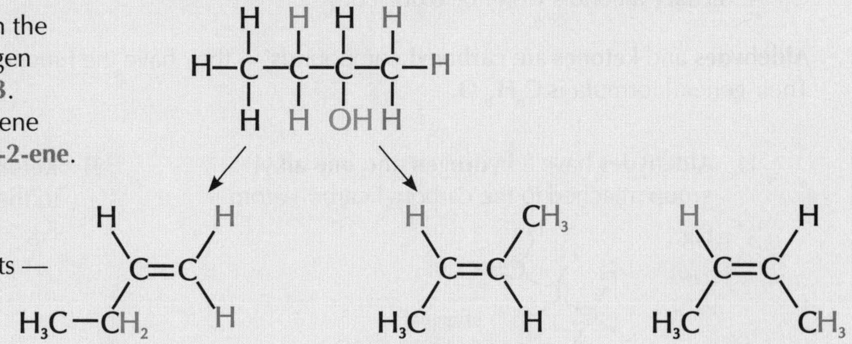

But-1-ene   E-But-2-ene   Z-But-2-ene

Practice Questions

Q1 What is the general formula for an alcohol?

Q2 How do the volatilities of alcohols compare with the volatilities of similarly sized alkanes?

Q3 What products are made when 2-methylpropan-2-ol is mixed with sodium bromide and concentrated sulfuric acid?

Exam Questions

Q1 a) Draw and name a primary alcohol, a secondary alcohol and a tertiary alcohol, each with the formula $C_5H_{12}O$. [3 marks]

b) Describe how ethanol could be converted into bromoethane [1 mark]

Q2 When 3-methyl-pentan-3-ol is heated with concentrated sulfuric acid, it reacts to form a mixture of organic products.

a) What is the name of this type of reaction? [1 mark]

b) How many organic compounds will be produced?

A 4 **B** 3 **C** 2 **D** 1 [1 mark]

Euuurghh, what a page... I think I need a drink...

Not too much to learn here — a few basic definitions, some fiddly explanations of their properties in terms of their polarity and intermolecular bonding, a tricky little dehydration reaction, a substitution reaction... As I was saying, not much here at all... Think I'm going to faint. *[THWACK]*

Oxidation of Alcohols

Another two pages of alcohol reactions. Probably not what you wanted for Christmas...

The Simplest way to Oxidise Alcohols is to **Burn Them**

It doesn't take much to set ethanol alight and it burns with a **pale blue flame**. The C–C and C–H bonds are broken as the ethanol is **completely oxidised** to make carbon dioxide and water. This is a **combustion** reaction.

$$C_2H_5OH_{(l)} + 3O_{2(g)} \rightarrow 2CO_{2(g)} + 3H_2O_{(g)}$$

If you burn any alcohol along with plenty of oxygen, you get carbon dioxide and water as products.
But if you want to end up with something more interesting, you need a more sophisticated way of oxidising...

How Much an Alcohol can be **Oxidised** Depends on its **Structure**

You can use the **oxidising agent acidified dichromate(VI)** ($Cr_2O_7^{2-}/H^+$, e.g. $K_2Cr_2O_7/H_2SO_4$) to **mildly** oxidise alcohols.

- **Primary** alcohols are oxidised to **aldehydes** and then to **carboxylic acids**.
- **Secondary** alcohols are oxidised to **ketones** only.
- **Tertiary** alcohols won't be oxidised.

The orange dichromate(VI) ion is reduced to the green chromium(III) ion, Cr^{3+}.

Aldehydes and **ketones** are **carbonyl** compounds — they have the functional group C=O.
Their general formula is $\mathbf{C_nH_{2n}O}$.

1) **Aldehydes** have a **hydrogen** and **one alkyl group** attached to the carbonyl carbon atom.
E.g.

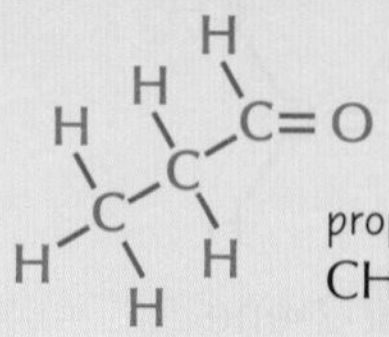

propanal
CH_3CH_2CHO

2) **Ketones** have **two alkyl groups** attached to the carbonyl carbon atom.
E.g.

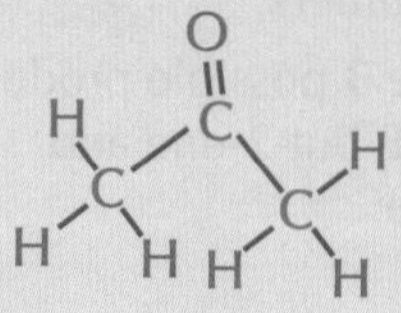

propanone
CH_3COCH_3

Primary Alcohols will Oxidise to **Aldehydes** and **Carboxylic Acids**

Primary alcohols can be oxidised **twice** — first to form **aldehydes** which can then be oxidised to form **carboxylic acids**.

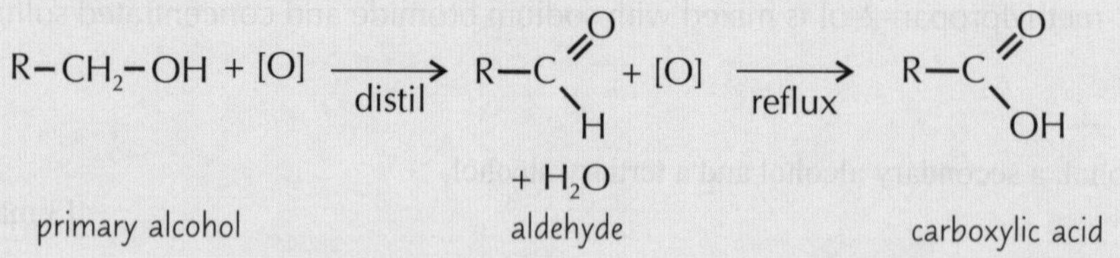

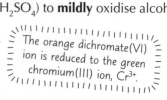

[O] = oxidising agent
e.g. potassium dichromate(VI)

Distil for an **Aldehyde**, and **Reflux** for a **Carboxylic Acid**

You can control how **far** the alcohol is oxidised by controlling the **reaction conditions**. For example...

1) Gently heating ethanol with potassium dichromate(VI) solution and sulfuric acid in a test tube should produce "apple" smelling **ethanal** (an aldehyde). However, it's **really tricky** to control the amount of heat and the aldehyde is usually oxidised to form "vinegar" smelling **ethanoic acid**.
2) To get just the **aldehyde**, you need to get it out of the oxidising solution **as soon** as it's formed. You can do this by gently heating excess alcohol with a **controlled** amount of oxidising agent in **distillation apparatus**, so the aldehyde (which boils at a lower temperature than the alcohol) is distilled off **immediately**.
3) To produce the **carboxylic acid**, the alcohol has to be **vigorously oxidised**. The alcohol is mixed with excess oxidising agent and heated under **reflux**.

There's loads more about distillation and reflux on page 112.

Oxidation of Alcohols

Secondary Alcohols will Oxidise to **Ketones**

1) Refluxing a secondary alcohol, e.g. propan-2-ol, with acidified dichromate(VI) will produce a **ketone**.
2) Ketones can't be oxidised easily, so even prolonged refluxing won't produce anything more.

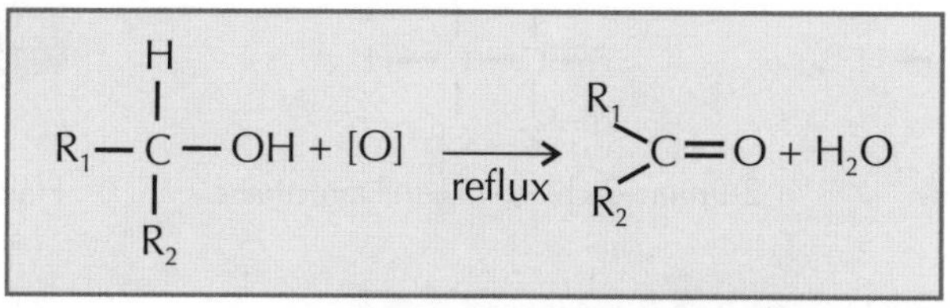

Monty and Bill were getting some much needed rest and refluxation.

Tertiary Alcohols can't be Oxidised Easily

1) Tertiary alcohols don't react with potassium dichromate(VI) at all — the solution stays orange.
2) The only way to oxidise tertiary alcohols is by **burning** them.

Practice Questions

Q1 What's the structural difference between an aldehyde and a ketone?

Q2 Why must you control the reaction conditions when oxidising a primary alcohol to an aldehyde?

Q3 How would you oxidise ethanol to ethanoic acid?

Q4 What will acidified potassium dichromate(VI) oxidise secondary alcohols to?

Q5 How would you oxidise a tertiary alcohol?

Exam Questions

Q1 A student wanted to produce the aldehyde propanal from propanol, and set up reflux apparatus using acidified potassium dichromate(VI) as the oxidising agent.

a) The student tested his product and found that he had not produced propanal.

i) What is the student's product? [1 mark]

ii) Write equations to show the two-stage reaction. You may use [O] to represent the oxidising agent. [2 marks]

iii) What technique should the student have used and why? [1 mark]

b) The student also tried to oxidise 2-methylpropan-2-ol, unsuccessfully.

i) Draw the full structural formula for 2-methylpropan-2-ol. [1 mark]

ii) Why is it not possible to oxidise 2-methylpropan-2-ol with an oxidising agent? [1 mark]

Q2 What will be produced if 2-methylbutan-2-ol is heated under reflux with acidified dichromate(VI)?

A an aldehyde **B** a carboxylic acid **C** a ketone **D** an unreacted alcohol [1 mark]

Q3 Plan an experiment to prepare 2-methylpropanal ($CH_3CH(CH_3)CHO$) from an appropriate alcohol. Your plan should include details of the chemicals (including an alcohol that could be used as a starting material) and procedure used for the reaction. [2 marks]

I've never been very good at singing — I'm always in the wrong key-tone...

These alcohols couldn't just all react in the same way, could they? Nope — it seems like they're out to make your life difficult. So close the book and write down all the different ways of oxidising primary, secondary and tertiary alcohols, and what the different products are. And don't get caught out by those pesky primary alcohols getting oxidised twice.

Haloalkanes

*If you haven't had enough of organic chemistry yet, there's more. If you **have** had enough — there's still more.*

Haloalkanes are Alkanes with Halogen Atoms

A **haloalkane** is an alkane with at least one **halogen atom** in place of a hydrogen atom.

E.g.

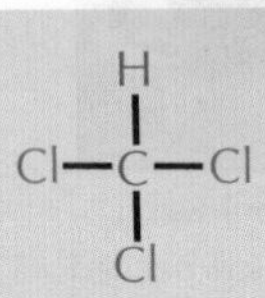

trichloromethane

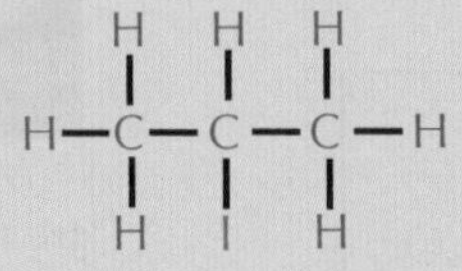

2-iodo-propane

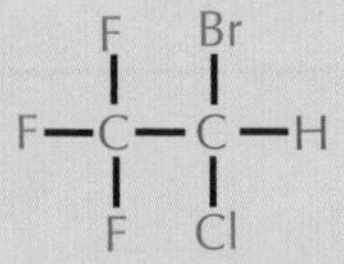

2-bromo-2-chloro-1,1,1-trifluoroethane

Haloalkanes are special amongst alkanes...

The Carbon–Halogen Bond in Haloalkanes is Polar

1) Halogens are generally much more **electronegative** than carbon. So, the **carbon–halogen bond** is **polar**.
2) The **δ+ carbon** is electron deficient. This means it can be attacked by a **nucleophile**.
3) A nucleophile's an **electron pair donor**. It could be a **negative ion** or an atom with a **lone pair** of electrons. It donates an **electron pair** to somewhere without enough electrons.
4) **OH^-**, **CN^-** and **NH_3** are all **nucleophiles** which react with haloalkanes. **Water's** a nucleophile too, but it reacts slowly.

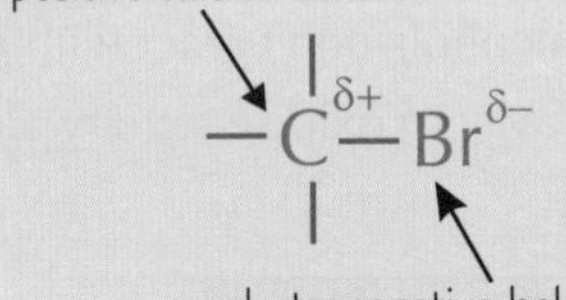

Haloalkanes can be Hydrolysed to make Alcohols

Haloalkanes can be **hydrolysed** to **alcohols**. This is a **nucleophilic substitution reaction**. You have to use a **warm aqueous alkali**, for example **sodium hydroxide** or **potassium hydroxide** or it won't work. The general equation is...

$$R\text{–}X + OH^- \xrightarrow[\text{reflux}]{OH^- / H_2O} R\text{–}OH + X^-$$

Hydrolysis is when water breaks bonds.

Here's what happens. It's a nice simple **one-step mechanism**.

(We've used bromoethane as an example, but the mechanism's the same for all haloalkanes.)

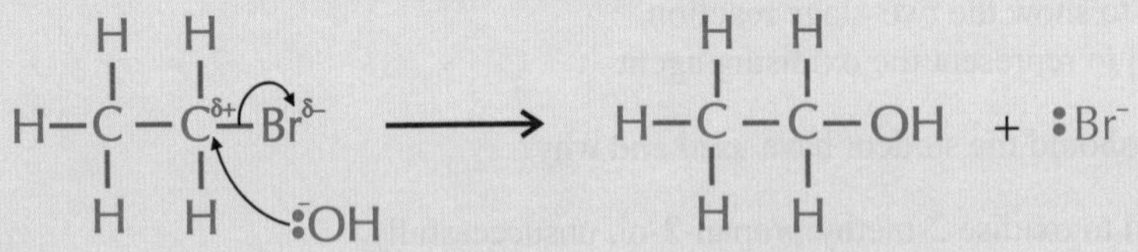

This is a nucleophilic substitution reaction.

1) OH^- is the **nucleophile** which provides a **pair of electrons** for the **$C^{\delta+}$**.
2) The C–Br bond breaks **heterolytically** — **both** electrons from the bond are taken by **Br^-**.
3) **Br^-** falls off as **OH^-** bonds to the carbon.

Water Can Act as a Nucleophile Too

1) The **water** molecule is a **weak nucleophile**, but it will eventually substitute for the halogen — it's just a much slower reaction than the one above.
2) You get an **alcohol** produced again. The general equation is:

$$R\text{–}X + H_2O \rightarrow R\text{–}OH + H^+ + X^-$$

3) Here's what would happen with bromoethane:

$$CH_3CH_2Br + H_2O \rightarrow C_2H_5OH + H^+ + Br^-$$

Haloalkanes

Iodoalkanes are Hydrolysed the Fastest

1) How quickly different haloalkanes are hydrolysed depends on **bond enthalpy** — see p.70 for more on this.
2) **Weaker** carbon-halogen bonds **break** more easily — so they react **faster**.
3) **Iodoalkanes** have the **weakest bonds**, so they hydrolyse the **fastest**.
4) **Fluoroalkanes** have the **strongest bonds**, so they're the **slowest** at hydrolysing.

bond	bond enthalpy kJ mol^{-1}
C–F	467
C–Cl	346
C–Br	290
C–I	228

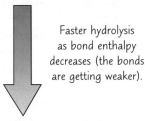

Faster hydrolysis as bond enthalpy decreases (the bonds are getting weaker).

5) You can **compare the reactivity** of chloroalkanes, bromoalkanes and iodoalkanes by doing an experiment:

1) When you mix a **haloalkane** with water, it reacts to form an **alcohol**.

$$R{-}X + H_2O \rightarrow R{-}OH + H^+ + X^-$$

2) If you put **silver nitrate solution** in the mixture too, the silver ions react with the **halide ions** as soon as they form, giving a **silver halide precipitate** (see page 63).

$$Ag^+_{(aq)} + X^-_{(aq)} \rightarrow AgX_{(s)}$$

3) To compare the reactivities, set up three test tubes each containing a different haloalkane, ethanol (as a solvent) and silver nitrate solution (this contains the water):

The haloalkanes should all have the same carbon skeleton to make it a fair test.

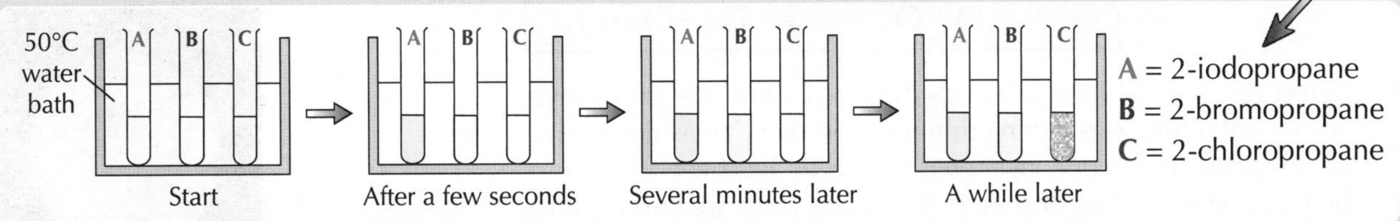

4) A pale yellow precipitate quickly forms with **2-iodopropane** — so iodoalkanes must be the **most reactive haloalkanes. Bromoalkanes** react slower than iodoalkanes to form a cream precipitate, and **chloroalkanes** form a white precipitate the slowest of all.

Practice Questions

Q1 Why is the carbon-halogen bond generally polar?

Q2 What is a nucleophile?

Q3 What is the product when bromoethane is reacted with warm aqueous sodium hydroxide?

Q4 Why does iodoethane react faster than chloro- or bromoethane with warm, aqueous sodium hydroxide?

Exam Questions

Q1 The haloalkane chloromethane is a substance that was formerly used as a refrigerant.

a) Draw the structure of this molecule. [1 mark]

b) Give the mechanism for the hydrolysis of this molecule by warm sodium hydroxide solution. [3 marks]

c) What would be observed if silver nitrate solution was added to the products of the reaction in part b)? [1 mark]

Q2 Which of the following compounds will react the fastest with aqueous potassium hydroxide?

A iodomethane **B** bromomethane **C** chloromethane [1 mark]

I got my tongue stuck on an ice cube last week...it was a polar bond...

Polar bonds manage to get in just about every area of Chemistry. If you still think they're something to do with either bears or mints, flick back and have a good read of page 48. Make sure you learn the mechanism of hydrolysis — including all the curly arrows and bond polarities— it could come up in exams. Ruin the examiner's day and get it right.

Haloalkanes and the Environment

Two pages on air pollution coming up, so take a deep breath...
unless you're hanging around somewhere with a lot of air pollution, that is...

CFCs are Haloalkanes

1) **Chlorofluorocarbons** (**CFCs**) are well-known haloalkanes.
2) They contain only chlorine, fluorine and carbon — all the hydrogens have been replaced.
3) They're very **stable**, **volatile**, **non-flammable** and **non-toxic**. They were used a lot — e.g. in **fridges**, **aerosol cans**, **dry cleaning** and **air-conditioning** — until scientists realised they were destroying the **ozone layer**.

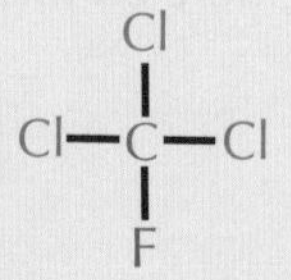

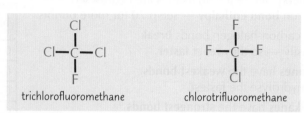

trichlorofluoromethane

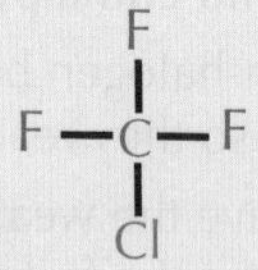

chlorotrifluoromethane

They're stable because of the strength of the carbon-halogen bonds.

Chlorine Atoms are Destroying The Ozone Layer

1) Ozone (O_3) in the upper atmosphere acts as a **chemical sunscreen**. It absorbs a lot of the **ultraviolet radiation** which can cause sunburn or even skin cancer.
2) Ozone's **formed naturally** when an **oxygen molecule** is **broken down** into **two free radicals** by **ultraviolet radiation**. The free radicals **attack** other oxygen molecules forming **ozone**. Just like this:

$$O_2 \xrightarrow{UV} O + O \Longrightarrow O_2 + O \rightarrow O_3$$

3) In the 1970s and 1980s, scientists discovered that the **ozone layer** above **Antarctica** was getting **thinner** — in fact, it was decreasing very rapidly. The ozone layer over the **Arctic** has been found to be thinning too. These 'holes' in the ozone layer are bad because they allow more harmful **UV radiation** to reach the Earth.
4) The 'holes' are formed because **CFCs** in the upper atmosphere absorb UV radiation and split to form **chlorine free radicals**. These free radicals **catalyse** the destruction of ozone — they **destroy ozone molecules** and are then **regenerated** to destroy more ozone. One chlorine atom can destroy 10 000 ozone molecules before it forms a stable compound. Here's what happens:

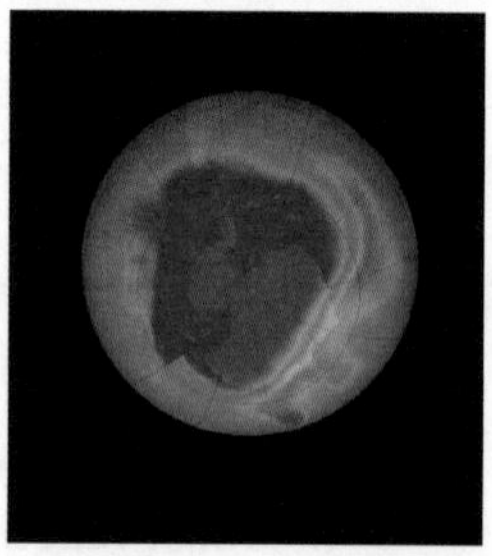

Here's a satellite map showing the 'hole' in the ozone layer over Antarctica. The 'hole' is shown by the blue area

- **Chlorine free radicals**, Cl•, are formed when the C–Cl bonds in **CFCs** are broken down by **ultraviolet radiation**. E.g. $CF_2Cl_{2(g)} \xrightarrow{UV} {\bullet}CF_2Cl_{(g)} + Cl{\bullet}_{(g)}$
- These free radicals are **catalysts**. They react with **ozone** to form an **intermediate** (ClO•) and an oxygen molecule.

$$Cl{\bullet}_{(g)} + O_{3\,(g)} \rightarrow O_{2\,(g)} + ClO{\bullet}_{(g)}$$
$$ClO{\bullet}_{(g)} + O_{(g)} \rightarrow O_{2\,(g)} + Cl{\bullet}_{(g)}$$

The O radical comes from the break down of oxygen by ultraviolet radiation.

The chlorine free radical is regenerated. It goes straight on to attack another ozone molecule. It only takes one little chlorine free radical to destroy loads of ozone molecules.

- So the **overall reaction** is... $O_{3\,(g)} + O_{(g)} \rightarrow 2O_{2\,(g)}$ ... and Cl• is the catalyst.

Nitrogen Oxides Can Also Break Ozone Down

1) **NO• free radicals** from **nitrogen oxides** destroy ozone too. Nitrogen oxides are produced by **car and aircraft engines** and **thunderstorms**. NO• free radicals affect ozone in the **same way** as chlorine radicals.
2) The reactions can be represented by these equations, where **R** represents either Cl• or NO•. In both cases, the free radicals act as **catalysts** for the destruction of the ozone. The overall reaction is: $O_3 + O \rightarrow 2O_2$

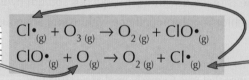

$$\mathbf{R} + O_3 \rightarrow \mathbf{RO} + O_2$$
$$\mathbf{RO} + O \rightarrow \mathbf{R} + O_2$$

Formed when UV breaks down O_2.

The harmful radical is regenerated.

NO• and Cl• aren't the only culprits — free radicals are produced from other haloalkanes too.

Haloalkanes and the Environment

Chemists Developed **Alternatives to CFCs**

1) In the 1970s scientists discovered that CFCs were causing **damage** to the **ozone layer**. The **advantages** of CFCs couldn't outweigh the **environmental problems** they were causing, so they were **banned**.
2) The **Montreal Protocol** of 1989 was an **international treaty** to phase out the use of CFCs and other ozone-destroying haloalkanes by the year 2000. There were a few **permitted uses** such as in medical inhalers and in fire extinguishers used in submarines.
3) Scientists supported the treaty, and worked on finding **alternatives** to CFCs.

- **HCFCs (hydrochlorofluorocarbons)** and **HFCs (hydrofluorocarbons)** are being used as temporary alternatives to CFCs until safer products are developed.
- **Hydrocarbons** are also used.
- **HCFCs** are broken down in the atmosphere in 10-20 years. They still damage the ozone layer, but their effect is much smaller than CFCs.
- **HFCs** are also broken down in the atmosphere. Unlike HCFCs, they **don't** contain **chlorine**, so they don't affect the ozone layer.
- Unfortunately, **HFCs and HCFCs are greenhouse gases** (see page 108) — they're 1000 times worse than carbon dioxide.
- Some **hydrocarbons** are being used in fridges but these are greenhouse gases too.
- Nowadays, most aerosols have been replaced by **pump spray systems** or use **nitrogen** as the propellant. Many industrial fridges and freezers now use **ammonia** as the coolant gas, and **carbon dioxide** is used to make foamed polymers.

4) These substances do have **drawbacks**, but they're currently the **least environmentally damaging** of all the alternatives.
5) The ozone holes **still** form in the spring but are slowly shrinking — so things are looking up.

Practice Questions

Q1 What is a CFC?

Q2 Describe how ozone is beneficial.

Q3 Write equations to show how ozone is formed.

Q4 Write out equations to show how ozone is destroyed, using R to represent the radical.

Q5 Name two alternatives to CFCs.

Exam Questions

Q1 Trichlorofluoromethane ($CFCl_3$) is a CFC that was once used widely as an aerosol propellant.

a) What are two useful properties of CFCs? [1 mark]

b) Give equations to show how trichlorofluoromethane catalyses the breakdown of ozone in the upper atmosphere. Your answer should include an equation for the overall reaction. [3 marks]

c) Name another species of free radical responsible for destroying ozone. [1 mark]

Q2 Nitric oxide radicals (NO•) are destructive radicals that can form in the atmosphere. These radicals act as catalysts in the breakdown of ozone. Give equations to show how nitric oxide radicals catalyse the break down of ozone. [2 marks]

WANTED for vandalism — CFCs. Highly volatile, approach with caution...

How scientists found the hole in the ozone layer and used their evidence to instigate government legislation is a great example of How Science Works. The alternatives to CFCs we use now are less stable, so they don't hang around for as long and are less likely to make it to the upper atmosphere. This gives the ozone layer a chance to replenish. Phew.

The Greenhouse Effect & Global Warming

The greenhouse effect keeps Earth warm, and that's great. Unfortunately, humans are pumping loads of greenhouse gases into the atmosphere, so the greenhouse effect is being enhanced. And that's where it all goes wrong.

The Greenhouse Effect Keeps Us Alive

1) Various gases in the atmosphere that contain C=O, C–H or O–H bonds are able to **absorb infrared radiation** (heat)... and **re-emit** it in **all directions** — including back towards Earth, keeping us warm. This is called the '**greenhouse effect**' (even though a real greenhouse doesn't actually work like this).
2) The main greenhouse gases are **water vapour**, **carbon dioxide** and **methane**.

An Enhanced Greenhouse Effect Causes Global Warming

1) Over the last 150 years or so, the world's **population** has increased, and we've become more **industrialised**. This means we've been **burning fossil fuels**, releasing tons of CO_2 and **chopping down forests** which absorb CO_2. We've also been growing more **food**, and cows and paddy fields release lots of **methane**.
2) Higher concentrations of greenhouse gases mean **more heat** is being trapped and the Earth is getting **warmer** — this is **global warming**. Global warming is thought to be responsible for recent **changes to climates** — such as the shrinking of the **polar ice caps** and **less predictable weather**.

There's Scientific Evidence for the Increase in Global Warming

1) Scientists have collected data to confirm whether or not climate change is happening, e.g. from analysing air samples and sea water samples.
2) The evidence shows that the Earth's average temperature has increased **dramatically** in the last 50 years, and that CO_2 levels have increased at the same time.
3) The **correlation** between CO_2 and temperature is pretty clear, but just showing a correlation doesn't prove that one thing **causes** another — there has to be a plausible mechanism for how one change causes the other (here, the explanation is the enhanced greenhouse effect).
4) There's now a consensus among climate scientists that the link **is** causal, and that recent warming is **anthropogenic** — **human activities** are to blame.

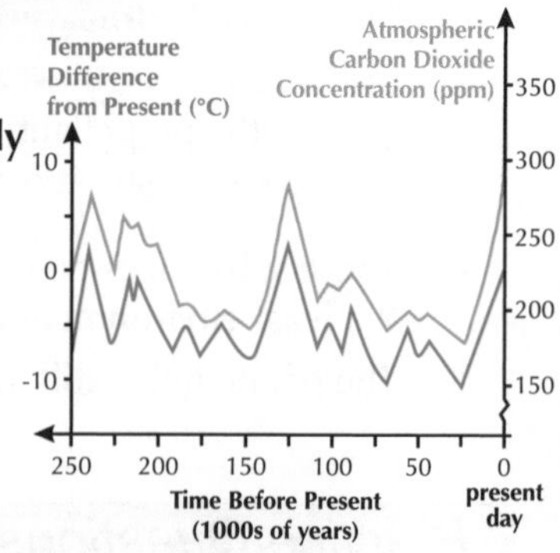

Governments are Working to Reduce their Greenhouse Gas Emissions

1) Scientific evidence has persuaded governments to form a **global agreement** that climate change could be damaging for people, the environment and economies, and that we should try to **limit** it.
2) In 1997 the **Kyoto protocol** was signed — industrialised countries (including the UK) promised to reduce their greenhouse gas emissions to agreed levels. This agreement came to an end in 2012, and currently has no replacement, though many governments agree that they need to reduce CO_2 emissions by around 50% by 2050.
3) The UK government has created policies to use more **renewable energy supplies**, such as wind and solar farms, in order to reduce their emissions.

Practice Questions

Q1 Name three greenhouse gases.

Q2 What's the difference between the greenhouse effect and global warming?

Exam Question

Q1 The concentration of carbon dioxide in the Earth's atmosphere has increased over the last 50 years.

a) Give two reasons for this increase. [2 marks]

b) How do governments know that global warming is happening? [1 mark]

c) Describe how governments are acting to reduce greenhouse gas emissions. [1 mark]

Eating ice cream causes sunburn (well, they correlate)...

Global warming doesn't just affect the temperature. The climate depends on a complicated system of ocean currents and winds etc. As the atmosphere warms up, these factors could change, leading to much less predictable weather.

Analytical Techniques

If you've got some stuff and don't know what it is, don't taste it. Stick it in an infrared spectrometer or a mass spectrometer instead. You'll wind up with some scary looking graphs. But just learn the basics, and you'll be fine.

Infrared Spectroscopy *Helps You* ***Identify Organic Molecules***

1) In infrared (IR) spectroscopy, a beam of **IR radiation** is passed through a sample of a chemical.
2) The IR radiation is absorbed by the **covalent bonds** in the molecules, increasing their **vibrational** energy (i.e. they vibrate more).
3) **Bonds between different atoms** absorb **different frequencies** of IR radiation. Bonds in different **places** in a molecule absorb different frequencies too — so the O–H bond in an **alcohol** and the O–H bond in a **carboxylic acid** absorb different frequencies. This table shows what **frequencies** different bonds absorb:

Functional Group	Where it's found	Frequency/ Wavenumber (cm^{-1})
C–H	alkyl groups, alkenes, arenes	2850 – 3100
O–H	alcohols	3200 – 3600
O–H	carboxylic acids	2500 – 3300 (broad)
C=O	aldehydes, ketones, carboxylic acids, esters	1630 – 1820

You don't need to learn this data, but you do need to understand how to use it.

4) An infrared spectrometer produces a **spectrum** that shows you what frequencies of radiation the molecules are absorbing. You can use it to identify the **functional groups** in a molecule:

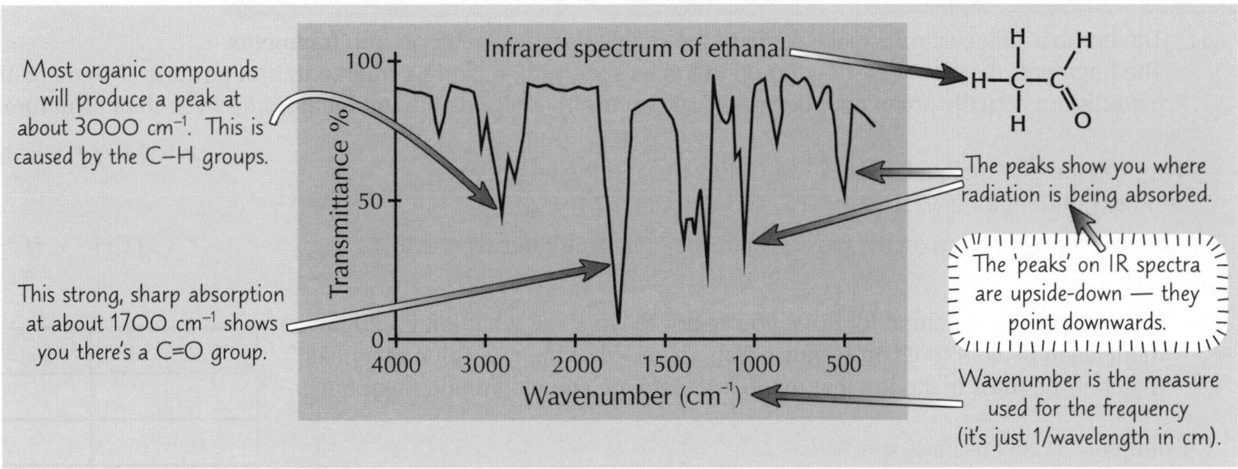
Infrared spectrum of ethanal
Most organic compounds will produce a peak at about 3000 cm⁻¹. This is caused by the C–H groups.
This strong, sharp absorption at about 1700 cm⁻¹ shows you there's a C=O group.
The peaks show you where radiation is being absorbed.
The 'peaks' on IR spectra are upside-down — they point downwards.
Wavenumber is the measure used for the frequency (it's just 1/wavelength in cm).
Transmittance %
100
50
0
4000
3000
2000
1500
1000
500
Wavenumber (cm⁻¹)

5) This also means that you can tell if a functional group has **changed** during a reaction. For example, if you **oxidise** an **alcohol** to an **aldehyde** you'll see the O–H absorption **disappear** from the spectrum, and a C=O absorption **appear**. If you then oxidise it further to a **carboxylic acid** an O–H peak at a slightly lower frequency than before will appear, alongside the C=O peak.

There Are ***Lots*** *of* ***Uses*** *for Infrared Spectroscopy*

1) Infrared spectroscopy is used in **breathalysers** to work out if a driver is over the drink-drive limit. The **amount** of **ethanol vapour** in the driver's breath is found by measuring the **intensity** of the peak corresponding to the **C–H bond** in the IR spectrum. It's chosen because it's **not affected** by any **water vapour** in the breath.
2) Infrared spectroscopy is also used to monitor the concentrations of **polluting gases** in the atmosphere. These include **carbon monoxide** (CO) and **nitrogen monoxide** (NO), which are both present in **car emissions**. The intensity of the peaks corresponding to the C≡O or N=O bonds can be studied to monitor their levels.

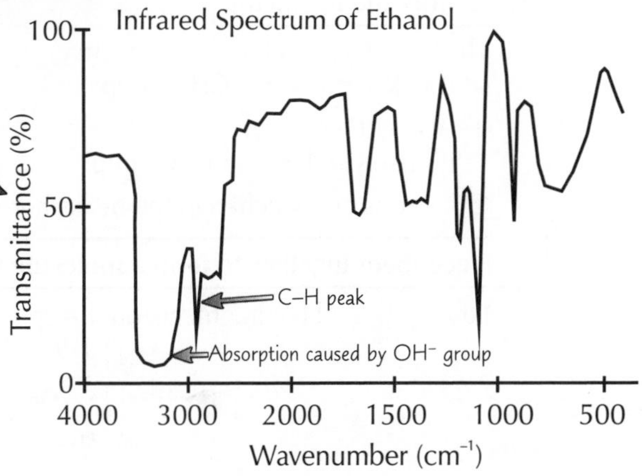

Analytical Techniques

Mass Spectrometry Can Help to Identify Compounds

1) You saw on page 19 how you can use a mass spectrum showing the relative isotopic abundances of an element to work out its relative atomic mass. You need to make sure you can remember how to do this. You can also get mass spectra for **molecular samples**.
2) A mass spectrum is produced by a mass spectrometer. The molecules in the sample are bombarded with electrons, which remove an electron from the molecule to form a **molecular ion, $M^+_{(g)}$**.
3) To find the relative molecular mass of a compound you look at the **molecular ion peak** (the **M peak**). The mass/charge value of the molecular ion peak is the **molecular mass**.

Assuming the ion has a 1+ charge, which it normally will have.

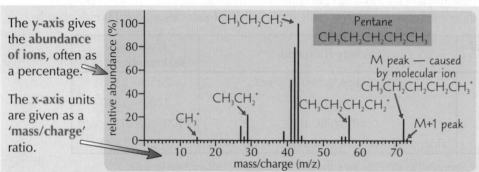

The **y-axis** gives the **abundance of ions**, often as a percentage.

The **x-axis** units are given as a **'mass/charge'** ratio.

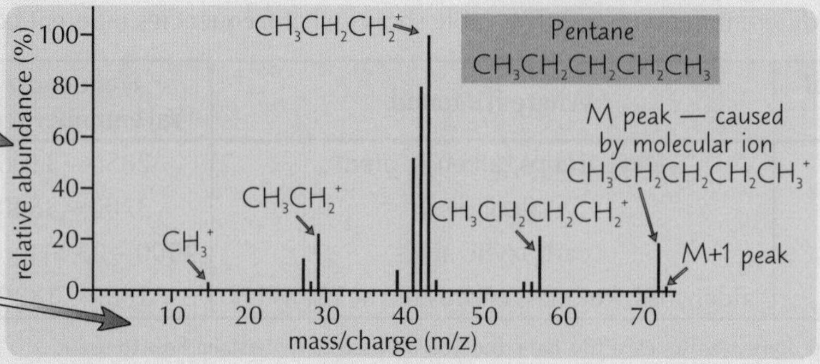

Here's the mass spectrum of pentane. Its M peak is at 72 — so the compound's M_r is 72.
For most organic compounds the M peak is the one with the second highest mass/charge ratio.
The smaller peak to the right of the M peak is called the M+1 peak — it's caused by the presence of the carbon isotope ^{13}C.

*The **Molecular Ion** can be **Broken** into **Smaller Fragments***

1) The bombarding electrons make some of the molecular ions break up into **fragments**. The fragments that are ions show up on the mass spectrum, making a **fragmentation pattern**. Fragmentation patterns are actually pretty cool because you can use them to identify **molecules** and even their **structure**.

For propane, the molecular ion is $CH_3CH_2CH_3^+$, and the fragments it breaks into include CH_3^+ (M_r = 15) and $CH_3CH_2^+$ (M_r = 29).
Only the **ions** show up on the mass spectrum — the **free radicals** are 'lost'.

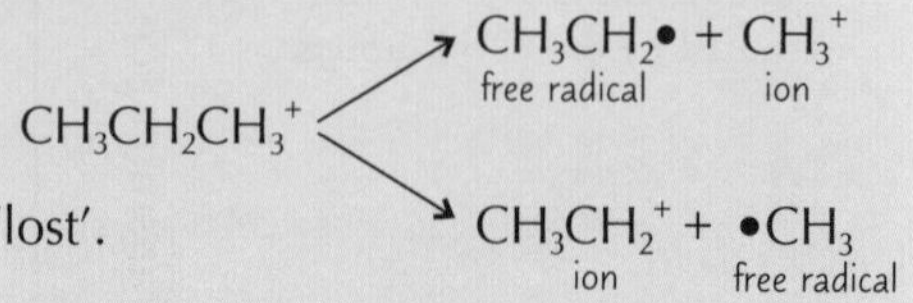

2) To work out the structural formula, you've got to work out what **ion** could have made each peak from its **m/z value**. (You assume that the m/z value of a peak matches the **mass** of the ion that made it.) Here are some common fragments:

Fragment	Molecular Mass
CH_3^+	15
$C_2H_5^+$	29
$CH_3CH_2CH_2^+$ or $CH_3CHCH_3^+$	43
OH^+	17

Example: Use this mass spectrum to work out the structure of the molecule:

It's only the m/z values you're interested in — ignore the heights of the bars.

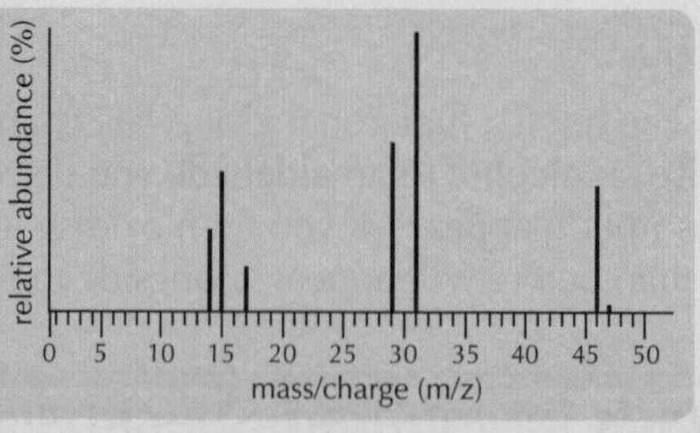

1. Identify the fragments

This molecule's got a peak at 15 m/z, so it's likely to have a **CH_3 group**.
It's also got a peak at 17 m/z, so it's likely to have an **OH group**.
Other ions are matched to the peaks here:

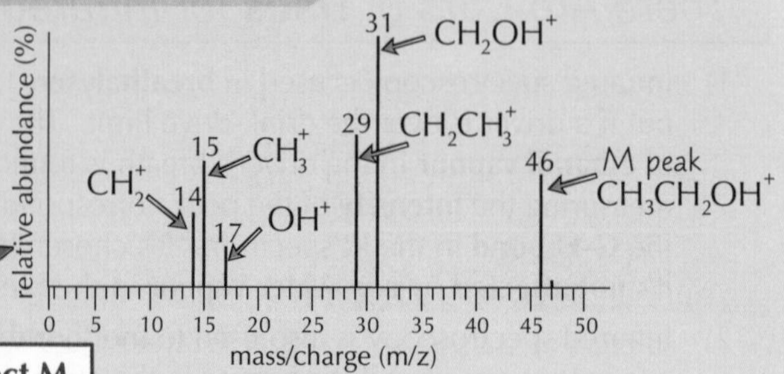

2. Piece them together to form a molecule with the correct M_r

Ethanol has all the fragments on this spectrum.

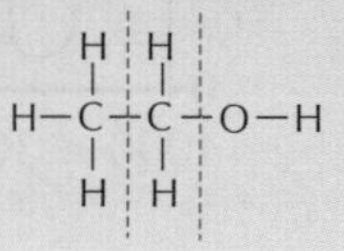

Ethanol's **molecular mass** is 46.
This should be the same as the m/z value of the M peak — it is.

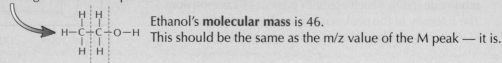

Analytical Techniques

Mass Spectrometry is Used to **Differentiate** Between **Similar Molecules**

1) Even if two **different compounds** contain **the same atoms**, you can still tell them apart with mass spectrometry because they won't produce exactly the same set of fragments.
2) The formulas of **propanal** and **propanone** are shown on the right. They've got the same M_r, but different structures, so they produce some **different fragments**. For example, propanal will have a C_2H_5 fragment but propanone won't.
3) Every compound produces a different mass spectrum — so the spectrum's like a **fingerprint** for the compound. Large computer **databases** of mass spectra can be used to identify a compound from its spectrum.

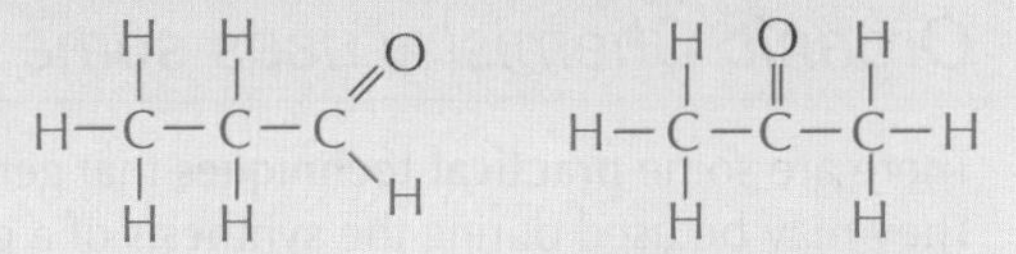

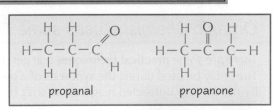

propanal   propanone

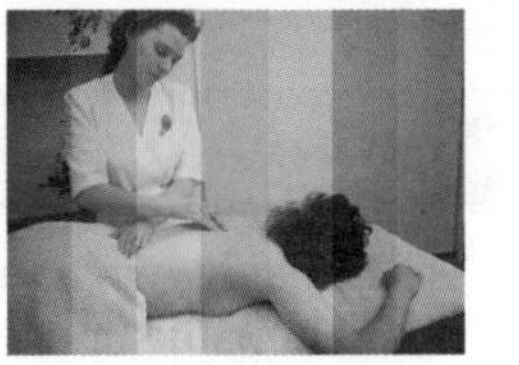

A massage spectrum

You Can **Combine Techniques** to **Identify** a Compound

In the exam, you may be asked to identify a compound from its **mass or percentage composition**, **IR spectrum** and **mass spectrum**. Here's what you should do:

1) Use the **composition** to work out the **molecular formula** of the compound.
2) Work out what **functional groups** are in the compound from its **infrared spectrum**.
3) Use the **mass spectrum** to work out the **structure** of the molecule.

Have a look at pages 22-23 if you're not sure how to work out a compound's molecular formula from its composition.

Practice Questions

Q1 Which parts of a molecule absorb infrared energy?

Q2 Why do most infrared spectra of organic molecules have a strong, sharp peak at around 3000 cm^{-1}?

Q3 Give two uses of infrared spectroscopy.

Q4 What is meant by the molecular ion?

Q5 What is the M peak?

Exam Questions

Use the infrared absorption data on p.109.

Q1 The molecule that produces the IR spectrum shown on the right has composition by mass of: C: 48.64%, H: 8.12%, O: 43.24%.

a) Which functional groups are responsible for peaks A and B? [2 marks]

b) Give the molecular formula and name of this molecule. Explain your answer. [3 marks]

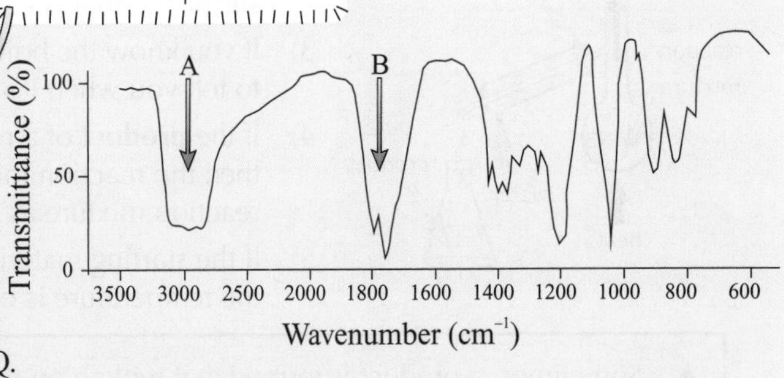

Q2 Below is the mass spectrum of an organic compound, Q.

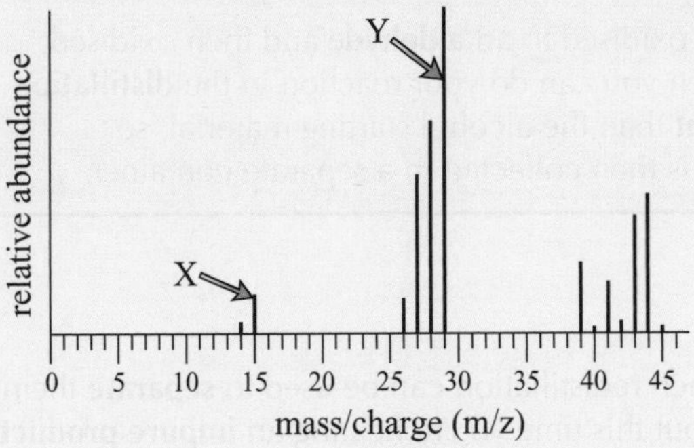

a) What is the M_r of compound Q? [1 mark]

b) What fragments are the peaks marked X and Y most likely to correspond to? [2 marks]

c) Suggest a structure for this compound. [1 mark]

d) Why is it unlikely that this compound is an alcohol? [1 mark]

Use the clues, identify a molecule — mass spectrometry my dear Watson...

Luckily you don't have to remember where any of the infrared peaks are. But you do need to be able to identify them using your data sheet. It's handy if you can learn the molecular masses of the common mass spec fragments, but if you do forget them, then you can just work them out from the relative atomic masses of the atoms in each fragment.

Organic Synthesis — Practical Skills

I'm sure learning all this organic chemistry has got you itching to get into the lab and do some experiments. Well, hold your horses and read these pages before you go throwing chemicals around willy-nilly...

Organic Chemistry uses some **Specific Techniques**

There are some **practical techniques** that get used a lot in organic chemistry. They may be used during the **synthesis** of a product, or to **purify** it from unwanted by-products or unreacted reagents once it's been made.

Refluxing Makes Sure You Don't Lose Any **Volatile** Organic Substances

1) **Organic reactions** are **slow** and the substances are usually **flammable** and **volatile** (they've got **low boiling points**). If you stick them in a beaker and heat them with a Bunsen burner they'll **evaporate** or **catch fire** before they have **time to react**.
2) You can **reflux** a reaction to get round this problem.
3) The mixture's **heated in a flask** fitted with a **vertical Liebig condenser** — this continuously boils, evaporates and condenses the vapours and **recycles** them back into the flask, giving them **time to react**.
4) The **heating** is usually **electrical** — hot plates, heating mantles, or electrically controlled water baths are normally used. This **avoids naked flames** that might ignite the compounds.

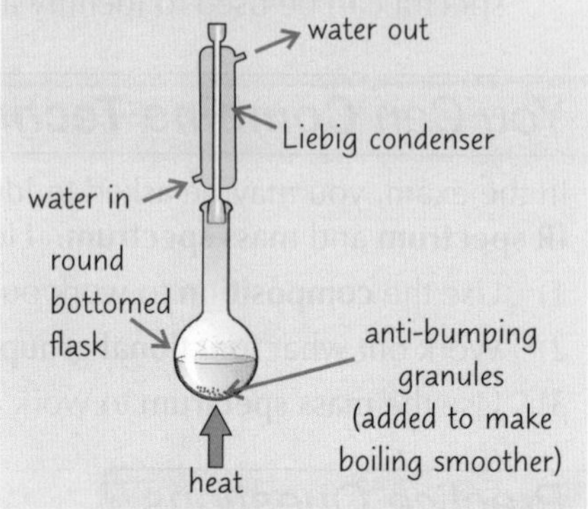

Distillation Separates Substances With Different **Boiling Points**

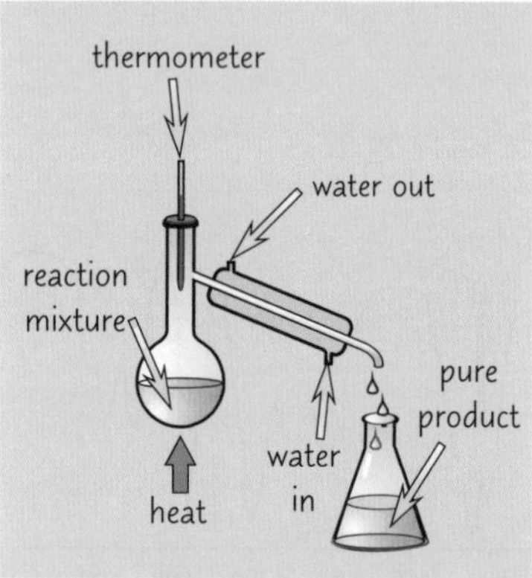

1) Distillation works by **gently heating** a mixture in a distillation apparatus. The substances will evaporate out of the mixture in order of **increasing boiling point**.
2) The thermometer shows the **boiling point** of the substance that is **evaporating** at any given time.
3) If you know the boiling point of your **pure product**, you can use the thermometer to tell you when it's evaporating and therefore when it's condensing.
4) If the **product** of a reaction has a **lower boiling point** than the **starting materials** then the reaction mixture can be **heated** so that the product **evaporates** from the reaction mixture as it forms.
5) If the starting material has a **higher boiling point** than the product, so as long as the temperature is controlled, it won't evaporate out from the reaction mixture.

- Sometimes, a product is formed that will go on to **react further** if it's left in the reaction mixture.
- For example, when you oxidise a **primary alcohol**, it is first oxidised to an **aldehyde** and then oxidised to a **carboxylic acid**. If you want the **aldehyde product**, then you can do your reaction in the **distillation equipment**. The aldehyde product has a **lower boiling point** than the alcohol starting material, so will distil out of the reaction mixture **as soon** as it forms. It is then collected in a separate container.

Volatile Liquids Can be Purified by **Redistillation**

1) If a product and its impurities have **different boiling points**, then redistillation can be used to **separate** them. You just use the same distillation apparatus as shown above, but this time you're heating an **impure product**, instead of the reaction mixture.
2) When the liquid you want **boils** (this is when the thermometer is at the boiling point of the liquid), you place a flask at the open end of the condenser ready to collect your product.
3) When the thermometer shows the temperature is changing, put another flask at the end of the condenser because a **different liquid** is about to be delivered.

Organic Synthesis — Practical Skills

Separation Removes Any **Water Soluble Impurities** From the Product

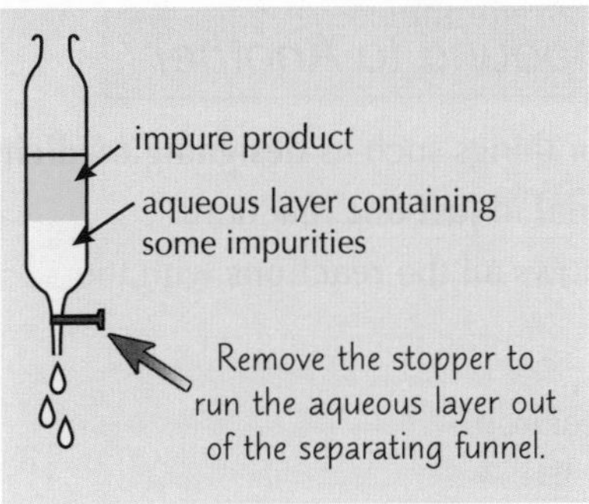

1) If the product is **insoluble** in water then you can use **separation** to remove any impurities that **do dissolve** in water, such as **salts** or water soluble organic compounds (e.g. alcohols).
2) Once the reaction is completed, the mixture is poured into a **separating funnel**, and **water** is added.
3) The funnel is **shaken** and then allowed to settle. The **organic layer** is **less dense** than the **aqueous layer** so should float on top. Any water soluble impurities should have dissolved in the lower **aqueous layer**. You can then open the stopper on the separating funnel, run off the aqueous layer and collect your product.

- If you use separation to purify a product, the organic layer will end up containing **trace amounts** of **water**, so it has to be **dried**.
- To do this you can add an **anhydrous salt** such as **magnesium sulfate** ($MgSO_4$) or **calcium chloride** ($CaCl_2$). The salt is used as a **drying agent** — it **binds** to any water present to become **hydrated**.
- When you first add the salt to the organic layer it will be **lumpy**. This means you need to add more. You know that all the water has been removed when you can swirl the mixture and it looks like a snow globe.
- You can **filter** the mixture to remove the solid **drying agent**.

Practice Questions

Q1 Draw a labelled diagram to show the apparatus used in a reflux reaction.

Q2 Why might you want to avoid naked flames when performing an experiment with organic substances?

Q3 Name two ways of purifying organic products.

Q4 Name two drying agents.

Exam Question

Q1 a) A student carried out an experiment to make hex-1-ene from hexan-1-ol using the following procedure:

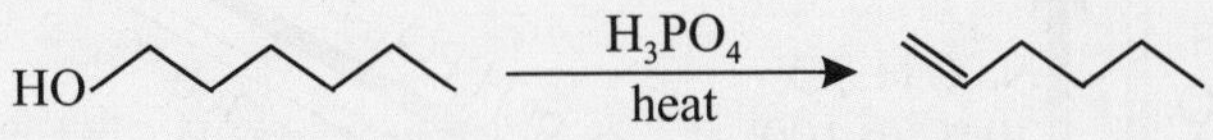

1) Mix 1 mL hexan-1-ol with concentrated phosphoric acid in a reflux apparatus, and reflux for 30 minutes.
2) Once the mixture has cooled, separate the alkene from any aqueous impurities.
3) Dry the organic layer. with anhydrous magnesium sulfate.

i) What is meant by reflux and why is it a technique sometimes used in organic chemistry? [2 marks]

ii) What organic compound is removed in the separating step? [1 mark]

iii) Describe, in detail, how the student would carry out the separation in step 2). [3 marks]

b) In another experiment, the student decides to make 1-hexen-6-ol by carrying out a single dehydration reaction of the diol 1,6-hexanediol.

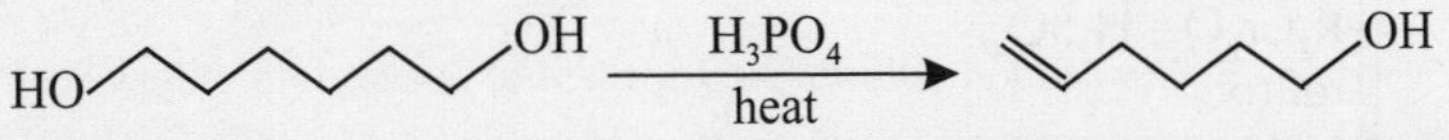

i) If the student follows the procedure in part a), why might he produce a mixture of products? [1 mark]

ii) How could the procedure in part a) be adapted to prevent a mixture of products being formed? [2 marks]

Thought this page couldn't get any drier? Try adding anhydrous $MgSO_4$...

Scientists need to know why they do the things they do — that way they can plan new experiments to make new compounds. Learning the fine details of how experiments are carried out may not be the most interesting thing in the world, but you should get to try out some of these methods in practicals, which is a lot more fun.

Organic Synthesis — Synthetic Routes

There's lots of information on these pages, but you've seen most of it before. It's really just a great big round-up of all the organic reactions you've met in this module. (Maybe not the most exciting thing in the world, but really useful).

Chemists Use **Synthetic Routes** to Get from One Compound to Another

1) Chemists need to be able to make one compound from another. It's vital for things such as **designing medicines**.
2) It's not always possible to synthesise a desired product from a starting material in **just one** reaction.
3) A **synthetic route** shows how you get from one compound to another. It shows all the **reactions** with the **intermediate products**, and the **reagents** needed for each reaction.

Example: You can't produce **propanone** from **2-bromopropane** via one reaction. Instead you first have to make **propan-2-ol**. The synthetic route is:

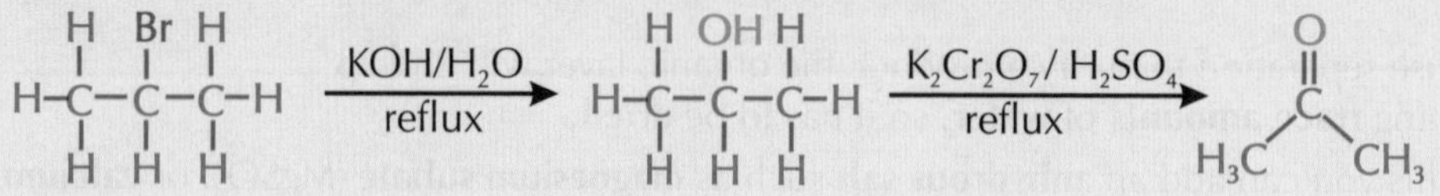

4) Here are all the **organic reactions** you've met so far:

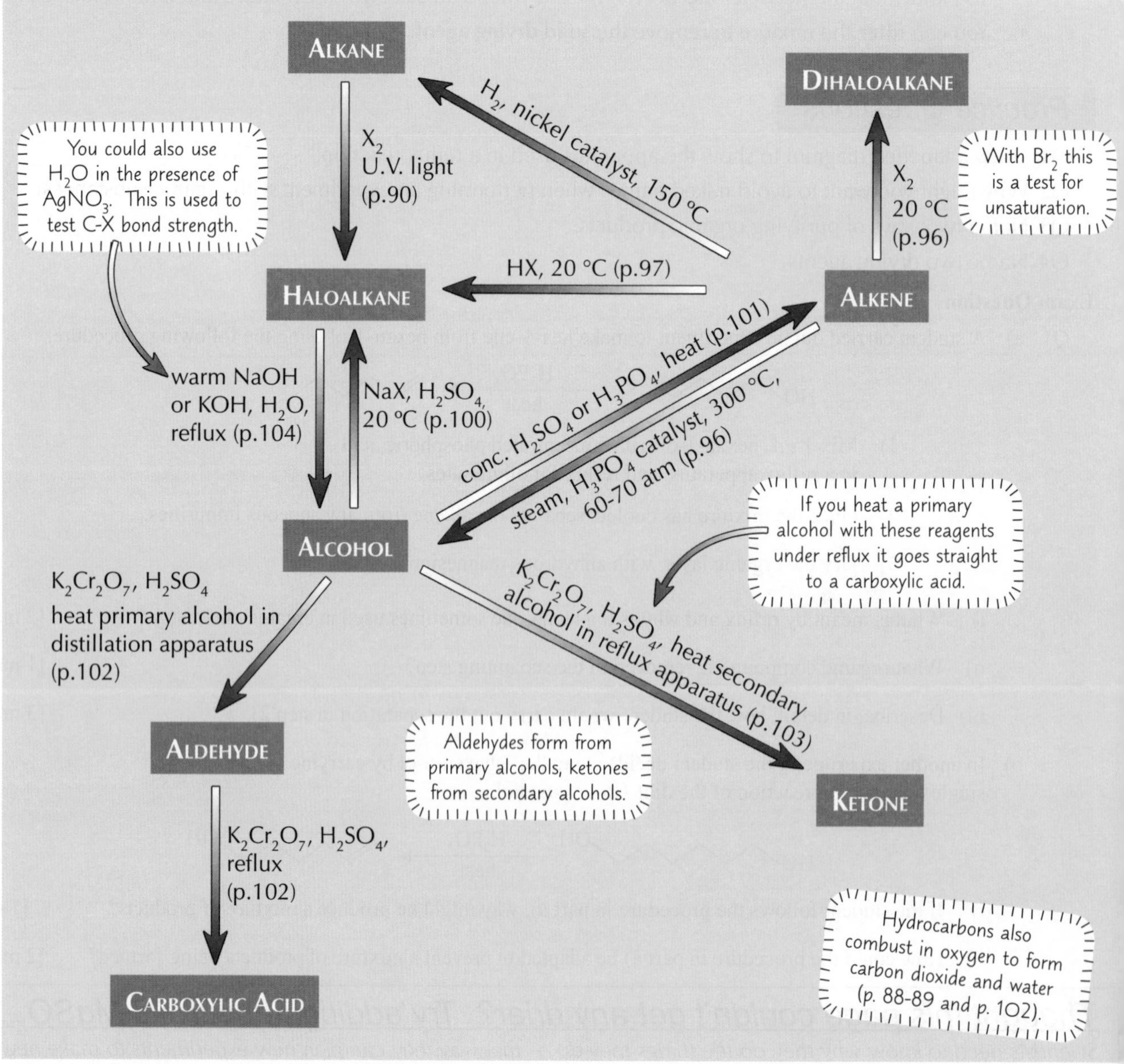

Organic Synthesis — Synthetic Routes

Different **Functional Groups** are Involved in Different **Types** of **Reactions**

1) The different **properties** of functional groups influence their **reactivity** — **nucleophiles** don't react with the **electron-rich double bond** in **alkenes**, but they do attack the **δ+ carbon** in **haloalkanes**.
2) Here are all the functional groups you've studied so far and how they'll typically react:

Homologous series	Functional group	Properties	Typical reactions
Alkane	C–C	Non-polar, unreactive	Radical substitution
Alkene	C=C	Non-polar, electron-rich double bond	Electrophilic addition
Alcohol	C–OH	Polar C–OH bond Lone pair on O can act as a nucleophile	Nucleophilic substitution Dehydration/elimination
Haloalkane	C–X	Polar C–X bond	Nucleophilic substitution
Aldehyde/Ketone	C=O	Polar C=O bond	Aldehydes will oxidise.
Carboxylic acid	-COOH	Electron deficient carbon centre	Esterification

3) Sometimes a compound will have **more than one** functional group. Make sure you can identify **all** of them.

Make Sure You Give **All** the Information

If you're asked how to make one compound from another in the exam, make sure you include:

1) Any **special procedures**, such as refluxing.
2) The **conditions** needed, e.g. high temperature or pressure, or the presence of a catalyst.

Practice Questions

Q1 Why might a chemist want to devise a synthetic route?

Q2 Write a reaction scheme to show how propanone could be formed from 2-bromopropane.

Q3 Name three types of compound that can react to form a haloalkane.

Q4 What is the name for the typical reaction of alkenes?

Exam Questions

Q1 The following flowchart shows some of the reactions of 2-methylpropan-1-ol:

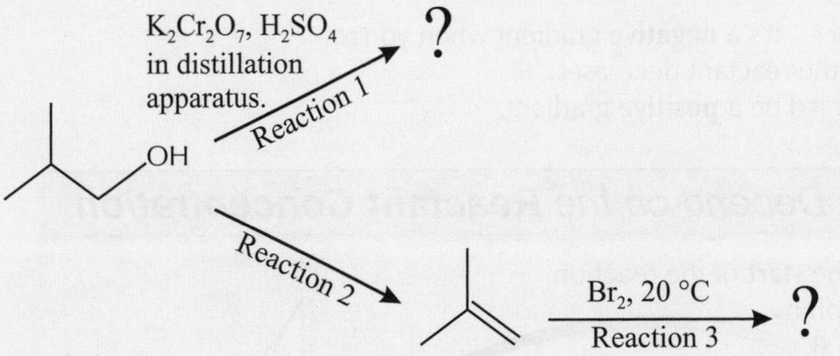

a) Give the skeletal formula of the product of Reaction 1. [1 mark]

b) What are the reagents and conditions needed for Reaction 2? [2 marks]

c) i) Draw the displayed formula of the product of Reaction 3. [1 mark]

ii) What would be observed during the reaction? [1 mark]

Q2 Devise a two step synthetic route for the formation of butanal from but-1-ene. Include all reagents and reaction conditions in your scheme. [3 marks]

Last week I dyed my hair bright pink... I've got synthetic roots...

Woah, there's a lot of information on these pages. But before you go for a well-deserved cuppa, have another look at that big spider diagram on the other page. It links up all the reactions and organic compounds you've met, and it'll be super useful to know in the exam. So draw it out with all the reagents and conditions. And then go and have a break.

Rates of Reaction

This section's a whole lot of fun. Well, it is if you like learning about speed of reactions anyway, and who doesn't...

The **Reaction Rate** tells you How Fast **Reactants** are Converted to **Products**

The **reaction rate** is the **change in the amount** of reactants or products **per unit time** (normally per second).

The units depend on **what** you're measuring. For example, if the reactants are in **solution**, the rate'll be **change in concentration per unit of time** and the units will be, e.g. **mol dm^{-3} s^{-1}**.

There are **Loads** of Ways to **Follow the Rate of a Reaction**

Although there are quite a few ways to follow reactions, not every method works for every reaction. You've got to **pick a property** that **changes** as the reaction goes on. Here are some methods you can use:

- Measure the **volume** of gas evolved.
- Measure the **loss in mass** as a gas is evolved.
- Use **colorimetry** to measure the colour change of a reaction.
- Measure the **pH change** of a reaction.

These are covered in Module 3 (p78).

Work Out **Reaction Rate** from a **Concentration-Time Graph**

1) By repeatedly taking **measurements** during a reaction (continuous monitoring) you can plot a **concentration-time** graph.
2) The rate at any point in the reaction is given by the **gradient** (slope) at that point on the graph.
3) If the graph is a curve, you'll have to draw a **tangent** to the curve and find the gradient of that.

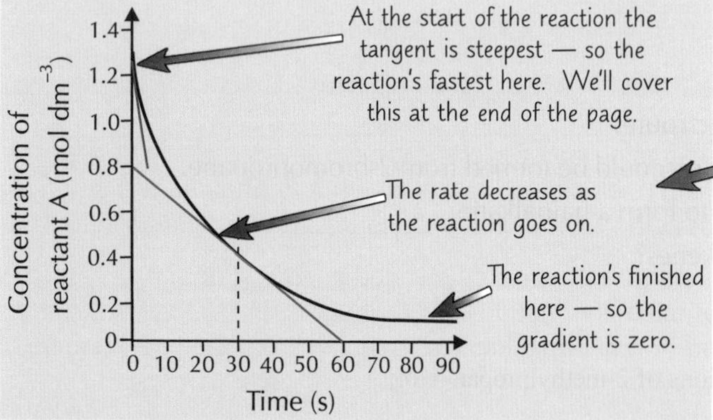
Concentration of reactant A (mol dm^{-3})
1.4
1.2
1.0
0.8
0.6
0.4
0.2
0
0 10 20 30 40 50 60 70 80 90
Time (s)
At the start of the reaction the tangent is steepest — so the reaction's fastest here. We'll cover this at the end of the page.
The rate decreases as the reaction goes on.
The reaction's finished here — so the gradient is zero.

A tangent is a line that just touches a curve and has the same gradient as the curve does at that point.

Here, the gradient of the blue tangent is the rate of the reaction after **30 seconds**.

$$\text{Gradient} = \frac{\text{change in } y}{\text{change in } x} = \frac{-0.8}{60} = \mathbf{-0.013\ mol\ dm^{-3}\ s^{-1}}$$

So, the rate after 30 seconds is **0.013 mol dm^{-3} s^{-1}**.

4) The **sign** of the gradient doesn't really matter — it's a **negative** gradient when you're measuring **reactant concentration** because the reactant decreases. If you measured the **product concentration**, it'd be a **positive** gradient.

Initial Rates Tell You How **Rates** Depend on the **Reactant Concentration**

The **initial rate of a reaction** is the rate right at the **start** of the reaction. You can find this from a **concentration-time** graph by calculating the **gradient** of the **tangent** at **time = 0**.

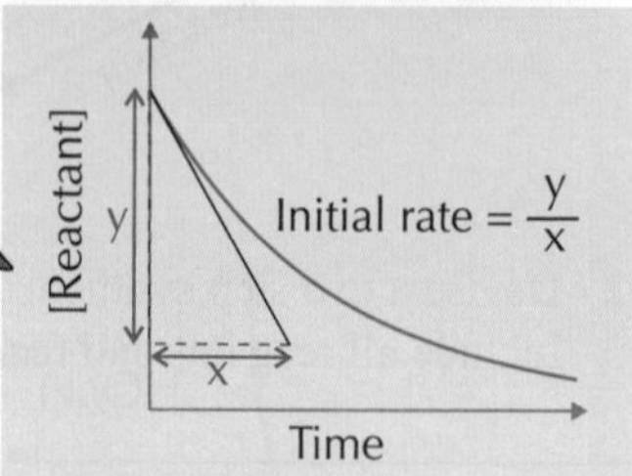
[Reactant]
y
x
Initial rate = y/x
Time

Here's how it works:

1) Carry out the reaction, continuously monitoring **one reactant**. Use this to draw a **concentration-time graph**.
2) Repeat the experiment using a **different initial concentration** of the reactant. Keep the concentrations of other reactants the same. Draw another **concentration-time graph**.
3) Use your graphs to calculate the **initial rate** for each experiment using the method above.
4) Repeat the process for **each reactant** (different reactants may affect the rate differently).
5) You'll see on p119 how you can go on to look at how the different **initial concentrations** affect the **overall rate**.

Rates of Reaction

Clock Reactions *can be used to* ***Simplify*** *the Initial Rate Method*

The method described at the bottom of the last page for working out initial rates is a bit of a faff — lots of measuring and drawing graphs. In clock reactions, the initial rate can be **easily estimated**.

1) In a clock reaction, you measure how the **time taken** for a **set amount** of **product** to form **changes** as you vary the concentration of **one** of the **reactants**.
2) There is usually an **easily observable endpoint**, such as a colour change, to tell you when the desired amount of product has formed.
3) The **quicker** the clock reaction finishes, the **faster** the initial rate of the reaction.
4) You need to make the following assumptions:
   - The **concentration** of each **reactant** doesn't change significantly over the time period of your clock reaction.
   - The **temperature** stays constant.
   - When the endpoint is seen, the reaction has not proceeded **too far**.
5) As long as these assumptions are **reasonable** for your experiment, you can assume that the **rate of reaction** stays **constant** during the time period of your measurement. So the rate of your clock reaction will be a **good estimate** for the **initial rate** of your reaction.

The most famous clock reaction is the **iodine clock reaction**. The reaction you're monitoring is:

$$H_2O_{2\,(aq)} + 2I^-_{(aq)} + 2H^+_{(aq)} \rightarrow 2H_2O_{(l)} + I_{2\,(aq)}$$

- A small amount of sodium thiosulfate solution and starch are added to **an excess** of hydrogen peroxide and iodide ions in acid solution. (Starch is used as an **indicator** — it turns blue-black in the presence of iodine.)
- The **sodium thiosulfate** that is added to the reaction mixture reacts **instantaneously** with any iodine that forms:

$$2S_2O_3{}^{2-}{}_{(aq)} + I_{2\,(aq)} \rightarrow 2I^-_{(aq)} + S_4O_6{}^{2-}{}_{(aq)}$$

- To begin with, all the iodine that forms in the **first reaction** is used up **straight away** in the second reaction. But once all the sodium thiosulfate is used up, any more iodine that forms will stay in solution, so the starch indicator will suddenly turn the solution blue-black. This is the **end** of the clock reaction.
- Varying iodide or hydrogen peroxide concentration while keeping the others constant will give **different times** for the colour change.

Colorimetry is a great way of monitoring this reaction due to the change in colour of the starch indicator when iodine is present.

Practice Questions

Q1 What is the rate of a reaction?

Q2 Give two ways of monitoring the rate of reaction in which a gas is evolved.

Q3 How would you work out the rate of a reaction from a concentration-time graph?

Q4 State two assumptions that you need to make when estimating the initial rate from a clock reaction.

Exam Question

Q1 A student investigates the rate of the following reaction by monitoring the concentration of HCl over time:

$$CH_3(CH_2)_2CHCH_{2\,(l)} + HCl_{(aq)} \rightarrow CH_3(CH_2)_2CHClCH_{3\,(l)}$$

His results are shown on the graph.

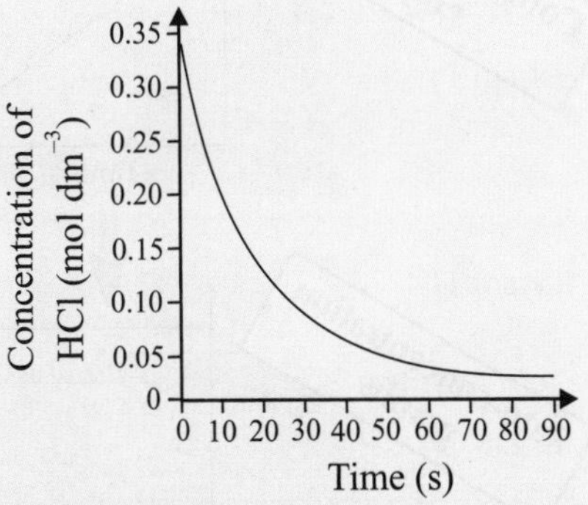

a) Suggest a way of monitoring the concentration of HCl. [1 mark]

b) i) What is the initial rate of the reaction? [2 marks]

ii) What is the rate after 40 seconds? [2 marks]

I hate mornings — I just have a really bad alarm clock reaction...

If you're asked to work out the rate of a reaction from a graph in the exam, make sure you show all your steps. Draw the tangent on the graph and write down the values you're using in your calculation. It shows the examiners you know what you're doing. And remember the units — they're always the units of whatever you're measuring per unit time.

Reaction Orders

A reaction order is not just a reaction being really demanding. Nope, instead it tells you how the rate of the reaction depends on the concentrations of the reactants. You can work them out with the help of a few experiments.

Orders Tell You How a Reactant's Concentration Affects the Rate

1) The **order of reaction** with respect to a particular reactant tells you how the **reactant's concentration** affects the **rate**.

If you double the reactant's concentration and the rate **stays the same**, the order with respect to that reactant is **0**.
If you double the reactant's concentration and the rate **also doubles**, the order with respect to that reactant is **1**.
If you double the reactant's concentration and the rate **quadruples**, the order with respect to that reactant is **2**.

2) A reaction will also have an **overall order**. This is the **sum** of the orders of all the different reactants.
3) You can only find **orders of reaction** from **experiments**. You **can't** work them out from chemical equations.

You Need to Monitor How Each Reactant Affects the Rate One by One

Think about the generic reaction: $A + B \rightarrow C$

Imagine you want to find out the **order** of the reaction with respect to the **concentration of A**.
You have to use **experimental data** to work out the order, and you've got two options:

- **Continuously monitor** the change in concentration of A against time to construct a **rate-concentration** graph.
- Use an **initial rates** method to find out how the initial rate changes as you vary the concentration of A.

Whichever way you choose, you have to make sure that the concentrations of any reactants you're **not investigating**, here it's just B, are in **excess** — there's loads more B than there is A. This means the concentration of B won't change much during the reaction (it will be pretty much constant, and the reaction is effectively zero order with respect to B). This means any change in the **rate** can **only** be due to the change in concentration of A (the reactant you're investigating).

The Shape of a Rate-Concentration Graph Tells You the Order

You can use your concentration-time graph to construct a **rate-concentration graph**, which you can then use to work out the order of the reaction. Here's how:

1) Find the **gradient** (which is the rate, remember) at various points along the concentration-time graph. This gives you a **set of points** for the rate-concentration graph.
2) Just **plot the points** and then **join them up** with a line or smooth curve, and you're done. The **shape** of the new graph tells you the **order**...

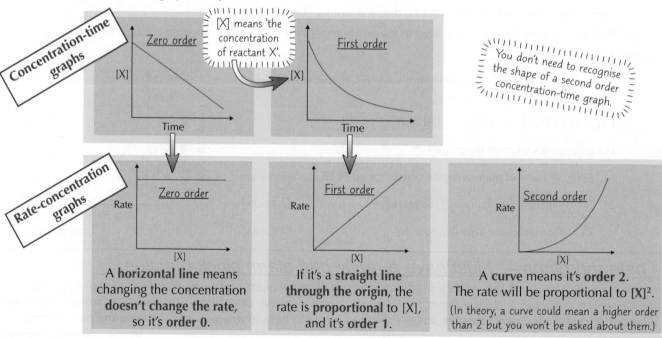

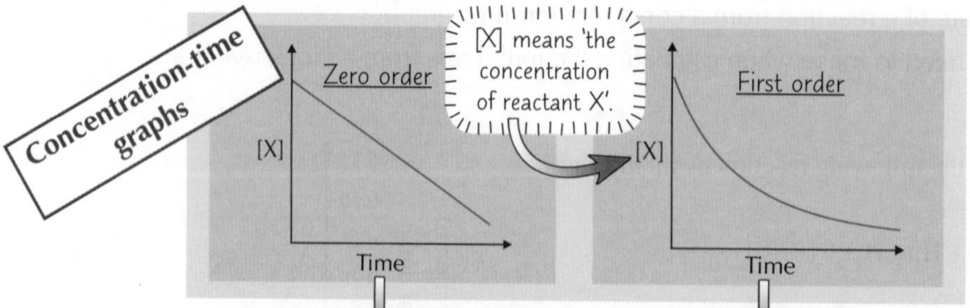

You don't need to recognise the shape of a second order concentration-time graph.

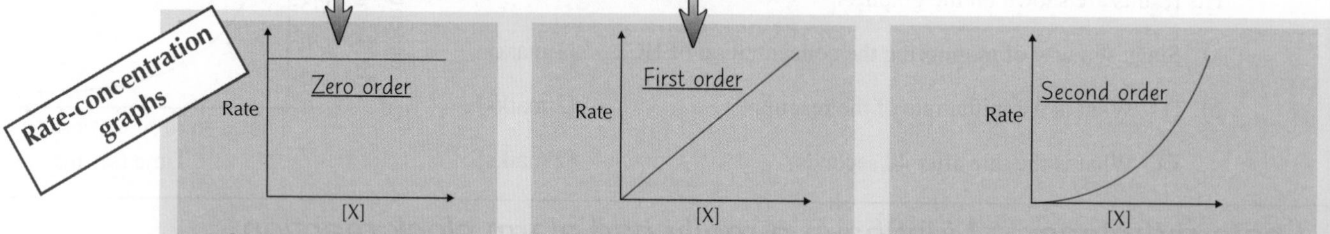

A **horizontal line** means changing the concentration **doesn't change the rate**, so it's **order 0**.

If it's a **straight line through the origin**, the rate is **proportional** to [X], and it's **order 1**.

A **curve** means it's **order 2**. The rate will be proportional to $[X]^2$. (In theory, a curve could mean a higher order than 2 but you won't be asked about them.)

Reaction Orders

The *Initial Rates Method* Can Be Used to Work Out *Orders* Too

You saw how to work out the initial rate of a reaction on page 116 — you often do this to see how the rate right at the **start** of a reaction changes if you change the concentration of one of the reactants.

The initial rates method is a great way of working out the **orders** of different reactants in a reaction.

Example: The table below shows the results of a series of initial rate experiments for the reaction:

$$NO_{(g)} + CO_{(g)} + O_{2(g)} \rightarrow NO_{2(g)} + CO_{2(g)}$$

Write down the order with respect to each reactant.

Experiment number	$[NO_{(g)}]$ (mol dm^{-3})	$[CO_{(g)}]$ (mol dm^{-3})	$[O_{2(g)}]$ (mol dm^{-3})	Initial rate (mol dm^{-3} s^{-1})
1	2.0×10^{-2}	1.0×10^{-2}	1.0×10^{-2}	0.176
2	4.0×10^{-2}	1.0×10^{-2}	1.0×10^{-2}	0.704
3	2.0×10^{-2}	2.0×10^{-2}	1.0×10^{-2}	0.176
4	1.0×10^{-2}	1.0×10^{-2}	2.0×10^{-2}	0.0440

1) Look at experiments 1 and 2 — when $[NO_{(g)}]$ doubles (but all the other concentrations stay constant), the rate **quadruples**. So the reaction is **second order** with respect to NO.
2) Look at experiments 1 and 3 — when $[CO_{(g)}]$ doubles (but all the other concentrations stay constant), the rate **stays the same**. So the reaction is **zero order** with respect to CO.
3) All that's left is to calculate the order for O_2. The only experiment where $[O_2]$ changes is experiment 4. Between experiments 1 and 4, $[NO_{(g)}]$ has **halved** and $[O_{2(g)}]$ has **doubled**.
   You've already worked out that the rate is second order with respect to NO so halving its concentration will cause the rate to be four times less than in experiment 1: **0.176 ÷ 4 = 0.0440.**
   This is the same as the reported rate of the reaction. So doubling the concentration of O_2 must have **no effect** on the rate. This means the reaction is **zero order** with respect to O_2.

Practice Questions

Q1 What does the order of a reaction with respect to a particular reactant tell you?

Q2 If you double the concentration of reactant X, the rate doubles.
What is the order of reaction with respect to reactant X?

Q3 How do you work out the overall order of a reaction?

Q4 Sketch a typical rate-concentration graph for a second order reaction.

Exam Questions

Q1 It takes 200 seconds to completely dissolve a 0.4 g piece of magnesium in 25 cm^3 of dilute hydrochloric acid. It takes 100 seconds if the concentration of the acid is doubled.

a) What is the order of the reaction with respect to the concentration of the acid? [1 mark]

b) Sketch a graph to show the relationship between the concentration of the acid and the overall rate of the reaction. [2 marks]

c) What physical parameter could be measured to follow the rate of this reaction in more detail? [1 marks]

Q2 A reaction between two compounds has an overall order of 2.
Which of the following could represent the order of reaction with respect to each of the reactants?

A Both reactants have an order of 2.

B One reactant has an order of 1, the other has an order of 2.

C Both reactants have an order of 1. [1 mark]

Look at those great curves...

...sorry, chemistry gets me a bit over-excited sometimes. I think I'm OK now. Remember that you can never (ever) tell the order of a reaction from its equation — you've got to do an experiment. And then you have to interpret your results, so make sure you know how the shapes of concentration-time graphs and rate-concentration graphs relate to the order.

The Rate Constant

The rate constant links the concentration of your reactants, their orders and the rate of your reaction. I'll warn you now — there's a little bit of maths involved. It's really not too bad though... promise...

The Rate Equation Links Reaction Rate to Reactant Concentrations

Rate equations look mean, but all they're really telling you is how the **rate** is affected by the **concentrations of reactants.** For a general reaction: **A + B → C + D**, the **rate equation** is:

$$\text{Rate} = k[A]^m[B]^n$$

The units of rate are mol dm^{-3} s^{-1}.

Remember — square brackets mean the concentration of whatever's inside them.

1) ***k*** is the **rate constant** — the bigger it is, the **faster** the reaction.
2) **m** and **n** are the **orders of the reaction** with respect to reactant A and reactant B. **m** tells you how the **concentration of reactant A** affects the **rate** and **n** tells you the same for **reactant B.**

Example: The chemical equation below shows the acid-catalysed reaction between propanone and iodine.

$$CH_3COCH_{3(aq)} + I_{2(aq)} \xrightarrow{H^+_{(aq)}} CH_3COCH_2I_{(aq)} + H^+_{(aq)} + I^-_{(aq)}$$

This reaction is first order with respect to propanone and $H^+_{(aq)}$ and zero order with respect to iodine. Write down the rate equation.

Even though $H^+_{(aq)}$ is a catalyst, rather than a reactant, it can still appear in the rate equation.

The **rate equation** is: rate = $k[CH_3COCH_{3(aq)}]^1[H^+_{(aq)}]^1[I_{2(aq)}]^0$

But $[X]^1$ is usually written as **[X]**, and $[X]^0$ equals **1** so is usually **left out** of the rate equation.

So you can **simplify** the rate equation to: **rate = $k[CH_3COCH_{3(aq)}][H^+_{(aq)}]$**

Think about the powers laws from maths.

You can Calculate the Rate Constant from the Orders and Rate of Reaction

Once the rate and the orders of the reaction have been found by experiment, you can work out the **rate constant, *k*.** The **units** of the rate constant vary, so you have to **work them out.**

Example: The reaction below was found to be second order with respect to NO and zero order with respect to CO and O_2. The rate is 1.76×10^{-3} mol dm^{-3} s^{-1} when $[NO_{(g)}] = [CO_{(g)}] = [O_{2(g)}] = 2.00 \times 10^{-3}$ mol dm^{-3}.

$$NO_{(g)} + CO_{(g)} + O_{2(g)} \rightarrow NO_{2(g)} + CO_{2(g)}$$

Find the value of the rate constant.

First write out the **rate equation:** Rate = $k[NO_{(g)}]^2[CO_{(g)}]^0[O_{2(g)}]^0 = k[NO_{(g)}]^2$

Next insert the **concentration** and the **rate. Rearrange** the equation and calculate the value of ***k*:**

Rate = $k[NO_{(g)}]^2$, so $1.76 \times 10^{-3} = k \times (2.00 \times 10^{-3})^2$ ⟹ $k = \dfrac{1.76 \times 10^{-3}}{(2.00 \times 10^{-3})^2} = 440$

Find the **units for *k*** by putting the other units in the rate equation:

Rate = $k[NO_{(g)}]^2$, so mol dm^{-3} s^{-1} = $k \times$ (mol dm^{-3})^2 ⟹ $k = \dfrac{\text{mol dm}^{-3}\text{ s}^{-1}}{(\text{mol dm}^{-3})^2} = \dfrac{\text{s}^{-1}}{\text{mol dm}^{-3}} = \text{dm}^3\text{ mol}^{-1}\text{ s}^{-1}$

So the answer is: **k = 440 dm^3 mol^{-1} s^{-1}**

Rate-Concentration Graphs Give the Rate Constants of First Order Reactions

If the overall reaction is **first order**, then the **rate constant** is equal to the **gradient** of the **rate-concentration graph** of that reactant.

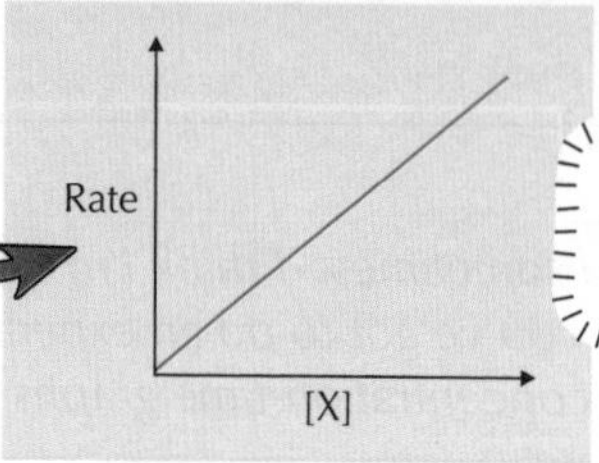

The rate equation of a first order reaction is: rate = k[X], so a graph of rate against [X] has a gradient equal to the rate constant, k.

The Rate Constant

Half-life is the Time for Half the Reactant to Disappear

Chocolate cake has a very short half-life.

1) The **half-life** of a reaction is the time it takes for **half of the reactant** to be used up.
2) The **half-life** of a **first order reaction** is **independent of the concentration**. So each half-life will be the **same length**.
3) This means the half-life of a first order reaction can be read off its **concentration-time graph** by seeing how long it takes to halve the reactant concentration.
4) If you know the **half-life** of a **first order reaction** you can work out the **rate constant** using the equation:

The units are: $\frac{\text{no units}}{\text{s}} = s^{-1}$

$$k = \frac{\ln 2}{t_{1/2}}$$

Example: This graph shows the decomposition of hydrogen peroxide, H_2O_2. Use the graph to measure the half-life at various points and work out the rate constant of the reaction.

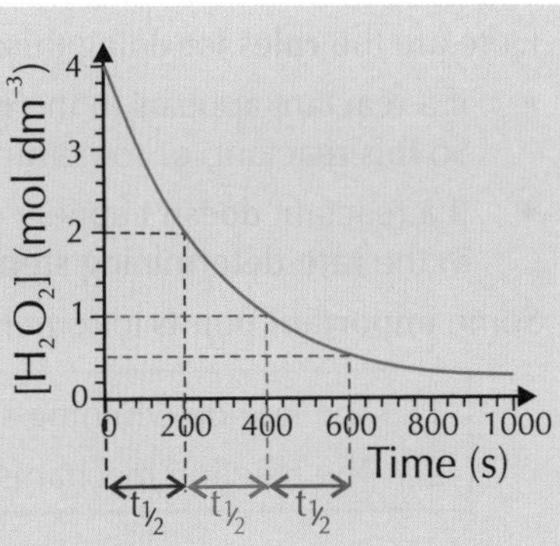

$[H_2O_2]$ from **4** to **2** mol dm^{-3} = **200 s**,
$[H_2O_2]$ from **2** to **1** mol dm^{-3} = **200 s**,
$[H_2O_2]$ from **1** to **0.5** mol dm^{-3} = **200 s**.

The half-life is always **200 s**, regardless of the concentration, so it's a **first order reaction** with respect to **$[H_2O_2]$**.

The rate constant is: $k = \frac{\ln 2}{t_{1/2}} = \frac{\ln 2}{200\text{ s}} = \mathbf{3.47 \times 10^{-3}\ s^{-1}}$

Practice Questions

Q1 How can you use a rate-concentration graph to work out the value of *k* for a first order reaction?

Q2 What's a half-life?

Exam Questions

Q1 The following reaction is second order with respect to NO and first order with respect to H_2.

$$2NO_{(g)} + 2H_{2(g)} \rightarrow 2H_2O_{(g)} + N_{2(g)}$$

a) Write a rate equation for the reaction. [1 mark]

b) The rate of the reaction at 800 °C is 0.00267 mol dm^{-3} s^{-1} when $[H_{2(g)}]$ = 0.00200 mol dm^{-3} and $[NO_{(g)}]$ = 0.00400 mol dm^{-3}. Calculate the value for the rate constant at 800 °C, including units. [2 marks]

Q2 The table shows the results of an experiment on the decomposition of nitrogen(V) oxide at constant temperature. The reaction is first order.

$$2N_2O_5 \rightarrow 4NO_2 + O_2$$

Time (s)	0	50	100	150	200	250	300
$[N_2O_5]$ (mol dm^{-3})	2.50	1.66	1.14	0.76	0.50	0.32	0.22

a) Plot a graph of these results. [3 marks]

b) Calculate the rate constant for the reaction at this temperature. [2 marks]

Q3 The graph on the right shows how the rate of the following reaction changes with the concentration of ester at 298 K:

$CH_3COOCH_3 + H_2O \rightarrow CH_3COOH + CH_3OH$

The reaction is first order with respect to CH_3COOCH_3. Calculate the rate constant of the reaction. [2 marks]

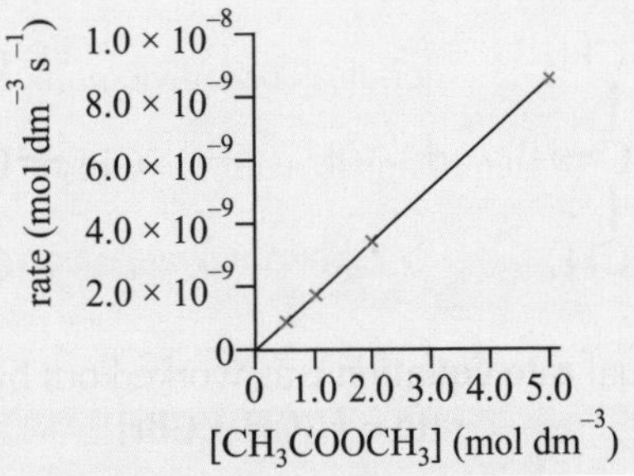

Spiffing page, that — really first rate...

What a lot of calculations and nasty-looking graphs. I'm sure you're thinking a cup of tea and a biscuit wouldn't go a miss after all that maths. I'm sorry to say we're only just getting started with rates though — there's much more to come...

The Rate-Determining Step

You know when you're trying to get out of a room to go to lunch, but it takes ages because not everyone can get through the door at the same time? Well getting through that door is the rate determining step. Talking about lunch...

The **Rate-Determining Step** is the **Slowest Step** in a Multi-Step Reaction

Reaction mechanisms can have **one step** or a **series of steps**.
In a series of steps, each step can have a **different rate**.
The **overall rate** is decided by the step with the **slowest** rate — the **rate-determining step**.

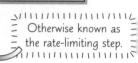

Otherwise known as the rate-limiting step.

Reactants in the **Rate Equation** Affect the **Rate**

The rate equation is handy for helping you work out the **mechanism** of a chemical reaction.
You need to be able to pick out which reactants from the chemical equation are involved in the **rate-determining step**.
Here are the **rules** for doing this:

- If a reactant appears in the **rate equation**, it must affect the **rate**.
  So this reactant, or something derived from it, must be in the **rate-determining step**.

- If a reactant **doesn't** appear in the **rate equation**, then it **isn't** involved
  in the **rate-determining step** (and neither is anything derived from it).

Catalysts can appear in rate equations, so they can be in rate-determining steps too.

Some **important points** to remember about rate-determining steps and mechanisms are:

1) The rate-determining step **doesn't** have to be the first step in a mechanism.
2) The reaction mechanism **can't** usually be predicted from **just** the chemical equation.

You Can Predict the **Rate Equation** from the **Rate-Determining Step**...

The **order of a reaction** with respect to a reactant shows the **number of molecules** of that reactant which are involved in the **rate-determining step**.

So, if a reaction's second order with respect to X, there'll be two molecules of X in the rate-determining step.

Example: The mechanism for the reaction between **chlorine free radicals** and **ozone**, O_3, consists of **two steps**:

$$Cl\bullet_{(g)} + O_{3(g)} \rightarrow ClO\bullet_{(g)} + O_{2(g)} \text{ — slow (rate-determining step)}$$
$$ClO\bullet_{(g)} + O_{(g)} \rightarrow Cl\bullet_{(g)} + O_{2(g)} \text{ — fast}$$

Predict the rate equation for this reaction.

$Cl\bullet$ and O_3 must both be in the rate equation, so the rate equation is of the form: $\text{rate} = k[Cl\bullet]^m[O_3]^n$.
There's only **one** $Cl\bullet$ radical and **one** O_3 molecule in the rate-determining step,
so the **orders**, m and n, are both **1**. So the rate equation is $\text{rate} = k[Cl\bullet][O_3]$.

...And You Can Predict the **Mechanism** from the **Rate Equation**

Knowing exactly which reactants are in the **rate-determining step** gives you an idea of the reaction **mechanism**.

For example, here are two possible mechanisms for the reaction $(CH_3)_3CBr + OH^- \rightarrow (CH_3)_3COH + Br^-$.

①
$$CH_3-\overset{\overset{\displaystyle CH_3}{|}}{\underset{\underset{\displaystyle CH_3}{|}}{C}}-Br + OH^- \rightarrow CH_3-\overset{\overset{\displaystyle CH_3}{|}}{\underset{\underset{\displaystyle CH_3}{|}}{C}}-OH + Br^-$$

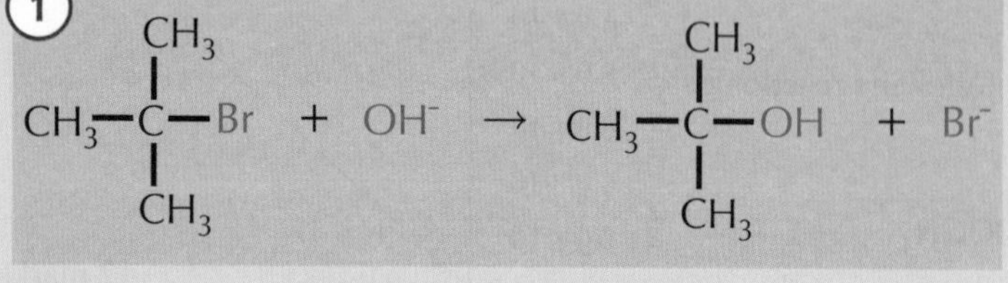

②
$$CH_3-\overset{\overset{\displaystyle CH_3}{|}}{\underset{\underset{\displaystyle CH_3}{|}}{C}}-Br \rightarrow CH_3-\overset{\overset{\displaystyle CH_3}{|}}{\underset{\underset{\displaystyle CH_3}{|}}{C^+}} + Br^-$$
— slow (rate-determining step)

$$CH_3-\overset{\overset{\displaystyle CH_3}{|}}{\underset{\underset{\displaystyle CH_3}{|}}{C^+}} + OH^- \rightarrow CH_3-\overset{\overset{\displaystyle CH_3}{|}}{\underset{\underset{\displaystyle CH_3}{|}}{C}}-OH$$
— fast

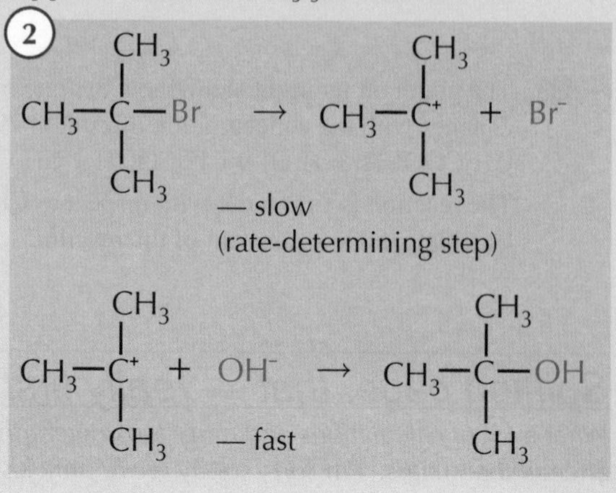

The actual **rate equation** was worked out by rate experiments:
$$\text{rate} = k[(CH_3)_3CBr]$$

OH⁻ isn't in the **rate equation**, so it **can't** be involved in the rate-determining step. So, **mechanism 2** is most likely to be correct — there is **1** molecule of $(CH_3)_3CBr$ (and **no molecules of OH⁻**) in the **rate determining step**. This agrees with the **rate equation**.

The Rate-Determining Step

You have to Take Care when Suggesting a Mechanism

If you're suggesting a mechanism, **watch out** — things might not always be what they seem.
For example, when nitrogen(V) oxide, N_2O_5, decomposes, it forms nitrogen(IV) oxide and oxygen:

$$2N_2O_{5(g)} \rightarrow 4NO_{2(g)} + O_{2(g)}$$

From the chemical equation, it looks like **two** N_2O_5 molecules react with each other.
So you might predict that the reaction is **second order** with respect to N_2O_5... but you'd be wrong.
Experimentally, it's been found that the reaction is **first order** with respect to N_2O_5 — the rate equation is:

$$\text{rate} = k[N_2O_5]$$

This shows that there's only one molecule of N_2O_5 in the rate-determining step.
One **possible mechanism** that fits the rate equation is:

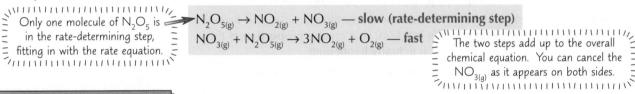

Only one molecule of N_2O_5 is in the rate-determining step, fitting in with the rate equation.

$N_2O_{5(g)} \rightarrow NO_{2(g)} + NO_{3(g)}$ — **slow (rate-determining step)**
$NO_{3(g)} + N_2O_{5(g)} \rightarrow 3NO_{2(g)} + O_{2(g)}$ — **fast**

The two steps add up to the overall chemical equation. You can cancel the $NO_{3(g)}$ as it appears on both sides.

Practice Questions

Q1 What is meant by the rate-determining step?

Q2 Is the rate-determining step always the first step in the reaction?

Q3 What is the connection between the rate equation and the rate-determining step?

Q4 How can the rate-determining step help you to understand the mechanism?

Exam Questions

Q1 The following reaction is first order with respect to H_2 and first order with respect to ICl.

$$H_{2(g)} + 2ICl_{(g)} \rightarrow I_{2(g)} + 2HCl_{(g)}$$

a) Write the rate equation for this reaction. [1 mark]

b) The mechanism for this reaction consists of two steps.

i) Identify the molecules that are in the rate-determining step. Justify your answer. [2 marks]

ii) A chemist suggested the following mechanism for the reaction.

$2ICl_{(g)} \rightarrow I_{2(g)} + Cl_{2(g)}$ slow

$H_{2(g)} + Cl_{2(g)} \rightarrow 2HCl_{(g)}$ fast

Suggest, with reasons, whether this mechanism is likely to be correct. [2 marks]

Q2 The reaction between HBr and oxygen gas occurs rapidly at 700 K.
It can be represented by the equation $4HBr_{(g)} + O_{2(g)} \rightarrow 2H_2O_{(g)} + 2Br_{2(g)}$
The rate equation found by experiment is: Rate = $k[HBr][O_2]$.

a) Explain why the reaction cannot be a one-step reaction. [2 marks]

b) Each of the 4 steps of this reaction involves the reaction of 1 molecule of HBr. Two of the steps are the same. The rate-determining step is the first one and results in the formation of $HBrO_2$. HBrO is formed in step 2. Suggest equations for the full set of 4 reactions. [4 marks]

I found rate-determining step aerobics a bit on the slow side...

These pages show you how rate equations, orders of reaction and reaction mechanisms all tie together and how each actually means something in the grand scheme of Chemistry. It's all very profound. So get it all learnt and answer the questions and then you'll have plenty of time to practise the quickstep for your Strictly Come Dancing routine.

The Arrhenius Equation

The Arrhenius Equation. As the name suggests, it's a bit heinous to learn I'm afraid, but super useful. It links together reaction constants, activation energies and temperatures — all pretty important in the world of reaction rates.

Temperature Changes Affect the Rate Constant

You learnt in Module 3 that increasing the **temperature** of a reaction will increase its **rate**.
Here's a quick recap of what goes on:

1) For a reaction to happen, the particles need to:
   - **Collide** with each other.
   - Have enough energy to react (i.e. have at least the **activation energy**).
   - Have the **right orientation**.

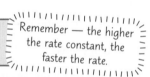

Rate constants are shape-shifters. Here's one in its true form.

2) Increasing the temperature gives the reactant particles more **kinetic energy**. This means the particles **speed up**, so they collide **more often**.
3) Increasing the temperature also means **more** reactant particles will have the required **activation energy** for the reaction, so a greater **proportion** of the collisions will result in the reaction **actually happening**.
4) In other words, **increasing temperature** increases the **reaction rate**.
5) According to the rate equation, reaction rate depends **only** on the rate constant and reactant concentrations.

$$\textbf{rate} = k[\text{A}]^{\text{m}}[\text{B}]^{\text{n}}$$

6) So changing the temperature must **change the rate constant**.

The **rate constant** applies to a **particular reaction** at a **certain temperature**.
At a **higher** temperature, the reaction will have a **higher** rate constant.

Remember — the higher the rate constant, the faster the rate.

The Arrhenius Equation *Links the* Rate Constant *and* Activation Energy

The **Arrhenius equation** (nasty-looking thing in the green box) links the **rate constant** (k) with **activation energy** (E_a, the minimum amount of kinetic energy particles need to react) and **temperature** (T).
This is probably the **worst** equation you're going to meet. Luckily, it'll be on your **data sheet** in the exam, so you don't have to learn it off by heart. But you do need to know what all the different bits **mean**, and how it works.
Here it is:

$$k = Ae^{\frac{-Ea}{RT}}$$

k = rate constant
E_a = activation energy (J mol^{-1})
T = temperature (K)
R = gas constant (8.31 J K^{-1} mol^{-1})
A = the pre-exponential factor (another constant)

It's an exponential relationship. This 'e' is the e^x button on your calculator.

1) As the activation energy, E_a, gets **bigger**, k gets **smaller**.
   You can **test** this out by trying **different numbers** for E_a in the equation... ahh go on, be a devil.
2) So, a **large E_a** will mean a **slow rate**. This **makes sense** when you think about it...
   If a reaction has a **high activation energy**, then not many of the reactant particles will have enough energy to react. So only a **few** of the collisions will result in the reaction actually happening, and the rate will be **slow**.
3) The equation also shows that as the temperature **rises**, **k increases**.

The Arrhenius Equation

Use the **Arrhenius Equation** to Calculate the **Activation Energy**

Putting the **Arrhenius equation** into **logarithmic form** makes it a bit easier to use.

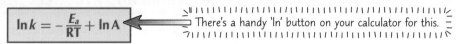

$$\ln k = -\frac{E_a}{RT} + \ln A$$

There's a handy 'ln' button on your calculator for this.

You can use this equation to create an **Arrhenius plot** by plotting **ln *k*** against $\frac{1}{T}$.
This will produce a graph with a **gradient** of $\frac{-E_a}{R}$ and a **y-intercept** of lnA.
So once you know the gradient, you can find both the **activation energy** and the **pre-exponential factor**.

Example: The graph below shows an Arrhenius plot for the decomposition of hydrogen iodide. Calculate the activation energy and the pre-exponential factor for this reaction. R = 8.31 J K^{-1} mol^{-1}.

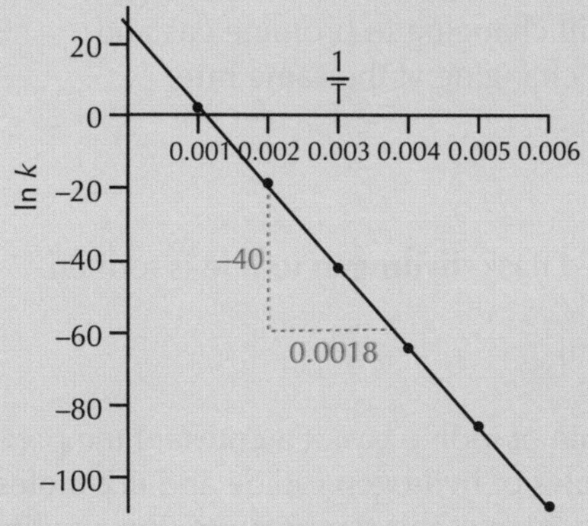

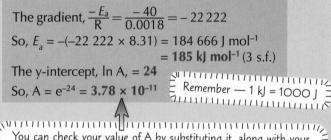

The gradient, $\frac{-E_a}{R} = \frac{-40}{0.0018} = -22\,222$
So, $E_a = -(-22\,222 \times 8.31) = 184\,666$ J mol^{-1}
$= \mathbf{185\ kJ\ mol^{-1}}$ (3 s.f.)
The y-intercept, ln A, = **24**
So, A = e^{-24} = **3.78×10^{-11}**

Remember — 1 kJ = 1000 J

You can check your value of A by substituting it, along with your value of E_a, into the equation ln k = $-E_a$/RT + ln A. You can use any data point from your graph to give you a value for ln k and 1/T.

Practice Questions

Q1 How does temperature affect the value of *k*?

Q2 In the Arrhenius equation, what do the terms *k*, T and R represent?

Q3 The Arrhenius equation is $k = Ae^{-E_a/RT}$. Which one of the following answers is true as E_a increases?
- **A** *k* increases and rate of reaction increases.
- **B** *k* increases and rate of reaction decreases.
- **C** *k* decreases and rate of reaction increases.
- **D** *k* decreases and rate of reaction decreases.

Q4 How would you find the activation energy from a graph of ln *k* against 1/T?

Exam Question

Q1 The table below gives values for the rate constant of the reaction between hydroxide ions and bromoethane at different temperatures.

a) Complete the table. [2 marks]

b) Use the table to plot a graph that would allow you to calculate the activation energy of the reaction. [3 marks]

c) Calculate the activation energy of the reaction. (R = 8.31 J K^{-1} mol^{-1}) [2 marks]

d) Calculate the value of the pre-exponential factor, A. [1 mark]

T (K)	*k*	1/T (K^{-1})	ln *k*
305	0.181	0.00328	–1.71
313	0.468		
323	1.34		
333	3.29	0.00300	1.19
344	10.1		
353	22.7	0.00283	3.13

Who knew rates of reaction could be such a pain in the ar...

...rhenius? That equation's fiddly to learn, but luckily you don't have to — it'll be on your data sheet in the exam. Hurrah. Be careful when you're plotting graphs to work out the activation energy though. There are lots of calculations to do before you get started, so check all your numbers before you draw anything so you don't make any silly mistakes.

The Equilibrium Constant

You met the equilibrium constant in Module 3 (pages 82 and 83) — charming fellow, I'm sure you'll agree. I realise that was a while ago though, so there's a quick recap before any of the new stuff.

At **Equilibrium** the Amounts of Reactants and Products **Stay the Same**

1) Lots of reactions are **reversible** — they can go **both ways**. To show a reaction is reversible, you stick in a $\rightleftharpoons$.
2) A system is said to be in **dynamic equilibrium** if the rate of the **forward reaction** is the **same** as the rate of the **reverse reaction**.
3) At dynamic equilibrium, the forwards and backwards reactions **cancel** each other out and there's no **overall change** in the concentrations of the reactants and products.
4) A **dynamic equilibrium** can only happen in a **closed system** at a **constant temperature**.
5) Equilibria can be set up in **physical systems**, e.g.:

A closed system just means nothing can get in or out.

When **liquid bromine** is shaken in a closed flask, some of it changes to orange **bromine gas**. After a while, **equilibrium** is reached — bromine liquid is **still** changing to bromine gas and bromine gas is still changing to bromine liquid, but they are changing at the **same rate**.

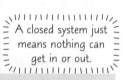

$Br_{2(l)} \rightleftharpoons Br_{2(g)}$

...and **chemical** systems, e.g.:

If **hydrogen gas** and **iodine gas** are mixed together in a closed flask, **hydrogen iodide** is formed.

$$H_{2(g)} + I_{2(g)} \rightleftharpoons 2HI_{(g)}$$

Imagine that **1.0 mole** of hydrogen gas is mixed with **1.0 mole** of iodine gas at a constant temperature of **640 K**. When this mixture reaches equilibrium, there will be **1.6 moles** of hydrogen iodide and **0.2 moles** of both hydrogen gas and iodine gas. No matter how long you leave them at this temperature, the **equilibrium** amounts **never change**. As with the physical system, it's all a matter of the forward and backward rates **being equal**.

6) The **ratio** of products and reactants at dynamic equilibrium is shown by the **equilibrium constant**, K_c.

For the general reaction **aA + bB $\rightleftharpoons$ dD + eE**,

$$K_c = \frac{[D]^d[E]^e}{[A]^a[B]^b}$$

molar concentration (mol dm^{-3})

stoichiometric quantity

The **Units** of K_c Depend on Your **Reaction**

1) You saw how to calculate K_c on page 82 — you just have to stick the **equilibrium concentrations** of the components into the **expression** for K_c.
2) You calculate the **units** of K_c just like you calculated the units of the rate constant — you have to plug all your units into your expression and **cancel** them as much as possible.

Example: Calculate K_c, including units, for the reaction: $PCl_{5(g)} \rightleftharpoons PCl_{3(g)} + Cl_{2(g)}$
At 600 K, the equilibrium concentrations are:
$[PCl_5] = 0.024$ mol dm^{-3}, $[PCl_3] = 0.016$ mol dm^{-3}, $[Cl_2] = 0.016$ mol dm^{-3}

From the expression above, you can see that $K_c = \frac{[PCl_3][Cl_2]}{[PCl_5]}$

So if you put your equilibrium concentrations into the expression, you get: $K_c = \frac{0.016 \times 0.016}{0.024} = \mathbf{0.011}$

Now work out the units for the rate constant by substituting the units for each component into the expression for K_c: $\frac{\cancel{(mol\,dm^{-3})}(mol\,dm^{-3})}{\cancel{(mol\,dm^{-3})}} = \frac{(mol\,dm^{-3})}{1} = \mathbf{mol\,dm^{-3}}$

So $K_c = \mathbf{0.011\ mol\ dm^{-3}}$

The Equilibrium Constant

Reactions Can be **Homogeneous** or **Heterogeneous**

If all the reactants and products in a reaction are in the same **state** (e.g. they're all gases, or all in solution) then the reaction is **homogeneous**. The dynamic equilibria you've met so far have all been homogeneous.

But if the reactants and products in a reaction are in **different states** the reaction is **heterogeneous**.
A **heterogeneous** reaction can change **what** you put in the **equilibrium constant expression**. The rule is:

- If the mixture is **homogeneous**, **all** the reactants and products are put into the expression for the equilibrium constant.
- If the mixture is **heterogeneous** only **gases** and **aqueous** substances go into the expression for the equilibrium constant (any solids or liquids get left out).

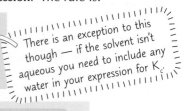

There is an exception to this though — if the solvent isn't aqueous you need to include any water in your expression for K_c.

Example: a) Write an expression for the equilibrium constant of the following reaction:
$Cu_{(s)} + 2Ag^+_{(aq)} \rightleftharpoons Cu^{2+}_{(aq)} + 2Ag_{(s)}$

The reactants and products are a **mixture** of **aqueous** and **solid**. So the reaction is **heterogeneous**. Only the **aqueous** substances go into the equilibrium constant.

So $K_c = \frac{[Cu^{2+}]}{[Ag^+]^2}$

b) At a certain temperature, there are 0.431 mol dm^{-3} Ag^+ and 0.193 mol dm^{-3} Cu^{2+} at equilibrium. Calculate K_c and give its units.

$$K_c = \frac{[Cu^{2+}]}{[Ag^+]^2} = \frac{0.193}{(0.431)^2} = 1.04$$

$$\text{The units are } \frac{(\text{mol dm}^{-3})}{(\text{mol dm}^{-3})^2} = \frac{1}{(\text{mol dm}^{-3})} = \textbf{mol}^{-1}\textbf{ dm}^3$$

So at 298 K, K_c = **1.04 mol^{-1} dm^3**

Practice Questions

Q1 Write the expression for K_c for the following reaction: $N_{2(g)} + O_{2(g)} \rightleftharpoons 2NO_{(g)}$

Q2 What are the units for K_c in the reaction in question 1?

Q3 What's a heterogeneous reaction?

Exam Questions

Q1 A sample of pure $N_2O_{4(g)}$ is placed in a sealed 6.00 dm^3 flask at 298 K and allowed to reach equilibrium with $NO_{2(g)}$.

$N_2O_{4(g)} \rightleftharpoons 2NO_{2(g)}$

At equilibrium there are 23.0 g $N_2O_{4(g)}$ and 0.389 g $NO_{2(g)}$.

Calculate K_c for the equilibrium at 298 K and give its units. [4 marks]

Hint: You'll first need to convert the masses into concentrations. You'll need the equations moles = $\frac{\text{mass}}{M_r}$ and concentration = $\frac{\text{moles}}{\text{volume}}$.

Q2 Hexaaqua cobalt(II) ($[Co(H_2O)_6]^{2+}$) and ammonia (NH_3) react to form the following equilibrium:

$[Co(H_2O)_6]^{2+}_{(aq)} + 6NH_{3(aq)} \rightleftharpoons [Co(NH_3)_6]^{2+}_{(aq)} + 6H_2O_{(l)}$

At 30 °C, the equilibrium concentrations are:
$[Co(NH_3)_6]^{2+}_{(aq)}$ = 2.19 mol dm^{-3}, $[Co(H_2O)_6]^{2+}_{(aq)}$ = 0.541 mol dm^{-3} and $[NH_{3(aq)}]$ = 0.234 mol dm^{-3}.

a) Write an expression for K_c for this reaction. [1 mark]

b) Calculate the value of K_c at 30 °C and give its units. [2 marks]

Understanding equilibria — it's a constant struggle...

Look carefully at the state symbols when you're writing out your expression for K_c. If the reaction is heterogeneous then liquids and solids never ever go in your expression for K_c. But in a homogeneous reaction you would put everything into your expression for K_c. Make sure you get that under your belt, so you don't end up in a pickle.

Equilibrium Concentrations

A few more calculations using K_c coming up. You'll need to look carefully at the reaction equations in each case — they can give you clues about the concentrations of different components at equilibrium.

K_c can be used to Work Out **Concentrations** in an **Equilibrium Mixture**

You may be given K_c and **some** of the equilibrium concentrations, and asked to **work out** the concentrations of the **other components**. You can do this by just **rearranging** your expression for K_c.

Example: When ethanoic acid was allowed to reach equilibrium with ethanol at 25 °C, it was found that the equilibrium mixture contained 2.0 mol dm^{-3} ethanoic acid and 3.5 mol dm^{-3} ethanol. The K_c of the equilibrium is 4.0 at 25 °C. What are the concentrations of the other components?

$$CH_3COOH_{(l)} + C_2H_5OH_{(l)} \rightleftharpoons CH_3COOC_2H_{5(l)} + H_2O_{(l)}$$

Write out the expression for K_c and substitute in all the values you know:

$$K_c = \frac{[CH_3COOC_2H_5][H_2O]}{[CH_3COOH][C_2H_5OH]} \Longrightarrow 4.0 = \frac{[CH_3COOC_2H_5][H_2O]}{2.0 \times 3.5}$$

Rearranging this gives: $[CH_3COOC_2H_5][H_2O] = 4.0 \times 2.0 \times 3.5 = 28.0$

But from the equation, $[CH_3COOC_2H_5] = [H_2O]$.

The equation tells you that for every mole of $CH_3COOC_2H_5$ produced, one mole of H_2O is also produced, so their concentrations will always be equal. (The reactant concentrations aren't the same since they were different at the start).

So: $[CH_3COOC_2H_5] = [H_2O] = \sqrt{28} = 5.3$ mol dm^{-3}

The concentration of $CH_3COOC_2H_5$ and H_2O is **5.3 mol dm^{-3}**.

The **Reaction Equation** Helps You Work Out **Equilibrium Concentrations**

If you know the initial concentrations of all of your reactants, and the equilibrium concentration of one of them, you can use the reaction equation to work out the concentrations of all the components at equilibrium. You can use this to calculate K_c.

Example: 500 cm^3 0.10 mol dm^{-3} iron(II) sulfate solution is added to 500 cm^3 0.10 mol dm^{-3} silver nitrate at 298 K to set up the following equilibrium reaction:

$$Fe^{2+}_{(aq)} + Ag^{+}_{(aq)} \rightleftharpoons Fe^{3+}_{(aq)} + Ag_{(s)}$$

Once the solution has reached equilibrium, a sample is taken and the concentration of Fe^{2+} ions is found by colorimetry. Given that at equilibrium, $[Fe^{2+}_{(aq)}] = 0.0439$ mol dm^{-3}, calculate K_c.

The **starting concentrations** of Ag^+ and Fe^{2+} are the same and equal to $(0.10 \div 2) =$ **0.05 mol dm^{-3}**.

500 cm^3 of each solution is diluted to 1000 cm^3, so the concentration of each reactant is halved.

The **colorimetry result** gives you an **equilibrium concentration** for **Fe^{2+}** of **0.0439 mol dm^{-3}**.

The equation tells you 1 mole of Fe^{2+} reacts with 1 mole of Ag^+ to form 1 mole of Fe^{3+} and 1 mole of Ag. In this particular reaction **solid** silver is formed, so you **don't** need to include it in the expression for K_c.

The equilibrium concentration of **Ag^+** will be the same as Fe^{2+} i.e. **0.0439 mol dm^{-3}**.
The equilibrium concentration of **Fe^{3+}** will be $0.05 - 0.0439 =$ **0.00610 mol dm^{-3}**.

So $K_c = \dfrac{[Fe^{3+}]}{[Fe^{2+}][Ag^+]} = \dfrac{0.00610}{0.0439 \times 0.0439} = \mathbf{3.17}$

The reaction is heterogeneous, so solids and liquids are omitted from the expression for K_c (see page 127).

The units of K_c are: $\dfrac{\text{mol dm}^{-3}}{(\text{mol dm}^{-3})(\text{mol dm}^{-3})} = \text{mol}^{-1}\text{ dm}^3$

At 298 K, K_c for this reaction = 3.17 mol^{-1} dm^3

Equilibrium Concentrations

Use the Equilibrium Concentration of a **Product** to Find the Others

You might have to figure out some of the **equilibrium concentrations** before you can find K_c. You can do this if you know the **initial concentrations** of your **reactants** and the **equilibrium concentration** of your product.

Example: 0.100 mol dm^{-3} Cu^{2+} ions are mixed with 0.300 mol dm^{-3} HCl to form the following equilibrium:

$$Cu^{2+}_{(aq)} + 4Cl^-_{(aq)} \rightleftharpoons [CuCl_4]^{2-}_{(aq)}$$

a) At equilibrium, there are x moles of $[CuCl_4]^{2-}_{(aq)}$. Write an expression for K_c in terms of x.

From the equation, you can see that for every mole of $[CuCl_4]^{2-}_{(aq)}$ formed, you will lose **1 mole $Cu^{2+}_{(aq)}$** and **4 moles $Cl^-_{(aq)}$** from your initial reactant concentrations.
So if x moles of $[CuCl_4]^{2-}_{(aq)}$ have **formed**, you will have **lost x** moles $Cu^{2+}_{(aq)}$ and **$4x$** moles $Cl^-_{(aq)}$.
So the equilibrium concentrations will be:
$Cu^{2+}_{(aq)}$ = (initial $Cu^{2+}_{(aq)}$ concentration) – x and **$Cl^-_{(aq)}$ = (initial $Cl^-_{(aq)}$ concentration) – $4x$**
You can use this information to construct a table:

Equilibrium component	$Cu^{2+}_{(aq)}$	$Cl^-_{(aq)}$	$[CuCl_4]^{2-}_{(aq)}$
Initial concentration (mol dm^{-3})	0.100	0.300	0
Equilibrium concentration (mol dm^{-3})	$0.100 - x$	$0.300 - 4x$	x

From your equilibrium concentrations, you can see that: $K_c = \frac{[[CuCl_4]^{2-}]}{[Cu^{2+}][Cl^-]^4} = \frac{x}{(0.100 - x)(0.300 - 4x)^4}$

b) At 291 K, the concentration of $[CuCl_4]^{2-}$ in solution is 0.0637 mol dm^{-3}. Calculate K_c.

You can work out K_c by substituting the concentration of $[CuCl_4]^{2-}$ at equilibrium for x:

x = 0.0637 mol dm^{-3}, so $K_c = \frac{0.0637}{(0.100 - 0.0637)(0.300 - 4 \times 0.0637)^4}$ = **4.20 × 10^5 mol^{-4} dm^{12}**

Practice Questions

Q1 Write down an expression you could use to work out [C] for the reaction $A + B \rightleftharpoons C$.

Q2 Calculate [C] given that at equilibrium [A] = 0.152 mol dm^{-3}, [B] = 0.586 mol dm^{-3} and K_c = 7.35 mol^{-1} dm^3.

Exam Questions

Q1 When 42.5 g nitrogen dioxide was heated in a vessel of volume 22.8 dm^3 at 500 °C, it dissociated to form x mol dm^{-3} of oxygen in the equilibrium mixture. $2NO_{2(g)} \rightleftharpoons 2NO_{(g)} + O_{2(g)}$.

a) Calculate the starting number of moles of nitrogen dioxide. [1 mark]

b) Write an expression for K_c in terms of x. [2 marks]

c) Calculate the value for K_c at 500 °C, and give its units, given that there were 14.1 g oxygen in the equilibrium mixture. [2 marks]

Q2 0.100 moles of dichromate(VI) ions and 0.100 moles of water were mixed together in a non-aqueous solvent and allowed to reach equilibrium at a fixed temperature: $Cr_2O_7^{2-}{}_{(aq)} + H_2O_{(l)} \rightarrow 2CrO_4^{2-}{}_{(aq)} + 2H^+_{(aq)}$

a) Write an expression for K_c for this reaction. [1 mark]

b) At equilibrium there were 0.0300 moles of $Cr_2O_7^{2-}$ ions.
If the total volume of the solution was 100 cm^3, calculate the equilibrium concentrations of:
i) H_2O ii) CrO_4^{2-} iii) H^+ [3 marks]

c) Calculate a value for K_c at this temperature. [2 marks]

Want to find K_c? It'll need your concentration...

Lots of maths on these pages, so make sure you've worked through all the examples and understand what's happening. Whatever question you're doing, always start by writing down an expression for K_c and all the concentrations you know.

Gas Equilibria

It's easier to talk about gases in terms of their pressures rather than their molar concentrations. If you want to do this, you need a slightly different equilibrium constant — it's called K_p (but I'm afraid it's got nothing to do with peanuts).

The **Total Pressure** is **Equal** to the **Sum** of the **Partial Pressures**

In a mixture of gases, each individual gas exerts its own pressure — this is called its **partial pressure**.

The **total pressure** of a gas mixture is the **sum** of all the **partial pressures** of the individual gases.

You might have to put this fact to use in pressure calculations:

Example: When 3.0 moles of the gas PCl_5 is heated, it decomposes into PCl_3 and Cl_2: $PCl_{5(g)} \rightleftharpoons PCl_{3(g)} + Cl_{2(g)}$
In a sealed vessel at 500 K, the equilibrium mixture contains chlorine with a partial pressure of 263 kPa. If the total pressure of the mixture is 714 kPa, what is the partial pressure of PCl_5?

From the equation you know that PCl_3 and Cl_2 are produced in equal amounts, so the partial pressures of these two gases are the **same** at equilibrium — they're both 263 kPa.

Total pressure = $p(PCl_5) + p(PCl_3) + p(Cl_2)$

p just means partial pressure.

$714 = p(PCl_5) + 263 + 263$

So the partial pressure of PCl_5 = 714 – 263 – 263 = **188 kPa**

Partial Pressures can be Worked Out from **Mole Fractions**

A '**mole fraction**' is just the **proportion** of a gas mixture that is a particular gas. So if you've got four moles of gas in total, and two of them are gas A, the mole fraction of gas A is ½. There are **two formulas** you've got to know:

1) Mole fraction of a gas in a mixture = $\dfrac{\textbf{number of moles of gas}}{\textbf{total number of moles of gas in the mixture}}$
2) Partial pressure of a gas = **mole fraction of gas × total pressure of the mixture**

Example: When 3.0 mol of PCl_5 is heated in a sealed vessel, the equilibrium mixture contains 1.75 mol of chlorine. If the total pressure of the mixture is 714 kPa, what is the partial pressure of PCl_5?

PCl_3 and Cl_2 are produced in equal amounts, so there'll be **1.75 moles** of PCl_3 too.
1.75 moles of PCl_5 must have decomposed so (3.0 – 1.75 =) **1.25 moles** of PCl_5 must be left at equilibrium.
This means that the total number of moles of gas at equilibrium = 1.75 + 1.75 + 1.25 = **4.75**
So the mole fraction of $PCl_5 = \dfrac{1.25}{4.75} = \mathbf{0.263}$
The partial pressure of PCl_5 = mole fraction × total pressure = 0.263 × 714 = **188 kPa**

The **Equilibrium Constant K_p** is Calculated from **Partial Pressures**

The expression for K_p is just like the one for K_c — except you use partial pressures instead of concentrations.

For the equilibrium $aA_{(g)} + bB_{(g)} \rightleftharpoons dD_{(g)} + eE_{(g)}$: $K_p = \dfrac{p(D)^d p(E)^e}{p(A)^a p(B)^b}$

There are no square brackets because they're partial pressures, not molar concentrations.

To **calculate K_p**, you just have to put the partial pressures in the expression. You work out the **units** like you did for K_c.

Example: Calculate K_p for the decomposition of PCl_5 gas at 500 K (as shown above).
The partial pressures of each gas are: $p(PCl_5)$ = 188 kPa, $p(PCl_3)$ = 263 kPa, $p(Cl_2)$ = 263 kPa

$$K_p = \frac{p(Cl_2)p(PCl_3)}{p(PCl_5)} = \frac{263\,\text{kPa} \times 263\,\text{kPa}}{188\,\text{kPa}} = 368$$

The units for K_p are worked out by putting the units into the expression instead of the numbers, and cancelling (like for K_c): $K_p = \dfrac{\text{kPa} \times \text{kPa}}{\text{kPa}} = \text{kPa}$. So, $\mathbf{K_p = 368\ kPa}$

Gas Equilibria

K_p can be Used to Find Partial Pressures

You might be given the K_p and have to use it to calculate **equilibrium partial pressures**.

Example: An equilibrium exists between ethanoic acid monomers, CH_3COOH, and dimers, $(CH_3COOH)_2$. At 160 °C the K_p for the reaction $(CH_3COOH)_{2(g)} \rightleftharpoons 2CH_3COOH_{(g)}$ is 180 kPa. At this temperature the partial pressure of the dimer, $(CH_3COOH)_2$, is 28.5 kPa. Calculate the partial pressure of the monomer in this equilibrium and state the total pressure exerted by the equilibrium mixture.

First, use the chemical equilibrium to write an expression for K_p: $K_p = \frac{p(CH_3COOH)^2}{p((CH_3COOH)_2)}$

This rearranges to give: $p(CH_3COOH)^2 = K_p \times p((CH_3COOH)_2) = 180 \times 28.5 = 5130$

$p(CH_3COOH) = \sqrt{5130} = 71.6$ kPa

So the total pressure of the equilibrium mixture = 28.5 + 71.6 = **100.1 kPa**

Add the two partial pressures together to get the total pressure.

K_p for Heterogeneous Equilibria Still Only Includes Gases

You met the idea of homogeneous and heterogeneous equilibria on page 127.
Up until now we've only thought about K_p expressions for **homogeneous equilibria**.
If you're writing an expression for K_p for a **heterogeneous equilibrium**, you don't include **solids** or **liquids**.

Example: Write an expression for K_p for the following reaction: $NH_4HS_{(s)} \rightleftharpoons NH_{3(g)} + H_2S_{(g)}$.

The equilibrium is **heterogeneous** — a solid decomposes to form two gases. Solids don't get included in K_p, so $K_p = p(NH_3)\,p(H_2S)$.

There's no bottom line as the reactant is a solid.

Practice Questions

Q1 What is meant by partial pressure?

Q2 How do you work out the mole fraction of a gas?

Q3 Write the expression for K_p for the following equilibrium: $NH_4HS_{(g)} \rightleftharpoons NH_{3(g)} + H_2S_{(g)}$

Exam Questions

Q1 At high temperatures, SO_2Cl_2 dissociates according to the equation $SO_2Cl_{2(g)} \rightleftharpoons SO_{2(g)} + Cl_{2(g)}$. When 1.50 moles of SO_2Cl_2 dissociates at 700 K, the equilibrium mixture contains SO_2 with a partial pressure of 60.2 kPa. The mixture has a total pressure of 141 kPa.

a) Write an expression for K_p for this reaction. [1 mark]

b) Calculate the partial pressure of Cl_2 and the partial pressure of SO_2Cl_2 in the equilibrium mixture. [2 marks]

c) Calculate a value for K_p for this reaction and give its units. [2 marks]

Q2 When nitric oxide and oxygen were mixed in a 2:1 mole ratio at a constant temperature in a sealed flask, an equilibrium was set up according to the equation $2NO_{(g)} + O_{2(g)} \rightleftharpoons 2NO_{2(g)}$. The partial pressure of the nitric oxide (NO) at equilibrium was 36 kPa and the total pressure in the flask was 99 kPa.

a) Deduce the partial pressure of oxygen in the equilibrium mixture. [1 mark]

b) Calculate the partial pressure of nitrogen dioxide in the equilibrium mixture. [1 mark]

c) Write an expression for the equilibrium constant, K_p, for this reaction and calculate its value at this temperature. State its units. [2 marks]

Pressure pushing down on me, pressing down on you... Under pressure...

Partial pressures are like concentrations for gases. The more of a substance you've got in a solution, the higher the concentration, and the more of a gas you've got in a container, the higher the partial pressure. It's all to do with how many molecules are crashing into the sides. With gases though, you've got to keep the lid on tight or they'll escape.

More on Equilibrium Constants

In Module 3 you saw how changing conditions can change the position of the equilibrium. That's great, but you also need to be able to predict what will happen to the equilibrium constant when you change conditions.

If ***Conditions Change*** *the* ***Position of Equilibrium*** *Will Move*

1) If you **change** the **concentration**, **pressure** or **temperature** of a reversible reaction, you're going to **alter** the **position of equilibrium**. This just means you'll end up with **different amounts** of reactants and products at equilibrium.
2) If the change causes **more product** to form, then you say that the equilibrium shifts to the **right**. If **less product** forms, then the equilibrium has shifted to the **left**.
3) In Module 3, you met Le Chatelier's principle, which lets you predict how the **position of equilibrium** will change if a **condition changes**. Here it is again:

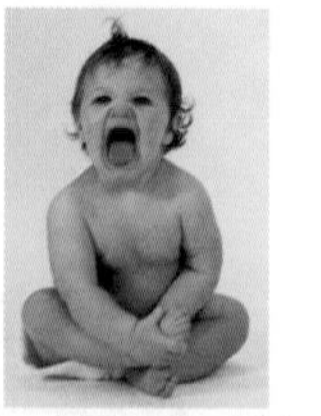
The removal of his dummy was a change that Maxwell always opposed.

> If there's a change in **concentration**, **pressure** or **temperature**, the equilibrium will move to help **counteract** the change.

4) So, basically, if you **raise the temperature**, the position of equilibrium will shift to try to **cool things down**. And if you **raise the pressure or concentration**, the position of equilibrium will shift to try to **reduce it again**.
5) The **size** of the equilibrium constant tells you where the equilibrium lies:
   - If the equilibrium constant is **greater than 1**, then there will be more **products** than reactants (the equilibrium will lie to the **right**). The **larger** the value of K_c, the further to the right the equilibrium lies.
   - If the equilibrium constant is **less than 1**, then there will be more **reactants** than products (the equilibrium will lie to the **left**). The **smaller** the value of K_c, the further to the left the equilibrium lies.

Temperature *Changes* ***Alter*** *the Equilibrium Constant*

1) From Le Chatelier's principle, you know that an **increase** in temperature causes more of the product of an **endothermic** reaction to form so that the extra heat is absorbed. Le Chatelier also states that a **decrease** in temperature causes more of the product of an **exothermic** reaction to form.
2) The equilibrium constant for a reaction depends on the **temperature**. Changing the temperature alters the position of equilibrium and the **value** of the equilibrium constant.

Example: The reaction below is exothermic in the forward direction. If you increase the temperature, the equilibrium shifts to the left to absorb the extra heat. What happens to K_p?

Exothermic ⟶

$$2SO_{2(g)} + O_{2(g)} \rightleftharpoons 2SO_{3(g)} \quad \Delta H = -197 \text{ kJ mol}^{-1}$$

⟵ Endothermic

An exothermic reaction releases heat and has a negative ΔH. An endothermic reaction absorbs heat and has a positive ΔH.

If the equilibrium shifts to the left, then less product will form. By looking at the expression for the equilibrium constant, you can see that if there's less product, the value of K_p will decrease.

This reaction is between gases, so it's easiest to use K_p, but it's exactly the same for K_c and the other equilibrium constants you'll meet in the next few pages.

$$K_p = \frac{p(SO_3)^2}{p(SO_2)^2 p(O_2)}$$

There's less product and more reactant, so the number on the top gets smaller and the number on the bottom gets bigger. This means K_p must have decreased.

3) The general rule for what happens to an equilibrium constant when you change the **temperature** of a reaction is that:

> - If changing the temperature causes **less product** to form, the equilibrium moves to the **left**, and the equilibrium constant **decreases**.
> - If changing the temperature causes **more product** to form, the equilibrium moves to the **right**, and the equilibrium constant **increases**.

More on Equilibrium Constants

Concentration and Pressure Changes Don't Affect the Equilibrium Constant

Concentration

The value of the **equilibrium constant** is **fixed** at a given temperature. So if the concentration of one thing in the equilibrium mixture **changes** then the concentrations of the others must change to keep the value of K_c the same.

E.g. $CH_3COOH_{(l)} + C_2H_5OH_{(l)} \rightleftharpoons CH_3COOC_2H_{5(l)} + H_2O_{(l)}$

If you **increase** the concentration of CH_3COOH then the equilibrium will move to the **right** to get rid of the extra CH_3COOH — so more $CH_3COOC_2H_5$ and H_2O are produced. This keeps the **equilibrium constant** the same.

Pressure

Increasing the pressure shifts the equilibrium to the side with **fewer** gas molecules — this **reduces** the pressure. **Decreasing** the pressure shifts the equilibrium to the side with **more** gas molecules. This **raises** the pressure again. K_p (or K_c) stays the **same**, no matter what you do to the pressure.

E.g. $2SO_{2(g)} + O_{2(g)} \rightleftharpoons 2SO_{3(g)}$

There are 3 moles on the left, but only 2 on the right.
So an **increase in pressure** would shift the equilibrium to the **right**.

So, to summarise, concentration and pressure **don't** affect the **values** of K_c or K_p, but they **do** change the **amounts** of products and reactants present at equilibrium. Changes in **temperature** not only alter the **amounts** of products and reactants present at equilibrium, but also **change** the **value** of the equilibrium constants.

Catalysts have **NO EFFECT** on the **position of equilibrium** or the value of K_c/K_p. They **can't** increase **yield** — but they **do** mean equilibrium is approached **faster**.

Practice Questions

Q1 If you raise the temperature of a reversible reaction, in which direction will the reaction move?

Q2 Does temperature change affect the equilibrium constant?

Q3 Why doesn't concentration affect the equilibrium constant?

Exam Questions

Q1 At temperature T_1, the equilibrium constant K_c for the following reaction is 0.67 mol^{-1} dm^3.

$$2SO_{2(g)} + O_{2(g)} \rightleftharpoons 2SO_{3(g)} \quad \Delta H = -196 \text{ kJmol}^{-1}.$$

a) When equilibrium was established at a different temperature, T_2, the value of K_c increased. State which of T_1 or T_2 is the lower temperature and explain why. [3 marks]

b) The experiment was repeated exactly the same in all respects at T_1, except a flask of smaller volume was used. How would this change affect the yield of sulfur trioxide and the value of K_c? [2 marks]

Q2 The reaction between methane and steam is used to produce hydrogen. The forward reaction is endothermic.

$$CH_{4(g)} + H_2O_{(g)} \rightleftharpoons CO_{(g)} + 3H_{2(g)}$$

a) Write an equation for K_p for this reaction. [1 mark]

b) Which of the following will cause the value of K_p to increase?

A Increasing the temperature. **B** Using a catalyst

C Decreasing the pressure. **D** Decreasing the temperature [1 mark]

It's just a jump to the left, and then a step to the right...

Hmm, sounds like there's a song in there somewhere. I've now got a vision of chemists in lab coats dancing at a Xmas party... Let's not go there. Instead make sure you really get your head round this concept of changing conditions and the equilibrium shifting to compensate. Reread until you've definitely got it — it makes this topic much easier to learn.

Acids and Bases

Remember this stuff? Well, it's all down to Brønsted and Lowry — they've got a lot to answer for.

An Acid **Releases** Protons — a Base **Accepts** Protons

Brønsted-Lowry acids are **proton donors** — they release **hydrogen ions** (H^+) when they're mixed with water. You never get H^+ ions by themselves in water though — they're always combined with H_2O to form **hydroxonium ions, H_3O^+**.

$$HA_{(aq)} + H_2O_{(l)} \rightarrow H_3O^+_{(aq)} + A^-_{(aq)}$$

Brønsted-Lowry bases are **proton acceptors**. When they're in solution, they grab **hydrogen ions** from water molecules.

$$B_{(aq)} + H_2O_{(l)} \rightarrow BH^+_{(aq)} + OH^-_{(aq)}$$

HA is any old acid and B is just a random base.

Some Acids Can Release **More than One** Proton

1) Acids like **HCl** and **HNO_3** only have **one proton** that they can release into solution. These are **monobasic** acids.
2) But some acids, such as sulfuric acid (H_2SO_4) or phosphoric acid (H_3PO_4), have **more than one** proton that they can release into solution.
3) **Sulfuric acid** can release **two protons** so it's a **dibasic acid:** $H_2SO_{4(aq)} \rightleftharpoons 2H^+_{(aq)} + SO_4^{2-}{}_{(aq)}$
4) **Phosphoric acid** is a **tribasic** acid. It can release **three protons** into solution: $H_3PO_{4(aq)} \rightleftharpoons 3H^+_{(aq)} + PO_4^{3-}{}_{(aq)}$

Monobasic acids are also known as monoprotic, dibasic as diprotic... etc.

Acids and Bases form **Conjugate Pairs**

A species is just any type of chemical — it could be an atom, a molecule, an ion...

1) Conjugate pairs are species that are linked by the **transfer** of a **proton**. They're always on opposite sides of the reaction equation.
2) The species that has **lost** a proton is the **conjugate base** and the species that has **gained** a proton is the **conjugate acid**.
3) When Brønsted-Lowry acids and bases react together, the equilibrium below is set up.

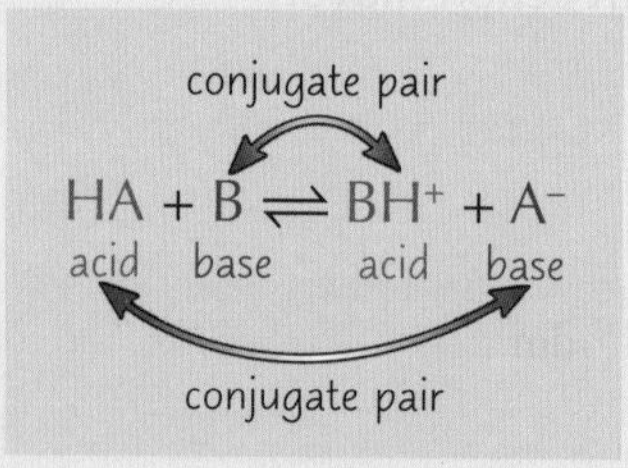

- In the **forward reaction**, HA acts as an **acid** as it **donates** a proton.
- In the **reverse reaction**, A^- acts as a **base** and **accepts** a proton from the BH^+ ion to form HA.
- HA and A^- are called a **conjugate pair** — HA is the **conjugate acid** of A^- and A^- is the **conjugate base** of the acid, HA.
- Similarly, B and BH^+ are a conjugate pair. The base B takes a proton to form **BH^+** — so B is the **conjugate base** of BH^+, and BH^+ is the **conjugate acid** of B.

4) **Water** is a special case — it reacts with acids to form a **conjugate acid** (H_3O^+), and reacts with **bases** to form a **conjugate base** (OH^-).

$$HA_{(aq)} + H_2O_{(l)} \rightleftharpoons A^-_{(aq)} + H_3O^+_{(aq)}$$

$$B_{(aq)} + H_2O_{(l)} \rightleftharpoons BH^+_{(aq)} + OH^-_{(aq)}$$

Acids React with **Metals** and **Bases**

You saw how acids can react in Module 2, but here's a quick recap:

1) **Reactive metals** react with acids releasing **hydrogen gas**. The metal atoms **donate electrons** to the **H^+ ions** in the acid solution. The metal atoms are **oxidised** and the H^+ ions are **reduced**. E.g. $Ca_{(s)} + 2H^+_{(aq)} \rightarrow Ca^{2+}_{(aq)} + H_{2(g)}$
2) **Carbonates** react with acids to produce **carbon dioxide** and **water**. $CO_3^{2-}{}_{(aq)} + 2H^+_{(aq)} \rightarrow H_2O_{(l)} + CO_{2(g)}$
3) **Alkalis** are bases that release **hydroxide ions** in water. They react with acids to form **water**. $H^+_{(aq)} + OH^-_{(aq)} \rightarrow H_2O_{(l)}$
4) Most insoluble bases are **metal oxides**. Like alkalis, they react with acids to form **water**. $2H^+_{(aq)} + O^{2-}_{(s)} \rightarrow H_2O_{(l)}$

These are ionic equations — they only include the reacting particles.

Acids and Bases

Acid-Base Theory Took Time to *Develop*

Scientific theories can take **years** to develop. A scientist will come up with an idea, and then someone else will find holes in the theory and make changes to **improve** it. This is how the **Brønsted-Lowry theory** of acids and bases came about.

Lavoisier thought it was all to do with oxygen...

Lavoisier came up with the first theory of acids and bases in the 18th century. He didn't know the formulas of compounds like hydrochloric acid but he did know that sulfuric acid had the formula H_2SO_4 and nitric acid had the formula HNO_3. So he proposed that acids had to have **oxygen** in them. It was later shown that acids like hydrochloric acid (HCl) and hydrogen sulfide (H_2S) don't have any oxygen in them at all.

Arrhenius thought it was about H^+ and OH^-...

At the end of the 19th century, a chemist called Arrhenius suggested that acids **release protons** in aqueous solution, whilst bases release **hydroxide ions**. He said that when acids and bases react together they form **water** and a **salt**. This is true for loads of examples, but doesn't work for bases such as **ammonia** (NH_3), which don't contain any hydroxide ions.

The Brønsted-Lowry theory is based on Arrhenius' work...

Brønsted and Lowry came up with their definition of acids and bases independently of one another. It's clearly based on Arrhenius' theory, but broadens the definition of a base to be a **proton acceptor**. They also came up with the idea that acids and bases react to form **conjugate pairs**, rather than a salt and water. This definition currently explains most of our observations, so is one of the theories we still use today — around 100 years later.

Brønsted and Lowry were off to make holes in other people's theories.

Practice Questions

Q1 Give the Brønsted-Lowry definitions of an acid and a base.

Q2 What's the difference between a monobasic, a dibasic and a tribasic acid?

Q3 What is the conjugate base of water? And the conjugate acid?

Q4 Write an ionic equation to show the reaction between copper(II) oxide and hydrochloric acid.

Exam Questions

Q1 Magnesium completely dissolves in aqueous sulfuric acid, $H_2SO_{4\,(aq)}$.

a) Which ions are present in a solution of sulfuric acid? [1 mark]

b) Write an ionic equation for the reaction of sulfuric acid and magnesium. [1 mark]

c) What is the conjugate base of sulfuric acid? [1 mark]

Q2 a) Write an equation to show the equilibrium set up when the acid hydrogen cyanide, HCN, is added to water. [1 mark]

b) From your equation, identify the two conjugate pairs formed. [2 marks]

c) Which ion links conjugate pairs? [1 mark]

Q3 a) Write an equation to show the equilibrium set up when ammonia, a weak base, is dissolved in water. [1 mark]

b) Is water behaving as an acid or a base in this equilibrium? Give a reason for your answer. [1 mark]

c) What species forms a conjugate pair with water in this reaction? [1 mark]

I do like bases — they're just so accepting...

Make sure you can identify conjugate pairs. Remember — they're always on opposite sides of the equation, and you can switch between them by adding or removing protons. And have another read of how the Brønsted-Lowry theory was thought up — the way it was developed over time from other theories is a prime example of How Science Works.

pH

Just when you thought it was safe to turn the page — it's even more about acids and bases. This page is positively swarming with calculations and constants...

*The **pH Scale** is a Measure of **Hydrogen Ion Concentration***

pH is a measure of how **acidic** or **basic** something is. It measures the **concentration** of **hydrogen** ions in solution. **Concentration of hydrogen ions** can vary enormously so a **logarithmic scale** called the **pH scale** is used.

$pH = -\log_{10}[H^+]$

The pH scale goes from **0** (very acidic) to **14** (very alkaline). **pH 7** is **neutral**.

The stronger the acid, the lower the pH.

1) If you know the **hydrogen ion concentration** of a solution, you can calculate its **pH** by sticking the numbers into the **formula**.

Example: A solution of hydrochloric acid has a hydrogen ion concentration of 0.01 mol dm^{-3}. What is the pH of the solution?

$pH = -\log_{10}[H^+] = -\log_{10}[0.01] = \mathbf{2}$

Use the 'log' button on your calculator for this.

Kelly's an expert at finding logs.

2) If you know the **pH** of a solution, and you want to find its **hydrogen ion concentration**, then you need the **inverse** of the pH formula: **$[H^+] = 10^{-pH}$**

Example: A solution of sulfuric acid has a pH of 1.52. What is the hydrogen ion concentration of this solution?

$[H^+] = 10^{-pH} = 10^{-1.52} = 0.0302$ mol dm^{-3} = **3.02×10^{-2} mol dm^{-3}**

*For Strong Monobasic Acids, **[H⁺] = [Acid]***

1) **Strong acids** such as hydrochloric acid and nitric acid **ionise fully** in solution.
2) They're also **monobasic**, which means **one mole of acid** produces **one mole of hydrogen ions**. So the H^+ concentration is the **same** as the acid concentration.

E.g. For **0.10 mol dm^{-3} HCl**, $[H^+]$ is also 0.10 mol dm^{-3}. So the **pH** $= -\log_{10}[H^+] = -\log_{10} 0.10 = \mathbf{1.00}$.
Or for **0.050 mol dm^{-3} HNO_3**, $[H^+]$ is also 0.050 mol dm^{-3}, giving **pH** $= -\log_{10} 0.050 = \mathbf{1.30}$.

*The Ionic Product of Water, K_w, Depends on the Concentration of **H⁺** and **OH⁻***

Water dissociates into **hydroxonium ions** and **hydroxide ions**. So the following equilibrium exists in water:

$H_2O_{(l)} + H_2O_{(l)} \rightleftharpoons H_3O^+_{(aq)} + OH^-_{(aq)}$ or more simply: $H_2O_{(l)} \rightleftharpoons H^+_{(aq)} + OH^-_{(aq)}$

And, just like for any other equilibrium reaction, you can write an expression for the **equilibrium constant**. It's such an important equilibrium constant, that it has it's own name — rather than K_c, the equilibrium constant for the dissociation of water is called the **ionic product** of water, and has the symbol $\boldsymbol{K_w}$.

The units of K_w are always mol^{2}dm^{-6}.

$K_w = [H^+][OH^-]$

It doesn't matter whether water is pure or part of a solution — this equilibrium is always happening, and K_w is always the same at the same temperature.

For **pure water**, there's a **1:1** ratio of H^+ and OH^- ions due to dissociation. This means **$[H^+] = [OH^-]$** and **$K_w = [H^+]^2$**. So if you know K_w of pure water at a certain temperature, you can calculate $[H^+]$ and use this to find the pH.

K_w behaves like other equilibrium constants:

- Changing the **concentration** of $[H^+]$ or $[OH^-]$ in solution has no effect on the **value** of K_w as the equilibrium will shift, changing the concentration of the other substances to keep the value of K_w the same..
- Changing the **temperature** of the solution changes the value of K_w — dissociation of water is an **endothermic** process, so for example, warming the solution shifts the equilibrium to the **right** and K_w increases.

The fact that K_w always has the **same value** for pure water or an aqueous solution at a **given temperature** is really useful, as you're about to discover...

pH

Use K_w to Find the pH of a Strong Base

1) Sodium hydroxide (NaOH) and potassium hydroxide (KOH) are **strong bases** that **fully ionise** in water:

$$NaOH_{(s)} \rightarrow Na^+_{(aq)} + OH^-_{(aq)} \qquad KOH_{(s)} \rightarrow K^+_{(aq)} + OH^-_{(aq)}$$

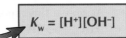

2) They donate **one mole of OH^- ions** per mole of base. This means that the concentration of OH^- ions is the **same** as the **concentration of the base**. So for 0.02 mol dm^{-3} sodium hydroxide solution, $[OH^-]$ is also **0.02 mol dm^{-3}**.
3) But to work out the **pH** you need to know **$[H^+]$** — luckily this is linked to **$[OH^-]$** through the **ionic product of water, K_w**:
4) So if you know K_w and $[OH^-]$ for a **strong aqueous base** at a certain temperature, you can work out **$[H^+]$** and then the **pH**.

$$K_w = [H^+][OH^-]$$

Example: Find the pH of 0.10 mol dm^{-3} NaOH at 298 K, given that K_w at 298 K is 1.0×10^{-14} mol^2 dm^{-6}.

1) First put all the values you know into the expression for the ionic product of water, K_w:

$$1.0 \times 10^{-14} = [H^+]\,[0.10]$$

2) Now rearrange the expression to find $[H^+]$:

$$[H^+] = \frac{1.0 \times 10^{-14}}{0.10} = 1.0 \times 10^{-13} \text{ mol dm}^{-3}$$

3) Use your value of $[H^+]$ to find the pH of the solution:

$$pH = -\log_{10}[H^+] = -\log_{10}(1.0 \times 10^{-13}) = \mathbf{13}$$

Practice Questions

Q1 Write the formula for calculating the pH of a solution.

Q2 What can you assume about $[H^+]$ for a strong monobasic acid?

Q3 Write the expression for the ionic product of water.

Q4 What are the units of K_w?

Q5 Explain how you'd find the pH of a strong base.

Exam Questions

Q1 a) What's the pH of a solution of the strong acid, hydrobromic acid (HBr), if it has a concentration of 0.32 mol dm^{-3}? [1 mark]

b) Hydrobromic acid is a stronger acid than hydrochloric acid. Explain what that means in terms of hydrogen ions and pH. [1 mark]

Q2 A solution of sodium hydroxide contains 2.50 g dm^{-3}. K_w at 298 K is 1.0×10^{-14} mol^2 dm^{-6}.

a) What is the molar concentration of the hydroxide ions in this solution? [2 marks]

b) Calculate the pH of this solution. [2 marks]

Q3 Calculate the pH of a 0.0370 mol dm^{-3} solution of sodium hydroxide at 298 K. K_w, the ionic product of water, is 1.0×10^{-14} mol^2 dm^{-6} at 298 K. [2 marks]

An ionic product — when your trousers have no creases in them...

You know things are getting serious when maths stuff like logs start appearing. It's fine really though, just practise a few questions and make sure you know how to use the log button on your calculator. And make sure you've learned the equation for K_w and both pH equations. And while you're up, go and make me a nice cup of tea, lots of milk, no sugar.

The Acid Dissociation Constant

More acid calculations to come, so you'll need to get that calculator warmed up... Either hold it for a couple of minutes in your armpit, or even better, warm it between your clenched buttocks. OK done that? Good stuff...

K_a is the Acid Dissociation Constant

1) Weak acids (like CH_3COOH) **don't** ionise fully in solution, so the $[H^+]$ **isn't** the same as the acid concentration. This makes it a **bit trickier** to find their pH. You have to use yet another **equilibrium constant**, K_a (the acid dissociation constant).

- For a weak aqueous acid, HA, you get the following equilibrium: $HA_{(aq)} \rightleftharpoons H^+_{(aq)} + A^-_{(aq)}$
- As only a **tiny amount** of HA dissociates, you can assume that $[HA_{(aq)}] >> [H^+_{(aq)}]$ so $[HA_{(aq)}]_{start} \approx [HA_{(aq)}]_{equilibrium}$.
- So if you apply the equilibrium law, you get: $K_a = \frac{[H^+][A^-]}{[HA]_{start}}$
- You can also assume that dissociation of the **acid** is much greater than dissociation of **water**. This means you can assume that all the H^+ ions in solution come from the **acid**, so $[H^+_{(aq)}] \approx [A^-_{(aq)}]$.

You can use this expression in calculations, but if you're asked to give an expression for K_a then make sure you write the one that includes $[A^-]$, don't use $[H^+]^2$.

So $K_a = \frac{[H^+]^2}{[HA]}$

The units of K_a are mol dm^{-3}.

2) The assumptions made above to find K_a only work for **weak acids**. Stronger acids **dissociate more** in solution, so the difference between $[HA_{(aq)}]_{start}$ and $[HA_{(aq)}]_{equilibrium}$ becomes **significant**, and the assumption that $[HA_{(aq)}]_{start} = [HA_{(aq)}]_{equilibrium}$ is no longer **valid**.

To Find the pH of a Weak Acid, You Use K_a

K_a is an **equilibrium constant** just like K_c or K_w. It applies to a particular acid at a **specific temperature** regardless of the **concentration**. You can use this fact to find the **pH** of a known concentration of a weak acid.

Example: Calculate the hydrogen ion concentration and the pH of a 0.02 mol dm^{-3} solution of propanoic acid (CH_3CH_2COOH). K_a for propanoic acid at this temperature is 1.30×10^{-5} mol dm^{-3}.

First, write down your expression for K_a and rearrange to find $[H^+]$.

$$K_a = \frac{[H^+]^2}{[CH_3CH_2COOH]} \Rightarrow [H^+]^2 = K_a[CH_3CH_2COOH] = 1.30 \times 10^{-5} \times 0.02 = 2.60 \times 10^{-7}$$

$$\Rightarrow [H^+] = \sqrt{(2.60 \times 10^{-7})} = \mathbf{5.10 \times 10^{-4}\ mol\ dm^{-3}}$$

You can now use your value for $[H^+]$ to find pH: $pH = -\log_{10} 5.10 \times 10^{-4} = \mathbf{3.29}$

You Might Have to Find the Concentration or K_a of a Weak Acid

You don't need to know anything new for this type of calculation. You usually just have to find $[H^+]$ from the pH, then fiddle around with the K_a **expression** to find the missing bit of information.

This bunny may look cute, but he can't help Horace with his revision.

Example: The pH of an ethanoic acid (CH_3COOH) solution was 3.02 at 298 K. Calculate the molar concentration of this solution. K_a of ethanoic acid is 1.75×10^{-5} mol dm^{-3} at 298 K.

First, use the pH to find $[H^+]$: $[H^+] = 10^{-pH} = 10^{-3.02} = \mathbf{9.55 \times 10^{-4}\ mol\ dm^{-3}}$

Then rearrange the expression for K_a and plug in your values to find $[CH_3COOH]$:

$$K_a = \frac{[H^+]^2}{[CH_3COOH]} \Rightarrow CH_3COOH = \frac{[H^+]^2}{K_a} = \frac{(9.55 \times 10^{-4})^2}{1.75 \times 10^{-5}} = \mathbf{0.0521\ mol\ dm^{-3}}$$

The Acid Dissociation Constant

$pK_a = -\log_{10} K_a$ and $K_a = 10^{-pK_a}$

pK_a is calculated from K_a in exactly the same way as pH is calculated from $[H^+]$ — and vice versa.

Example: a) If an acid has a K_a value of 1.50×10^{-7} mol dm³, what is its pK_a?

$pK_a = -\log_{10}(1.50 \times 10^{-7}) = \mathbf{6.82}$

b) What is the K_a value of an acid if its pK_a is 4.32?

$K_a = 10^{-4.32} = \mathbf{4.79 \times 10^{-5}\ mol\ dm^{-3}}$

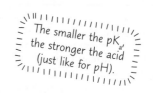

The smaller the pK_a, the stronger the acid (just like for pH).

Just to make things that bit more complicated, you might be given a **pK_a** value in a question to work out concentrations or pH. If so, you just need to convert it to K_a so that you can use the **K_a expression**.

Example: Calculate the pH of 0.0500 mol dm⁻³ methanoic acid (HCOOH).
Methanoic acid has a pK_a of 3.75 at this temperature.

$K_a = 10^{-pK_a} = 10^{-3.75} = 1.78 \times 10^{-4}$ mol dm⁻³ ⟸ First you have to convert the pK_a to K_a.

$K_a = \frac{[H^+]^2}{[COOH]} \Longrightarrow [H^+]^2 = K_a \times [HCOOH] = 1.78 \times 10^{-4} \times 0.0500 = 8.90 \times 10^{-6}$

$[H^+] = \sqrt{(8.90 \times 10^{-6})} = 2.98 \times 10^{-3}$ mol dm⁻³

$pH = -\log_{10} 2.98 \times 10^{-3} = \mathbf{2.53}$

You might also be asked to work out a **pK_a** value from concentrations or pH. In this case, you just work out the K_a value as usual and then convert it to **pK_a** — and Bob's a revision goat.

Bob the revision goat.

Practice Questions

Q1 What are the units of K_a?

Q2 What assumptions do you have to make when calculating K_a for a weak acid?
Why aren't these assumptions true for a strong acid?

Q3 Describe how you would calculate the pH of a weak acid from its acid dissociation constant.

Q4 How is pK_a defined?

Q5 Would you expect strong acids to have higher or lower K_a values than weak acids?

Exam Questions

Q1 The value of K_a for the weak acid HA, at 298 K, is 5.60×10^{-4} mol dm⁻³.

a) Write an expression for K_a for HA. [1 mark]

b) Calculate the pH of a 0.280 mol dm⁻³ solution of HA at 298 K. [2 marks]

Q2 The pH of a 0.150 mol dm⁻³ solution of a weak monobasic acid, HX, is 2.65 at 298 K.

a) Calculate the value of K_a for the acid HX at 298 K. [2 marks]

b) Calculate pK_a for this acid. [1 mark]

Q3 Benzoic acid is a weak acid that is used as a food preservative. It has a pK_a of 4.2 at 298 K.
Find the pH of a 1.6×10^{-4} mol dm⁻³ solution of benzoic acid at 298 K. [3 marks]

Fluffy revision animals... aaawwwww...

Strong acids have high K_a values and weak acids have low K_a values. For pK_a values, it's the other way round — the stronger the acid, the lower the pK_a. If something's got p in front of it, like pH, pK_w or pK_a, it'll mean –log10 of whatever. Oh and did you like the cute animals on this page? Did it really make your day? Good, I'm really pleased about that.

Buffers

I always found buffers a bit mind-boggling. How is it possible that a solution can resist becoming more acidic if you add acid to it? And why on earth would it want to? Here's where you find out...

Buffers Resist Changes in **pH**

A **buffer** is a solution that **minimises** changes in pH when **small** amounts of acid or base are added.

A buffer **doesn't** stop the pH from changing completely — it does make the changes **very slight** though. Buffers only work for small amounts of acid or base — put too much in and they won't be able to cope. You can get **acidic buffers** and **basic buffers**, but you only need to know about acidic ones.

Acidic Buffers Contain a **Weak Acid** and its **Conjugate Base**

Acidic buffers have a pH of less than 7 — they're made by setting up an equilibrium between a **weak acid** and its **conjugate base**. This can be done in two ways:

1) **Mix a weak acid with the salt of its conjugate base.**
   e.g. ethanoic acid and sodium ethanoate:
   - The salt **fully** dissociates into its ions when it dissolves:
     $CH_3COO^-Na^+_{(aq)} \rightarrow CH_3COO^-_{(aq)} + Na^+_{(aq)}$
   - The **weak acid** only **slightly** dissociates:
     $CH_3COOH_{(aq)} \rightleftharpoons H^+_{(aq)} + CH_3COO^-_{(aq)}$

2) **Mix an excess of weak acid with a strong alkali.**
   e.g. ethanoic acid and sodium hydroxide:
   - **All** the base reacts with the acid:
     $CH_3COOH_{(aq)} + OH^-_{(aq)} \rightarrow CH_3COO^- + H_2O$
   - The weak acid was in **excess**, so there's still some left in solution once all the base has reacted. This acid **slightly dissociates**:
     $CH_3COOH_{(aq)} \rightleftharpoons H^+_{(aq)} + CH_3COO^-_{(aq)}$

In both cases, the following equilibrium is set up between the weak acid and its conjugate base:

Lots of undissociated weak acid → $CH_3COOH_{(aq)} \rightleftharpoons H^+_{(aq)} + CH_3COO^-_{(aq)}$ ← Lots of CH_3COO^-

The equilibrium solution contains:

- Lots of undissociated acid (HA).
- Lots of the acid's conjugate base (A^-).
- Enough H^+ ions to make the solution acidic.

Conjugate Pairs Set Up an **Equilibrium** that **Resists** Changes in pH

It's the job of the conjugate pair to control the pH of a buffer solution. The **conjugate base** mops up an excess of H^+, while the **conjugate acid releases** H^+ if there's too much base around.

If you add a **small** amount of **acid** the **H^+ concentration** increases. Most of the extra H^+ ions combine with CH_3COO^- ions to form CH_3COOH. This shifts the equilibrium to the **left**, reducing the H^+ concentration to close to its original value. So the **pH** doesn't change much.

The large number of CH_3COO^- ions make sure the buffer can cope with the addition of acid.

If a **small** amount of **alkali** (e.g. NaOH) is added, the **OH^- concentration** increases. Most of the extra OH^- ions react with H^+ ions to form water — removing H^+ ions from the solution. This causes more CH_3COOH to **dissociate** to form H^+ ions — shifting the equilibrium to the **right**. The H^+ concentration increases until it's close to its original value, so the **pH** doesn't change much.

This isn't a problem as there's loads of spare CH_3COOH molecules.

Buffer Solutions are Important in **Blood**

1) In our bodies, **blood** needs to be kept between pH 7.35 and 7.45. The pH is controlled using a **carbonic acid-hydrogen carbonate** buffer system. Two equilibrium reactions occur.

   $H_2CO_{3(aq)} \rightleftharpoons H^+_{(aq)} + HCO_3^-{}_{(aq)}$
   and $H_2CO_{3(aq)} \rightleftharpoons H_2O_{(l)} + CO_{2(aq)}$

2) The levels of $\mathbf{H_2CO_3}$ are controlled by **respiration**. By **breathing out CO_2** the level of H_2CO_3 is reduced as it moves this **equilibrium** to the **right**.
3) The levels of HCO_3^- are controlled by the **kidneys** with excess being **excreted** in the urine.

Buffers

Here's How to Calculate the pH of a Buffer Solution

Calculating the **pH** of an acidic buffer isn't too tricky. You just need to know the K_a of the weak acid and the **concentrations** of the weak acid and its salt. Your calculation requires the following assumptions to be made:

- The **salt** of the **conjugate base** is **fully dissociated**, so assume that the equilibrium concentration of A^- is the **same** as the initial concentration of the salt.
- **HA** is only **slightly dissociated**, so assume that its equilibrium concentration is the **same** as its initial concentration.

The conjugate base doesn't only come from dissociation of the weak acid so $[H^+] \neq [A^-]$.

Here's how you calculate the pH of a buffer solution:

Example: A buffer solution contains 0.40 mol dm^{-3} methanoic acid, HCOOH, and 0.60 mol dm^{-3} sodium methanoate, $HCOO^-Na^+$. For methanoic acid, $K_a = 1.8 \times 10^{-4}$ mol dm^{-3}. What is the pH of this buffer?

Firstly, write the expression for K_a of the weak acid:

$$HCOOH_{(aq)} \rightleftharpoons H^+_{(aq)} + HCOO^-_{(aq)} \Longrightarrow K_a = \frac{[H^+][HCOO^-]}{[HCOOH]}$$

Remember — these are all equilibrium concentrations.

Then rearrange the expression and stick in the data to calculate $[H^+]$:

$$[H^+] = K_a \times \frac{[HCOOH]}{[HCOO^-]}$$

$$\Longrightarrow [H^+] = 1.8 \times 10^{-4} \times \frac{0.4}{0.6} = 1.20 \times 10^{-4} \text{ mol dm}^{-3}$$

Finally, convert $[H^+_{(aq)}]$ to pH:

$$pH = -\log_{10}[H^+_{(aq)}] = -\log_{10}(1.20 \times 10^{-4}) = \mathbf{3.92}$$

And that's your answer.

Nobody's gonna change my pH.

Acids and bases didn't mess with Jeff after he became buffer.

Practice Questions

Q1 What's a buffer solution?

Q2 Name two ways of preparing buffer solutions.

Q3 Describe how a mixture of ethanoic acid and sodium ethanoate act as a buffer.

Q4 Describe how the pH of the blood is buffered.

Exam Questions

Q1 A buffer solution contains 0.40 mol dm^{-3} benzoic acid, C_6H_5COOH, and 0.20 mol dm^{-3} sodium benzoate, $C_6H_5COO^-Na^+$. At 25 °C, K_a for benzoic acid is 6.4×10^{-5} mol dm^{-3}.

a) Calculate the pH of the buffer solution. [2 marks]

b) Explain the effect on the buffer of adding a small quantity of dilute sulfuric acid. [1 mark]

Q2 A buffer was prepared by mixing solutions of butanoic acid, $CH_3(CH_2)_2COOH$, and sodium butanoate, $CH_3(CH_2)_2COO^-Na^+$, so that they had the same concentration.

a) Write a balanced chemical equation to show butanoic acid acting as a weak acid. [1 mark]

b) Given that K_a for butanoic acid is 1.5×10^{-5} mol dm^{-3} at 298 K, calculate the pH of the buffer solution. [2 marks]

Old buffers are often resistant to change...

So that's how buffers work. There's a pleasing simplicity and neatness about it that I find rather elegant. Like a fine glass of red wine with a nose of berry and undertones of raspberries, oak and... OK, I'll shut up now.

pH Curves and Titrations

If you add alkali to an acid, the pH changes in a squiggly sort of way.

*You Can **Measure** the pH of a Solution Using a **pH Meter***

1) A **pH meter** does what it says on the tin — it's an electronic gadget you can use to tell you the **pH** of a solution.
2) pH meters have a **probe** that you put into your solution and a **digital display** that shows the reading. At the bottom of the probe is a bulb that's very **delicate**, so be careful when handling it.
3) Before you use a pH meter, you need to make sure it's **calibrated correctly**. To do this...
   - Place the bulb of the pH meter into **distilled water** and allow the reading to settle. Now **adjust** the reading so that it reads **7.0**.
   - Do the same with a standard solution of pH 4 and another of pH 10. Make sure you **rinse** the probe with **distilled water** in between each reading.
4) You're now ready to take your actual measurement. Place the probe in the liquid you're measuring and let the reading settle before you record the result. After each measurement, you should rinse the probe in **distilled water**.

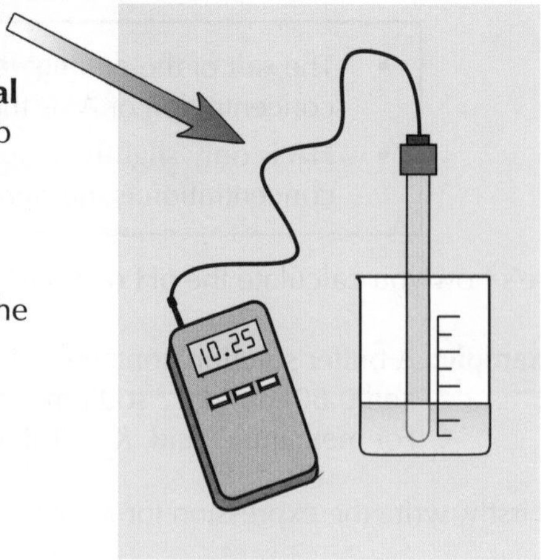

***pH Curves** Plot **pH** Against **Volume** of **Acid** or **Base** Added*

1) **Titrations** let you find out **exactly** how much alkali is needed to **neutralise** a quantity of acid.
2) All you have to do is plot the **pH** of the titration mixture against the **amount of base** added as the titration goes on. The pH of the mixture can be measured using a pH meter and the scale on the burette can be used to see how much base has been added.
3) The **shape** of your plot looks a bit different depending on the **strengths** of the acid and base that are used.
4) Here are the graphs of the pH curves for the different combinations of strong and weak monobasic acids and bases:

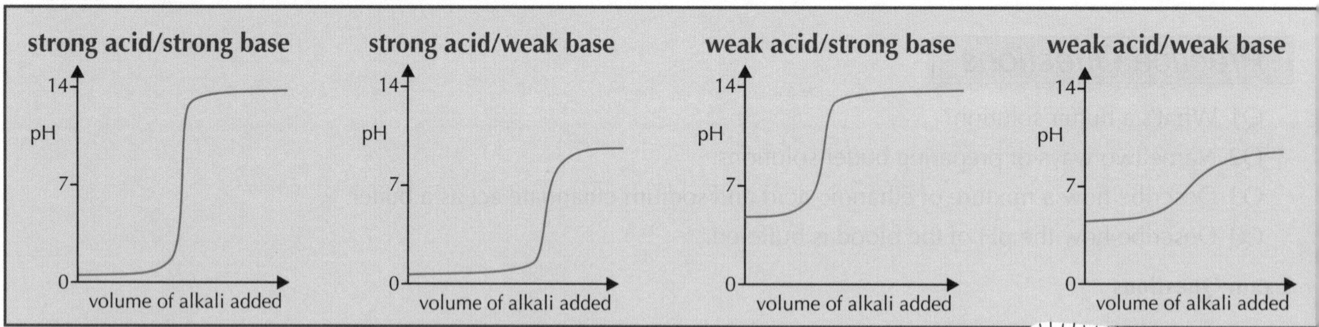

You can explain why each graph has a particular shape:

- The **initial** pH depends on the **strength** of the **acid**. So a strong acid titration will start at a much **lower** pH than a weak acid.
- To start with, addition of **small** amounts of base have **little impact** on the pH of the solution.
- All the graphs (apart from the weak acid/weak base graph) have a bit that's almost vertical — this is the **equivalence point** or **end point**. At this point **$[H^+] \approx [OH^-]$** — it's here that all the acid is just **neutralised.** When this is the case, a tiny amount of base causes a sudden, big change in pH.
- You need to add **more weak base** than strong base to a **strong acid** to cause a pH change, and the change is less **pronounced.** On the other hand, you need to add **less strong base** to a **weak acid** to see a large change in pH.
- The **final** pH depends on the strength of the **base** — the **stronger** the base, the **higher** the final pH.

If you titrate a base with an acid instead, the shapes of the curves stay the same, but they're reversed.

pH Curves and Titrations

pH Curves can Help you Decide which Indicator to Use

1) You've met **titrations** before — they're experiments that let you work out the **concentrations** of different solutions.
2) You can use titrations instead of pH meters to work out the **concentration** of an acid or base. You'll need an **indicator** that changes **colour** to show you when your sample has been **neutralised**.
3) You need your indicator to change colour exactly at the **end point** of your titration. So you need to pick one that changes colour over a **narrow pH range** that lies entirely on the **vertical part** of the pH curve.

E.g. For this titration, the curve is vertical between **pH 8** and **pH 11** — so a very small amount of base will cause the pH to **change** from 8 to 11.

So you want an indicator that changes **colour** somewhere between pH 8 and pH 11.

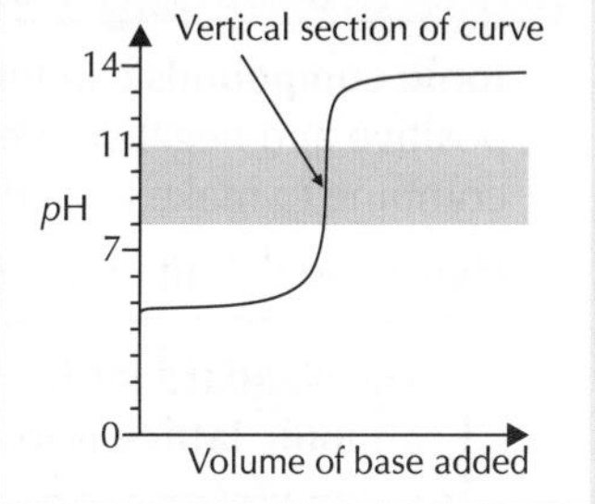

4) **Methyl orange** and **phenolphthalein** are **indicators** that are often used for acid-base titrations. They each change colour over a **different pH range**:

Name of indicator	Colour at low pH	Approx. pH of colour change	Colour at high pH
Methyl orange	red	3.1 – 4.4	yellow
Phenolphthalein	colourless	8.3 – 10	pink

- For a **strong acid/strong base** titration, you can use **either** of these indicators — there's a rapid pH change over the range for **both** indicators.
- For a **strong acid/weak base** only **methyl orange** will do. The pH changes rapidly across the range for methyl orange, but not for phenolphthalein.
- For a **weak acid/strong base**, **phenolphthalein** is the stuff to use. The pH changes rapidly over phenolphthalein's range, but not over methyl orange's.
- For **weak acid/weak base** titrations there's no sharp pH change, so **neither** of these indicators works. In fact, there aren't **any** indicators you can use in weak acid/weak base titrations, so you should just use a pH meter.

Indicators can be thought of as **weak acids**. They work because they have differently coloured **conjugate pairs**. As the pH of the solution changes during a titration, the equilibrium concentrations of the conjugate pairs will also change. The colour will **change** depending on whether the indicator is mainly **protonated** or **deprotonated.**

E.g. **Phenolphthalein-H $\rightleftharpoons$ Phenolphthalein$^-$ + H^+**
colourless — pink

Methylorange-H $\rightleftharpoons$ Methylorange$^-$ + H^+
red — yellow

Practice Questions

Q1 Sketch the pH curve for a weak acid/strong alkali titration.

Q2 What indicator should you use for a strong acid/weak alkali titration — methyl orange or phenolphthalein?

Q3 What colour is methyl orange at pH 2?

Exam Questions

Q1 1.0 mol dm^{-3} NaOH (a strong base) is added separately to 25 cm^3 samples of 1.0 mol dm^{-3} nitric acid (a strong acid) and 1.0 mol dm^{-3} ethanoic acid (a weak acid). Sketch the pH curves for each of these titrations. [2 marks]

Q2 A sample of ethanoic acid (a weak acid) was titrated against potassium hydroxide (a strong base).

From the table on the right, select the best indicator for this titration, and explain your choice. [2 marks]

Name of indicator	pH range
bromophenol blue	3.0 – 4.6
methyl red	4.2 – 6.3
bromothymol blue	6.0 – 7.6
thymol blue	8.0 – 9.6

I'll burette your bottom dollar that you're bored of pH by now...

Titrations involve playing with big bits of glassware that you're told not to break as they're really expensive — so you instantly become really clumsy. If you manage not to smash the burette, you'll find it easier to get accurate results if you use a dilute acid or alkali — drops of dilute acid and alkali contain fewer particles so you're less likely to overshoot.

Lattice Enthalpy and Born-Haber Cycles

On these pages you can learn about lattice enthalpy, not lettuce enthalpy, which is the enthalpy change when 1 mole consumes salad from a veggie patch. Bu–dum cha... (that was meant to be a drum — work with me here).

Lattice Enthalpy is a Measure of *Ionic Bond Strength*

Ionic compounds can form regular structures called **giant ionic lattices** where the positive and negative ions are held together by **electrostatic attractions**. When **gaseous ions** combine to make a solid lattice, energy is given out — this is called the **lattice enthalpy**.

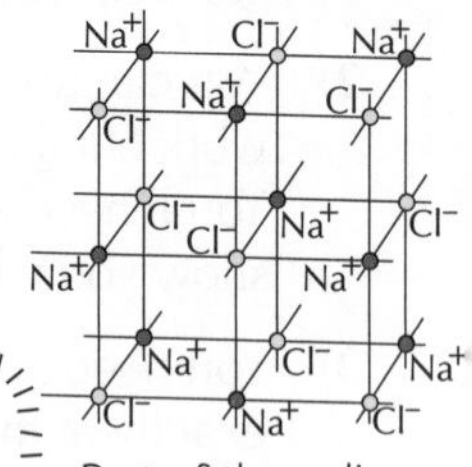

Part of the sodium chloride lattice

Here's the definition of **standard lattice enthalpy** that you need to know:

> The **standard lattice enthalpy**, $\Delta_{LE}H^\ominus$, is the enthalpy change when **1 mole** of an **ionic lattice** is formed from its **gaseous ions** under standard conditions.

Standard conditions are 298 K (25 °C) and 100 kPa.

The standard lattice enthalpy is a measure of **ionic bond strength**. The more **negative** the lattice enthalpy, the **stronger** the bonding. E.g. out of NaCl and MgO, MgO has stronger bonding.

$Na^+_{(g)} + Cl^-_{(g)} \rightarrow NaCl_{(s)}$ $\Delta_{LE}H^\ominus = -787\ kJ\,mol^{-1}$

$Mg^{2+}_{(g)} + O^{2-}_{(g)} \rightarrow MgO_{(s)}$ $\Delta_{LE}H^\ominus = -3791\ kJ\,mol^{-1}$

Ionic Charge and *Size* Affects *Lattice Enthalpy*

1) The **higher the charge** on the ions, the **more energy** is released when an ionic lattice forms. This is due to the **stronger electrostatic forces** between the ions.
2) More energy released means that the lattice enthalpy will be **more negative**. So the lattice enthalpies for compounds with **2+** or **2– ions** (e.g. Mg^{2+} or S^{2-}) are **more exothermic** than those with **1+** or **1– ions** (e.g. Na^+ or Cl^-).

   > E.g. the lattice enthalpy of **NaCl** is only –787 kJ mol⁻¹, but the lattice enthalpy of **$MgCl_2$** is –2526 kJ mol⁻¹. **MgS** has an even **higher** lattice enthalpy (–3299 kJ mol⁻¹) because both Mg and S ions have **double charges**.

3) The **smaller** the **ionic radii** of the ions involved, the **more exothermic** (more negative) the **lattice enthalpy**. Smaller ions have a higher **charge density** and their **smaller ionic radii** mean that the ions can sit **closer together** in the lattice. Both these things mean that the attractions between the ions are **stronger**.

Born-Haber Cycles can be Used to Calculate *Lattice Enthalpies*

Hess's law says that the **total enthalpy change** of a reaction is always the **same**, no matter which route is taken — this is known as the conservation of energy.

You can't calculate a lattice enthalpy **directly**, so you have to use a **Born-Haber cycle** to figure out what the enthalpy change would be if you took **another, less direct, route**.

Here's a Born-Haber cycle you could use to calculate the lattice enthalpy of **NaCl**:

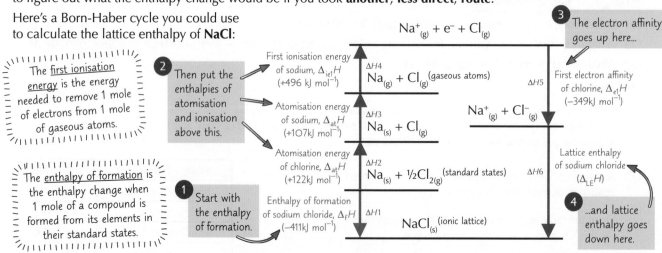

The first ionisation energy is the energy needed to remove 1 mole of electrons from 1 mole of gaseous atoms.

The enthalpy of formation is the enthalpy change when 1 mole of a compound is formed from its elements in their standard states.

1 Start with the enthalpy of formation.

2 Then put the enthalpies of atomisation and ionisation above this.

3 The electron affinity goes up here...

4 ...and lattice enthalpy goes down here.

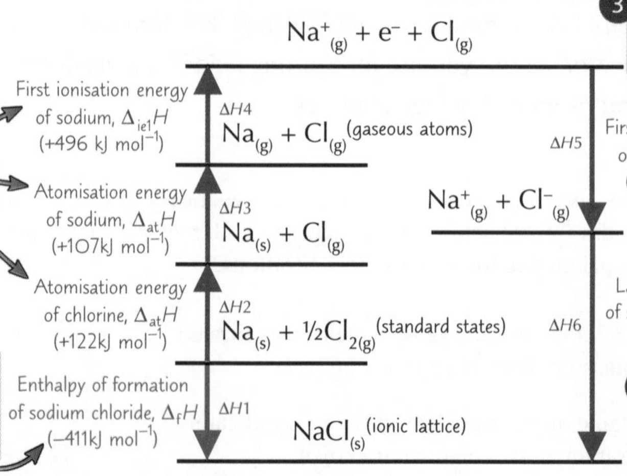

There are **two routes** you can follow to get from the elements in their **standard states** to the **ionic lattice**. The green arrow shows the **direct route** and the purple arrows show the **indirect route**. The enthalpy change for each is the **same**.

> From Hess's law: $\Delta H6 = -\Delta H5 - \Delta H4 - \Delta H3 - \Delta H2 + \Delta H1$
> $= -(-349) - (+496) - (+107) - (+122) + (-411) = \mathbf{-787\ kJ\,mol^{-1}}$

You need a minus sign if you go the wrong way along an arrow.

Lattice Enthalpy and Born-Haber Cycles

Calculations involving **Group 2 Elements** are a Bit **Different**

Born-Haber cycles for compounds containing **Group 2 elements** have a few **changes** from the one on the previous page. Make sure you understand what's going on so you can handle whatever compound they throw at you.

Here's the Born-Haber cycle for calculating the lattice enthalpy of **magnesium chloride** ($MgCl_2$):

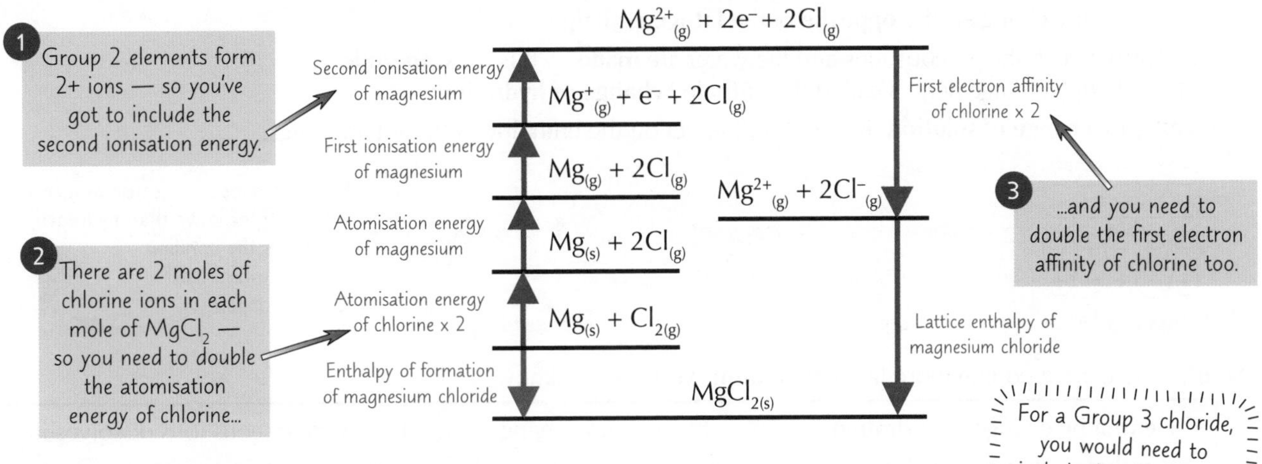

1 Group 2 elements form 2+ ions — so you've got to include the second ionisation energy.
2 There are 2 moles of chlorine ions in each mole of MgCl2 — so you need to double the atomisation energy of chlorine...
3 ...and you need to double the first electron affinity of chlorine too.
Mg2+(g) + 2e− + 2Cl(g)
Second ionisation energy of magnesium
Mg+(g) + e− + 2Cl(g)
First ionisation energy of magnesium
Mg(g) + 2Cl(g)
Atomisation energy of magnesium
Mg(s) + 2Cl(g)
Atomisation energy of chlorine x 2
Mg(s) + Cl2(g)
Enthalpy of formation of magnesium chloride
MgCl2(s)
First electron affinity of chlorine x 2
Mg2+(g) + 2Cl−(g)
Lattice enthalpy of magnesium chloride

For a Group 3 chloride, you would need to include three ionisation energies and triple the enthalpies of chlorine.

Practice Questions

Q1 What is the definition of standard lattice enthalpy?

Q2 What does a large, negative lattice enthalpy mean, in terms of bond stength?

Q3 Why does magnesium chloride have a more negative lattice enthalpy than sodium chloride?

Q4 Why would lithium chloride have a more negative lattice enthalpy than sodium chloride?

Exam Questions

Q1 Using this data:

$\Delta_f H^\ominus$[potassium bromide] = –394 kJ mol^{-1} $\Delta_{at} H^\ominus$[bromine] = +112 kJ mol^{-1} $\Delta_{at} H^\ominus$[potassium] = +89 kJ mol^{-1}
$\Delta_{ie1} H^\ominus$[potassium] = +419 kJ mol^{-1} $\Delta_{e1} H^\ominus$[bromine] = –325 kJ mol^{-1}

a) Construct a Born-Haber cycle for potassium bromide (KBr). [3 marks]

b) Use your Born-Haber cycle to calculate the lattice enthalpy of potassium bromide. [2 marks]

Q2 Using this data:

$\Delta_f H^\ominus$[aluminium chloride] = –706 kJ mol^{-1} $\Delta_{at} H^\ominus$[chlorine] = +122 kJ mol^{-1} $\Delta_{at} H^\ominus$[aluminium] = +326 kJ mol^{-1}
$\Delta_{e1} H^\ominus$[chlorine] = –349 kJ mol^{-1} $\Delta_{ie1} H^\ominus$[aluminium] = +578 kJ mol^{-1}
$\Delta_{ie2} H^\ominus$[aluminium] = +1817 kJ mol^{-1} $\Delta_{ie3} H^\ominus$[aluminium] = +2745 kJ mol^{-1}

a) Construct a Born-Haber cycle for aluminium chloride ($AlCl_3$). [3 marks]

b) Use your cycle to calculate the lattice enthalpy of aluminium chloride. [2 marks]

Q3 Using this data:

$\Delta_f H^\ominus$[aluminium oxide] = –1676 kJ mol^{-1} $\Delta_{at} H^\ominus$[oxygen] = +249 kJ mol^{-1} $\Delta_{at} H^\ominus$[aluminium] = +326 kJ mol^{-1}
$\Delta_{ie1} H^\ominus$[aluminium] = +578 kJ mol^{-1} $\Delta_{ie2} H^\ominus$[aluminium] = +1817 kJ mol^{-1} $\Delta_{ie3} H^\ominus$[aluminium] = +2745 kJ mol^{-1}
$\Delta_{e1} H^\ominus$[oxygen] = –141 kJ mol^{-1} $\Delta_{e2} H^\ominus$[oxygen] = +844 kJ mol^{-1}

a) Construct a Born-Haber cycle for aluminium oxide (Al_2O_3). [3 marks]

b) Use your cycle to calculate the lattice enthalpy of aluminium oxide. [2 marks]

Using Born-Haber cycles — it's just like riding a bike...

All this energy going in and out can get a bit confusing. Remember these simple rules: 1) It takes energy to break bonds, but energy is given out when bonds are made. 2) A negative ΔH means energy is given out (it's exothermic). 3) A positive ΔH means energy is taken in (it's endothermic). 4) Never return to a firework once lit.

Enthalpies of Solution

Once you know what's happening when you stir sugar into your tea, your cuppa'll be twice as enjoyable.

Dissolving** Involves **Enthalpy Changes

When a solid **ionic lattice** dissolves in water these **two** things happen:

1) The bonds between the ions **break** to give gaseous ions — this is **endothermic**. The enthalpy change is the **opposite** of the **lattice enthalpy**.
2) Bonds between the gaseous ions and the water are **made** — this is **exothermic**. The enthalpy change here is called the **enthalpy change of hydration**.

The **enthalpy change of solution**, is the overall effect on the enthalpy of these two things.

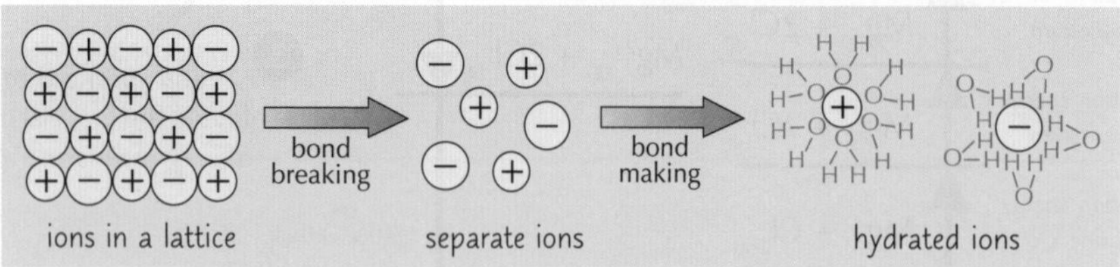

This effect happens because oxygen is more electronegative than hydrogen, so it draws the bonding electrons toward itself, creating a dipole.

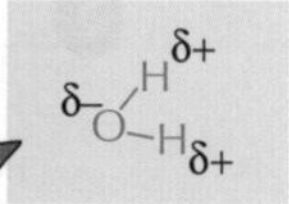

So now, here are a couple more fancy **definitions** you need to know:

The **enthalpy change of hydration**, $\Delta_{hyd}H^{\ominus}$, is the enthalpy change when 1 mole of gaseous ions dissolves in water.
The **enthalpy change of solution**, $\Delta_{sol}H^{\ominus}$, is the enthalpy change when 1 mole of solute dissolves in water.

Substances generally **only** dissolve if the energy released is roughly the same, or **greater than** the energy taken in. So soluble substances tend to have **exothermic** enthalpies of solution.

***Enthalpy Change of Solution** can be Calculated*

You can work out the enthalpy change of solution using a Born-Haber cycle — but one drawn a bit differently from those on pages 144 and 145.
You just need to know the **lattice enthalpy** of the compound and the **enthalpies of hydration** of the ions.

Here's how to draw the enthalpy cycle for working out the **enthalpy change of solution** for **sodium chloride**.

1. Put the ionic lattice and the dissolved ions on the top — connect them by the enthalpy change of solution. This is the direct route.
2. Connect the ionic lattice to the gaseous ions by the reverse of the lattice enthalpy. The breakdown of the lattice has the opposite enthalpy change to the formation of the lattice.

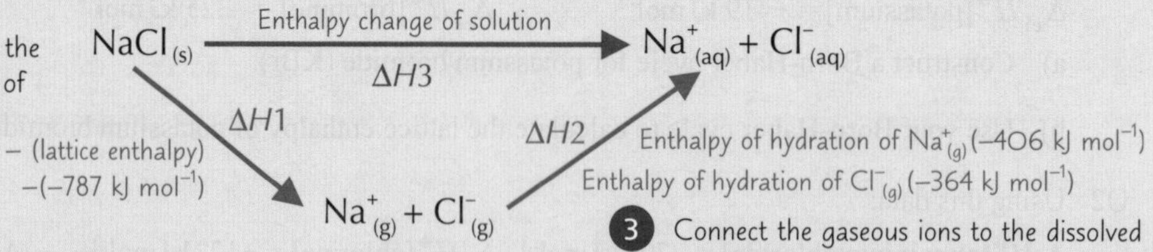

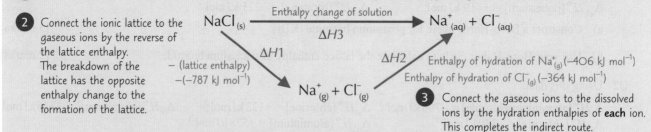

3. Connect the gaseous ions to the dissolved ions by the hydration enthalpies of **each** ion. This completes the indirect route.

From Hess's law: $\Delta H3 = \Delta H1 + \Delta H2 = +787 + (-406 + -364) = \mathbf{+17\ kJ\ mol^{-1}}$

The enthalpy change of solution is **slightly endothermic**, but there are other factors at work that mean that sodium chloride still dissolves in water.

Here's another. This one's for working out the **enthalpy change of solution** for **silver chloride**:

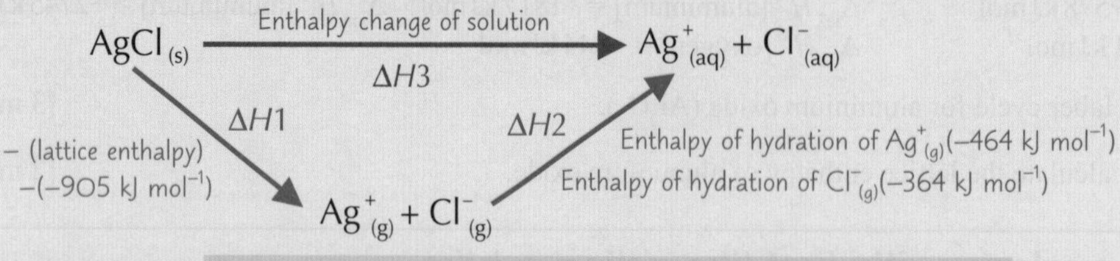

From Hess's law: $\Delta H3 = \Delta H1 + \Delta H2 = +905 + (-464 + -364) = \mathbf{+77\ kJ\ mol^{-1}}$

This is much **more endothermic** than the enthalpy change of solution for sodium chloride. As such, silver chloride is **insoluble** in water.

As long as there's only one unknown enthalpy value, you can use these cycles to work out any value on the arrows. For example, if you know the enthalpy change of solution and the enthalpy changes of hydration, you can use those values to work out the lattice enthalpy.

Enthalpies of Solution

Ionic Charge and Ionic Radius Affect the Enthalpy of Hydration

The **two** things that can affect the lattice enthalpy (see page 144) can also affect the enthalpy of hydration. They are the **size** and the **charge** of the ions.

Ions with a greater charge have a greater enthalpy of hydration.

Ions with a **higher charge** are better at **attracting** water molecules than those with lower charges — the electrostatic attraction between the ion and the water molecules is **stronger**. This means **more energy** is released when the bonds are **made** giving them a **more exothermic** enthalpy of hydration.

Smaller ions have a greater enthalpy of hydration.

Smaller ions have a **higher** charge density than bigger ions. They **attract** the water molecules **better** and have a **more exothermic** enthalpy of hydration.

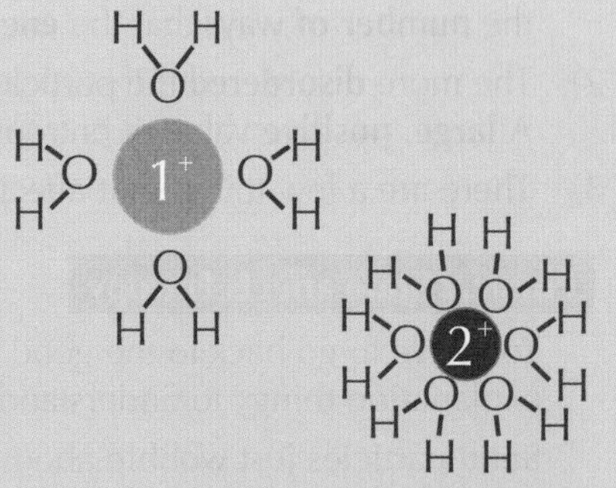

The higher charge and smaller size of the 2+ ion create a higher charge density than the 1+ ion. This creates a stronger attraction for the water molecules and gives a more exothermic enthalpy of hydration.

E.g. a magnesium ion is smaller and more charged than a sodium ion, which gives it a much bigger enthalpy of hydration.

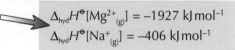

$\Delta_{hyd}H^{\ominus}[Mg^{2+}_{(g)}] = -1927\ kJ\,mol^{-1}$

$\Delta_{hyd}H^{\ominus}[Na^{+}_{(g)}] = -406\ kJ\,mol^{-1}$

Practice Questions

Q1 Describe the two steps that occur when an ionic lattice dissolves in water.

Q2 Define the enthalpy change of solution.

Q3 Do soluble substances have exothermic or endothermic enthalpies of solution in general?

Q4 Sketch a Born-Haber cycle to calculate the enthalpy change of solution of silver chloride.

Q5 Name two factors that affect the enthalpy of hydration of an ion.

Exam Questions

Q1 a) Draw an enthalpy cycle for the enthalpy change of solution of $AgF_{(s)}$. Label each enthalpy change. [2 marks]

b) Calculate the enthalpy change of solution for AgF from the following data: [2 marks]

$\Delta_{latt}H^{\ominus}[AgF_{(s)}] = -960\,kJ\,mol^{-1}$, $\Delta_{hyd}H^{\ominus}[Ag^{+}_{(g)}] = -464\,kJ\,mol^{-1}$, $\Delta_{hyd}H^{\ominus}[F^{-}_{(g)}] = -506\,kJ\,mol^{-1}$.

Q2 a) Draw an enthalpy cycle for the enthalpy change of solution of $SrF_{2(s)}$. Label each enthalpy change. [2 marks]

b) Calculate the enthalpy change of solution for SrF_2 from the following data: [2 marks]

$\Delta_{latt}H^{\ominus}[SrF_{2(s)}] = -2492\ kJ\,mol^{-1}$, $\Delta_{hyd}H^{\ominus}[Sr^{2+}_{(g)}] = -1480\ kJ\,mol^{-1}$, $\Delta_{hyd}H^{\ominus}[F^{-}_{(g)}] = -506\ kJ\,mol^{-1}$.

Q3 Show that the enthalpy of hydration of $Cl^{-}_{(g)}$ is $-364\ kJ\,mol^{-1}$, given that: [3 marks]

$\Delta_{latt}H^{\ominus}[MgCl_{2(s)}] = -2526\ kJ\,mol^{-1}$, $\Delta_{hyd}H^{\ominus}[Mg^{2+}_{(g)}] = -1920\ kJ\,mol^{-1}$, $\Delta_{sol}H^{\ominus}[MgCl_{2(s)}] = -122\ kJ\,mol^{-1}$.

Q4 Which of these ions will have a greater enthalpy of hydration — Ca^{2+} or K^{+}?
Explain your answer. [3 marks]

Enthalpy change of solution of the Wicked Witch of the West = 939 kJ mol^{-1}...

Compared to the ones on the previous two pages, these enthalpy cycles are an absolute breeze. You've got to make sure the definitions are firmly fixed in your mind though. You only need to know the lattice enthalpy and the enthalpy of hydration of your lattice ions, and you're well on your way to finding out the enthalpy change of solution.

Entropy

If you were looking for some random chemistry pages, you've just found them.

Entropy *Tells you How Much* ***Disorder*** *there is*

Squirrels do not teach Chemistry. But if they did, this is what a demonstration of increasing entropy would look like.

1) Entropy is a measure of the **number of ways** that **particles** can be **arranged** and the **number of ways** that the **energy** can be shared out between the particles.
2) The more **disordered** the particles are, the higher the entropy is. A **large**, **positive** value of entropy shows a **high** level of disorder.
3) There are a few things that affect entropy:

Physical State affects Entropy

You have to go back to the good old **solid-liquid-gas** particle explanation thingy to understand this.

Solid particles just wobble about a fixed point — there's **hardly any** randomness, so they have the **lowest entropy**.

Gas particles whizz around wherever they like. They've got the most **random arrangements** of particles, so they have the **highest entropy**.

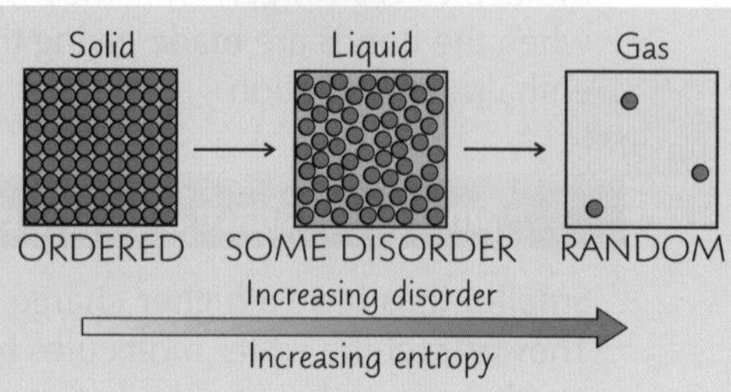

More Particles means More Entropy

It makes sense — the more particles you've got, the **more ways** they and their energy can be **arranged** — so in a reaction like $N_2O_{4(g)} \rightarrow 2NO_{2(g)}$, entropy increases because the **number of moles** increases.

More ***Arrangements*** *Means More* ***Stability***

1) Substances really **like** disorder — they're actually more **energetically stable** when there's more disorder. So particles will move to try to **increase their entropy**.
2) This is why some reactions are **feasible** (they just happen by themselves — without the addition of energy) even when the enthalpy change is **endothermic**.

Example: The reaction of sodium hydrogencarbonate with hydrochloric acid is an **endothermic reaction** — but it is **feasible**. This is due to an **increase in entropy** as the reaction produces carbon dioxide gas and water. Liquids and gases are **more disordered** than solids and so have a **higher entropy**. This increase in entropy **overcomes** the change in enthalpy.

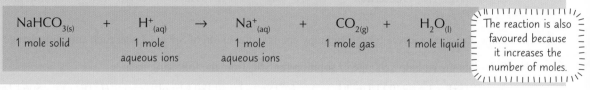

$NaHCO_{3(s)}$	+	$H^+_{(aq)}$	$\rightarrow$	$Na^+_{(aq)}$	+	$CO_{2(g)}$	+	$H_2O_{(l)}$
1 mole solid		1 mole aqueous ions		1 mole aqueous ions		1 mole gas		1 mole liquid

The reaction is also favoured because it increases the number of moles.

3) When a substance reaches its maximum entropy state (its lowest energy state), it's said to be **thermodynamically stable**. This means it won't react any further without the input of energy.

You Can ***Calculate*** *the* ***Entropy Change*** *of a Reaction*

You can calculate the **entropy change** of a reaction if you know the entropies of the **products** and of the **reactants**.

The units of entropy are $J\,K^{-1}mol^{-1}$.

$$\Delta S = S_{products} - S_{reactants}$$

Reactions with a positive value of ΔS are more likely to be feasible.

Entropy

Example: Calculate the entropy change for the reaction of ammonia and hydrogen chloride under standard conditions.

$$NH_{3(g)} + HCl_{(g)} \rightarrow NH_4Cl_{(s)}$$

$S^{\ominus}[NH_{3(g)}] = 192.3\ J K^{-1} mol^{-1}$, $S^{\ominus}[HCl_{(g)}] = 186.8\ J K^{-1} mol^{-1}$, $S^{\ominus}[NH_4Cl_{(s)}] = 94.60\ J K^{-1} mol^{-1}$

1) First find the entropy of the **products**:

$S^{\ominus}_{products} = S^{\ominus}[NH_4Cl] = 94.60\ J\ K^{-1}\ mol^{-1}$

2) Now find the entropy change of the **reactants**:

$S^{\ominus}_{reactants} = S^{\ominus}[NH_3] + S^{\ominus}[HCl] = 192.3\ J K^{-1}\ mol^{-1} + 186.8\ J K^{-1} mol^{-1} = 379.1\ J K^{-1} mol^{-1}$

3) Finally you can subtract the entropy of the reactants from the entropy of the products to find the **entropy change** for the reaction:

$\Delta S^{\ominus} = S^{\ominus}_{products} - S^{\ominus}_{reactants} = 94.60 - 379.1 = \mathbf{-284.5\ J K^{-1} mol^{-1}}$

This shows a negative change in entropy. It's not surprising as 2 moles of gas have combined to form 1 mole of solid.

A positive entropy change of reaction means that a reaction is likely to be feasible, but a negative change in entropy of reaction **doesn't gurantee** the reaction **can't** happen — **enthalpy**, **temperature** and **kinetics** also play a part in whether or not a reaction occurs.

There's more about this on the next page...

Practice Questions

Q1 What does the term 'entropy' mean?

Q2 In each of the following pairs choose the one with the greater entropy value.
  a) 1 mole of $NaCl_{(aq)}$ and 1 mole of $NaCl_{(s)}$
  b) 1 mole of $Br_{2(l)}$ and 1 mole of $Br_{2(g)}$
  c) 1 mole of $Br_{2(g)}$ and 2 moles of $Br_{2(g)}$

Q3 Write down the formula for the entropy change of a reaction.

Exam Questions

Q1 a) Based on just the equation below, predict whether the reaction is likely to be feasible. Give a reason for your answer.

$Mg_{(s)} + \frac{1}{2}O_{2(g)} \rightarrow MgO_{(s)}$ [2 marks]

b) Use the data on the right to calculate the entropy change for the reaction above. [2 marks]

Substance	Entropy — standard conditions ($J\ K^{-1}\ mol^{-1}$)
$Mg_{(s)}$	32.7
$O_{2(g)}$	205.0
$MgO_{(s)}$	26.9

c) Does the result of the calculation indicate that the reaction will be feasible? Give a reason for your answer. [1 mark]

Q2 For the reaction $H_2O_{(l)} \rightarrow H_2O_{(s)}$:

$S^{\ominus}[H_2O_{(l)}] = 70\ J K^{-1} mol^{-1}$, $S^{\ominus}[H_2O_{(s)}] = 48\ J K^{-1} mol^{-1}$

a) Calculate the entropy change for this reaction. [2 marks]

b) Explain why this reaction might be feasible. [1 mark]

Being neat and tidy is against the laws of nature...

Well, there you go. Entropy in all its glory. You haven't seen the back of it yet though, oh no. There's more where this came from. Which is why, if random disorder has left you in a spin, I'd suggest reading it again and making sure you've got your head round this lot before you turn over. You'll thank me for it, you will... Chocolates are always welcome...

Free Energy

Free energy — I could do with a bit of that. My gas bill is astronomical.

For Feasible Reactions ΔG must be **Negative** or **Zero**

1) The tendency of a process to take place is dependent on three things — the **entropy**, **ΔS**, the **enthalpy**, **ΔH**, and the **temperature**, **T**. When you put all these things **together** you get the **free energy change**, **ΔG**.
ΔG tells you if a reaction is **feasible** or not — the more negative the value of ΔG, the more feasible the reaction.
Of course, there's a formula for it:

$$\Delta G = \Delta H - T\Delta S$$

ΔH = enthalpy change (in $J\,mol^{-1}$)
T = temperature (in K)
ΔS = entropy change (in $J\,K^{-1}mol^{-1}$)

The units of ΔG are $J\,mol^{-1}$.

Example: Calculate the free energy change for the following reaction at 298 K.

$MgCO_{3(g)} \rightarrow MgO_{(s)} + CO_{2(g)}$ $\Delta H^{\circ} = +117\,000\ J\,mol^{-1}$, $\Delta S^{\circ}_{system} = +175\ J\,K^{-1}\,mol^{-1}$

$\Delta G = \Delta H - T\Delta S_{system} = +117\,000 - (298 \times (+175)) =$ **$+64\,900\ J\,mol^{-1}$** (3 s.f.)

ΔG is positive — so the reaction isn't feasible at this temperature.

2) When $\Delta G = 0$, the reaction is **just feasible**. So the temperature at which the reaction becomes feasible can be calculated by rearranging the equation like this:

$$\Delta H - T\Delta S = 0, \text{ so } T = \frac{\Delta H}{\Delta S}$$

Example: At what temperature does the reaction $MgCO_{3(g)} \rightarrow MgO_{(s)} + CO_{2(g)}$ become feasible?

$$T = \frac{\Delta H}{\Delta S} = \frac{+117\,000}{+175} = \mathbf{669\ K}$$

3) You can use ΔG to **predict** whether or not a reaction is **feasible**.
By looking at the equation $\Delta G = \Delta H - T\Delta S$, you can see that:

When ΔH is **negative** and ΔS is **positive**, ΔG will always be **negative** and the reaction is **feasible**.
When ΔH is **positive** and ΔS is **negative**, ΔG will always be **positive** and the reaction is **not feasible**.

In other situations, the feasibility of the reaction is dependent on the temperature.

Negative ΔG does not **Guarantee** a Reaction

The value of the free energy change doesn't tell you anything about the reaction's **rate**.
Even if ΔG shows that a reaction is theoretically feasible, it might have a really high activation energy or happen so slowly that you wouldn't notice it happening at all. For example:

$H_{2(g)} + ½O_{2(g)} \rightarrow H_2O_{(g)}$ $\Delta H^{\circ} = -242\,000\ J\,mol^{-1}$, $\Delta S^{\circ} = -44.4\ J\,K^{-1}\,mol^{-1}$
At 298 K, $\Delta G = -242\,000 - (298 \times (-44.4)) =$ **$-229\,000\ J\,mol^{-1}$** (3 s.f.)
But this reaction is **not** feasible at 298 K — it needs a spark to start it off due to its **high activation energy**.

You Might Need to Work Out ΔH

Sometimes, to find ΔG for a reaction, you may first need to work out the **enthalpy change** of the reaction.
You can calculate **ΔH** from the **temperature change** of a **known volume** of water (or solution) using this equation:

energy change = mass × specific heat capacity × change in temperature

More often, you'll probably see it written in symbols: $q = mc\Delta T$

You may remember this equation from way back in Module 3 (p. 71).

q is the energy change in J (it's the same as ΔH (in $J\,mol^{-1}$) if the pressure is constant).
m is the mass of water or solution in g and ΔT is the temperature change in K or °C.
c is the specific heat capacity of the substance (usually the specific heat capacity of water, 4.18 $J\,g^{-1}K^{-1}$).

To find **ΔH** (the energy change per mole), just **divide** the value of q by the **number of moles** of reactant.
Once you've worked out the enthalpy change, you can go on to work out ΔG...

Free Energy

Example: When 30.0 g of solid ammonium chloride ($NH_4Cl_{(s)}$) is dissolved in water, the temperature of the water decreases from 293 K to 291 K. The total mass of the solution is 980 g. What is the free energy change in $J\,mol^{-1}$ for this reaction at 25.0 °C? Assume the specific heat capacity of the solution is 4.18 $J\,g^{-1}K^{-1}$.

$$NH_4Cl_{(s)} \rightarrow NH_4{}^+{}_{(aq)} + Cl^-{}_{(aq)}$$

$S^{\ominus}[NH_4Cl_{(s)}] = 94.6\ J\,K^{-1}\,mol^{-1}$ $S^{\ominus}[NH_4{}^+{}_{(aq)}] = 113.4\ J\,K^{-1}\,mol^{-1}$ $S^{\ominus}[Cl^-] = 56.5\ J\,K^{-1}\,mol^{-1}$

1. First work out the **enthalpy change**, ΔH:

$q = mc\Delta T = 980 \times 4.18 \times (293 - 291) = 8192.8\ J$

$M_r(NH_4Cl) = 14.0 + (4 \times 1.0) + 35.5 = 53.5$

$30.0 \div 53.5 = 0.561$ moles of NH_4Cl ← This is the number of moles of NH_4Cl that have dissolved to give q.

The balanced reaction involves 1 mole of NH_4Cl, so:

$\Delta H = 8192.8 \div 0.561 \approx$ **+14 600 $J\,mol^{-1}$** ← The reaction is endothermic, so ΔH is positive.

2. Then work out the **entropy change**, ΔS:

$\Delta S = \Delta S_{products} - \Delta S_{reactants} = (113.4 + 56.5) - 94.6 =$ **75.3 $J\,K^{-1}\,mol^{-1}$**

3. Now you can find ΔG:

First, convert the temperature to Kelvin:

$T = 25.0 + 273 = 298\ K$

$\Delta G = \Delta H - T\Delta S = 14\,600 - (298 \times 75.3)$

$\approx$ **−7840 $J\,mol^{-1}$** (3 s.f.)

ΔG is negative, so the reaction is feasible at 25 °C.

Practice Questions

Q1 What are the three things that determine the value of ΔG?

Q2 If the free energy change of a reaction is positive, what can you conclude about the reaction?

Q3 Why might a reaction with a negative ΔG value not always be feasible?

Q4 What equation links the energy change of a reaction with the specific heat capacity, temperature and mass?

Exam Questions

Q1 a) Use the equation below and the table on the right to calculate the free energy change for the complete combustion of methane at 298 K. [2 marks]

$$CH_{4(g)} + 2O_{2(g)} \rightarrow CO_{2(g)} + 2H_2O_{(l)} \qquad \Delta H^{\ominus} = -730\ kJ\,mol^{-1}$$

b) Explain whether the reaction is feasible at 298 K. [1 mark]

c) What is the maximum temperature at which the reaction is feasible? [2 marks]

Substance	$S^{\ominus}(J\,K^{-1}\,mol^{-1})$
$CH_{4(g)}$	186
$O_{2(g)}$	205
$CO_{2(g)}$	214
$H_2O_{(l)}$	69.9
$C_3H_7OH_{(l)}$	193

Q2 In an experiment to determine ΔG for the complete combustion of propanol, the heat produced by burning 48.5g of propanol raised the temperature of 100 ml of water by 3.50 °C.

The balanced equation for this reaction is: $C_3H_7OH_{(l)} + 4\frac{1}{2}O_{2(g)} \rightarrow 3CO_{2(g)} + 4H_2O_{(l)}$

Use the equation and the values in the table to calculate the free energy change of the combustion of propanol at 298 K. The specific heat capacity of water is 4.18 $J\,g^{-1}\,K^{-1}$. [5 marks]

ΔG for chemistry revision definitely has a positive value...

Okay, so ΔG won't tell you for definite whether a reaction will happen, but it will tell you if the reaction is at least theoretically feasible. Make sure you know the formula for ΔG, as well as how to work out the numbers to plonk in it. And I know I've said it before, but I'll say it again now... check your units, check your units, check your units.

Redox Equations

And now for something a bit different. Read on to learn more about redox...

*In a **Redox Reaction,** Electrons are **Transferred***

In case you've forgotten all of that stuff on page 38, here's a brief recap of redox reactions:

1) **Oxidation** is a **loss** of electrons. **Reduction** is a **gain** of electrons.
2) In a redox reaction, reduction and oxidation happen **simultaneously**.
3) An **oxidising agent accepts** electrons and gets **reduced**.
4) A **reducing agent donates** electrons and gets **oxidised**.

$$Na + \frac{1}{2}Cl_2 \rightarrow Na^+ Cl^-$$

($-e^-$ from Na to Na^+; $+e^-$ from Cl_2 to Cl^-)

Na is oxidised.
Cl in reduced.

I couldn't find a red ox, so you'll have to make do with a multicoloured donkey instead.

*You can Separate Redox Reactions into **Half-Reactions***

1) A redox reaction is made up of an **oxidation half-reaction** and a **reduction half-reaction**.
2) You can write an **ionic half-equation** for each of these **half-reactions**.
For example, the half-equations for the oxidation of sodium and the reduction of chlorine look like this:

$$Na \rightarrow Na^+ + e^-$$

$$Cl_2 + 2e^- \rightarrow 2Cl^-$$

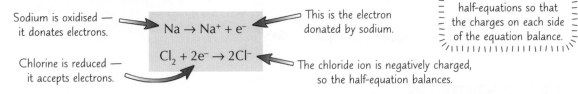

Sodium is oxidised — it donates electrons.

This is the electron donated by sodium.

Chlorine is reduced — it accepts electrons.

The chloride ion is negatively charged, so the half-equation balances.

Electrons are shown in half-equations so that the charges on each side of the equation balance.

3) An oxidation half-equation can be **combined** with a reduction half-equation to make a **full redox equation**.

Example: **Zinc metal** displaces **silver ions** from silver nitrate solution to form **zinc nitrate** and a deposit of **silver metal**.

The zinc atoms each lose 2 electrons (oxidation): $Zn_{(s)} \rightarrow Zn^{2+}_{(aq)} + 2e^-$

The silver ions each gain 1 electron (reduction): $Ag^+_{(aq)} + e^- \rightarrow Ag_{(s)}$

Two silver ions are needed to accept the **two electrons** released by each zinc atom.
So you need to **double** the silver half-equation before the two half-equations can be combined:

$$2Ag^+_{(aq)} + 2e^- \rightarrow 2Ag_{(s)}$$

Now the number of electrons lost and gained **balance**, so the half-equations can be combined:

$$Zn_{(s)} + 2Ag^+_{(aq)} + 2e^- \rightarrow Zn^{2+}_{(aq)} + 2e^- + 2Ag_{(s)}$$

The electrons **cancel each other out**, so they aren't included in the full equation:

$$Zn_{(s)} + 2Ag^+_{(aq)} \rightarrow Zn^{2+}_{(aq)} + 2Ag_{(s)}$$

The charges on each side of the equation should be balanced — the charge on each side of this equation is +2.

4) Apart from multiplying up the reactants and products, **electrons**, **H^+** ions and **water** are the **only** things that you're allowed to add to balance half-equations.
5) If your oxidising agent contains **oxygen**, you might have to add some H^+ ions and H_2O to your half-equations to make them balance.
6) Once you've balanced the **atoms** in the half-equation, don't forget to also balance the **charges**. Read on to find out more...

Redox Equations

Use e^-, H^+ and H_2O to Balance Half-Equations

Example: Acidified manganate(VII) ions (MnO_4^-) can be reduced to Mn^{2+} by Fe^{2+} ions. Write the two half-equations for this reaction.

Iron is being oxidised. The half equation for this is: $Fe^{2+}_{(aq)} \rightarrow Fe^{3+}_{(aq)} + e^-$

The second half-equation is a little bit trickier...

1) Manganate is being reduced. Start by writing this down: $MnO_4^-{}_{(aq)} \rightarrow Mn^{2+}_{(aq)}$
2) To balance the **oxygens**, you need to add **water** to the right hand side of the equation:

$$MnO_4^-{}_{(aq)} \rightarrow Mn^{2+}_{(aq)} + 4H_2O_{(l)}$$

3) Now you need to add some **H^+ ions** to the left hand side to balance the **hydrogens**:

$$MnO_4^-{}_{(aq)} + 8H^+_{(aq)} \rightarrow Mn^{2+}_{(aq)} + 4H_2O_{(l)}$$

This is why oxidising agents containing oxygen often have to be acidified — the oxygen needs those H+ ions for somewhere to go.

4) Finally, balance the **charges** by adding some **electrons**:

$$MnO_4^-{}_{(aq)} + 8H^+_{(aq)} + 5e^- \rightarrow Mn^{2+}_{(aq)} + 4H_2O_{(l)}$$

Charges: (–1) (+8) (–5) (+2) 0

The charges on each side now add up to +2.

The transfer of $5e^-$ makes sense: Mn in manganate(VII) has an oxidation state of +7. It needs to gain five electrons for it to change to an oxidation state of +2.

Practice Questions

Q1 Does an oxidising agent lose or gain electrons during a redox reaction?

Q2 Identify which species is being oxidised in this reaction: $Zn + 2Ag^+ \rightarrow Zn^{2+} + 2Ag$

Q3 Which of these half-equations shows a reduction reaction? A $Fe^{2+} \rightarrow Fe^{3+} + e^-$ B $Cl_2 + 2e^- \rightarrow 2Cl^-$

Exam Questions

Q1 Give the two half-equations for this reaction: $Cl_2 + 2Fe^{2+} \rightarrow 2Cl^- + 2Fe^{3+}$ [2 marks]

Q2 The two half-equations for the reaction between aluminium and oxygen are:

$Al \rightarrow Al^{3+} + e^-$ and $O_2 + e^- \rightarrow O^{2-}$

a) Balance these two half-equations. [1 mark]

b) Combine these half-equations to give the full redox equation for this reaction. [1 mark]

Q3 Acidified manganate(VII) ions will react with aqueous iodide ions to form iodine. The two half-equations for the changes that occur are:

$MnO_4^- + 8H^+ + 5e^- \rightarrow Mn^{2+} + 4H_2O$ and $2I^- \rightarrow I_2 + 2e^-$

Write a balanced equation to show the reaction taking place. [1 mark]

Q4 Dichromate ions ($Cr_2O_7^{2-}$) are reduced to Cr^{3+} by zinc. One of the half-equations for this reaction is: $Zn \rightarrow Zn^{2+} + 2e^-$.

a) Write the other half-equation. [2 marks]

b) Give the full redox equation for this reaction. [1 mark]

Sodium's lost an electron — it was an oxidant waiting to happen...

Just when you thought you knew all there is to know about redox, now you've got to figure out the equations too. Don't get all up in a tizzy about it, just make sure you've got the half-equations balanced before you stick them together — and remember to check the charges when you're done. The overall charge should be the same on both sides.

Redox Titrations

Redox titrations work like acid-base titrations but they're used to find out how much oxidising agent is needed to exactly react with a quantity of reducing agent (or vice versa). You don't need to use an indicator though...

Transition Elements are Used as Oxidising and Reducing Agents

Transition (d-block) elements are good at changing **oxidation state** (see p. 166). This makes them useful as oxidising and reducing agents as they'll readily **give out** or **receive** electrons. What's more, as they change oxidation state they often also change **colour**, so it's easy to spot when the reaction is finished. Here are a couple of examples:

Acidified **potassium manganate(VII)** solution, $KMnO_{4\,(aq)}$, is used as an **oxidising agent**.
It contains **manganate(VII) ions** (MnO_4^-), in which manganese has an oxidation state of **+7**.
They can be reduced to Mn^{2+} ions during a **redox reaction**.

Example: The oxidation of Fe^{2+} to Fe^{3+} by manganate(VII) ions in solution.

Half equations:

$$MnO_4^- + 8H^+ + 5e^- \rightarrow Mn^{2+} + 4H_2O \quad \text{Manganese is reduced}$$

$$5Fe^{2+} \rightarrow 5Fe^{3+} + 5e^- \quad \text{Iron is oxidised}$$

$$MnO_4^- + 8H^+ + 5Fe^{2+} \rightarrow Mn^{2+} + 4H_2O + 5Fe^{3+}$$

$MnO_{4\,(aq)}^-$ is purple. $[Mn(H_2O)_6]^{2+}_{(aq)}$ is colourless. During this reaction, you'll see a colour change from purple to colourless.

Acidified **potassium dichromate** solution, $K_2Cr_2O_{7\,(aq)}$, is another **oxidising agent**.
It contains **dichromate(VI) ions** ($Cr_2O_7^{2-}$) in which chromium has an oxidation state of **+6**.
They can be reduced to Cr^{3+} ions during a **redox reaction**.

Example: The oxidation of Zn to Zn^{2+} by dichromate(VI) ions in solution.

Half equations:

$$Cr_2O_7^{2-} + 14H^+ + 6e^- \rightarrow 2Cr^{3+} + 7H_2O \quad \text{Chromium is reduced}$$

$$3Zn \rightarrow 3Zn^{2+} + 6e^- \quad \text{Zinc is oxidised}$$

$$Cr_2O_7^{2-} + 14H^+ + 3Zn \rightarrow 2Cr^{3+} + 7H_2O + 3Zn^{2+}$$

$Cr_2O_{7\,(aq)}^{2-}$ is orange. $[Cr(H_2O)_6]^{3+}_{(aq)}$ is violet, but usually looks green. During this reaction, you'll see a colour change from orange to green.

Titrations Using Transition Element Ions are Redox Titrations

To work out the **concentration** of a reducing agent, you just need to titrate a **known volume** of it against an oxidising agent of **known concentration**. This allows you to work out how much oxidising agent is needed to **exactly react** with your sample of reducing agent.

To find out how many **manganate(VII) ions** (MnO_4^-) are needed to react with a reducing agent:

You can also work out the concentration of an oxidising agent by titrating it with a reducing agent of known concentration.

1) First you measure out a quantity of the **reducing agent**, e.g. aqueous Fe^{2+} ions, using a pipette, and put it in a conical flask.
2) You then add some **dilute sulfuric acid** to the flask — this is an excess, so you don't have to be too exact.
   The acid is added to make sure there are plenty of H^+ ions to allow the oxidising agent to be reduced.
3) Now you gradually add the aqueous MnO_4^- (the **oxidising agent**) to the reducing agent using a **burette**, **swirling** the conical flask as you do so.
4) You stop when the mixture in the flask **just** becomes tainted with the colour of the MnO_4^- (the **end point**) and record the volume of the oxidising agent added.
5) Run a few **titrations** and then calculate the **mean volume** of MnO_4^-.

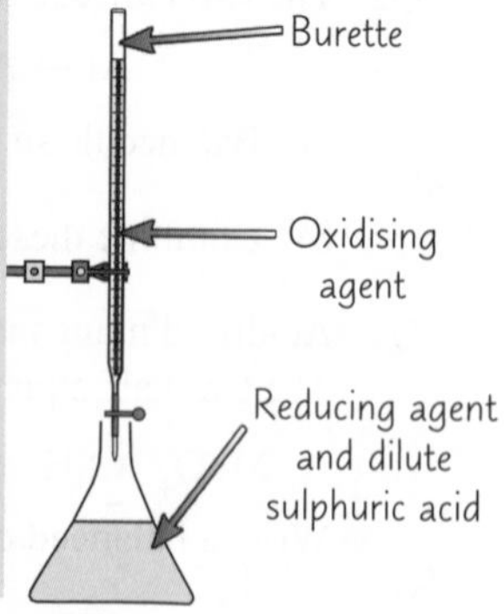

You can also do titrations the **other way round** — adding the reducing agent to the oxidising agent.
The rule tends to be that you add the substance of **known** concentration to the substance of **unknown** concentration.

Watch Out For the Sharp Colour Change

1) **Manganate(VII) ions** (MnO_4^-) in **aqueous potassium manganate(VII)** ($KMnO_4$) are **purple**. When they're added to the reducing agent, they start reacting. This reaction will continue until **all** of the reducing agent is used up.
2) The **very next drop** into the flask will give the mixture the **purple colour of the oxidising agent**. The trick is to spot **exactly** when this happens. (You could use a coloured reducing agent and a colourless oxidising agent instead — then you'd be watching for the moment that the colour in the flask disappears.)
3) Doing the reaction in front of a white surface can make colour changes easier to spot.

Redox Titrations

You Can **Calculate** the **Concentration** of a Reagent from the **Titration Results**

Example: 27.5 cm^3 of 0.0200 mol dm^{-3} aqueous potassium manganate(VII) reacted with 25.0 cm^3 of acidified iron(II) sulfate solution. Calculate the concentration of Fe^{2+} ions in the solution.

$$MnO_4^-{}_{(aq)} + 8H^+{}_{(aq)} + 5Fe^{2+}{}_{(aq)} \rightarrow Mn^{2+}{}_{(aq)} + 4H_2O_{(l)} + 5Fe^{3+}{}_{(aq)}$$

1) Work out the number of **moles of MnO_4^- ions** added to the flask.

$$\text{Number of moles } MnO_4^- \text{ added} = \frac{\text{concentration} \times \text{volume}}{1000} = \frac{0.0200 \times 27.5}{1000} = 5.50 \times 10^{-4} \text{ moles}$$

2) Look at the balanced equation to find how many moles of **Fe^{2+}** react with **one mole** of MnO_4^-. Then you can work out the **number of moles of Fe^{2+}** in the flask.

5 moles of Fe^{2+} react with 1 mole of MnO_4^-. So moles of Fe^{2+} = $5.50 \times 10^{-4} \times 5 = 2.75 \times 10^{-3}$ moles.

3) Work out the **number of moles of Fe^{2+}** that would be in 1000 cm^3 (1 dm^3) of solution — this is the **concentration.**

25.0 cm^3 of solution contained 2.75×10^{-3} moles of Fe^{2+}.

1000 cm^3 of solution would contain $\frac{(2.75 \times 10^{-3}) \times 1000}{25.0} = 0.110$ moles of Fe^{2+}.

So the concentration of Fe^{2+} is **0.110 mol dm^{-3}**.

Practice Questions

Q1 Write a half equation to show manganate(VII) ions acting as an oxidising agent.

Q2 Why is dilute acid added to the reaction mixture in redox titrations involving MnO_4^- ions?

Q3 If you carry out a redox titration by slowly adding aqueous MnO_4^- ions to aqueous Fe^{2+} ions, how can you tell that you've reached the end point?

Exam Questions

Q1 A 10 cm^3 sample of $SnCl_2$ solution was titrated with acidified potassium manganate(VII) solution. Exactly 20 cm^3 of 0.10 mol dm^{-3} potassium manganate(VII) solution was needed to fully oxidise the tin(II) chloride.

a) How many moles of potassium manganate(VII) were needed to fully oxidise the tin(II) chloride? [1 mark]

b) The equation for this reaction is: $2MnO_4^- + 16H^+ + 5Sn^{2+} \rightarrow 2Mn^{2+} + 8H_2O + 5Sn^{4+}$
How many moles of tin(II) chloride were present in the 10 cm^3 sample? [1 mark]

c) Calculate the concentration of Sn^{2+} ions in the sample solution. [1 mark]

Q2 Steel wool contains a high percentage of iron, and a small amount of carbon.
A 1.30 g piece of steel wool was completely dissolved in 50.0 cm^3 of aqueous sulfuric acid.
The resulting solution was titrated with 0.400 mol dm^{-3} of potassium manganate(VII) solution.
11.5 cm^3 of the potassium manganate(VII) solution was needed to oxidise all of the iron(II) ions to iron(III).

a) Write a balanced equation for the reaction between the manganate(VII) ions and the iron(II) ions. [1 mark]

b) Calculate the concentration of iron(II) ions present in the original solution. [3 marks]

c) Calculate the percentage of iron present in the steel wool. Give your answer to one decimal place. [2 marks]

And how many moles does it take to change a light bulb...

...two, one to change the bulb, and another to ask "Why do we need light bulbs? We're moles — most of the time that we're underground, we keep our eyes shut. And the electricity costs a packet. We haven't thought this through..."

Iodine-Thiosulfate Titrations

This is another example of a redox titration — it's a nifty little reaction that you can use to find the concentration of an oxidising agent. And since it's a titration, that also means a few more calculations to get to grips with...

Iodine-Sodium Thiosulfate Titrations *are Dead Handy*

Iodine-sodium thiosulfate titrations are a way of finding the concentration of an **oxidising agent**.

The **more concentrated** an oxidising agent is, the **more ions will be oxidised** by a certain volume of it.
So here's how you can find out the concentration of a solution of the oxidising agent **potassium iodate(V)**:

STAGE 1: Use a sample of oxidising agent to oxidise as much iodide as possible.

1) Measure out a certain volume of **potassium iodate(V)** solution (**KIO_3**) (the oxidising agent) — say **25.0 cm³**.
2) Add this to an excess of acidified **potassium iodide** solution (**KI**).
The iodate(V) ions in the potassium iodate(V) solution **oxidise** some of the **iodide ions** to **iodine**.

$$IO_3^-{}_{(aq)} + 5I^-{}_{(aq)} + 6H^+{}_{(aq)} \rightarrow 3I_{2(aq)} + 3H_2O_{(l)}$$

STAGE 2: Find out how many moles of iodine have been produced.

You do this by **titrating** the resulting solution with **sodium thiosulfate** (**$Na_2S_2O_3$**).
(You need to know the concentration of the sodium thiosulfate solution.)

The iodine in the solution reacts with **thiosulfate ions** like this:

$$I_{2\,(aq)} + 2S_2O_3^{2-}{}_{(aq)} \rightarrow 2I^-{}_{(aq)} + S_4O_6^{2-}{}_{(aq)}$$

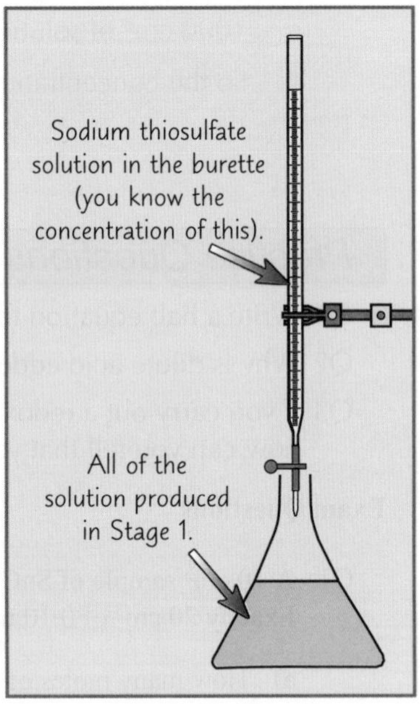
Sodium thiosulfate solution in the burette (you know the concentration of this).
All of the solution produced in Stage 1.

Titration of Iodine with Sodium Thiosulfate

1) Take the flask containing the solution that was produced in Stage 1.
2) From a burette, add sodium thiosulfate solution to the flask **drop by drop**.
3) It's hard to see the end point, so when the iodine colour fades to a **pale yellow** (this is close to the end point), add 2 cm³ of **starch solution** (to detect the presence of iodine). The solution in the conical flask will go **dark blue**, showing there's still some iodine there.
4) Add sodium thiosulfate **one drop at a time** until the blue colour disappears.
5) When this happens, it means all the iodine has **just** been reacted.
6) Now you can **calculate** the number of moles of iodine in the solution.

Here's how you'd do the titration calculation to find the **number of moles of iodine** produced in Stage 1.

Example: The iodine in the solution produced in Stage 1 reacted fully with 11.0 cm³ of 0.120 mol dm⁻³ thiosulfate solution. Work out the number of moles of iodine present in the starting solution.

$$I_2 + 2S_2O_3^{2-} \rightarrow 2I^- + S_4O_6^{2-}$$

11.0 cm³
0.120 mol dm⁻³

Number of moles of thiosulfate $= \frac{\text{concentration} \times \text{volume (cm}^3)}{1000} = \frac{0.120 \times 11.0}{1000} = \mathbf{1.32 \times 10^{-3}}$ **moles**

1 mole of iodine reacts with **2 moles** of thiosulfate.

So number of **moles of iodine** in the solution = $1.32 \times 10^{-3} \div 2 = \mathbf{6.60 \times 10^{-4}}$ **moles**

Iodine-Thiosulfate Titrations

STAGE 3: Calculate the concentration of the oxidising agent.

1) Now you look back at your original equation: $IO_3^-{}_{(aq)} + 5I^-{}_{(aq)} + 6H^+{}_{(aq)} \rightarrow 3I_{2(aq)} + 3H_2O_{(l)}$

2) 25.0 cm³ of potassium iodate(V) solution produced **6.60 × 10⁻⁴ moles of iodine.** The equation shows that **one mole** of iodate(V) ions will produce **three moles** of iodine.

3) That means there must have been **6.60 × 10⁻⁴ ÷ 3 = 2.20 × 10⁻⁴ moles of iodate(V) ions** in the original solution. So now it's straightforward to find the **concentration** of the potassium iodate(V) solution, which is what you're after:

$$\text{number of moles} = \frac{\text{concentration} \times \text{volume}(\text{cm}^3)}{1000} \Rightarrow 2.20 \times 10^{-4} = \frac{\text{concentration} \times 25.0}{1000}$$

⇒ concentration of potassium iodate(V) solution = **0.00880 mol dm⁻³**

Practice Questions

Q1 How can an iodine-sodium thiosulfate titration help you to work out the concentration of an oxidising agent?

Q2 How many moles of thiosulfate ions react with one mole of iodine molecules?

Q3 What is added during an iodine-sodium thiosulfate titration to make the end point easier to see?

Q4 Describe the colour change at the end point of the iodine-sodium thiosulfate titration.

Exam Questions

Q1 10.0 cm³ of potassium iodate(V) solution was reacted with excess acidified potassium iodide solution. All of the resulting solution was titrated with 0.150 mol dm⁻³ sodium thiosulfate solution. It fully reacted with 24.0 cm³ of the sodium thiosulfate solution.

a) Write an equation showing how iodine is formed in the reaction between iodate(V) ions and iodide ions in acidic solution. [1 mark]

b) How many moles of thiosulfate ions were there in 24.0 cm³ of the sodium thiosulfate solution? [1 mark]

c) In the titration, iodine reacted with sodium thiosulfate according to this equation:

$$I_{2(aq)} + 2Na_2S_2O_{3(aq)} \rightarrow 2NaI_{(aq)} + Na_2S_4O_{6(aq)}$$

Calculate the number of moles of iodine that reacted with the sodium thiosulfate solution. [1 mark]

d) How many moles of iodate(V) ions produce 1 mole of iodine from potassium iodide? [1 mark]

e) What was the concentration of the potassium iodate(V) solution? [2 marks]

Q2 An 18.0 cm³ sample of potassium manganate(VII) solution was reacted with an excess of acidified potassium iodide solution. The resulting solution was titrated with 0.300 mol dm⁻³ sodium thiosulfate solution. 12.5 cm³ of sodium thiosulfate solution were needed to fully react with the iodine.

When they were mixed, the manganate(VII) ions reacted with the iodide ions according to this equation:

$$2MnO_4^-{}_{(aq)} + 10I^-{}_{(aq)} + 16H^+ \rightarrow 5I_{2(aq)} + 8H_2O_{(aq)} + 2Mn^{2+}{}_{(aq)}$$

During the titration, the iodine reacted with sodium thiosulfate according to this equation:

$$I_{2(aq)} + 2Na_2S_2O_{3(aq)} \rightarrow 2NaI_{(aq)} + Na_2S_4O_{6(aq)}$$

Calculate the concentration of the potassium manganate(VII) solution. [4 marks]

Two vowels went out for dinner — they had an iodate...

This might seem like quite a faff — you do a redox reaction to release iodine, titrate the iodine solution, do a sum to find the iodine concentration, write an equation, then do another sum to work out the concentration of something else. The thing is though, it does work, and you do have to know how. If you're rusty on the calculations, look back to page 31.

Electrochemical Cells

There are electrons toing and froing in redox reactions. And when electrons move, you get electricity.

Electrochemical Cells Make Electricity

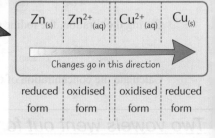

Electrochemical cells can be made from **two different metals** dipped in salt solutions of their **own ions** and connected by a wire (the **external circuit**).

There are always **two** reactions within an electrochemical cell — one's an oxidation and one's a reduction — so it's a **redox process** (see page 152).

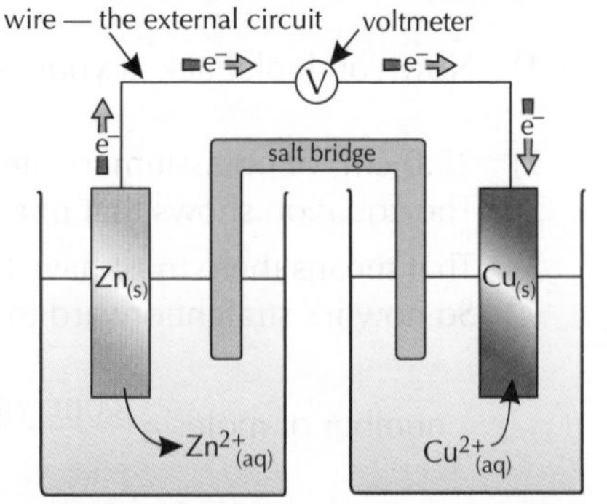

The solutions are connected by a **salt bridge** made from filter paper soaked in $KNO_{3(aq)}$. This allows ions to flow through and balance out the charges.

Here's what happens in the **zinc/copper** electrochemical cell on the right:

1) Zinc **loses electrons** more easily than copper. So in the half-cell on the left, zinc (from the zinc electrode) is **oxidised** to form $\mathbf{Zn^{2+}_{(aq)}}$ ions. This releases electrons into the external circuit.
2) In the other half-cell, the **same number of electrons** are taken from the external circuit, **reducing** the Cu^{2+} ions to copper atoms.

So **electrons** flow through the wire from the most reactive metal to the least.

A voltmeter in the external circuit shows the **voltage** between the two half-cells. This is the **cell potential** or **e.m.f.**, E_{cell}

You can also have half-cells involving **solutions of two aqueous ions of the same element**, such as $\mathbf{Fe^{2+}_{(aq)}/Fe^{3+}_{(aq)}}$. The conversion from Fe^{2+} to Fe^{3+}, or vice versa, happens on the surface of a platinum **electrode**.

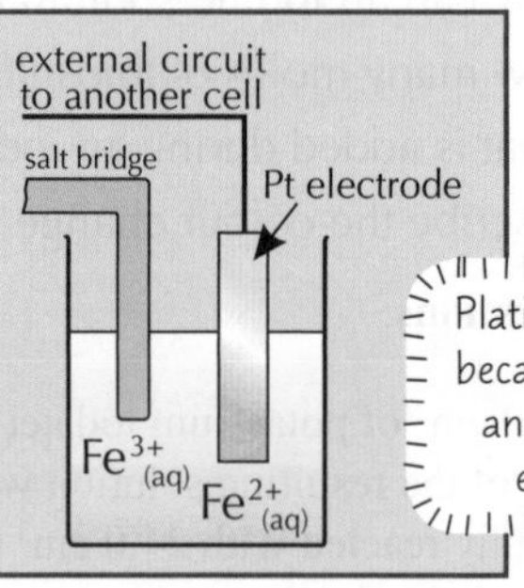

Platinum is used because it's inert and conducts electricity.

Electrochemical cells can also be made from **non-metals**.
For systems involving a **gas** (e.g. chlorine), the gas can be **bubbled over** a platinum electrode sitting in a solution of its **aqueous ions** (e.g. Cl^-).

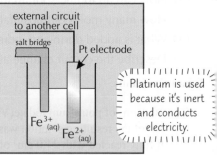

The Reactions at Each Electrode are Reversible

1) The **reactions** that occur at each electrode in the **zinc/copper cell** above are:

$$Zn^{2+}_{(aq)} + 2e^- \rightleftharpoons Zn_{(s)}$$
$$Cu^{2+}_{(aq)} + 2e^- \rightleftharpoons Cu_{(s)}$$

2) The **reversible arrows** show that both reactions can go in **either direction**. **Which direction** each reaction goes in depends on **how easily** each metal **loses electrons** (i.e. how easily it's **oxidised**).
3) How easily a metal is oxidised is measured using **electrode potentials**. A metal that's **easily oxidised** has a very **negative electrode potential**, while one that's harder to oxidise has a less negative or **a positive electrode potential**.

Half-cell	Electrode potential E°(V)
$Zn^{2+}_{(aq)}/Zn_{(s)}$	–0.76
$Cu^{2+}_{(aq)}/Cu_{(s)}$	+0.34

4) The table on the left shows the electrode potentials for the copper and zinc half-cells. The **zinc half-cell** has a **more negative** electrode potential, so **zinc is oxidised** (the reaction goes **backwards**), while **copper is reduced** (the reaction goes **forwards**). Remember, the little ⊖ symbol next to the *E* means it's under standard conditions — 298 K and 100 kPa.

There's a Convention for Drawing Electrochemical Cells

It's a bit of a faff drawing pictures of electrochemical cells. There's a **shorthand** way of representing them though — for example, this is the **Zn/Cu cell**:

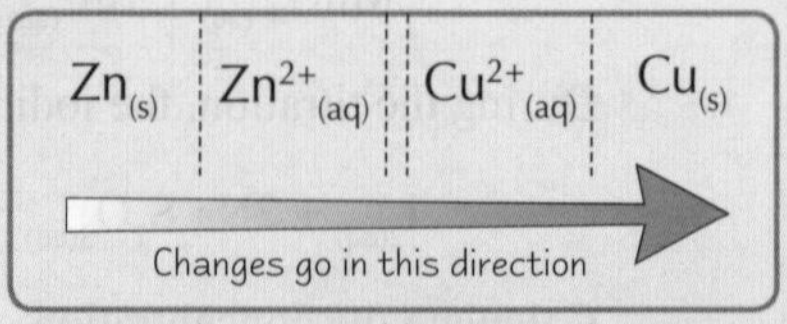

There are a couple of important **conventions** when drawing cells:

1) The **half-cell** with the **more negative** potential goes on the **left**.
2) The **oxidised forms** go in the **centre** of the cell diagram.

If you follow the conventions, you can use the electrode potentials to calculate the overall cell potential.

$$E^{\circ}_{cell} = E^{\circ}_{\text{right hand side}} - E^{\circ}_{\text{left hand side}}$$

The symbol for electrode potential is E°.

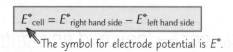

The cell potential will always be a **positive voltage**, because the more negative E° value is being subtracted from the more positive E° value. For example, the cell potential for the Zn/Cu cell = +0.34 – (–0.76) = **+1.1 V**.

Electrochemical Cells

Electrode Potentials are Measured Against Standard Hydrogen Electrodes

You measure the electrode potential of a half-cell against a **standard hydrogen electrode**.

> The **standard electrode potential**, E°, of a half-cell is the **voltage measured** under **standard conditions** when the **half-cell** is connected to a **standard hydrogen electrode**.

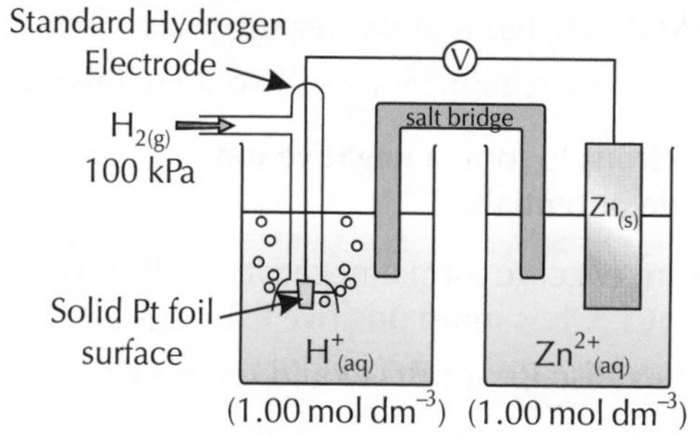

Standard conditions are:

1) Any solutions must have a concentration of **1.00 mol dm^{-3}** or be **equimolar** (i.e. contain the same number of moles of ions).
2) The temperature must be **298 K (25 °C)**.
3) The pressure must be **100 kPa**.

1) The **standard hydrogen electrode** is always shown on the **left** — it doesn't matter whether or not the other half-cell has a more positive value. The standard hydrogen electrode half-cell has a value of **0.00 V**.
2) The whole cell potential = $E^{\circ}_{\text{right hand side}} - E^{\circ}_{\text{left hand side}}$.
$E^{\circ}_{\text{left hand side}}$ = 0.00 V, so the **voltage reading** will be equal to $E^{\circ}_{\text{right hand side}}$.
This reading could be **positive** or **negative**, depending which way the **electrons flow**.

Conditions Affect the Value of the Electrode Potential

Just like any other reversible reaction, the **equilibrium position** in a half-cell is affected by changes in **temperature**, **pressure** and **concentration**. Changing the equilibrium position changes the **cell potential**.
To get around this, **standard conditions** are used to measure electrode potentials — using these conditions means you always get the **same value** for the electrode potential and you can **compare values** for different cells.

Practice Questions

Q1 $Zn^{2+}_{(aq)} + 2e^- \rightleftharpoons Zn_{(s)}$, $E^{\circ} = -0.76$ V $Cu^{2+}_{(aq)} + 2e^- \rightleftharpoons Cu_{(s)}$, $E^{\circ} = +0.34$ V
Draw a diagram to show the set up of a zinc/copper electrochemical cell, including the direction of electrons.

Q2 What's the definition of standard electrode potential?

Q3 What is the voltage of the standard hydrogen electrode half-cell?

Exam Questions

Q1 A cell is made up of a lead and an iron plate, dipped in solutions of lead(II) nitrate and iron(II) nitrate respectively and connected by a salt bridge. The electrode potentials for the two electrodes are:

$Fe^{2+}_{(aq)} + 2e^- \rightleftharpoons Fe_{(s)}$ $E^{\circ} = -0.44$ V $Pb^{2+}_{(aq)} + 2e^- \rightleftharpoons Pb_{(s)}$ $E^{\circ} = -0.13$ V

a) Which metal becomes oxidised in the cell? Explain your answer. [2 marks]

b) Find the standard cell potential of this cell. [1 mark]

Q2 An electrochemical cell containing a zinc half-cell and a silver half-cell was set up using a potassium nitrate salt bridge. The cell potential at 25 °C was measured to be 1.40 V.

$Zn^{2+}_{(aq)} + 2e^- \rightleftharpoons Zn_{(s)}$ $E^{\circ} = -0.76$ V $Ag^{+}_{(aq)} + e^- \rightleftharpoons Ag_{(s)}$ $E^{\circ} = +0.80$ V

a) Use the standard electrode potentials given to calculate the standard cell potential for a zinc-silver cell. [1 mark]

b) Suggest two possible reasons why the actual cell potential was different from the value calculated in part (a). [2 marks]

Cells aren't just for Biologists, you know...

You've just got to think about this stuff. The metal on the left-hand electrode disappears off into the solution, leaving its electrons behind. This makes the left-hand electrode the negative one. So the right-hand electrode's got to be the positive one. It makes sense if you think about it. This electrode gives up electrons to turn the positive ions into atoms.

The Electrochemical Series

The electrochemical series is like a pop chart of the most reactive metals – except without the pop so it's really just a char

*The **Electrochemical Series** Shows You What's **Reactive** and What's Not*

1) The **more reactive** a **metal** is, the **more** it wants to **lose electrons** to form a **positive ion**.
More reactive metals have **more negative standard electrode potentials**.

> **Example:** Magnesium is **more reactive** than zinc — so it's more eager to form 2+ ions than zinc is.
> The list of standard electrode potentials shows that Mg^{2+}/Mg has a **more negative** value than Zn^{2+}/Zn.
> In terms of oxidation and reduction, magnesium would **reduce** Zn^{2+} (or Zn^{2+} would **oxidise** Mg).

2) The more reactive a **non-metal** is, the **more** it wants to **gain electrons** to form a **negative ion**.
More reactive non-metals have **more positive standard electrode potentials**.

> **Example:** Chlorine is **more reactive** than bromine — so it's more eager to form a negative ion than bromine is.
> The list of standard electrode potentials shows that $\frac{1}{2}Cl_2/Cl^-$ is **more positive** than $\frac{1}{2}Br_2/Br^-$.
> In terms of oxidation and reduction, chlorine would **oxidise** Br^- (or Br^- would **reduce** Cl).

3) Here's an **electrochemical series** showing some standard electrode potentials:

More positive electrode potentials mean that:
1. The left-hand substances are more easily reduced.
2. The right-hand substances are more stable.

Half-reaction	$E^\ominus$/V
$Mg^{2+}_{(aq)} + 2e^- \rightleftharpoons Mg_{(s)}$	–2.37
$Zn^{2+}_{(aq)} + 2e^- \rightleftharpoons Zn_{(s)}$	–0.76
$H^+_{(aq)} + e^- \rightleftharpoons \frac{1}{2}H_{2(g)}$	0.00
$Cu^{2+}_{(aq)} + 2e^- \rightleftharpoons Cu_{(s)}$	+0.34
$Fe^{3+}_{(aq)} + e^- \rightleftharpoons Fe^{2+}_{(aq)}$	+0.77
$\frac{1}{2}Br_{2(aq)} + e^- \rightleftharpoons Br^-_{(aq)}$	+1.07
$\frac{1}{2}Cl_{2(aq)} + e^- \rightleftharpoons Cl^-_{(aq)}$	+1.36

More negative electrode potentials mean that:
1. The right-hand substances are more easily oxidised.
2. The left-hand substances are more stable.

*Use **Electrode Potentials** to **Predict** Whether a Reaction Will Happen*

To figure out if a metal will react with the aqueous ions of another metal, you can use their E° values.

Example: Predict whether:
a) Zinc reacts with aqueous copper ions.

First you write the two **half-equations** down as reduction reactions:

$Zn^{2+}_{(aq)} + 2e^- \rightleftharpoons Zn_{(s)}$ $E^\circ = -0.76$ V

$Cu^{2+}_{(aq)} + 2e^- \rightleftharpoons Cu_{(s)}$ $E^\circ = +0.34$ V

The half-reactions are written as reduction reactions but one will always have to move in the direction of oxidation. Zn^{2+}/Zn has a more negative electrode potential than Cu^{2+}/Cu, so the zinc will be oxidised.

Then you look at the standard electrode potentials.
The half-equation with the **more negative** electrode potential will move to the **left**: $Zn_{(s)} \rightarrow Zn^{2+}_{(aq)} + 2e^-$
The half-equation with the **more positive** electrode potential will move to the **right**: $Cu^{2+}_{(aq)} + 2e^- \rightarrow Cu_{(s)}$

The two half-equations combine to give: $Zn_{(s)} + Cu^{2+}_{(aq)} \rightarrow Zn^{2+}_{(aq)} + Cu_{(s)}$

This is the **feasible** direction of the two half-reactions and it matches the reaction described in the question.
So zinc **will** react with aqueous copper ions.

b) Copper reacts with dilute sulfuric acid.

Again, write the two **half-equations** down: $Cu^{2+}_{(aq)} + 2e^- \rightleftharpoons Cu_{(s)}$ $E^\circ = +0.34$ V

$2H^+_{(aq)} + 2e^- \rightleftharpoons H_{2(g)}$ $E^\circ = 0.00$ V

For the acid, use the hydrogen half-equation.

The hydrogen half-equation has the **more negative** E°, so it will move to the **left**: $H_{2(g)} \rightarrow 2H^+_{(aq)} + 2e^-$

The two half-equations combine to give: $H_{2(g)} + Cu^{2+}_{(aq)} \rightarrow 2H^+_{(aq)} + Cu_{(s)}$

This equation shows the **feasible** direction of the two half-equations but shows gaseous hydrogen reacting with copper ions, not solid copper reacting with sulfuric acid. So copper **won't** react with sulfuric acid.

The Electrochemical Series

Sometimes the Prediction is Wrong

A **prediction** using E° only states if a reaction is **possible** under **standard conditions**. The prediction might be **wrong if**...

...the conditions are not standard.

1) Changing the **concentration** (or temperature) of the solution can cause the electrode potential to **change**.
2) For example the zinc/copper cell has these half equations in equilibrium...

$Zn_{(s)} \rightleftharpoons Zn^{2+}_{(aq)} + 2e^-$ $E^\circ = -0.76\ V$
$Cu^{2+}_{(aq)} + 2e^- \rightleftharpoons Cu_{(s)}$ $E^\circ = +0.34\ V$

$Zn_{(s)} + Cu^{2+}_{(aq)} \rightleftharpoons Zn^{2+}_{(aq)} + Cu_{(s)}$ $E_{cell} = +1.10\ V$

3) ...if you **increase** the concentration of Zn^{2+}, the **equilibrium** will shift to the **left**, **reducing** the ease of **electron loss**. The electrode potential of Zn/Zn^{2+} becomes **less negative** and the whole cell potential will be lower.
4) ...if you **increase** the concentration of Cu^{2+}, the **equilibrium** will shift to the **right**, **increasing** the ease of **electron gain**. The electrode potential of Cu^{2+}/Cu becomes **more positive** and the whole cell potential will be higher.

...the reaction kinetics are not favourable.

1) The **rate of a reaction** may be so **slow** that the reaction might **not appear** to happen.
2) If a reaction has a **high activation energy**, this may stop it happening.

Practice Questions

Q1 Cu is less reactive than Pb. Predict which half-reaction has the more negative standard electrode potential.
A $Pb^{2+} + 2e^- \rightleftharpoons Pb$ B $Cu^{2+} + 2e^- \rightleftharpoons Cu$

Q2 Use electrode potentials to show that magnesium will reduce Zn^{2+}.

Q3 Use the table on the opposite page to predict whether or not Zn^{2+} ions can oxidise Fe^{2+} ions to Fe^{3+} ions.

Exam Questions

Q1 Use the $E^\ominus$ values in the table on the right and on the previous page to determine the outcome of mixing the following solutions. If there is a reaction, determine the $E^\ominus$ value and write the equation. If there isn't a reaction, state this and explain why.

a) Zinc metal and Ni^{2+} ions. [2 marks]

b) Acidified MnO_4^- ions and Sn^{2+} ions. [2 marks]

c) $Br_{2(aq)}$ and acidified $Cr_2O_7^{2-}$ ions. [2 marks]

Half-reaction	$E^\ominus$/V
$MnO_4^-{}_{(aq)} + 8H^+_{(aq)} + 5e^- \rightleftharpoons Mn^{2+}_{(aq)} + 4H_2O_{(l)}$	+1.51
$Cr_2O_7^{2-}{}_{(aq)} + 14H^+_{(aq)} + 6e^- \rightleftharpoons 2Cr^{3+}_{(aq)} + 7H_2O_{(l)}$	+1.33
$Sn^{4+}_{(aq)} + 2e^- \rightleftharpoons Sn^{2+}_{(aq)}$	+0.14
$Ni^{2+}_{(aq)} + 2e^- \rightleftharpoons Ni_{(s)}$	–0.25

Q2 Potassium manganate(VII), $KMnO_4$, and potassium dichromate $K_2Cr_2O_7$, are both used as oxidising agents. From their electrode potentials (given in the table above), which would you predict is the stronger oxidising agent? Explain why. [2 marks]

Q3 A cell is set up with copper and nickel electrodes in $1\ mol\ dm^{-3}$ solutions of their ions, Cu^{2+} and Ni^{2+}, connected by a salt bridge.

a) Write equations for the reactions that occur in each half-cell. [2 marks]

b) Find the voltage of the cell. Use the $E^\ominus$ values in the table above and on the previous page. [1 mark]

c) What is the overall equation for this reaction? [1 mark]

d) How would the voltage of the cell change if a more dilute copper solution was used? [1 mark]

My mam always said I had potential...

To see if a reaction will happen, you basically find the two half-equations in the electrochemical series and check that the one you are predicting to go backwards is the one with the more negative electrode potential. Alternatively, you could calculate the cell potential for the reaction — if it's negative, it's never going to happen.

Storage and Fuel Cells

Yet more electrochemical reactions on these pages, but you're nearly at the end of the section so keep going...

Energy Storage Cells are Like Electrochemical Cells

Energy storage cells (fancy name for a battery) have been around for ages and modern ones **work** just like an **electrochemical cell**. For example the nickel-iron cell was developed way back at the start of the 1900s and is often used as a back-up power supply because it can be repeatedly charged and is very robust. You can work out the **voltage** produced by these **cells** by using the **electrode potentials** of the substances used in the cell.

There are **lots** of different cells and you **won't** be asked to remember the E° for the reactions, but you might be **asked** to work out the **cell potential** or **cell voltage** for a given cell... so here's an example I prepared earlier.

Example: The nickel-iron cell has a nickel oxide hydroxide (NiO(OH)) cathode and an iron (Fe) anode with potassium hydroxide as the electrolyte. Using the half equations given:

a) write out the full equation for the reaction.

b) calculate the cell voltage produced by the nickel-iron cell.

$Fe + 2OH^- \rightleftharpoons Fe(OH)_2 + 2e^-$ $\quad E^\circ = -0.44V$

$NiO(OH) + H_2O + e^- \rightleftharpoons Ni(OH)_2 + OH^-$ $\quad E^\circ = +0.76V$

You have to double everything in the second equation so that the electrons balance those in the first equation.

For the first part you have to **combine** the two half-equations together. The e^- and the OH^- are not shown because they get cancelled out.

The **overall** reaction is...

$2NiO(OH) + 2H_2O + Fe \rightarrow 2Ni(OH)_2 + Fe(OH)_2$

To calculate the **cell voltage** you use the **same formula** for working out the **cell potential** (page 158).

So the **cell voltage** $= E^\circ_{\text{right hand side}} - E^\circ_{\text{left hand side}}$

$= +0.76 - (-0.44)$

$= 1.2V$

Remember, $E^\circ_{\text{left hand side}}$ is the more negative electrode potential.

Fuel Cells Generate Electricity from Reacting a Fuel with an Oxidant

A **fuel cell** produces electricity by reacting a **fuel**, usually hydrogen, with an **oxidant**, which is most likely to be oxygen.

1) At the **anode** the platinum catalyst **splits** the H_2 into protons and electrons.

2) The **polymer electrolyte membrane** (PEM) **only** allows the H^+ across and this **forces** the e^- to travel **around** the circuit to get to the cathode.

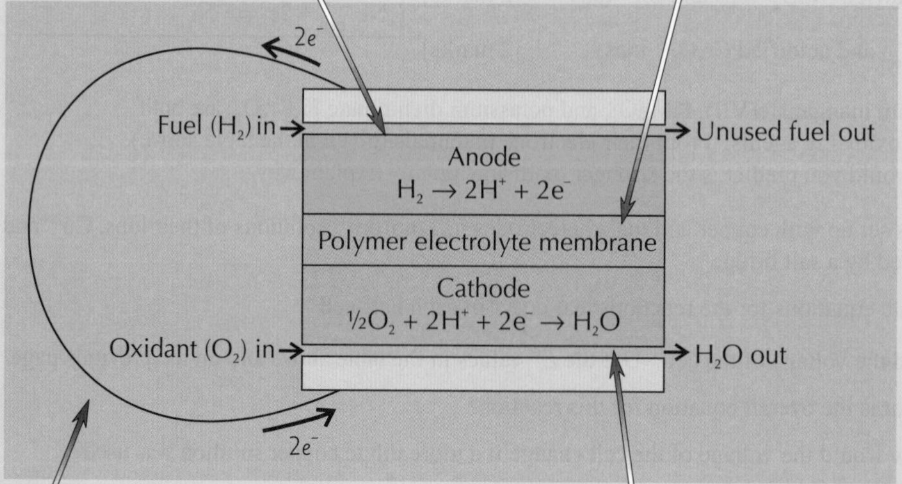

3) An **electric current** is created in the circuit, which is used to **power** something like a car or a bike or a dancing Santa.

4) At the **cathode**, O_2 **combines** with the H^+ from the anode and the e^- from the circuit to make H_2O. This is the only waste product.

Storage and Fuel Cells

Electrochemical Cells Have Some **Important Advantages**

- They are more **efficient** at producing energy than conventional combustion engines. This is because energy is wasted during combustion as **heat**.
- They produce a lot **less pollution** (such as CO_2). For hydrogen fuel cells, the only waste product is water.

Cuteness is an important advantage of electrochemical seals.

However, there are also drawbacks to using electrochemical cells for energy:

1) The production of the cells involves the use of **toxic chemicals**, which need to be **disposed of** once the cell has reached the end of its life span.
2) The chemicals used to make the cells are also often very **flammable**. E.g. lithium (commonly used in rechargeable batteries), is **highly reactive** and will catch fire if a fault causes it to overheat.

Practice Questions

Q1 How does a fuel cell produce electricity?

Q2 What particle travels through the electrolyte in a hydrogen-oxygen fuel cell?

Q3 Give one advantage and one disadvantage of electrochemical cells over conventional combustion engines.

Exam Questions

Q1 The diagram below shows the structure of a hydrogen-oxygen fuel cell.

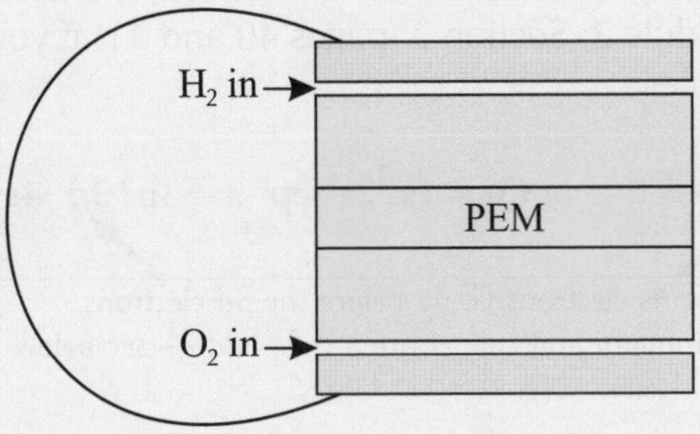

a) i) Label the site of oxidation and the site of reduction on the diagram. [2 marks]

ii) Draw an arrow to show the direction of the flow of electrons. [1 mark]

b) Write a half-equation for the reaction at each electrode. [2 marks]

c) Explain the purpose of the polymer electrolyte membrane (PEM) in the fuel cell. [2 marks]

Q2 The two half-equations for the reaction that happen in a nickel/cadmium battery are shown below.

$$Cd(OH)_{2(s)} + 2e^- \rightleftharpoons Cd_{(s)} + 2OH^-_{(aq)} \qquad E^\ominus = -0.88\text{ V}$$

$$NiO(OH)_{(s)} + H_2O_{(l)} + e^- \rightleftharpoons Ni(OH)_{2(s)} + OH^-_{(aq)} \qquad E^\ominus = +0.52\text{ V}$$

a) Calculate the cell voltage for a nickel/cadmium cell. [1 mark]

b) Write an equation for the overall reaction occurring in this cell. [1 mark]

In the past they used donkey-powered mills. They were called...wait for it...

...mule cells. Buddum tish. Oh dear, I'm really struggling today. Anyway, the hydrogen future is not upon us yet. It may have some advantages over the oil we use today but there are a few things to overcome first. So maybe it will happen and maybe it won't. All we really know is it's the end of the section and that's got to be a good thing. Hurrah!!

The d-block

The d-block can be found slap bang in the middle of the periodic table. It's here you'll find the transition elements. The most precious metals in the world are found in the d-block. That's got to make it worth a look...

Transition Elements are Found in the d-Block

Transition elements can also be called transition metals.

1) The **d-block** is the block of elements in the middle of the periodic table.
2) Most of the elements in the d-block are **transition elements**.
3) You only need to know about the transition elements in the first row of the d-block (period 4) — the ones from **titanium to copper**.

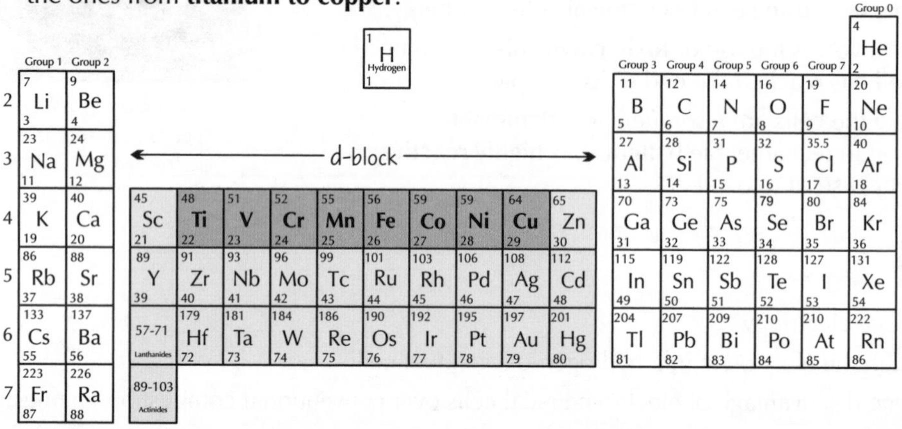

"A'm tellin' ya boy — there's gold in that thar d-block."

You Need to Know the Electron Configurations of the Transition Elements

1) Make sure you can write down the **electron configurations** of **all** the **period 4, d-block elements** in sub-shell notation. Have a look back at Module 2: Section 2 (pages 40 and 41) if you've forgotten how to do this. Here are a couple of examples:

$V = 1s^2\ 2s^2\ 2p^6\ 3s^2\ 3p^6\ 3d^3\ 4s^2$

$Co = 1s^2\ 2s^2\ 2p^6\ 3s^2\ 3p^6\ 3d^7\ 4s^2$

The 4s electrons fill up before the 3d electrons. But chromium and copper are a trifle odd — see below.

2) Here's the definition of a transition element:

> A **transition element** is a d-block element that can form **at least one stable ion** with an **incomplete d sub-shell**.

3) A d sub-shell can hold **10** electrons. So transition elements must form **at least one ion** that has **between 1 and 9 electrons** in the d sub-shell. All the period 4 d-block elements are transition elements apart from **scandium** and **zinc**. The diagram below shows the 3d and 4s sub-shells of these elements:

The **3d** orbitals are occupied **singly** at first. The electrons only **double up** when they have to.

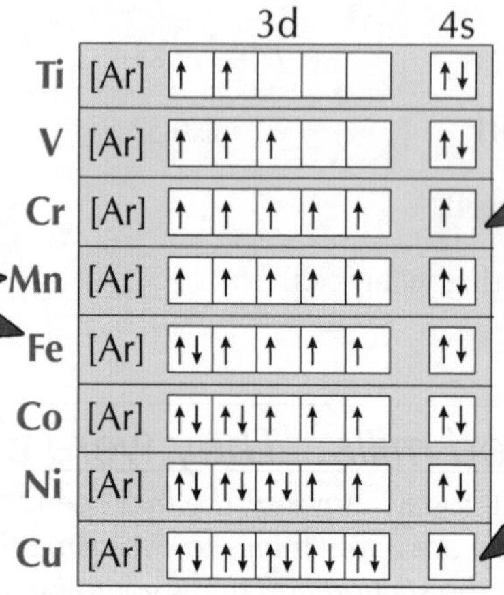

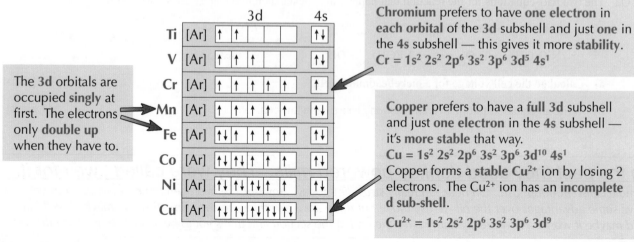

Chromium prefers to have **one electron** in **each orbital** of the **3d** subshell and just **one** in the **4s** subshell — this gives it more **stability**.
$Cr = 1s^2\ 2s^2\ 2p^6\ 3s^2\ 3p^6\ 3d^5\ 4s^1$

Copper prefers to have a **full 3d** subshell and just **one electron** in the **4s** subshell — it's **more stable** that way.
$Cu = 1s^2\ 2s^2\ 2p^6\ 3s^2\ 3p^6\ 3d^{10}\ 4s^1$
Copper forms a **stable** Cu^{2+} ion by losing 2 electrons. The Cu^{2+} ion has an **incomplete d sub-shell**.
$Cu^{2+} = 1s^2\ 2s^2\ 2p^6\ 3s^2\ 3p^6\ 3d^9$

The d-block

When **Ions** are Formed, the **s Electrons** are **Removed First**

When transition elements form **positive** ions, the **s electrons** are removed **first**, then the d electrons.

1) Iron can form Fe^{2+} ions and Fe^{3+} ions.
2) When it forms 2+ ions, it loses **both its 4s electrons.**
   $Fe = 1s^2\ 2s^2\ 2p^6\ 3s^2\ 3p^6\ 3d^6\ 4s^2 \rightarrow Fe^{2+} = 1s^2\ 2s^2\ 2p^6\ 3s^2\ 3p^6\ 3d^6$
3) Only once the 4s electrons are removed can a **3d electron** be removed.
   E.g. **$Fe^{2+} = 1s^2\ 2s^2\ 2p^6\ 3s^2\ 3p^6\ 3d^6 \rightarrow Fe^{3+} = 1s^2\ 2s^2\ 2p^6\ 3s^2\ 3p^6\ 3d^5$**

Scandium and Zinc **Aren't** Transition Elements

Scandium and zinc can't form **stable ions** with **incomplete d sub-shells**.
So neither of them fits the definition of a **transition element**.

Scandium only forms one ion, Sc^{3+}, which has an **empty d sub-shell.**
Scandium has the electron configuration **$1s^2\ 2s^2\ 2p^6\ 3s^2\ 3p^6\ 3d^1\ 4s^2$**.
It loses three electrons to form Sc^{3+}, which has the electron configuration **$1s^2\ 2s^2\ 2p^6\ 3s^2\ 3p^6$**.

Zinc only forms one ion, Zn^{2+}, which has a **full d sub-shell.**
Zinc has the electron configuration **$1s^2\ 2s^2\ 2p^6\ 3s^2\ 3p^6\ 3d^{10}\ 4s^2$**.
When it forms Zn^{2+} it loses 2 electrons, both from the 4s sub-shell — so it keeps its full 3d sub-shell.

Practice Questions

Q1 Name two transition elements in period 4 of the periodic table.

Q2 What's the definition of a transition element?

Q3 Name two period 4 elements that aren't transition elements.

Exam Questions

Q1 Which of the following shows an incorrect electron configuration for the transition element atom?

A vanadium: $1s^2\ 2s^2\ 2p^6\ 3s^2\ 3p^6\ 3d^3\ 4s^2$

B chromium: $1s^2\ 2s^2\ 2p^6\ 3s^2\ 3p^6\ 3d^5\ 4s^1$

C manganese: $1s^2\ 2s^2\ 2p^6\ 3s^2\ 3p^6\ 3d^6\ 4s^1$

D iron: $1s^2\ 2s^2\ 2p^6\ 3s^2\ 3p^6\ 3d^6\ 4s^2$ [1 mark]

Q2 Write electron configurations using sub-shell notation for the following atoms and ions.

a) Ni b) Fe^{2+} c) Cu^{2+} d) Mn^{6+} [4 marks]

Q3 How many unpaired electrons are there in each of the following atoms and ions?

a) Co b) Cr c) Cr^{3+} d) V^{5+} [4 marks]

Q4 A student states that scandium and titanium are both period 4 transition elements.

Comment on the student's statement. [2 marks]

Scram Sc and Zn — we don't take kindly to your types round these parts...

As long as you're up to speed with your electron configuration rules, these pages are a bit of a breeze. Chromium and copper do throw a couple of spanners in the works (those banterous scamps), so make sure you don't get complacent.

Properties of Transition Elements

Thanks to their interesting electronic structures, the transition elements make pretty coloured solutions and get involved in all sorts of fancy reactions. Some of them make pretty good catalysts too. What a great bunch of lads.

Transition Elements have Special Chemical Properties

1) Transition elements can exist in **variable oxidation states**.
For example, iron can exist in the **+2** oxidation state as Fe^{2+} ions and in the **+3** oxidation state as Fe^{3+} ions.
2) They also form **coloured ions**. E.g. Fe^{2+} ions are **pale green** and Fe^{3+} ions are **yellow**.
Some common **coloured** ions and **oxidation states** are shown below. The colours refer to the **aqueous ions**.

Oxidation state	+7	+6	+5	+4	+3	+2
Titanium					Ti^{3+} (purple)	Ti^{2+} (violet)
Vanadium			VO_2^+ (yellow)	VO^{2+} (blue)	V^{3+} (green)	V^{2+} (violet)
Chromium		$Cr_2O_7^{2-}$ (orange)			Cr^{3+} (green)	
Manganese	MnO_4^- (purple)	MnO_4^{2-} (green)				Mn^{2+} (pale pink)
Iron					Fe^{3+} (yellow)	Fe^{2+} (pale green)
Cobalt						Co^{2+} (pink)
Nickel						Ni^{2+} (green)
Copper						Cu^{2+} (pale blue)

These elements show **variable** oxidation states because the **energy levels** of the 4s and the 3d sub-shells are **very close** to one another. So different numbers of electrons can be gained or lost using fairly **similar** amounts of energy.

Transition Elements and their Compounds make Good Catalysts

1) Transition elements and their compounds make **good catalysts** because they can **change oxidation states** by gaining or losing electrons within their **d orbitals**. This means they can **transfer electrons** to **speed up** reactions.
2) Transition **metals** are also good at **adsorbing** substances onto their **surfaces** to lower the activation energy of reactions.
Here are a few examples of transition element catalysts:

- **$CuSO_4$** (oxidation state of copper = +2) catalyses the reaction of **zinc** with **acids**. → $Zn_{(s)} + H_2SO_{4(aq)} \xrightarrow{CuSO_{4(s)}} ZnSO_{4(aq)} + H_{2(g)}$
- **MnO_2** (oxidation state of manganese = +4) catalyses the **decomposition of hydrogen peroxide**. → $2H_2O_{2(aq)} \xrightarrow{MnO_{2(s)}} 2H_2O_{(l)} + O_{2(g)}$
- **Iron** (oxidation state = 0) is the catalyst in the **Haber process** to produce **ammonia**. → $N_{2(g)} + 3H_{2(g)} \xrightarrow{Fe_{(s)}} 2NH_{3(g)}$

3) Catalysts are good for **industry** and for the **environment** as they allow reactions to happen **faster** and at **lower temperatures** and pressures, **reducing energy useage**.
4) Using transition element catalysts can pose health **risks** as many of the metals and their compounds are **toxic**. For example, long term exposure to **copper** can damage the **liver** and **kidneys**, and exposure to **manganese** can cause **psychiatric problems**.

Properties of Transition Elements

Transition Element **Hydroxides** are **Brightly Coloured Precipitates**

1) When you mix an aqueous solution of **transition element ions** with aqueous **sodium hydroxide** (NaOH) or aqueous **ammonia** (NH_3) you get a **coloured hydroxide precipitate**.
2) In **aqueous solutions**, transition elements take the form $[M(H_2O)_6]^{n+}$. They can also be written as $M^{n+}_{(aq)}$, as long as the metal ion is **only** bonded to **water**. If it's bonded to anything else you need to write out the whole formula.
3) You need to know the **equations** for the following reactions, and the **colours** of the hydroxide precipitates:

copper(II): $[Cu(H_2O)_6]^{2+}_{(aq)} + 2OH^-_{(aq)} \rightarrow [Cu(OH)_2(H_2O)_4]_{(s)} + 2H_2O_{(l)}$

this can also be written as: $Cu^{2+}_{(aq)} + 2OH^-_{(aq)} \rightarrow Cu(OH)_{2(s)}$

$[Cu(H_2O)_6]^{2+}_{(aq)} + 2NH_{3(aq)} \rightarrow [Cu(OH)_2(H_2O)_4]_{(s)} + 2NH_4^+{}_{(aq)}$

In excess NH_3, $[Cu(OH)_2(H_2O)_4]_{(s)}$ reacts further to form $[Cu(NH_3)_4(H_2O)_2]^{2+}_{(aq)}$ which is a **dark blue** colour.

This goes from a **pale blue solution** to a **blue precipitate**.

iron(II): $[Fe(H_2O)_6]^{2+}_{(aq)} + 2OH^-_{(aq)} \rightarrow [Fe(OH)_2(H_2O)_4]_{(s)} + 2H_2O_{(l)}$

$[Fe(H_2O)_6]^{2+}_{(aq)} + 2NH_{3(aq)} \rightarrow [Fe(OH)_2(H_2O)_4]_{(s)} + 2NH_4^+{}_{(aq)}$

This goes from a **pale green solution** to a **green precipitate**, which **darkens** on standing.

iron(III): $[Fe(H_2O)_6]^{3+}_{(aq)} + 3OH^-_{(aq)} \rightarrow [Fe(OH)_3(H_2O)_3]_{(s)} + 3H_2O_{(l)}$

$[Fe(H_2O)_6]^{3+}_{(aq)} + 3NH_{3(aq)} \rightarrow [Fe(OH)_3(H_2O)_3]_{(s)} + 3NH_4^+{}_{(aq)}$

This goes from a **yellow solution** to an **orange precipitate**, which **darkens** on standing.

manganese(II): $[Mn(H_2O)_6]^{2+}_{(aq)} + 2OH^-_{(aq)} \rightarrow [Mn(OH)_2(H_2O)_4]_{(s)} + 2H_2O_{(l)}$

$[Mn(H_2O)_6]^{2+}_{(aq)} + 2NH_{3(aq)} \rightarrow [Mn(OH)_2(H_2O)_4]_{(s)} + 2NH_4^+{}_{(aq)}$

This goes from a pale pink solution to a pink/buff precipitate, which **darkens** on standing.

chromium(III): $[Cr(H_2O)_6]^{3+}_{(aq)} + 3OH^-_{(aq)} \rightarrow [Cr(OH)_3(H_2O)_3]_{(s)} + 3H_2O_{(l)}$

In excess NaOH, $[Cr(OH)_3(H_2O)_3]_{(s)}$ reacts further to form $Cr(OH)_6^{3-}{}_{(aq)}$ which is a **dark green** colour.

$[Cr(H_2O)_6]^{3+}_{(aq)} + 3NH_{3(aq)} \rightarrow [Cr(OH)_3(H_2O)_3]_{(s)} + 3NH_4^+{}_{(aq)}$

In excess NH_3, $[Cr(OH)_3(H_2O)_3]_{(s)}$ reacts further to form $[Cr(NH_3)_6]^{3+}_{(aq)}$ which is a **purple** colour.

This goes from a **green solution** to a **grey-green precipitate**.

If you know which **transition element** ion produces which **colour** precipitate, you can use these reactions to **identify** a transition element ion solution (see page 173).

Practice Questions

Q1 State three chemical properties which are characteristic of transition elements.

Q2 Write an equation for the reaction of iron(II) ions with hydroxide ions. Describe the colour change that occurs during this reaction.

Exam Question

Q1 Identify the following transition elements from the descriptions below:

a) Forms a yellow aqueous solution when its ions have an oxidation state of +3. [1 mark]

b) A grey-green precipitate is formed when aqueous ammonia is added to an aqueous solution of its 3+ ions. [1 mark]

c) One of its oxides catalyses the decomposition of hydrogen peroxide. [1 mark]

Oi you — get off my property...

Learning the colour changes and equations on this page might seem like a pain in the neck but there's a decent chance you'll have to recall some of the stuff here in the exam. So it's worth spending a bit of time memorising them...

Ligands and Complex Ions

Transition elements are always forming complex ions. These aren't as complicated as they sound, though. Honest.

Complex Ions *are* ***Metal Ions*** *Surrounded by* ***Ligands***

1) Transition elements can form **complex ions**. E.g, iron forms a **complex ion with water** — $[Fe(H_2O)_6]^{2+}$.

> A **complex ion** is a **metal ion** surrounded by **coordinately bonded ligands**.

2) A **coordinate bond** (or dative covalent bond) is a covalent bond in which **both electrons** in the shared pair come from the **same atom**.
3) So a **ligand** is an atom, ion or molecule that **donates a pair of electrons** to a central metal atom or ion.
4) The **coordination number** is the **number** of **coordinate bonds** that are formed with the central metal atom/ion.
5) In most of the complex ions that you need to know about, the coordination number will be **4** or **6**. If the ligands are **small**, like H_2O, CN^- or NH_3, **6** can fit around the central metal atom/ion. But if the ligands are **larger**, like Cl^-, **only 4** can fit around the central metal atom/ion.

6 coordinate bonds mean an octahedral shape

Here are a few examples:

The different types of bond arrow show that the complex is 3-D. The wedge-shaped arrows represent bonds coming towards you and the dashed arrows represent bonds sticking out behind the molecule.

The ligands don't always have to be the same.

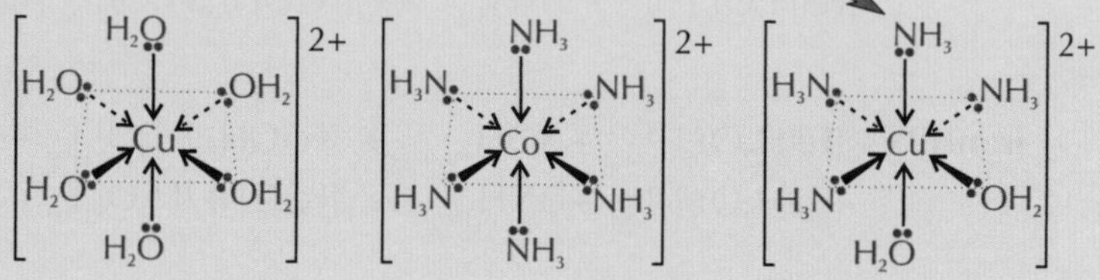

$[Cu(H_2O)_6]^{2+}_{(aq)}$ $[Co(NH_3)_6]^{2+}_{(aq)}$ $[Cu(NH_3)_4(H_2O)_2]^{2+}_{(aq)}$

4 coordinate bonds usually mean a tetrahedral shape...

E.g. $[CoCl_4]^{2-}$, which is blue, and $[CuCl_4]^{2-}$, which is yellow and shown here.

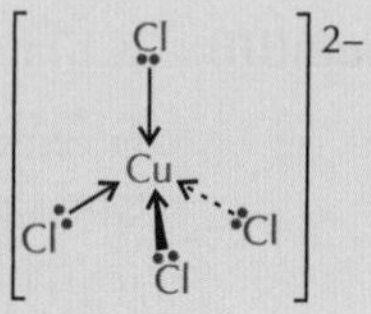

$[CuCl_4]^{2-}_{(aq)}$

...but not always

In a **few** complexes, **4 coordinate bonds** form a **square planar** shape.
E.g. $[NiCl_2(NH_3)_2]$ — see the next page.

A Ligand Must Have ***at Least One Lone Pair of Electrons***

A ligand must have **at least one lone pair of electrons**, or it won't have anything to form a **coordinate bond** with.

- Ligands that have **one lone pair** available for bonding are called **monodentate** — e.g. $H_2\ddot{O}$, $\ddot{N}H_3$, $\ddot{C}l^-$, $\ddot{C}N^-$
- Ligands with **two lone pairs** are called **bidentate** — e.g. ethane-1,2-diamine: $\ddot{N}H_2CH_2CH_2\ddot{N}H_2$
  Bidentate ligands can each form **two coordinate bonds** with a metal ion.
- Ligands that form **two or more coordinate bonds** are called **multidentate**.

You might see ethane-1,2-diamine abbreviated to "en".

Complex Ions Can Show ***Optical Isomerism***

Optical isomerism is a type of **stereoisomerism**. With complex ions, it happens when an ion can exist in **two non-superimposable mirror images**.

This happens in octahedral complexes when **three bidentate ligands**, are attached to the central ion. E.g $[Ni(NH_2CH_2CH_2NH_2)_3]^{2+}$.

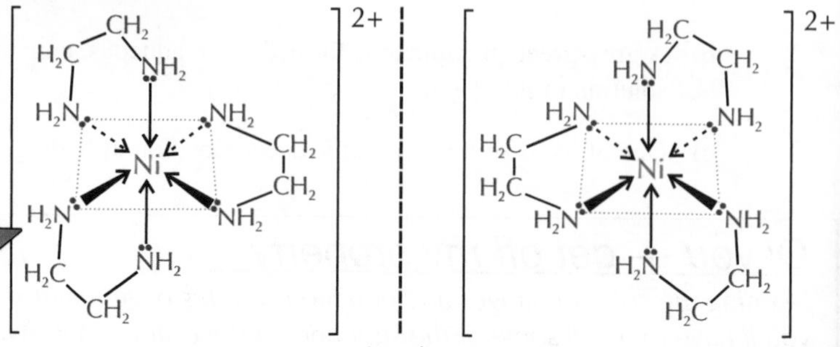

mirror line

Ligands and Complex Ions

Complex Ions Can Show *Cis/Trans Isomerism*

E/Z is another type of stereoisomerism. In stereoisomerism, the atoms are joined together in the same way, but they have different orientations in space.

Cis/trans isomerism is a special case of **E/Z isomerism** (see page 94). When there are only **two different groups** involved, you can use the **cis/trans naming system. Square planar** and **octahedral** complex ions that have at least **two pairs** of ligands show **cis/trans isomerism. Cis** isomers have the **same groups** on the **same side**, **trans** have the **same groups opposite** each other. Here are a couple of examples:

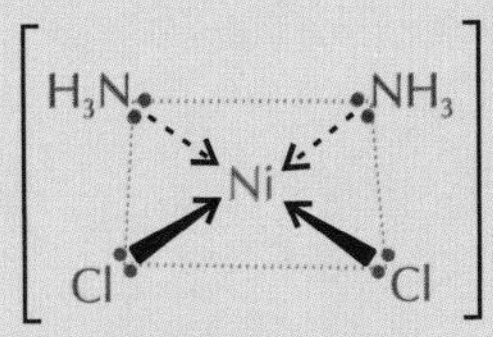

cis-$[NiCl_2(NH_3)_2]$

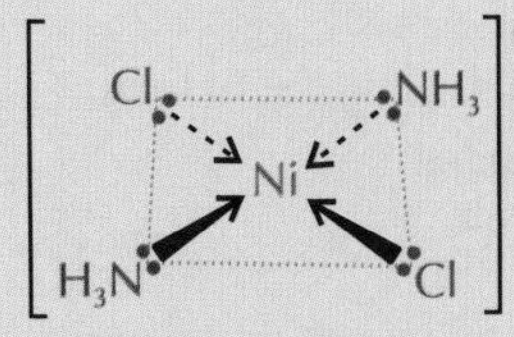

trans-$[NiCl_2(NH_3)_2]$

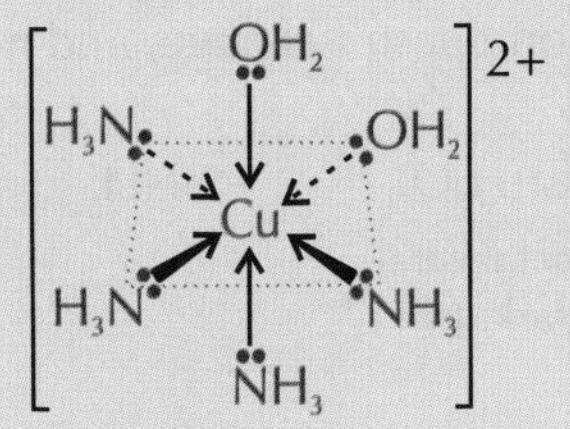

cis-$[Cu(NH_3)_4(H_2O)_2]^{2+}$

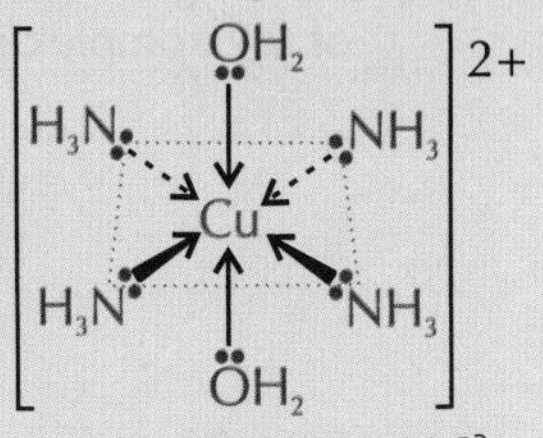

trans-$[Cu(NH_3)_4(H_2O)_2]^{2+}$

Cis-platin Can *Bind to DNA* in *Cancer Cells*

Cis-platin is a complex of platinum(II) with two chloride ions and two ammonia molecules in a square planar shape. It is used as an **anti-cancer** drug.

This is how it works:

1) The two **chloride ligands** are very easy to displace. So the cis-platin loses them, and bonds to two **nitrogen atoms** on the **DNA molecule** inside the **cancerous cell** instead.

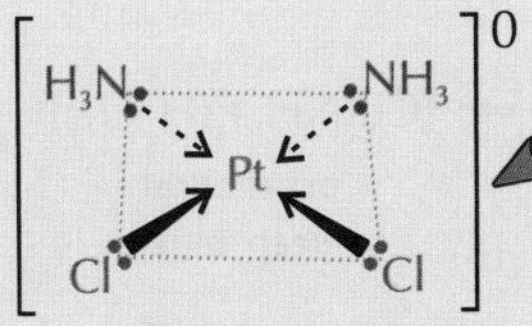

The two chloride ions are **next to each other**, so this complex is **cis-platin**. If they were **opposite** each other you would have **trans-platin**, which has different biological effects.

2) This **block** on its DNA prevents the cancerous cell from **reproducing** by division. The cell will **die**, since it is unable to repair the damage.
3) The downside is that cis-platin also prevents **normal cells** from reproducing, including blood, which can suppress the **immune system** and increase the risk of infection. Cis-platin may also cause **damage** to the **kidneys**.

Practice Questions

Q1 Explain what the term 'coordination number' means in relation to a complex ion.

Q2 Draw the shape of the complex ion $[Co(NH_3)_6]^{2+}$. Name the shape.

Q3 What is meant by the term 'bidentate ligand'? Give an example of one.

Q4 Draw the cis and trans isomers of the complex $[NiCl_2(NH_3)_2]$.

Exam Questions

Q1 Iron(III) can form the complex ion $[Fe(C_2O_4)_3]^{3-}$ with three ethanedioate ions. The ethanedioate ion is a bidentate ligand. Its structure is shown on the right.

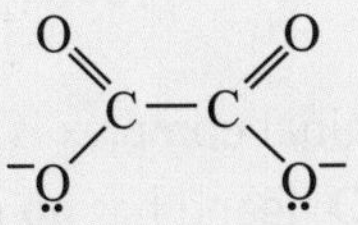

a) Draw a diagram to show a possible structure of the $[Fe(C_2O_4)_3]^{3-}$ complex ion. [1 mark]

b) The $[Fe(C_2O_4)_3]^{3-}$ complex displays optical isomerism. Explain what optical isomerism is. [1 mark]

Q2 Cis-platin is a platinum-based complex ion that is used as an anti-cancer drug.

a) Draw the structure of cis-platin. [1 mark]

b) Explain how cis-platin works as a cancer treatment. [2 marks]

Put your hands up — we've got you surrounded...

You'll never get transition element ions floating around by themselves in a solution — they'll always be surrounded by other molecules. It's kind of like what'd happen if you put a dish of sweets in a room of eight (or eighteen) year-olds. When you're drawing complex ions, you should always include some wedge-shaped bonds to show that it's 3-D.

Substitution Reactions

There are more substitutions on this page than the number of elephants you can fit in a mini.

Ligands can Exchange Places with One Another

One ligand can be **swapped** for another ligand — this is **ligand substitution**. It usually causes a **colour change**.

1) If the ligands are of **similar size**, e.g. H_2O, NH_3 or CN^-, then the **coordination number** of the complex ion **doesn't change**, and neither does the **shape**.

$$[Cr(H_2O)_6]^{3+}_{(aq)} + 6NH_{3(aq)} \rightleftharpoons [Cr(NH_3)_6]^{3+}_{(aq)} + 6H_2O_{(l)}$$

octahedral, dark green → octahedral, purple

2) If the ligands are **different sizes**, e.g. H_2O and Cl^-, there's a **change of coordination number** and a **change of shape**.

$$[Cu(H_2O)_6]^{2+}_{(aq)} + 4Cl^-_{(aq)} \rightleftharpoons [CuCl_4]^{2-}_{(aq)} + 6H_2O_{(l)}$$

octahedral, pale blue → tetrahedral, yellow

3) Sometimes the substitution is only **partial**.

$$[Cu(H_2O)_6]^{2+}_{(aq)} + 4NH_{3(aq)} \rightleftharpoons [Cu(NH_3)_4(H_2O)_2]^{2+}_{(aq)} + 4H_2O_{(l)}$$

octahedral, pale blue → octahedral, deep blue

This reaction only happens when you add an excess of ammonia — if you just add a bit, you get a blue precipitate of $[Cu(H_2O)_4(OH)_2]$ instead (see page 167).

As it's in solution and contains ligands that aren't water, you need to include all the water ligands when writing the formula of a complex like $[Cu(NH_3)_4(H_2O)_2]^{2+}$. But if you're writing out the formula of a precipitate, such as $[Cu(H_2O)_4(OH)_2]$, you can leave out the water ligands and just write $Cu(OH)_2$.

You Might be Asked to Predict the Products of Unfamiliar Substitution Reactions

Example: A student has a solution of $[Co(H_2O)_6]^{2+}$ ions. She adds excess $KCN_{(aq)}$ to a sample of the solution. Write an equation for this ligand substitution reaction and predict the shape of the complex ion formed.

The CN^- ligand is of a similar size to the H_2O ligand so CN^- replaces H_2O with **no change** in coordination number or shape of the complex ion.

$$[Co(H_2O)_6]^{2+}_{(aq)} + 6CN^-_{(aq)} \rightleftharpoons [Co(CN)_6]^{4-}_{(aq)} + 6H_2O_{(l)}$$

The original complex is octahedral so $[Co(CN)_6]^{4-}$ is **octahedral**.
The $\mathbf{H_2O}$ ligand has **no charge** and $\mathbf{CN^-}$ has a **1–** charge, so the **overall charge** of the complex **changes**.

Example continued: The student then adds excess $HCl_{(aq)}$ to a sample of the $[Co(H_2O)_6]^{2+}$ solution. Write an equation for this ligand substitution reaction and predict the shape of the complex ion formed.

The Cl^- ligand is larger than the H_2O ligand so when Cl^- replaces H_2O it results in a **change** in coordination number and shape of the complex ion.

$$[Co(H_2O)_6]^{2+}_{(aq)} + 4Cl^-_{(aq)} \rightleftharpoons [CoCl_4]^{2-}_{(aq)} + 6H_2O_{(l)}$$

$[Co(Cl)_4]^{2-}$ is **tetrahedral.**

Substitution Reactions

Fe^{2+} in Haemoglobin Allows Oxygen to be Carried in the Blood

Haem is a multidentate ligand.

1) **Haemoglobin** contains Fe^{2+} ions. The Fe^{2+} ions form **6 coordinate bonds.** Four of the **lone pairs** come from nitrogen atoms within a circular part of a molecule called **'haem'**. A fifth lone pair comes from a nitrogen atom on a protein (**globin**). The last position is the important one — this has a **water ligand** attached to the **iron**.
2) In the lungs the oxygen concentration is high, so the water ligand is **substituted** for an **oxygen molecule (O_2)**, forming **oxyhaemoglobin**. This is carried around the body and when it gets to a place where oxygen is needed, the oxygen molecule is exchanged for a water molecule again.
3) If **carbon monoxide (CO)** is inhaled, the **haemoglobin** swaps its **water** ligand for a **carbon monoxide** ligand, forming **carboxyhaemoglobin**. This is bad news because carbon monoxide is a **strong** ligand and **doesn't** readily exchange with oxygen or water ligands, meaning the haemoglobin **can't transport oxygen** any more.

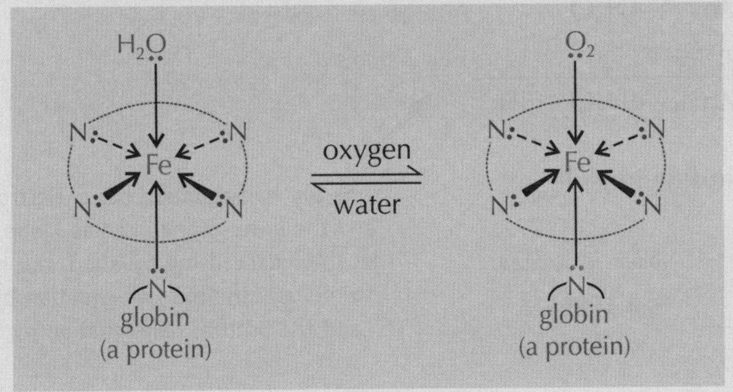

Gary thinks he's a haemoglobin molecule. This is him carrying 'O_2' around. He takes his job quite seriously. Just don't mention carbon monoxide to him.

Practice Questions

Q1 Give an example of a ligand substitution reaction that involves a change of coordination number.

Q2 What is the coordination number of the Fe^{2+} ion in the haemoglobin complex?

Exam Questions

Q1 A sample of copper(II) sulfate powder is dissolved in pure water, giving a pale blue solution.

a) Give the formula of the complex ion that is present in the pale blue solution. [1 mark]

b) An excess of ammonia is added to the solution.

i) Write a balanced equation for the ligand substitution reaction that takes place. [2 marks]

ii) Give the colour of the new solution. [1 mark]

iii) What shape is the new complex ion formed? [1 mark]

Q2 Haemoglobin is a complex ion that is found in the blood. It consists of an Fe^{2+} ion bonded to four nitrogen atoms from a haem ring, one nitrogen atom from a protein called globin, and one water molecule.

a) When blood passes through the lungs, a ligand substitution reaction occurs.

i) Which of the ligands in the haemoglobin complex is replaced, and by what? [1 mark]

ii) Why is this ligand substitution reaction important? [1 mark]

b) Explain how inhaling carbon monoxide can damage the human body. [2 marks]

There's no hard work for substitution — well, not that much anyway ...

Three things to do with this page — One: learn what a ligand substitution reaction is and how to predict their products. Two: learn why haemoglobin's an important example of one. Three: fold it into a mad-looking origami chimp.

Reactions of Ions

Transition elements love to swap electrons around, so they're always getting involved in redox reactions.

Transition Elements** Take Part in **Redox Reactions

1) Transition elements can exist in many different **oxidation states** (see page 166).
2) They can **change** oxidation state by **gaining** or **losing electrons** in **redox reactions**.
3) For complex ions in solution, a change in oxidation state is often accompanied by a **colour change**.
   Here are a few examples:

If it's been a while since you've looked at redox reactions, now might be a good time to flick back to p38 and 39 and brush up a bit.

Interconversion between Fe^{2+} and Fe^{3+}

$Fe^{2+}_{(aq)}$ (pale green) is **oxidised** to $Fe^{3+}_{(aq)}$ (yellow) by **acidified potassium manganate(VII)** solution, $KMnO_{4(aq)}$.

Half equations:	$MnO_4^- + 8H^+ + 5e^- \rightarrow Mn^{2+} + 4H_2O$	Manganese is reduced.
	$Fe^{2+} \rightarrow Fe^{3+} + e^-$	Iron is oxidised.
Full equation:	$MnO_4^- + 8H^+ + 5Fe^{2+} \rightarrow Mn^{2+} + 4H_2O + 5Fe^{3+}$	

The top half-equation has 5 electrons and the bottom one just has 1. So, to get the balanced full equation, you need to multiply the top half-equation by 1 and the bottom half-equation by 5.

$Fe^{3+}_{(aq)}$ (yellow) is **reduced** to $Fe^{2+}_{(aq)}$ (pale green) by **iodide** ions, $I^-_{(aq)}$.

Half equations:	$2I^- \rightarrow I_2 + 2e^-$	Iodide is oxidised.
	$Fe^{3+} + e^- \rightarrow Fe^{2+}$	Iron is reduced.
Full equation:	$2I^- + 2Fe^{3+} \rightarrow 2Fe^{2+} + I_2$	

Interconversion between Cr^{3+} and $Cr_2O_7^{2-}$

$[Cr(OH)_6]^{3-}$ is formed by adding excess $NaOH_{(aq)}$ to $[Cr(H_2O)_6]^{3+}$.

The Cr^{3+} ion in $[Cr(OH)_6]^{3-}$ (dark green) is oxidised to the yellow chromate(VI) solution, $CrO_4^{2-}{}_{(aq)}$, by warming with **hydrogen peroxide** solution, $H_2O_{2(aq)}$, in **alkaline** conditions.

Half equations:	$H_2O_2 + 2e^- \rightarrow 2OH^-$	Oxygen is reduced.
	$2Cr(OH)_6^{3-} + 4OH^- \rightarrow 2CrO_4^{2-} + 8H_2O + 6e^-$	Chromium is oxidised.
Full equation	$3H_2O_2 + 2Cr(OH)_6^{3-} \rightarrow 2OH^- + 2CrO_4^{2-} + 8H_2O$	

Adding dilute sulfuric acid to the chromate(VI) solution produces the orange dichromate(VI) solution, $Cr_2O_7^{2-}{}_{(aq)}$.

$$2CrO_4^{2-} + 2H^+ \rightarrow Cr_2O_7^{2-} + H_2O$$

$Cr_2O_7^{2-}{}_{(aq)}$ (orange) is reduced to $Cr^{3+}_{(aq)}$ (green) by **acidified zinc**.

Half equations:	$Zn \rightarrow Zn^{2+} + 2e^-$	Zinc is oxidised.
	$Cr_2O_7^{2-} + 14H^+ + 6e^- \rightarrow 2Cr^{3+} + 7H_2O$	Chromium is reduced.
Full equation:	$Cr_2O_7^{2-} + 14H^+ + 3Zn \rightarrow 2Cr^{3+} + 7H_2O + 3Zn^{2+}$	

You don't need to memorise the equations on this page — if you're asked to construct a full equation you'll be given the half-equations.

Reduction of Cu^{2+} and disproportionation of Cu^+

$Cu^{2+}_{(aq)}$ (pale blue) is reduced to the off-white precipitate copper(I) iodide by **iodide ions**, $I^-_{(aq)}$.

$$2Cu^{2+}_{(aq)} + 4I^-_{(aq)} \rightarrow 2CuI_{(s)} + I_{2(aq)}$$

$Cu^+_{(aq)}$ is unstable and **spontaneously disproportionates** (oxidises and reduces itself) to produce $Cu_{(s)}$ and $Cu^{2+}_{(aq)}$.

$$2Cu^+_{(aq)} \rightarrow Cu_{(s)} + Cu^{2+}_{(aq)}$$

Reactions of Ions

Transition Element Ions can be Identified Using Sodium Hydroxide

1) Many transition element ions form **coloured precipitates** when **aqueous sodium hydroxide** is added (see page 167).
2) This is a good way to **identify** which transition element ions might be in a **mixture**.
3) Add $NaOH_{(aq)}$ solution, dropwise from a pipette, to a test tube containing the unknown solution and **record the colour** of any precipitate formed.
4) The table on the right shows some of the ions that can be identified using this method.

ION	OBSERVATION
Cu^{2+}	blue precipitate
Fe^{2+}	green precipitate
Fe^{3+}	orange precipitate
Mn^{2+}	pink/buff precipitate
Cr^{3+}	grey-green precipitate

Some Ligands can be Identified Using Simple Tests

1) The tests for some **common ligands** can be carried out using **simple apparatus** in the lab.
2) The tests for these ions are covered in more detail in Module 3: Section 1 (pages 66 and 67). But here's a quick summary of the tests and results for some common ligands:

ION	TEST	OBSERVATION
CO_3^{2-} (carbonate)	Add nitric acid to the test compound. Bubble any gas given off through limewater.	Limewater turns from clear to cloudy if carbonate is present, due to $CO_{2(g)}$.
Cl^- (chloride)	add silver nitrate to test compound	white precipitate forms
Br^- (bromide)	add silver nitrate to test compound	cream precipitate forms
I^- (iodide)	add silver nitrate to test compound	pale yellow precipitate forms
SO_4^{2-} (sulfate)	add barium nitrate or barium chloride to test compound	white precipitate forms
NH_4^+ (ammonium)	Add cold NaOH to the test compound and warm. Hold damp, red litmus paper over the solution.	Red litmus paper turns blue in presence of ammonia.

You need to be careful what reagents you add so that you don't introduce ions that could interfere with any later tests. E.g. in the test for CO_3^{2-} ions you could use $HCl_{(aq)}$ instead of $HNO_{3(aq)}$, but doing this would add chloride ions to the sample, so you wouldn't be able to find out whether or not the initial solution contained chloride ions — you'd definitely get a white ppt. with silver nitrate.

Practice Questions

Q1 Write a half equation showing $Cr_2O_7^{2-}$ being reduced to Cr^{3+}.

Q2 Describe a test to determine whether or not a mixture contains carbonate ions.

Exam Questions

Q1 Manganate(VII) ions, MnO_4^-, oxidise the oxygen in H_2O_2 to oxygen gas in a redox reaction. The half equations for this reaction are:

$$MnO_4^- + 8H^+ + 5e^- \rightarrow Mn^{2+} + 4H_2O \quad \text{and} \quad H_2O_2 \rightarrow O_2 + 2H^+ + 2e^-$$

Give the balanced full equation for the reaction. [1 mark]

Q2 A student is given a sample of an unknown solution containing a transition element complex. The student carries out two tests:

1. Acidified silver nitrate is added to the compound. A pale yellow precipitate forms.

2. Aqueous sodium hydroxide is added to a sample of the solution and a blue precipitate forms.

Give a likely formula of the unknown transition element complex. [1 mark]

If only all tests were as simple as adding a few drops of NaOH...

Make sure you know how to interpret unfamiliar redox reactions and reserve a little space in the old dome for those ion tests. Heaven forbid you should lose marks in the exam for confusing your white and pale yellow precipitates.

Benzene and Aromatic Compounds

We begin this unit with a fantastical tale of the discovery of the magical rings of Benzene.
Our story opens in a shire where four hobbits are getting up to mischief... Actually no, that's something else.

Benzene has a **Ring Of Carbon Atoms**

Benzene has the formula $\mathbf{C_6H_6}$. It has a cyclic structure, with its six carbon atoms joined together in a ring. There are two ways of representing it — the **Kekulé model** and the **delocalised model**.

The **Kekulé Model** Came First

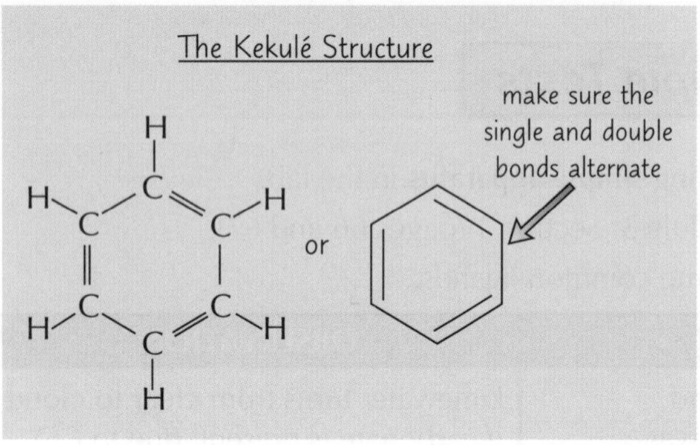

1) In 1865, the German chemist Friedrich August Kekulé proposed that **benzene** was made up of a **planar** (flat) **ring** of **carbon** atoms with **alternating single** and **double** bonds between them.
2) In Kekulé's model, each carbon atom is also bonded to **one hydrogen** atom.
3) He later adapted the model to say that the benzene molecule was constantly **flipping** between two forms (**isomers**) by switching over the double and single bonds.

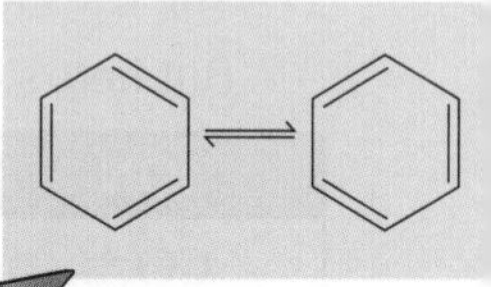

4) If the Kekulé model was correct, you'd expect there to always be three bonds with the length of a **C–C bond** (154 pm) and three bonds with the length of a **C=C bond** (134 pm).
5) However **X-ray diffraction studies** have shown that all the carbon-carbon bonds in benzene have the **same length** of 140 pm — i.e. they are **between** the length of a single bond and a double bond.
6) So the Kekulé structure **can't** be completely right. Chemists still **draw** the Kekulé structure of benzene though, as it's useful when drawing **reaction mechanisms**.

Apparently Kekulé imagined benzene as a snake catching its own tail. So here's a picture of a man charming some snakes.

The **Delocalised Model** Replaced Kekulé's Model

The bond-length observations are explained with the **delocalised** model.

1) The delocalised model says that the **p-orbitals** of all six carbon atoms **overlap** to create a **π-system**.
2) The π-system is made up of two **ring-shaped** clouds of electrons — one above and one below the plane of the six carbon atoms.
3) All the bonds in the ring are the **same length** because all the bonds are the same.
4) The electrons in the rings are said to be **delocalised** because they don't belong to a **specific** carbon atom. They are represented as a **circle** inside the ring of carbons rather than as double or single bonds.

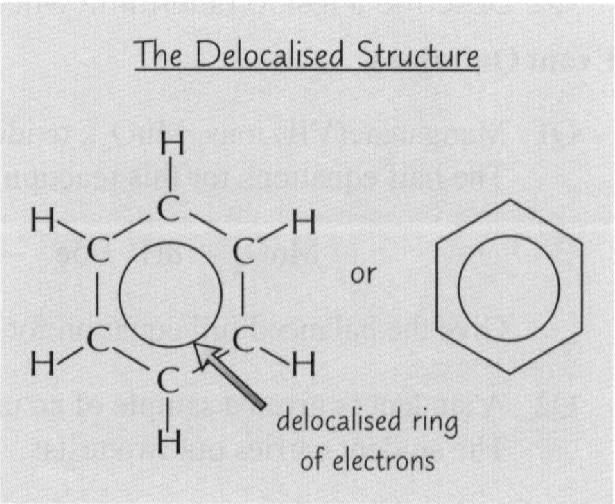

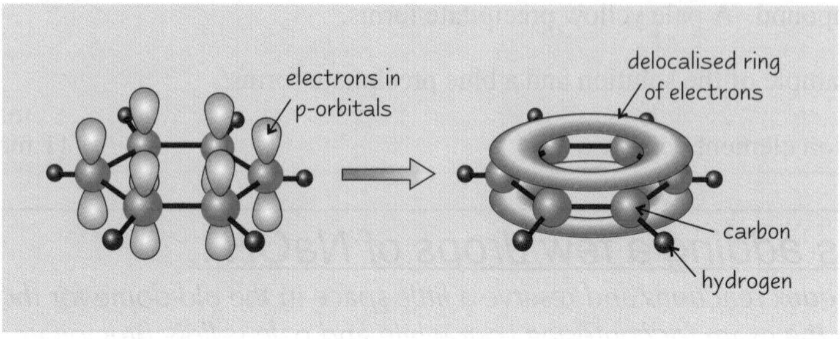

Benzene is a planar (flat) molecule — it's got a ring of carbon atoms with their hydrogens sticking out all on a flat plane.

Benzene and Aromatic Compounds

Enthalpy Changes of Hydrogenation Give More Evidence for Delocalisation

1) If you react an **alkene** with **hydrogen gas**, two atoms of hydrogen add across the **double bond**. This is called **hydrogenation**, and the enthalpy change of the reaction is the **enthalpy change of hydrogenation**.
2) Cyclohexene has **one** double bond. When it's hydrogenated, the enthalpy change is **-120 kJ mol^{-1}**. If benzene had three double bonds (as in the Kekulé structure), you'd expect the enthalpy of hydrogenation to be $(3 \times 120) = -360$ kJ mol^{-1}.
3) But the **experimental** enthalpy of hydrogenation of benzene is **-208 kJ mol^{-1}** — far **less exothermic** than expected.
3) Energy is put in to break bonds and released when bonds are made. So **more energy** must have been put in to break the bonds in benzene than would be needed to break the bonds in the Kekulé structure.

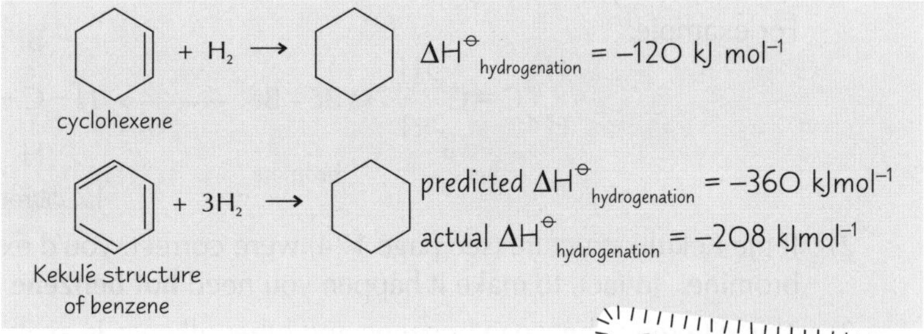

See p68-70 for more about enthalpy changes.

4) This difference indicates that benzene is **more stable** than the Kekulé structure would be. Benzene's **resistance to reaction** gives more evidence for it being **more stable** than the Kekulé structure suggests (see page 176). The stability is thought to be due to the **delocalised ring of electrons**.

Aromatic Compounds are Derived from Benzene

1) Compounds containing a **benzene ring** are called **arenes** or **'aromatic compounds'**. There are **two** ways of **naming** arenes, but there's no easy rule to know which name to give them. Here are some examples:

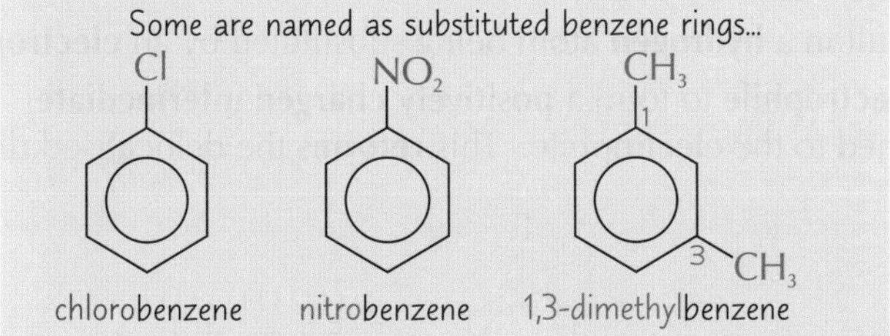

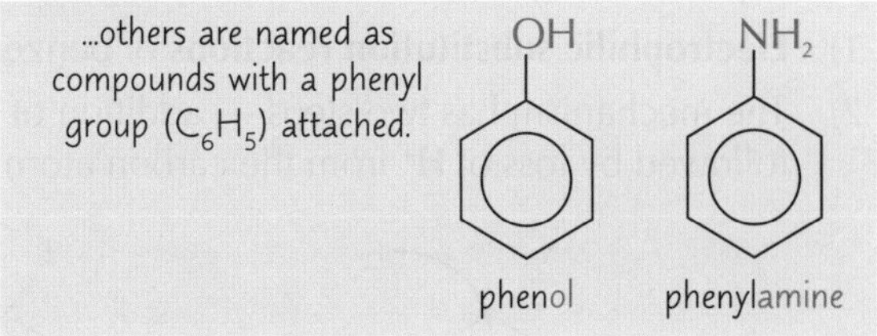

2) If there's **more than one** functional group attached to the benzene ring you have to **number** the **carbons** to show where the groups are.
   - If all the functional groups are the **same**, pick any group to start from and count round the way that gives the **smallest** numbers.
   - If the functional groups are **different**, start from whichever functional group gives the molecule its **suffix** (e.g. the –OH group for a phenol) and continue counting round the way that gives the **smallest** numbers.

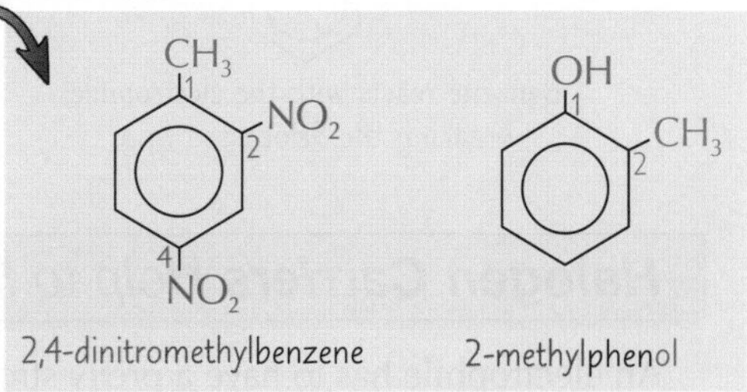

Practice Questions

Q1 Draw the Kekulé and delocalised models of benzene.

Q2 What are the two ways of naming aromatic compounds? Give an example of each.

Exam Question

Q1 a) In 1865, Friedrich Kekulé proposed the structure for benzene shown on the right. What does this model imply about the C–C bond lengths in the molecule? [1 mark]

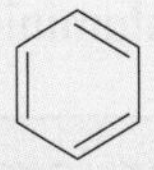

b) How was it shown that the bond lengths suggested by the Kekulé structure are incorrect? [1 mark]

c) Describe another piece of evidence that shows that the Kekulé structure is incorrect. [2 marks]

Everyone needs a bit of stability in their life...

The structure of benzene is bizarre — even top scientists struggled to find out what its molecular structure looked like. Make sure you can draw all the different representations of benzene given on this page, including the ones showing the Cs and Hs. Yes, and don't forget there's a hydrogen at every point on the ring — it's easy to forget they're there.

Electrophilic Substitution

Benzene is an alkene but it often doesn't behave like one — whenever this is the case, you can pretty much guarantee that our kooky friend Mr Delocalised Electron Ring is up to his old tricks again...

Alkenes usually like **Addition** Reactions, but **Not Benzene**

1) **Alkenes** react easily with **bromine** water at room temperature. This **decolourises** the orange bromine water. It's an **electrophilic addition reaction** — the bromine atoms are added across the double bond of the alkene. For example:

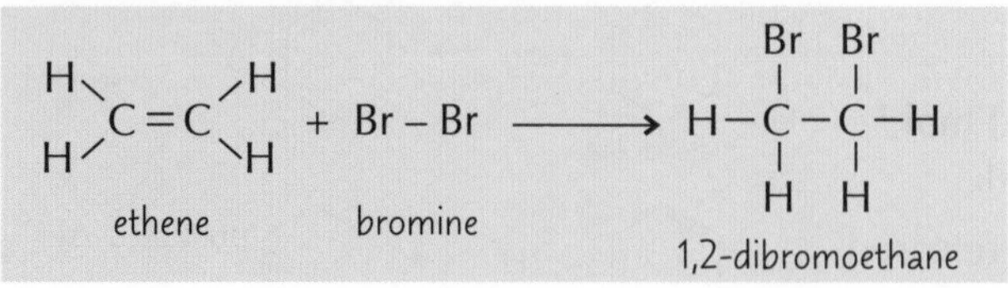

Remember — electrophiles are positively charged ions, or polar molecules, that are attracted to areas of negative charge.

2) If the Kekulé structure (see page 174) were correct, you'd expect a **similar reaction** between benzene and bromine. In fact, to make it happen you need **hot benzene** and **ultraviolet light** — and it's still a real **struggle**.
3) This difference between benzene and other alkenes is explained by the π-system in benzene — the **delocalised electron rings** above and below the plane of carbon atoms. They **spread out** the negative charge and make the benzene ring very **stable**. So benzene is **unwilling** to undergo **addition reactions** which would destroy the stable ring. The **reluctance** of benzene to undergo addition reactions is **more evidence** supporting the **delocalised model**.
4) In alkenes, the **π-bond** in the C=C double bond is an area of localised **high electron density** which strongly attracts **electrophiles**. In benzene, this attraction is reduced due to the negative charge being spread out.
5) So benzene prefers to react by **electrophilic substitution**.

Arenes Undergo **Electrophilic Substitution** Reactions

1) **Electrophilic substitution reactions** of benzene result in a **hydrogen** atom being substituted by an **electrophile**.
2) The mechanism has two steps — addition of the **electrophile** to form a **positively charged intermediate**, followed by loss of **H^+** from the carbon atom attached to the electrophile. This **reforms** the delocalised ring.

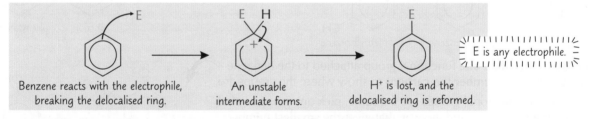

Benzene reacts with the electrophile, breaking the delocalised ring. An unstable intermediate forms. H^+ is lost, and the delocalised ring is reformed.

E is any electrophile.

Halogen Carriers Help to Make **Good Electrophiles**

An electrophile has to have a pretty strong **positive charge** to be able to attack the stable benzene ring. Most compounds just **aren't polarised enough** — but some can be made into **stronger electrophiles** using a catalyst called a **halogen carrier**.

A halogen carrier accepts a **lone pair of electrons** from a **halogen** atom on an **electrophile**. As the lone pair of electrons is pulled away, the **polarisation** in the molecule **increases** and sometimes a **carbocation** forms. This makes the electrophile **stronger**. Halogen carriers include **aluminium halides**, **iron halides** and **iron**.

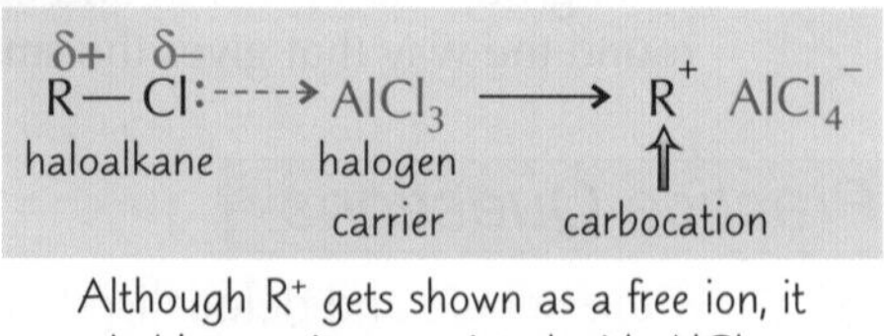

Although R^+ gets shown as a free ion, it probably remains associated with $AlCl_4^-$ — this doesn't affect how R^+ reacts though.

Halogen Carriers Help **Halogens Substitute** into the Benzene Ring

1) Benzene will react with **halogens** (e.g. Br_2) in the presence of an **aluminium chloride catalyst**, $AlCl_3$.
2) The catalyst **polarises** the halogen, allowing one of the halogen atoms to act as an **electrophile**.
3) During the reaction, a halogen atom is **substituted** in place of a H atom — this is called **halogenation**.

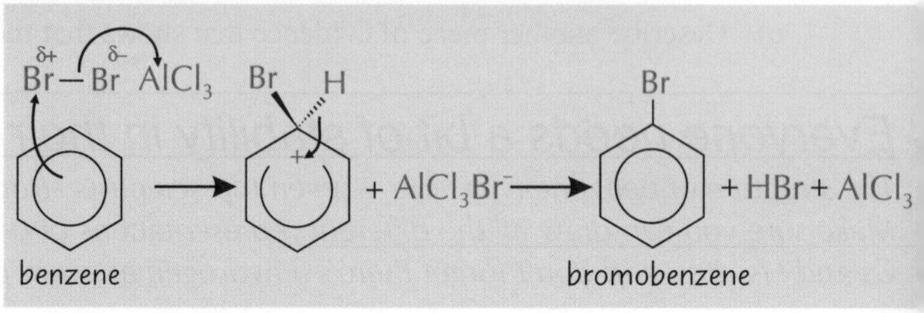

Electrophilic Substitution

Friedel-Crafts Reactions Form *C–C* Bonds

Friedel-Crafts reactions are really useful for forming C–C bonds in organic synthesis. They are carried out by refluxing benzene with a halogen carrier and either a **haloalkane** or an **acyl chloride**. There are two types:

1) **Friedel-Crafts alkylation** puts **any alkyl group** onto a benzene ring using a **haloalkane** and a halogen carrier. The general reaction is:

$$C_6H_6 + R\text{-}X \xrightarrow[\text{Reflux}]{AlCl_3} C_6H_5R + HX$$

Example: To make methylbenzene:

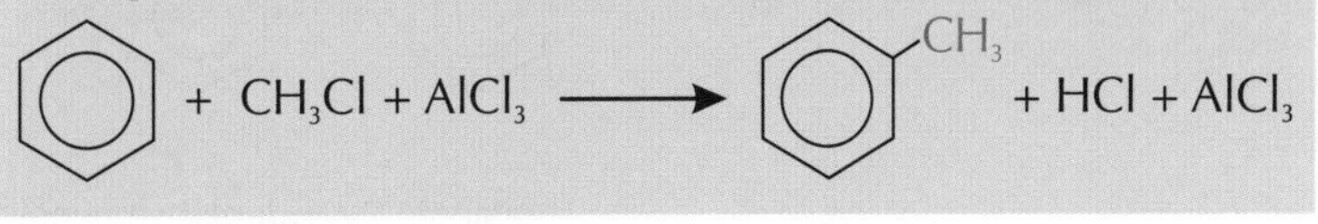

2) **Friedel-Crafts acylation** substitutes an **acyl group** for an H atom on benzene. You have to reflux benzene with an **acyl chloride** instead of a chloroalkane. This produces **phenylketones** (unless R = H, in which case an aldehyde called benzenecarbaldehyde, or benzaldehyde, is formed). The general reaction is:

Acyl groups contain a C=O double bond.

$$C_6H_6 + RCOCl \xrightarrow[\text{Reflux}]{AlCl_3} C_6H_5COR + HCl$$

Example: To make phenylethanone:

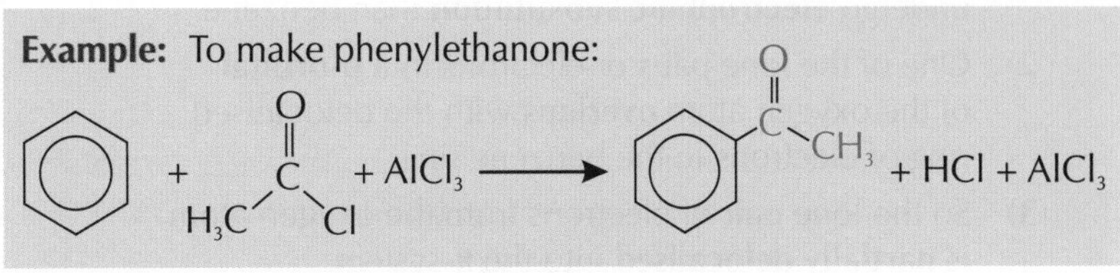

Nitric Acid Acts as an *Electrophile* with a *Sulfuric Acid Catalyst*

When you warm **benzene** with **concentrated nitric acid** and **concentrated sulfuric acid**, you get nitrobenzene. Sulfuric acid is a **catalyst** — it helps make the nitronium ion, $\mathbf{NO_2^+}$, which is the **electrophile**. It's then regenerated at the end of the reaction mechanism.

$$HNO_3 + H_2SO_4 \rightarrow H_2NO_3^+ + HSO_4^-$$
$$H_2NO_3^+ \rightarrow NO_2^+ + H_2O$$

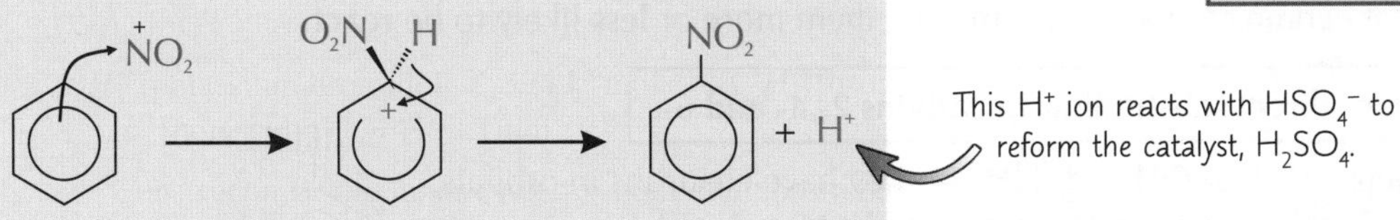

If you only want one NO_2 group added (**mononitration**), you need to keep the temperature **below 55 °C**. Above this temperature you'll get lots of substitutions.

Practice Questions

Q1 What type of reaction does benzene tend to undergo?

Q2 Name two substances that are used as halogen carriers in substitution reactions of benzene.

Q3 Describe two ways of making C–C bonds with benzene.

Q4 Which two acids are used in the production of nitrobenzene?

Exam Question

Q1 a) A student takes two test tubes, each containing bromine water. He adds cyclohexene to one of the test tubes and benzene to the other. Describe and explain what the student will see. [3 marks]

b) To make bromine and benzene react, they are heated together with iron(III) chloride.

i) What is the function of the iron(III) chloride? [1 mark]

ii) Draw a mechanism for this reaction. [3 marks]

Shhhh... Don't disturb The Ring...

Arenes really like Mr Delocalised Electron Ring and they won't give him up for nobody, at least not without a fight. They'd much rather get tangled up in an electrophilic substitution — anything not to bother The Ring.

Substituted Benzene Rings

On its own benzene is quite reluctant to react — you have to use catalysts and often high temperatures for anything to happen. But substituted benzene rings have other functional groups on them, and this changes their reactivity.

Phenols Have Benzene Rings with –OH Groups Attached

Phenol has the formula C_6H_5OH.

Other phenols have various groups attached to the benzene ring:

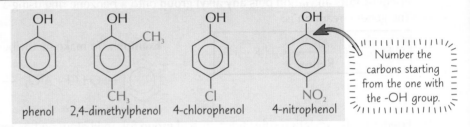

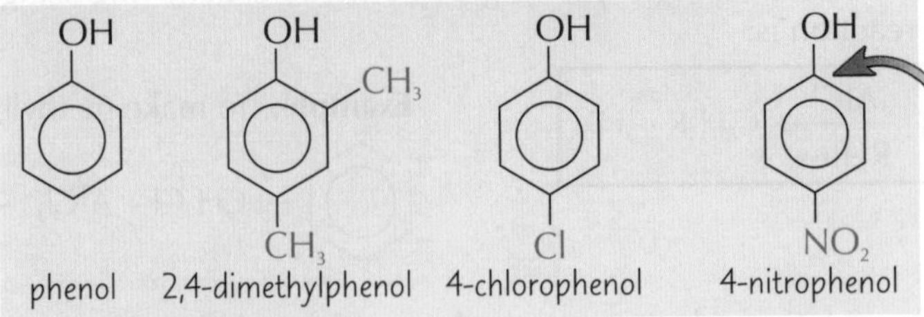

Number the carbons starting from the one with the -OH group.

Phenol is More Reactive than Benzene

1) The -OH group means that phenol is more likely to undergo **electrophilic substitution** than benzene.
2) One of the lone pairs of electrons in a **p-orbital** of the oxygen atom **overlaps** with the delocalised ring of electrons in the benzene ring.
3) So the lone pair of electrons from the oxygen atom is **partially delocalised** into the π-system.
4) This increases the **electron density** of the ring, making it more likely to be attacked by electrophiles.

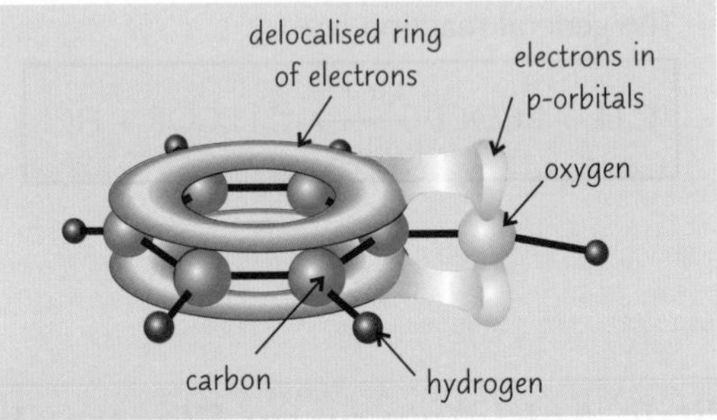

Functional Groups Can Affect the Position of Substitution

1) In an unsubstituted **benzene** ring, all the carbon atoms are the **same** so electrophiles can react with **any** of them.
2) If you have a **substituted** benzene ring, such as **phenol**, the functional group can change the **electron density** at certain carbon atoms, making them **more** or **less** likely to be **react**.

Electron donating groups direct substitution to carbons 2-,4- and 6-.

Electron-donating groups include **-OH** and **$-NH_2$** — they have electrons in orbitals that **overlap** with the delocalised ring and increase its **electron density**.

In particular, they increase the electron density at carbons **2-**, **4-** and **6-**, so electrophiles are **most likely** to react at these positions.

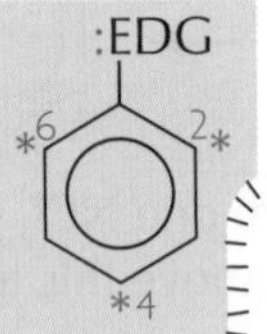

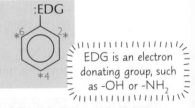

EDG is an electron donating group, such as -OH or $-NH_2$

Electron withdrawing groups direct substitution to carbons 3- and 5-.

$-NO_2$ is an **electron withdrawing group**. It doesn't have any orbitals that can overlap with the delocalised ring and it's **electronegative**, so it **withdraws** electron density from the ring.

In particular, it withdraws electron density at carbons 2-,4- and 6-, so electrophiles are **unlikely** to react at these positions. This has the effect of **directing** electrophilic substitution to the **3-** and **5-** positions.

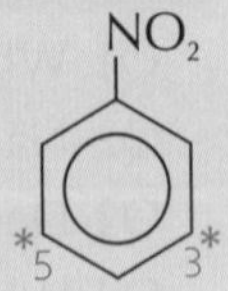

3) So you can **predict** the products of electrophilic substitution reactions.

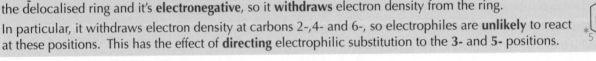

Example: Predict the product of the following reaction:

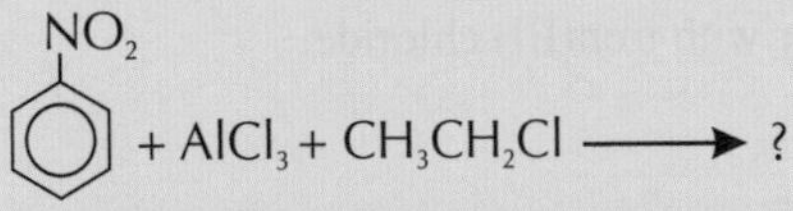

The benzene ring's only substituted once, so it doesn't matter whether you number the carbons clockwise or anticlockwise. This means the 3- and the 5- positions are the same.

$-NO_2$ is **electron withdrawing**, so directs electrophilic substitution to **carbon 3**.

The product is **3-ethylnitrobenzene**:

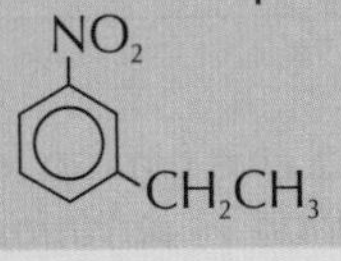

Angela and Sue weren't entirely sure of their direction

Substituted Benzene Rings

Phenol Reacts with **Bromine Water**

1) Phenol is **more reactive** than **benzene**, so if you shake phenol with orange bromine water, it will **react**, **decolourising** it.
2) The -OH group is **electron donating** so directs substitution to carbons **2-**, **4-** and **6-**. The product is called **2,4,6-tribromophenol** — it's insoluble in water and **precipitates** out of the mixture. It smells of antiseptic.

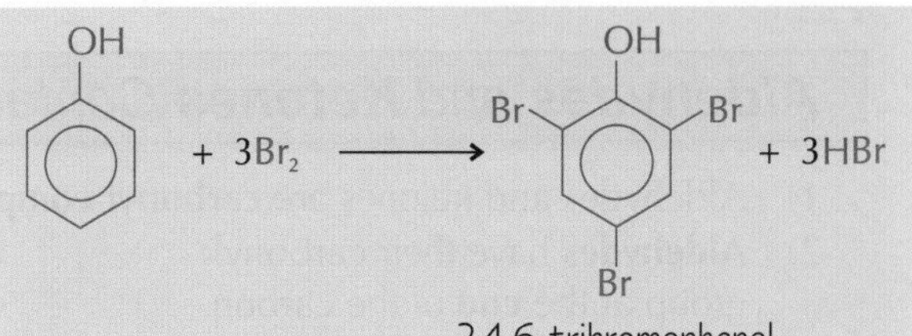

2,4,6-tribromophenol

Phenol Can be **Nitrated** Using **Dilute Nitric Acid**

1) Phenol reacts with **dilute nitric acid** to give two **isomers** of **nitrophenol**, and water.
2) Nitrating phenol is much **easier** than nitrating benzene — that requires **concentrated** nitric acid and a concentrated sulfuric acid **catalyst**.
3) The difference is due to the **activating** effect of the **OH group** again — and that's also why you're most likely to get NO_2 groups at positions 2 and 4 on the carbon ring.

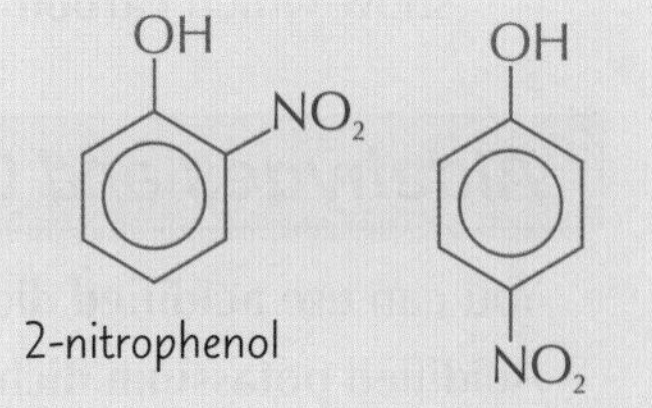

2-nitrophenol

4-nitrophenol

Phenol reacts with **Bases** and **Sodium** to form **Salts**

Phenol is weakly acidic, so will undergo typical acid-base reactions.

1) Phenol reacts with **sodium hydroxide solution** at room temperature in a **neutralisation reaction** to form **sodium phenoxide** and **water**.
2) It **doesn't react** with **sodium carbonate** solution though — phenol is not a **strong enough** acid.

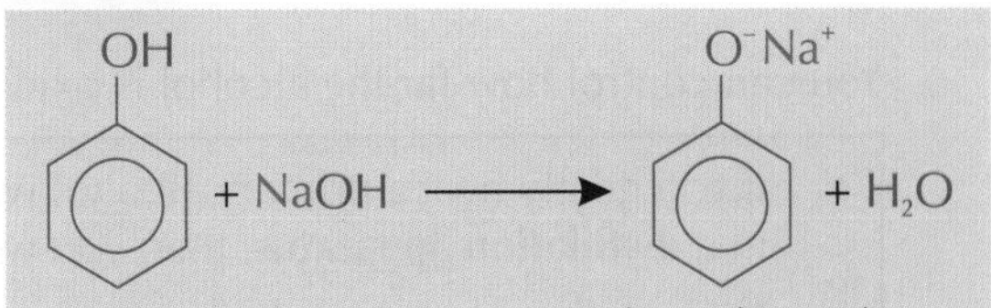

phenol

sodium phenoxide

Practice Questions

Q1 What is the formula and structure of phenol?

Q2 Which of the carbon atoms in phenol are electrophiles most likely to react with?

Q3 Write a balanced equation for the reaction between phenol and bromine (Br_2).

Q4 Write a balanced equation for the reaction between phenol and sodium hydroxide solution.

Exam Questions

Q1 a) Draw the structure of 2-methylphenol. [1 mark]

b) When 2-methylphenol reacts with dilute nitric acid, two isomers are formed. Draw both these isomers and give their systematic names. [2 marks]

Q2 a) Bromine water can be used to distinguish between benzene and phenol. Describe what you would observe in each case and name any products formed. [2 marks]

b) Explain why phenol reacts differently from benzene. [2 marks]

c) Name the type of reaction that occurs between phenol and bromine. [1 mark]

Phenol Destination 4 — more compounds, more equations, more horror...

The reactions of phenol are all pretty similar to benzene — phenol's just more reactive so the reaction conditions can be a bit milder. Of course there's the added confusion of predicting which carbon the electrophilic substitution will happen at, so have another look at that bit and make sure you've got it completely under your belt.

Aldehydes and Ketones

Aldehydes and ketones are both carbonyl compounds. You met them in Module 4 — they're made from oxidising alcohols. Well now you get to learn a whole load more reactions and mechanisms. I bet you can't wait to get started...

Aldehydes and Ketones Contain a Carbonyl Group

1) Aldehydes and ketones are **carbonyl compounds** — they contain the **carbonyl** functional group, **C=O**.
2) **Aldehydes** have their carbonyl group at the **end** of the carbon chain. Their names end in **–al**.

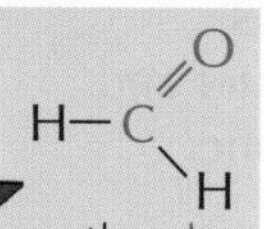

methanal

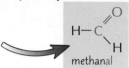

3) **Ketones** have their carbonyl group in the **middle** of the carbon chain. Their names end in **–one**, and often have a number to show which **carbon** the carbonyl group is on.

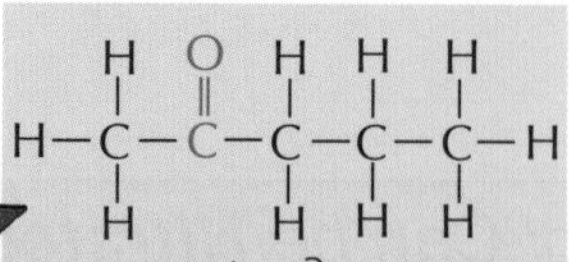

pentan-2-one

Aldehydes and Carboxylic Acids are Made by Oxidising Primary Alcohols

You can use **acidified dichromate(VI) ions** ($Cr_2O_7^{2-}$) to **mildly** oxidise alcohols.
Acidified **potassium dichromate(VI)** ($K_2Cr_2O_7$ / H_2SO_4) is often used.

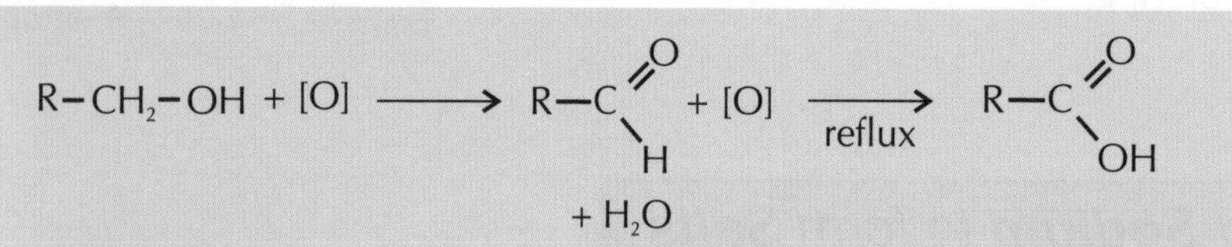

primary alcohol — aldehyde — carboxylic acid

[O] = oxidising agent

The orange dichromate(VI) ion is reduced to the green chromium(III) ion, Cr^{3+}.

You can control how **far** the alcohol is oxidised by controlling the **reaction conditions**:

- If you gently heat a primary alcohol with acidified potassium dichromate(VI) in a **distillation apparatus**, then you will form the **aldehyde**.
- If you **reflux** a primary alcohol (or an aldehyde) with acidified potassium dichromate(VI), then you'll oxidise the aldehyde further and form a **carboxylic acid**.

Ketones are made by oxidising secondary alcohols with acidified potassium dichromate(VI). They can't be oxidised any further.

You Can Reduce Aldehydes and Ketones Back to Alcohols

Using a **reducing agent** [H] you can:

1) reduce an **aldehyde** to a **primary alcohol**.

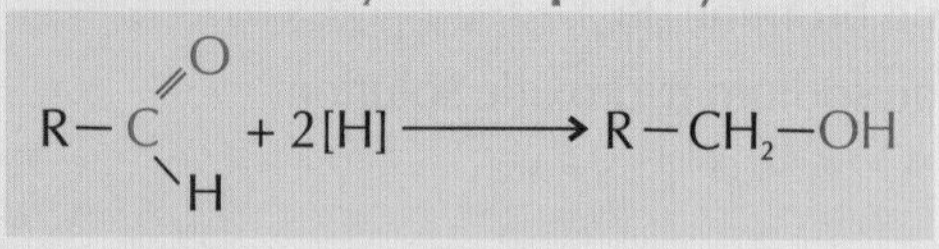

2) reduce a **ketone** to a **secondary alcohol**.

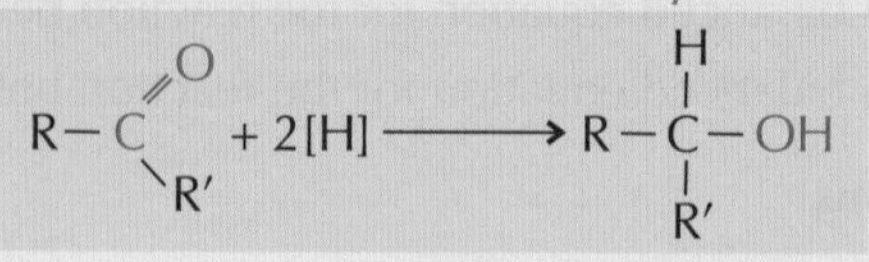

The reducing agent is normally **$NaBH_4$** (sodium tetrahydriborate(III) or sodium borohydride) dissolved in water with methanol.

It's a **nucleophilic addition reaction** — a **nucleophile** attacks the molecule, and an extra group is **added** to it.

The reducing agent, e.g. $NaBH_4$, supplies **hydride ions**, H^-. H^- has a **lone pair** of electrons, so it's a **nucleophile** and can attack the δ+ carbon on the **carbonyl group** of an aldehyde or ketone:

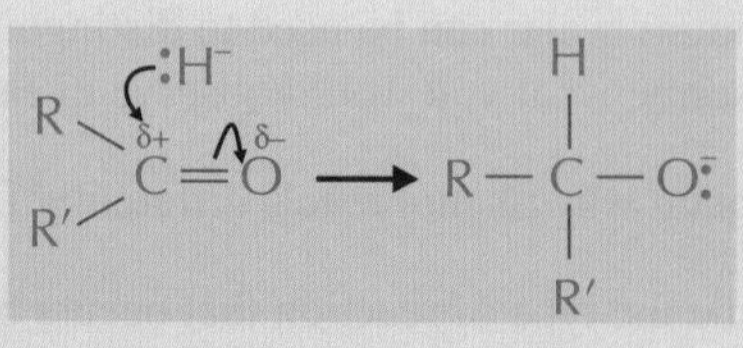

Addition of water then gives...

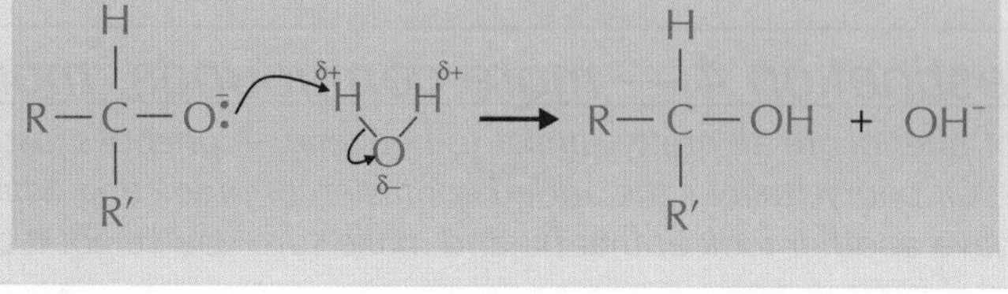

Nucleophiles are electron pair donors. They react with atoms that don't have enough electrons

Aldehydes and Ketones

Hydrogen Cyanide will React with Carbonyls by Nucleophilic Addition

Hydrogen cyanide reacts with carbonyl compounds to produce **hydroxynitriles** (molecules with a CN and OH group). It's a **nucleophilic addition reaction**.

Hydrogen cyanide is a **weak acid** — it partially dissociates in water to form H^+ and CN^- ions. $HCN \rightleftharpoons H^+ + CN^-$

1) The CN^- ion **attacks** the slightly positive carbon atom and **donates** a pair of electrons to it. Both electrons from the double bond transfer to the oxygen.
2) H^+ (from hydrogen cyanide or water) bonds to the oxygen to form the **hydroxyl group** (OH).

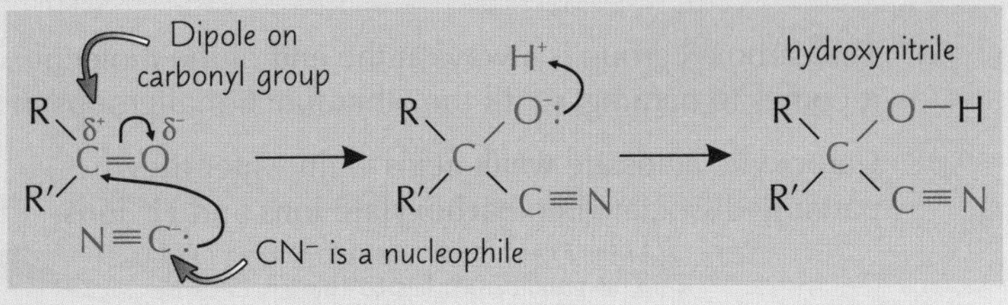

Hydrogen cyanide is a **highly toxic** gas. When this reaction is done in the laboratory, a solution of **acidified sodium cyanide** is used instead, to reduce the risk. Even so, the reaction should be done in a **fume cupboard**.

2,4-dinitrophenylhydrazine Tests for Aldehydes and Ketones

1) When **2,4-dinitrophenylhydrazine** (2,4-DNP or Brady's reagent) is dissolved in methanol and concentrated sulfuric acid it will react with **carbonyl groups** to form a **bright orange precipitate**. This only happens with **C=O groups**, not with ones like COOH, so it only tests for **aldehydes** and **ketones**.
2) The orange precipitate is a **derivative** of the carbonyl compound. Each different carbonyl compound produces a crystalline derivative with a **different melting point**. So if you measure the melting point of the crystals and compare it against the **known** melting points of the derivatives, you can **identify** the carbonyl compound.

Use Tollens' Reagent to Test for an Aldehyde

This test lets you distinguish between an aldehyde and a ketone. It uses the fact that an **aldehyde** can be **easily oxidised** to a carboxylic acid, but a ketone can't.

- Tollens' reagent is a **colourless** solution of **silver nitrate** dissolved in **aqueous ammonia**.
- When heated together in a test tube, the aldehyde is **oxidised** and the silver ions in the Tollens' reagent are **reduced** to silver causing a **silver mirror** to form.
- The test tube should be heated in a beaker of hot water, rather than directly over a flame.

$$Ag(NH_3)_2^+{}_{(aq)} + e^- \rightarrow Ag_{(s)} + 2NH_{3(aq)}$$

colourless — silver

Tollens' reagent can also be called ammoniacal silver nitrate.

Practice Questions

Q1 Give the reagents and conditions for oxidising an aldehyde to a carboxylic acid.

Q2 Draw the reaction mechanism for reducing a ketone to an alcohol.

Q3 Describe how you could determine the identity of an aldehyde or ketone using 2,4-dinitrophenylhydrazine.

Exam Question

Q1 Compounds X and Y are unknown compounds both with the molecular formula C_3H_6O.
When compounds X and Y are reacted separately with 2,4-dinitrophenylhydrazine, both form an orange precipitate.
When heated gently with Tollens' reagent, compound Y forms a silver mirror. No change is observed for compound X.

a) Identify, with reasoning, compounds X and Y. [3 marks]

b) Draw a mechanism to show how compound X reacts with HCN. [2 marks]

c) Which of the compounds would oxidise to form a carboxylic acid? [1 mark]

Silver mirror, silver mirror on the wall, who's the fairest carbonyl of them all...

You've got to be a pro at recognising different functional groups from a mile off. Make sure you know how aldehydes differ from ketones and what happens if you try to oxidise them. And how to reduce them. And don't forget the details of those pesky tests. Phew, it's hard work some of this chemistry. Don't worry, it'll only make you stronger.

Carboxylic Acids and Acyl Chlorides

Carboxylic acids — the clue's in the name. They're weak acids, so expect some acid-base reactions to come your way...

Carboxylic Acids contain -COOH

1) **Carboxylic acids** contain the **carboxyl** functional group **-COOH**. To name them, you find and name the longest alkane chain, take off the 'e' and add **'–oic acid'**.

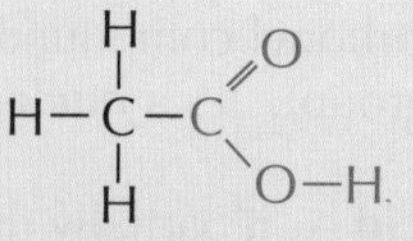

ethanoic acid

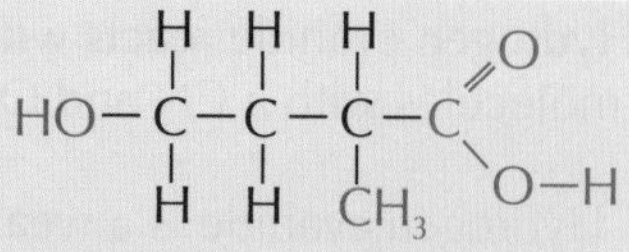

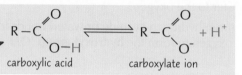

4-hydroxy-2-methylbutanoic acid

2) The carboxyl group is always at the **end** of the molecule. It's more important than other functional groups (when it comes to naming) so all the other functional groups in the molecule are numbered starting from this carbon.
3) Carboxylic acids are **weak acids** — in water they partially dissociate into **carboxylate ions** and **H^+ ions**.

This equilibrium lies to the left because most of the molecules don't dissociate.

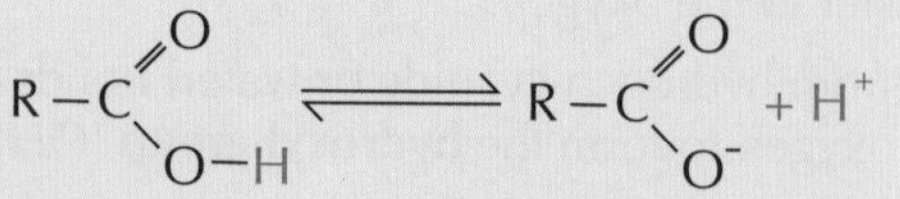

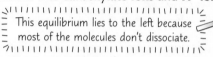

carboxylic acid carboxylate ion

Carboxylic Acids Form Hydrogen Bonds

Carboxylic acids are polar molecules, since electrons are drawn towards the O atoms. **Hydrogen bonds** are able to form between the **highly polarised** $H^{\delta+}$ atom and $O^{\delta-}$ atoms on other molecules. This makes small carboxylic acids **very soluble** in water — they form hydrogen bonds with the water molecules.

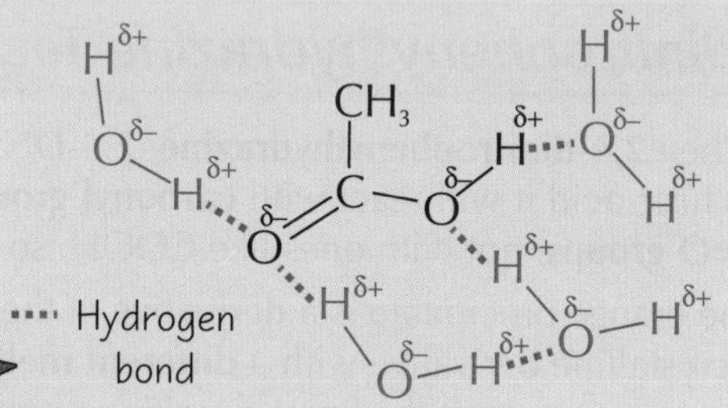

Carboxylic Acids React with Metals, Carbonates and Bases

1) Carboxylic acids react with the more **reactive metals** in a **redox reaction** to form a **salt** and **hydrogen gas**.

$$2CH_3COOH_{(aq)} + Mg_{(s)} \rightarrow (CH_3COO)_2Mg_{(aq)} + H_{2(g)}$$

ethanoic acid → magnesium ethanoate

Salts of carboxylic acids are called carboxylates and their names end with –oate.

2) Carboxylic acids react with **carbonates CO_3^{2-}** to form a **salt, carbon dioxide** and **water**.

$$2CH_3COOH_{(aq)} + Na_2CO_{3(s)} \rightarrow 2CH_3COONa_{(aq)} + H_2O_{(l)} + CO_{2(g)}$$

ethanoic acid → sodium ethanoate

In reactions 1 and 2, the gas fizzes out of the solution.

3) Carboxylic acids are neutralised by other **bases** to form **salts** and **water**.

With **alkalis**: $CH_3COOH_{(aq)} + NaOH_{(aq)} \rightarrow CH_3COONa_{(aq)} + H_2O_{(l)}$

With **metal oxides**: $2CH_3COOH_{(aq)} + MgO_{(s)} \rightarrow (CH_3COO)_2Mg_{(aq)} + H_2O_{(l)}$

Acyl Chlorides are Formed by Reacting Carboxylic Acids with $SOCl_2$

Acyl (or **acid**) **chlorides** have the functional group **-COCl** — their general formula is **$C_nH_{2n-1}OCl$**.

All their names end in **'–oyl chloride'**, e.g.:

The carbon atoms are numbered from the end with the acyl functional group. (This is the same as with carboxylic acids.)

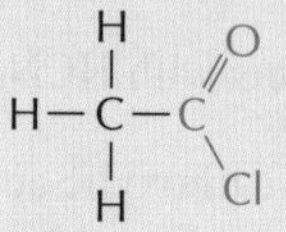

ethanoyl chloride

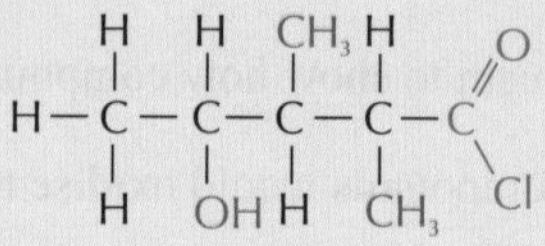

4-hydroxy-2,3-dimethylpentanoyl chloride

They're made by reacting **carboxylic acids** with **$SOCl_2$** (thionyl chloride) — the **-OH** group in the acid is replaced by **-Cl**. For example:

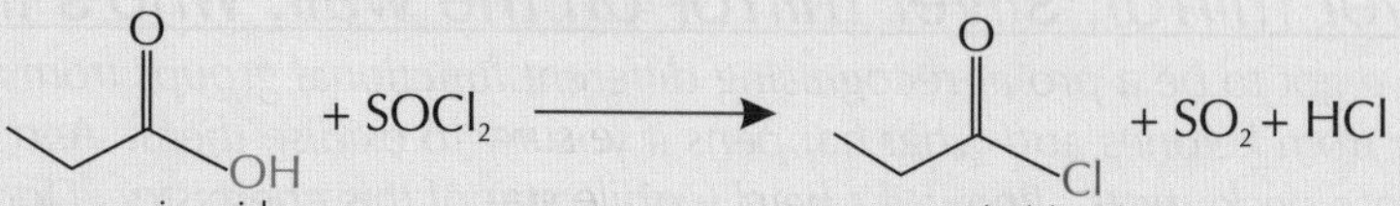

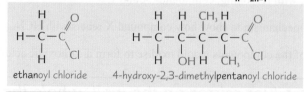

propanoic acid + $SOCl_2$ → propanoyl chloride + SO_2 + HCl

Carboxylic Acids and Acyl Chlorides

Acyl Chlorides Easily **Lose** Their **Chlorine**

This irreversible reaction is a much easier, faster way to produce an ester than reacting an alcohol with a carboxylic acid (see page 184).

Acyl chlorides react with...

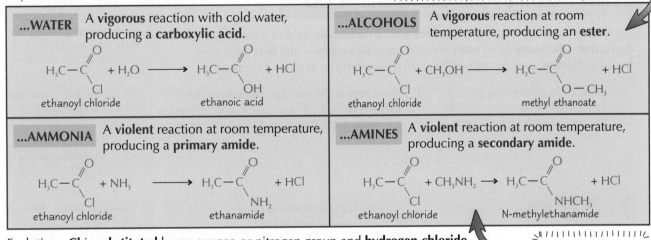

...WATER A **vigorous** reaction with cold water, producing a **carboxylic acid**.

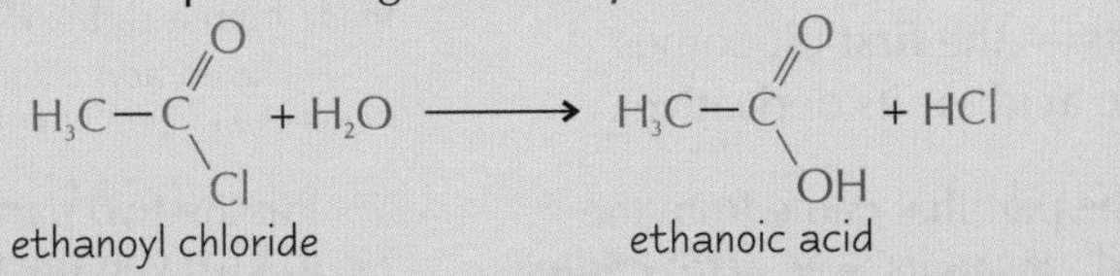

...ALCOHOLS A **vigorous** reaction at room temperature, producing an **ester**.

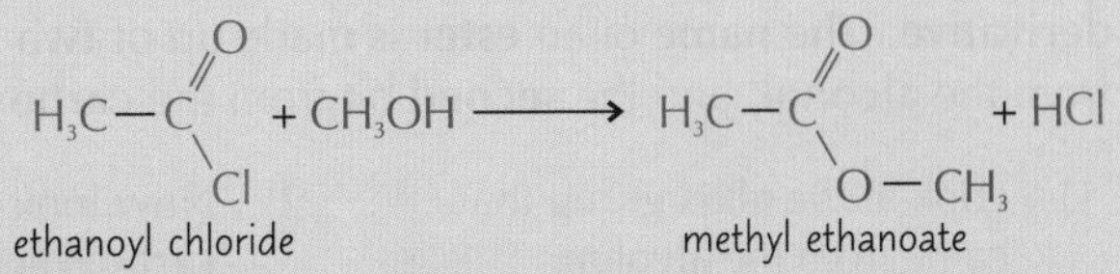

...AMMONIA A **violent** reaction at room temperature, producing a **primary amide**.

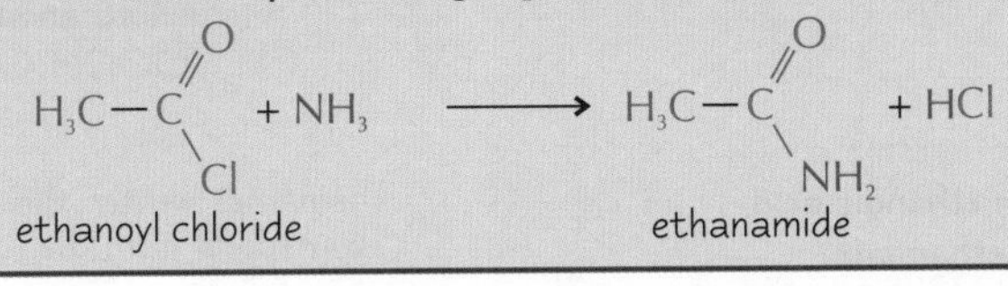

...AMINES A **violent** reaction at room temperature, producing a **secondary amide**.

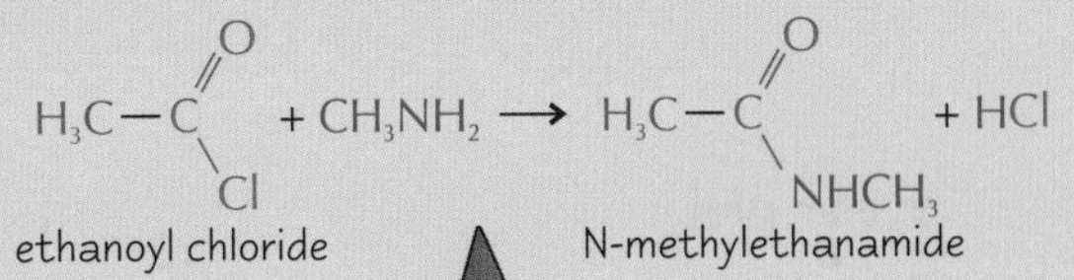

Each time, **Cl** is **substituted** by an oxygen or nitrogen group and **hydrogen chloride** fumes are given off — they're **nucleophilic addition-elimination** reactions.

See p.186 for amines and amides.

Acyl Chlorides React with **Phenol** to Form **Esters**

You can normally make **esters** by reacting an **alcohol** with a **carboxylic acid**. Phenols react **very** slowly with carboxylic acids, so it's faster to use an **acyl chloride**, such as ethanoyl chloride.

Ethanoyl chloride reacts slowly with phenol at room temperature, producing the ester **phenyl ethanoate** and **hydrogen chloride** gas.

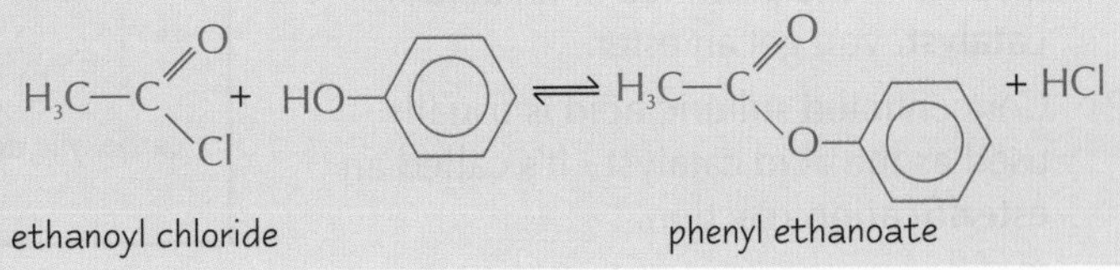

Practice Questions

Q1 Draw an equilibrium to show the dissociation of a carboxylic acid in water.

Q2 Explain why small carboxylic acids are soluble in water.

Q3 What products are formed when a carboxylic acid is reacted with magnesium?

Q4 What's the functional group in an acyl chloride?

Exam Question

Q1 The reaction scheme below shows some of the reactions of an acyl chloride and its derivatives.

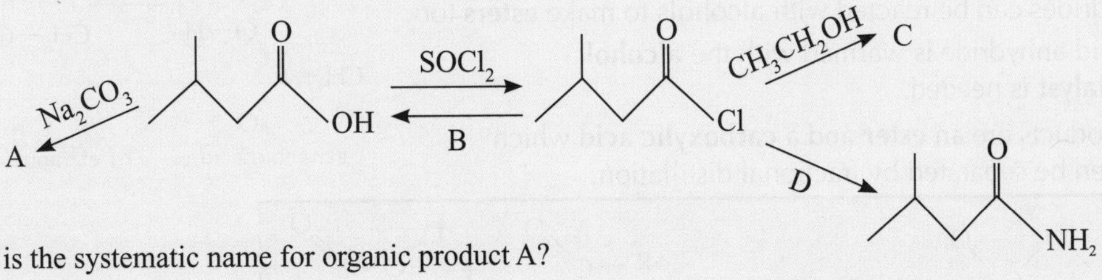

a) What is the systematic name for organic product A? [1 mark]

b) Give the reagent(s) in reaction B. [1 mark]

c) Give the skeletal formula of organic product C. [1 mark]

d) Give the reagent(s) in reaction D. [1 mark]

Acyl Chlorides — ace by name, ace by nature....

Acyl chlorides are really reactive — they'll react with most nucleophiles and the chlorine atom gets replaced. This is really useful in organic synthesis. So make sure you've got all those reactions learnt. You should know them so well that you're able to recite them backwards while standing on your head and trying to solve a 1000 piece jigsaw puzzle.

Esters

Esther's a sweet girl. Her favourite colour's green and she's got a weakness for hob nobs. That's all you need to know. Esters, however, are yet another type of organic compound. You need to know how to make 'em and how to break 'em.

Esters have the Functional Group –COO–

A carboxylic acid derivative is just something that can be made from a carboxylic acid — like an acyl chloride.

An **ester** is made by reacting an **alcohol** with a **carboxylic acid** or a carboxylic acid **derivative**. The **name** of an **ester** is made up of **two parts** — the **first** bit comes from the **alcohol**, and the **second** bit from the **carboxylic acid** (or its derivative).

1) Look at the **alkyl group** that came from the **alcohol**. This is the first bit of the ester's name.

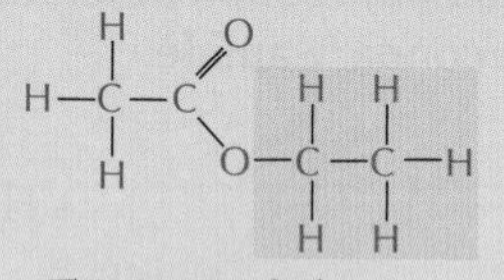

This is an **ethyl** group.

2) Now look at the part that came from the **carboxylic acid**. Swap its '-oic acid' ending for 'oate' to get the second bit of the name.

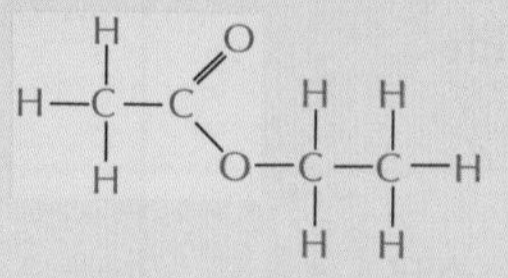

This came from **ethanoic acid**, so it's an **ethanoate**.

3) Put the two parts together to give you the full systematic name.

It's **ethyl ethanoate**
$CH_3COOCH_2CH_3$

The name's written the opposite way round from the formula.

You can make Esters...

1) From Alcohols and Carboxylic Acids

1) If you heat a **carboxylic acid** with an **alcohol** in the presence of an **acid catalyst**, you get an ester.
2) Concentrated sulfuric acid is usually used as the acid catalyst. It's called an **esterification** reaction.

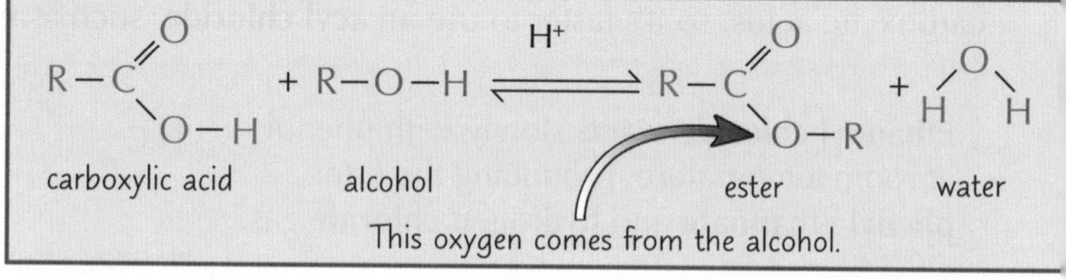

3) The reaction is **reversible**, so you need to separate out the product **as it's formed**.
4) For small esters, you can warm the mixture and just **distil off** the ester, because it's more volatile than the other compounds.
5) Larger esters are harder to form so it's best to heat them under **reflux** and use **fractional distillation** to separate the ester from the other compounds.

It's an example of a condensation reaction — where molecules combine by releasing a small molecule.

2) From Alcohols and Acid Anhydrides

An **acid anhydride** is made from two carboxylic acid molecules.

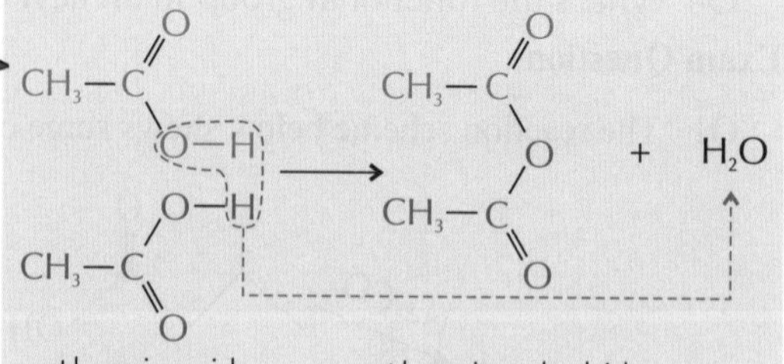

Acid anhydrides can be reacted with alcohols to make **esters** too.

1) The acid anhydride is warmed with the **alcohol**. **No catalyst** is needed.
2) The products are an **ester** and a **carboxylic acid** which can then be separated by fractional distillation.

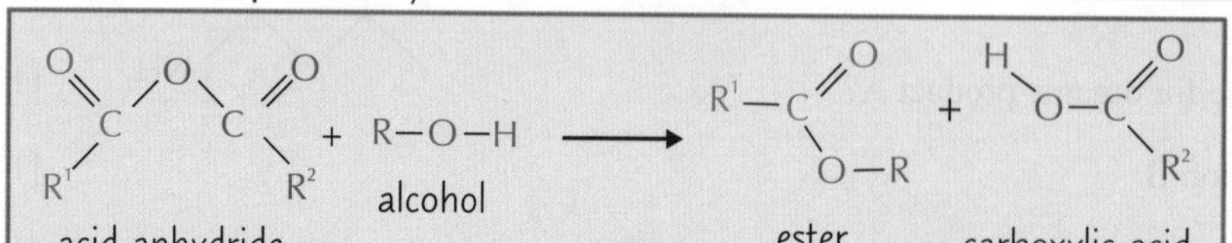

3) From Alcohols and Acyl Chlorides

When alcohols react with acyl chlorides, an ester is formed along with hydrogen chloride gas.

There's more about acyl chlorides on p.182-183.

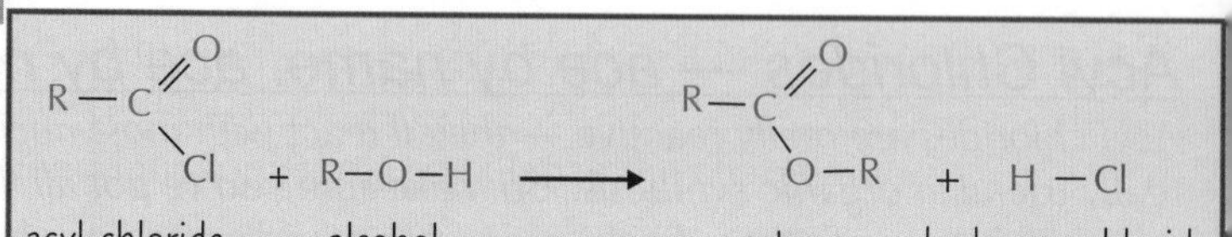

Esters

Esters are **Hydrolysed** to Form **Alcohols**

There are two ways to hydrolyse esters — using **acid hydrolysis** or **base hydrolysis**. With both types you get an **alcohol**, but the second product in each case is different.

Acid Hydrolysis

Acid hydrolysis splits the ester into a **carboxylic acid** and an **alcohol**. You have to **reflux** the ester with a **dilute acid**, such as hydrochloric or sulfuric.

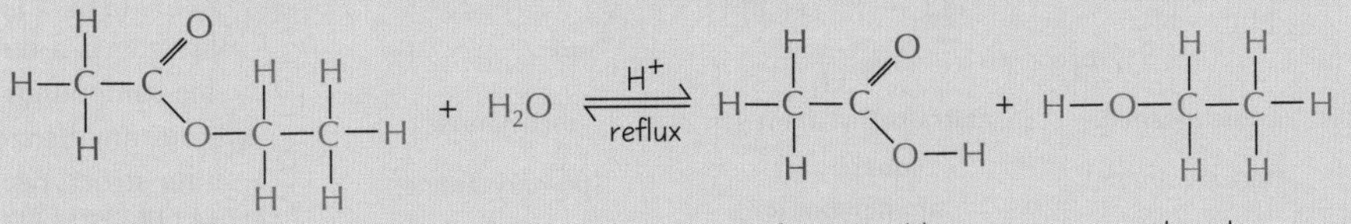

ethyl ethanoate — ethanoic acid — ethanol

As it's a reversible reaction, you need to use lots of water to push the equilibrium over to the right.

We are never, ever, ever getting back together
Like, ever?

Esther's break up was completely irreversible.

Base Hydrolysis

This time you have to **reflux** the ester with a **dilute alkali**, such as sodium hydroxide. You get a **carboxylate salt** and an **alcohol**.

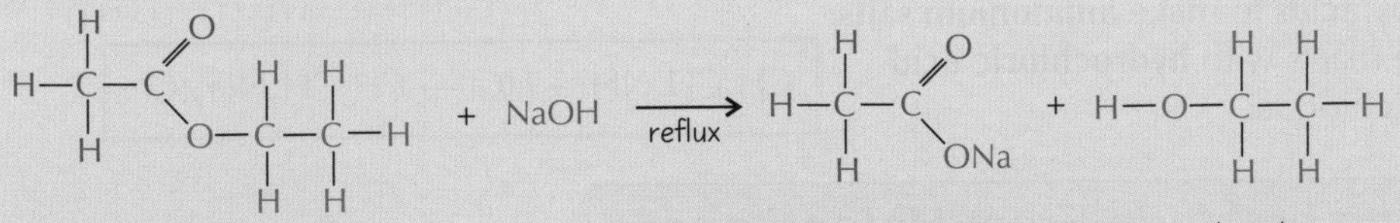

ethyl ethanoate — sodium ethanoate — ethanol

Practice Questions

Q1 What is the functional group of an ester?

Q2 Give two ways of making esters using an alcohol.

Q3 What are the products when you hydrolyse an ester in acidic conditions?

Q4 Under what conditions is the hydrolysis of an ester a reversible reaction?

Exam Questions

Q1 Propyl ethanoate is a pear-scented oil. It is used as a solvent and as a flavouring.

a) Name the alcohol that it can be made from. [1 mark]

b) Name and draw two different organic substances that could be added to the alcohol to produce the propyl ethanoate. [2 marks]

Q2 a) Choose the two compounds that will react together under acidic conditions to form the ester 2-methylpropylpentanoate:

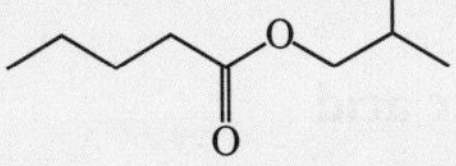

A 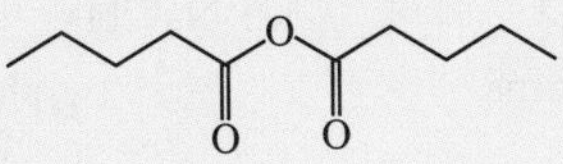 **B** 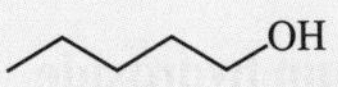 **C** 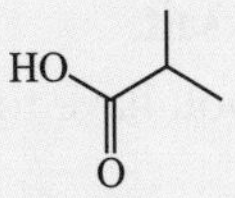 **D** 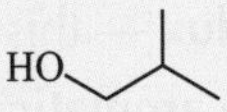 [1 mark]

b) What are the products when this ester is warmed with aqueous sodium hydroxide? [1 mark]

Esters están terminandos...

Those two ways of hydrolysing esters are just similar enough that it's easy to get in a muddle. Remember — hydrolysis in acidic conditions is reversible, and you get a carboxylic acid as well as an alcohol. Hydrolysis with a base is a one way reaction that gives you an alcohol and a carboxylate salt. Now we've got that sorted, I think it's time for a cuppa.

Amines and Amides

We start this section with a few more types of compounds for you to learn about — these ones all contain nitrogen.

Amines are Organic Derivatives of Ammonia

If one or more of the **hydrogens** in **ammonia** (NH_3) is replaced with an organic group, you get an **amine**. Amines can be **primary**, **secondary** or **tertiary** depending on how many **alkyl** groups the nitrogen atom is bonded to. If the nitrogen atom is bonded to **four** alkyl groups, you get a **positively** charged **quaternary ammonium** ion.

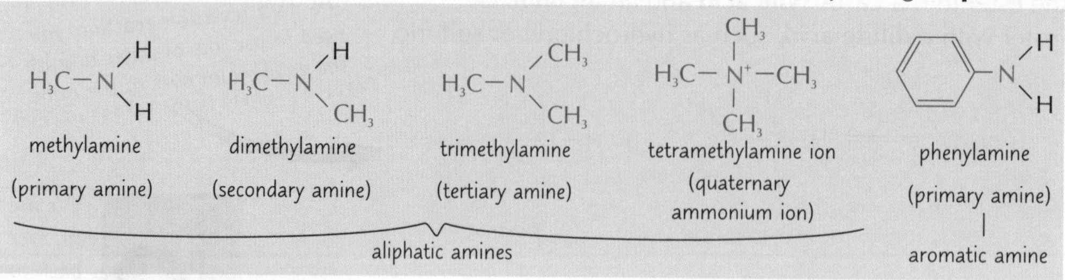

'Aliphatic' is a term for compounds without any benzene ring structures.

Amines Are Bases

1) There's a **lone pair of electrons** on the **nitrogen** atom of an amine that's able to accept **protons (H^+ ions)**. This means that amines are **bases**.
2) Amines are **neutralised** by **acids** to make **ammonium salts**. For example, **ethylamine** reacts with **hydrochloric acid** to form ethylammonium chloride:

$$CH_3CH_2NH_2 + HCl \rightarrow CH_3CH_2NH_3^+Cl^-$$

Acids are proton donors, and bases are proton acceptors. It's all there on page 134 if you need a reminder.

Aliphatic Amines *can be Made From* Haloalkanes

Amines can be made by heating a **haloalkane** with an excess of **ethanolic ammonia** (ammonia dissolved in ethanol). You'll get a **mixture** of primary, secondary and tertiary amines, and quaternary ammonium salts, as more than one hydrogen is likely to be substituted. You can separate the products using **fractional distillation**.

For example, **bromoethane** will react with ammonia to form **ethylamine**:

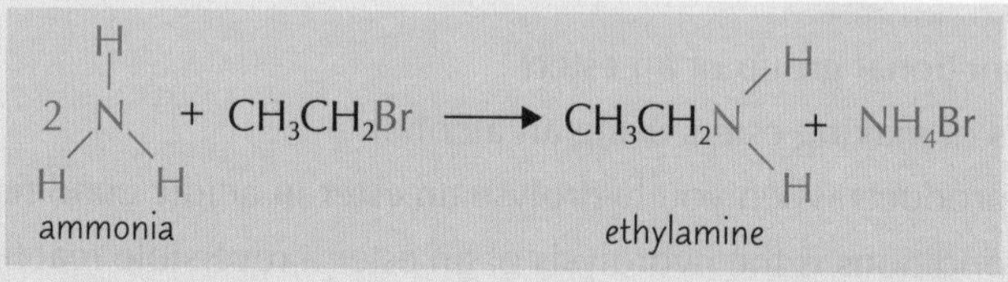

This is a nucleophilic substitution reaction.

Ethylamine can **also** react with **bromoethane** to form **diethylamine**:

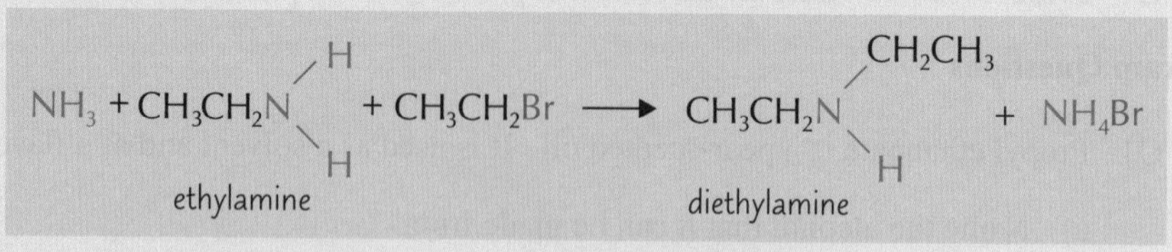

And so on.

Aromatic *Amines are Made by* Reducing *a* Nitro Compound

Nitro compounds, such as **nitrobenzene**, are reduced in two steps:
1) Heat a mixture of a **nitro compound**, **tin metal** and **concentrated hydrochloric acid** under **reflux** — this makes a **salt**.
2) To get the **aromatic amine**, you have to add **sodium hydroxide**.

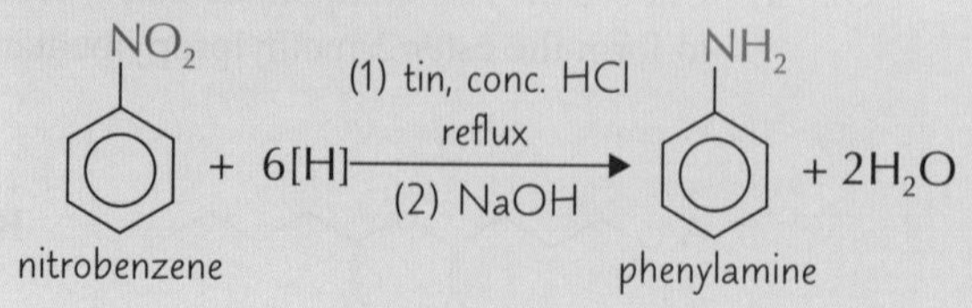

Amides *are Carboxylic Acid Derivatives*

Amides contain the functional group **$-CONH_2$**.

The **carbonyl group** pulls electrons away from the rest of the $-CONH_2$ group, so amides behave differently from amines.

You get **primary** and **secondary** amides depending on how many **carbon atoms** the nitrogen is bonded to.

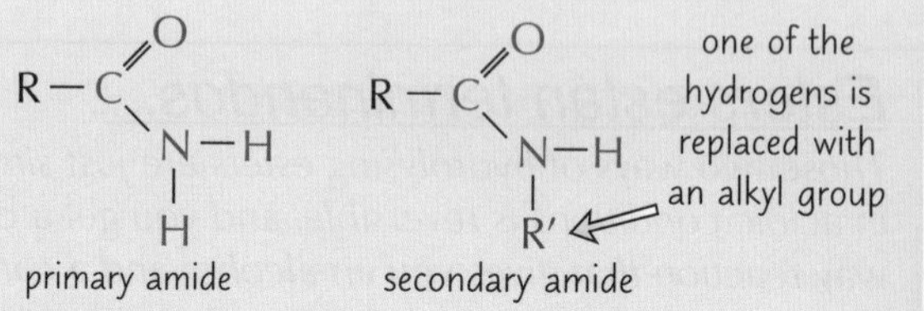

Amines and Amides

Amino Acids have an **Amino Group** and a **Carboxyl Group**

1) An **amino acid** has a **basic amino group** (NH_2) and an **acidic carboxyl group** (COOH).
2) In an α–**amino acid**, both groups are attached to the **same** carbon atom — the 'α carbon'. The **general formula** of an α–amino acid is **$RCH(NH_2)COOH$**.

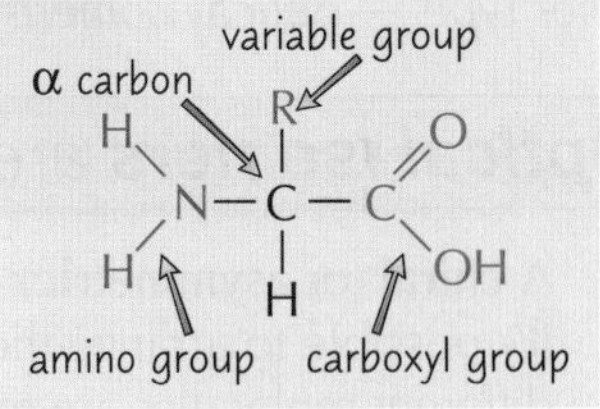

Amino Acids Can **React** with **Acids** and **Alkalis**

1) The **carboxylic acid group** in an amino acid can react with an **alkali** to form a **conjugate base** — $RCH(NH_2)COO^-$. This can combine with a positive ion to form a **salt**. For example:

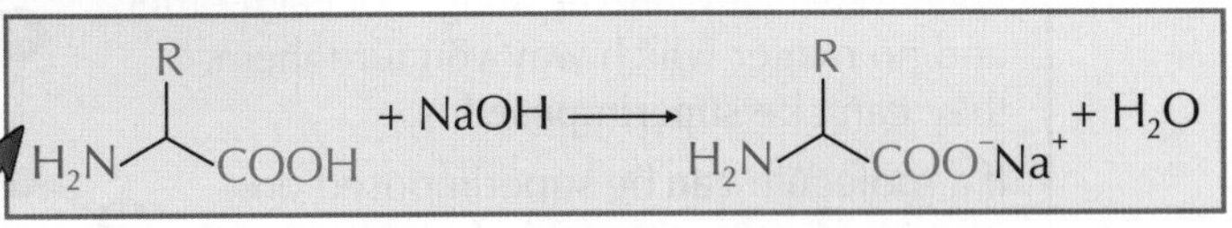

2) The **amino group** meanwhile can react with an **acid** to form a **salt** of the **conjugate acid**. For example:

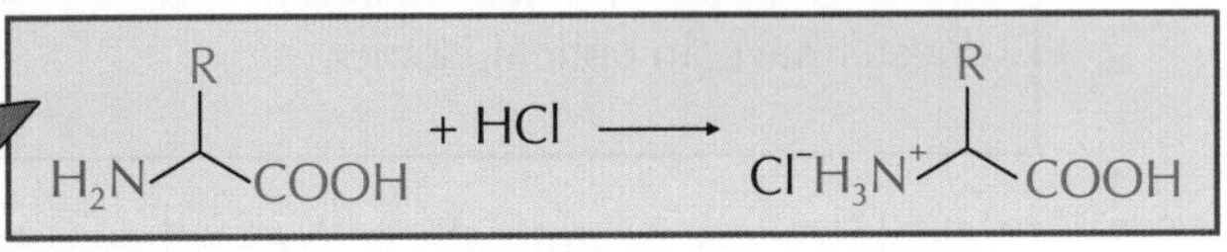

Amino Acids React with **Alcohols** to Form **Esters**

Just like other carboxylic acids, the **carboxylic acid group** in an amino acid can react with an **alcohol** in the presence of a **strong acid catalyst** (normally sulfuric acid) to form an **ester**.

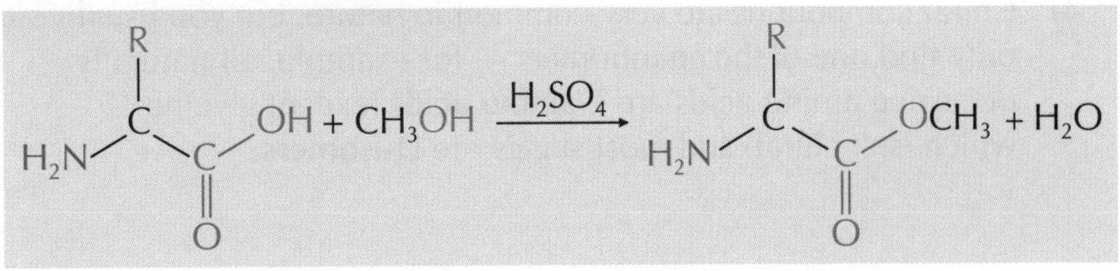

Practice Questions

Q1 Draw examples of a primary, secondary and tertiary amine, and a quaternary ammonium ion.

Q2 Why do amines act as bases?

Q3 Draw the general structure of a primary amide and a secondary amide.

Q4 What's the general formula of an α-amino acid?

Exam Questions

Q1 When 1-chloropropane is reacted with ammonia, a mixture of different amines are produced.

a) Name two of the amines produced in the reaction. [2 marks]

b) What technique could you use to separate the mixture? [1 mark]

c) Outline the steps needed to reduce nitrobenzene to make phenylamine. [2 marks]

Q2 The organic compound shown on the right is leucine.
Which of the following statements is incorrect?

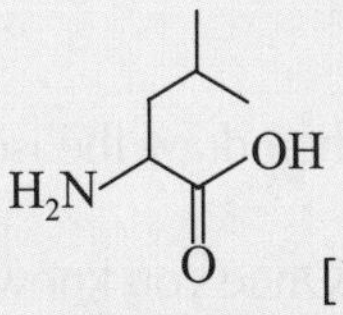

A Leucine is an α-amino acid.

B Leucine contains an amino group.

C Leucine reacts with sodium hydroxide to form the salt of its conjugate acid.

D Leucine reacts with alcohols to form esters.

[1 mark]

This topic was quite amine one...

Amino acids don't just pop up in Chemistry. They're the building blocks of proteins in your body, so they're really quite important for life as well as for your exams. Make sure you understand the different ways they react — with acids, alkalis and alcohols. And while you're at it, you may as well go through the reactions for making amines as well.

Chirality

Stereoisomers have the same molecular formula and their atoms are arranged in the same way. The only difference is the orientation of their bonds in space. You met E/Z stereoisomerism in Module 4. Now it's time to find out about another type — optical isomerism. Something called chirality is the key here, as you're about to discover.

Optical Isomers are Mirror Images of Each Other

1) A **chiral** (or **asymmetric**) carbon atom is one which has **four different** groups attached to it. It's possible to arrange the groups in **two** different ways around the carbon atom so that two different molecules are made — these molecules are called **enantiomers** or **optical isomers**.

Enantiomers are **mirror images** of each other and no matter which way you turn them, they can't be **superimposed**.

If a molecule **can** be superimposed on its mirror image, it's **achiral** and it doesn't have an optical isomer.

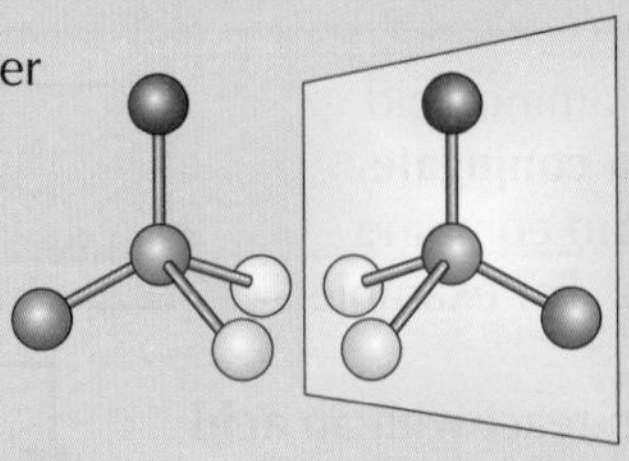

You might use a molecular modelling kit in class to see for yourself how enantiomers are non-superimposable.

2) Optical isomers are **optically active** — they **rotate plane-polarised light**. One enantiomer rotates it in a **clockwise** direction, the other rotates it the **same amount** but in an **anticlockwise** direction.

Normal light vibrates in all directions, but plane-polarised light only vibrates in one direction.

3) The enantiomers are sometimes identified as the **D** isomer or the **L** isomer — luckily you don't have to worry about which is which.

4) Chiral compounds are very common in nature, but you usually only find **one** of the enantiomers — for example, all naturally occurring amino acids are **L-amino acids** (except glycine which isn't chiral) and most sugars are **D-isomers**.

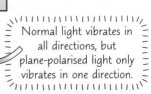

An anteateriomer.

Make Sure You Can Spot Chiral Centres

You have to be able to draw optical isomers. To do this you need to be able to identify the chiral centre...

Example: Draw the optical isomers for 2-hydroxypropanoic acid:

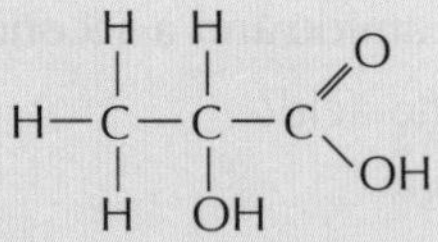

First locate the chiral centre:

Look for the carbon atom with **four** different groups attached. Here it's the carbon with the four groups H, OH, COOH and CH_3 attached.

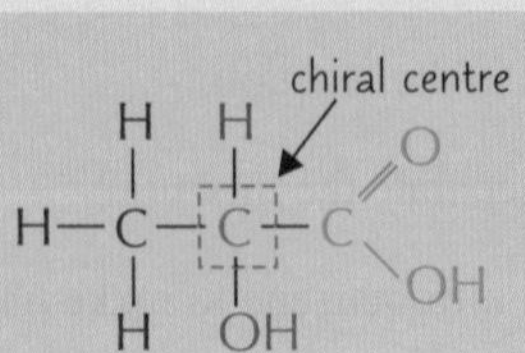

Then draw the isomers:

Once you know the chiral carbon, **draw** one enantiomer in a **tetrahedral** shape. Don't try to draw the full structure of each group — it gets confusing. Then draw a **mirror image** beside it.

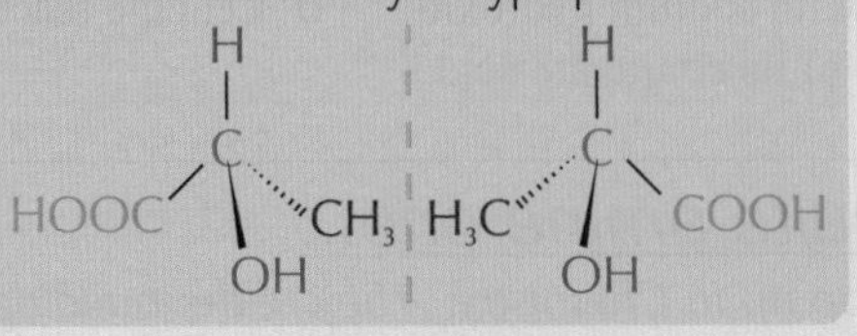

Chirality

Some Molecules Have **More Than One** Chiral Centre

Some molecules have **more than one** chiral centre — you need to be able to spot them **all**.

Example: Label all the chiral centres in the following organic molecule:

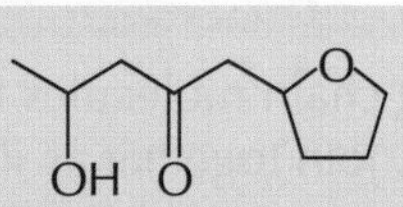

The structure shown is a **skeletal formula** — to find the carbon atoms that have **four different groups** attached, it can be helpful to show all the **hydrogen atoms** as well.

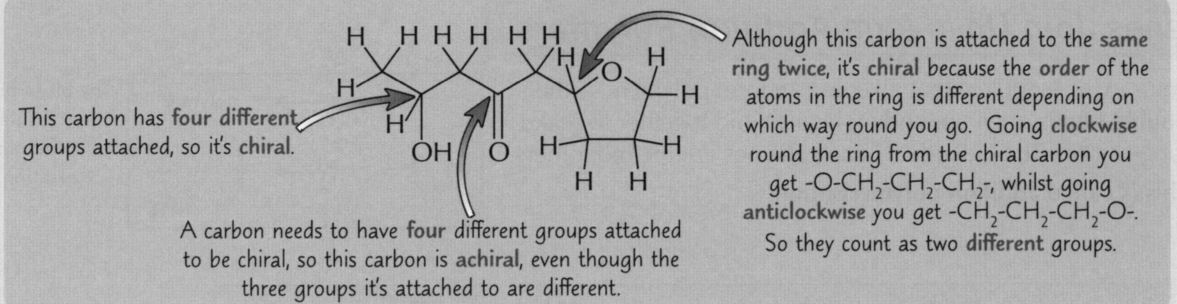
This carbon has four different groups attached, so it's chiral.
A carbon needs to have four different groups attached to be chiral, so this carbon is achiral, even though the three groups it's attached to are different.
Although this carbon is attached to the same ring twice, it's chiral because the order of the atoms in the ring is different depending on which way round you go. Going clockwise round the ring from the chiral carbon you get -O-CH2-CH2-CH2-, whilst going anticlockwise you get -CH2-CH2-CH2-O-. So they count as two different groups.

The chiral centres are:

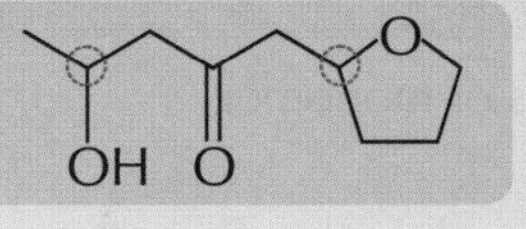

If a molecule has **more** than **one chiral centre**, it will have **more** than **two optical isomers**.

Example: The molecule 3-methylpentan-2-ol is shown on the right. It contains two chiral carbons, which are marked with asterisks. Draw all the optical isomers of the molecule.

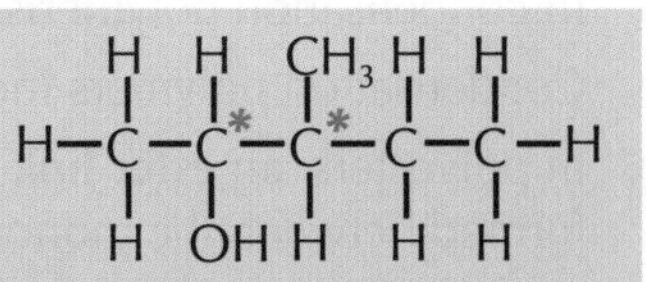

The molecule has **two** chiral centres, so there are **four** different optical isomers of this molecule:

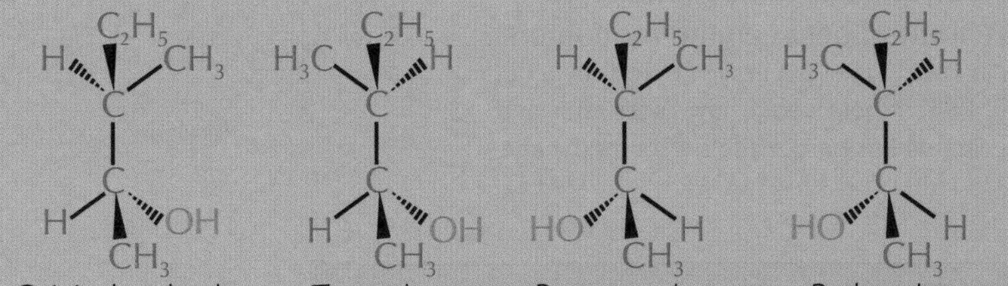

Original molecule. | Top carbon mirror-imaged. | Bottom carbon mirror-imaged. | Both carbons mirror-imaged.

Practice Questions

Q1 What makes a carbon atom chiral?

Q2 What are enantiomers?

Q3 How do optical isomers affect plane polarised light?

Exam Question

Q1 The skeletal formula of 3-ethyl-4-phenylhexan-2-one is shown on the right.

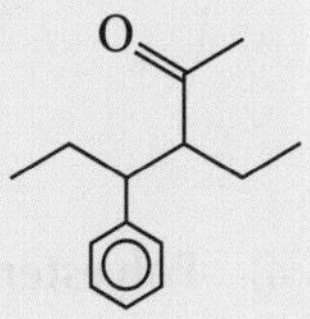

a) Mark each chiral centre with an asterisk. [1 mark]

b) Draw all the optical isomers of the molecule. [4 marks]

Mirror, mirror on the wall, who's the fairest molecule of them all...

This isomer stuff's not all bad — you get to draw little pretty pictures of molecules. If you're having difficulty picturing them as 3D shapes, you could always make models with Blu-tack® and those matchsticks that're propping your eyelids open. Blu® Tack's very therapeutic anyway and squishing it about'll help relieve all that revision stress. It's great stuff.

Polymers

You met polymers for the first time in Module 4, and I bet you thought you'd never have to see their ugly faces again. You were wrong — they're back. Unlike those pesky polymers, I'll try not to be too long, or repeat myself too much.

There are **Two Types** of Polymerisation — **Addition** and **Condensation**

1) **Polymers** are long chain molecules formed when lots of small molecules, called **monomers**, join together as if they're holding hands.

2) There are two ways of **making** polymers — by **addition polymerisation**, or **condensation polymerisation**.

Alkenes **Join Up** to form **Addition Polymers**

1) You saw in Module 4 that alkenes can form polymers — the **double bonds** open up, and molecules join together to make long chains. The individual, small alkenes are the monomers.

2) This is called **addition polymerisation**.

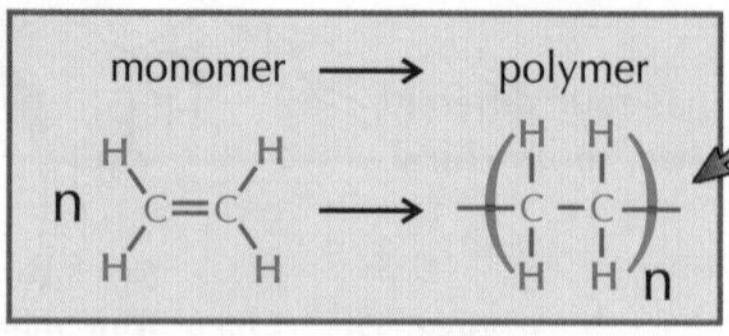

The bit in brackets is the 'repeating unit'. n is the number of repeating units.

Condensation Polymers are formed as **Water** is **Removed**...

1) Condensation polymers are normally formed from **two types** of monomer, each of which has at least **two functional groups**.

2) The functional group on one monomer reacts with a group on the other type of monomer to form a **link**, creating the polymer **chain**.

3) In condensation polymerisation, each time a link is formed, a small molecule is lost (often it's **water**).

4) Condensation polymers include **polyesters** and **polyamides**.

5) In polyesters, an **ester link** (–COO–) is formed between the monomers.

6) In polyamides, **amide links** (–CONH–) are formed between the monomers.

There's more about how these ester and amide links are made on the next page.

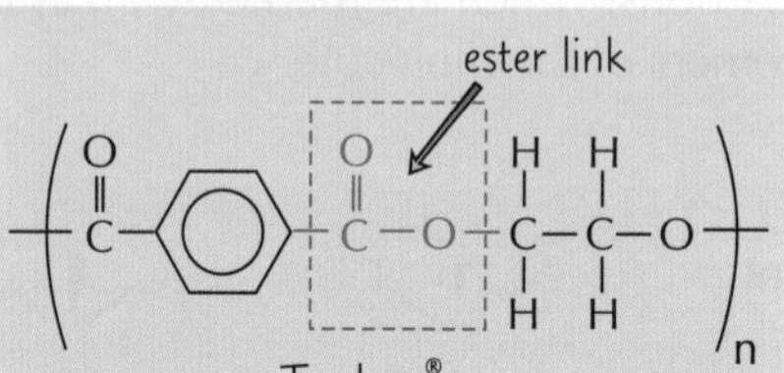

Terylene®   nylon 6,6

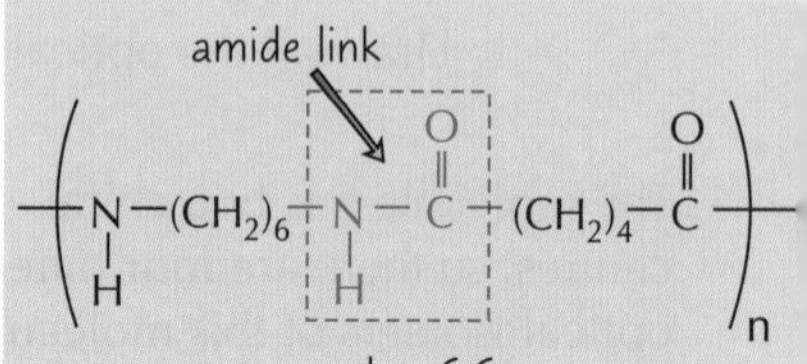

...and **Broken Down** by **Adding It**

1) Condensation polymerisation can be reversed by **hydrolysis** — water molecules are added back in and the links are broken.

2) In practice, hydrolysis with just water is far too **slow**, so the reaction is done with an **acid** or **base**.

3) **Polyamides** will hydrolyse more easily with an **acid** than a base:

amide link

polyamide   + $2n\,H_2O$ $\xrightarrow{\ H^+\ }$ $n\ HO$—C—R—C—OH   + $n\ H$—N—R'—N—H

dicarboxylic acid   diamine

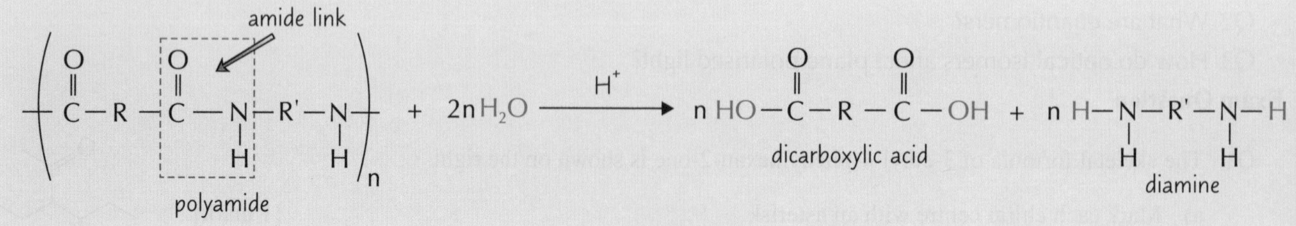

4) **Polyesters** will hydrolyse more easily with a **base**. A **metal salt** of the carboxylic acid is formed.

ester link

polyester   + $2n\,NaOH$ $\longrightarrow$ $n\ Na^+O^-$—C—R—C—O^-Na^+ + $n\ H$—O—R'—O—H

dicarboxylic acid salt   diol

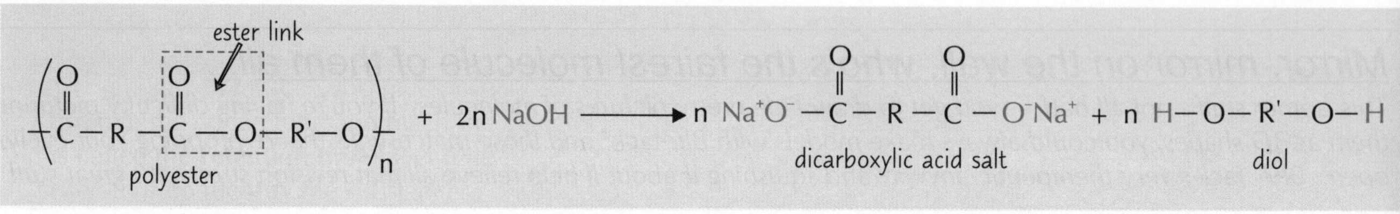

Polymers

Reactions Between **Dicarboxylic Acids** and **Diamines** Make **Polyamides**

1) **Carboxyl** (–COOH) groups react with **amino** (–NH_2) groups to form **amide** (–CONH–) links.
2) A water molecule is lost each time an amide link is formed — it's a **condensation** reaction.
3) The condensation polymer formed is a **polyamide**.

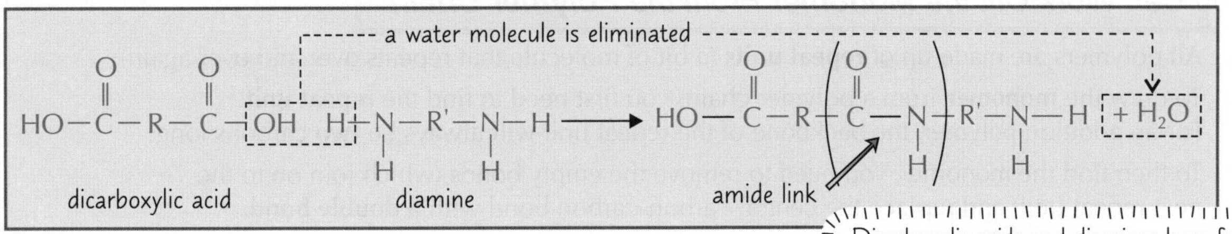

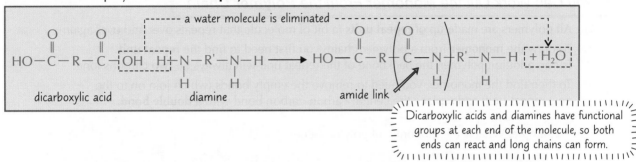

Dicarboxylic acids and diamines have functional groups at each end of the molecule, so both ends can react and long chains can form.

Reactions Between **Dicarboxylic Acids** and **Diols** Make **Polyesters**

Carboxyl groups (–COOH) react with **hydroxyl** (–OH) groups to form **ester links** (–COO–).
It's another **condensation** reaction, and the polymer formed is a **polyester**

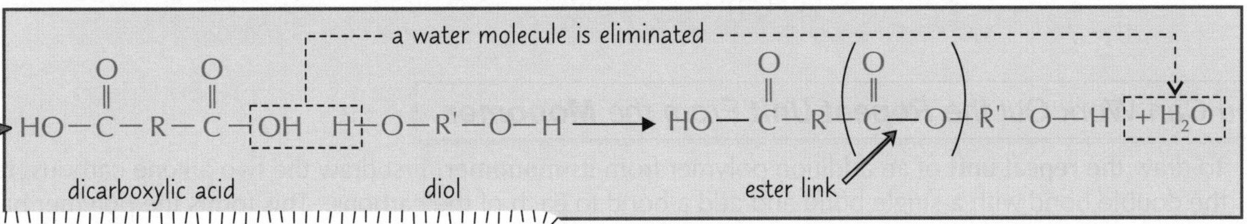

Compounds where one of the carboxylic acid groups is changed to an acyl chloride will also react to form polyesters and polyamides. Instead of water, hydrochloric acid is eliminated in the condensation reaction.

Practice Questions

Q1 Name the two types of polymerisation reaction.

Q2 What type of link forms between monomers in a polyester? And in a polyamide?

Q3 What is a polyamide made from?

Q4 What functional groups react together to form the link in a polyester?

Exam Question

Q1 Kevlar® is a polymer used in bulletproof vests. Its repeating unit is shown below.

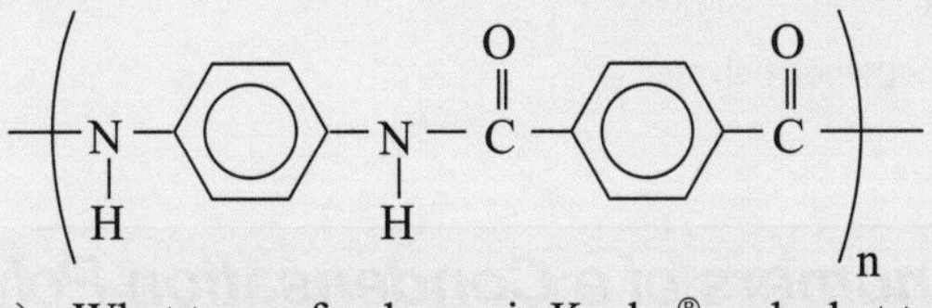

a) What type of polymer is Kevlar® and what type of reaction is used to make it? [2 marks]

b) Kevlar® is made by reacting two different monomers together.
What type of compounds are these monomers? [1 mark]

c) How could you break up Kevlar® into its constituent monomers? [1 mark]

Conversation polymerisation — when someone just goes on and on and on...

Condensation polymers are like those friends who are in an on-off relationship. They get together, then they hydrolyse apart, only to get back together again. And you have to keep up with it — monomers, polymers, amides, esters and all.

More on Polymers

So, you know the basics of polymerisation, but you also need to be able to look at a polymer and work out what the monomers that made it are. Or look at some monomers and work out how they join together to form a polymer.

The Repeat Units of **Addition** Polymers are Based Around the **Double Bond**

You Can Work Out the **Monomer** From the **Polymer Chain**

1) All polymers are made up of **repeat units** (a bit of molecule that repeats over and over again).
2) To draw the **monomer** from a polymer chain, you first need to find the **repeat unit**. For an addition polymer, the backbone of the repeat unit will always be **two** carbons long.
3) To then find the monomer, you need to remove the empty bonds (which join on to the next repeat unit) and replace the central carbon-carbon bond with a **double bond**.

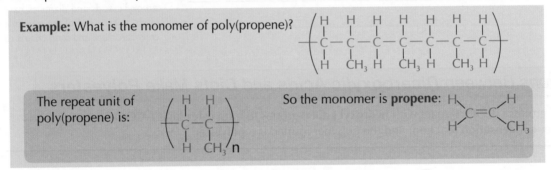

Example: What is the monomer of poly(propene)?

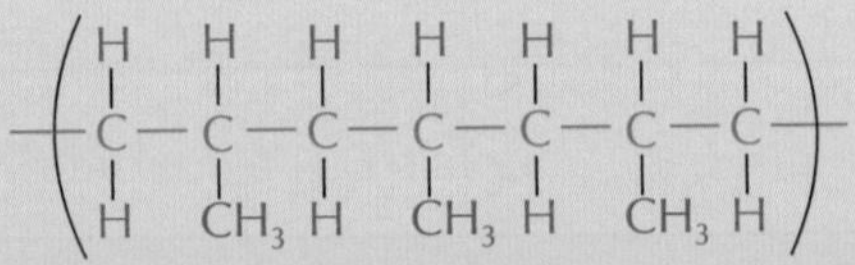

The repeat unit of poly(propene) is:

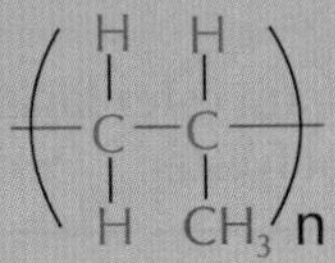

So the monomer is **propene**:

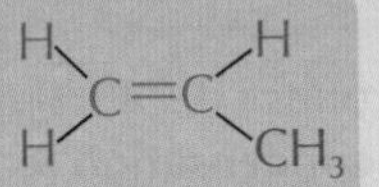

You Can Work Out the **Repeat Unit** From the **Monomer**

1) To draw the **repeat unit** of an addition polymer from its **monomer**, first draw the two alkene carbons, replace the double bond with a single bond and add a bond to each of the carbons. This forms the polymer backbone.
2) Then just fill in the rest of the groups in the same way they surrounded the double bond.

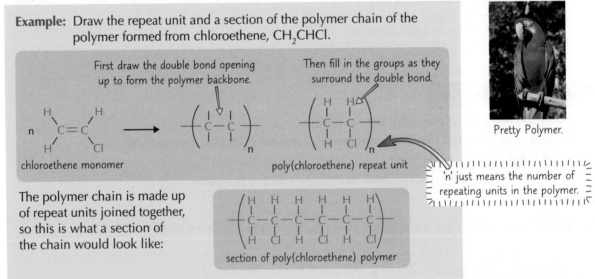

Example: Draw the repeat unit and a section of the polymer chain of the polymer formed from chloroethene, CH_2CHCl.

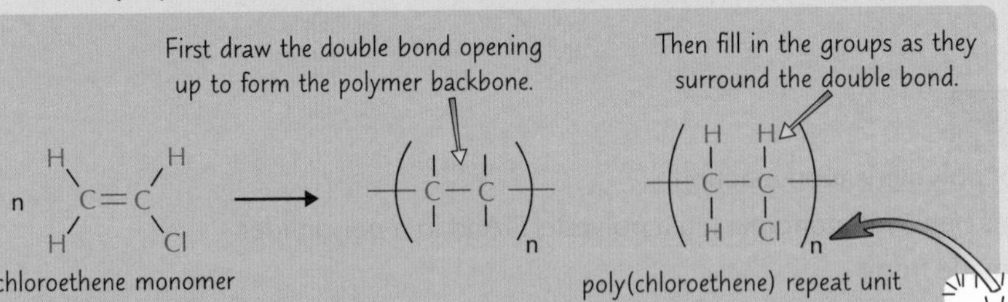
First draw the double bond opening up to form the polymer backbone.
Then fill in the groups as they surround the double bond.
chloroethene monomer
poly(chloroethene) repeat unit

'n' just means the number of repeating units in the polymer.

Pretty Polymer.

The polymer chain is made up of repeat units joined together, so this is what a section of the chain would look like:

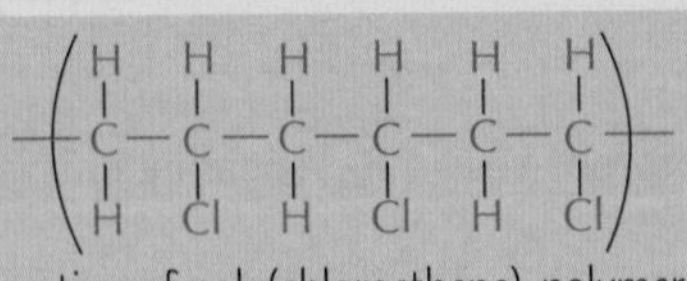

section of poly(chloroethene) polymer

Break the **Amide** or **Ester** Link to Find the **Monomers** of a **Condensation** Polymer

You can find the formulas of the **monomers** used to make a condensation polymer by looking at its formula.

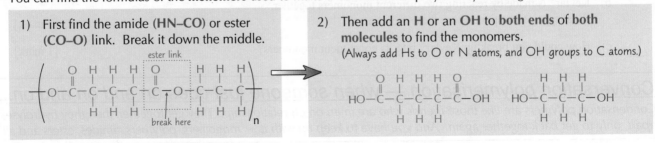

1) First find the amide (**HN–CO**) or ester (**CO–O**) link. Break it down the middle.

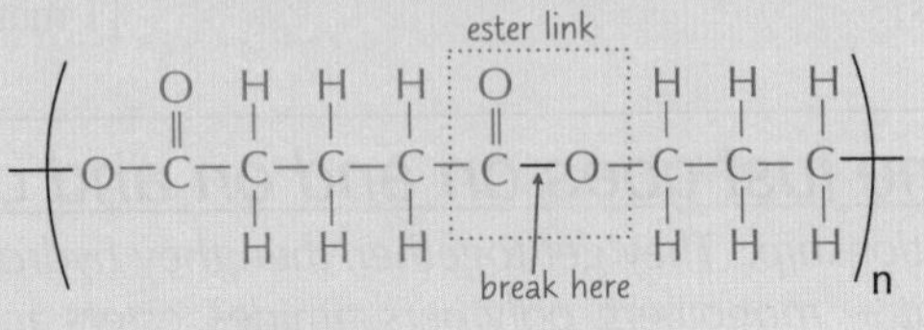
ester link
break here

2) Then add an **H** or an **OH** to **both ends of both molecules** to find the monomers. (Always add Hs to O or N atoms, and OH groups to C atoms.)

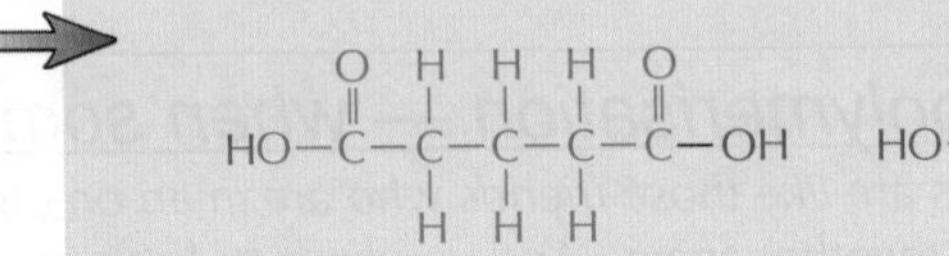

More on Polymers

Join the Monomer Functional Groups to Find a Condensation Polymer

If you know the **formulas** of a pair of **monomers** that react together in a **condensation polymerisation** reaction, you can work out the **repeat unit** of the condensation polymer that they would form.

Example: A condensation polymer is made from 1,4-diaminobutane, $H_2N(CH_2)_4NH_2$, and decanedioic acid, $HOOC(CH_2)_8COOH$. Draw the repeat unit of the polymer that is formed.

1) Draw out the two **monomer** molecules next to each other.
2) Remove an **OH** from the **dicarboxylic acid**, and an **H** from the **diamine** — that gives you a water molecule.
3) Join the C and the N together to make an **amide link**.
4) Take another **H** and **OH** off the ends of your molecule. Draw brackets around it, and there's your **repeat unit**.

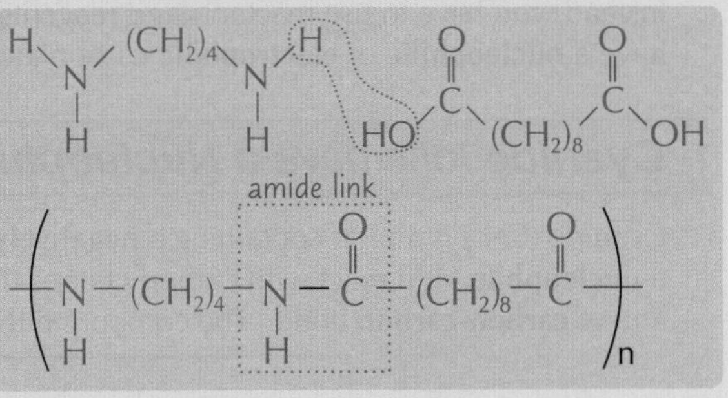
amide link

If the monomer molecules are a **dicarboxylic acid** and a **diol**, then you take an **H** atom from the **diol** and an **OH** group from the **dicarboxylic acid**, and form an **ester** link instead.

Watch Out for More Complex Condensation Polymers

1) Molecules that contain **both** an **amine** and an **alcohol** group can react with **dicarboxylic acids** in a condensation polymerisation reaction. The polymers they form contain both **amide** and **ester** links.

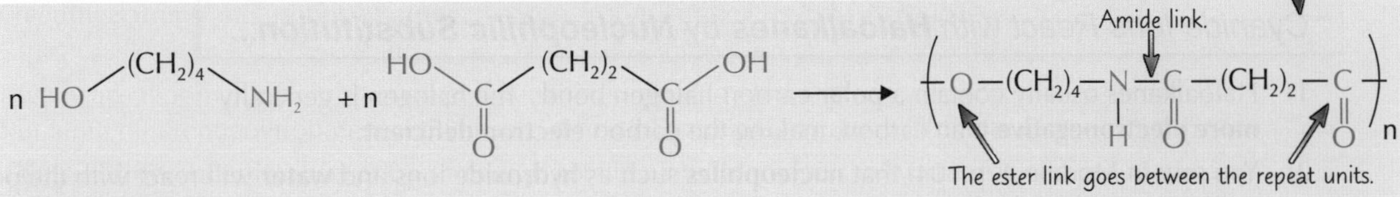
Amide link.
The ester link goes between the repeat units.

2) If a molecule contains a **carboxylic acid** group and either an **alcohol** or an **amine** group, it can polymerise with **itself** to from a condensation polymer with only **one monomer**.

Practice Questions

Q1 Draw the monomer of poly(propene), $(-CH_2CH(CH_3)-)_n$.

Q2 Name two functional groups a molecule could contain in order to form a condensation polymer with itself.

Exam Questions

Q1 PET is a polymer used in the making of plastic bottles. The repeat unit of the polymer is shown on the right.

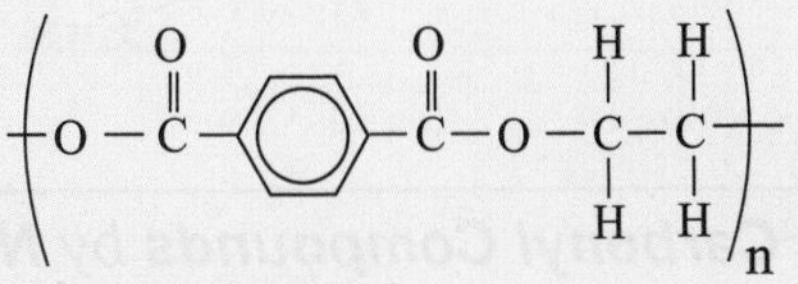

a) Draw the monomers that make up this poylmer. [1 mark]

b) Name the type of polymerisation reaction by which this polymer is formed. [1 mark]

Q2 Polystyrene is a polymer that is commonly used in packaging materials. Its monomer is shown on the right.

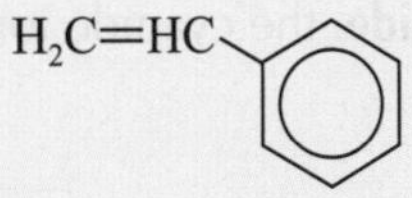

a) Draw the repeat unit of polystyrene. [1 mark]

b) Draw a section of the polymer chain of polystyrene that is three repeat units long. [1 mark]

All this stuff on polymers is really quite repetitive...

Condensation polymers can look quite confusing when there are lots of groups in the repeating unit, but all you need to worry about is finding the amide or ester link. Once you've found that, split the repeating unit in two, play around with a few Hs and Os and hey presto — you've got your monomers. Have a practice with the example on page 192.

Carbon-Carbon Bond Synthesis

The whole of Organic Chemistry revolves around carbon compounds and how they react, but getting one carbon to react with another and form a new carbon-carbon bond is surprisingly hard. Here are some reactions that let you do it.

You Use Carbon-Carbon Bond Synthesis to ***Extend*** the ***Carbon Chain***

In organic synthesis, it's useful to have ways of making a carbon chain **longer**. You can't just put two carbon chains together and expect them to react though. Instead, you have to use reactants and reagents that have a **nucleophilic** or **electrophilic** carbon atom.

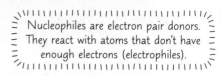

Nucleophiles are electron pair donors. They react with atoms that don't have enough electrons (electrophiles).

Cyanide Ions have a ***Nucleophilic*** Carbon

Cyanide (CN^-) is an ion containing a **negatively charged** carbon atom, so it's a **nucleophile**. It'll react with carbon centres that have a **slight positive charge** to create a new **carbon-carbon** bond. The compound that's initially produced is a **nitrile**.

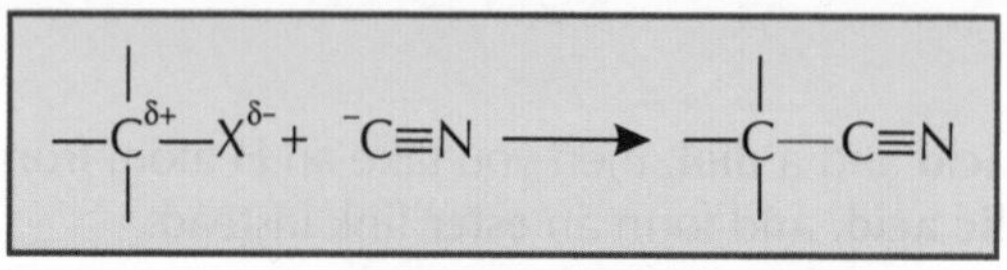

If the electron withdrawing group (X) is a carbonyl group (=O), then the double bond opens up and the product is:

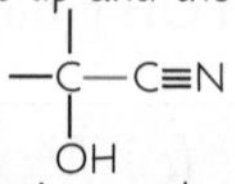

(See the reaction mechanism below.)

So you can **increase** the length of a carbon chain by reacting an organic compound that contains a **slightly positive carbon centre** with a **cyanide** reagent such as **potassium cyanide** (KCN), **sodium cyanide** (NaCN) or **hydrogen cyanide** (HCN).

Cyanide Ions React with ***Haloalkanes*** by ***Nucleophilic Substitution...***

1) Haloalkanes usually contain a **polar** carbon-halogen bond. The halogen is generally **more electronegative** than carbon, making the carbon **electron deficient**.
2) You saw in Module 4 (p.104) that **nucleophiles** such as **hydroxide** ions and **water** will react with the positive carbon centre in haloalkanes to **replace** the **halogen** atom. This is a **nucleophilic substitution reaction**.
3) Well, if you **reflux** a haloalkane with **potassium** (or sodium) **cyanide** in **ethanol**, then the cyanide ions will also react with the haloalkane by **nucleophilic substitution** to form a **nitrile**.

$$R\text{–}X + CN^- \xrightarrow[\text{reflux}]{\text{ethanol}} R\text{–}C\equiv N + X^-$$

4) The mechanism is:

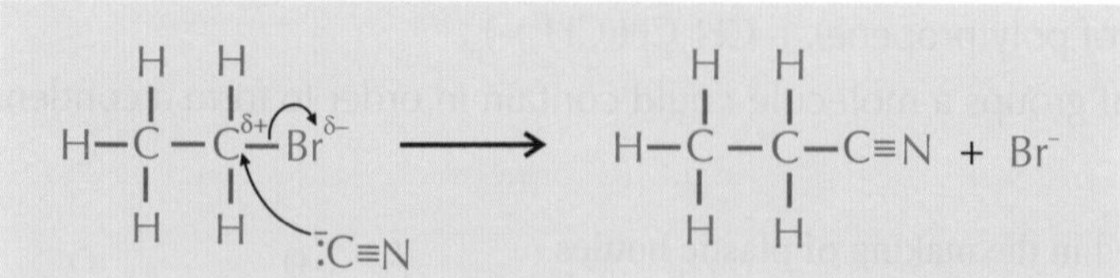

...and with ***Carbonyl Compounds*** by ***Nucleophilic Addition***

Aldehydes and **ketones** are both carbonyl compounds — they contain a **polar C=O** bond. If you mix them with **hydrogen cyanide**, the cyanide ion will react with the **positive carbon centre** to form a **hydroxynitrile**.

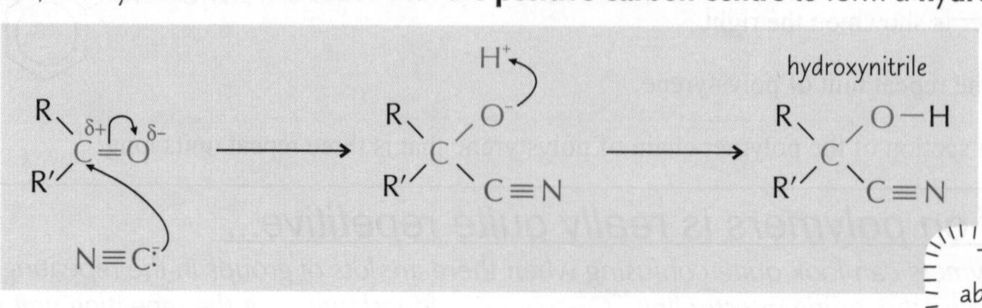

There's loads more about the reactions of carbonyls on p.180-181.

Carbon-Carbon Bond Synthesis

Nitriles Can React to Form **New** Functional Groups

1) Once you've added another carbon atom onto the carbon chain and formed a **nitrile** (or a **hydroxynitrile**), it's easy to **convert** the nitrile into a new functional group. This is because nitrile groups are very **reactive**.
2) This is really **useful** in **synthesis** — you can make a number of different compounds from the nitrile.

Nitriles Can Be **Reduced** to Form **Amines**

You can **reduce** a nitrile to a **primary amine** by a number of different methods.

1) You can use **lithium aluminium hydride** (**$LiAlH_4$** — a strong reducing agent), followed by some **dilute acid**.
E.g.

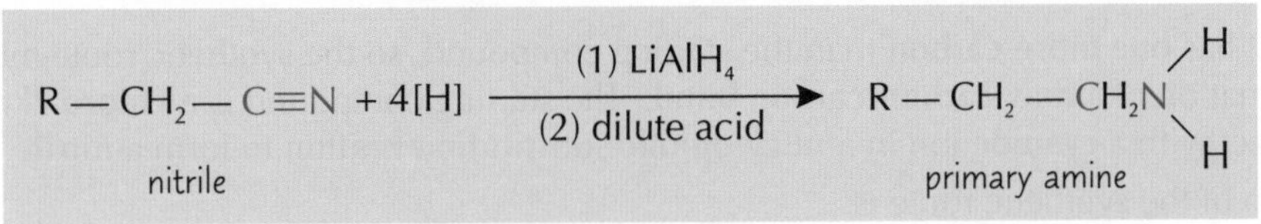

You can also reduce **hydroxynitriles** using this method.
E.g.

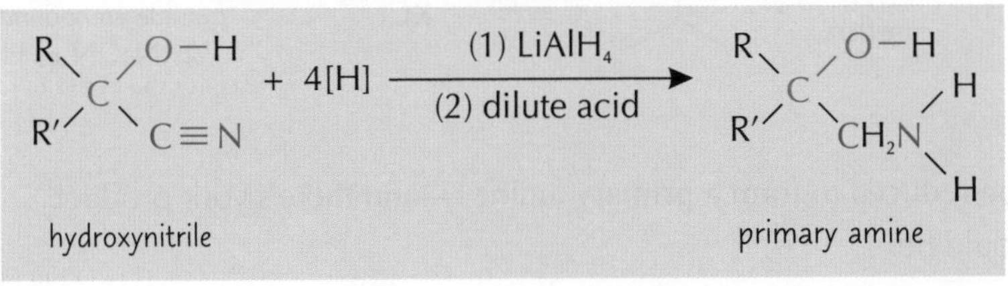

Knight Rile

Knight Rile reduction

2) You can also reduce the nitrile (or hydroxynitrile) with **sodium** metal and **ethanol**.
3) The two methods above are great in the lab, but $LiAlH_4$ and sodium are too **expensive** for industrial use. In industry, nitriles are reduced using **hydrogen gas** with a **metal catalyst** such as platinum or nickel at a high temperature and pressure — this is called **catalytic hydrogenation**.
E.g.

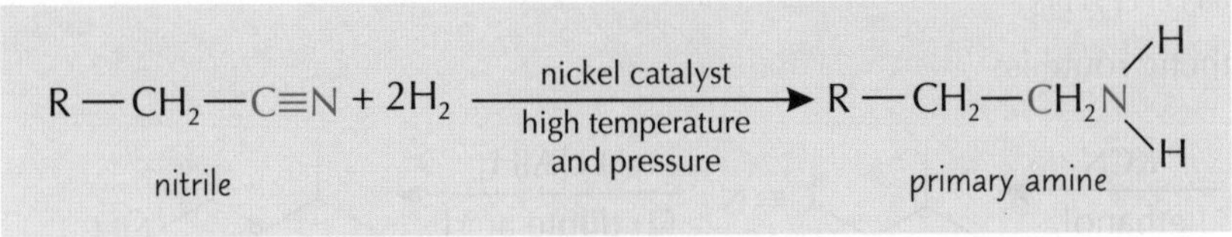

This method also works for hydroxynitriles — the product is the same as above.

Nitriles Can Be **Hydrolysed** to Form **Carboxylic Acids**

If you reflux a nitrile in dilute hydrochloric acid, then the nitrile group will be **hydrolysed** to form a **carboxylic acid**. The **carbon** of the **nitrile** starting material becomes the carbon of the carboxyl group in the product.

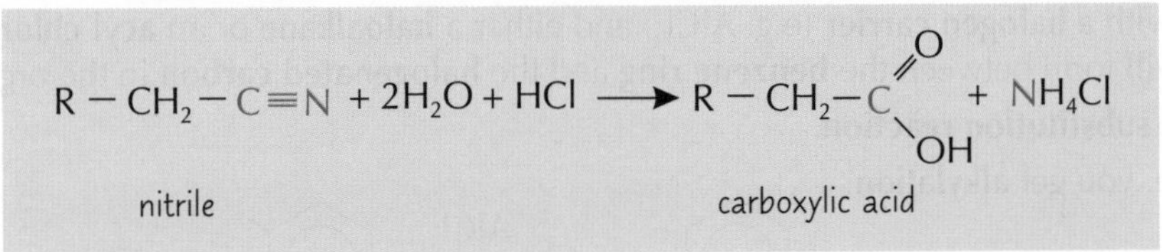

Hydrolysis means using water to break up a compound. Here, the -C≡N bond reacts with water to break up and form $-COO^-$ and NH_4^+.

You can do the same with a hydroxynitrile:

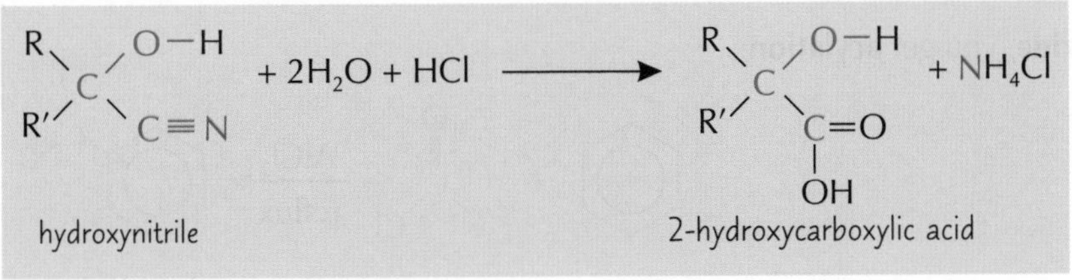

Carbon-Carbon Bond Synthesis

Think About **Nitrile Reactions** When You're Planning **Synthetic Routes**

If the product of a synthesis reaction contains one more carbon in the chain than the starting compound had, then it's likely that the synthetic route will include formation of a **nitrile** or **hydroxynitrile**.

Example: Plan a two-step synthetic route to synthesise 3-methylbutamine from 1-chloro-2-methylpropane. You should include all reagents and conditions as well as showing any intermediate products.

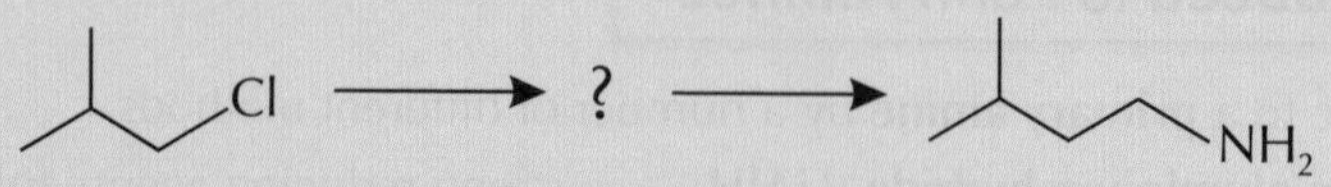

The **product** has **one more carbon** than the starting compound, so the synthetic route must include formation of a **new carbon-carbon bond**. The starting compound is a **chloroalkane** so it can react with a **cyanide** ion in a **nucleophilic substitution reation** to form a **nitrile**.

The first step of the synthetic route is:

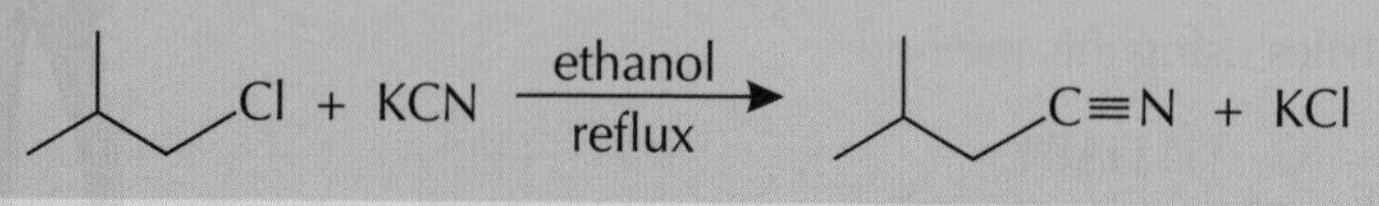

You could also use other cyanide compounds, such as NaCN or HCN.

The nitrile can then be **reduced** to form a **primary amine** — and there's your product.

So the second step could be:

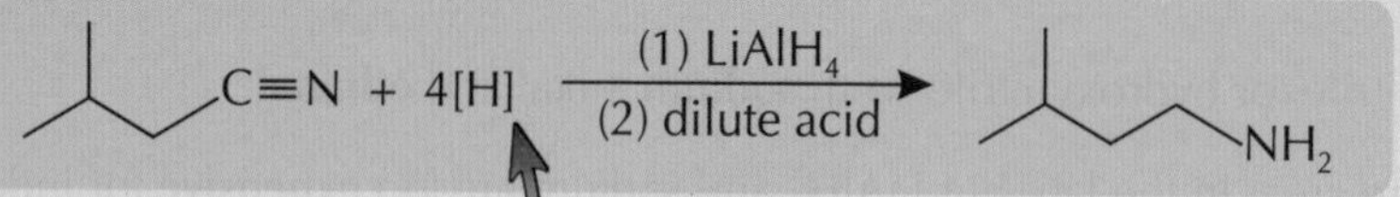

Remember to balance the reaction equation using [H].

There are other ways to reduce a nitrile on page 195.

Overall the synthetic route is:

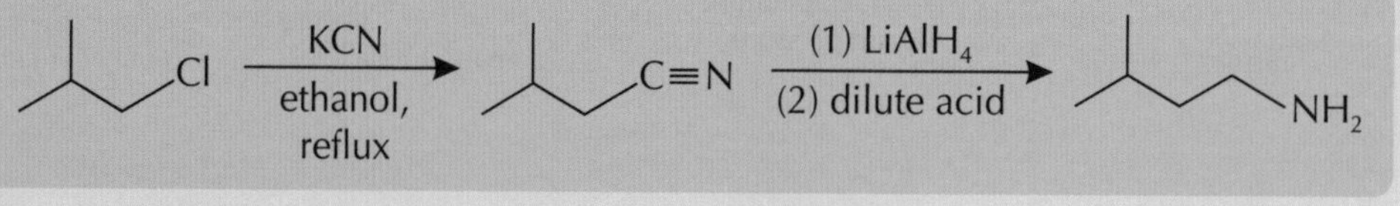

Friedel-Crafts Reactions Form Carbon-Carbon Bonds with **Benzene Rings**

1) If you reflux benzene with a **halogen carrier** (e.g. $AlCl_3$) and either a **haloalkane** or an **acyl chloride** then a new carbon-carbon bond will form between the **benzene ring** and the **halogenated carbon** in the organic reactant.
2) This is an **electrophilic substitution reaction.**
3) If you use a **haloalkane**, you get **alkylation**:

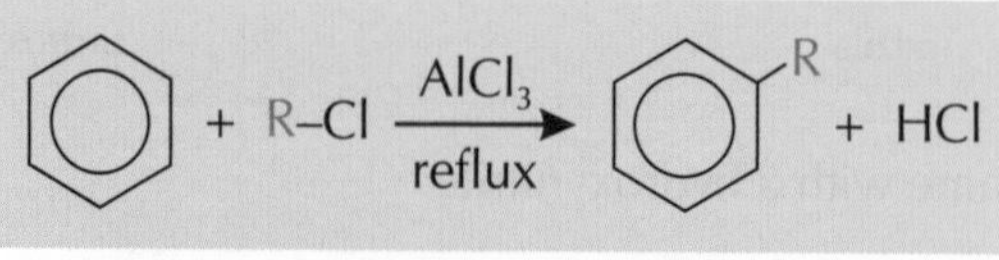

See page 177 for more on Friedel-Crafts reactions.

4) If you use an **acyl chloride**, you get **acylation**:

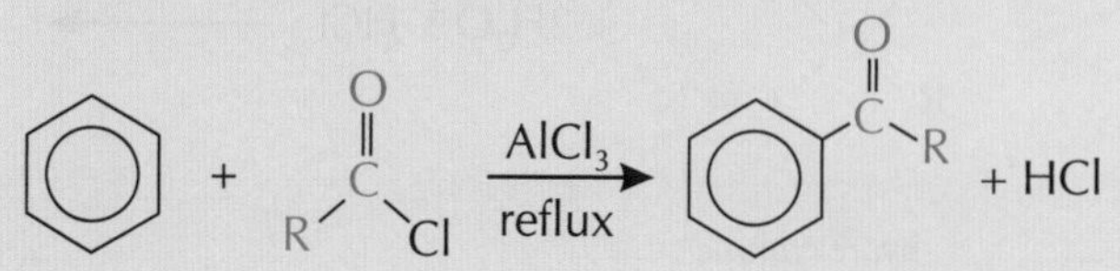

Carbon-Carbon Bond Synthesis

Friedel-Crafts Reactions May be Useful in *Synthetic Routes*

You may have to design a synthetic route that includes using a **Friedel-Crafts** reaction.

Example: Consider the following reaction scheme:

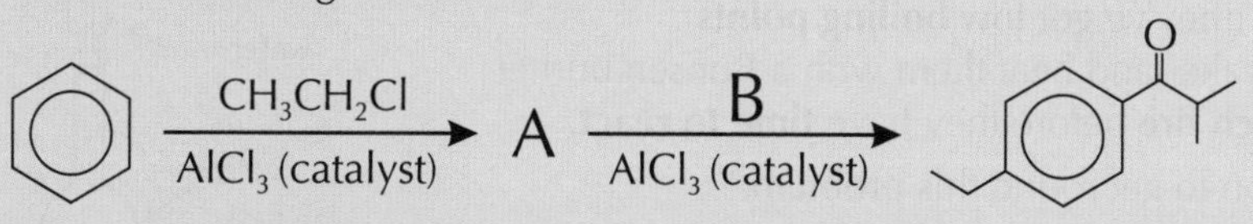

a) What is A, the organic product of the first step?

In the first step, benzene is reacted with **chloroethane** and a halogen carrier. It's a **Friedel-Crafts alkylation** reaction, so the product is **ethylbenzene:**

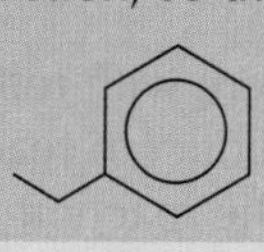

b) What is the reagent, B, in the second step?

Ethylbenzene (the product from the first step) is **acylated** in the second step, so the reaction will be a **Friedel-Crafts acylation.**

The reagent is **2-methylpropanoylchloride:**

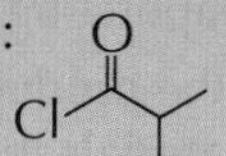

Practice Questions

Q1 What type of reaction is the reaction between potassium cyanide and a haloalkane?

Q2 What is the organic product of the reaction between hydrogen cyanide and a carbonyl compound?

Q3 Give the reagents and conditions for two different methods of converting a nitrile to an amine.

Q4 What are the reagents and conditions needed to put an acyl group onto a benzene ring?

Exam Questions

Q1 Consider the following reaction scheme:

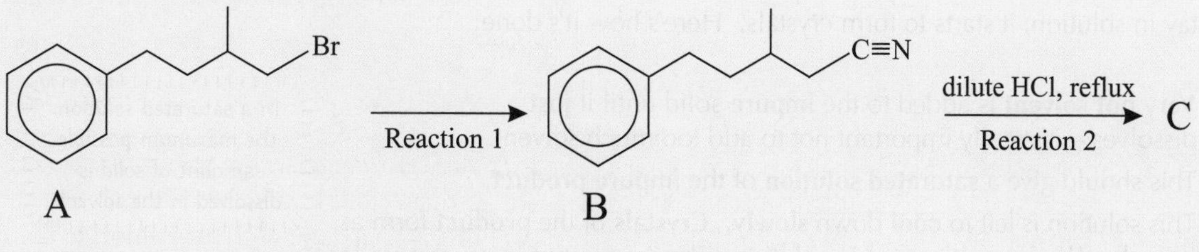

a) What are the reagents and conditions needed for Reaction 1? [2 marks]

b) Draw the skeletal formula of compound C, the organic product of Reaction 2. [1 mark]

c) Compound A can be made in one step from benzene.
What are the reagents and conditions needed for this reaction? [2 marks]

Q2 Draw the structure of the organic product that is formed when butanone is reacted with hydrogen cyanide. [1 mark]

My friends are really creative — Aisling likes drawing and Friedel crafts...

Most of these reactions have come up before, but now we're using them for a specific purpose. Making new carbon-carbon bonds is really useful — new drug molecules are often based on compounds found in nature, which chemists then tweak so they work better. Often they'll need to extend a carbon chain, so they'll use reactions like these.

Organic Synthesis — Practical Techniques

You can't call yourself a chemist unless you know these practical techniques. Not unless your name's Boots.

Reactions Often Need to be Heated to Work

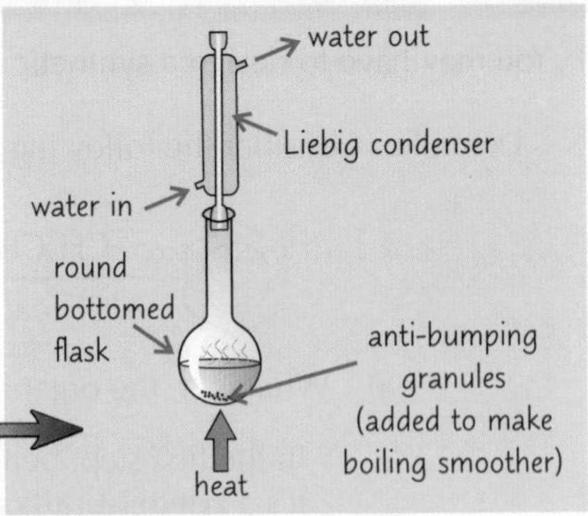

1) **Organic reactions** are **slow** and the substances are usually **flammable** and **volatile** (they've got **low boiling points**). If you stick them in a beaker and heat them with a Bunsen burner they'll **evaporate** or **catch fire** before they have **time to react**.
2) You can **reflux** a reaction to get round this problem.
3) The mixture's **heated in a flask** fitted with a **vertical Liebig condenser** — so when the mixture boils, the vapours are condensed and **recycled** back into the flask. This stops reagents being **lost** from the flask, and gives them **time to react**.

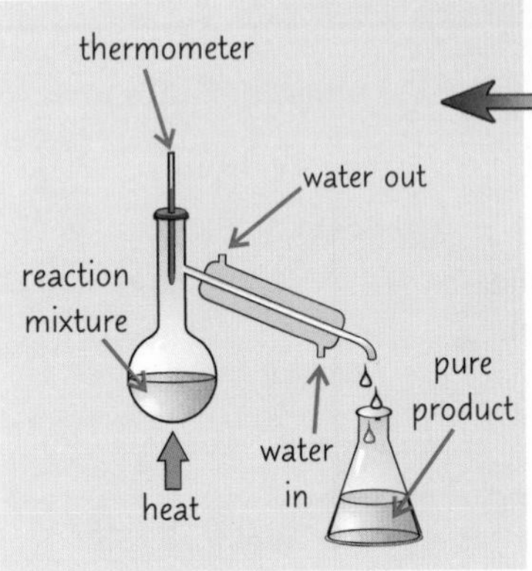

4) One problem with **refluxing** a reaction is that it can cause the desired product to **react further**. If this is the case you can carry out the reaction in a **distillation apparatus** instead.
5) The mixture is **gently heated** and substances **evaporate** out of the mixture in order of **increasing boiling point**.
6) If you know the boiling point of your **pure product**, you can use the thermometer to tell you when it's evaporating, and therefore when it's condensing.
7) If the **product** of a reaction has a **lower boiling point** than the **starting materials** then the reaction mixture can be **heated** so that the product **evaporates** from the reaction mixture as it forms. The **starting materials** will stay in the reaction mixture as long as the temperature is **controlled**.

There's more about distillation and reflux, as well as other organic techniques, back in Module 4 — see pages 112 and 113.

Organic Solids can be Purified by Recrystallisation

If the product of an organic reaction is a solid, then the simplest way of purifying it is a process called **recrystallisation**. First you dissolve your solid in a solvent to make a **saturated** solution. Then you let it cool. As the solution cools, the solubility of the product falls. When it reaches the point where it can't stay in solution, it starts to form crystals. Here's how it's done:

1) **Very hot solvent** is added to the **impure** solid until it **just** dissolves – it's really important not to add too much solvent.
2) This should give a **saturated solution** of the **impure product**.
3) This solution is left to **cool** down **slowly**. **Crystals** of the **product** form as it cools. The **impurities** stay in solution. They're present in much smaller amounts than the product, so they'd take much longer to crystallise out.
4) The crystals are removed by **filtration** under **reduced pressure** (see next page) and **washed** with ice-cold solvent. Then they are dried — leaving you with crystals of your product that are **much purer** than the original solid.

In a saturated solution, the maximum possible amount of solid is dissolved in the solvent.

The Choice of Solvent for Recrystallisation is Very Important

1) When you **recrystallise** a product, you must use an **appropriate solvent** for that particular substance. It will only work if the solid is **very soluble** in the **hot** solvent, but **nearly insoluble** when the solvent is **cold**.
2) If your product **isn't soluble enough** in the hot solvent you **won't** be able to dissolve it at all.
3) If your product **is too soluble** in the cold solvent, most of it will **stay in the solution** even after cooling. When you filter it, you'll **lose** most of your product, giving you a very low **yield**.

Organic Synthesis — Practical Techniques

You Can *Filter* an Organic Solid Under *Reduced Pressure*

1) If your **product** is a **solid**, you can separate it from any **liquid** impuritites by filtering it under **reduced pressure**.
2) The reaction mixture is poured into a **Büchner funnel** with a piece of **filter paper** in it. The Büchner funnel is on top of a sealed sidearm flask which is connected to a **vacuum line**, causing it to be under **reduced pressure**.
3) The reduced pressure causes **suction** through the funnel which causes the liquid to pass **quickly** into the flask, leaving behind **dry crystals** of your product.

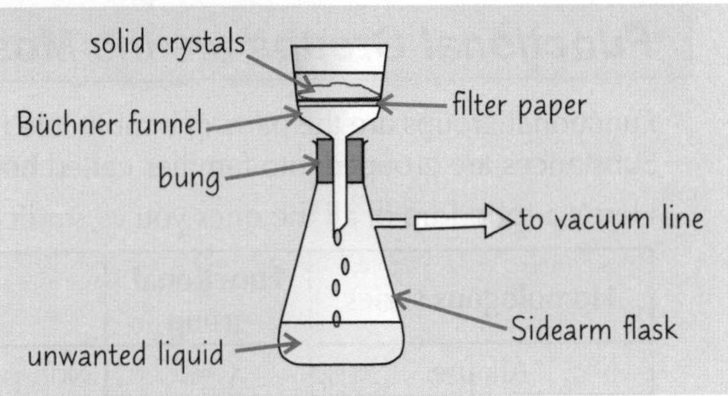

Melting and *Boiling* Points are Good Indicators of *Purity*

Most **pure substances** have a **specific melting** and **boiling point**. If they're **impure**, the **melting point's lowered** and the **boiling point is raised**. If they're **very impure**, melting and boiling will occur across a wide range of temperatures.

To accurately measure the melting point:
Put a small amount of the solid in a **capillary tube** and place it in a beaker of oil with a very sensitive thermometer. **Slowly heat**, with constant stirring, until the solid **just melts** and read the temperature on the thermometer.

Once you've measured the melting point of your sample, you can **compare** it to the **known** melting point of the substance to determine its purity. If the melting points are **similar** then your sample is quite pure, but if your value is much **lower** than the standard value, your sample contains impurities.

Practice Questions

Q1 Why is refluxing needed in many organic reactions?

Q2 Give two factors you should consider when choosing a solvent for recrystallisation.

Q3 How could you separate a solid product from liquid impurities?

Q4 Why is the melting point of a substance helpful in deciding its purity?

Exam Questions

Q1 Two samples of impure stearic acid melt at 69 °C and 64 °C respectively.
Stearic acid dissolves in hot propanone but not in water.

a) Explain which sample is purer. [1 mark]

b) Write a method for how the impure sample could be purified. [3 marks]

c) How could the sample from b) be tested for purity? [1 mark]

Q2 A student is carrying out an experiment using the apparatus shown on the right.
What type of experiment is she doing?

A reflux **B** filtration under reduced pressure

C distillation **D** recrystallisation [1 mark]

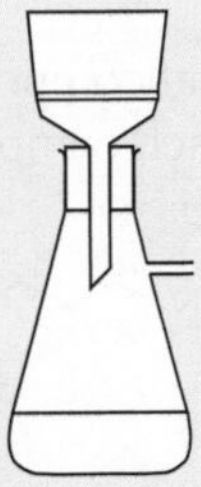

I hope that everything's now crystal clear...

You'll probably have a chance to use these techniques in practicals. The key to a good recrystallisation is patience. You have to add as little solvent as possible, so the solution is completely saturated. Then slowly cool the solution and leave it a while to make sure as much of your product as possible has crystallised. The longer you wait, the better your yield.

Functional Groups

It's been a bit of a hard slog of equations and reaction conditions and dubious puns to get this far. But with a bit of luck it should all be starting to come together now. If not, don't panic — there's always revision bunny.

***Functional Groups** are the **Most Important Parts** of a Molecule*

Functional groups are the parts of a molecule that are responsible for the way the molecule reacts. Substances are grouped into families called **homologous series** based on what functional groups they contain. Here's a round-up of all the ones you've studied:

Homologous series	Functional group	Properties	Typical reactions
Alkane	C–C	Non-polar, unreactive.	Radical substitution
Alkene	C=C	Non-polar, electron-rich double bond.	Electrophilic addition
Aromatic compounds	C_6H_5-	Stable delocalised ring of electrons.	Electrophilic substitution
Alcohol	C–OH	Polar C–OH bond.	Nucleophilic substitution Dehydration/elimination
		Lone pair on oxygen can act as a nucleophile.	Esterification Nucleophilic substitution
Haloalkane	C–X	Polar C–X bond.	Nucleophilic substitution Elimination
Amine	C–NR_2	Lone pair on nitrogen is basic and can act as a nucleophile.	Neutralisation Nucleophilic substitution
Nitrile	C—C≡N	Electron deficient carbon centre.	Reduction Hydrolysis
Aldehyde/Ketone	C=O	Polar C=O bond.	Nucleophilic addition Reduction Aldehydes will oxidise.
Carboxylic acid	-COOH	Electron deficient carbon centre.	Neutralisation Esterification
Ester	RCOOR′	Electron deficient carbon centre.	Hydrolysis
Acyl chloride	-COCl	Electron deficient carbon centre.	Nucleophilic addition-elimination Condensation (lose HCl) Friedel-Crafts acylation
Acid anhydride	RCOOCOR′	Electron deficient carbon centre.	Esterification

The functional groups in a molecule give you clues about its **properties** and **reactions**. For example, a **–COOH group** will (usually) make the molecule **acidic** and mean it will **form esters** with alcohols. Molecules containing **ester groups** will have **distinctive smells**.

*You May Have to **Identify** Functional Groups*

You need to be able to **recognise** functional groups.

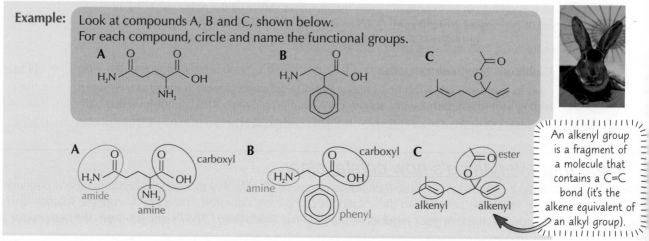

Example: Look at compounds A, B and C, shown below.
For each compound, circle and name the functional groups.

A
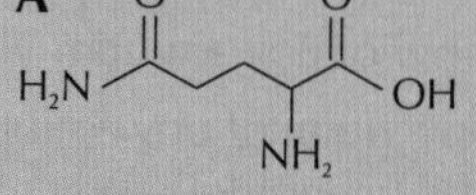

B
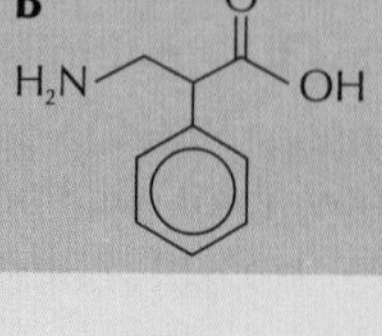

C
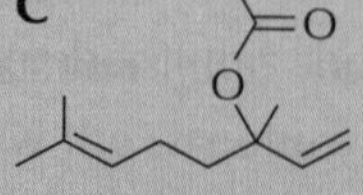

A
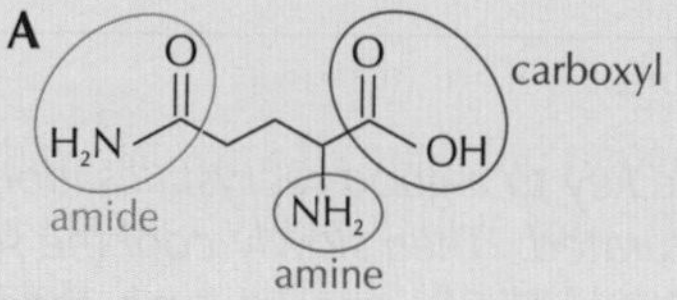

B
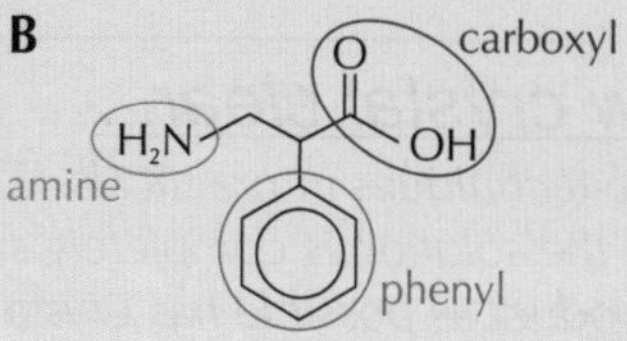

C
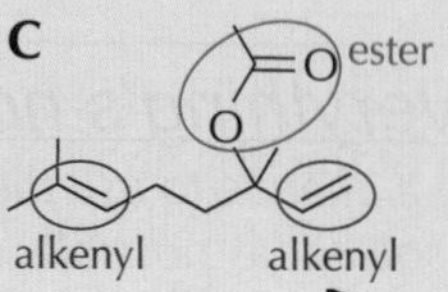

An alkenyl group is a fragment of a molecule that contains a C=C bond (it's the alkene equivalent of an alkyl group).

Functional Groups

Organic Chemistry **Reactions** can be Classified into **Seven Types**

In organic chemistry you can **classify** all the different reactions based on what happens to the molecules involved. All of the reactions you've met will fit into one of these seven types.

Reaction Type	Description	Functional groups that undergo this type of reaction
Addition	Two molecules join together to form a single product. Involves breaking a double bond.	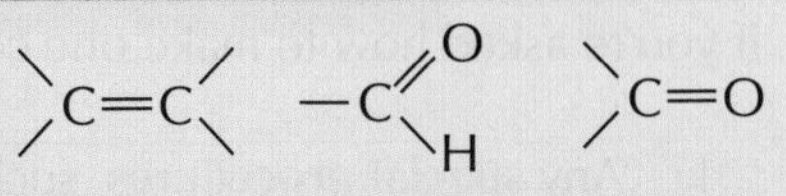
Elimination / Dehydration	Involves removing a functional group which is released as part of a small molecule. Often a double bond is formed.	—X (H–X eliminated) —OH (H_2O eliminated) X = halogen
Substitution	A functional group on a molecule is swapped for a new one.	—X —OH 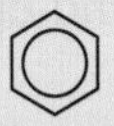 (H replaced)
Condensation	Two molecules get joined together with the loss of a small molecule, e.g. water or HCl.	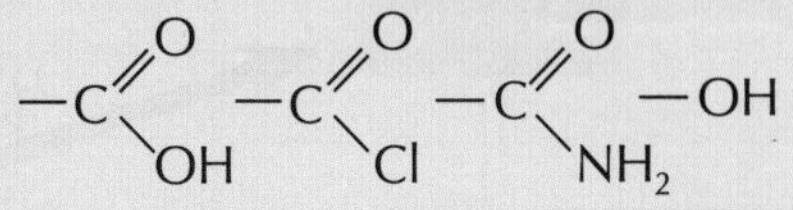
Hydrolysis	Water is used to split apart a molecule, creating two smaller ones. Opposite of condensation.	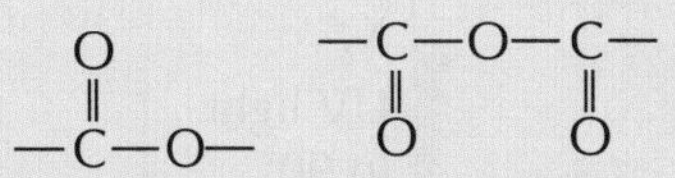 polyamides and polyesters
Oxidation	Oxidation is loss of electrons. In organic chemistry, it usually means gaining an oxygen atom or losing a hydrogen atom.	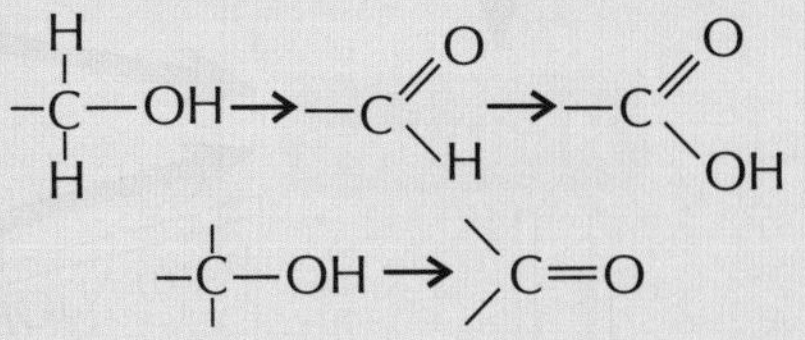
Reduction	Reduction is gain of electrons. In organic chemistry, it usually means gaining a hydrogen atom or losing an oxygen atom.	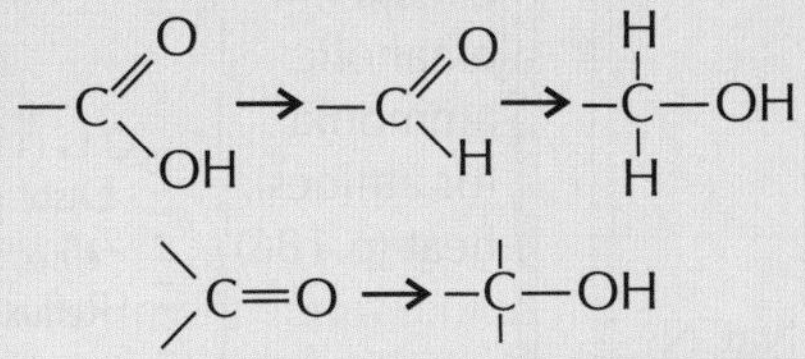

Practice Questions

Q1 Name these functional groups:
a) –COCl, b) –COOCO–, c) –COO–.

Q2 Draw the functional group of each of these families of compounds:
a) amines, b) aromatic compounds, c) nitriles.

Exam Question

Q1 a) Name the reactive functional groups in molecules A–C. [3 marks]

A $CH_3CH_2CH_2OH$ **B** CH_3—C(OH)=CH—CH_3 **C** 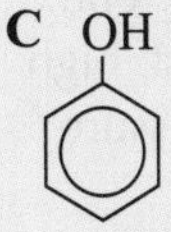

b) Which molecule(s) are aromatic? [1 mark]

c) Which molecule(s) can be oxidised to an aldehyde? [1 mark]

d) Which molecule(s) take part in addition reactions? [1 mark]

The Alcohols have lots of properties — a flat in London, a house in France...

There's lots of information on these pages, but you've seen it all before. If some of it's been eliminated from your brain, or substituted by more interesting things (like what's for tea) you can find more detail in this Module and in Module 4. Have another look at those functional groups — being able to identify them quickly will make life a whole lot easier.

Synthetic Routes

In your exam you may be asked to suggest a pathway for the synthesis of a particular molecule. These pages contain a summary of some of the reactions you should know.

Chemists use **Synthesis Routes** to Get from One Compound to Another

Chemists have got to be able to make one compound from another. It's vital for things like **designing medicines**. It's also good for making imitations of **useful natural substances** when the real things are hard to extract.

If you're asked how to make one compound from another in the exam, make sure you include:

1) Any **special procedures**, such as refluxing.
2) The **conditions** needed, e.g. high temperature or pressure, or the presence of a catalyst.
3) Any **safety** precautions, e.g. do it in a fume cupboard.

Here's a round-up of the reactions you've covered in this Module and also in Module 4:

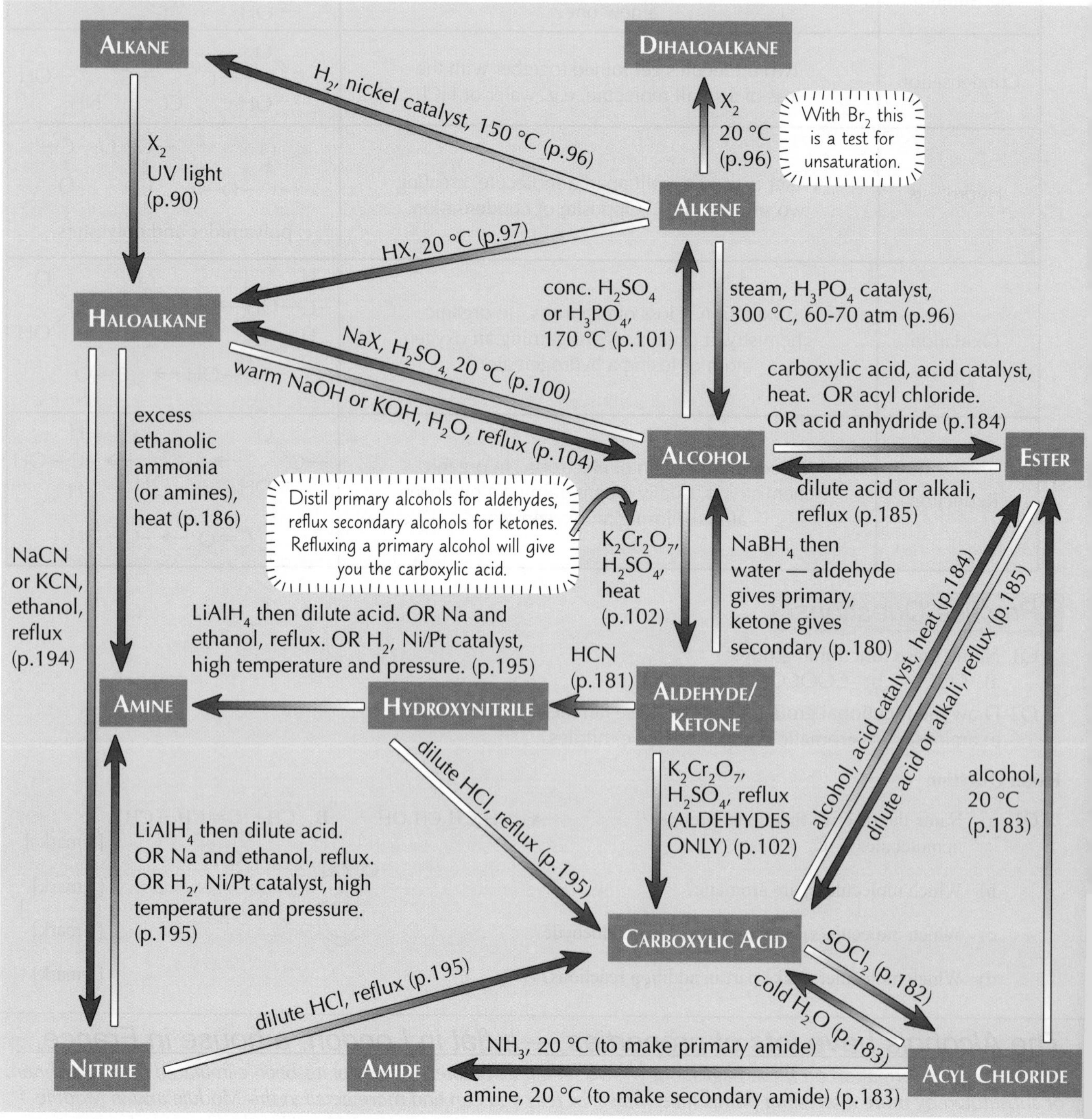

Synthetic Routes

Synthesis Route for Making **Aromatic Compounds**

There aren't so many of these reactions to learn — so make sure you know all the itty-bitty details.
If you can't remember any of the reactions, look back to the relevant pages and take a quick peek over them.

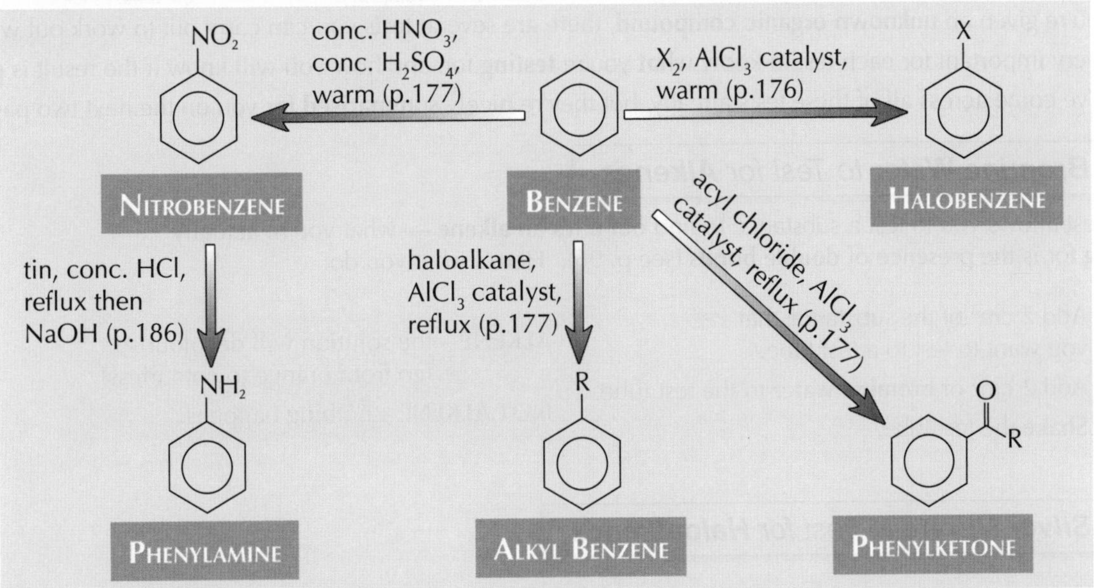

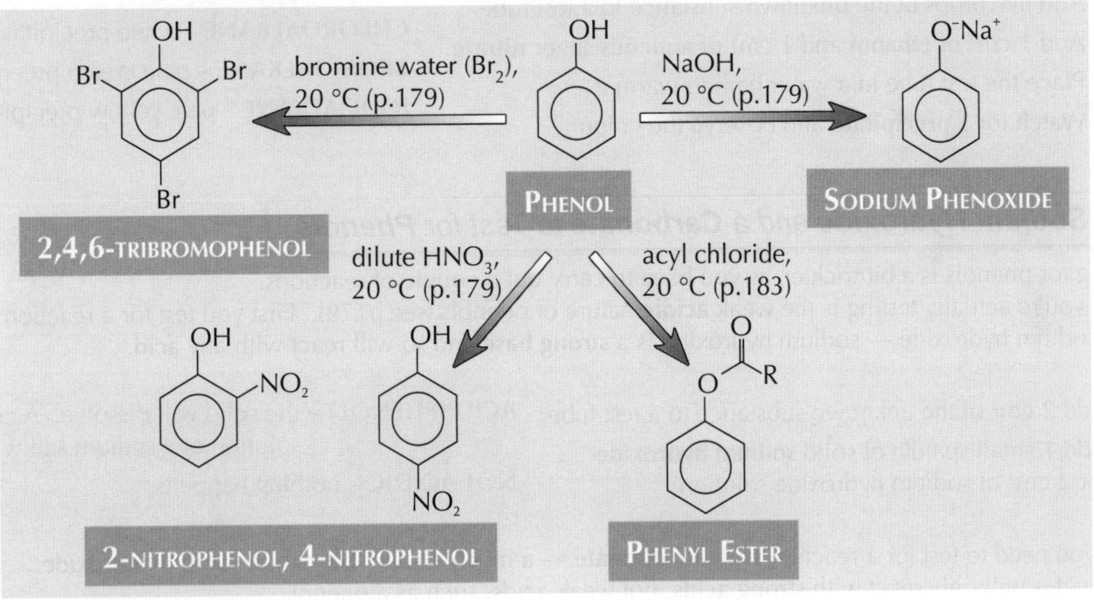

Practice Questions

Q1 How do you make an alkene from an aldehyde?

Q2 How do you make phenylamine from benzene?

Exam Questions

Q1 Ethyl methanoate is one of the compounds responsible for the smell of raspberries.
Outline, with reaction conditions, how it could be synthesised in the laboratory from methanol. [2 marks]

Q2 How would you synthesise propanol starting with propane?
State the reaction conditions and reagents needed for each step. [2 marks]

Big red buses are great at Organic Synthesis — they're Route Masters...

There's loads of information here. Tons and tons of it. But you've covered pretty much all of it before, so it shouldn't be too hard to make sure it's firmly embedded in your head. If it's not, you know what to do — go back over it again. Then cover the diagrams up and try to draw them out from memory. Keep going until you can do it perfectly.

Tests for Organic Functional Groups

Now it's time for a spot of qualitative analysis. Don't be put off by those posh words though — all it really means is testing to see whether a particular substance is present in a sample. Couldn't be easier...

You Can Carry Out Tests to Identify Unknown Organic Compounds

1) If you're given an **unknown organic compound**, there are several tests you can carry out to work out what it is.
2) It's very important for each test to know **what** you're **testing** for, and how you will know if the result is **positive**.
3) You've come across all of these tests already, but they're nicely **summarised** for you on the next two pages.

Use Bromine Water to Test for Alkenes

This test allows you to test a substance to find out if it's an **alkene** — what you're actually testing for is the presence of **double bonds** (see p. 96). Here's what you do:

1) Add 2 cm^3 of the substance that you want to test to a test tube.
2) Add 2 cm^3 of **bromine water** to the test tube.
3) **Shake** the test tube.

ALKENE – the solution will decolourise (go from orange to colourless).
NOT ALKENE – nothing happens.

Use Silver Nitrate to Test for Haloalkanes

1) Add five drops of the unknown substance to a test tube.
2) Add 1 cm^3 of **ethanol** and 1 cm^3 of **aqueous silver nitrate**.
3) Place the test tube in a water bath to warm it.
4) Watch for a **precipitate** and observe the colour.

CHLOROALKANE – white precipitate.
BROMOALKANE – pale cream precipitate.
IODOALKANE – pale yellow precipitate.

Use Sodium Hydroxide and a Carbonate to Test for Phenols

Testing for phenols is a bit trickier, as you have to carry out a couple of reactions. What you're actually testing is the **weak acidic** nature of phenols (see p179). First you test for a reaction with sodium hydroxide — sodium hydroxide is a **strong base** and so will react with any **acid**.

1) Add 2 cm^3 of the unknown substance to a test tube.
2) Add 1 small spatula of solid **sodium hydroxide** (or 2 cm^3 of sodium hydroxide solution).

ACID (PHENOL) – the solid will dissolve. A colourless solution of a sodium salt will form.
NOT ACIDIC – nothing happens.

Next you need to test for a reaction with a **carbonate** — a much weaker base than sodium hydroxide. Carbonates will only react with **strong acids**, not weak acids, such as a phenol.

1) Add 2 cm^3 of the unknown substance to a test tube.
2) Add 1 small spatula of a solid **carbonate** or 2 cm^3 of a carbonate solution (**sodium carbonate** will work nicely).

PHENOL/BASE – nothing happens.
STRONG ACID – effervescence.

Effervescence is just another way to describe fizzing and bubbling.

Use Sodium Carbonate to Test for Carboxylic Acids

Unlike phenols, **carboxylic acids** do react with carbonates to form a salt, **carbon dioxide** and water (see page 182). You can use this reaction to test whether a substance is a carboxylic acid.

1) Add 2 cm^3 of the substance that you want to test to a test tube.
2) Add 1 small spatula of a solid **carbonate** (or 2 cm^3 of a carbonate solution) e.g. **sodium carbonate**.
3) If the solution begins to **fizz**, bubble the gas that it produces through some **limewater** in a second test tube.

CARBOXYLIC ACID – the solution will fizz. The carbon dioxide gas that is produced will turn limewater cloudy.
NOT CARBOXYLIC ACID – nothing happens.

Tests for Organic Functional Groups

Use 2,4-DNP to Test for a Carbonyl Group

With this test, you need to use the reagent **2,4-dinitrophenylhydrazine** (2,4-DNP).
It may be a bit of a mouthful to say, but it's great for testing for **aldehydes** and **ketones** (see page 181).

1) Dissolve 0.2 g of **2,4-DNP** in 1 cm^3 of sulfuric acid, 2 cm^3 of water and 5 cm^3 of methanol.
2) In a different test tube, add 5 drops of the unknown substance to 2 cm^3 of your solution from 1).
3) **Shake** the test tube and watch for a **precipitate**.

ALDEHYDE/ KETONE – bright orange precipitate.

NOT ALDEHYDE/ KETONE – nothing happens.

The solution you've made at the end of step 1) is known as Brady's reagent.

Use Tollens' Reagent to Test for Aldehydes

This is another test for **aldehydes** (see page 181) but this time it allows you to tell aldehydes and ketones apart. Unfortunately you have to prepare the reagent yourself. Mean.

1) Put 2 cm^3 of 0.10 mol dm^{-3} **silver nitrate solution** in a test tube.
2) Add 5 drops of 0.80 mol dm^{-3} sodium hydroxide solution. A **light brown precipitate** should form.
3) Add drops of dilute ammonia solution until the brown precipitate **dissolves** completely.
4) Place the test tube in a hot water bath and add 10 drops of **aldehyde** or **ketone**. Wait for a few minutes.

ALDEHYDE – a silver mirror (a thin coating of silver) forms on the walls of the test tube.

KETONE/NOT ALDEHYDE – nothing happens.

The solution you've made at the end of step 3) is Tollens' reagent.

Use Acidified Dichromate to Test for Primary and Secondary Alcohols

1) Add 10 drops of the alcohol to 2 cm^3 of **acidified potassium dichromate** solution in a test tube.
2) Warm the mixture gently in a hot water bath.
3) Then watch for a **colour change**:

The colour change is the orange dichromate(VI) ion ($Cr_2O_7^{2-}$) being reduced to the green chromium(III) ion (Cr^{3+}).

PRIMARY – the orange solution slowly turns green as an aldehyde forms. (If you carry on heating, the aldehyde will be oxidised further to give a carboxylic acid.)

SECONDARY – the orange solution slowly turns green as a ketone forms.

TERTIARY – nothing happens — boring, but easy to remember.

Practice Questions

Q1 Describe how you would test a sample of a compound to find out if it contained a haloalkene.

Q2 What reagent would you use to test if a solution contained either a primary or secondary alcohol?

Exam Questions

Q1 Which one of these statements about cyclohexene is correct?

A It produces a bright orange precipitate with 2,4-DNP solution.

B It decolourises bromine water.

C It turns limewater cloudy.

D It forms a silver mirror with Tollens' reagent. [1 mark]

Q2 Describe a chemical test you could use to show that a solution is a carboxylic acid.
Include any reagents, conditions and expected observations in your answer. [3 marks]

It's not the winning that counts, but the precipitation...

There are a fair few precipitates on this page — they can give a clear indication of what mystery compound you've got. But remember — when testing something, you might need to work through several tests before you can identify it.

Chromatography

You've probably tried chromatography with a spot of ink on a piece of filter paper — it's a classic experiment.

Chromatography is Good for **Separating** and **Identifying** Things

1) Chromatography is used to **separate** stuff in a mixture — once the mixture's separated out, you can often **identify** the different components, for example, different organic compounds.
2) There are quite a few different types of chromatography — you might have tried paper chromatography before — but the ones you need to know about are **thin-layer chromatography** (TLC) and **gas chromatography** (GC).

Thin-Layer Chromatography Separates Components by **Adsorption**

In **thin-layer chromatography** (TLC) a **solvent**, such as ethanol, moves over a **glass or plastic plate** which is covered in a **thin layer of solid** (e.g. silica gel or aluminium powder).

Here's the method for setting it up:

1) Draw a **pencil line** near the bottom of the plate and put a **spot** of the mixture to be separated on the line.
2) Dip the bottom of the plate (not the spot) into a **solvent**.
3) As the solvent spreads up the plate, the different substances in the mixture move with it, but **different distances** — so they separate out.
4) When the solvent's **nearly** reached the top of the plate, take the plate out and **mark** the distance that the solvent has moved (**solvent front**) in pencil.

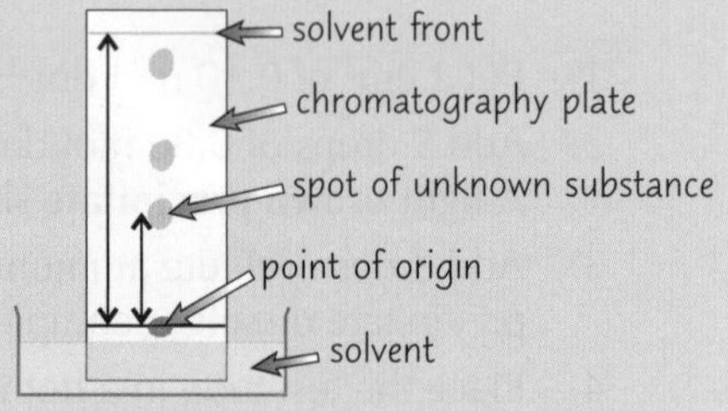

R_f **Values** Help to **Identify** Organic Molecules

You can work out what was in the mixture by calculating an R_f **value** for each spot on the TLC plate and looking them up in a **table of known values**.

$$R_f \text{ value} = \frac{\text{distance travelled by spot}}{\text{distance travelled by solvent}}$$

1) **How far** an organic molecule travels up the plate depends on **how strongly** it's **attracted** to the **layer of solid** on the surface of the plate.
2) The **attraction** between a substance and the surface of the plate is called **adsorption**.
3) A substance that is **strongly adsorbed** will move **slowly**, so it **won't travel as far** as one that's only **weakly adsorbed**. This means it will have a **different** R_f **value**.
4) Chemical properties, such as **polarity**, affect how strongly adsorbed a particular substance is to the plate.
5) The distance a particular substance moves up the plate also depends on the **solid coating** on the plate, the **solvent** used, and external variables such as **temperature**. This means small changes in the TLC set-up can cause changes in the R_f value. So once you've identified what you think an unknown compound is, it's best to check you're right by **running a pure sample** of the **known substance alongside** your **unknown compound** on a TLC plate. Identical substances should travel the same distance up the plate, i.e. have the **same** R_f **value**.

Gas Chromatography is a Bit More **High-Tech**

1) In **gas chromatography** (GC) the **sample** to be analysed is **injected** into a stream of **gas**, which carries it through a coiled **tube** coated with a **viscous liquid** (such as an oil) or a **solid**.
2) The components of the mixture constantly **dissolve in the oil** or **onto the solid**, **evaporate back** into the gas and then **redissolve** as they travel through the tube.
3) The time taken for the substances to pass through the coiled tube and reach the detector is called the **retention time**. It can be used to help **identify** the substances.

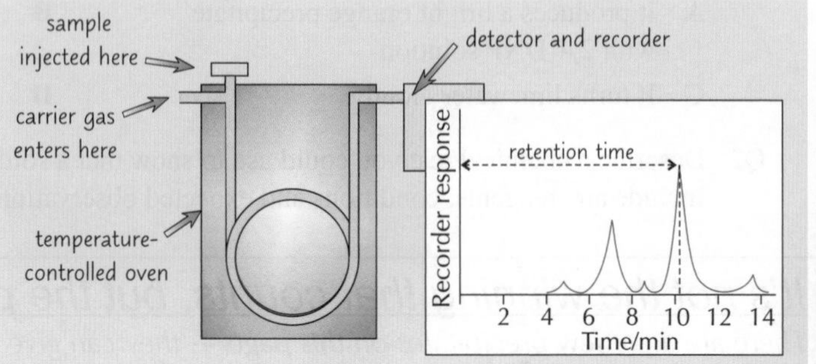

Chromatography

***GC Chromatograms** Show the **Proportions** of the Components in a Mixture*

A **gas chromatogram** shows a **series of peaks** at the times when the **detector** senses something other than the carrier gas **leaving the tube**. They can be used to **identify the substances** within a sample and their **relative proportions**.

1) Each **peak** on a chromatogram corresponds to a substance with a particular **retention time**.
2) **Retention times** are measured from **zero** to the **centre** of each peak, and can be looked up in a **reference table** to **identify** the **substances** present.
3) The **area** under each peak is proportional to the relative **amount of each substance** in the original mixture. Remember, it's **area**, not height, that's important — the **tallest** peak on the chromatogram **won't always** represent the **most abundant substance**.

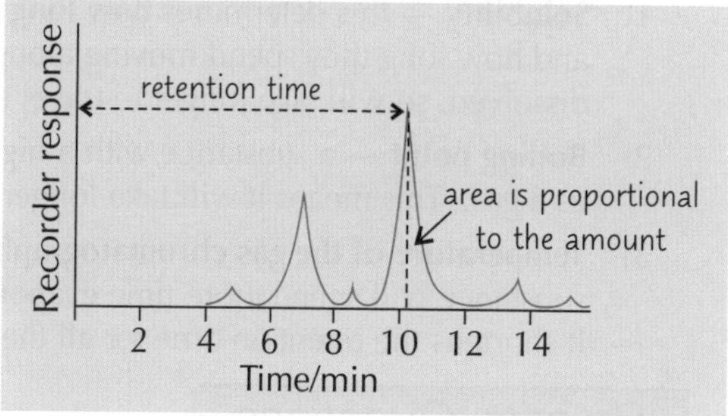

External Calibration Curves** Help Find **Concentation

The **area** under the peak of a GC chromatogram gives you the **relative amount** of a substance, but finding the exact concentration is a bit trickier. To work out the **concentration** of a particular substance in a sample you need create an **external calibration curve**. Here's how:

1) Create a series of **standard solutions** of **different concentrations** of analyte — this is just the substance you've chosen to detect for your calibration.
2) One by one, inject your standard solutions into a gas chromatography instrument and **record** the **result**.
3) Calculate the **area** under the peak of each response for each standard solution.
4) Plot these values on a graph of **area vs concentration**.
5) **Join your points** up to create an external calibration curve.

Your calibration curve can be a straight line or a curve.

It's a good idea to run a **blank** when you're making a callibration curve.
A **blank** is just a solution containing all the solvents and reagents used when making the standard solutions, but **no analyte**. By **subtracting** the response of the blank from each of the responses of your standard solutions, you can find a **corrected peak value** — one that takes into account the effect of reagents and solvents on the peak areas.

Example: On a chromatogram, the area under the peak for substance X is 360 units. Estimate the concentration of substance X in the sample by drawing an external calibration curve, using the data in the table below. The areas have been corrected using a blank.

Concentration (mol dm^{-3})	0.00	0.25	0.50	0.75
Area (units)	0	190	410	625

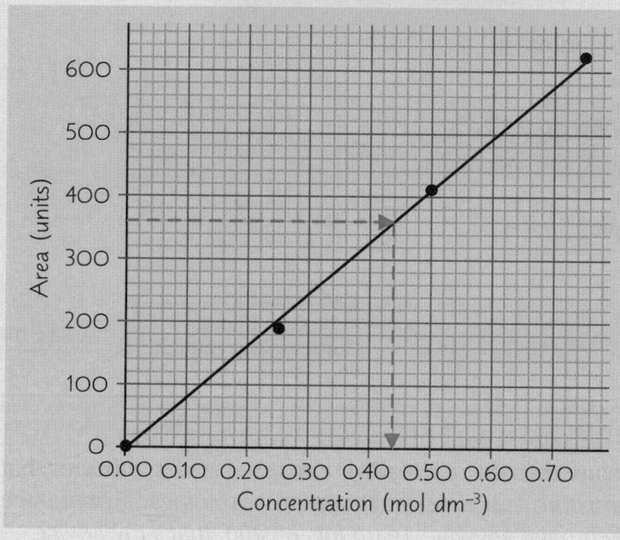

1) First, plot the points from the table on a graph. Concentration is always plotted on the *x*-axis and area on the *y*-axis.
2) Draw a line (or curve) of best fit.
3) Now work out what concentration corresponds to an area of **360 units** by drawing a line from 360 on the *y*-axis to where it meets the line of best fit, and then drawing a line from this point, down to the *x*-axis.
4) Read off the result on the *x*-axis.
5) So the concentration of substance X is **0.44 mol dm^{-3}**.

Your answer is only an estimate — you don't know exactly what the concentration is.

Chromatography

Retention Time Helps **Identify** Different Molecules

You saw on the last page that retention times can be used to identify the presence of different substances in a mixture. There are several factors that affect retention times:

1) **Solubility** — this determines **how long** each component of the mixture spends **dissolved in the oil** or **on the solid** and how long they spend **moving along** the tube in the **gas**. A highly soluble substance will spend more time dissolved, so will take longer to travel through the tube to the detector than one with a lower solubility.
2) **Boiling point** — a substance with a **high boiling point** will spend more time **condensed** as a liquid in the tube than as a gas. This means it will take longer to travel through the tube than one with a lower boiling point.
3) **Temperature of the gas chromatography instrument** — a **high temperature** means the substance will spend more time **evaporated** in the gas and so will move along the tube quickly. It shortens the retention time for **all** the substances in the tube.

Practice Questions

Q1 Describe how you would calculate the R_f value of a substance on a TLC plate.

Q2 Give three factors that affect the retention time in gas chromatography.

Exam Questions

Q1 Look at this diagram of a chromatogram produced using TLC on a mixture of substances A and B.

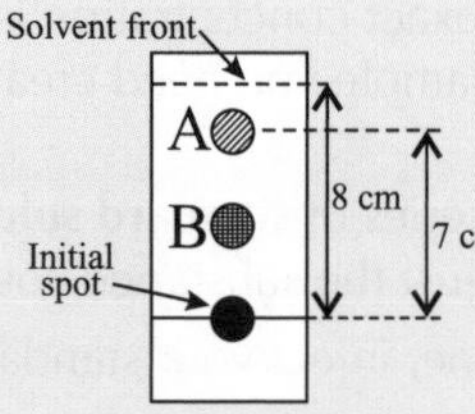

a) Calculate the R_f value of spot A. [2 marks]

b) Explain why substance A has moved further up the plate than substance B. [1 mark]

Q2 A scientist has a mixture of several organic chemicals. He wants to know if it contains any hexene. He runs a sample of pure hexene through a GC machine and finds that its retention time is 5 minutes. Then he runs a sample of his mixture through the same machine, under the same conditions,and produces the chromatogram shown on the right.

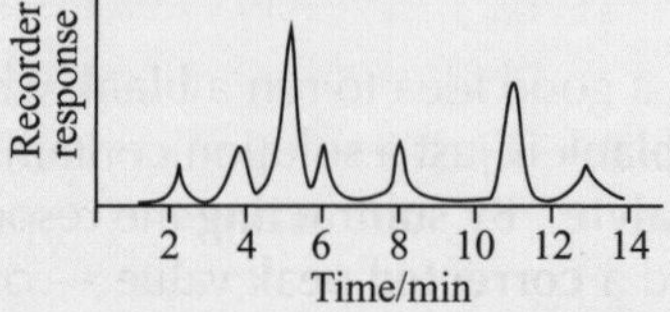

a) What feature of the chromatogram suggests that the sample contains hexene? [1 mark]

b) The mixture is also found to contain small amounts of ethene. How would you expect the retention time of ethene to compare with that of hexene? Explain your answer. [2 marks]

Q3 A mixture of 25% ethanol and 75% benzene is run through a GC apparatus.

a) Describe what happens to the mixture in the apparatus. [4 marks]

b) Given that ethanol and benzene have very similar boiling points, explain why the substances separate. [2 marks]

c) How will the resulting chromatogram show the proportions of ethanol and benzene present in the mixture? [1 mark]

Q4 The graph on the right is an external calibration curve for substance A. On a chromatogram for a sample containing substance A, the area under the peak for substance A is 16 units. Estimate the concentration of substance A in the sample?

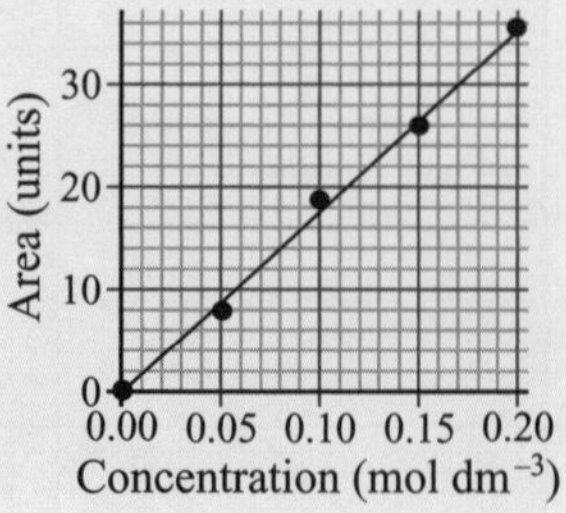

A 0.06 mol dm^{-3} **B** 0.28 mol dm^{-3}

C 0.09 mol dm^{-3} **D** 0.16 mol dm^{-3} [1 mark]

A little bit of TLC is what you need...

If you only remember one thing about chromatography, remember that it's really good at separating mixtures, but not so reliable at identifying the substances that make up the mixture. Or does that count as two things? Hmm... well it's probably not the best idea to only learn one thing from each page anyway. Learn lots of stuff, that's my advice.

NMR Spectroscopy

NMR isn't the easiest of things, so ingest this information one piece at a time — a bit like eating a bar of chocolate.

NMR Gives You Information about the Structure of Molecules

Nuclear magnetic resonance (**NMR**) **spectroscopy** is an analytical technique that you can use to work out the **structure** of an organic molecule. The way that NMR works is pretty **complicated**, but here are the **basics**:

1) A sample of a compound is placed in a **strong magnetic field** and exposed to a range of different **frequencies** of **radio waves**.
2) The **nuclei** of certain atoms within the molecule **absorb energy** from the radio waves.
3) The amount of energy that a nucleus absorbs at each frequency will depend on the **environment** that it's in — there's more about this further down the page.
4) The **pattern** of these absorptions gives you information about the **positions** of certain atoms within the molecule, and about **how many** atoms of that type the molecule contains.
5) You can piece these bits of information together to work out the **structure of the molecule**.

The two types of NMR spectroscopy you need to know about are **carbon-13 NMR** and **high resolution proton NMR**.

Carbon-13 (or ^{13}C) **NMR** gives you information about the **number of carbon atoms** that are in a molecule, and the **environments** that they are in.

High resolution proton NMR gives you information about the **number of hydrogen atoms** that are in a molecule, and the **environments** that they're in.

Nuclei in Different Environments Absorb Different Amounts of Energy

1) A nucleus is partly **shielded** from the effects of external magnetic fields by its **surrounding electrons**.
2) Any **other atoms** and **groups of atoms** that are around a nucleus will also affect its amount of electron shielding. E.g. If a carbon atom bonds to a more electronegative atom (like oxygen) the amount of electron shielding around its nucleus will decrease.
3) This means that the nuclei in a molecule feel different magnetic fields depending on their **environments**. Nuclei in different environments will absorb **different amounts** of energy at **different frequencies**.
4) It's these **differences in absorption** of energy between environments that you're looking for in **NMR spectroscopy**.
5) An atom's **environment** depends on **all** the groups that it's connected to, going **right along the molecule** — not just the atoms it's actually bonded to. To be in the **same environment**, two atoms must be joined to **exactly the same things**.

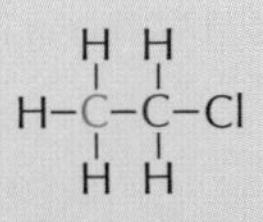

Chloroethane has **2** carbon environments — its carbons are bonded to different atoms.

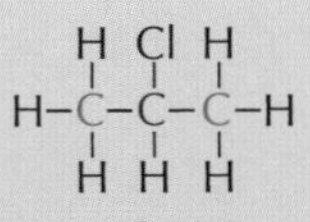

2-chloropropane has **2** carbon environments:
- **1 C** in a CHCl group, bonded to $(CH_3)_2$
- **2 Cs** in CH_3 groups, bonded to $CHCl(CH_3)$

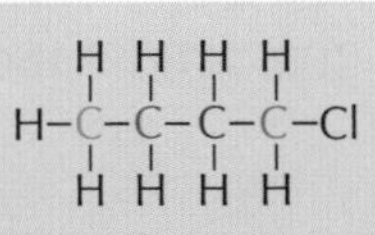

1-chlorobutane has **4** carbon environments. (The two carbons in CH_2 groups are **different distances** from the **electronegative** Cl atom — so their **environments** are **different**.)

Tetramethylsilane is Used as a Standard

The diagram below shows a typical **carbon-13 NMR spectrum**. The **peaks** show the **frequencies** at which **energy was absorbed** by the carbon nuclei. **Each peak** represents one **carbon environment** — so this molecule has two.

1) The **differences in absorption** are measured relative to a **standard substance** — **tetramethylsilane** (**TMS**).
2) TMS produces a **single absorption peak** in both types of NMR because all its carbon and hydrogen nuclei are in the **same environment**.
3) It's chosen as a standard because the **absorption peak** is at a **lower frequency** than just about everything else.
4) This peak is given a value of **0** and all the peaks in other substances are measured as **chemical shifts** relative to this.

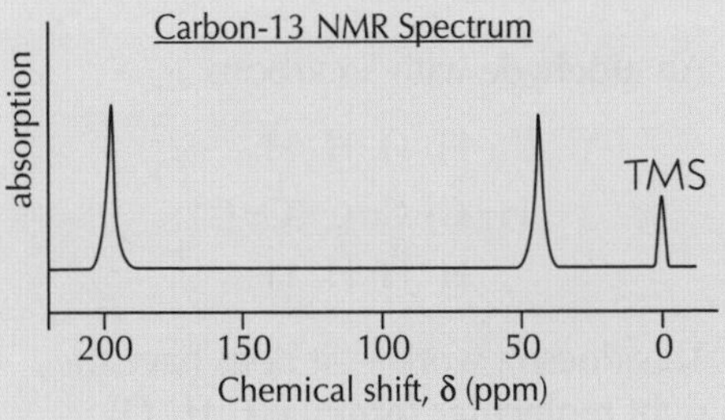

Chemical shift is the **difference in the radio frequency** absorbed by the nuclei (hydrogen or carbon) in the molecule being analysed and that absorbed by the same nuclei in **TMS**. They're given the symbol δ and are measured in **parts per million**, or **ppm**. A small amount of TMS is often added to samples to give a **reference peak** on the spectrum.

The chemical formula for TMS is $Si(CH_3)_4$.

NMR Spectroscopy

^{13}C NMR Spectra Tell You About Carbon Environments

It's very likely that you'll be given an **NMR spectrum** to **interpret** in your exam. It might be a **carbon-13 NMR spectrum** or a **proton NMR spectrum** (you might even see both if you're really lucky), so you need to have both kinds sussed. First, here's a **step-by-step guide** to interpreting carbon-13 spectra.

1) Count the Number of Carbon Environments

First, count the **number of peaks** in the spectrum — this is the **number of carbon environments** in the molecule. If there's a peak at **δ = 0**, **don't count it** — it's the reference peak from **TMS**.

The spectrum on the right has **three peaks** — so the molecule must have **three different carbon environments**. This **doesn't** necessarily mean it only has **three carbons**, as it could have **more than one** in the **same environment**. In fact the molecular formula of this molecule is **$C_5H_{10}O$**, so it must have **several carbons** in the **same environment**.

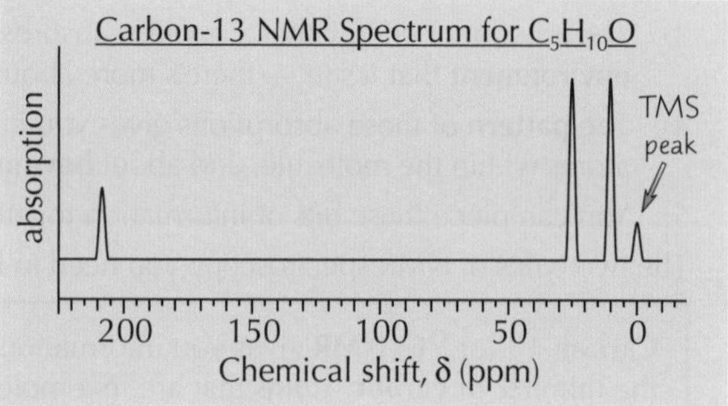

2) Look Up the Chemical Shifts in a Shift Diagram

In your exam you'll get a **data sheet** that will include a **diagram** like the one below. The diagram shows the **chemical shifts** experienced by **carbon nuclei** in **different environments**. The boxes show the range of shift values a carbon in that environment could have, e.g. **C=O** could have a shift value anywhere between 160 – 220 ppm.

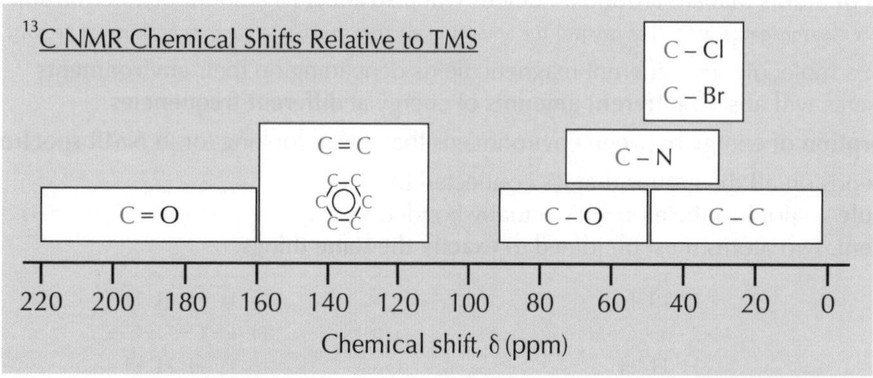

Matching peaks to the groups that cause them isn't always straightforward, because the chemical shifts can overlap. For example, a peak at δ ≈ 40 might be caused by C–C, C–Cl, C–N or C–Br.

You need to **match up** the **peaks** in the spectrum with the **chemical shifts** in the diagram to work out which **carbon environments** they could represent. For example, the peak at **δ ≈ 10** in the spectrum above represents a **C–C** bond. The peak at **δ ≈ 25** is also due to a **C–C** bond. The carbons causing this peak have a different chemical shift to those causing the first peak — so they must be in a slightly different environment. The peak at **δ ≈ 210**, is due to a **C=O** group, but you don't know whether it could be an aldehyde or a ketone (you know it can't be a carboxylic acid as the molecular formula only contains one **O**).

3) Try Out Possible Structures

An **aldehyde** with 5 carbons:

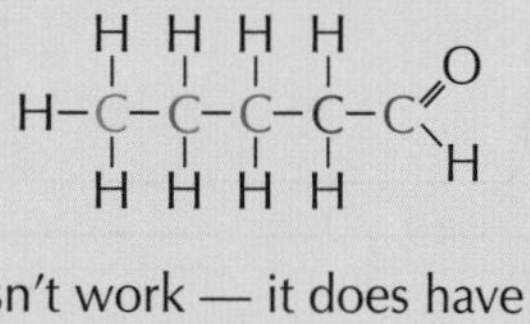

This doesn't work — it does have the right **molecular formula** (**$C_5H_{10}O$**), but it also has **five carbon environments**.

A **ketone** with five carbons:

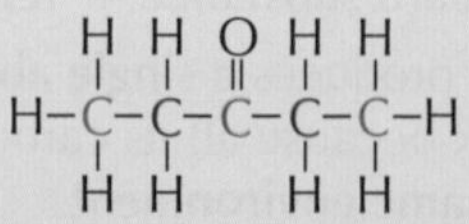

This works. **Pentan-3-one** has **three** carbon environments — two CH_3 carbons, each bonded to $CH_2COCH_2CH_3$, two CH_2 carbons, each bonded to CH_3 and $COCH_2CH_3$, and one CO carbon bonded to $(CH_2CH_3)_2$. It has the right **molecular formula** (**$C_5H_{10}O$**) too.

It can't be pentan-2-one — that has 5 carbon environments.

So, the molecule analysed was **pentan-3-one**.

NMR Spectroscopy

Interpreting NMR Spectra Gets Easier with *Practice*

Example: The diagram shows the carbon-13 NMR spectrum of an alcohol with the molecular formula $C_4H_{10}O$. Analyse and interpret the spectrum to identify the structure of the alcohol.

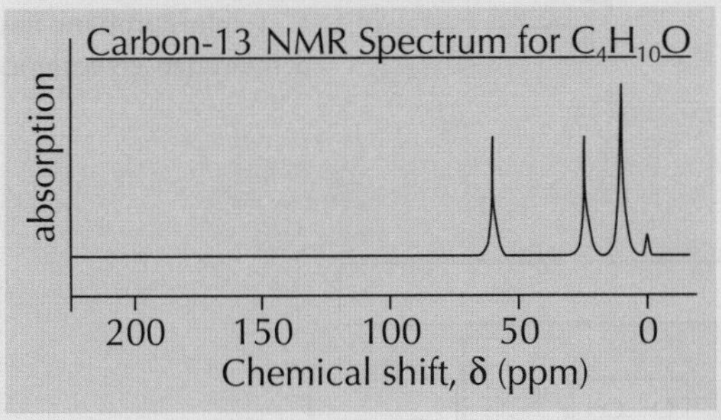

1) Looking at the **diagram** on the **previous page**, the peak with a **chemical shift** of **δ ≈ 65** is likely to be due to a **C–O** bond.
2) The two peaks around **δ ≈ 20** probably both represent carbons in **C–C** bonds, but with slightly different environments. Remember the alcohol doesn't contain any **chlorine**, **bromine** or **nitrogen** so you know the peak can't be caused by C–Cl, C–Br or C–N bonds.
3) The spectrum has **three peaks**, so the alcohol must have three **carbon environments**. There are **four carbons** in the alcohol, so two of the carbons must be in the **same environment**.
4) Put together all the **information** you've got so far, and try out some **structures**:

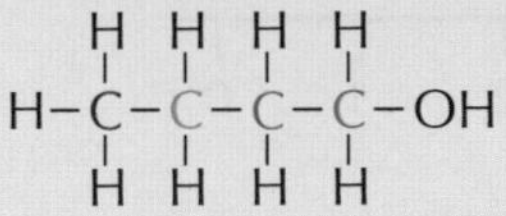

This has a C–O bond, and some C–C bonds, which is right. But all four carbons are in different environments.

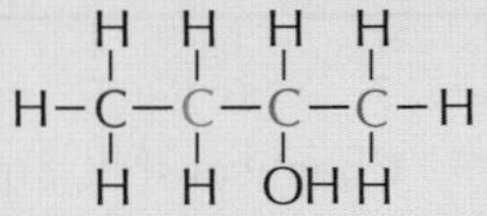

Again, this has a C–O bond, and some C–C bonds. But the carbons are still all in different environments.

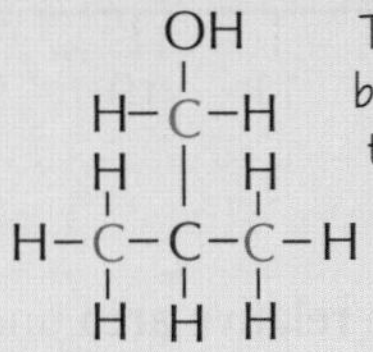

This molecule has a C–O bond and C–C bonds and two of the carbons are in the same environment. So this must be the correct structure.

You'll also need to be able to predict what the carbon-13 NMR spectum of a molecule may look like. This isn't as hard as it sounds — just identify the number of unique carbon environments, then use your data sheet to work out where the peaks of each carbon environment would appear.

Practice Questions

Q1 What part of the electromagnetic spectrum does NMR spectroscopy use?

Q2 What is meant by chemical shift? What compound is used as a reference for chemical shifts?

Q3 How can you tell from a carbon-13 NMR spectrum how many carbon environments a molecule contains?

Q4 Which types of bond could a shift of δ ≈ 150 correspond to?

For these questions, use the shift values from the diagram on p.210.

Exam Questions

Q1 The carbon-13 NMR spectrum shown on the right was produced by a compound with the molecular formula C_3H_9N.

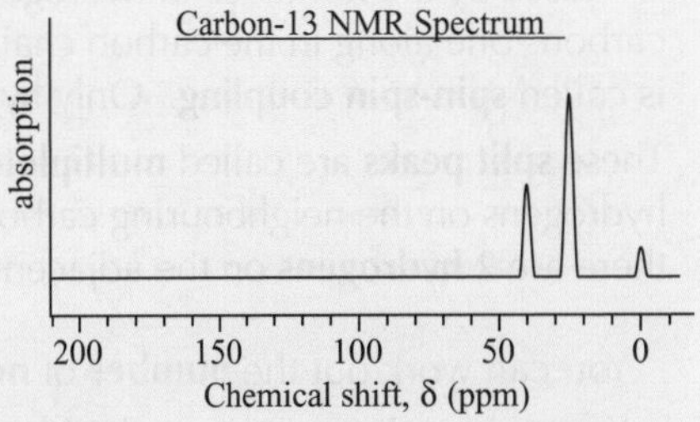

a) Explain why there is a peak at δ = 0. [1 mark]

b) The compound does not have the formula $CH_3CH_2CH_2NH_2$. Explain how the spectrum shows this. [2 marks]

c) Suggest and explain a possible structure for the compound. [4 marks]

Q2 Look at the molecule X, on the right. Which of the following statements is/are true?

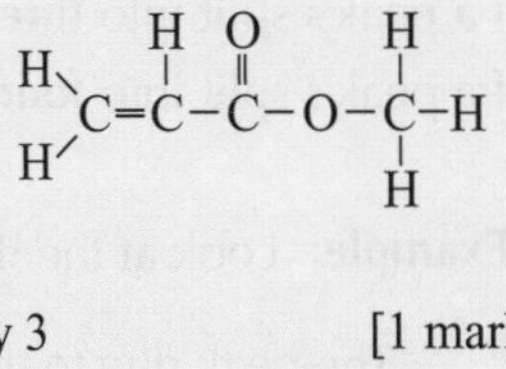

1. The carbon-13 NMR spectrum of X has a peak in the region of 160 - 220.
2. Molecule X has three different carbon environments.
3. The carbon-13 NMR spectrum of X shows four peaks.

A 1, 2 and 3 **B** Only 1 and 2 **C** Only 1 and 3 **D** Only 3 [1 mark]

Why did the carbon peak? Because it saw the radio wave...

The ideas behind NMR are difficult, but don't worry too much if you don't really understand them. The important thing is to know how to interpret a spectrum — that's what will get you marks in the exam. If you're having trouble, go over the examples and practice questions a few more times. You should have the "ahh... I get it" moment sooner or later.

Proton NMR

So, you know how to interpret carbon-13 NMR spectra — now it's time to get your teeth into some proton NMR spectra.

¹H NMR Spectra Tell You About Hydrogen Environments

Interpreting **proton NMR spectra** is similar to interpreting carbon-13 NMR spectra:

1) Each peak represents one **hydrogen environment**.
2) Look up the **chemical shifts** on a **data diagram** to identify possible environments. They're different from ^{13}C NMR, so make sure you're looking at the **correct data diagram**.

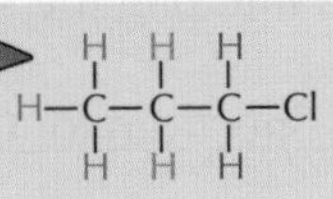

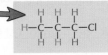

For example, **1-chloropropane** has **3 hydrogen environments**.

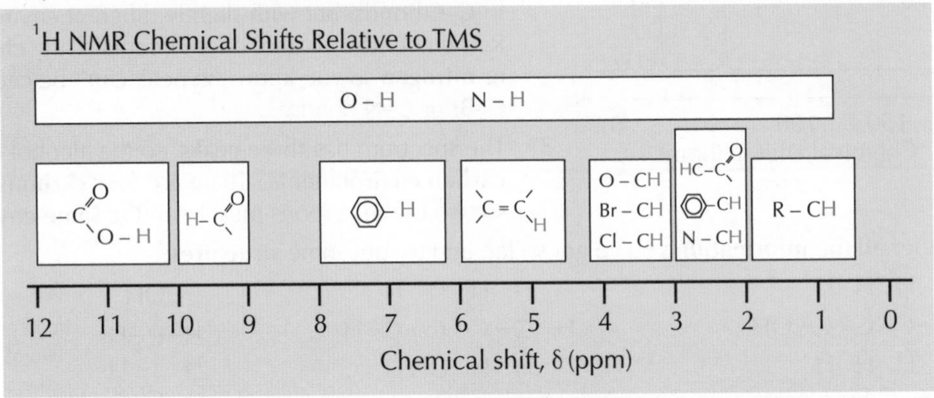

3) In ^{1}H NMR, the **relative area** under each peak tells you the relative number of H atoms in each environment. For example, if the area under two peaks is in the **ratio** 2:1, there will be **two** H atoms in the first environment for every **one** in the second environment.
4) Areas can be shown using **numbers** above the peaks or with an **integration trace**.

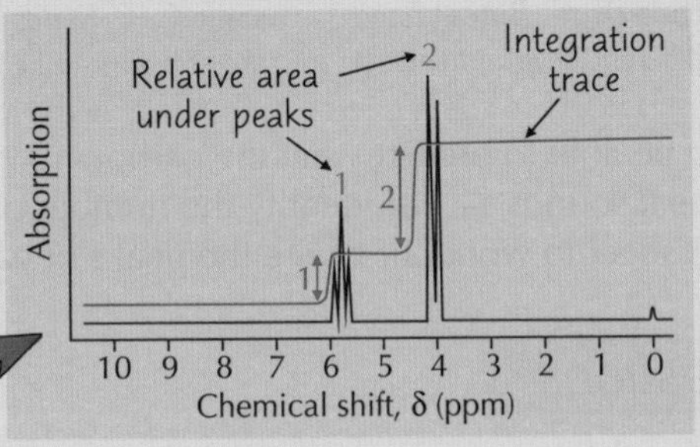

The **integration trace** is the **red line**. The **height increases** are proportional to the **area under** each peak.

The big difference between carbon-13 NMR and proton NMR spectra is that the peaks in a spectrum **split** according to how the **hydrogen environments are arranged**. Putting all this info together should let you work out the structure.

Spin-Spin Coupling Splits the Peaks in a Proton NMR Spectrum

In a proton NMR spectrum, a peak that represents a hydrogen environment can be **split**. The splitting is caused by the influence of hydrogen atoms that are bonded to **neighbouring carbons** — these are carbons one along in the carbon chain from the carbon the hydrogen's attached to. This effect is called **spin-spin coupling**. Only hydrogen nuclei on **adjacent** carbon atoms affect each other.

The splitting of the peak for this H...

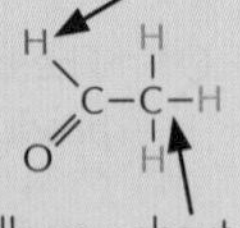

...tells you about the hydrogens on this adjacent carbon.

These **split peaks** are called **multiplets**. They always split into one more than the number of hydrogens on the neighbouring carbon atoms — it's called the **n + 1 rule**. For example, if there are **2 hydrogens** on the adjacent carbon atoms, the peak will be split into 2 + 1 = 3.

You can work out the **number** of **neighbouring hydrogens** by looking at how many the peak splits into:
If a peak's split into **two** (a **doublet**) then there's **one hydrogen** on the neighbouring carbon atoms.
If a peak's split into **three** (a **triplet**) then there are **two hydrogens** on the neighbouring carbon atoms.
If a peak's split into **four** (a **quartet**) then there are **three hydrogens** on the neighbouring carbon atoms.

Example: Look at the ^{1}H NMR spectrum of **1,1,2-trichloroethane**:

The peak due to the blue hydrogens is split into **two** because there's **one hydrogen** on the adjacent carbon atom.
The peak due to the red hydrogen is split into **three** because there are **two hydrogens** on the adjacent carbon atom.

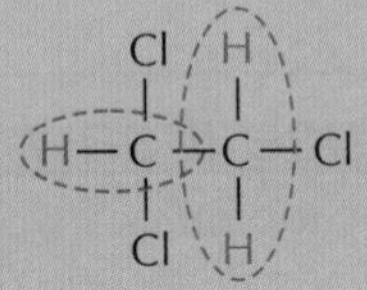

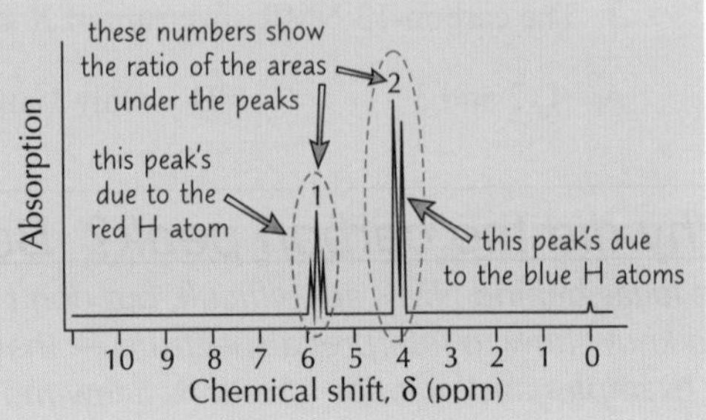

Proton NMR

Deuterated Solvents are used in Proton NMR Spectroscopy

NMR spectra are recorded with the molecule that is being analysed in **solution**. But if you used a ordinary solvent like water or ethanol, the **hydrogen nuclei** in the solvent would **add peaks** to the spectrum and confuse things. To overcome this, the **hydrogen nuclei** in the solvent are **replaced** with **deuterium** (D) — an **isotope** of hydrogen with **one proton** and **one neutron**. Deuterium nuclei don't absorb the radio wave energy, so they don't add peaks to the spectrum. A commonly used example of a '**deuterated solvent**' is **deuterated chloroform, $CDCl_3$**.

OH and NH Protons can be Identified by Proton Exchange Using D_2O

The **chemical shift** due to protons attached to oxygen (OH) or nitrogen (NH) is very **variable** — check out the huge **ranges** given in the **table** on the previous page. They make quite a **broad** peak that isn't usually split. Don't panic, though, as there's a clever little trick chemists use to identify OH and NH protons:

1) Run **two** spectra of the molecule — one with a little **deuterium oxide**, D_2O, added.
2) If an OH or NH proton is present it'll swap with deuterium and, hey presto, the peak will **disappear**. (This is because deuterium doesn't absorb the radio wave energy). This can help you to identify the presence of hydroxyl or N–H groups.

Proton NMR spectrum of ethanol

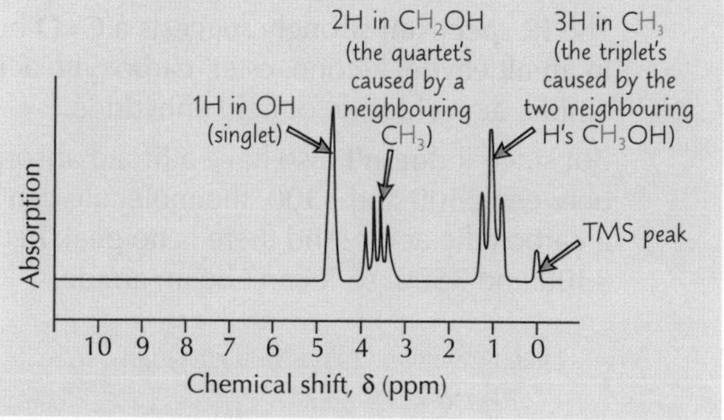

Proton NMR spectrum of ethanol run with D_2O added

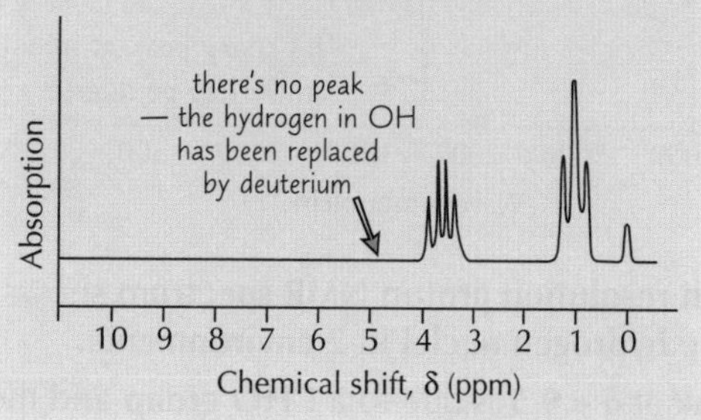

Practice Questions

Q1 What causes the peaks on a high resolution proton NMR spectrum to split?

Q2 What causes a triplet of peaks on a high resolution proton NMR spectrum?

Q3 What are deuterated solvents? Why are they needed?

Q4 How can you get rid of a peak caused by an OH group?

You might also be asked to predict the proton NMR spectrum for a molecule.

Exam Question

Q1 The proton NMR spectrum on the right is for an alkyl halide.
Use the diagram of chemical shifts on page 212 to answer this question.

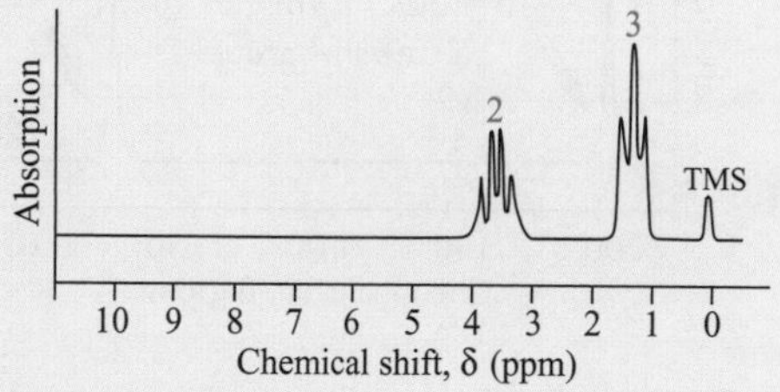

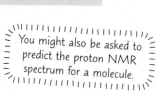

a) What is the likely environment of the two protons with a shift of 3.6 ppm? [1 mark]

b) What is the likely environment of the three protons with a shift of 1.3 ppm? [1 mark]

c) The molecular mass of the molecule is 64.5.
Suggest a possible structure and explain your suggestion. [2 marks]

d) Explain the splitting patterns of the two peaks. [2 marks]

Never mind splitting peaks — this stuff's likely to cause splitting headaches...

Is your head spinning yet? I know mine is. Round and round like a merry-go-round. It's a hard life when you're tied to a desk trying to get NMR spectroscopy firmly fixed in your head. You must be looking quite peaky by now... so go on, learn this stuff, take the dog around the block, then come back and see if you can still remember it all.

More on Spectra

Yes, I know, it's yet another page on spectra — but it's the last one (alright, two) I promise.

*You Can Use **Data From Several Spectra** to **Work Out a Structure***

All the **spectroscopy techniques** in this section will **give clues** to the **identity of a mystery molecule**, but you can be more **certain** about a structure (and avoid jumping to wrong conclusions) if you look at **data from several different types of spectrum**. Look back at page 110 for a reminder about mass spectroscopy, and page 109 for IR spectra.

Example: The following spectra are all of the same molecule. Deduce the molecule's structure.

The **mass spectrum** tells you the molecule's got a **mass of 44** and it's likely to contain a **CH_3 group**.

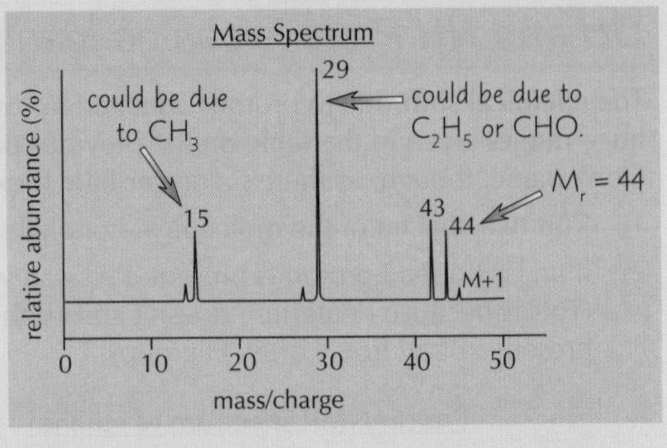

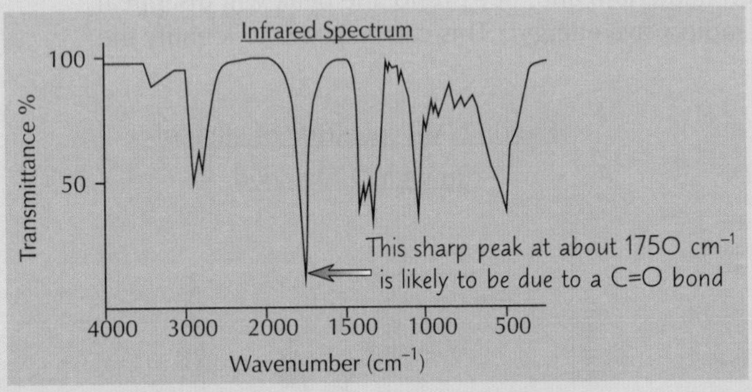

The **IR spectrum** strongly suggests a **C=O** bond in an aldehyde, ketone, ester, carboxylic acid, amide, acyl chloride or acid anhydride.

But since it **doesn't** also have a broad absorption between 2500 and 3300, the molecule **can't** be a carboxylic acid. And there is no peak between 3300 and 3500, so it can't be an amide.

The **high resolution proton NMR spectrum** shows that there are **hydrogen nuclei in 2 environments**.

The peak at $\delta \approx$ **9.5** is due to a **CHO group** and the one at $\delta \approx$ **2.5** is probably the hydrogen atoms in **$COCH_3$**.

(You know that these can't be any other groups with similar chemical shifts thanks to the mass spectrum and IR spectrum.)

The **area** under the peaks is in the ratio **1 : 3**, which makes sense as there's **1 hydrogen in CHO** and **3 in $COCH_3$**.

The **splitting pattern** shows that the protons are on **adjacent carbon atoms**, so the group must be **$HCOCH_3$**.

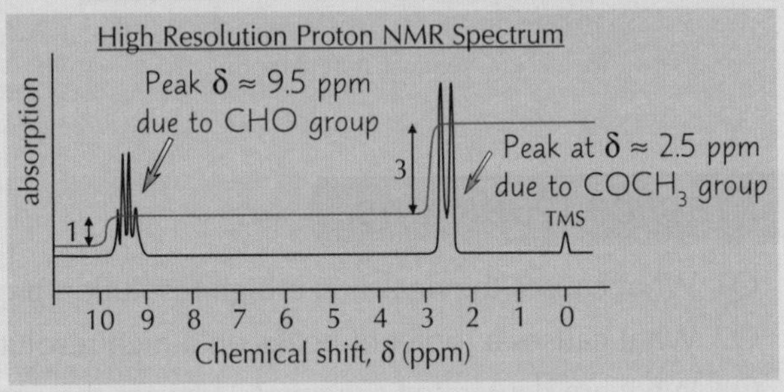

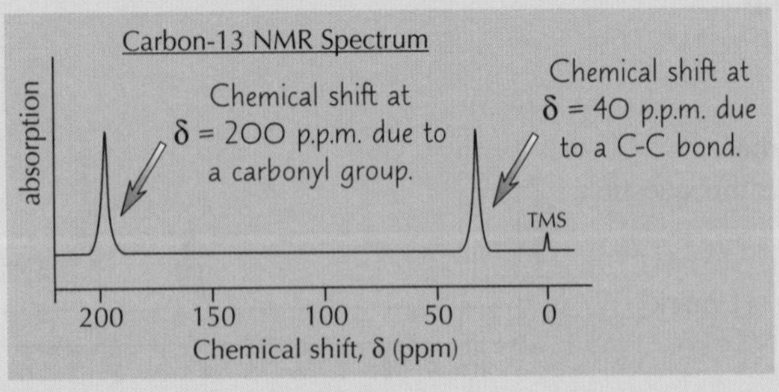

The **carbon-13 NMR spectrum** shows that the molecule has carbon nuclei in **2 different environments**.

The peak at **δ = 200** corresponds to a carbon in a **carbonyl group** and the other peak is due to a **C–C bond**.

Putting all this together we have a molecule with a **mass of 44**, which contains a **CH_3** group, a **C=O** bond, and an **$HCOCH_3$** group.

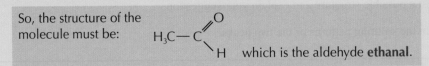

So, the structure of the molecule must be:

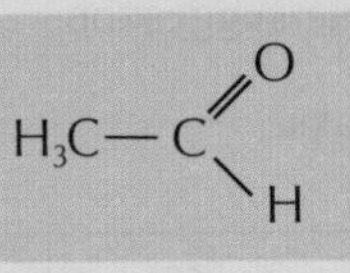

which is the aldehyde **ethanal**.

You probably could have worked the molecule's structure out **without** using all the spectra, but in more **complex examples** you might well need all of them, so it's good practice. And while we're on the subject, there are a couple **more examples** for you to practise on the next page — enjoy.

More on Spectra

Elemental Analysis also Helps to Work Out a Structure

1) In elemental analysis, experiments determine the **masses** or percentage compositions of different elements in a compound.
2) This data can help you to work out the **empirical** and **molecular formulae** of a compound. See pages 22 and 23 to remind yourself how to do this.
3) Knowing the molecular formula is useful in working out the **structure** of the compound from different spectra.

Practice Questions

Q1 Which type of spectrum gives you the mass of a molecule?

Q2 Which spectrum can tell you how many carbon environments are in a molecule?

Q3 Which spectrum can tell you how many different hydrogen environments there are in a molecule?

Q4 Which spectrum involves radio wave radiation?

Exam Questions

Q1 The four spectra shown were produced by running different tests on samples of the same pure organic compound. Use them to work out:

a) The molecular mass of the compound. [1 mark]

b) The probable structure of the molecule. Explain your reasoning. [6 marks]

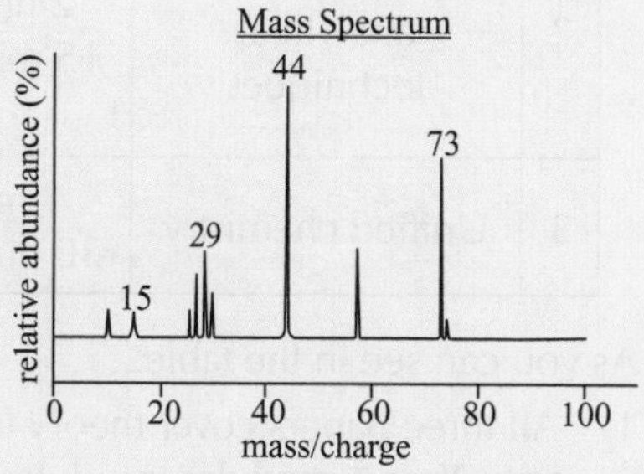

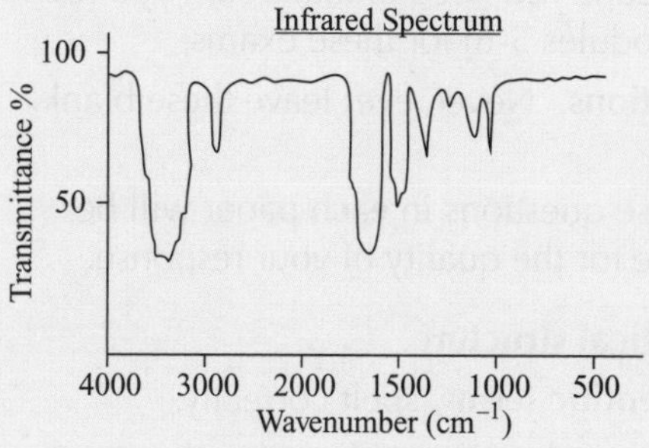

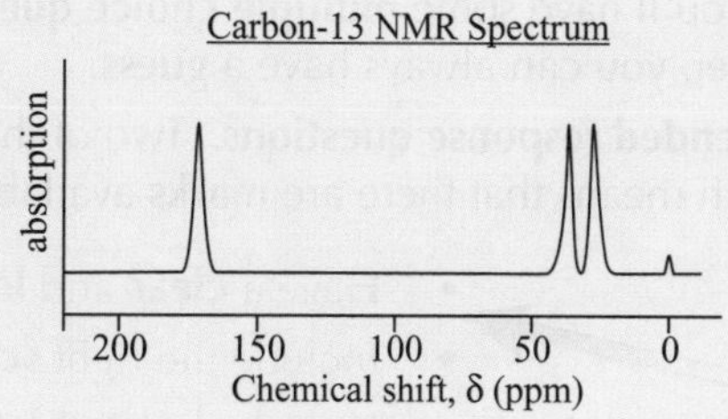

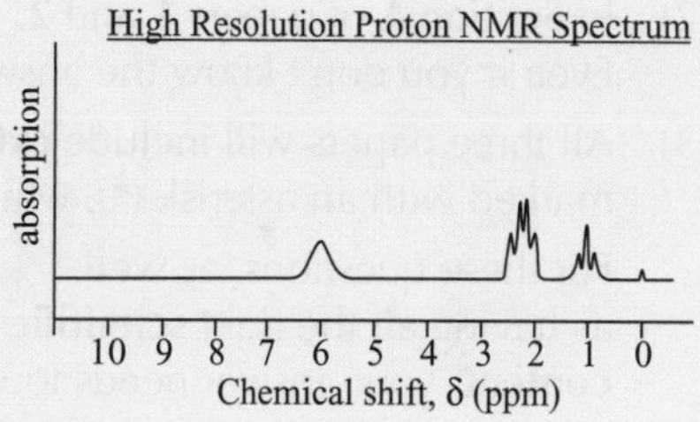

Q2 The four spectra shown were produced by running different tests on samples of the same pure organic compound. Use them to work out:

a) The molecular mass of the compound. [1 mark]

b) The probable structure of the molecule. Explain your reasoning. [6 marks]

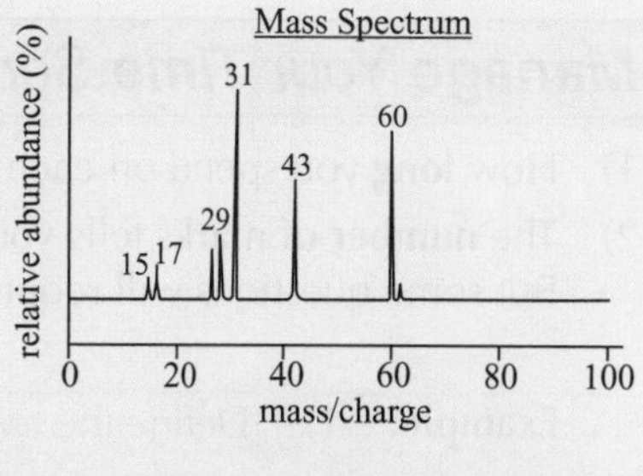

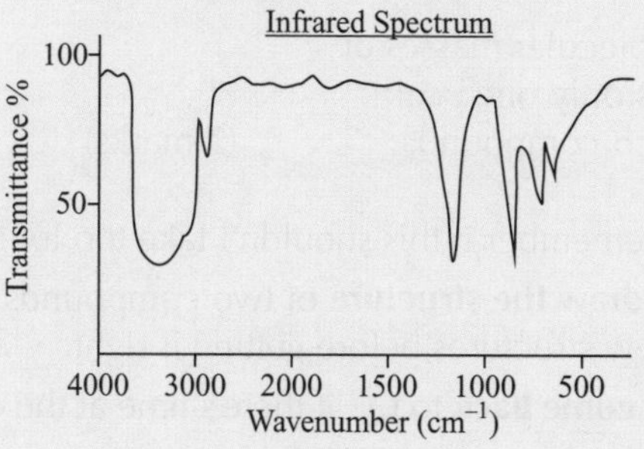

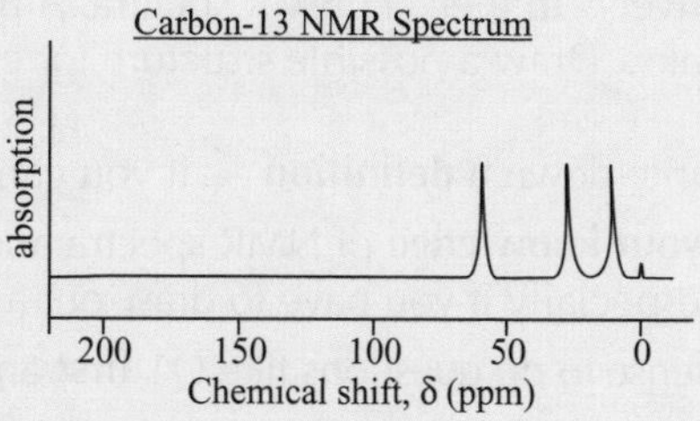

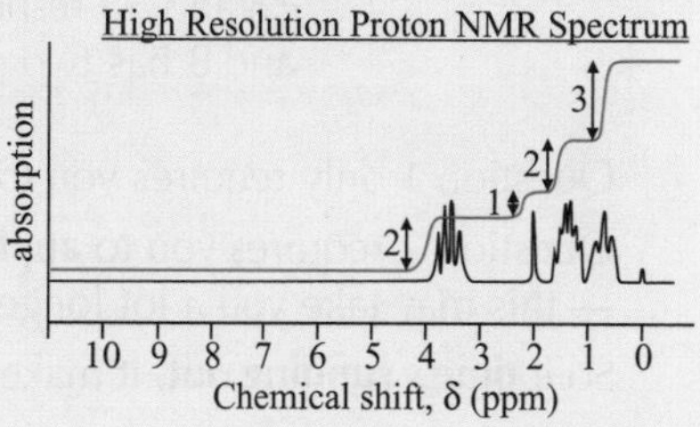

Spectral analysis — psychology for ghosts...

So that's analysis done and dusted, you'll be pleased to hear. Actually, that's pretty much the whole book done and dusted. Hurrah, huzzah and other joyful exclamations. But don't go scooting off to enjoy yourself just yet — take a moment to check that you really have got everything lodged in your brain. Then go forth and be examined. Good luck.

Do Well In Your Exams

Passing exams isn't all about revision — it really helps if you know how the exam is structured and have got your exam technique nailed so that you pick up every mark you can.

Make Sure You Know the **Structure** of Your **Exams**

If you're sitting AS-Level Chemistry, you'll be doing different papers so this info isn't relevant to you.

For **A-Level Chemistry**, you'll be sitting **three papers**. Knowing what's going to come up in each paper and how much time you'll have will be really useful when you're preparing for your exams, so here's what you'll be up against:

Paper		Time	No. of Marks	Modules assessed	Paper details	
1	Periodic table, elements and physical chemistry	2 hrs 15 mins	100	1, 2, 3 and 5	Section A — multiple choice questions (15 marks)	Section B — short answer and extended response questions (85 marks)
2	Synthesis and analytical techniques	2 hrs 15 mins	100	1, 2, 4 and 6	Section A — multiple choice questions (15 marks)	Section B — short answer and extended response questions (85 marks)
3	Unified chemistry	1 hr 30 mins	70	All modules	Short answer and extended response questions.	

As you can see in the table...

1) All three papers cover theory from **both years** of your course — this means you need to make sure you revise your **Year 1 modules** (modules 1-4) as well as your **Year 2 modules** (modules 5-6) for these exams.
2) In **Section A** of papers **1** and **2**, you'll have some **multiple choice questions**. Never, ever leave these blank. Even if you don't know the answer, you can always have a **guess**.
3) All three papers will include **extended response questions**. Two of these questions in each paper will be marked with an asterisk (*), which means that there are **marks** available for the quality of your response.

   For these questions, as well as having all the right **scientific content**, your answer needs to:
   - Have a **clear** and **logical structure**.
   - Include the right **scientific terms**, spelt correctly.
   - Include **detailed information** that's **relevant** to the question.

Manage Your **Time** Sensibly

1) How **long** you spend on each question is important in an exam — it could make all the difference to your grade.
2) The **number of marks** tells you **roughly** how long to spend on a question. But some questions will require lots of work for a few marks while others will be quicker.

Example: 1) Define the term 'enthalpy change of neutralisation'. (2 marks)

2) Compounds A and B are hydrocarbons with relative molecular masses of 78 and 58 respectively. In their ^1H NMR spectra, A has only one peak and B has two peaks. Draw a possible structure for each compound. (2 marks)

Question 1 only requires you to write down a **definition** — if you can remember it this shouldn't take too long.

Question 2 requires you to **apply your knowledge** of NMR spectra and **draw the structure** of two compounds — this may take you a lot longer, especially if you have to draw out a few structures before getting it right.

So if **time's running out**, it makes sense to do questions like Q1 **first** and **come back** to Q2 if there's time at the end.

3) If you get stuck on a question for too long, it may be best to **move on** and come back to it later.
4) You **don't** have to work through the paper **in order** — for example, you might decide **not** to do the multiple choice questions first, or leave questions on the topics you find hard till the end.
5) But if you **skip** any questions the first time round, don't forget to **go back** to do them.

Do Well In Your Exams

Make Sure You Read the Question

1) It sounds obvious, but it's really important you read each question **carefully**, and give an answer that fits.
2) **Command words** in the question give you an idea of the kind of answer you should write. You'll find answering exam questions much easier if you understand exactly what they mean. Here's a summary of the common ones:

Command word:	What to do:
Give / Name / State	Give a brief one or two word answer, or a short sentence.
Identify	Say what something is.
Describe (an observation)	Write about what you would expect to happen in a reaction, e.g. a colour change or the formation of a precipitate.
Explain	Give reasons for something.
Suggest / Predict	Use your scientific knowledge to work out what the answer might be.
Outline / Describe (an experiment)	Write about each step you would take in an experiment — including any equipment you would use, the reagents required and any reaction conditions (e.g. temperature, presence of a catalyst). If you are identifying a substance, you should also include any physical changes you would expect to see, such as a precipitate being formed.
Calculate	Work out the solution to a mathematical problem.
Deduce / Determine	Use the information given in the question to work something out.

From the looks on his classmates' faces, Ivor deduced that he had gone a bit overboard when decorating his lucky exam hat.

Some Questions Will Test Your Knowledge of Practical Skills

Some of the marks in your A-Level Chemistry exams will focus on **practical skills**. This means you will be given questions where you're asked to do things like comment on the **design** of **experiments**, make **predictions**, **draw graphs**, **calculate** percentage **errors** — basically, anything related to planning experiments or analysing results. These skills are covered in the Practical Skills section of this book on pages 4 to 13.

Remember to Use the Exam Data Sheet

When you sit your exams, you'll be given a **data sheet**. It will contain lots of useful information, including: the **characteristic infrared absorptions**, **^{13}C NMR shifts** and **^{1}H NMR shifts** of some common functional groups, some useful **constants** and **equations** and a copy of the **periodic table**.

Be Careful With Calculations

20% of the marks up for grabs in A-Level Chemistry will require maths skills, so make sure you know your stuff.

1) In calculation questions you should always **show your working** — you may get some marks for your **method** even if you get the answer wrong.
2) Don't **round** your answer until the **very end**. Some of the calculations in A-Level chemistry can be quite **long**, and if you round too early you could introduce errors to your final answer.
3) Be careful with **units**. Lots of formulas require quantities to be in specific units (e.g. temperature in Kelvin), so it's best to **convert** any numbers you're given into these before you start. And obviously, if the question **tells** you which units to give your **answer** in, don't throw away marks by giving it in different ones.
4) You should give your final answer to the correct number of **significant figures**. This is usually the same as the data with the **lowest number** of significant figures in the question — see page 9 for more on significant figures.
5) It can be easy to mis-type numbers into your calculator when you're under pressure in an exam, so always **double-check** your calculations and make sure that your answer looks **sensible**.

I'd tell you another Chemistry joke, but I'm not sure it'd get a good reaction...

The key to preparing for your exams is to practise, practise, practise. Get your hands on some practice papers and try to do each of them in the time allowed. This'll flag up any topics that you're a bit shaky on, so you can go back and revise.

Answers

Module 1 — Development of Practical Skills

Page 5 — Planning Experiments

1 Using litmus paper is not a particularly accurate method of measuring pH / not very sensitive equipment ***[1 mark]***. It would be better to use a pH meter ***[1 mark]***.

Page 7 — Practical Techniques

1 a) The student measured the level of the liquid from the top of the meniscus, when he should have measured it from the bottom ***[1 mark]***.
b) B ***[1 mark]***.

Page 9 — Presenting Results

1 a) mean volume$= \frac{7.30 + 7.25 + 7.25}{3} = 7.26666...$ cm^3
= **0.00727 dm^3** or **7.27 × 10^{-3} dm^3** (3 s.f.) ***[1 mark]***
b) 0.50 ÷ 1000 = **0.00050 mol cm^{-3}** or **5.0 × 10^{-4} mol cm^{-3}** ***[1 mark]***

Page 11 — Analysing Results

1 a) 15 °C and 25 °C ***[1 mark]***.
b) Positive correlation ***[1 mark]***.
c) C ***[1 mark]***

Page 13 — Evaluating Experiments

1 a) The volumetric flask reads to the nearest 0.5 cm^3, so the uncertainty is ±0.25 cm^3.
$$\text{percentage error} = \frac{\text{uncertainty}}{\text{reading}} \times 100 = \frac{0.25}{25} \times 100 = \mathbf{1.0\ \%}$$
[1 mark]
b) E.g. The student should add the thermometer to the citric acid solution and allow it to stabilise before adding the sodium bicarbonate to give an accurate value for the initial temperature ***[1 mark]***. The student should then measure the temperature change until the solution stops reacting to give a valid result for the temperature change of the entire reaction ***[1 mark]***.

Module 2: Section 1 — Atoms and Reactions

Page 15 — The Atom

1 a) Similarity — They've all got the same number of protons/electrons ***[1 mark]***. Difference — They all have different numbers of neutrons ***[1 mark]***.
b) 1 proton, 1 neutron (2 – 1), 1 electron ***[1 mark]***.
c) ^{3}H ***[1 mark]***
Since tritium has 2 neutrons in the nucleus and also 1 proton, it has a mass number of 3. You could also write $^3_1$H but you don't really need the atomic number.

2 a) i) They both have 18 electrons ***[1 mark]***.
ii) They both have 16 protons (the atomic number of S must always be the same) ***[1 mark]***.
iii) They both have 22 neutrons ***[1 mark]***.
b) **A** and **C** ***[1 mark]***. They have the same number of protons but different numbers of neutrons ***[1 mark]***.
It doesn't matter that they have a different number of electrons because they are still the same element.

Page 17 — Atomic Models

1 a) Bohr knew that if an electron was freely orbiting the nucleus it would spiral into it, causing the atom to collapse ***[1 mark]***. His model only allowed electrons to be in fixed shells and not in between them ***[1 mark]***.
b) When an electron moves from one shell to another electromagnetic radiation is emitted or absorbed ***[1 mark]***.
c) Atoms react in order to gain full shells of electrons ***[1 mark]***. Noble gases have full shells and so do not react ***[1 mark]***. (Alternatively: a full shell of electrons makes an atom stable ***[1 mark]***; noble gases have full shells and do not react because they are stable ***[1 mark]***.)

Page 19 — Relative Mass

1 a) First multiply each relative abundance by the relative mass —
120.8 × 63 = 7610.4, 54.0 × 65 = 3510.0
Next add up the products: 7610.4 + 3510.0 = 11 120.4 ***[1 mark]***
Now divide by the total abundance (120.8 + 54.0 = 174.8)
$A_r(\text{Cu}) = \frac{11120.4}{174.8} \approx$ **63.6** ***[1 mark]***
You can check your answer by seeing if A_r(Cu) is in between 63 and 65 (the lowest and highest relative isotopic masses).
b) A sample of copper is a mixture of 2 isotopes in different abundances ***[1 mark]***. The relative atomic mass is an average mass of these isotopes which isn't a whole number ***[1 mark]***.

2 You use pretty much the same method here as for question 1 a).
93.1 × 39 = 3630.9, 0.120 × 40 = 4.8, 6.77 × 41 = 277.57
3630.9 + 4.8 + 277.57 = **3913.27** ***[1 mark]***
This time you divide by 100 because they're percentages.
$A_r(\text{K}) = \frac{3913.27}{100} \approx$ **39.1** ***[1 mark]***
Again check your answer's between the lowest and highest relative isotopic masses, 39 and 41. A_r(K) is closer to 39 because most of the sample (93.1 %) is made up of this isotope.

Page 21 — The Mole

1 Molar mass of HCl = 1.0 + 35.5 = 36.5 g mol^{-1}
No. moles in 7.3 g HCl = $\frac{7.3}{36.5}$ = 0.2 mol
No. molecules of HCl in 0.2 mol = 0.2 × 6.02 × 10^{23} = 1.204 × 10^{23} ***[1 mark]***
There are 2 atoms in each molecule of HCl, so
No. atoms = 2 × 1.204 × 10^{23} = **2.4 × 10^{23} atoms** (2 s.f) ***[1 mark]***

2 M(CH_3COOH) = (2 × 12.0) + (4 × 1.0) + (2 × 16.0) = 60.0 g mol^{-1} ***[1 mark]*** so mass of 0.360 moles = 60.0 × 0.360 = **21.6 g** ***[1 mark]***

3 Moles of Cl_2 = $\frac{1.28}{35.5 \times 2}$ = 0.0180 moles ***[1 mark]***
Rearranging pV = nRT to find T gives $T = \frac{pV}{nR}$.
So, $T = \frac{175 \times (98.6 \times 10^{-3})}{0.0180 \times 8.314}$ = **115 K** ***[1 mark]***

4 M of C_3H_8 = (3 × 12.0) + (8 × 1.0) = 44.0 g mol^{-1}
No. of moles of C_3H_8 = $\frac{88}{44.0}$ = 2 moles ***[1 mark]***
At r.t.p. 1 mole of gas occupies 24 dm^3, so 2 moles of gas occupies 2 x 24 = **48 dm^3** ***[1 mark]***
You could also use the equation pV = nRT to answer this question, where at r.t.p, T = 298 K, and p = 101 300 Pa. In this case, your answer would be $V = \frac{nRT}{p} = \frac{2 \times 8.314 \times 298}{101300}$ = 0.0489 m^3 = 49 dm^3.

Page 23 — Empirical and Molecular Formulae

1 Assume you've got 100 g of the compound so you can turn the % straight into mass.
No. of moles of C = $\frac{92.3}{12}$ =7.69 moles
No. of moles of H = $\frac{7.7}{1}$ = 7.7 moles ***[1 mark]***
Divide both by the smallest number, in this case 7.69.
So ratio C : H = 1 : 1
So, the empirical formula = CH ***[1 mark]***
The empirical mass = 12.0 + 1.0 = 13.0
No. of empirical units in molecule = $\frac{78}{13}$ = 6
So the molecular formula = **C_6H_6** ***[1 mark]***

Answers

The magnesium is burning, so it's reacting with oxygen and the product is magnesium oxide. First work out the number of moles of each element.
No. of moles Mg = $\frac{1.2}{24.3}$ = 0.05 moles
Mass of O is everything that isn't Mg: 2 – 1.2 = 0.8 g
No. of moles O = $\frac{0.8}{16}$ = 0.05 moles ***[1 mark]***
Ratio Mg : O = 0.05 : 0.05
Divide both by the smallest number, in this case 0.05.
So ratio Mg : O = 1 : 1
So the empirical formula is **MgO** ***[1 mark]***

First calculate the no. of moles of each product and then the mass of C and H:
No. of moles of CO_2 = $\frac{33}{44.0}$ = 0.75 moles
Mass of C = 0.75 × 12.0 = 9 g
No. of moles of H_2O = $\frac{10.8}{18.0}$ = 0.6 moles
0.6 moles H_2O = 1.2 moles H
Mass of H = 1.2 × 1.0 = 1.2 g ***[1 mark]***
Organic acids contain C, H and O,
so the rest of the mass must be O.
Mass of O = 19.8 – (9 + 1.2) = 9.6 g
No. of moles of O = $\frac{9.6}{16.0}$ = 0.6 moles ***[1 mark]***
Mole ratio = C : H : O = 0.75 : 1.2 : 0.6
Divide by smallest 1.25 : 2 : 1
This isn't a whole number ratio, so you have to multiply them all up until it is. Multiply them all by 4.
So, mole ratio = C : H : O = 5 : 8 : 4
Empirical formula = $C_5H_8O_4$ ***[1 mark]***
Empirical mass = (5 × 12.0) + (8 × 1.0) + (4 × 16.0) = 132 g
This is the same as what we're told the molecular mass is, so the molecular formula is also $\mathbf{C_5H_8O_4}$ ***[1 mark]***.

Page 25 — Equations and Calculations

1 $2KI_{(aq)} + Pb(NO_3)_{2\,(aq)} \rightarrow PbI_{2\,(s)} + 2KNO_{3\,(aq)}$ ***[1 mark]***
In this equation, the NO_3 group remains unchanged, so it makes balancing much easier if you treat it as one indivisible lump.

2 M of C_2H_5Cl = (2 × 12) + (5 × 1) + (1 × 35.5) = 64.5 g mol^{-1}
Number of moles of C_2H_5Cl = $\frac{258}{64.5}$ = 4 moles ***[1 mark]***
From the equation, 1 mole C_2H_5Cl is made from 1 mole C_2H_4
so, 4 moles C_2H_5Cl is made from 4 moles C_2H_4.
M of C_2H_4 = (2 × 12) + (4 × 1) = 28 g mol^{-1}
so, the mass of 4 moles C_2H_4 = 4 × 28 = **112 g** ***[1 mark]***

3 Start by writing the balanced equation for the combustion of butane:
$C_4H_{10} + 6\tfrac{1}{2}O_2 \rightarrow 4CO_2 + 5H_2O$ ***[1 mark]***
So, moles of O_2 required = 3.50 × 10^{-2} × 6.5 = 0.2275 mol
At room temperature and pressure, 1 mole of gas occupies 24 dm^3.
So 0.2275 × 24 = **5.46 dm^3** ***[1 mark]***.

4 a) M of $CaCO_3$ = 40.1 + 12 + (3 × 16) = 100.1 g mol^{-1}
Number of moles of $CaCO_3$ = $\frac{15.0}{100.1}$ = 0.150 moles
From the equation, 1 mole $CaCO_3$ produces 1 mole CaO
so, 0.150 moles of $CaCO_3$ produces 0.150 moles of CaO ***[1 mark]***.
M of CaO = 40.1 + 16 = 56.1 g mol^{-1} so, mass of 0.150 moles of CaO = 56.1 × 0.150 = **8.42 g** ***[1 mark]***

b) From the equation, 1 mole $CaCO_3$ produces 1 mole CO_2
so, 0.150 moles of $CaCO_3$ produces 0.150 moles of CO_2.
1 mole gas occupies 24.0 dm^3, so, 0.150 moles occupies 24.0 × 0.150 = **3.60 dm^3** ***[1 mark]***

Page 27 — Formulae of Ionic Compounds

1 $Sc_2(SO_4)_3$ ***[1 mark]***
Scandium has a charge of +3. Sulfate has a charge of –2. So, for every 2 scandium atoms, you will need three sulfate ions to balance the charge.

2 Na_2O ***[1 mark]***
Sodium is in group 1, so forms ions with a charge of +1.
In compounds, oxygen usually has a charge of –2.

3 a) M of $CaSO_4$ = 40.1 + 32.1 + (4 × 16.0) = 136.2 g mol^{-1} ***[1 mark]***
no. moles = $\frac{1.133}{136.2}$ = **0.008319 moles** ***[1 mark]***

b) mass of water = difference in mass between hydrated and anhydrous salt = 1.883 – 1.133 = 0.7500 g ***[1 mark]***
no. moles of water = $\frac{\text{mass}}{\text{molar mass}}$ = $\frac{0.7500}{18.0}$ = 0.04167 ***[1 mark]***
X = ratio of no. moles water to no. moles salt = $\frac{0.04167}{0.008319}$ = 5.009.
Rounded to nearest whole number, X = **5** ***[1 mark]***

Page 29 — Acids and Bases

1 a) One of: magnesium ($Mg_{(s)}$), magnesium hydroxide ($Mg(OH)_2$), magnesium oxide (MgO) or magnesium carbonate ($MgCO_3$) ***[1 mark]***

b) One of: $Mg + 2HCl \rightarrow MgCl_2 + H_2$,
$Mg(OH)_2 + 2HCl \rightarrow MgCl_2 + 2H_2O$,
$MgO + 2HCl \rightarrow MgCl_2 + H_2O$,
$MgCO_3 + 2HCl \rightarrow MgCl_2 + CO_2 + H_2O$ ***[1 mark]***

2 a) $NaOH_{(aq)} + HNO_{3\,(aq)} \rightarrow H_2O_{(l)} + NaNO_{3\,(aq)}$ ***[1 mark]***

b) neutralisation ***[1 mark]***

Page 31 — Titrations

1 n = 0.600 × ($\frac{250}{1000}$) = 0.150 moles ***[1 mark]***
M($NaHSO_4$) = (23 + 1 + 32.1 + (4 × 16)) = 120.1
So mass of $NaHSO_4$ needed = 0.150 × 120.1 = **18.0 g** ***[1 mark]***.

2 ***5-6 marks:***
The answer explains how indicators are used and includes at least one suitable and one unsuitable indictor for acid/alkali titrations, with reasoning. The answer has a clear and logical structure. The information given is relevant and detailed.
3-4 marks:
The answer explains how indicators are used and includes one example of a suitable or unsuitable indicator for acid/alkali titrations. The answer has some structure. Most of the information given is relevant and there is some detail involved.
1-2 marks:
The answer contains some explanation of how indicators are used but gives no examples of indicators for acid/alkali titrations. The answer has no clear structure. The information given is basic and lacking in detail. It may not all be relevant.
0 marks:
No relevant information is given.
Here are some points your answer may include:
Indicators change colour at an end point. They are used in acid/alkali titrations to mark an end point. Indicators used in titrations need to change colour quickly over a very small pH range. A few drops of indicator solution are added to the analyte. The analyte/indicator solution can be placed on a white surface to make a colour change easy to see. Methyl orange turns from yellow to red when adding acid to alkali. Phenolphthalein turns from pink to colourless when adding acid to alkali. Universal indicator is a poor indicator to use for titrations as the colour changes gradually over a wide pH range.

Page 33 — Titration Calculations

1 First write down what you know:

CH_3COOH	+	$NaOH$	→	CH_3COONa	+	H_2O
25.4 cm^3		14.6 cm^3				
?		0.500 mol dm^{-3}				

No. of moles of NaOH = $\frac{0.500 \times 14.6}{1000}$ = 0.00730 moles ***[1 mark]***
From the equation, you know 1 mole of NaOH neutralises 1 mole of CH_3COOH, so if you've used 0.00730 moles NaOH you must have neutralised 0.00730 moles CH_3COOH ***[1 mark]***.
Concentration of CH_3COOH = $\frac{0.00730 \times 1000}{25.4}$ = 0.287 mol dm^{-3} ***[1 mark]***

Answers

2 First write down what you know again:

$$CaCO_3 + H_2SO_4 \rightarrow CaSO_4 + H_2O + CO_2$$

0.750 g   0.250 mol dm^{-3}

M of $CaCO_3$ = 40.1 + 12.0 + (3 × 16.0) = 100.1 g mol^{-1}

Number of moles of $CaCO_3 = \frac{0.750}{100.1} = 7.49 \times 10^{-3}$ moles ***[1 mark]***

From the equation, 1 mole $CaCO_3$ reacts with 1 mole H_2SO_4 so, 7.49×10^{-3} moles $CaCO_3$ reacts with 7.49×10^{-3} moles H_2SO_4 ***[1 mark]***.

The volume needed is $= \frac{(7.49 \times 10^{-3}) \times 1000}{0.250}$ = **30.0 cm^3** ***[1 mark]***

If the question mentions concentration or molarities, you can bet your last clean pair of underwear that you'll need to use the formula number of moles $= \frac{\text{concentration} \times \text{volume}}{1000}$. Just make sure the volume's in cm^3 though.

3 a) $Ca(OH)_2 + 2HCl \rightarrow CaCl_2 + 2H_2O$ ***[1 mark]***

b) Number of moles of HCl $= \frac{0.250 \times 17.1}{1000}$
$= 4.275 \times 10^{-3}$ moles ***[1 mark]***
From the equation in a), 2 moles HCl reacts with 1 mole $Ca(OH)_2$, so, 4.275×10^{-3} moles HCl reacts with 2.1375×10^{-3} moles $Ca(OH)_2$ ***[1 mark]***.
So concentration of $Ca(OH)_2$ solution =
$\frac{2.1375 \times 10^{-3} \times 1000}{25.0}$ = **0.0855 mol dm^{-3}** ***[1 mark]***.

Page 35 — Atom Economy and Percentage Yield

1 a) 2 is an addition reaction ***[1 mark]***

b) For reaction 1: % atom economy
$= M_r(C_2H_5Cl) \div [M_r(C_2H_5Cl) + M_r(POCl_3) + M_r(HCl)] \times 100\%$ ***[1 mark]***
= [(2 × 12.0) + (5 × 1.0) + 35.5] ÷ [(2 × 12.0) + (5 × 1.0) + 35.5 + 31.0 + 16.0 + (3 × 35.5) + 1.0 + 35.5] × 100%
= (64.5 ÷ 254.5) × 100% = **25.3%** ***[1 mark]***

c) The atom economy is 100% because there is only one product (there are no by-products) ***[1 mark]***

2 a) Number of moles = mass ÷ molar mass
Moles PCl_3 = 0.275 ÷ 137.5 = 0.002 moles
Chlorine is in excess, so there must be 0.002 moles of product ***[1 mark]***. Mass of PCl_5 = 0.002 × 208.5 = 0.417 g ***[1 mark]***

b) percentage yield = (0.198 ÷ 0.417) × 100% = **47.5%** ***[1 mark]***

c) Changing reaction conditions will have no effect on atom economy ***[1 mark]***. Since the equation shows that there is only one product, the atom economy will always be 100% ***[1 mark]***.
Atom economy is related to the type of reaction — addition, substitution, etc. — not to the quantities of products and reactants.

Page 37 — Oxidation Numbers

1 SO_4^{2-} contains sulfur and oxygen so it's a sulfate.
It has an overall charge of –2.
Total charge from the SO_4^{2-} ions = 3 × –2 = –6.
For the overall charge to be 0, the total charge from chromium ions = +6. 6 ÷ 2 = +3.
So the systematic name is **chromium(III) sulfate** ***[1 mark]***.

2 Oxidation number of iron = +2. Charge of nitrate = –1.
You will need a ratio of 1 : 2 of iron : nitrate to make the compound neutral. So the formula is **$Fe(NO_3)_2$** ***[1 mark]***.

3 a) Since lead oxide and sulfuric acid react in a ratio of 1:1, the formula for lead sulfate must be **$PbSO_4$** ***[1 mark]***.

b) i) Oxygen has an oxidation number of –2, so lead must be **+2** ***[1 mark]***.

ii) Sulfate has a charge of –2, so lead must have an oxidation number of **+2**. ***[1 mark]***

Page 39 — Redox Reactions

1 redox reaction ***[1 mark]***

2 D ***[1 mark]***

3 a) When metals and acids react, they produce hydrogen and a salt.
$Fe_{(s)} + H_2SO_{4(aq)} \rightarrow FeSO_{4(aq)} + H_{2(g)}$ ***[1 mark]***

b) Hydrogen has been reduced from oxidation number +1 to 0.
Hydrogen is the oxidising agent.
Iron has been oxidised from oxidation number 0 to +2.
Iron is the reducing agent ***[1 mark]***.

4 At the start of the reaction, Al has an oxidation number of 0.
In AlI_3, each I ion has an oxidation number of –1. Therefore, Al has an oxidation number of +3 (since (–1 × 3) + 3 = 0).
Al has lost electrons, so it has been oxidised ***[1 mark]***.

Module 2: Section 2 — Electrons, Bonding & Structure

Page 41 — Electronic Structure

1 a) K atom: $1s^2\ 2s^2\ 2p^6\ 3s^2\ 3p^6\ 4s^1$ ***[1 mark]***.
K^+ ion: $1s^2\ 2s^2\ 2p^6\ 3s^2\ 3p^6$ ***[1 mark]***.

b) O^{2-} ion: 1s [↑↓] 2s [↑↓] 2p [↑↓][↑↓][↑↓] ***[1 mark]***.

2 a) Germanium ($1s^2\ 2s^2\ 2p^6\ 3s^2\ 3p^6\ 3d^{10}\ 4s^2\ 4p^2$) ***[1 mark]***.

b) Ar (atom) ***[1 mark]***, K^+ (positive ion) ***[1 mark]***, Cl^- (negative ion) ***[1 mark]***. You also could have suggested Ca^{2+}, S^{2-} or P^{3-}.

c) $1s^2\ 2s^2\ 2p^6$ ***[1 mark]***

3 a) $1s^22s^22p^63s^23p^2$ ***[1 mark]***

b) Two ***[1 mark]***

Page 43 — Ionic Bonding

1 a) Giant ionic lattice ***[1 mark]***

b) You'd expect it to have a high melting point ***[1 mark]***, because a lot of energy is required to overcome the strong electrostatic attraction between the positive and negative ions ***[1 mark]***.

2 a)

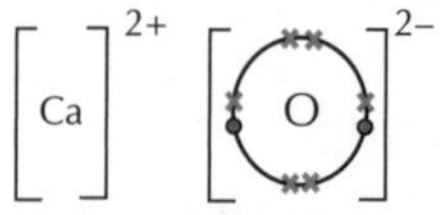

Ca^{2+} calcium ion O^{2-} oxide ion

[2 marks]

1 mark for correct electron arrangement, 1 mark for correct charges

b) In a solid, ions are held in place by strong ionic bonds ***[1 mark]***. When molten, the ions are mobile ***[1 mark]*** and so carry charge (and hence electricity) through the substance ***[1 mark]***.

Page 45 — Covalent Bonding

1 a) The electrostatic attraction between a shared pair of electrons and the nuclei of the bonded atoms. ***[1 mark]***

b)

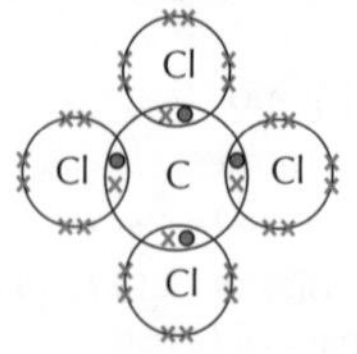

Your diagram should show the following —
- a completely correct electron arrangement ***[1 mark]***
- all 4 overlaps correct (one dot + one cross in each) ***[1 mark]***

2 a) Covalent bonding and dative covalent/coordinate bonding ***[1 mark]***

b) One atom donates a pair of/both the electrons to the bond ***[1 mark]***.

Answers

Page 47 — Shapes of Molecules

a) i) 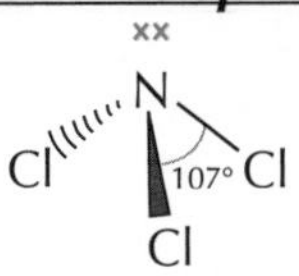

[1 mark]

shape: pyramidal ***[1 mark]***,
bond angle: 107° (accept between 106° and 108°) ***[1 mark]***.

ii) 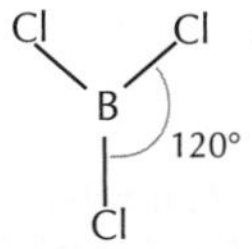

[1 mark]

shape: trigonal planar ***[1 mark]***
bond angle: 120° exactly ***[1 mark]***.

b) BCl_3 has three electron pairs only around B. ***[1 mark]***
NCl_3 has four electron pairs around N ***[1 mark]***, including one lone pair. ***[1 mark]***
Atom A: shape: trigonal planar, bond angle: 120° ***[1 mark]***
Atom B: shape: tetrahedral, bond angle: 109.5° ***[1 mark]***
Atom C: shape: non-linear/bent, bond angle: 104.5° ***[1 mark]***

Page 51 — Polarity and Intermolecular Forces

a) An atom's ability to attract the electron pair in a covalent bond ***[1 mark]***.

b) i) Br — Br ***[1 mark]***

ii) 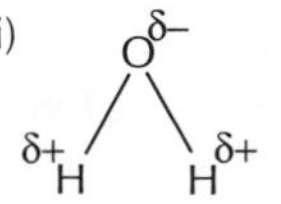

[1 mark]

iii) 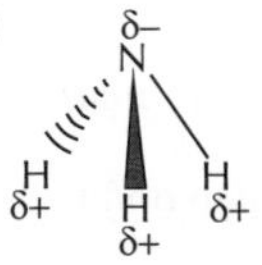

[1 mark]

a) Induced dipole-dipole OR London (dispersion) forces. ***[1 mark]***
Permanent dipole-dipole interactions/forces. ***[1 mark]***
Hydrogen bonding. ***[1 mark]***

b) i) Water contains hydrogen covalently bonded to oxygen, so it is able to form hydrogen bonds ***[1 mark]***. These hydrogen bonds are stronger than the other types of intermolecular forces, so more energy is needed to break them ***[1 mark]***.

ii) 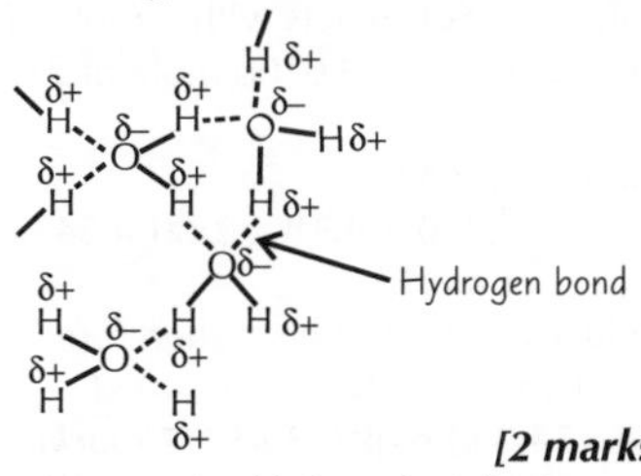

[2 marks]

Your diagram should show the following —

- Labelled hydrogen bonds between the water molecules.
- At least two hydrogen bonds between an oxygen atom and a hydrogen atom on adjacent molecules.

Module 3: Section 1 — The Periodic Table

Page 53 — The Periodic Table

B ***[1 mark]***
D ***[1 mark]***
The p-block ***[1 mark]***.
Aluminium atoms have one more proton than magnesium atoms ***[1 mark]***.

Page 56 — Ionisation Energies

1 a) Group 3 ***[1 mark]***
There are three electrons removed before the first big jump in energy.

b) The electrons are being removed from an increasingly positive ion ***[1 mark]*** so more energy is needed to remove an electron / the force of attraction that has to be broken is greater ***[1 mark]***.

c) When an electron is removed from a different shell there is a big increase in the energy required (since that shell is closer to the nucleus) ***[1 mark]***.

d) There are 3 shells (because there are 2 big jumps in energy) ***[1 mark]***.

2 ***5-6 marks:***
The answer correctly describes the general trend in the first ionisation energies across Period 3 and gives an explanation AND the exceptions to the trend are also described and explained.
The answer has a clear and logical structure. The information given is relevant and detailed.

3-4 marks:
The answer describes the general trend in the first ionisation energies across Period 3 with some explanation of the trend. Exceptions to the trend are referenced briefly. The answer has some structure. Most of the information given is relevant and there is some detail involved.

1-2 marks:
The answer describes the general trend in the first ionisation energies across Period 3 . Exceptions to the trend are not mentioned. The answer has no clear structure. The information given is basic and lacking in detail. It may not all be relevant.

0 marks:
No relevant information is given.

Here are some points your answer may include:
Generally the first ionisation energy increases across Period 3. The number of protons / positive charge of the nucleus increases, so the atomic radius decreases. Also, the number of electrons in the outer shell increases but there is no extra shielding. Both of these factors strengthen the attraction between the nucleus and the outer electrons. The first ionisation energy decreases slightly between magnesium and aluminium. This is because aluminium's outer electron is in a p orbital rather than an s orbital, so it is slightly further away from the nucleus (so it is less strongly attracted). The first ionisation energy also decreases slightly between phosphorous and sulfur. This is because sulfur's outer electron is being removed from an orbital containing two electrons. The (p orbital) repulsion between the electrons makes it easier to remove one of them.

Page 59 — Structure, Bonding and Properties

1 Mg has more delocalised electrons per atom ***[1 mark]*** and a smaller ionic radius ***[1 mark]***. So the electrostatic attraction between the metal ions and the delocalised electrons is stronger ***[1 mark]***.

2 a) Si has a giant covalent lattice structure ***[1 mark]*** consisting of lots of very strong covalent bonds ***[1 mark]***.

b) Sulfur (S_8) is a larger molecule than phosphorus (P_4) ***[1 mark]*** which results in stronger induced dipole-dipole forces of attraction between molecules ***[1 mark]***.

3 ***5-6 marks:***
The answer describes in detail the relative abilities of diamond, graphite and graphene to conduct electricity AND includes correct references to their structure and its impact on the availability of delocalised electrons. The answer has a clear and logical structure. The information given is relevant.

3-4 marks:
The answer describes in some detail the abilities of diamond, graphite and graphene to conduct electricity. Their structures are described AND delocalised electrons are identified. The answer has some structure and most of the information given is relevant.

Answers

1-2 marks:
The answer describes briefly the ability of diamond, graphite or graphene to conduct electricity. There is some link to their structure. The information given is basic and lacking in detail. It may not all be relevant.
0 marks:
No relevant information is given.
Here are some points your answer may include:
Diamond has all of its outer electrons in localised covalent bonds, so it is a poor electrical conductor. Graphite has delocalised electrons between the sheets which can flow, so it is a good electrical conductor. Graphene also has delocalised electrons which can flow. It is a better electrical conductor than graphite because it has no other layers to slow the electrons down.

Page 61 — Group 2 — The Alkaline Earth Metals

1 $CaCO_{3(s)} + 2HCl_{(aq)} \rightarrow CaCl_{2(aq)} + CO_{2\,(g)} + H_2O_{(l)}$ ***[1 mark]***
2 a) $2Ba_{(s)} + O_{2(g)} \rightarrow 2BaO_{(s)}$ ***[1 mark]***
b) From 0 to +2 ***[1 mark]***
c) Strongly alkaline / pH 12-13 ***[1 mark]***
3 a) Z ***[1 mark]***
b) Z has the largest radius ***[1 mark]*** so it will be furthest down the group / have the smallest ionisation energy ***[1 mark]***.

Page 63 — Group 7 — The Halogens

1 a) $I_2 + 2At^- \rightarrow 2I^- + At_2$ ***[1 mark]***
b) astatide ***[1 mark]***
2 A ***[1 mark]***
3 C ***[1 mark]***

Page 65 — Disproportionation and Water Treatment

1 a) $2OH^- + Br_2 \rightarrow OBr^- + Br^- + H_2O$ ***[1 mark]***
b) A disproportionation reaction ***[1 mark]***.
2 a) $2I^- + ClO^- + H_2O \rightarrow I_2 + Cl^- + 2OH^-$ ***[1 mark]***
b) Iodine: −1 to 0 — oxidation
Chlorine: +1 to −1 — reduction ***[1 mark]***

Page 67 — Tests for Ions

1 B ***[1 mark]***
2 ***5-6 marks:***
The answer describes all of the tests and provides observations to correctly identify each compound. The answer has a clear and logical structure. The information given is relevant and detailed.
3-4 marks:
The answer describes most of the tests with some detail and provides observations to correctly identify each compound. The answer has some structure. Most of the information given is relevant and there is some detail involved.
1-2 marks:
The answer describes some of the tests but lacks description of any observations. The answer has no clear structure. The information given is basic and lacking in detail. It may not all be relevant.
0 marks:
No relevant information is given.
Here are some points your answer may include:
Add dilute hydrochloric acid to a sample of each solution to identify the carbonates. Two solutions should produce a gas/ CO_2 which turns limewater cloudy. Add sodium hydroxide to samples of these two solutions, warm them and test for ammonia with damp red litmus paper. One solution should turn the litmus paper blue — this is ammonium carbonate, and the other solution is calcium carbonate. Add barium chloride solution to each of the remaining samples to identify sodium sulfate — it should form a white precipitate. Add silver nitrate solution to identify magnesium chloride — it should form a white precipitate.

Module 3: Section 2 — Physical Chemistry

Page 69 — Enthalpy Changes

1

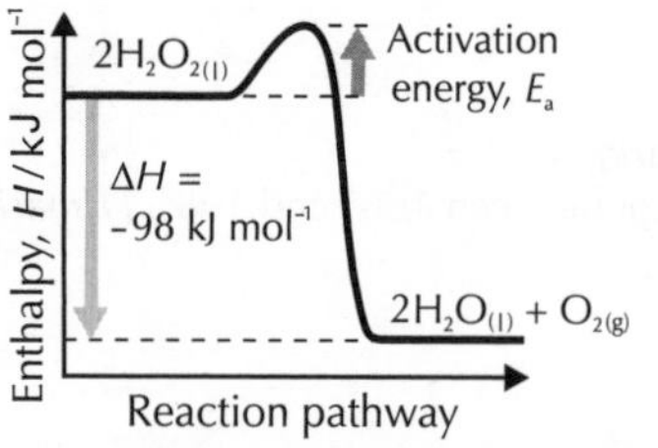

[1 mark for having reactants lower in energy than products. 1 mark for labelling activation energy correctly. 1 mark for labelling ΔH correctly, with arrow pointing downwards.]
For an exothermic reaction, the ΔH arrow points downwards, but for an endothermic reaction it points upwards. The activation energy arrow always points upwards though.

2 a) $CH_3OH_{(l)} + 1\frac{1}{2}O_{2(g)} \rightarrow CO_{2(g)} + 2H_2O_{(l)}$ ***[1 mark]***
Make sure that only 1 mole of CH_3OH is combusted, as it says in the definition for $\Delta_c H^\circ$.
b) $C_{(s)} + 2H_{2(g)} + \frac{1}{2}O_{2(g)} \rightarrow CH_3OH_{(l)}$ ***[1 mark]***
c) Only 1 mole of C_3H_8 should be shown according to the definition of $\Delta_c H^\circ$ ***[1 mark]***.
You really need to know the definitions of the standard enthalpy changes off by heart. There are loads of nit-picky little details they could ask you questions about.

3 a) $C_{(s)} + O_{2(g)} \rightarrow CO_{2(g)}$ ***[1 mark]***
b) It has the same value because it is the same reaction ***[1 mark]***.
c) 1 tonne = 1 000 000 g
1 mole of carbon is 12.0 g
so 1 tonne is 1 000 000 ÷ 12.0 = 83 333 moles ***[1 mark]***
1 mole releases 393.5 kJ
so 1 tonne will release 83 333 × 393.5 = **32 800 000 kJ** (3 s.f.) ***[1 mark]***
The final answer is rounded to 3 significant figures because the number with the fewest significant figures in the whole calculation is 12.0.

Page 71 — More on Enthalpy Changes

1 No. of moles of $CuSO_4$ = (0.200 × 50.0) ÷ 1000 = 0.0100 mole ***[1 mark]***
From the equation, 1 mole of $CuSO_4$ reacts with 1 mole of Zn.
So, 0.0100 mole of $CuSO_4$ reacts with 0.0100 mole of Zn ***[1 mark]***.
Heat produced by reaction $= mc\Delta T$
$= 50.0 \times 4.18 \times 2.60 = 543.4$ J ***[1 mark]***
0.0100 mole of zinc produces 543.4 J of heat, therefore 1 mole of zinc produces 543.4 ÷ 0.0100 = 54 340 J = 54.340 kJ
So the enthalpy change is **−54.3 kJ mol⁻¹** (3 s.f.) ***[1 mark]***
You need the minus sign because it's exothermic.

2 a) A chemical reaction always involves bond breaking which needs energy / is endothermic and bond making which releases energy / is exothermic ***[1 mark]***. Whether the reaction is exothermic or endothermic depends on whether more energy is used to break bonds or released by forming new bonds over the whole reaction ***[1 mark]***.
b) $q = mc\Delta T$
m = 1.000 kg = 1000 g
no. of moles carbon = m ÷ M_r = 6.000 ÷ 12.0 = 0.5000 mole ***[1 mark]***
So q = 0.5000 × 393.5 = 196.75 kJ = 196 750 J ***[1 mark]***
So 196 750 = 1000 × 4.18 × ΔT
ΔT = 196 750 ÷ (1000 × 4.18) = **47.1 K** (3 s.f.) ***[1 mark]***

Answers

Page 73 — Enthalpy Calculations

1 $\Delta_r H^{\circ}$ = sum of $\Delta_f H^{\circ}$(products) – sum of $\Delta_f H^{\circ}$(reactants) ***[1 mark]***
$\Delta_r H^{\circ}$ = [0 + (3 × –602)] – [–1676 + 0]
$\Delta_r H^{\circ}$ = **–130 kJ mol^{-1}** ***[1 mark]***
Don't forget the units. It's a daft way to lose marks.

2 $\Delta_f H^{\circ}$ = $\Delta_c H^{\circ}$(glucose) – 2 × $\Delta_c H^{\circ}$(ethanol) ***[1 mark]***
$\Delta_f H^{\circ}$ = [–2820] – [(2 × –1367)]
$\Delta_f H^{\circ}$ = **–86 kJ mol^{-1}** ***[1 mark]***

3 $\Delta_f H^{\circ}$ = sum of $\Delta_c H^{\circ}$(reactants) – $\Delta_c H^{\circ}$(propane) ***[1 mark]***
$\Delta_f H^{\circ}$ = [(3 × –394) + (4 × –286)] – [–2220]
$\Delta_f H^{\circ}$ = **–106 kJ mol^{-1}** ***[1 mark]***

4 Total energy required to break bonds = (4 × 435) + (2 × 498) = 2736 kJ
Energy released when bonds form = (2 × 805) + (4 × 464) = 3466 kJ ***[1 mark]***
Net energy change = 2736 + (–3466) = **–730 kJ mol^{-1}** ***[1 mark]***

Page 75 — Reaction Rates

1 Increasing the pressure will increase the rate of reaction ***[1 mark]*** because the molecules will be closer together, so they will collide more frequently and therefore are more likely to react ***[1 mark]***.

2 a) X ***[1 mark]***
The X curve shows the same total number of molecules as the 25 °C curve, but more of them have lower energy.

b) The shape of the curve shows fewer molecules have the required activation energy ***[1 mark]***.

Page 77 — Catalysts

1 a)
$$2SO_{2(g)} + O_{2(g)} \xrightarrow{V_2O_{5(s)}} 2SO_{3(g)}$$
[1 mark]
You could also write the reaction as $SO_{2(g)} + \frac{1}{2}O_{2(g)} \longrightarrow SO_{2(g)}$.

b) A ***[1 mark]***
A catalyst only lowers activation energy. It doesn't affect the enthalpy change.

c) The vanadium(V) oxide catalyst is heterogenous because it's in a different physical state to the reactants ***[1 mark]***.

Page 79 — Calculating Reaction Rates

1 a) E.g.

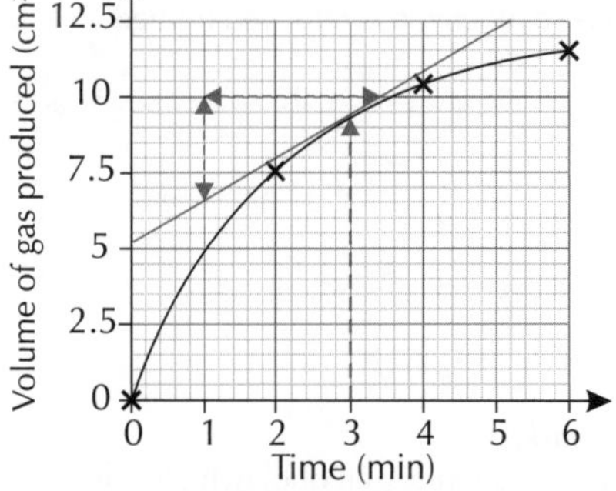

[1 mark for tangent drawn at 3 mins.]
rate of reaction = gradient of tangent at 3 mins
gradient = change in y ÷ change in x
e.g. = (10.00 – 6.50) ÷ (3.40 – 1.00)
= **1.46 (± 0.3) cm^3 min^{-1}**
[1 mark for answer within margin of error. 1 mark for units.]
Different people will draw slightly different tangents and pick different spots on the tangent so there's a margin of error in this answer.
1.45 (± 0.3) cm^3 min^{-1} means any answer between 1.15 cm^3 min^{-1} and 1.75 cm^3 min^{-1} is worth the mark.

b) E.g. the volume of gas produced could be measured using a gas syringe ***[1 mark]***.

c) One of the reactants is a gas ***[1 mark]***.

Page 81 — Dynamic Equilibrium

1 a) i) There's no change as there's the same number of molecules/moles on each side of the equation ***[1 mark]***.

ii) Reducing temperature removes heat. The equilibrium shifts in the exothermic direction to release heat, so the position of equilibrium shifts left ***[1 mark]***.

iii) Removing nitrogen monoxide reduces its concentration. The equilibrium position shifts right to try and increase the nitrogen monoxide concentration again ***[1 mark]***.

b) No effect ***[1 mark]***.
Catalysts don't affect the equilibrium position.
They just help the reaction to get there sooner.

2 For an exothermic reaction, a low temperature means a high yield ***[1 mark]***. But a low temperature also means a slow reaction rate, so moderate temperatures are chosen as a compromise ***[1 mark]***.

Page 83 — The Equilibrium Constant

1 a) $K_c = [NH_3]^2 \div ([N_2] \times [H_2]^3)$ ***[1 mark]***
$= (1.190)^2 \div ((0.890) \times (1.412)^3)$
= **0.565 mol^{-2} dm^6** ***[1 mark]***
To work out the units...
$(\text{mol dm}^{-3})^2 \div (\text{mol dm}^{-3})^4$
$= (\text{mol}^2\ \text{dm}^{-6}) \div (\text{mol}^4\ \text{dm}^{-12})$
$= \text{mol}^{-2}\ \text{dm}^6$ (but you don't need to give units with this answer to get the marks)

b) The concentration of NH_3 would increase ***[1 mark]***. Exothermic reactions speed up when the temperature in decreased ***[1 mark]***.

2 E.g. equal amounts of the equilibrium mixture should be added to three test tubes. The first test tube is a control and should be orangey/yellow in colour. Add some chromate solution to test tube 2 and note any colour change. Add some dichromate solution to test tube 3 and note any colour change ***[1 mark for description of experiment]***. Test tube 2 should turn more orange as the forward reaction speeds up to produce more dichromate ions, pushing equilibrium to the right ***[1 mark]***. Test tube 3 should turn more yellow as the reverse reaction speeds up to produce more chromate ions, pushing equilibrium to the left ***[1 mark]***.

Module 4: Section 1 — Basic Concepts and Hydrocarbons

Page 87 — Organic Chemistry — The Basics

1 a)

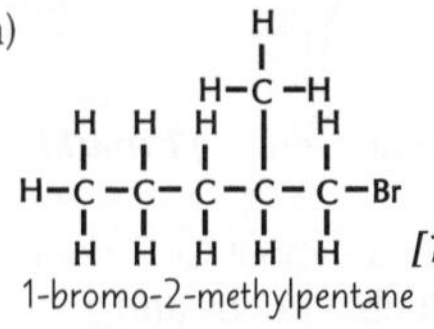

[1 mark]
1-bromo-2-methylpentane

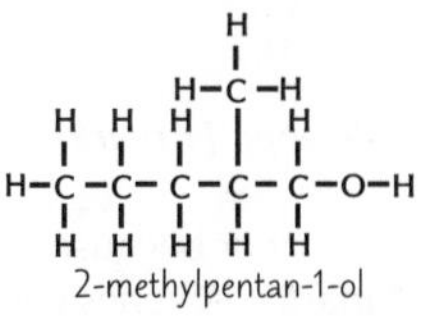

[1 mark]
2-methylpentan-1-ol

b) –OH (hydroxyl) ***[1 mark]***.
It could be attached to any of the five carbons OR because the position of the –OH group affects its chemistry ***[1 mark]***.

2 a) 4-chloro-pentanoic acid ***[1 mark]***

b) methylbutane ***[1 mark]***
There's only actually one type of methylbutane. You can't have 1-methylbutane — it'd be exactly the same as pentane.

c) Dimethylpropane ***[1 mark]***
There's only one type of dimethylpropane — 1,1-dimethylpropane and 1,2-dimethylpropane are actually methylbutane.

3 a) B ***[1 mark]***

b) The same molecular formula ***[1 mark]*** but different arrangements of the carbon skeleton ***[1 mark]***.

Answers

Page 89 — Alkanes

1 a) One with no double bonds OR all the carbon-carbon bonds are single bonds ***[1 mark]***. It contains only hydrogen and carbon atoms ***[1 mark]***.

b) $C_2H_{6(g)} + 3½O_{2(g)} \rightarrow 2CO_{2(g)} + 3H_2O_{(g)}$ ***[2 marks]***
1 mark for correct symbols, 1 mark for balancing

2 a) Nonane will have a higher boiling point than 2,2,3,3-tetramethylpentane ***[1 mark]*** because the molecules of branched-chain alkanes like 2,2,3,3-tetramethylpentane are less closely packed together than their straight-chain isomers, so they have fewer induced dipole-dipole interactions holding them together ***[1 mark]***.

b) i) $C_9H_{20} + 9½O_2 \rightarrow 9CO + 10H_2O$ ***[1 mark]***
ii) Carbon monoxide binds to haemoglobin in the blood in preference to oxygen ***[1 mark]***, so less oxygen can be carried around the body, leading to oxygen deprivation ***[1 mark]***.

Page 91 — Reactions of Alkanes

1 a) Free radical substitution. ***[1 mark]***

b) $CH_4 + Br_2 \xrightarrow{U.V.} CH_3Br + HBr$ ***[1 mark]***

c) $Br\bullet + CH_4 \rightarrow HBr + \bullet CH_3$ ***[1 mark]***
$\bullet CH_3 + Br_2 \rightarrow CH_3Br + Br\bullet$ ***[1 mark]***

d) i) Two methyl radicals bond together to form an ethane molecule. ***[1 mark]***
ii) Termination step ***[1 mark]***
iii) $\bullet CH_3 + \bullet CH_3 \rightarrow CH_3CH_3$ ***[1 mark]***

e) Tetrabromomethane ***[1 mark]***

Page 92 — Alkenes

1 a) Ethane is an alkane, so has a single C–C bond made up of a σ bond ***[1 mark]***. Ethene is an alkene, so has a C=C double bond made up of a σ bond and a π bond ***[1 mark]***.

b) Ethene will be more reactive than ethane because the double bond has a high electron density / the π bond sticks out above and below the plane of the molecule, so it attracts electrophiles ***[1 mark]*** and because the π bond has a low bond enthalpy so is more easily broken than the C–C σ bond in ethane ***[1 mark]***.

Page 95 — Stereoisomerism

1 a)

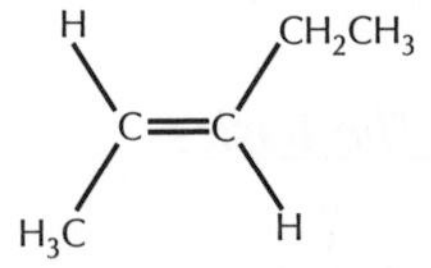

E-pent-2-ene ***[1 mark]***

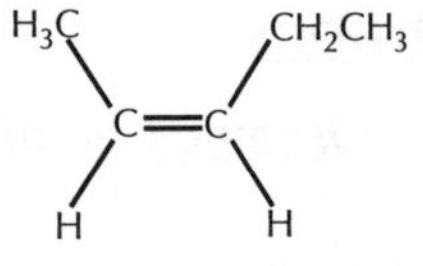

Z-pent-2-ene ***[1 mark]***

b) E/Z isomers occur because atoms can't rotate about C=C double bonds ***[1 mark]***. Alkenes contain C=C double bonds and alkanes don't, so alkenes can form E/Z isomers and alkanes can't ***[1 mark]***.

2 B ***[1 mark]***

Page 97 — Reactions of Alkenes

1 a) Shake the alkene with bromine water ***[1 mark]***, and the solution goes colourless if a double bond is present ***[1 mark]***.

b) Electrophilic addition ***[1 mark]***.

c)

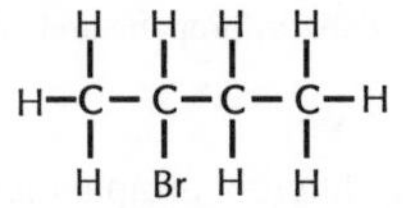

2-bromobutane ***[1 mark]***

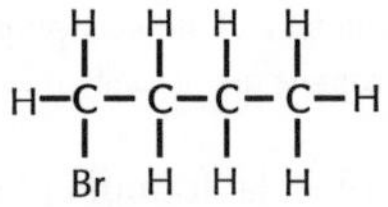

1-bromobutane ***[1 mark]***

The major product will be 2-bromobutane ***[1 mark]***.

Page 99 — Polymers

1 a) Energy can be used to generate electricity ***[1 mark]***

b) Toxic gases produced ***[1 mark]***.

2 Used as an organic feedstock to produce plastics and other organic chemicals ***[1 mark]*** or melted and remoulded ***[1 mark]***.

3

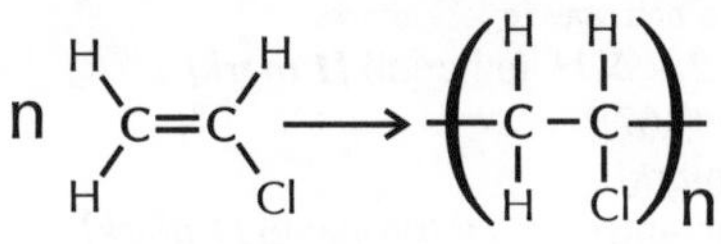

[1 mark] ***[1 mark]***

Module 4: Section 2 — Alcohols, Haloalkanes & Analysis

Page 101 — Alcohols

1 a) primary: e.g.

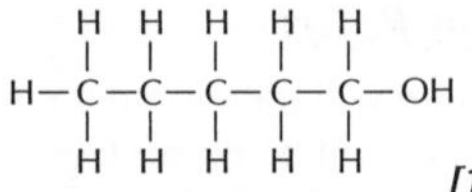

pentan-1-ol ***[1 mark]***

secondary: e.g

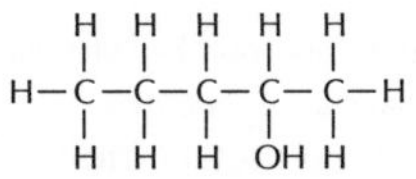

pentan-2-ol ***[1 mark]***

tertiary:

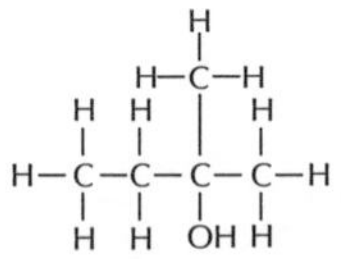

2-methylbutan-2-ol ***[1 mark]***

b) React ethanol with sodium bromide (NaBr) with a concentrated sulfuric acid catalyst ***[1 mark]***.

2 a) Elimination reaction OR dehydration reaction ***[1 mark]***.

b) C ***[1 mark]***

Page 103 — Oxidation of Alcohols

1 a) i) Propanoic acid (CH_3CH_2COOH) ***[1 mark]***
ii) $CH_3CH_2CH_2OH + [O] \rightarrow CH_3CH_2CHO + H_2O$ ***[1 mark]***
$CH_3CH_2CHO + [O] \rightarrow CH_3CH_2COOH$ ***[1 mark]***
iii) Distillation. This is so aldehyde is removed immediately as it forms ***[1 mark]***.
If you don't get the aldehyde out quick-smart, it'll be a carboxylic acid before you know it.

b) i)

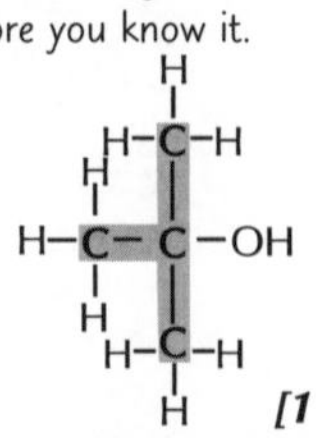

[1 mark]

ii) 2-methylpropan-2-ol is a tertiary alcohol (which is more stable) ***[1 mark]***.

2 D ***[1 mark]***

3 React 2-methylpropan-1-ol ($CH_3CH(CH_3)CH_2OH$) ***[1 mark]*** with a controlled amount of acidified potassium dichromate(VI) and heat gently in distillation apparatus to distil off the aldehyde ***[1 mark]***.

Answers

Page 105 — Haloalkanes

1 a) 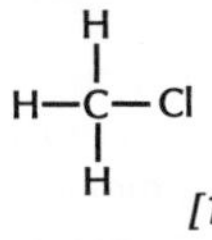 *[1 mark]*

b) 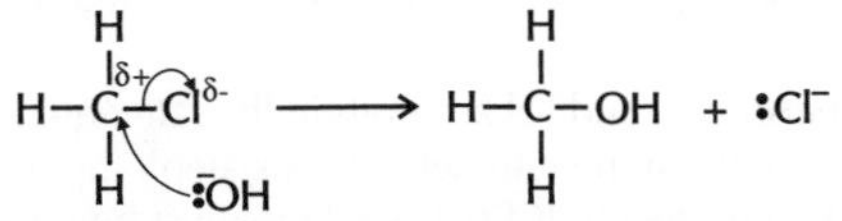

Your diagram should show:
- Curly arrow from lone pair on OH^- to δ+ on carbon ***[1 mark]***.
- Curly arrow and dipole on C–Cl bond ***[1 mark]***.
- Correct products ***[1 mark]***.

c) A white precipitate ***[1 mark]***.

2 A ***[1 mark]***

Page 107 — Haloalkanes and the Environment

1 a) Any two from: stable/volatile/non-flammable/non-toxic ***[1 mark]***.

b) $CFCl_{3(g)} \xrightarrow{U.V.} \cdot CFCl_{2(g)} + Cl\cdot_{(g)}$ ***[1 mark]***

$Cl\cdot_{(g)} + O_{3(g)} \rightarrow O_{2(g)} + ClO\cdot_{(g)}$ and

$ClO\cdot_{(g)} + O_{(g)} \rightarrow O_{2(g)} + Cl\cdot_{(g)}$ ***[1 mark]***

Overall reaction: $O_{3(g)} + O_{(g)} \rightarrow 2O_{2(g)}$ ***[1 mark]***

c) $NO\cdot$ free radicals ***[1 mark]***

2 $NO\cdot + O_3 \rightarrow NO_2 + O_2$ ***[1 mark]***

$NO_2 + O \rightarrow NO\cdot + O_2$ ***[1 mark]***

Page 108 — The Greenhouse Effect & Global Warming

1 a) Any two from: increased use of fossil fuels/increased deforestation/increased food production ***[2 marks]***.

b) Scientists collected data which shows that the Earth's average temperature has dramatically increased in recent years ***[1 mark]***.

c) Creating policies to use more renewable energy sources, such as wind and solar farms ***[1 mark]***.

Page 111 — Analytical Techniques

1 a) A: O–H group in a carboxylic acid ***[1 mark]***.
B: C=O as in an aldehyde, ketone, carboxylic acid, ester or acid anhydride ***[1 mark]***.

b) From the percentage composition data, the ratio of elements in the compound, C:H:O is 3:6:2 ***[1 mark]*** so the empirical formula is $C_3H_6O_2$ ***[1 mark]***. The spectrum suggests that the compound is a carboxylic acid, so it must be propanoic acid (CH_3CH_2COOH) ***[1 mark]***.

2 a) 44 ***[1 mark]***

b) X has a mass of 15. It is probably a methyl group/CH_3^+ ***[1 mark]***.
Y has a mass of 29. It is probably an ethyl group/$C_2H_5^+$ ***[1 mark]***.

c) 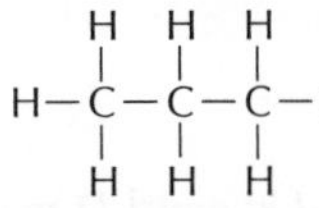 ***[1 mark]***

d) If the compound was an alcohol, you would expect a peak with m/z ratio of 17, caused by the OH fragment ***[1 mark]***.

Page 113 — Organic Synthesis — Practical Skills

1 a) i) Reflux is continuous boiling/evaporation and condensation ***[1 mark]***. It's done to prevent loss of volatile liquids while heating ***[1 mark]***.

ii) Unreacted hexan-1-ol ***[1 mark]***

iii) Pour the reaction mixture into a separating funnel and add water ***[1 mark]***. Shake the funnel and allow the layers to settle. The lower layer is the denser aqueous layer and contains water soluble impurities ***[1 mark]***. This can be run off, so only the organic layer, containing the product and other organic impurities, remains ***[1 mark]***.

b) i) The alkene product may dehydrate again to form a diene ***[1 mark]***.

ii) Carry out the experiment in a distillation apparatus ***[1 mark]*** so the singly dehydrated product is removed immediately from the reaction mixture and doesn't react a second time ***[1 mark]***.

Page 115 — Organic Synthesis — Synthetic Routes

1 a) 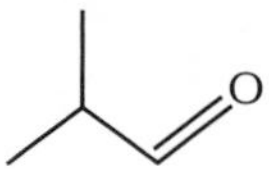 ***[1 mark]***

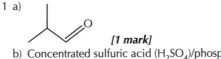

b) Concentrated sulfuric acid (H_2SO_4)/phosphoric acid (H_3PO_4) ***[1 mark]***, heat ***[1 mark]***.

c) i) 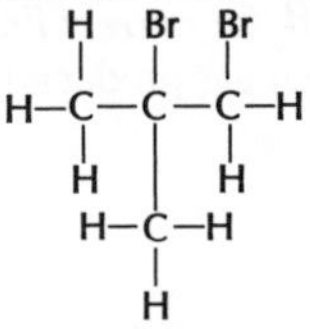 ***[1 mark]***

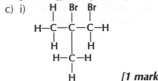

ii) The mixture would turn from orange/brown to colourless ***[1 mark]***.

2 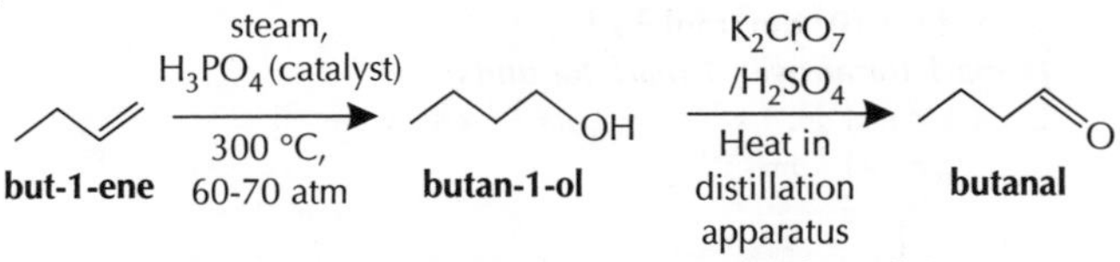

[3 marks — 2 marks for correct reagents and conditions, 1 mark for intermediate butan-1-ol product.]

Answers

Module 5: Section 1 — Rates, Equilibrium & pH

Page 117 — Rates of Reaction

1 a) e.g. monitoring pH / monitoring conductivity ***[1 mark]***.

b) i) Initial rate is the gradient when time
$= \frac{\text{change in } y}{\text{change in } x} = \frac{0.25}{10} =$ **0.025 mol dm^{-3} s^{-1}**
(± 0.0050 mol dm^{-3} s^{-1})
[1 mark for correct value, 1 mark for correct units]

ii) After 40 seconds, gradient $= \frac{\text{change in } y}{\text{change in } x} = \frac{0.14}{66}$
0.0020 mol dm^{-3} s^{-1} (± 0.0005 mol dm^{-3} s^{-1})
[1 mark for correct value, 1 mark for correct units]

Page 119 — Reaction Orders

1 a) 1st order ***[1 mark]***

b)

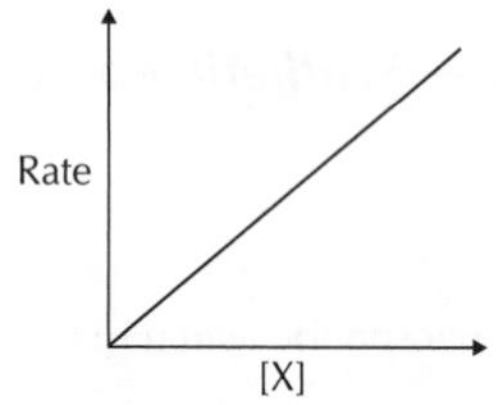

[1 mark for correctly labelled axes, 1 mark for correct line]

c) You could measure the volume of hydrogen gas produced in a unit of time ***[1 mark]***.

2 C ***[1 mark]***

Page 121 — The Rate Constant

1 a) Rate = k[$NO_{(g)}$]^2 [$H_{2(g)}$] ***[1 mark]***

b) 0.00267 = k × (0.00400)^2 × 0.00200
k = **8.34 × 10^4 dm^6 mol^{-2} s^{-1}**
[1 mark for answer, 1 mark for units].
Units: k = mol dm^{-3} s^{-1} ÷ [(mol dm^{-3})^2 × (mol dm^{-3})]
= mol^{-2} dm^6 s^{-1}.

2 a)

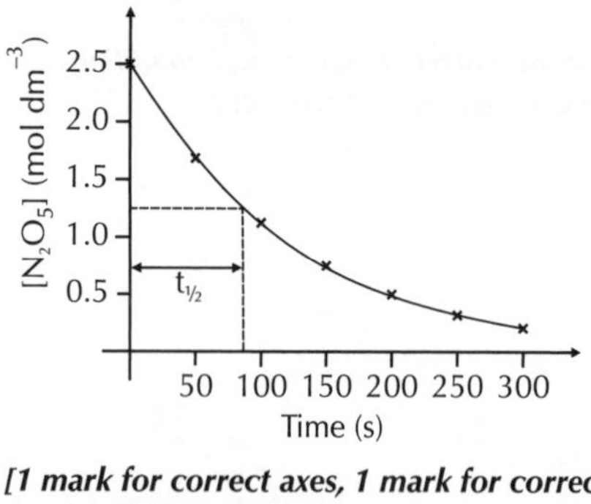

[1 mark for correct axes, 1 mark for correctly plotted points, 1 mark for best-fit curve]

b) From graph, half-life = 85 s ***[1 mark, allow 85 ± 2]***
$k = \frac{\ln 2}{t_{1/2}} = \frac{\ln 2}{85\text{ s}} =$ **8.2 × 10^{-3} s^{-1}** ***[1 mark, allow 8.2 ± 0.2 × 10^{-3}]***

3 The reaction is first order with respect to CH_3COOCH_3, so rate = k[CH_3COOH], and the gradient of the graph = k ***[1 mark]***.

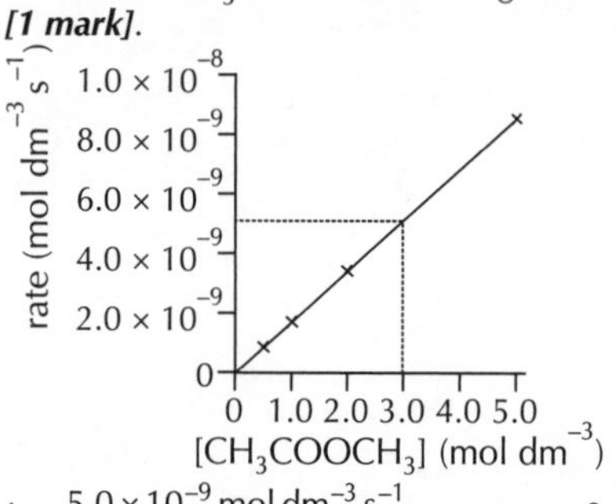

$k = \frac{5.0 \times 10^{-9}\text{ mol dm}^{-3}\text{ s}^{-1}}{3.0\text{ mol dm}^{-3}} =$ **1.7 × 10^{-9} s^{-1}** ***[1 mark]***

Page 123 — The Rate-Determining Step

1 a) rate = k[H_2][ICl] ***[1 mark]***

b) i) If the molecule is in the rate equation, it must be in the rate-determining step ***[1 mark]***. The reaction is first order with respect to both H_2 and ICl. So there will be one molecule of H_2 and one molecule of ICl in the rate determining step ***[1 mark]***.

ii) Incorrect ***[1 mark]***. H_2 and ICl are both in the rate equation, so they must both be in the rate-determining step / the order of the reaction with respect to ICl is 1, so there must be only one molecule of ICl in the rate-determining step ***[1 mark]***.

2 a) The rate equation is first order with respect to HBr and O_2 so only 1 molecule of HBr (and O_2) is involved in the rate-determining step ***[1 mark]***. There must be more steps as 4 molecules of HBr are in the equation ***[1 mark]***.

b) HBr + O_2 → $HBrO_2$ (rate-determining step) ***[1 mark]***
HBr + $HBrO_2$ → 2HBrO ***[1 mark]***
HBr + HBrO → H_2O + Br_2 ***[1 mark]***
HBr + HBrO → H_2O + Br_2 ***[1 mark]***
Part b) is pretty tricky — you need to do a fair bit of detective work and some trial and error. Make sure you use all of the clues in the question...

Page 125 — The Arrhenius Equation

1 a)

T (K)	*k*	1/T (K^{-1})	ln *k*
305	0.181	0.00328	–1.71
313	0.468	**0.00319**	**–0.759**
323	1.34	**0.00310**	**0.293**
333	3.29	0.00300	1.19
344	10.1	**0.00291**	**2.31**
353	22.7	0.00283	3.12

[1 mark for all 3 1/T values, 1 mark for all 3 ln k values]

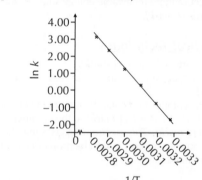

b)

[1 mark for correct axes, 1 mark for correctly plotted points, 1 mark for line of best fit]

c) Gradient = –10 750 ± 250 ***[1 mark]***
$\frac{-E_a}{R} = -10\,750$
E_a = 10 750 × 8.31 = **89 300 J mol^{-1}** OR **89.3 kJ mol^{-1}** ***[1 mark]***

d) By substituting values into the expression $\ln k = \frac{-E_a}{RT} + \ln A$
–0.76 = –10 750 × 0.00319 + ln A
ln A = 33.5 ± 0.1
A = e$^{33.5}$ = **3.54 × 10^{14}** ***[1 mark]***
You can't use the graph to find the value of ln A (by extrapolation to find the y-intercept) because the x axis has a broken scale — it isn't all shown.

Answers

Page 127 — The Equilibrium Constant

PQs 1 $K_c = \frac{[NO_2]^2}{[N_2][O_2]}$

2 units = $\frac{(\text{mol dm}^{-3})^2}{\text{mol dm}^{-3} \times \text{mol dm}^{-3}}$ = no units

moles of N_2O_4 = mass ÷ M_r = 23.0 ÷ 92.0 = 0.250 mol
concentration N_2O_4 = moles ÷ volume = 0.250 ÷ 6.00
= 0.0417 mol dm^{-3} ***[1 mark]***.
moles NO_2 = mass ÷ M_r = 0.389 ÷ 46 = 8.46 × 10^{-3} mol
concentration NO_2 = moles ÷ volume = 8.46 × 10^{-3} ÷ 6.00
= 1.41 × 10^{-3} mol dm^{-3} ***[1 mark]***.

$K_c = \frac{[NO_2]^2}{[N_2O_4]} = \frac{(1.41 \times 10^{-3})^2}{0.0417}$ = **4.77 × 10^{-5}** ***[1 mark]***

units = $\frac{(\text{mol dm}^{-3})^{\not 2}}{(\not{\text{mol dm}^{-3}})}$ = **mol dm^{-3}** ***[1 mark]***

1 a) $K_c = \frac{[[Co(NH_3)_6]^{2+}]}{[[Co(H_2O)_6]^{2+}][NH_3]^6}$ ***[1 mark]***

b) $K_c = \frac{(2.19)}{(0.541) \times (0.234)^6}$ = **2.47 × 10^4** ***[1 mark]***

units = $\frac{(\not{\text{mol dm}^{-3}})}{(\not{\text{mol dm}^{-3}}) \times (\text{mol dm}^{-3})^6}$ = **mol^{-6} dm^{18}** ***[1 mark]***

Page 129 — Equilibrium Concentrations

PQs 1 $K_c = \frac{[C]}{[A][B]}$ so $[C] = K_c[A][B]$

2 [C] = 7.35 × 0.152 × 0.586 = **0.655 mol^{-1} dm^3**

1 a) moles = mass ÷ M_r = 42.5 ÷ 46 = **0.924 mol** ***[1 mark]***

b) Initial concentration NO_2 = moles ÷ volume = 0.924 ÷ 22.8
= 0.0405 mol dm^{-3}
So the component concentrations are as follows:

Equilibrium component	$NO_{2(g)}$	$NO_{(g)}$	$O_{2(g)}$
Initial concentration (mol dm^{-3})	0.0405	0	0
Equilibrium concentration (mol dm^{-3})	0.0405 – 2x	2x	x

[1 mark]

$K_c = \frac{[NO]^2[O_2]}{[NO_2]^2} = \frac{(2x)^2(x)}{(0.0405-2x)^2}$ ***[1 mark]***

c) moles of O_2 = mass ÷ M_r = 14.1 ÷ 32 = 0.441 mol ***[1 mark]***
concentration O_2 = moles ÷ volume = 0.441 ÷ 22.8
= 0.0193 mol dm^{-3}.
So x = 0.0193 mol dm^{-3} ***[1 mark]***

$K_c = \frac{(2x)^2(x)}{(0.0405-2x)^2} = \frac{(2 \times 0.0193)^2 \times (0.0193)}{(0.0405-(2 \times 0.0193))^2}$ = **7.97 mol dm^{-3}**

[1 mark]

(Units = (mol dm^{-3})^2 × (mol dm^{-3}) ÷ (mol dm^{-3})^2 = mol dm^{-3})

2 a) $K_c = \frac{[CrO_4^{2-}]^2[H^+]^2}{[Cr_2O_7^{2-}][H_2O]}$ ***[1 mark]***

b) i) Since there's 0.0300 moles of $Cr_2O_7^{2-}$ at equilibrium, from the equation there must also be 0.0300 moles of H_2O.
$[H_2O]$ = 0.0300 ÷ 0.100 = **0.300 mol dm^{-3}** ***[1 mark]***

ii) 0.0700 moles of $Cr_2O_7^{2-}$ must have reacted, which will give 0.140 moles of CrO_4^{2-}.
$[CrO_4^{2-}]$ = 0.140 ÷ 0.100 = **1.40 mol dm^{-3}** ***[1 mark]***

iii) $[CrO_4^{2-}]$ = $[H^+]$ = 0.140 ÷ 0.100 = **1.40 mol dm^{-3}** ***[1 mark]***
You can see from molar ratios in the equation that $Cr_2O_7^{2-}$ reacts to produce double the amount of CrO_4^{2-} and H^+.

c) Concentration of $Cr_2O_7^{2-}$ = 0.0300 ÷ 0.100 = 0.300 mol dm^{-3}

$K_c = \frac{1.4^2 \times 1.4^2}{0.3 \times 0.3}$ = **42.7 mol^2 dm^{-6}**

[1 mark for correct numerical value, 1 mark for correct units]

Page 131 — Gas Equilibria

1 a) $K_p = \frac{p(SO_2)p(Cl_2)}{p(SO_2Cl_2)}$ ***[1 mark]***

b) Cl_2 and SO_2 are produced in equal amounts so
$p(Cl_2) = p(SO_2)$ = 60.2 kPa ***[1 mark]***
Total pressure = $p(SO_2Cl_2) + p(Cl_2) + p(SO_2)$ so
$p(SO_2Cl_2)$ = 141 – 60.2 – 60.2 = **20.6 kPa** ***[1 mark]***

c) $K_p = \frac{60.2\,\text{kPa} \times 60.2\,\text{kPa}}{20.6\,\text{kPa}}$ = 176 ***[1 mark]*** kPa ***[1 mark]***
(Units = (kPa × kPa)/ kPa = kPa)

2 a) $p(O_2)$ = ½ × 36 = 18 kPa ***[1 mark]***

b) $p(NO_2)$ = total pressure – $p(NO)$ – $p(O_2)$
= 99 – 36 – 18 = **45 kPa** ***[1 mark]***

c) $K_p = \frac{p(NO_2)^2}{p(NO)^2 p(O_2)}$ ***[1 mark]***

$= \frac{(45\,\text{kPa})^2}{(36\,\text{kPa})^2 \times (18\,\text{kPa})}$ = **0.087 kPa^{-1}** ***[1 mark]***

(Units = kPa^2/(kPa^2 × kPa) = kPa^{-1})

Page 133 — More on Equilibrium Constants

1 a) T_2 is lower than T_1 ***[1 mark]***.
A decrease in temperature shifts the position of equilibrium in the exothermic direction, producing more product ***[1 mark]***.
More product means K_c increases ***[1 mark]***.
A negative ΔH means the forward reaction is exothermic — it gives out heat.

b) The yield of SO_3 increases ***[1 mark]***. (A decrease in volume means an increase in pressure.) This shifts the equilibrium position to the right where there are fewer moles of gas. K_c is unchanged ***[1 mark]***.

2 a) $K_p = \frac{p(CO)p(H_2)^3}{p(CH_4)p(H_2O)}$ ***[1 mark]***

b) A ***[1 mark]***

Page 135 — Acids and Bases

1 a) H^+ or H_3O^+ and SO_4^{2-} ***[1 mark]***

b) $2H^+_{(aq)} + Mg_{(s)} \rightarrow Mg^{2+}_{(aq)} + H_{2(g)}$ ***[1 mark]***

c) HSO_4^- ***[1 mark]***

2 a) $HCN_{(aq)} + H_2O_{(l)} \rightleftharpoons H_3O^+_{(aq)} + CN^-_{(aq)}$ ***[1 mark]***

b) The pairs are HCN and CN^- ***[1 mark]***
AND H_2O and H_3O^+ ***[1 mark]***.

c) H^+ ***[1 mark]***

3 a) $NH_3 + H_2O \rightleftharpoons NH_4^+ + OH^-$ ***[1 mark]***

b) An acid as it donates a proton ***[1 mark]***

c) OH^- ***[1 mark]***

Page 137 — pH

1 a) It's a strong monobasic acid, so $[H^+]$ = [HBr] = 0.32 mol dm^{-3}.
pH = $-\log_{10}$ 0.32 = **0.49** ***[1 mark]***

b) HBr is a stronger acid than HCl, so will be more dissociated in solution. This means the concentration of hydrogen ions will be higher, so the pH will be lower. ***[1 mark]***.

2 a) Moles of NaOH = 2.50 ÷ 40.0 = 0.0625 moles ***[1 mark]***
1 mole of NaOH gives 1 mole of OH^-.
So $[OH^-]$ = [NaOH] = **0.0625 mol dm^{-3}** ***[1 mark]***.

b) $K_w = [H^+][OH^-]$
$[H^+]$ = 1 × 10^{-14} ÷ 0.0625 = 1.60 × 10^{-13} ***[1 mark]***
pH = $-\log_{10}$(1.60 × 10^{-13}) = **12.80** ***[1 mark]***

3 $K_w = [H^+][OH^-]$
$[OH^-]$ = [NaOH] = 0.0370
$[H^+] = K_w \div [OH^-]$ = (1 × 10^{-14}) ÷ 0.0370 = 2.70 × 10^{-13} ***[1 mark]***
pH = $-\log_{10}[H^+]$ = $-\log_{10}$(2.70 × 10^{-13}) = **12.57** ***[1 mark]***

Answers

Page 139 — The Acid Dissociation Constant

1 a) $K_a = \frac{[H^+][A^-]}{[HA]}$ ***[1 mark]***

b) $K_a = \frac{[H^+]^2}{[HA]}$ [HA] is 0.280 because only a small amount of HA will dissociate

$[H^+] = \sqrt{(5.60 \times 10^{-4}) \times (0.280)} = 0.0125 \text{ mol dm}^{-3}$ ***[1 mark]***

pH = $-\log_{10}[H^+] = -\log_{10}(0.0125)$ = **1.90** ***[1 mark]***

2 a) $[H^+] = 10^{-2.65}$ = **2.24×10^{-3} mol dm^{-3}** ***[1 mark]***

$K_a = \frac{[H^+]^2}{[HX]} = \frac{(2.24 \times 10^{-3})^2}{0.150}$

= **3.35×10^{-5} mol dm^{-3}** ***[1 mark]***

b) $pK_a = -\log_{10}K_a = -\log_{10}(3.35 \times 10^{-5})$ = **4.47** ***[1 mark]***

3 $K_a = 10^{-pK_a} = 10^{-4.2} = 6.3 \times 10^{-5}$ ***[1 mark]***

$K_a = \frac{[H^+]^2}{[HA]}$ so $[H^+] = \sqrt{K_a \times [HA]}$

$\sqrt{(6.3 \times 10^{-5}) \times (1.6 \times 10^{-4})} = \sqrt{1.0 \times 10^{-8}}$

= 1.0 × 10–4 mol dm–3 ***[1 mark]***

pH = $-\log_{10}[H^+] = -\log_{10} 1.0 \times 10^{-4}$ = **4.00** ***[1 mark]***

Page 141 — Buffers

1 a) $K_a = \frac{[C_6H_5COO^-][H^+]}{[C_6H_5COOH]}$

$[H^+] = 6.4 \times 10^{-5} \times \frac{0.40}{0.20} = 1.28 \times 10^{-4} \text{ mol dm}^{-3}$ ***[1 mark]***

pH = $-\log_{10}[1.28 \times 10^{-4}]$ = **3.89** ***[1 mark]***

b) $C_6H_5COOH \rightleftharpoons H^+ + C_6H_5COO^-$

Adding H_2SO_4 increases the concentration of H^+.

The equilibrium shifts left to reduce the concentration of H^+, so the pH will only change very slightly ***[1 mark]***.

2 a) $CH_3(CH_2)_2COOH \rightleftharpoons H^+ + CH_3(CH_2)_2COO^-$ ***[1 mark]***

b) $[CH_3(CH_2)_2COOH] = [CH_3(CH_2)_2COO^-]$,
so $[CH_3(CH_2)_2COOH] \div [CH_3(CH_2)_2COO^-] = 1$ ***[1 mark]***
and $K_a = [H^+]$.

pH = $-\log_{10}[1.5 \times 10^{-5}]$ = **4.82** ***[1 mark]***

If the concentrations of the weak acid and the salt are equal, they cancel from the K_a expression and the buffer pH = pK_a.

Page 143 — pH Curves and Titrations

1 Nitric acid:

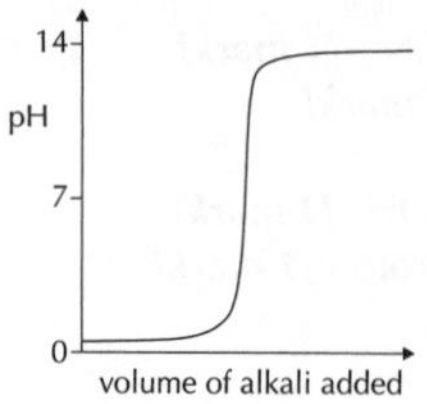

[1 mark]

Ethanoic acid:

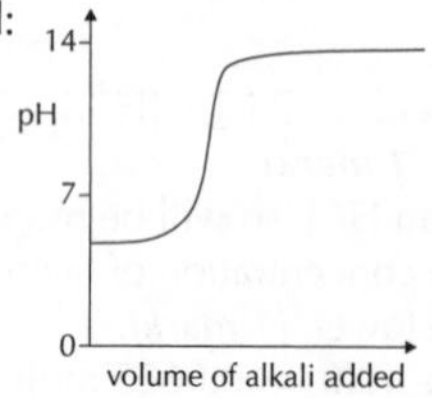

[1 mark]

2 Thymol blue ***[1 mark]***. It's a weak acid/strong base titration so the equivalence point is above pH 8 ***[1 mark]***.

Module 5: Section 2 — Energy

Page 145 — Lattice Enthalpy and Born-Haber Cycles

1 a)

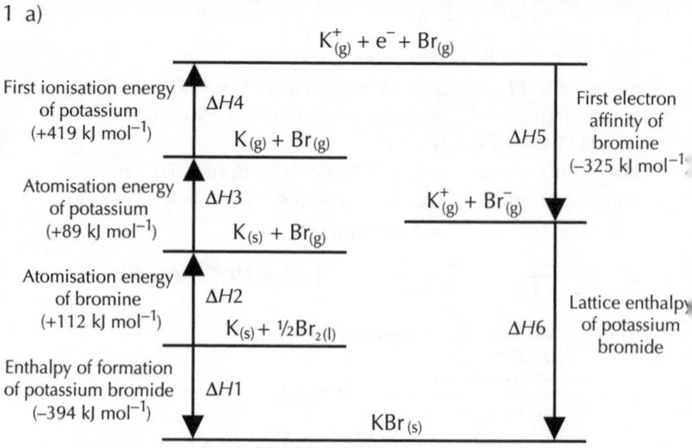

[1 mark for correct enthalpy changes. 1 mark for formulas/state symbols. 1 mark for correct directions of arrows.]

b) Lattice enthalpy, $\Delta H6 = -\Delta H5 - \Delta H4 - \Delta H3 - \Delta H2 + \Delta H1$
= –(–325) – (+419) – (+89) – (+112) + (–394) ***[1 mark]***
= **–689 kJ mol^{-1}** ***[1 mark]***

2 a)

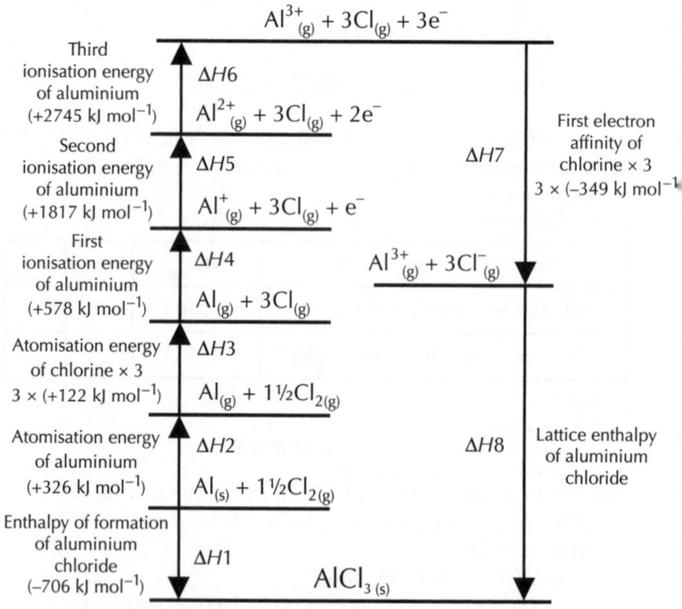

[1 mark for correct enthalpy changes and correctly multiplying all the enthalpies. 1 mark for formulas/state symbols. 1 mark for correct directions of arrows.]

b) Lattice enthalpy, $\Delta H8$
$= -\Delta H7 - \Delta H6 - \Delta H5 - \Delta H4 - \Delta H3 - \Delta H2 + \Delta H1$
= –3(–349) – (+2745) – (+1817) – (+578) – 3(+122) – (+326) + (–706) ***[1 mark]***
= **–5491 kJ mol^{-1}** ***[1 mark]***

Answers

a)

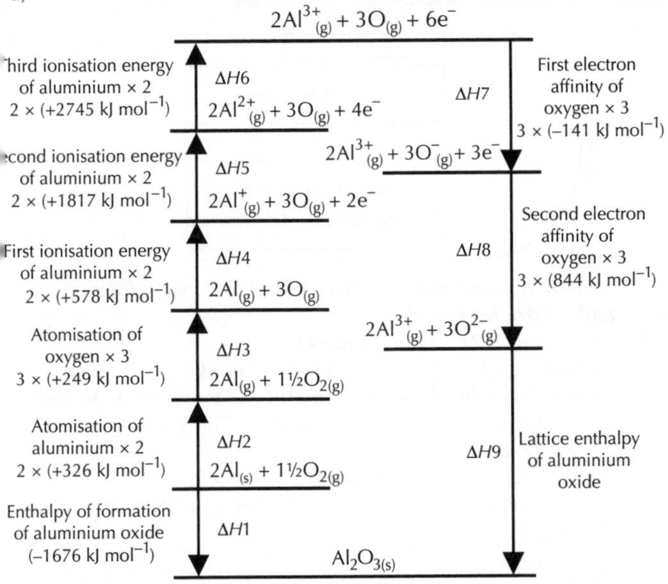

[1 mark for correct enthalpy changes and correctly multiplying all the enthalpies. 1 mark for formulas/state symbols. 1 mark for correct directions of arrows.]

b) Lattice enthalpy, $\Delta H9$
$= -\Delta H8 - \Delta H7 - \Delta H6 - \Delta H5 - \Delta H4 - \Delta H3 - \Delta H2 + \Delta H1$
$= -3(+844) - 3(-141) - 2(+2745) - 2(+1817) - 2(+578)$
$- 3(+249) - 2(+326) + (-1676)$ ***[1 mark]***
$=$ **–15 464 kJ mol⁻¹** ***[1 mark]***

age 147 — Enthalpies of Solution

a)

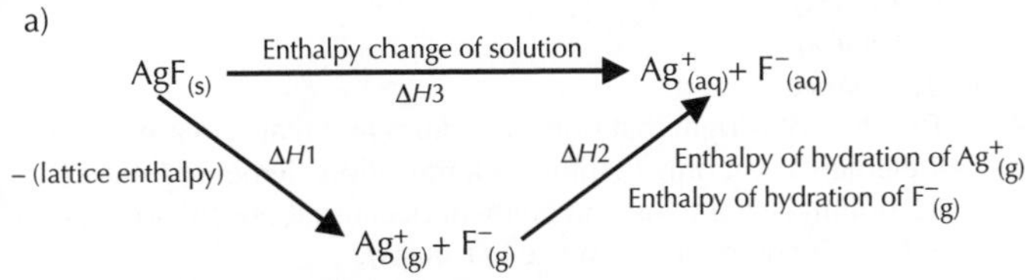

[1 mark for a complete correct cycle, 1 mark for correctly labelled arrows.]

b) $\Delta H3 = \Delta H1 + \Delta H2$
$= -(-960) + (-506) + (-464)$ ***[1 mark]*** $=$ **–10 kJ mol⁻¹** ***[1 mark]***

a)

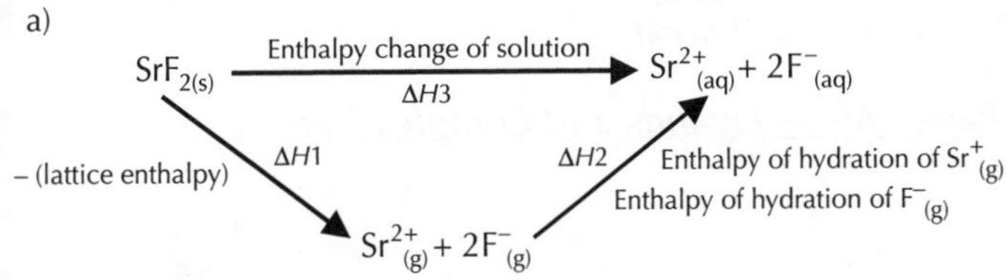

[1 mark for a complete correct cycle, 1 mark correctly labelled arrows.]

b) $-(-2492) + (-1480) + (2 \times -506)$ ***[1 mark]*** $=$ **0 kJ mol⁻¹** ***[1 mark]***
Don't forget — you have to double the enthalpy of hydration for F^- because there are two F^- ions in SrF_2.

By Hess's law:
Enthalpy change of solution ($MgCl_{2(s)}$)
= –lattice enthalpy ($MgCl_{2(s)}$) + enthalpy of hydration ($Mg^{2+}_{(g)}$)
+ [2 × enthalpy of hydration ($Cl^-_{(g)}$)] ***[1 mark]***
So enthalpy of hydration ($Cl^-_{(g)}$)
= [enthalpy change of solution ($MgCl_{2(s)}$) +
lattice enthalpy ($MgCl_{2(s)}$) – enthalpy of hydration ($Mg^{2+}_{(g)}$)] ÷ 2
= [(–122) + (–2526) – (–1920)] ÷ 2 ***[1 mark]***
= –728 ÷ 2 = **–364 kJ mol⁻¹** ***[1 mark]***

Ca^{2+} will have a greater enthalpy of hydration ***[1 mark]*** because it is smaller and has a higher charge / has a higher charge density than K^+ ***[1 mark]***. This means there is a stronger attraction between Ca^{2+} and the water molecules, so more energy is released when bonds are formed between them ***[1 mark]***.

Page 149 — Entropy

1 a) The reaction is not likely be feasible ***[1 mark]*** because there are fewer moles of product than moles of reactants and therefore a decrease in entropy ***[1 mark]***.
Remember — more particles means more entropy.
There's 1½ moles of reactants and only 1 mole of product.

b) $\Delta S = 26.9 - [32.7 + (\frac{1}{2} \times 205)]$ ***[1 mark]***
= **–108 J K⁻¹ mol⁻¹** ***[1 mark]***

c) The reaction is not likely to be feasible because ΔS is negative/there is a decrease in entropy ***[1 mark]***.

2 a) $\Delta S = 48 - 70 = -22\ J\,K^{-1}\,mol^{-1}$ ***[1 mark]***

b) Despite the negative entropy change, the reaction might still be feasible because other factors such as enthalpy, temperature and kinetics also play a part in whether or not a reaction occurs ***[1 mark]***.

Page 151 — Free Energy

1 a) $\Delta S = [214 + (2 \times 69.9)] - [186 + (2 \times 205)]$
$= -242.2\ J\,K^{-1}\,mol^{-1}$ ***[1 mark]***
$\Delta G = -730\,000 - (298 \times -242.2)$
≈ **–658 000 J mol⁻¹** (3 s.f.) (= **–658 kJ mol⁻¹**) ***[1 mark]***

b) The reaction is feasible at 298 K because ΔG is negative ***[1 mark]***.

c) $T = \frac{\Delta H}{\Delta S} = -730\,000 \div -242.2$ ***[1 mark]*** = **3010 K** ***[1 mark]***

2 First find ΔH:
$q = mc\Delta T = 100 \times 4.18 \times 3.5 = 1463$ J ***[1 mark]***
$M_r(C_3H_7OH) = (3 \times 12.0) + (8 \times 1.0) + 16.0 = 60.0$
So, number of moles of $C_3H_7OH = 48.5 \div 60.0 = 0.808$ ***[1 mark]***
$\Delta H = -1463 \div 0.808 = -1810\ J\,mol^{-1}$ ***[1 mark]***
ΔH is negative because the combustion reaction is exothermic.
Now find ΔS:
$\Delta S = [(3 \times 214) + (4 \times 69.9)] - [193 + (4\frac{1}{2} \times 205)]$
$= -193.9\ J\,K^{-1}\,mol^{-1}$ ***[1 mark]***
Finally, find ΔG:
$\Delta G = \Delta H - T\Delta S = -1810 - (298 \times -193.9)$
≈ **56 000 J mol⁻¹** (3 s.f.) (= **56 kJ mol⁻¹**) ***[1 mark]***

Page 153 — Redox Equations

1 $Cl_2 + 2e^- \rightarrow 2Cl^-$ ***[1 mark]***
$Fe^{2+} \rightarrow Fe^{3+} + e^-$ ***[1 mark]***

2 a) $Al \rightarrow Al^{3+} + 3e^-$ and $O_2 + 4e^- \rightarrow 2O^{2-}$ ***[1 mark for both correct]***

b) $4Al \rightarrow 4Al^{3+} + 12e^-$
$3O_2 + 12e^- \rightarrow 6O^{2-}$
$\mathbf{4Al + 3O_2 \rightarrow 4Al^{3+} + 6O^{2-}}$ OR $\mathbf{4Al + 3O_2 \rightarrow 2Al_2O_3}$ ***[1 mark]***
You have to balance the number of electrons before you can combine the half-equations. And always double-check that your equation definitely balances. It's easy to slip up and throw away marks.

3 $2MnO_4^- + 16H^+ + 10e^- \rightarrow 2Mn^{2+} + 8H_2O$
$10I^- \rightarrow 5I_2 + 10e^-$
$2MnO_4^- + 16H^+ + 10I^- \rightarrow 2Mn^{2+} + 8H_2O + 5I_2$ ***[1 mark]***

4 a) $Cr_2O_7^{2-} \rightarrow 2Cr^{3+}$
$Cr_2O_7^{2-} \rightarrow 2Cr^{3+} + 7H_2O$
$Cr_2O_7^{2-} + 14H^+ \rightarrow 2Cr^{3+} + 7H_2O$ ***[1 mark]***
$Cr_2O_7^{2-} + 14H^+ + 6e^- \rightarrow 2Cr^{3+} + 7H_2O$ ***[1 mark]***
$Cr_2O_7^{2-} + 14H^+ \rightarrow 2Cr^{3+} + 7H_2O$
(–2) (+14) (+6) O
The total charge is +12 on the left hand side and +6 on the right hand side, so you need to add 6 electrons to the left hand side to balance the charges.

b) $Cr_2O_7^{2-} + 14H^+ + 3Zn \rightarrow 2Cr^{3+} + 7H_2O + 3Zn^{2+}$ ***[1 mark]***
Six electrons are needed to reduce each dichromate ion. Each zinc atom loses two electrons, so you need to multiply the zinc half-equation by three: $3Zn \rightarrow 3Zn^{2+} + 6e^-$. When the two half-equations are combined, the electrons cancel each other out.

Page 155 — Redox Titrations

1 a) Number of moles = (concentration × volume) ÷ 1000
= (20 × 0.10) ÷ 1000 = **0.0020 mol** ***[1 mark]***

Answers

b) 2 moles of MnO_4^- react with 5 moles of Sn^{2+}.
$(0.0020 \div 2) \times 5 =$ **0.0050 mol** ***[1 mark]***

c) Concentration = (number of moles ÷ volume) × 1000
$= (0.0050 \div 10) \times 1000 =$ **0.50 mol dm⁻³** ***[1 mark]***

2 a) $MnO_4^- + 8H^+ + 5Fe^{2+} \rightarrow Mn^{2+} + 4H_2O + 5Fe^{3+}$ ***[1 mark]***

b) Number of moles = (concentration × volume) ÷ 1000
$= (0.400 \times 11.5) \div 1000 = 0.00460$ ***[1 mark]***
Moles of Fe^{2+} = moles of $MnO_4^- \times 5 = 0.0230$ ***[1 mark]***
Concentration = (number of moles ÷ volume) × 1000
$= (0.0230 \div 50.0) \times 1000 =$ **0.460 mol dm⁻³** ***[1 mark]***

c) Mass of substance = moles × relative atomic mass
Mass of iron in solution $= (0.0230) \times 55.8 = 1.2834$ g ***[1 mark]***
% iron in steel wool $= (1.2834 \div 1.30) \times 100 =$ **98.7 %** ***[1 mark]***

Page 157 — Iodine Thiosulfate Titrations

1 a) $IO_3^- + 5I^- + 6H^+ \rightarrow 3I_2 + 3H_2O$ ***[1 mark]***

b) Number of moles = (concentration × volume) ÷ 1000
Number of moles of thiosulfate $= (0.150 \times 24.0) \div 1000$
$=$ **3.60×10^{-3}** ***[1 mark]***

c) 2 moles of thiosulfate react with 1 mole of iodine, so there were $(3.60 \times 10^{-3}) \div 2 =$ **1.80×10^{-3}** moles of iodine ***[1 mark]***.

d) 1/3 mole ***[1 mark]***

e) There must be $1.80 \times 10^{-3} \div 3 = 6.00 \times 10^{-4}$ moles of iodate(V) in the solution ***[1 mark]***.
So concentration of potassium iodate(V) =
$(6.00 \times 10^{-4}) \div (10.0 \div 1000) =$ **0.0600 mol dm⁻³** ***[1 mark]***.

2 Number of moles = (concentration × volume) ÷ 1000
Number of moles of thiosulfate $= (0.300 \times 12.5) \div 1000$
$= 3.75 \times 10^{-3}$ ***[1 mark]***
2 moles of thiosulfate react with 1 mole of iodine.
So there must have been $(3.75 \times 10^{-3}) \div 2 = 1.875 \times 10^{-3}$ moles of iodine produced ***[1 mark]***.
2 moles of manganate(VII) ions produce 5 moles of iodine molecules
So there must have been $(1.875 \times 10^{-3}) \times (2 \div 5)$
$= 7.50 \times 10^{-4}$ moles of manganate(VII) in the solution ***[1 mark]***.
Concentration of potassium manganate(VII)
$= (7.50 \times 10^{-4}$ moles$) \div (18.0 \div 1000) =$ **0.0417 mol dm⁻³** ***[1 mark]***

Page 159 — Electrochemical Cells

1 a) Iron ***[1 mark]*** as it has a more negative electrode potential/ it loses electrons more easily than lead ***[1 mark]***.

b) Standard cell potential $= -0.13 - (-0.44) =$ **+0.31 V** ***[1 mark]***

2 a) $+0.80\text{ V} - (-0.76\text{ V}) =$ **+1.56 V** ***[1 mark]***

b) The concentration of Zn^{2+} ions or Ag^+ ions was not 1.00 mol dm⁻³ or equimolar ***[1 mark]***. The pressure wasn't 100 kPa ***[1 mark]***.

Page 161 — The Electrochemical Series

1 a) $Zn_{(s)} + Ni^{2+}_{(aq)} \rightleftharpoons Zn^{2+}_{(aq)} + Ni_{(s)}$ ***[1 mark]***
$E^\ominus = (-0.25) - (-0.76) =$ **+0.51 V** ***[1 mark]***

b) $2MnO^-_{4\,(aq)} + 16H^+_{(aq)} + 5Sn^{2+}_{(aq)} \rightleftharpoons$
$2Mn^{2+}_{(aq)} + 8H_2O_{(l)} + 5Sn^{4+}_{(aq)}$ ***[1 mark]***
$E^\ominus = (+1.51) - (+0.14) =$ **+1.37 V** ***[1 mark]***

c) No reaction ***[1 mark]***. Both reactants are in their oxidised form ***[1 mark]***.

2 $KMnO_4$ ***[1 mark]*** because it has a more positive/less negative electrode potential ***[1 mark]***.

3 a) $Cu^{2+}_{(aq)} + 2e^- \rightleftharpoons Cu_{(s)}$ ***[1 mark]***
$Ni^{2+}_{(aq)} + 2e^- \rightleftharpoons Ni_{(s)}$ ***[1 mark]***

b) $0.34 - (-0.25) =$ **+0.59 V** ***[1 mark]***

c) $Cu^{2+}_{(aq)} + Ni_{(s)} \rightleftharpoons Cu_{(s)} + Ni^{2+}_{(aq)}$ ***[1 mark]***

d) If the copper solution was more dilute, the $E^\ominus$ of the copper half-cell would be lower (the equilibrium will shift to the left/ the copper will lose electrons more easily), so the overall cell potential would be lower ***[1 mark]***.

Page 163 — Storage and Fuel Cells

1 a)

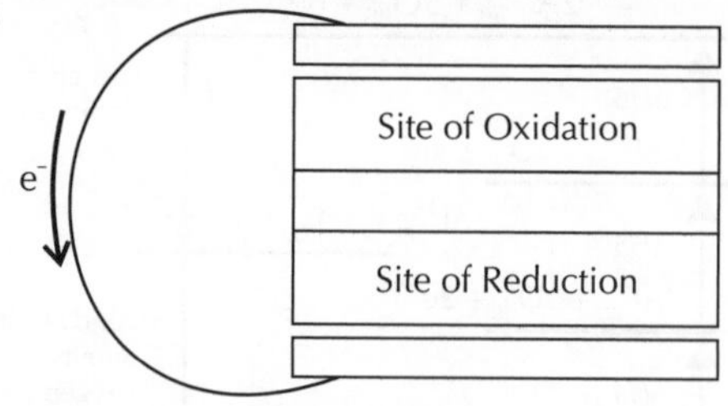

[1 mark for each correct label — total of 2 marks for part i) and 1 mark for part ii).]

b) Anode: $H_2 \rightarrow 2H^+ + 2e^-$ ***[1 mark]***
Cathode: $\frac{1}{2}O_2 + 2H^+ + 2e^- \rightarrow H_2O$ ***[1 mark]***

c) It only allows the H^+ across ***[1 mark]*** and forces the e^- to travel around the circuit to get to the cathode. This creates an electrica current ***[1 mark]***.

2 a) $+0.52 - (-0.88) =$ **1.4 V** ***[1 mark]***

b) $Cd_{(s)} + 2NiO(OH)_{(s)} + 2H_2O_{(l)} \rightarrow Cd(OH)_{2(s)} + 2Ni(OH)_{2(s)}$
[1 mark]

Module 5: Section 3 — Transition Elements

Page 165 — The d-block

1 C ***[1 mark]***

2 a) $1s^2\ 2s^2\ 2p^6\ 3s^2\ 3p^6\ 3d^8\ 4s^2$ ***[1 mark]***

b) $1s^2\ 2s^2\ 2p^6\ 3s^2\ 3p^6\ 3d^6$ ***[1 mark]***

c) $1s^2\ 2s^2\ 2p^6\ 3s^2\ 3p^6\ 3d^9$ ***[1 mark]***

d) $1s^2\ 2s^2\ 2p^6\ 3s^2\ 3p^6\ 3d^1$ ***[1 mark]***

3 a) 3 ***[1 mark]***

b) 6 ***[1 mark]***

c) 3 ***[1 mark]***

d) 0 ***[1 mark]***

4 The student is right that both scandium and titanium are period 4 elements, but only titanium is a transition element ***[1 mark]***. Scandium isn't a transition element because it doesn't form an ior with an incomplete d sub-shell ***[1 mark]***.

Page 167 — Properties of Transition Elements

1 a) iron ***[1 mark]***

b) chromium ***[1 mark]***

c) manganese ***[1 mark]***

Page 169 — Ligands and Complex Ions

1 a)

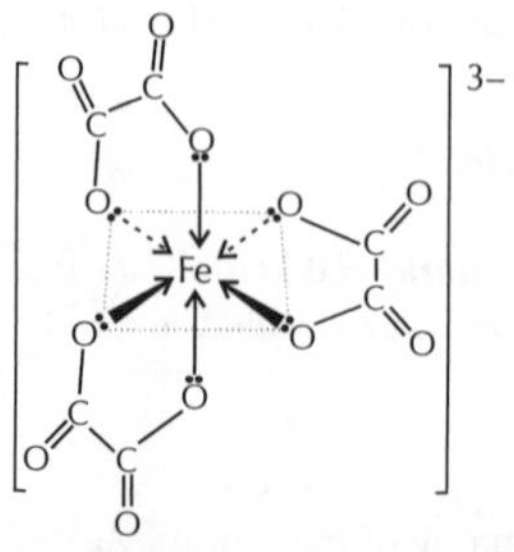

or

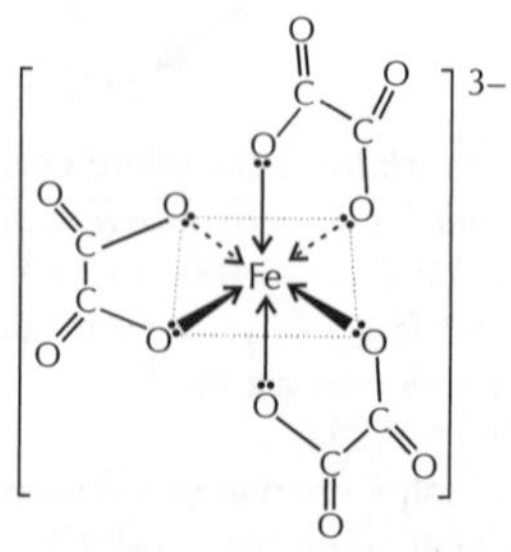

[1 mark]

b) Optical isomerism is a type of stereoisomerism that happens wher a molecule can exist in two non-superimposable mirror images ***[1 mark]***.

2 a)

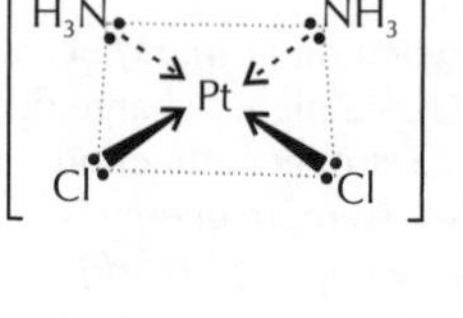

[1 mark]

Answers

b) The two chloride ligands are displaced and their places taken by two nitrogen atoms from the cancer cell's DNA ***[1 mark]***. This stops the cell from reproducing. The cell is unable to repair the damage, and dies ***[1 mark]***.

Page 171 — Substitution Reactions

a) $[Cu(H_2O)_6]^{2+}$ ***[1 mark]***

b) i) $[Cu(H_2O)_6]^{2+}{}_{(aq)} + 4NH_{3(aq)} \rightleftharpoons$ $[Cu(NH_3)_4(H_2O)_2]^{2+}{}_{(aq)} + 4H_2O_{(l)}$
[1 mark for correct formula of new complex formed, 1 mark for the rest of the equation being correctly balanced.]

ii) Deep blue ***[1 mark]***

iii) Octahedral ***[1 mark]***

a) i) The water ligand is replaced with an oxygen ligand ***[1 mark]***.

ii) It is the basis of the oxygen transportation mechanism in the bloodstream ***[1 mark]***.

b) Carbon monoxide will bind to the haemoglobin complex and will not exchange with an oxygen (or water) ligand ***[1 mark]***. The haemoglobin can't transport oxygen any more, so cells of the body will get less oxygen ***[1 mark]***.

Page 173 — Reactions of Ions

$2MnO_4^- + 6H^+ + 5H_2O_2 \rightarrow 2Mn^{2+} + 8H_2O + 5O_2$ ***[1 mark]***

The electrons have to be cancelled out by multiplying the manganate half-equation by 2 and the H_2O_2 half-equation by 5.

E.g. CuI_2 ***[1 mark]***

Module 6: Section 1 — Aromatic Compounds & Carbonyls

Page 175 — Benzene and Aromatic Compounds

a) The model suggests that there should be two different bond lengths in the molecule, corresponding to C=C and C–C ***[1 mark]***.

b) X-ray diffraction shows that all the carbon–carbon bond lengths in benzene are actually the same, which doesn't fit the Kekulé model ***[1 mark]***.

c) E.g. If the Kekulé model were true, and benzene contained three double bonds, you'd expect the enthalpy of hydrogenation to be three times that of cyclohexene ***[1 mark]***. The enthalpy of hydrogenation is in fact less exothermic than expected, implying that benzene is actually more stable than the Kekulé model predicts. This is thought to be due to the delocalised ring of electrons ***[1 mark]***.

Page 177 — Electrophilic Substitution

a) Cyclohexene would decolorise bromine water, benzene would not ***[1 mark]***. This is because orange bromine reacts in an electrophilic addition reaction with cyclohexene, due to the localised electrons in the double bond, ***[1 mark]*** to form a colourless dibromocycloalkane, leaving a clear solution. Benzene has a delocalised π system which spreads out the negative charge and makes it very stable, so it doesn't react with bromine water and the solution stays orange ***[1 mark]***.

b) i) It acts as a halogen carrier ***[1 mark]***

ii)

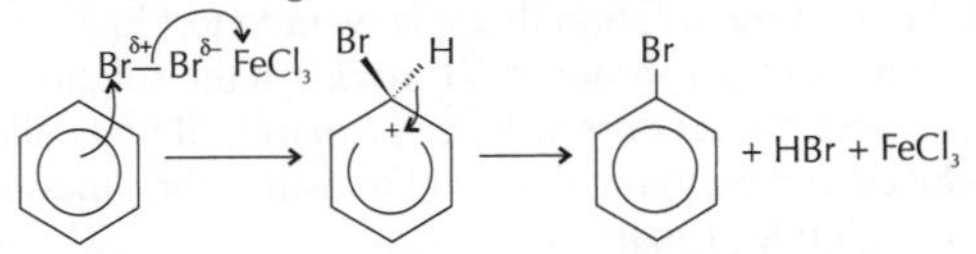

[3 marks available — 1 mark for each stage above.]

Page 179 — Substituted Benzene Rings

1 a)

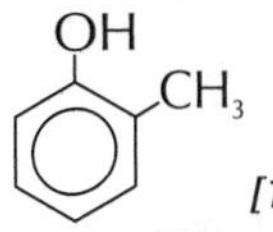

[1 mark]

b)

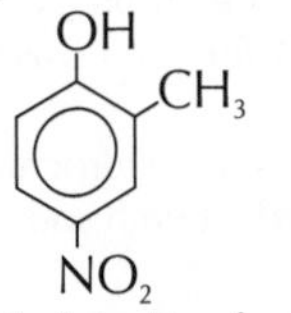

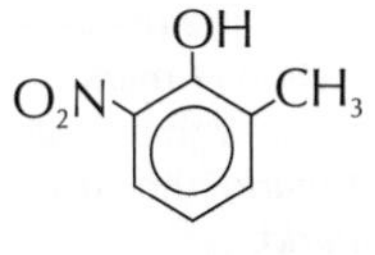

2-methyl-4-nitrophenol   2-methyl-6-nitrophenol

[2 marks — 1 mark for each correct structure and name.]

2 a) With benzene, there will be no reaction but with phenol a reaction will occur which decolorises the bromine water and forms a precipitate ***[1 mark]***. The product from the reaction with phenol is 2,4,6-tribromophenol ***[1 mark]***.

b) Electrons from one of oxygen's p-orbitals overlap with the benzene ring's delocalised system, increasing its electron density ***[1 mark]***. This makes the ring more likely to be attacked by electrophiles. ***[1 mark]***

c) Electrophilic substitution ***[1 mark]***

Page 181 — Aldehydes and Ketones

1 a) Both compounds react with 2,4-dinitrophenylhydrazine to form an orange precipitate, so they must both be carbonyl compounds ***[1 mark]***. The only carbonyl compounds with the molecular formula C_3H_6O are propanone (CH_3COCH_3) and propanal (CH_3CH_2CHO). Compound Y reacts with Tollens' reagent to form a silver mirror, so must be the aldehyde propanal ***[1 mark]***. Compound X has no reaction with Tollens' reagent so it is the ketone propanone ***[1 mark]***.

b)

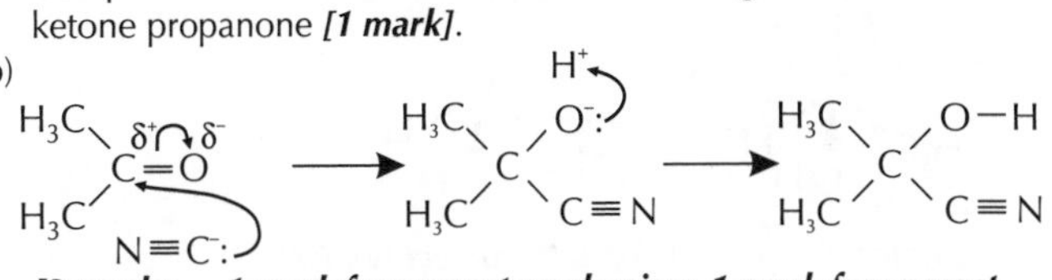

[2 marks — 1 mark for correct mechanism, 1 mark for correct product]

c) Compound Y (propanal) ***[1 mark]***

Page 183 — Carboxylic Acids and Acyl Chlorides

1 a) Sodium 3-methylbutanoate ***[1 mark]***.

b) cold water ***[1 mark]***.

c)

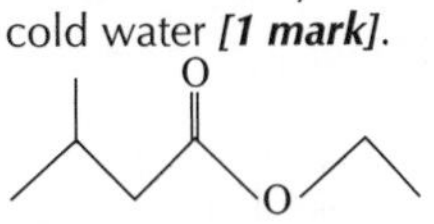

[1 mark].

d) Ammonia ***[1 mark]***.

Page 185 — Esters

1 a) Propan-1-ol ***[1 mark]***

b) Any two from:

Ethanoic acid:

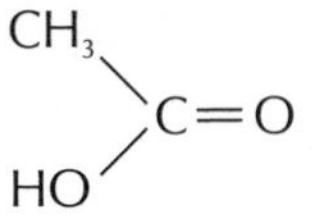

Ethanoyl chloride:

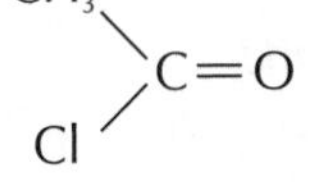

Ethanoic anhydride:

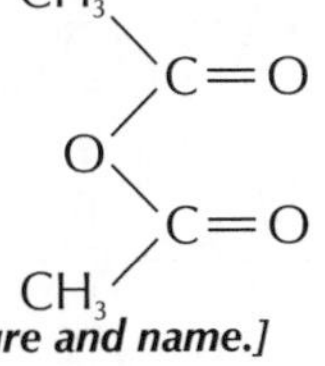

[2 marks — 1 mark for each correct structure and name.]

2 a) A and D ***[1 mark]***.

b) 2-methylpropanol and sodium pentanoate ***[1 mark]***.

Answers

Module 6: Section 2 — Nitrogen Compounds, Polymers & Synthesis

Page 187 — Amines and Amides

1 a) Any two from: propylamine / dipropylamine / tripropylamine / tetrapropylamine ion ***[2 marks — 1 mark for each correct name]***.
b) fractional distillation ***[1 mark]***
c) React nitrobenzene with tin and concentrated hydrochloric acid under reflux ***[1 mark]***, then react the product with sodium hydroxide ***[1 mark]***.

2 C ***[1 mark]***

Page 189 — Chirality

1 a)

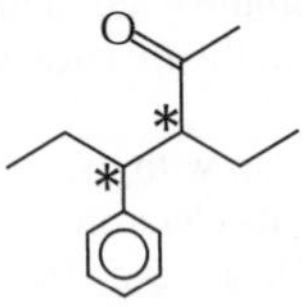

[1 mark]

b)

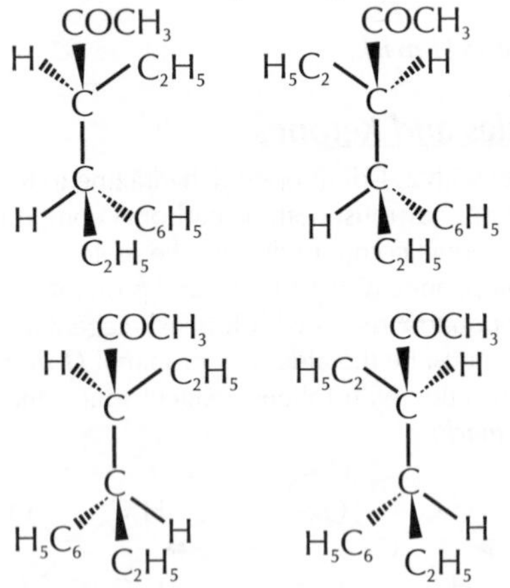

[4 marks — 1 mark for each correct isomer]

Page 191 — Polymers

1 a) It's a polyamide ***[1 mark]*** and it's made by condensation polymerisation ***[1 mark]***.
b) A dicarboxylic acid and a diamine ***[1 mark]***.
c) Hydrolysis with an acid / base ***[1 mark]***.

Page 193 — More on Polymers

1 a)

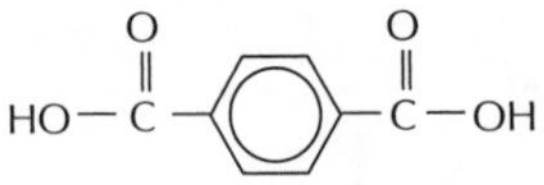

and

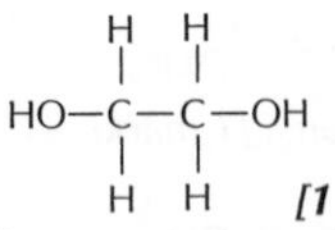

[1 mark]

b) condensation polymerisation ***[1 mark]***

2 a)

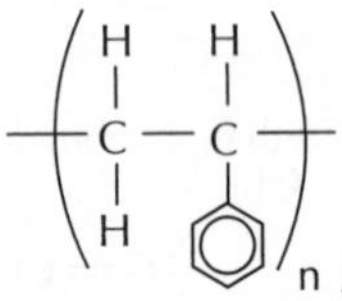

[1 mark]

b)

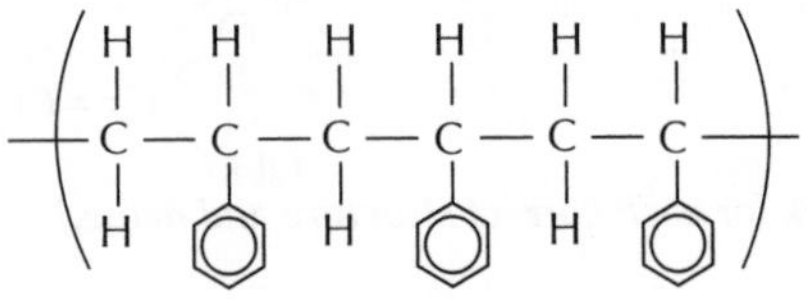

[1 mark]

Page 197 — Carbon-Carbon Bond Synthesis

1 a) KCN or NaCN ***[1 mark]***, ethanol, reflux ***[1 mark]***.
b)

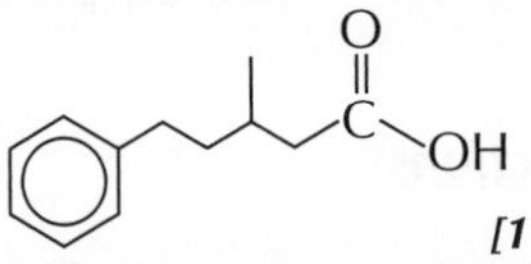

[1 mark]

c) Reflux benzene with $AlCl_3$ (or any other appropriate halogen carrier, e.g. $FeCl_3$) ***[1 mark]*** and 1-bromo-4-chloro-2-methylbutane ***[1 mark]***.
This is the structure of 1-bromo-4-chloro-2-methylbutane:

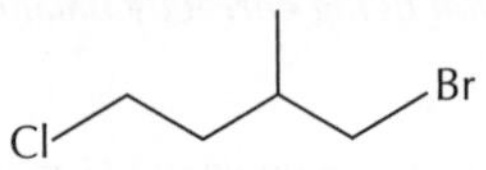

2

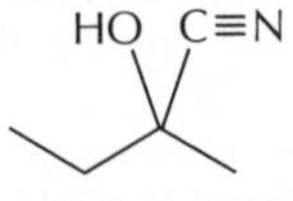

[1 mark]

Page 199 — Organic Synthesis — Practical Techniques

1 a) The purer sample will have the higher melting point, so the sample that melts at 69 °C is purer ***[1 mark]***.
b) To purify the sample you could dissolve it in hot propanone to make a saturated solution ***[1 mark]*** and cool the solution slowly so that the product recrystallises ***[1 mark]***. You'd then filter the crystals under reduced pressure, wash them with very cold propanone ***[1 mark]*** and dry them.
c) E.g. the purity could be checked by measuring the melting point and comparing it against the known melting point of stearic acid ***[1 mark]***.

2 B ***[1 mark]***

Page 201 — Functional Groups

1 a) A — alcohol / hydroxyl ***[1 mark]***
B — alcohol / hydroxyl and alkene / alkenyl ***[1 mark]***
C — alcohol / hydroxyl and aromatic ring / phenyl ***[1 mark]***
b) C ***[1 mark]***
c) A ***[1 mark]***
d) B ***[1 mark]***

Page 203 — Synthetic Routes

1 E.g. Step 1: The methanol is refluxed with $K_2Cr_2O_7$ and acid to form methanoic acid ***[1 mark]***.
Step 2: The methanoic acid is heated with ethanol using an acid catalyst to make ethyl methanoate ***[1 mark]***.

2 E.g. Step 1: React propane with bromine in the presence of UV light to form bromopropane ***[1 mark]***.
Step 2: Bromopropane is then refluxed with aqueous sodium hydroxide solution to form propanol ***[1 mark]***.

Module 6: Section 3 — Analysis

Page 205 — Tests for Organic Functional Groups

1 B ***[1 mark]***
Cyclohexene is an alkene so it decolourises bromine water.

2 E.g. put 2 cm^3 of the solution that you want to test in a test tube and add some sodium carbonate ***[1 mark]***. If the solution is a carboxylic acid, the mixture will fizz ***[1 mark]***. If you collect the gas produced and bubble it through limewater, the limewater should turn cloudy ***[1 mark]***.

Answers

Page 208 — Chromatography

1 a) R_f value = $\frac{\text{Distance travelled by spot}}{\text{Distance travelled by solvent}}$ ***[1 mark]***

R_f value of spot A = 7 ÷ 8 = 0.875 ***[1 mark]***

The R_f value has no units, because it's a ratio.

b) Substance A has moved further up the plate because it's less strongly adsorbed onto the surface than substance B ***[1 mark]***.

2 a) The peak at 5 minutes ***[1 mark]***.

b) The retention time for ethene will be shorter ***[1 mark]*** because it has a lower boiling point that hexene, so will spend less time condensed as a liquid and will travel faster through the tube ***[1 mark]***.

3 a) The mixture is injected into a stream of carrier gas, which takes it through a tube over the oil / solid ***[1 mark]***. The components of the mixture dissolve in the oil / on the solid ***[1 mark]***, evaporate into the gas ***[1 mark]***, and redissolve, gradually travelling along the tube to the detector ***[1 mark]***.

b) The substances separate because they have different solubilities in the oil / on the solid ***[1 mark]***, so they take different amounts of time to move through the tube ***[1 mark]***.

c) The areas under the peaks will be proportional to the relative amount of each substance in the mixture OR the area under the benzene peak will be three times greater than the area under the ethanol peak ***[1 mark]***.

4 C ***[1 mark]***

Page 211 — NMR Spectroscopy

1 a) The peak at δ = 0 is produced by the reference compound, tetramethylsilane/TMS ***[1 mark]***.

b) All three carbon atoms in the molecule $CH_3CH_2CH_2NH_2$ are in different environments ***[1 mark]***. There are only two peaks on the carbon-13 NMR spectrum shown ***[1 mark]***.

The ^{13}C NMR spectrum of $CH_3CH_2CH_2NH_2$ would have three peaks because this molecule has three carbon environments.

c) The peak at δ ≈ 25 represents carbons in C–C bonds ***[1 mark]***.
The peak at δ ≈ 40 represents a carbon in a C–N bond ***[1 mark]***.
The spectrum has two peaks, so the molecule must have two carbon environments ***[1 mark]***.
So the structure of the molecule must be:

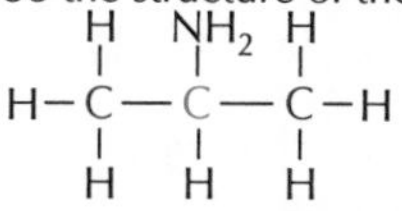

[1 mark].

The two carbon environments are CH_3–$CH(NH_2)$–CH_3 and $CH(NH_2)$–$(CH_3)_2$.

2 C ***[1 mark]***

Page 213 — Proton NMR

1 a) A CH_2 group adjacent to a halogen ***[1 mark]***.

You've got to read the question carefully — it tells you it's an alkyl halide. So the group at 3.6 ppm. can't have oxygen in it. It can't be halogen-CH_3 either, as this has 3 hydrogens in it.

b) A CH_3 group ***[1 mark]***.

c) CH_2 added to CH_3 gives a mass of 29.0, so the halogen must be chlorine with a mass of 35.5. ***[1 mark]***.
So a likely structure is CH_3CH_2Cl ***[1 mark]***.

d) The quartet at 3.6 ppm. is caused by 3 protons on the adjacent carbon. The n + 1 rule tells you that 3 protons give 3 + 1 = 4 peaks ***[1 mark]***. Similarly the triplet at 1.3 ppm. is due to 2 adjacent protons giving 2 + 1 = 3 peaks ***[1 mark]***.

Page 215 — More on Spectra

1 a) Mass of molecule = 73 ***[1 mark]***
You can tell this from the mass spectrum — the mass of the molecular ion is 73.

b) Structure of the molecule:

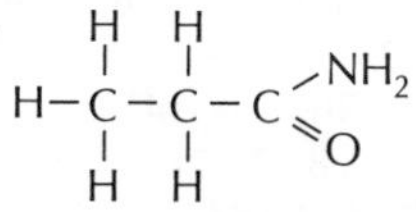

[1 mark]

Explanation: ***[Award 1 mark each for the following pieces of reasoning, up to a total of 5 marks]***:
The infrared spectrum of the molecule shows a strong absorbance at about 3200 cm^{-1}, which suggests that the molecule contains an amine or amide group.
It also has a trough at about 1700 cm^{-1}, which suggests that the molecule contains a C=O group.
The ^{13}C NMR spectrum tells you that the molecule has three carbon environments.
One of the ^{13}C NMR peaks has a chemical shift of about 170, which corresponds to a carbonyl group in an amide.
The ^1H NMR spectrum has a quartet at δ ≈ 2, and a triplet at δ ≈ 1 — to give this splitting pattern the molecule must contain a CH_2CH_3 group.
The ^1H NMR spectrum has a singlet at δ ≈ 6, corresponding to H atoms in an amine or amide group.
The mass spectrum shows a peak at m/z = 15 which corresponds to a CH_3 group.
The mass spectrum shows a peak at m/z = 29 which corresponds to a CH_2CH_3 group.
The mass spectrum shows a peak at m/z = 44 which corresponds to a $CONH_2$ group.

2 a) Mass of molecule = 60 ***[1 mark]***
You can tell this from the mass spectrum — the mass of the molecular ion is 60.

b) Structure of the molecule:

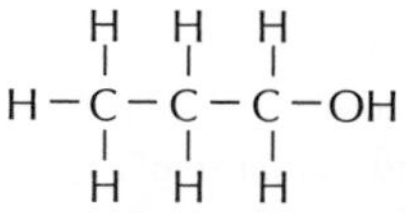

[1 mark]

Explanation: ***[Award 1 mark each for the following pieces of reasoning, up to a total of 5 marks]***:
The ^{13}C NMR spectrum tells you that the molecule has three carbon environments.
One of the ^{13}C NMR peaks has a chemical shift of 60 — which corresponds to a C–O group.
The infrared spectrum of the molecule has a trough at about 3300 cm^{-1}, which suggests that the molecule contains an alcoholic OH group.
It also has a trough at about 1200 cm^{-1}, which suggests that the molecule also contains a C–O group.
The mass spectrum shows a peak at m/z = 15 which corresponds to a CH_3 group.
The mass spectrum shows a peak at m/z = 17 which corresponds to an OH group.
The mass spectrum shows a peak at m/z = 29 which corresponds to a C_2H_5 group.
The mass spectrum shows a peak at m/z = 31 which corresponds to a CH_2OH group.
The mass spectrum shows a peak at m/z = 43 which corresponds to a C_3H_7 group.
The ^1H NMR spectrum has 4 peaks, showing that the molecule has 4 proton environments.
The ^1H NMR spectrum has a singlet at δ ≈ 2, corresponding to H atoms in an OH group.
The ^1H NMR spectrum has a sextuplet with an integration trace of 2 at δ ≈ 1.5, a quartet with an integration trace of 2 at δ ≈ 3.5, and a triplet with an integration trace of 3 at δ ≈ 1 — to give this splitting pattern the molecule must contain a $CH_3CH_2CH_2$ group.

Index

Index

Index